CATHO

SUNDAY AND DAILY MAS

MW01134386

CATHOLIC SUNDAY AND DAILY MASS READINGS FOR 2024 WITH THE PRINCIPAL
CELEBRATIONS OF THE LITURGICAL YEAR B, 2024

Compiled by

Catholic Lectionary Publishers

CONTENTS
Section A
PRINCIPAL CELEBRATIONS OF THE LITURGICAL YEAR B, 2024   - 4
Section B

PRINCIPAL CELEBRATIONS OF THE LITURGICAL YEAR B, 2024

CELEBRATIONS	DATE
First Sunday of Advent, Year B	December 3, 2023
Ash Wednesday	February 14, 2024
Easter Sunday	March 31, 2024
The Ascension of the Lord	May 12, 2024
Pentecost Sunday	May 19, 2024
The Most Holy Body and Blood of Christ (*Corpus Christi*)	June 16, 2022
First Sunday of Advent, Year C	December 1, 2024

Solemnity of Blessed Virgin Mary, Mother of God
First Reading: Numbers 6:22-27

22The LORD said to Moses: 23 "Speak to Aaron and his sons and tell them: This is how you shall bless the Israelites. Say to them:

24The LORD bless you and keep you!

25The LORD let his face shine upon you, and be gracious to you!

26The LORD look upon you kindly and give you peace!

27So shall they invoke my name upon the Israelites, and I will bless them."

Responsorial Psalm: Psalms 67:2-3, 5, 6, 8.

R. (2a) *May God bless us in his mercy.*

2 May God have pity on us and bless us;
    may he let his face shine upon us.
3 So may your way be known upon earth;
    among all nations, your salvation.
R. *May God bless us in his mercy.*

5 May the nations be glad and exult
    because you rule the peoples in equity;
    the nations on the earth you guide.
R. *May God bless us in his mercy.*
6 May the peoples praise you, O God;
    may all the peoples praise you!
8 May God bless us,
    and may all the ends of the earth fear him!
R. May God bless us in his mercy.

Second Reading: Galatians 4:4-7

Brothers and sisters: 4When the fullness of time had come, God sent his Son, born of a woman, born under the law, 5 to ransom those under the law, so that we might receive adoption as sons. 6As proof that you are sons, God sent the Spirit of his Son into our hearts, crying out, "Abba, Father!" 7So you are no longer a slave but a son, and if a son then also an heir, through God.

Alleluia: Hebrews 1:1-2

R. Alleluia, alleluia.

1In the past God spoke to our ancestors

through the prophets;
2 in these last days, he has spoken to us
through the Son.
R. Alleluia, alleluia.

Gospel: Luke 2:16-21

16 The shepherds went in haste to Bethlehem and found Mary and Joseph, and the infant lying in the manger. 17 When they saw this, they made known the message that had been told them about this child. 18All who heard it were amazed by what had been told them by the shepherds. 19And Mary kept all these things, reflecting on them in her heart. 20Then the shepherds returned, glorifying and praising God for all they had heard and seen, just as it had been told to them.

21When eight days were completed for his circumcision, he was named Jesus, the name given him by the angel before he was conceived in the womb.

Tuesday January 2, 2024

Memorial of Saints Basil the Great and Gregory Nazianzen, Bishops and Doctors

First Reading: 1 John 2:22-28

Beloved: 22Who is the liar? Whoever denies that Jesus is the Christ. Whoever denies the Father and the Son, this is the antichrist. 23Anyone who denies the Son does not have the Father, but whoever confesses the Son has the Father as well.

24Let what you heard from the beginning remain in you. If what you heard from the beginning remains in you, then you will remain in the Son and in the Father. 25And this is the promise that he made us: eternal life. 26I write you these things about those who would deceive you. 27As for you, the anointing that you received from him remains in you, so that you do not need anyone to teach you. But his anointing teaches you about everything and is true and not false; just as it taught you, remain in him.

28And now, children, remain in him, so that when he appears we may have confidence and not be put to shame by him at his coming.

Responsorial Psalm: Psalms 98:1, 2-3AB, 3CD-4

R. (3cd) *All the ends of the earth have seen the*
saving power of God.

1 Sing to the LORD a new song,
for he has done wondrous deeds;
His right hand has won victory for him,
his holy arm.
R. All the ends of the earth have seen the saving
power of God.

² The LORD has made his salvation known:
>in the sight of the nations he has revealed
>>his justice.
³ᴬᴮ He has remembered his kindness and his
>>faithfulness
>>toward the house of Israel.
R. All the ends of the earth have seen the saving
>>**power of God.**

³ᶜᴰAll the ends of the earth have seen
>>the salvation by our God.
⁴ Sing joyfully to the LORD, all you lands;
>>break into song; sing praise.
R. All the ends of the earth have seen the saving
>>**power of God.**

Alleluia: Hebrews 1:1-2
R. Alleluia, alleluia.
¹ In the past God spoke to our ancestors
>>through the prophets:
² in these last days, he has spoken to us
>>through the Son.
R. Alleluia, alleluia.

Gospel: John 1:19-28
¹⁹This is the testimony of John. When the Jews from Jerusalem sent priests and Levites to him to ask him, "Who are you?" ²⁰ he admitted and did not deny it, but admitted, "I am not the Christ." ²¹So they asked him, "What are you then? Are you Elijah?" And he said, "I am not." "Are you the Prophet?" He answered, "No." ²²So they said to him, "Who are you, so we can give an answer to those who sent us? What do you have to say for yourself?" ²³He said: "I am *the voice of one crying out in the desert, 'Make straight the way of the Lord,'* as Isaiah the prophet said." ²⁴Some Pharisees were also sent. ²⁵They asked him, "Why then do you baptize if you are not the Christ or Elijah or the Prophet?" ²⁶John answered them, "I baptize with water; but there is one among you whom you do not recognize, ²⁷the one who is coming after me, whose sandal strap I am not worthy to untie." ²⁸This happened in Bethany across the Jordan, where John was baptizing.

Wednesday January 3, 2024

Wednesday of the Christmas Weekday
First Reading: 1 John 2:29-3:6
²⁹If you consider that God is righteous, you also know that everyone who acts in righteousness is begotten by him.

[1]See what love the Father has bestowed on us that we may be called the children of God. Yet so we are. The reason the world does not know us is that it did not know him. [2]Beloved, we are God's children now; what we shall be has not yet been revealed. We do know that when it is revealed we shall be like him, for we shall see him as he is. [3]Everyone who has this hope based on him makes himself pure, as he is pure.

[4]Everyone who commits sin commits lawlessness, for sin is lawlessness. [5]You know that he was revealed to take away sins, and in him there is no sin. [6]No one who remains in him sins; no one who sins has seen him or known him.

Responsorial Psalm: Psalms 98:1, 3CD-4,5-6

R. [3cd] *All the ends of the earth have seen the saving power of God.*

[1] Sing to the LORD a new song,
    for he has done wondrous deeds;
His right hand has won victory for him,
    his holy arm.
R. *All the ends of the earth have seen the saving power of God.*

[3CD] All the ends of the earth have seen
    the salvation by our God.
[4] Sing joyfully to the LORD, all you lands;
    break into song; sing praise.
R. *All the ends of the earth have seen the saving power of God.*

[5] Sing praise to the LORD with the harp,
    with the harp and melodious song.
[6] With trumpets and the sound of the horn
    sing joyfully before the King, the LORD.
R. *All the ends of the earth have seen the saving power of God.*

Alleluia: John 1:14A, 12A

R. Alleluia, alleluia.
[14A]The Word of God became flesh and dwelt
    among us.
[12A]To those who accepted him
he gave power to become the children of
    God.
R. Alleluia, alleluia.

Gospel: John 1:29-34

[29]John the Baptist saw Jesus coming toward him and said, "Behold, the Lamb of God, who takes away the sin of the world. [30]He is the one of whom I said, 'A man is coming after me who ranks ahead of me because he existed before me.' [31]I did not know him, but the reason why I came baptizing with water was that he might be made known to Israel." [32]John testified further, saying, "I saw the Spirit come down like a dove from the sky and remain upon him. [33]I did not know him, but the one who sent me to baptize with water told me, 'On whomever you see the Spirit come down and remain, he is the one who will baptize with the Holy Spirit.' [34]Now I have seen and testified that he is the Son of God."

Thursday January 4, 2024

Memorial of Saint Elizabeth Ann Seton, Religious

First Reading: 1 John 3:7-10

[7]Children, let no one deceive you. The person who acts in righteousness is righteous, just as he is righteous. [8]Whoever sins belongs to the Devil, because the Devil has sinned from the beginning. Indeed, the Son of God was revealed to destroy the works of the Devil. [9]No one who is begotten by God commits sin, because God's seed remains in him; he cannot sin because he is begotten by God. [10]In this way, the children of God and the children of the Devil are made plain; no one who fails to act in righteousness belongs to God, nor anyone who does not love his brother.

Responsorial Psalm: Psalms 98:1, 7-8, 9

R. [3cd] *All the ends of the earth have seen the saving power of God.*

[1] Sing to the LORD a new song,
    for he has done wondrous deeds;
His right hand has won victory for him,
    his holy arm.
R. *All the ends of the earth have seen the saving power of God.*

[7] Let the sea and what fills it resound,
    the world and those who dwell in it;
[8] Let the rivers clap their hands,
    the mountains shout with them for joy
        before the LORD.
R. *All the ends of the earth have seen the saving power of God.*

[9] The LORD comes;
    he comes to rule the earth;
He will rule the world with justice
    and the peoples with equity.

R. *All the ends of the earth have seen the saving power of God.*

Alleluia: Hebrews 1:1-2

R. Alleluia, alleluia.

[1] In the past God spoke to our ancestors
   through the prophets:
[2] in these last days, he has spoken to us
   through the Son.

R. Alleluia, alleluia.

Gospel: John 1:35-42

[35]John was standing with two of his disciples, [36]and as he watched Jesus walk by, he said, "Behold, the Lamb of God." [37]The two disciples heard what he said and followed Jesus. [38]Jesus turned and saw them following him and said to them, "What are you looking for?" They said to him, "Rabbi" (which translated means Teacher), "where are you staying?" [39]He said to them, "Come, and you will see." So they went and saw where he was staying, and they stayed with him that day. It was about four in the afternoon. [40]Andrew, the brother of Simon Peter, was one of the two who heard John and followed Jesus. [41]He first found his own brother Simon and told him, "We have found the Messiah," which is translated Christ. [42]Then he brought him to Jesus. Jesus looked at him and said, "You are Simon the son of John; you will be called Cephas," which is translated Peter.

Friday January 5, 2024

Memorial of Saint John Neumann, Bishop

First Reading: 1 John 3:11-21

Beloved: [11]This is the message you have heard from the beginning: we should love one another, [12]unlike Cain who belonged to the Evil One and slaughtered his brother. Why did he slaughter him? Because his own works were evil, and those of his brother righteous. [13]Do not be amazed, then, brothers and sisters, if the world hates you. [14]We know that we have passed from death to life because we love our brothers. Whoever does not love remains in death. [15]Everyone who hates his brother is a murderer, and you know that no murderer has eternal life remaining in him. [16]The way we came to know love was that he laid down his life for us; so we ought to lay down our lives for our brothers. [17]If someone who has worldly means sees a brother in need and refuses him compassion, how can the love of God remain in him? [18]Children, let us love not in word or speech but indeed and truth.

[19]Now this is how we shall know that we belong to the truth and reassure our hearts before him [20]in whatever our hearts condemn, for God is greater than our hearts and knows everything. [21]Beloved, if our hearts do not condemn us, we have confidence in God.

Responsorial Psalm: Psalms 100:1B-2, 3, 4, 5

R. *(2a)* **Let all the earth cry out to God with joy.**

[1B] Sing joyfully to the LORD, all you lands;
   [2]serve the LORD with gladness;
   come before him with joyful song.

R. **Let all the earth cry out to God with joy.**

[3] Know that the LORD is God;
   he made us, his we are;
   his people, the flock he tends.

R. **Let all the earth cry out to God with joy.**

[4] Enter his gates with thanksgiving,
   his courts with praise;
Give thanks to him; bless his name.

R. **Let all the earth cry out to God with joy.**

[5] The LORD is good:
   the LORD, whose kindness endures
      forever,
   and his faithfulness, to all generations.

R. **Let all the earth cry out to God with joy.**

Alleluia

R. **Alleluia, alleluia.**

A holy day has dawned upon us.

Come, you nations, and adore the Lord.

Today a great light has come upon the earth.

R. **Alleluia, alleluia.**

Gospel: John 1:43-51

[43]Jesus decided to go to Galilee, and he found Philip. And Jesus said to him, "Follow me." [44]Now Philip was from Bethsaida, the town of Andrew and Peter. [45] Philip found Nathanael and told him, "We have found the one about whom Moses wrote in the law, and also the prophets, Jesus, son of Joseph, from Nazareth." [46] But Nathanael said to him, "Can anything good come from Nazareth?" Philip said to him, "Come and see." [47]Jesus saw Nathanael coming toward him and said of him, "Here is a true child of Israel. There is no duplicity in him." [48]Nathanael said to him, "How do you know me?" Jesus answered and said to him, "Before Philip called you, I saw you under the fig tree." [49]Nathanael answered him, "Rabbi, you are the Son of God; you are the King of Israel." [50]Jesus answered and said to him, "Do you believe because I told you that I saw you under the fig tree? You will see greater things than this." [51]And he said to him, "Amen, amen, I say to you, you will see the sky opened and the angels of God ascending and descending on the Son of Man."

Memorial of Saint Andre Bessette

First Reading: 1 John 5:5-13

Beloved: [5]Who indeed is the victor over the world but the one who believes that Jesus is the Son of God?

[6]This is the one who came through water and Blood, Jesus Christ, not by water alone, but by water and Blood. [7]The Spirit is the one who testifies, and the Spirit is truth. So there are three that testify, [8]the Spirit, the water, and the Blood, and the three are of one accord. [9]If we accept human testimony, the testimony of God is surely greater. Now the testimony of God is this, that he has testified on behalf of his Son. [10]Whoever believes in the Son of God has this testimony within himself. Whoever does not believe God has made him a liar by not believing the testimony God has given about his Son. [11]And this is the testimony: God gave us eternal life, and this life is in his Son. [12] Whoever possesses the Son has life; whoever does not possess the Son of God does not have life.

[13]I write these things to you so that you may know that you have eternal life, you who believe in the name of the Son of God.

Responsorial Psalm: Psalms 147:12-13, 14-15, 19-20

R. [12a] *Praise the Lord, Jerusalem. or: R. Alleluia.*

[12] Glorify the LORD, O Jerusalem;
    praise your God, O Zion.
[13] For he has strengthened the bars of your
        gates;
    he has blessed your children within you.
R. *Praise the Lord, Jerusalem. or: R. Alleluia.*

[14] He has granted peace in your borders;
    with the best of wheat he fills you.
[15] He sends forth his command to the earth;
    swiftly runs his word!
R. *Praise the Lord, Jerusalem. or: R. Alleluia.*

[19] He has proclaimed his word to Jacob,
    his statutes and his ordinances to Israel.
[20] He has not done thus for any other nation;
        his ordinances he has not made known to
        them. Alleluia.
R. *Praise the Lord, Jerusalem. or: R. Alleluia.*

Alleluia: Mark 9:6

R. Alleluia, alleluia.

[6] The heavens were opened and the voice of
        the Father thundered:
This is my beloved Son. Listen to him.

R. Alleluia, alleluia.

Gospel: Mark 1:7-11

[7] This is what John the Baptist proclaimed: "One mightier than I is coming after me. I am not worthy to stoop and loosen the thongs of his sandals. [8] I have baptized you with water; he will baptize you with the Holy Spirit."

[9] It happened in those days that Jesus came from Nazareth of Galilee and was baptized in the Jordan by John. [10] On coming up out of the water he saw the heavens being torn open and the Spirit, like a dove, descending upon him. [11] And a voice came from the heavens, "You are my beloved Son; with you I am well pleased."

or Luke 3:23-38

[23] When Jesus began his ministry he was about thirty years of age. He was the son, as was thought, of Joseph, the son of Heli, [24] the son of Matthat, the son of Levi, the son of Melchi, the son of Jannai, the son of Joseph, [25] the son of Mattathias, the son of Amos, the son of Nahum, the son of Esli, the son of Naggai, [26] the son of Maath, the son of Mattathias, the son of Semein, the son of Josech, the son of Joda, [27] the son of Joanan, the son of Rhesa, the son of Zerubbabel, the son of Shealtiel, the son of Neri, [28] the son of Melchi, the son of Addi, the son of Cosam, the son of Elmadam, the son of Er, [29] the son of Joshua, the son of Eliezer, the son of Jorim, the son of Matthat, the son of Levi, [30] the son of Simeon, the son of Judah, the son of Joseph, the son of Jonam, the son of Eliakim, [31] the son of Melea, the son of Menna, the son of Mattatha, the son of Nathan, the son of David, [32] the son of Jesse, the son of Obed, the son of Boaz, the son of Sala, the son of Nahshon, [33] the son of Amminadab, the son of Admin, the son of Arni, the son of Hezron, the son of Perez, the son of Judah, [34] the son of Jacob, the son of Isaac, the son of Abraham, the son of Terah, the son of Nahor, [35] the son of Serug, the son of Reu, the son of Peleg, the son of Eber, the son of Shelah, [36] the son of Cainan, the son of Arphaxad, the son of Shem, the son of Noah, the son of Lamech, [37] the son of Methuselah, the son of Enoch, the son of Jared, the son of Mahalaleel, the son of Cainan, [38] the son of Enos, the son of Seth, the son of Adam, the son of God.

OR Luke 3:23, 31-34, 36, 38

[23] When Jesus began his ministry he was about thirty years of age. He was the son, as was thought, of Joseph, the son of Heli, [31] the son of Melea, the son of Menna, the son of Mattatha, the son of Nathan, the son of David, [32] the son of Jesse, the son of Obed, the son of Boaz, the son of Sala, the son of Nahshon, [33] the son of Amminadab, the son of Admin, the son of Arni, the son of Hezron, the son of Perez, the son of Judah, [34] the son of

Jacob, the son of Isaac, the son of Abraham, the son of Terah, the son of Nahor, [36]the son of Cainan, the son of Arphaxad, the son of Shem, the son of Noah, the son of Lamech, [38]the son of Enos, the son of Seth, the son of Adam, the son of God.

Sunday January 7 2024

Solemnity of the Epiphany of the Lord

First Reading: Isaiah 60:1-6

[1]Rise up in splendor, Jerusalem! Your light
       has come,
    the glory of the Lord shines upon you.
[2]See, darkness covers the earth,
     and thick clouds cover the peoples;
but upon you the LORD shines,
    and over you appears his glory.
[3] Nations shall walk by your light,
    and kings by your shining radiance.
[4]Raise your eyes and look about;
     they all gather and come to you:
your sons come from afar,
    and your daughters in the arms of their
       nurses.

[5] Then you shall be radiant at what you see,
    your heart shall throb and overflow,
for the riches of the sea shall be emptied out
      before you,
    the wealth of nations shall be brought to
      you.
[6]Caravans of camels shall fill you,
    dromedaries from Midian and Ephah;
all from Sheba shall come
    bearing gold and frankincense,
    and proclaiming the praises of the LORD.

Responsorial Psalm: Psalms 72:1-2, 7-8, 10-11, 12-13.

R. (cf. 11) *Lord, every nation on earth will adore you.*
[1] O God, with your judgment endow the king,
     and with your justice, the king's son;
[2] He shall govern your people with justice
     and your afflicted ones with judgment.
R. *Lord, every nation on earth will adore you.*
[7] Justice shall flower in his days,

and profound peace, till the moon be no
   more.
[8] May he rule from sea to sea,
      and from the River to the ends of the
      earth.
R. Lord, every nation on earth will adore you.

[10] The kings of Tarshish and the Isles shall
         offer gifts;
         the kings of Arabia and Seba shall bring
         tribute.
[11] All kings shall pay him homage,
      all nations shall serve him.
R. Lord, every nation on earth will adore you.

[12] For he shall rescue the poor when he cries
         out,
         and the afflicted when he has no one to
         help him.
[13] He shall have pity for the lowly and the
         poor;
         the lives of the poor he shall save.
R. Lord, every nation on earth will adore you.

Second Reading: Ephesians 3:2-3A, 5-6
Brothers and sisters: [2]You have heard of the stewardship of God's grace that was given to me for your benefit, [3A]namely, that the mystery was made known to me by revelation. [5]It was not made known to people in other generations as it has now been revealed to his holy apostles and prophets by the Spirit: [6]that the Gentiles are coheirs, members of the same body, and copartners in the promise in Christ Jesus through the gospel.

Alleluia: Matthew 2:2
R. Alleluia, alleluia.
[2]We saw his star at its rising
and have come to do him homage.
R. Alleluia, alleluia.

Gospel: Matthew 2:1-12
[1]When Jesus was born in Bethlehem of Judea, in the days of King Herod, behold, magi from the east arrived in Jerusalem, [2]saying, "Where is the newborn king of the Jews? We saw his star at its rising and have come to do him homage." [3]When King Herod heard this,

he was greatly troubled, and all Jerusalem with him. ⁴Assembling all the chief priests and the scribes of the people, He inquired of them where the Christ was to be born. ⁵They said to him, "In Bethlehem of Judea, for thus it has been written through the prophet:

⁶*And you, Bethlehem, land of Judah,*
are by no means least among the rulers of
Judah;
since from you shall come a ruler,
who is to shepherd my people Israel."

⁷Then Herod called the magi secretly and ascertained from them the time of the star's appearance. ⁸He sent them to Bethlehem and said, "Go and search diligently for the child. When you have found him, bring me word, that I too may go and do him homage." ⁹After their audience with the king they set out. And behold, the star that they had seen at its rising preceded them, until it came and stopped over the place where the child was. ¹⁰They were overjoyed at seeing the star, ¹¹and on entering the house they saw the child with Mary his mother. They prostrated themselves and did him homage. Then they opened their treasures and offered him gifts of gold, frankincense, and myrrh. ¹²And having been warned in a dream not to return to Herod, they departed for their country by another way.

Monday January 8, 2024
Feast of the Baptism of the Lord

First Reading: Isaiah 42:1-4, 6-7

Thus says the LORD:
¹Here is my servant whom I uphold,
my chosen one with whom I am
pleased,
upon whom I have put my spirit;
he shall bring forth justice to the
nations,
²not crying out, not shouting,
not making his voice heard in the
street.
³A bruised reed he shall not break,
and a smoldering wick he shall not
quench,
⁴until he establishes justice on the earth;
the coastlands will wait for his
teaching.

⁶I, the LORD, have called you for the
victory of justice,

I have grasped you by the hand;
I formed you, and set you
    as a covenant of the people,
    a light for the nations,
[7]to open the eyes of the blind,
    to bring out prisoners from
        confinement,
    and from the dungeon, those who
        live in darkness.

Or Isaiah 55:1-11

Thus says the LORD:
[1]All you who are thirsty,
    come to the water!
You who have no money,
    come, receive grain and eat;
come, without paying and without cost,
    drink wine and milk!
[2]Why spend your money for what is not
        bread,
    your wages for what fails to satisfy?
Heed me, and you shall eat well,
    you shall delight in rich fare.
[3]Come to me heedfully,
    listen, that you may have life.
I will renew with you the everlasting
        covenant,
    the benefits assured to David.
[4]As I made him a witness to the peoples,
    a leader and commander of nations,
[5]so shall you summon a nation you knew
        not,
    and nations that knew you not shall
        run to you,
because of the LORD, your God,
    the Holy One of Israel, who has
        glorified you.

[6] Seek the LORD while he may be found,
    call him while he is near.[7]
Let the scoundrel forsake his way,
    and the wicked man his thoughts;

let him turn to the LORD for mercy;
to our God, who is generous in
forgiving.
[8]For my thoughts are not your thoughts,
nor are your ways my ways, says the
LORD.
[9]As high as the heavens are above the
earth
so high are my ways above your
ways
and my thoughts above your
thoughts.

[10] For just as from the heavens
the rain and snow come down
and do not return there
till they have watered the earth,
making it fertile and fruitful,
giving seed to the one who sows
and bread to the one who eats,
[11]so shall my word be
that goes forth from my mouth;
my word shall not return to me void,
but shall do my will,
achieving the end for which I sent it.

Responsorial Psalm: Psalms 29:1-2, 3-4, 3, 9-10.

R. [(11b)] **The Lord will bless his people with peace.**
[1] Give to the LORD, you sons of God,
give to the LORD glory and praise,
[2] Give to the LORD the glory due his name;
adore the LORD in holy attire.
R. **The Lord will bless his people with peace.**

[3AC] The voice of the LORD is over the waters,
the LORD, over vast waters.
[4] The voice of the LORD is mighty;
the voice of the LORD is majestic.
R. **The Lord will bless his people with peace.**

[3B] The God of glory thunders,
[9C] and in his temple all say, "Glory!"

[10] The LORD is enthroned above the flood;
  the LORD is enthroned as king forever.
R. The Lord will bless his people with peace.

Or Isaiah 12:2-3, 4BCD, 5-6

R. *[3] You will draw water joyfully from the*
    springs of salvation.

[2] God indeed is my savior;
  I am confident and unafraid.
My strength and my courage is the LORD,
  and he has been my savior.
[3] With joy you will draw water
  at the fountain of salvation.
R. You will draw water joyfully from the
  springs of salvation.

[4BCD] Give thanks to the LORD, acclaim his
    name;
  among the nations make known his deeds,
  proclaim how exalted is his name.
R. You will draw water joyfully from the
  springs of salvation.

[5] Sing praise to the LORD for his glorious
    achievement;
  let this be known throughout all the earth.
[6] Shout with exultation, O city of Zion,
  for great in your midst
  is the Holy One of Israel!
R. You will draw water joyfully from the
  springs of salvation.

Second Reading: Acts 10:34-38

[34]Peter proceeded to speak to those gathered in the house of Cornelius, saying: "In truth, I see that God shows no partiality. [35]Rather, in every nation whoever fears him and acts uprightly is acceptable to him. [36]You know the word that he sent to the Israelites as he proclaimed peace through Jesus Christ, who is Lord of all, [37]what has happened all over Judea, beginning in Galilee after the baptism that John preached, [38]how God anointed Jesus of Nazareth with the Holy Spirit and power. He went about doing good and healing all those oppressed by the devil, for God was with him."

Or 1 John 5:1-9

Beloved:

[1]Everyone who believes that Jesus is the Christ is begotten by God, and everyone who loves the Father loves also the one begotten by him. [2]In this way we know that we love the children of God when we love God and obey his commandments. [3]For the love of God is this, that we keep his commandments. And his commandments are not burdensome, [4]for whoever is begotten by God conquers the world. And the victory that conquers the world is our faith. [5]Who indeed is the victor over the world but the one who believes that Jesus is the Son of God?

[6]This is the one who came through water and blood, Jesus Christ, not by water alone, but by water and blood. [7]The Spirit is the one who testifies, and the Spirit is truth. [8]So there are three that testify, the Spirit, the water, and the blood, and the three are of one accord. [9]If we accept human testimony, the testimony of God is surely greater. Now the testimony of God is this, that he has testified on behalf of his Son.

Alleluia: cf. John 1:29

R. Alleluia, alleluia.

[29]John saw Jesus approaching him, and said: Behold the Lamb of God who takes away the sin of

the world.

R. Alleluia, alleluia.

Gospel: Mark 1:7-11

[7]This is what John the Baptist proclaimed: "One mightier than I is coming after me. I am not worthy to stoop and loosen the thongs of his sandals. [8] I have baptized you with water; he will baptize you with the Holy Spirit."

[9]It happened in those days that Jesus came from Nazareth of Galilee and was baptized in the Jordan by John. [10]On coming up out of the water he saw the heavens being torn open and the Spirit, like a dove, descending upon him. [11]And a voice came from the heavens, "You are my beloved Son; with you I am well pleased."

Tuesday January 9, 2024

Tuesday of the First Week in Ordinary Time
First Reading: 1 Samuel 1:9-20

[9] Hannah rose after a meal at Shiloh, and presented herself before the LORD; at the time, Eli the priest was sitting on a chair near the doorpost of the LORD's temple. [10] In her bitterness she prayed to the LORD, weeping copiously, [11] and she made a vow, promising: "O LORD of hosts, if you look with pity on the misery of your handmaid, if you remember me and do not forget me, if you give your handmaid a male child, I will give him to the LORD for as long as he lives; neither wine nor liquor shall he drink, and no razor shall ever touch his head." [12] As she remained long at prayer before the LORD, Eli watched her mouth, [13] for Hannah was praying silently; though her lips were moving, her voice could

not be heard. Eli, thinking her drunk, [14] said to her, "How long will you make a drunken show of yourself? Sober up from your wine!" [15] "It isn't that, my lord," Hannah answered. "I am an unhappy woman. I have had neither wine nor liquor; I was only pouring out my troubles to the LORD. [16] Do not think your handmaid a ne'er-do-well; my prayer has been prompted by my deep sorrow and misery." [17] Eli said, "Go in peace, and may the God of Israel grant you what you have asked of him." [18] She replied, "Think kindly of your maidservant," and left. She went to her quarters, ate and drank with her husband, and no longer appeared downcast. [19] Early the next morning they worshiped before the LORD, and then returned to their home in Ramah.

When Elkanah had relations with his wife Hannah, the LORD remembered her. [20] She conceived, and at the end of her term bore a son whom she called Samuel, since she had asked the LORD for him.

Responsorial Psalm: 1 Samuel 2:1, 4-5, 6-7, 8ABCD

R. *(See 1)* **My heart exults in the Lord, my Savior.**

[1] "My heart exults in the LORD,
    my horn is exalted in my God.
I have swallowed up my enemies;
    I rejoice in my victory."
R. **My heart exults in the Lord, my Savior.**

[4] "The bows of the mighty are broken,
    while the tottering gird on strength.
[5] The well-fed hire themselves out for bread,
    while the hungry batten on spoil.
The barren wife bears seven sons,
    while the mother of many languishes."
R. **My heart exults in the Lord, my Savior.**

[6] "The LORD puts to death and gives life;
    he casts down to the nether world;
    he raises up again.
[7] The LORD makes poor and makes rich;
    he humbles, he also exalts."
R. **My heart exults in the Lord, my Savior.**

[8] "He raises the needy from the dust;
    from the dung heap he lifts up the poor,
To seat them with nobles
    and make a glorious throne their
        heritage."
R. **My heart exults in the Lord, my Savior.**

Alleluia: 1 Thessalonians 2:13

R. Alleluia, alleluia.

[13] Receive the word of God, not as the word of
men,
but as it truly is, the word of God.

R. Alleluia, alleluia.

Gospel: Mark 1:21-28

[21] Jesus came to Capernaum with his followers, and on the sabbath he entered the synagogue and taught. [22] The people were astonished at his teaching, for he taught them as one having authority and not as the scribes. [23] In their synagogue was a man with an unclean spirit; [24] he cried out, "What have you to do with us, Jesus of Nazareth? Have you come to destroy us? I know who you are the Holy One of God!" [25] Jesus rebuked him and said, "Quiet! Come out of him!" [26] The unclean spirit convulsed him and with a loud cry came out of him. [27] All were amazed and asked one another, "What is this? A new teaching with authority. He commands even the unclean spirits and they obey him." [28] His fame spread everywhere throughout the whole region of Galilee.

Wednesday January 10, 2024

Wednesday of the First Week in Ordinary Time
First Reading: 1 Samuel 3:1-10, 19-20

[1] During the time young Samuel was minister to the LORD under Eli, a revelation of the LORD was uncommon and vision infrequent. [2] One day Eli was asleep in his usual place. His eyes had lately grown so weak that he could not see. [3] The lamp of God was not yet extinguished, and Samuel was sleeping in the temple of the LORD where the ark of God was. [4] The LORD called to Samuel, who answered, "Here I am."

[5] Samuel ran to Eli and said, "Here I am. You called me." "I did not call you," Eli said. "Go back to sleep." So he went back to sleep. [6] Again the LORD called Samuel, who rose and went to Eli. "Here I am," he said. "You called me." But Eli answered, "I did not call you, my son. Go back to sleep." [7] At that time Samuel was not familiar with the LORD, because the LORD had not revealed anything to him as yet. [8] The LORD called Samuel again, for the third time. Getting up and going to Eli, he said, "Here I am. You called me." Then Eli understood that the LORD was calling the youth. [9] So Eli said to Samuel, "Go to sleep, and if you are called, reply, 'Speak, LORD, for your servant is listening.'" When Samuel went to sleep in his place, [10] the LORD came and revealed his presence, calling out as before, "Samuel, Samuel!" Samuel answered, "Speak, for your servant is listening."

[19] Samuel grew up, and the LORD was with him, not permitting any word of his to be without effect. [20] Thus all Israel from Dan to Beersheba came to know that Samuel was an accredited prophet of the LORD.

Responsorial Psalm: Psalms 40:2 AND 5, 7-8A, 8B-9, 10

R. [8a and 9a] **Here am I, Lord; I come to do your will.**

[2] I have waited, waited for the LORD,
    and he stooped toward me and heard my
        cry.
[5] Blessed the man who makes the LORD his
        trust;
    who turns not to idolatry
    or to those who stray after falsehood.
R. Here am I, Lord; I come to do your will.

[7] Sacrifice or oblation you wished not,
    but ears open to obedience you gave me.
Burnt offerings or sin-offerings you sought
        not;
    [8A] then said I, "Behold I come."
R. Here am I, Lord; I come to do your will.

[8B] "In the written scroll it is prescribed for me.
[9] To do your will, O my God, is my delight,
    and your law is within my heart!"
R. Here am I, Lord; I come to do your will.

[10] I announced your justice in the vast
        assembly;
    I did not restrain my lips, as you, O LORD,
        know.
R. Here am I, Lord; I come to do your will.

Alleluia: John 10:27

R. Alleluia, alleluia.
[27] My sheep hear my voice, says the Lord.
I know them, and they follow me.
R. Alleluia, alleluia.

Gospel: Mark 1:29-39

[29] On leaving the synagogue Jesus entered the house of Simon and Andrew with James and John. [30] Simon's mother-in-law lay sick with a fever. They immediately told him about her. [31] He approached, grasped her hand, and helped her up. Then the fever left her and she waited on them.

[32] When it was evening, after sunset, they brought to him all who were ill or possessed by demons. [33] The whole town was gathered at the door. [34] He cured many

who were sick with various diseases, and he drove out many demons, not permitting them to speak because they knew him.

³⁵Rising very early before dawn, he left and went off to a deserted place, where he prayed. ³⁶ Simon and those who were with him pursued him ³⁷ and on finding him said, "Everyone is looking for you." ³⁸ He told them, "Let us go on to the nearby villages that I may preach there also. For this purpose have I come." ³⁹ So he went into their synagogues, preaching and driving out demons throughout the whole of Galilee.

Thursday of the First Week in Ordinary Time
First Reading: 1 Samuel 4:1-11

¹The Philistines gathered for an attack on Israel. Israel went out to engage them in battle and camped at Ebenezer, while the Philistines camped at Aphek. ²The Philistines then drew up in battle formation against Israel. After a fierce struggle Israel was defeated by the Philistines, who slew about four thousand men on the battlefield. ³ When the troops retired to the camp, the elders of Israel said, "Why has the LORD permitted us to be defeated today by the Philistines? Let us fetch the ark of the LORD from Shiloh that it may go into battle among us and save us from the grasp of our enemies."

⁴So the people sent to Shiloh and brought from there the ark of the LORD of hosts, who is enthroned upon the cherubim. The two sons of Eli, Hophni and Phinehas, were with the ark of God. ⁵ When the ark of the LORD arrived in the camp, all Israel shouted so loudly that the earth resounded. ⁶ The Philistines, hearing the noise of shouting, asked, "What can this loud shouting in the camp of the Hebrews mean?" On learning that the ark of the LORD had come into the camp, ⁷ the Philistines were frightened. They said, "Gods have come to their camp." They said also, "Woe to us! This has never happened before. ⁸ Woe to us! Who can deliver us from the power of these mighty gods? These are the gods that struck the Egyptians with various plagues and with pestilence. ⁹ Take courage and be manly, Philistines; otherwise you will become slaves to the Hebrews, as they were your slaves. So fight manfully!" ¹⁰ The Philistines fought and Israel was defeated; every man fled to his own tent. It was a disastrous defeat, in which Israel lost thirty thousand foot soldiers. ¹¹ The ark of God was captured, and Eli's two sons, Hophni and Phinehas, were among the dead.

Responsorial Psalm: Psalms 44:10-11, 14-15, 24-25
R. ⁽²⁷ᵇ⁾ *Redeem us, Lord, because of your mercy.*
¹⁰ Yet now you have cast us off and put us in
        disgrace,
        and you go not forth with our armies.
¹¹ You have let us be driven back by our foes;
        those who hated us plundered us at will.
R. *Redeem us, Lord, because of your mercy.*

¹⁴ You made us the reproach of our neighbors,

the mockery and the scorn of those
around us.
[15] You made us a byword among the nations,
a laughingstock among the peoples
R. Redeem us, Lord, because of your mercy.

[24] Why do you hide your face,
forgetting our woe and our oppression?
[25] For our souls are bowed down to the dust,
our bodies are pressed to the earth.
R. Redeem us, Lord, because of your mercy.

Alleluia: Matthew 4:23
R. Alleluia, alleluia.
[23] Jesus preached the Gospel of the Kingdom and cured every disease among the people.
R. Alleluia, alleluia.

Gospel: Mark 1:40-45
[40]A leper came to him and kneeling down begged him and said, "If you wish, you can make me clean." [41] Moved with pity, he stretched out his hand, touched the leper, and said to him, "I do will it. Be made clean." [42] The leprosy left him immediately, and he was made clean. [43] Then, warning him sternly, he dismissed him at once. [44] Then he said to him, "See that you tell no one anything, but go, show yourself to the priest and offer for your cleansing what Moses prescribed; that will be proof for them." [45] The man went away and began to publicize the whole matter. He spread the report abroad so that it was impossible for Jesus to enter a town openly. He remained outside in deserted places, and people kept coming to him from everywhere.

Friday January 12, 2024

Friday of the First Week in Ordinary Time
First Reading: 1 Samuel 8:4-7, 10-22A
[4]All the elders of Israel came in a body to Samuel at Ramah [5] and said to him, "Now that you are old, and your sons do not follow your example, appoint a king over us, as other nations have, to judge us."

[6]Samuel was displeased when they asked for a king to judge them. He prayed to the LORD, [7] however, who said in answer: "Grant the people's every request. It is not you they reject, they are rejecting me as their king."

[10]Samuel delivered the message of the LORD in full to those who were asking him for a king. [11] He told them: "The rights of the king who will rule you will be as follows: He will take your sons and assign them to his chariots and horses, and they will run before his chariot. [12] He will also appoint from among them his commanders of groups of a thousand and of a hundred soldiers. He will set them to do his plowing and his harvesting, and to

make his implements of war and the equipment of his chariots. [13] He will use your daughters as ointment makers, as cooks, and as bakers. [14] He will take the best of your fields, vineyards, and olive groves, and give them to his officials. [15] He will tithe your crops and your vineyards, and give the revenue to his eunuchs and his slaves. [16] He will take your male and female servants, as well as your best oxen and your asses, and use them to do his work. [17] He will tithe your flocks and you yourselves will become his slaves. [18] When this takes place, you will complain against the king whom you have chosen, but on that day the LORD will not answer you."

[19]The people, however, refused to listen to Samuel's warning and said, "Not so! There must be a king over us. [20] We too must be like other nations, with a king to rule us and to lead us in warfare and fight our battles." [21] When Samuel had listened to all the people had to say, he repeated it to the LORD, who then said to him, [22] "Grant their request and appoint a king to rule them."

Responsorial Psalm: Psalms 89:16-17, 18-19
R. [(2)] *For ever I will sing the goodness of the Lord.*
[16] Blessed the people who know the joyful
        shout;
            in the light of your countenance, O LORD,
                they walk.
[17] At your name they rejoice all the day,
        and through your justice they are exalted.
R. *For ever I will sing the goodness of the Lord.*

[18] For you are the splendor of their strength,
        and by your favor our horn is exalted.
[19] For to the LORD belongs our shield,
        and to the Holy One of Israel, our King.
R. *For ever I will sing the goodness of the Lord.*

Alleluia: Luke 7:16
R. Alleluia, alleluia.
[16] A great prophet has arisen in our midst and God has visited his people.
R. Alleluia, alleluia.

Gospel: Mark 2:1-12
[1]When Jesus returned to Capernaum after some days, it became known that he was at home. [2] Many gathered together so that there was no longer room for them, not even around the door, and he preached the word to them. [3] They came bringing to him a paralytic carried by four men. [4] Unable to get near Jesus because of the crowd, they opened up the roof above him. After they had broken through, they let down the mat on which the paralytic was lying. [5] When Jesus saw their faith, he said to him, "Child, your

sins are forgiven." [6] Now some of the scribes were sitting there asking themselves, [7] "Why does this man speak that way? He is blaspheming. Who but God alone can forgive sins?" [8] Jesus immediately knew in his mind what they were thinking to themselves, so he said, "Why are you thinking such things in your hearts? [9] Which is easier, to say to the paralytic, 'Your sins are forgiven,' or to say, 'Rise, pick up your mat and walk'? [10] But that you may know that the Son of Man has authority to forgive sins on earth" [11] —he said to the paralytic, "I say to you, rise, pick up your mat, and go home." [12] He rose, picked up his mat at once, and went away in the sight of everyone. They were all astounded and glorified God, saying, "We have never seen anything like this."

Saturday January 13, 2024

Saturday of the First Week in Ordinary Time
First Reading: 1 Samuel 9:1-4, 17-19; 10:1

[1] There was a stalwart man from Benjamin named Kish, who was the son of Abiel, son of Zeror, son of Becorath, son of Aphiah, a Benjaminite. [2] He had a son named Saul, who was a handsome young man. There was no other child of Israel more handsome than Saul; he stood head and shoulders above the people.

[3] Now the asses of Saul's father, Kish, had wandered off. Kish said to his son Saul, "Take one of the servants with you and go out and hunt for the asses." [4] Accordingly they went through the hill country of Ephraim, and through the land of Shalishah. Not finding them there, they continued through the land of Shaalim without success. They also went through the land of Benjamin, but they failed to find the animals.

[17] When Samuel caught sight of Saul, the LORD assured him, "This is the man of whom I told you; he is to govern my people."

[18] Saul met Samuel in the gateway and said, "Please tell me where the seer lives." [19] Samuel answered Saul: "I am the seer. Go up ahead of me to the high place and eat with me today. In the morning, before dismissing you, I will tell you whatever you wish."

[1] Then, from a flask he had with him, Samuel poured oil on Saul's head; he also kissed him, saying: "The LORD anoints you commander over his heritage. You are to govern the LORD's people Israel, and to save them from the grasp of their enemies roundabout.

"This will be the sign for you that the LORD has anointed you commander over his heritage."

Responsorial Psalm: Psalms 21:2-3, 4-5, 6-7

R. [2a] **Lord, in your strength the king is glad.**

[2] O LORD, in your strength the king is glad;
    in your victory how greatly he rejoices!
[3] You have granted him his heart's desire;
    you refused not the wish of his lips.
R. **Lord, in your strength the king is glad.**

[4] For you welcomed him with goodly
    blessings,

27

you placed on his head a crown of pure
   gold.
[5] He asked life of you: you gave him
   length of days forever and ever.
R. Lord, in your strength the king is glad.

[6] Great is his glory in your victory;
   majesty and splendor you conferred
      upon him.
[7] For you made him a blessing forever;
   you gladdened him with the joy of your
      face.
R. Lord, in your strength the king is glad.

Alleluia: Luke 4:18
R. Alleluia, alleluia.
[18]The Lord sent me to bring glad tidings to the
      poor
and to proclaim liberty to captives.
R. Alleluia, alleluia.

Gospel: Mark 2:13-17
[13]Jesus went out along the sea. All the crowd came to him and he taught them. [14]As he passed by, he saw Levi, son of Alphaeus, sitting at the customs post. Jesus said to him, "Follow me." And he got up and followed Jesus. [15]While he was at table in his house, many tax collectors and sinners sat with Jesus and his disciples; for there were many who followed him. [16] Some scribes who were Pharisees saw that Jesus was eating with sinners and tax collectors and said to his disciples, "Why does he eat with tax collectors and sinners?" [17] Jesus heard this and said to them, "Those who are well do not need a physician, but the sick do. I did not come to call the righteous but sinners."

Sunday January 14, 2024

Second Sunday in Ordinary Time Year B
First Reading: 1 Samuel 3:3B-10, 19
[3B]Samuel was sleeping in the temple of the LORD where the ark of God was.[4]The LORD called to Samuel, who answered, "Here I am."[5]Samuel ran to Eli and said, "Here I am. You called me." "I did not call you," Eli said. "Go back to sleep." So he went back to sleep.[6]Again the LORD called Samuel, who rose and went to Eli. "Here I am, " he said. "You called me." But Eli answered, "I did not call you, my son. Go back to sleep."

   [7]At that time Samuel was not familiar with the LORD, because the LORD had not revealed anything to him as yet. [8]The LORD called Samuel again, for the third time. Getting up and going to Eli, he said, "Here I am. You called me." Then Eli understood that

the LORD was calling the youth.[9]So he said to Samuel, "Go to sleep, and if you are called, reply, Speak, LORD, for your servant is listening." When Samuel went to sleep in his place,[10]the LORD came and revealed his presence, calling out as before, "Samuel, Samuel!" Samuel answered, "Speak, for your servant is listening."

[19]Samuel grew up, and the LORD was with him, not permitting any word of his to be without effect.

Responsorial Psalm: Psalms 40:2, 4, 7-8, 8-9, 10

R. (8a and 9a) *Here am I, Lord; I come to do your will.*

[2] I have waited, waited for the LORD,
    and he stooped toward me and heard my
        cry.
[4AB] And he put a new song into my mouth,
    a hymn to our God.
R. *Here am I, Lord; I come to do your will.*

[7] Sacrifice or offering you wished not,
    but ears open to obedience you gave me.
Holocausts or sin-offerings you sought not;
    [8A] then said I, "Behold I come."
R. *Here I am, Lord; I come to do your will.*

[8B1] "In the written scroll it is prescribed for me,
    [9]to do your will, O my God, is my delight,
and your law is within my heart!"
R. *Here am I, Lord; I come to do your will.*
[10] I announced your justice in the vast
        assembly;
    I did not restrain my lips, as you, O LORD,
        know.
R. *Here am I, Lord; I come to do your will.*

Second Reading: 1 Corinthians 6:13C-15A, 17-20

Brothers and sisters: [13C]The body is not for immorality, but for the Lord, and the Lord is for the body; [14]God raised the Lord and will also raise us by his power.

[15A] Do you not know that your bodies are members of Christ? [17]But whoever is joined to the Lord becomes one Spirit with him.[18]Avoid immorality. Every other sin a person commits is outside the body, but the immoral person sins against his own body.[19]Do you not know that your body is a temple of the Holy Spirit within you, whom you have from God, and that you are not your own? [20]For you have been purchased at a price. Therefore glorify God in your body.

Alleluia: John 1:41, 17B
R. Alleluia, alleluia.
[41] We have found the Messiah:
[17B] Jesus Christ, who brings us truth and grace.
R. Alleluia, alleluia.

Gospel: John 1:35-42
[35]John was standing with two of his disciples,[36]and as he watched Jesus walk by, he said, "Behold, the Lamb of God." [37]The two disciples heard what he said and followed Jesus.[38]Jesus turned and saw them following him and said to them, "What are you looking for?" They said to him, "Rabbi" – which translated means Teacher, "where are you staying?" [39]He said to them, "Come, and you will see." So they went and saw where Jesus was staying, and they stayed with him that day. It was about four in the afternoon.[40]Andrew, the brother of Simon Peter, was one of the two who heard John and followed Jesus. [41]He first found his own brother Simon and told him, "We have found the Messiah" – which is translated Christ. [42]Then he brought him to Jesus. Jesus looked at him and said, "You are Simon the son of John; you will be called Cephas" – which is translated Peter.

Monday January 15, 2024

Monday of Second Week in Ordinary Time
First Reading: 1 Samuel 15:16-23
[16]Samuel said to Saul: "Stop! Let me tell you what the LORD said to me last night." Saul replied, "Speak!" [17]Samuel then said: "Though little in your own esteem, are you not leader of the tribes of Israel? The LORD anointed you king of Israel [18]and sent you on a mission, saying, 'Go and put the sinful Amalekites under a ban of destruction. Fight against them until you have exterminated them.' [19]Why then have you disobeyed the LORD? You have pounced on the spoil, thus displeasing the LORD." [20] Saul answered Samuel: "I did indeed obey the LORD and fulfill the mission on which the LORD sent me. I have brought back Agag, and I have destroyed Amalek under the ban. [21] But from the spoil the men took sheep and oxen, the best of what had been banned, to sacrifice to the LORD their God in Gilgal." [22]But Samuel said:

"Does the LORD so delight in burnt offerings
	and sacrifices
	as in obedience to the command of the
		LORD?
Obedience is better than sacrifice,
	and submission than the fat of rams.
[23]For a sin like divination is rebellion,
	and presumption is the crime of idolatry.
Because you have rejected the command of

the LORD,
    he, too, has rejected you as ruler."

Responsorial Psalm: Psalms 50:8-9, 16BC-17, 21 AND 23

R.[23b] *To the upright I will show the saving power
          of God.*

[8]"Not for your sacrifices do I rebuke you,
    for your burnt offerings are before me
        always.
[9]I take from your house no bullock,
    no goats out of your fold."

R. *To the upright I will show the saving power of
        God.*

[16BC]"Why do you recite my statutes,
    and profess my covenant with your
        mouth,
[17]Though you hate discipline
    and cast my words behind you?"

R. *To the upright I will show the saving power of
        God.*

[21]"When you do these things, shall I be deaf to
      it?
    Or do you think that I am like yourself?
    I will correct you by drawing them up
        before your eyes.
[23]He that offers praise as a sacrifice glorifies
      me;
    and to him that goes the right way I will
      show the salvation of God."

R. *To the upright I will show the saving power of
        God.*

Alleluia: Hebrews 4:12

R. Alleluia, alleluia.

[12]The word of God is living and effective,
able to discern reflections and thoughts of
        the heart.

R. Alleluia, alleluia.

Gospel: Mark 2:18-22

[18]The disciples of John and of the Pharisees were accustomed to fast. People came to Jesus and objected, "Why do the disciples of John and the disciples of the Pharisees fast, but your disciples do not fast?" [19]Jesus answered them, "Can the wedding guests fast

while the bridegroom is with them? As long as they have the bridegroom with them they cannot fast. [20]But the days will come when the bridegroom is taken away from them, and then they will fast on that day. [21]No one sews a piece of unshrunken cloth on an old cloak. If he does, its fullness pulls away, the new from the old, and the tear gets worse. [22]Likewise, no one pours new wine into old wineskins. Otherwise, the wine will burst the skins, and both the wine and the skins are ruined. Rather, new wine is poured into fresh wineskins."

Tuesday January 16, 2024

Tuesday of Second Week in Ordinary Time
First Reading: 1 Samuel 16:1-13

[1]The LORD said to Samuel: "How long will you grieve for Saul, whom I have rejected as king of Israel? Fill your horn with oil, and be on your way. I am sending you to Jesse of Bethlehem, for I have chosen my king from among his sons." [2]But Samuel replied: "How can I go? Saul will hear of it and kill me." To this the LORD answered: "Take a heifer along and say, 'I have come to sacrifice to the LORD.' [3]Invite Jesse to the sacrifice, and I myself will tell you what to do; you are to anoint for me the one I point out to you."

[4]Samuel did as the LORD had commanded him. When he entered Bethlehem, the elders of the city came trembling to meet him and inquired, "Is your visit peaceful, O seer?" [5]He replied: "Yes! I have come to sacrifice to the LORD. So cleanse yourselves and join me today for the banquet." He also had Jesse and his sons cleanse themselves and invited them to the sacrifice. [6]As they came, he looked at Eliab and thought, "Surely the LORD's anointed is here before him." [7]But the LORD said to Samuel: "Do not judge from his appearance or from his lofty stature, because I have rejected him. Not as man sees does God see, because he sees the appearance but the LORD looks into the heart." [8]Then Jesse called Abinadab and presented him before Samuel, who said, "The LORD has not chosen him." [9]Next Jesse presented Shammah, but Samuel said, "The LORD has not chosen this one either." [10]In the same way Jesse presented seven sons before Samuel, but Samuel said to Jesse, "The LORD has not chosen any one of these." [11]Then Samuel asked Jesse, "Are these all the sons you have?" Jesse replied, "There is still the youngest, who is tending the sheep." Samuel said to Jesse, "Send for him; we will not begin the sacrificial banquet until he arrives here." [12]Jesse sent and had the young man brought to them. He was ruddy, a youth handsome to behold and making a splendid appearance. The LORD said, "There—anoint him, for this is he!" [13]Then Samuel, with the horn of oil in hand, anointed him in the midst of his brothers; and from that day on, the Spirit of the LORD rushed upon David. When Samuel took his leave, he went to Ramah.

Responsorial Psalm: Psalms 89:20, 21-22, 27-28
R. [21a] *I have found David, my servant.*
[20]Once you spoke in a vision,
     and to your faithful ones you said:
"On a champion I have placed a crown;

over the people I have set a youth."
R. I have found David, my servant.

[21]"I have found David, my servant;
    with my holy oil I have anointed him,
[22]That my hand may be always with him,
    and that my arm may make him strong."
R. I have found David, my servant.

[27]"He shall say of me, 'You are my father,
    my God, the Rock, my savior.'
[28]And I will make him the first-born,
    highest of the kings of the earth."
R. I have found David, my servant.

Alleluia: Ephesians 1:17-18
R. Alleluia, alleluia.
[17]May the Father of our Lord Jesus Christ enlighten the eyes of our hearts,
that we may know what is the hope that belongs to our call.
R. Alleluia, alleluia.

Gospel: Mark 2:23-28
[23]As Jesus was passing through a field of grain on the sabbath, his disciples began to make a path while picking the heads of grain. [24]At this the Pharisees said to him, "Look, why are they doing what is unlawful on the sabbath?" [25]He said to them, "Have you never read what David did when he was in need and he and his companions were hungry? [26]How he went into the house of God when Abiathar was high priest and ate the bread of offering that only the priests could lawfully eat, and shared it with his companions?" [27]Then he said to them, "The sabbath was made for man, not man for the sabbath. [28]That is why the Son of Man is lord even of the sabbath."

Wednesday January 17, 2024

Memorial of Saint Anthony, Abbot
First Reading: 1 Samuel 17:32-33, 37, 40-51
[32]David spoke to Saul: "Let your majesty not lose courage. I am at your service to go and fight this Philistine." [33]But Saul answered David, "You cannot go up against this Philistine and fight with him, for you are only a youth, while he has been a warrior from his youth."

[37]David continued: "The LORD, who delivered me from the claws of the lion and the bear, will also keep me safe from the clutches of this Philistine." Saul answered David, "Go! the LORD will be with you."

[40]Then, staff in hand, David selected five smooth stones from the wadi and put them in the pocket of his shepherd's bag. [41]With his sling also ready to hand, he approached the Philistine.

With his shield bearer marching before him, the Philistine also advanced closer and closer to David. [42]When he had sized David up, and seen that he was youthful, and ruddy, and handsome in appearance, the Philistine held David in contempt. [43]The Philistine said to David, "Am I a dog that you come against me with a staff?" Then the Philistine cursed David by his gods [44]and said to him, "Come here to me, and I will leave your flesh for the birds of the air and the beasts of the field." [45]David answered him: "You come against me with sword and spear and scimitar, but I come against you in the name of the LORD of hosts, the God of the armies of Israel that you have insulted. [46]Today the LORD shall deliver you into my hand; I will strike you down and cut off your head. This very day I will leave your corpse and the corpses of the Philistine army for the birds of the air and the beasts of the field; thus the whole land shall learn that Israel has a God. [47]All this multitude, too, shall learn that it is not by sword or spear that the LORD saves. For the battle is the LORD's and he shall deliver you into our hands."

[48]The Philistine then moved to meet David at close quarters, while David ran quickly toward the battle line in the direction of the Philistine. [49]David put his hand into the bag and took out a stone, hurled it with the sling, and struck the Philistine on the forehead. The stone embedded itself in his brow, and he fell prostrate on the ground. [50]Thus David overcame the Philistine with sling and stone; he struck the Philistine mortally, and did it without a sword. [51]Then David ran and stood over him; with the Philistine's own sword which he drew from its sheath he dispatched him and cut off his head.

Responsorial Psalm: Psalms 144:1B, 2, 9-10

R. [(1)] *Blessed be the Lord, my Rock!*

[1B]Blessed be the LORD, my rock,
  who trains my hands for battle,
    my fingers for war.
R. *Blessed be the Lord, my Rock!*

[2]My refuge and my fortress,
  my stronghold, my deliverer,
My shield, in whom I trust,
  who subdues my people under me.
R. *Blessed be the Lord, my Rock!*

[9]O God, I will sing a new song to you;
  with a ten-stringed lyre I will chant your
    praise,
[10]You who give victory to kings,
  and deliver David, your servant from the

evil sword.
R. Blessed be the Lord, my Rock!

Alleluia: Matthew 4:23
R. Alleluia, alleluia.
[23]Jesus preached the Gospel of the Kingdom and cured every disease among the people.
R. Alleluia, alleluia.

Gospel: Mark 3:1-6
[1]Jesus entered the synagogue. There was a man there who had a withered hand. [2]They watched Jesus closely to see if he would cure him on the sabbath so that they might accuse him. [3]He said to the man with the withered hand, "Come up here before us." [4]Then he said to the Pharisees, "Is it lawful to do good on the sabbath rather than to do evil, to save life rather than to destroy it?" But they remained silent. [5]Looking around at them with anger and grieved at their hardness of heart, Jesus said to the man, "Stretch out your hand." He stretched it out and his hand was restored. [6] The Pharisees went out and immediately took counsel with the Herodians against him to put him to death.

Thursday January 18, 2024

Thursday of Second Week in Ordinary Time
First Reading: 1 Samuel 18:6-9; 19:1-7
[6]When David and Saul approached (on David's return after slaying the Philistine), women came out from each of the cities of Israel to meet King Saul, singing and dancing, with tambourines, joyful songs, and sistrums. [7]The women played and sang:
"Saul has slain his thousands, and David his ten thousands."
[8]Saul was very angry and resentful of the song, for he thought: "They give David ten thousands, but only thousands to me. All that remains for him is the kingship." [9]And from that day on, Saul was jealous of David.
[1]Saul discussed his intention of killing David with his son Jonathan and with all his servants. But Saul's son Jonathan, who was very fond of David, [2]told him: "My father Saul is trying to kill you. Therefore, please be on your guard tomorrow morning; get out of sight and remain in hiding. [3]I, however, will go out and stand beside my father in the countryside where you are, and will speak to him about you. If I learn anything, I will let you know."
[4]Jonathan then spoke well of David to his father Saul, saying to him: "Let not your majesty sin against his servant David, for he has committed no offense against you, but has helped you very much by his deeds. [5]When he took his life in his hands and slew the Philistine, and the LORD brought about a great victory for all Israel through him, you were glad to see it. Why, then, should you become guilty of shedding innocent blood by killing David without cause?" [6]Saul heeded Jonathan's plea and swore, "As the LORD lives, he shall not be killed." [7]So Jonathan summoned David and repeated the whole conversation to him. Jonathan then brought David to Saul, and David served him as before.

Responsorial Psalm: Psalms 56:2-3, 9-10A, 10B-11, 12-13

R. [5b] *In God I trust; I shall not fear.*

[2]Have mercy on me, O God, for men trample
        upon me;
    all the day they press their attack against me.
[3]My adversaries trample upon me all the day;
    yes, many fight against me.
R. In God I trust; I shall not fear.

[9]My wanderings you have counted;
        my tears are stored in your flask;
        are they not recorded in your book?
[10A]Then do my enemies turn back,
        when I call upon you.
R. In God I trust; I shall not fear.
[10B]Now I know that God is with me.
        [11]In God, in whose promise I glory,
        in God I trust without fear;
        what can flesh do against me?
R. In God I trust; I shall not fear.

[12]I am bound, O God, by vows to you;
        your thank offerings I will fulfill.
[13]For you have rescued me from death,
        my feet, too, from stumbling;
        that I may walk before God in the light of
            the living.
R. In God I trust; I shall not fear.

Alleluia: 2 Timothy 1:10

R. Alleluia, alleluia.
[10]Our Savior Jesus Christ has destroyed death and brought life to light through the Gospel.
R. Alleluia, alleluia.

Gospel: Mark 3:7-12

[7]Jesus withdrew toward the sea with his disciples. A large number of people followed from Galilee and from Judea. [8]Hearing what he was doing, a large number of people came to him also from Jerusalem, from Idumea, from beyond the Jordan, and from the neighborhood of Tyre and Sidon. [9]He told his disciples to have a boat ready for him because of the crowd, so that they would not crush him. [10]He had cured many and, as a result, those who had diseases were pressing upon him to touch him. [11]And whenever

unclean spirits saw him they would fall down before him and shout, "You are the Son of God." [12]He warned them sternly not to make him known.

Friday of Second Week in Ordinary Time
First Reading: 1 Samuel 24:3-21

[3]Saul took three thousand picked men from all Israel and went in search of David and his men in the direction of the wild goat crags. [4]When he came to the sheepfolds along the way, he found a cave, which he entered to relieve himself. David and his men were occupying the inmost recesses of the cave.

[5]David's servants said to him, "This is the day of which the LORD said to you, 'I will deliver your enemy into your grasp; do with him as you see fit.'" So David moved up and stealthily cut off an end of Saul's mantle. [6]Afterward, however, David regretted that he had cut off an end of Saul's mantle. [7]He said to his men, "The LORD forbid that I should do such a thing to my master, the LORD's anointed, as to lay a hand on him, for he is the LORD's anointed." [8]With these words David restrained his men and would not permit them to attack Saul. Saul then left the cave and went on his way. [9]David also stepped out of the cave, calling to Saul, "My lord the king!" When Saul looked back, David bowed to the ground in homage [10]and asked Saul: "Why do you listen to those who say, 'David is trying to harm you'? [11]You see for yourself today that the LORD just now delivered you into my grasp in the cave. I had some thought of killing you, but I took pity on you instead. I decided, 'I will not raise a hand against my lord, for he is the LORD's anointed and a father to me.' [12]Look here at this end of your mantle which I hold. Since I cut off an end of your mantle and did not kill you, see and be convinced that I plan no harm and no rebellion. I have done you no wrong, though you are hunting me down to take my life. [13]The LORD will judge between me and you, and the LORD will exact justice from you in my case. I shall not touch you. [14]The old proverb says, 'From the wicked comes forth wickedness.' So I will take no action against you. [15]Against whom are you on campaign, O king of Israel? Whom are you pursuing? A dead dog, or a single flea! [16]The LORD will be the judge; he will decide between me and you. May he see this, and take my part, and grant me justice beyond your reach!" [17]When David finished saying these things to Saul, Saul answered, "Is that your voice, my son David?" And Saul wept aloud. [18]Saul then said to David: "You are in the right rather than I; you have treated me generously, while I have done you harm. [19]Great is the generosity you showed me today, when the LORD delivered me into your grasp and you did not kill me. [20]For if a man meets his enemy, does he send him away unharmed? May the LORD reward you generously for what you have done this day. [21]And now, I know that you shall surely be king and that sovereignty over Israel shall come into your possession."

Responsorial Psalm: Psalms 57:2, 3-4, 6 AND 11
R. [(2a)] *Have mercy on me, God, have mercy.*
[2]Have mercy on me, O God; have mercy on
      me,
        for in you I take refuge.

In the shadow of your wings I take refuge,
    till harm pass by.
R. Have mercy on me, God, have mercy.

[3]I call to God the Most High,
    to God, my benefactor.
[4]May he send from heaven and save me;
    may he make those a reproach who
        trample upon me;
    may God send his mercy and his
        faithfulness.
R. Have mercy on me, God, have mercy.

[6]Be exalted above the heavens, O God;
    above all the earth be your glory!
[11]For your mercy towers to the heavens,
    and your faithfulness to the skies.
R. Have mercy on me, God, have mercy.

Alleluia: 2 Corinthians 5:19
R. Alleluia, alleluia.
[19]God was reconciling the world to himself in
        Christ,
and entrusting to us the message of
        reconciliation.
R. Alleluia, alleluia.

Gospel: Mark 3:13-19
[13]Jesus went up the mountain and summoned those whom he wanted and they came to him. [14]He appointed Twelve, whom he also named Apostles, that they might be with him and he might send them forth to preach [15]and to have authority to drive out demons: [16]He appointed the Twelve: Simon, whom he named Peter; [17]James, son of Zebedee, and John the brother of James, whom he named Boanerges, that is, sons of thunder; [18]Andrew, Philip, Bartholomew, Matthew, Thomas, James the son of Alphaeus; Thaddeus, Simon the Cananean, [19]and Judas Iscariot who betrayed him.

Saturday January 20, 2024
Saturday of Second Week in Ordinary Time
First Reading: 2 Samuel 1:1-4,11-12,19, 23-27
[1]David returned from his defeat of the Amalekites and spent two days in Ziklag. [2]On the third day a man came from Saul's camp, with his clothes torn and dirt on his head. Going to David, he fell to the ground in homage. [3]David asked him, "Where do you come from?"

He replied, "I have escaped from the camp of the children of Israel." [4]"Tell me what happened," David bade him. He answered that many of the soldiers had fled the battle and that many of them had fallen and were dead, among them Saul and his son Jonathan.

[11]David seized his garments and rent them, and all the men who were with him did likewise. [12]They mourned and wept and fasted until evening for Saul and his son Jonathan, and for the soldiers of the LORD of the clans of Israel, because they had fallen by the sword.

[19]"Alas! the glory of Israel, Saul,
      slain upon your heights;
how can the warriors have fallen!

[23]"Saul and Jonathan, beloved and cherished,
      separated neither in life nor in death,
      swifter than eagles, stronger than lions!
[24]Women of Israel, weep over Saul,
      who clothed you in scarlet and in finery,
      who decked your attire with ornaments
            of gold.

[25] "How can the warriors have fallen-
      in the thick of the battle,
      slain upon your heights!

[26]"I grieve for you, Jonathan my brother!
      most dear have you been to me;
      more precious have I held love for you
            than love for women.

[27]"How can the warriors have fallen,
      the weapons of war have perished!"

Responsorial Psalm: Psalms 80:2-3, 5-7
R. [(4b)]*Let us see your face, Lord, and we shall be
            saved.*
[2]O shepherd of Israel, hearken,
      O guide of the flock of Joseph!
From your throne upon the cherubim, shine
            forth
      [3]before Ephraim, Benjamin and Manasseh.
Rouse your power,
      and come to save us.

R. *Let us see your face, Lord, and we shall be saved.*

[5]O LORD of hosts, how long will you burn with
    anger
        while your people pray?
[6]You have fed them with the bread of tears
        and given them tears to drink in ample
        measure.
[7]You have left us to be fought over by our
        neighbors,
        and our enemies mock us.

R. *Let us see your face, Lord, and we shall be saved.*

Alleluia: cf. Acts 16:14B

R. Alleluia, alleluia.

[14B] Open our hearts, O Lord,
to listen to the words of your Son.

R. Alleluia, alleluia

Gospel: Mark 3:20-21

[20]Jesus came with his disciples into the house. Again the crowd gathered, making it impossible for them even to eat. [21]When his relatives heard of this they set out to seize him, for they said, "He is out of his mind."

Sunday January 21, 2024

Third Sunday in Ordinary Time, Year B

First Reading: Jonah 3:1-5, 10

[1]The word of the LORD came to Jonah, saying: [2]"Set out for the great city of Nineveh, and announce to it the message that I will tell you." [3]So Jonah made ready and went to Nineveh, according to the LORD'S bidding. Now Nineveh was an enormously large city; it took three days to go through it.[4]Jonah began his journey through the city, and had gone but a single day's walk announcing, "Forty days more and Nineveh shall be destroyed," [5]when the people of Nineveh believed God; they proclaimed a fast and all of them, great and small, put on sackcloth.

[10]When God saw by their actions how they turned from their evil way, he repented of the evil that he had threatened to do to them; he did not carry it out.

Responsorial Psalm: Psalms 25:4-5, 6-7, 8-9

R. [(4a)] *Teach me your ways, O Lord.*

[4] Your ways, O LORD, make known to me;

teach me your paths,
⁵ Guide me in your truth and teach me,
for you are God my savior.
R. Teach me your ways, O Lord.

⁶ Remember that your compassion, O LORD,
and your love are from of old.
⁷ In your kindness remember me,
because of your goodness, O LORD.
R. Teach me your ways, O Lord.

⁸ Good and upright is the LORD;
thus he shows sinners the way.
⁹ He guides the humble to justice
and teaches the humble his way.
R. Teach me your ways, O Lord.

Second Reading: 1 Corinthians 7:29-31

²⁹I tell you, brothers and sisters, the time is running out. From now on, let those having wives act as not having them, ³⁰those weeping as not weeping, those rejoicing as not rejoicing, those buying as not owning,³¹those using the world as not using it fully. For the world in its present form is passing away.

Alleluia: Mark 1:15

R. Alleluia, alleluia.
¹⁵The kingdom of God is at hand.
Repent and believe in the Gospel.
R. Alleluia, alleluia.

Gospel: Mark 1:14-20

¹⁴After John had been arrested, Jesus came to Galilee proclaiming the gospel of God: ¹⁵ "This is the time of fulfillment. The kingdom of God is at hand. Repent, and believe in the gospel."

¹⁶As he passed by the Sea of Galilee, he saw Simon and his brother Andrew casting their nets into the sea; they were fishermen. ¹⁷Jesus said to them, "Come after me, and I will make you fishers of men." ¹⁸Then they abandoned their nets and followed him. ¹⁹He walked along a little farther and saw James, the son of Zebedee, and his brother John. They too were in a boat mending their nets. ²⁰Then he called them. So they left their father Zebedee in the boat along with the hired men and followed him.

Monday of Third Week in Ordinary Time
First Reading: 2 Samuel 5:1-7, 10

[1]All the tribes of Israel came to David in Hebron and said: "Here we are, your bone and your flesh. [2]In days past, when Saul was our king, it was you who led the children of Israel out and brought them back. And the LORD said to you, 'You shall shepherd my people Israel and shall be commander of Israel.'" [3]When all the elders of Israel came to David in Hebron, King David made an agreement with them there before the LORD, and they anointed him king of Israel. [4]David was thirty years old when he became king, and he reigned for forty years: [5]seven years and six months in Hebron over Judah, and thirty-three years in Jerusalem over all Israel and Judah.

[6]Then the king and his men set out for Jerusalem against the Jebusites who inhabited the region. David was told, "You cannot enter here: the blind and the lame will drive you away!" which was their way of saying, "David cannot enter here." [7]But David did take the stronghold of Zion, which is the City of David.

[10]David grew steadily more powerful, for the LORD of hosts was with him.

Responsorial Psalm: Psalms 89:20, 21-22, 25-26

R. [25a]*My faithfulness and my mercy shall be with him.*

[20]Once you spoke in a vision,
    and to your faithful ones you said:
"On a champion I have placed a crown;
    over the people I have set a youth."
R. *My faithfulness and my mercy shall be with him.*

[21]"I have found David, my servant;
    with my holy oil I have anointed him,
[22]That my hand may be always with him,
    and that my arm may make him strong."
R. *My faithfulness and my mercy shall be with him.*

[25]"My faithfulness and my mercy shall be with him,
    and through my name shall his horn be exalted.
[26]I will set his hand upon the sea,
    his right hand upon the rivers."

R. *My faithfulness and my mercy shall be with*

42

him.

Alleluia: 2 Timothy 1:10
R. Alleluia, alleluia.
[10]Our Savior Jesus Christ has destroyed death and brought life to light through the Gospel.
R. Alleluia, alleluia.

Gospel: Mark 3:22-30
[22]The scribes who had come from Jerusalem said of Jesus, "He is possessed by Beelzebul," and "By the prince of demons he drives out demons."

[23]Summoning them, he began to speak to them in parables, "How can Satan drive out Satan? [24]If a kingdom is divided against itself, that kingdom cannot stand. [25]And if a house is divided against itself, that house will not be able to stand. [26]And if Satan has risen up against himself and is divided, he cannot stand; that is the end of him. [27]But no one can enter a strong man's house to plunder his property unless he first ties up the strong man. Then he can plunder his house. [28]Amen, I say to you, all sins and all blasphemies that people utter will be forgiven them. [29]But whoever blasphemes against the Holy Spirit will never have forgiveness, but is guilty of an everlasting sin." [30]For they had said, "He has an unclean spirit."

Tuesday January 23, 2024

Tuesday of Third Week in Ordinary Time
First Reading: 2 Samuel 6:12B-15, 17-19
[12B]David went to bring up the ark of God from the house of Obed-edom into the City of David amid festivities.[13]As soon as the bearers of the ark of the LORD had advanced six steps, he sacrificed an ox and a fatling.[14]Then David, girt with a linen apron, came dancing before the LORD with abandon,[15]as he and all the house of Israel were bringing up the ark of the LORD with shouts of joy and to the sound of the horn.[17]The ark of the LORD was brought in and set in its place within the tent David had pitched for it. Then David offered burnt offerings and peace offerings before the LORD. [18]When he finished making these offerings, he blessed the people in the name of the LORD of hosts.[19]He then distributed among all the people, to each man and each woman in the entire multitude of Israel, a loaf of bread, a cut of roast meat, and a raisin cake. With this, all the people left for their homes.

Responsorial Psalm: Psalms 24:7, 8, 9, 10
R. [8] Who is this king of glory? It is the Lord!
[7] Lift up, O gates, your lintels;
    reach up, you ancient portals,
    that the king of glory may come in!
R. Who is this king of glory? It is the Lord!

[8] Who is this king of glory?
    The LORD, strong and mighty,

the LORD, mighty in battle.
R. Who is this king of glory? It is the Lord!

⁹ Lift up, O gates, your lintels;
  reach up, you ancient portals,
  that the king of glory may come in!
R. Who is this king of glory? It is the Lord!

¹⁰ Who is this king of glory?
  The LORD of hosts; he is the king of glory.
R. Who is this king of glory? It is the Lord!

Alleluia: Matthew 11:25
R. Alleluia, alleluia.
²⁵ Blessed are you, Father, Lord of heaven and
   earth;
you have revealed to little ones the
   mysteries of the Kingdom.
R. Alleluia, alleluia.

Gospel: Mark 3:31-35
³¹The mother of Jesus and his brothers arrived at the house. Standing outside, they sent word to Jesus and called him. ³²A crowd seated around him told him, "Your mother and your brothers and your sisters are outside asking for you." ³³But he said to them in reply, "Who are my mother and my brothers?" ³⁴And looking around at those seated in the circle he said, "Here are my mother and my brothers.³⁵For whoever does the will of God is my brother and sister and mother."

Wednesday January 24, 2024

Wednesday of Third Week in Ordinary Time
First Reading: 2 Samuel 7:4-17
⁴That night the LORD spoke to Nathan and said: ⁵"Go, tell my servant David, 'Thus says the LORD: Should you build me a house to dwell in? ⁶I have not dwelt in a house from the day on which I led the children of Israel out of Egypt to the present, but I have been going about in a tent under cloth. ⁷In all my wanderings everywhere among the children of Israel, did I ever utter a word to any one of the judges whom I charged to tend my people Israel, to ask: Why have you not built me a house of cedar?'

  ⁸"Now then, speak thus to my servant David, 'The LORD of hosts has this to say: It was I who took you from the pasture and from the care of the flock to be commander of my people Israel. ⁹I have been with you wherever you went, and I have destroyed all your enemies before you. And I will make you famous like the great ones of the earth. ¹⁰I will fix a place for my people Israel; I will plant them so that they may dwell in their place

without further disturbance. Neither shall the wicked continue to afflict them as they did of old, [11]since the time I first appointed judges over my people Israel. I will give you rest from all your enemies. The LORD also reveals to you that he will establish a house for you. [12]And when your time comes and you rest with your ancestors, I will raise up your heir after you, sprung from your loins, and I will make his Kingdom firm. [13]It is he who shall build a house for my name. And I will make his royal throne firm forever. [14]I will be a father to him, and he shall be a son to me. And if he does wrong, I will correct him with the rod of men and with human chastisements; [15]but I will not withdraw my favor from him as I withdrew it from your predecessor Saul, whom I removed from my presence. [16]Your house and your kingdom shall endure forever before me; your throne shall stand firm forever.'"

[17]Nathan reported all these words and this entire vision to David.

Responsorial Psalm: Psalms 89:4-5, 27-28, 29-30

R. [(29a)] *For ever I will maintain my love for my servant.*

[4]"I have made a covenant with my chosen
one;
I have sworn to David my servant:
[5]I will make your dynasty stand forever
and establish your throne through all
ages."

R. *For ever I will maintain my love for my servant.*

[27]"He shall cry to me, 'You are my father,
my God, the Rock that brings me victory!'
[28]I myself make him firstborn,
Most High over the kings of the earth."

R. *For ever I will maintain my love for my servant.*

[29]"Forever I will maintain my love for him;
my covenant with him stands firm.
[30]I will establish his dynasty forever,
his throne as the days of the heavens."

R. *For ever I will maintain my love for my servant.*

Alleluia

R. Alleluia, alleluia.
The seed is the word of God, Christ is the
sower;

all who come to him will live for ever.
R. Alleluia, alleluia.

Gospel: Mark 4:1-20

[1]On another occasion, Jesus began to teach by the sea. A very large crowd gathered around him so that he got into a boat on the sea and sat down. And the whole crowd was beside the sea on land. [2]And he taught them at length in parables, and in the course of his instruction he said to them, [3]"Hear this! A sower went out to sow. [4]And as he sowed, some seed fell on the path, and the birds came and ate it up. [5]Other seed fell on rocky ground where it had little soil. It sprang up at once because the soil was not deep. [6]And when the sun rose, it was scorched and it withered for lack of roots. [7]Some seed fell among thorns, and the thorns grew up and choked it and it produced no grain. [8]And some seed fell on rich soil and produced fruit. It came up and grew and yielded thirty, sixty, and a hundredfold." [9]He added, "Whoever has ears to hear ought to hear."

[10]And when he was alone, those present along with the Twelve questioned him about the parables. [11]He answered them, "The mystery of the Kingdom of God has been granted to you. But to those outside everything comes in parables, [12]so that

they may look and see but not perceive,
and hear and listen but not understand,
in order that they may not be converted and
be forgiven."

[13]Jesus said to them, "Do you not understand this parable? Then how will you understand any of the parables? [14]The sower sows the word. [15]These are the ones on the path where the word is sown. As soon as they hear, Satan comes at once and takes away the word sown in them. [16]And these are the ones sown on rocky ground who, when they hear the word, receive it at once with joy. [17]But they have no roots; they last only for a time. Then when tribulation or persecution comes because of the word, they quickly fall away. [18]Those sown among thorns are another sort. They are the people who hear the word, [19]but worldly anxiety, the lure of riches, and the craving for other things intrude and choke the word, and it bears no fruit. [20]But those sown on rich soil are the ones who hear the word and accept it and bear fruit thirty and sixty and a hundredfold."

Thursday January 25, 2024

Feast of Conversion of Saint Paul, Apostle

First Reading: Acts 22:3-16

[3]Paul addressed the people in these words: "I am a Jew, born in Tarsus in Cilicia, but brought up in this city. At the feet of Gamaliel I was educated strictly in our ancestral law and was zealous for God, just as all of you are today. [4]I persecuted this Way to death, binding both men and women and delivering them to prison. [5]Even the high priest and the whole council of elders can testify on my behalf. For from them I even received letters

to the brothers and set out for Damascus to bring back to Jerusalem in chains for punishment those there as well.

[6]"On that journey as I drew near to Damascus, about noon a great light from the sky suddenly shone around me. [7]I fell to the ground and heard a voice saying to me, 'Saul, Saul, why are you persecuting me?' [8]I replied, 'Who are you, sir?' And he said to me, 'I am Jesus the Nazorean whom you are persecuting.' [9]My companions saw the light but did not hear the voice of the one who spoke to me. [10]I asked, 'What shall I do, sir?' The Lord answered me, 'Get up and go into Damascus, and there you will be told about everything appointed for you to do.' [11]Since I could see nothing because of the brightness of that light, I was led by hand by my companions and entered Damascus.

[12]"A certain Ananias, a devout observer of the law, and highly spoken of by all the Jews who lived there, [13]came to me and stood there and said, 'Saul, my brother, regain your sight.' And at that very moment I regained my sight and saw him. [14]Then he said, 'The God of our ancestors designated you to know his will, to see the Righteous One, and to hear the sound of his voice; [15]for you will be his witness before all to what you have seen and heard. [16]Now, why delay? Get up and have yourself baptized and your sins washed away, calling upon his name.'"

Or Acts 9:1-22

[1]Saul, still breathing murderous threats against the disciples of the Lord, went to the high priest [2]and asked him for letters to the synagogues in Damascus, that, if he should find any men or women who belonged to the Way, he might bring them back to Jerusalem in chains. [3]On his journey, as he was nearing Damascus, a light from the sky suddenly flashed around him. [4]He fell to the ground and heard a voice saying to him, "Saul, Saul, why are you persecuting me?" [5]He said, "Who are you, sir?" The reply came, "I am Jesus, whom you are persecuting. [6]Now get up and go into the city and you will be told what you must do." [7]The men who were traveling with him stood speechless, for they heard the voice but could see no one. [8]Saul got up from the ground, but when he opened his eyes he could see nothing; so they led him by the hand and brought him to Damascus. [9]For three days he was unable to see, and he neither ate nor drank.

[10]There was a disciple in Damascus named Ananias, and the Lord said to him in a vision, Ananias." He answered, "Here I am, Lord." [11]The Lord said to him, "Get up and go to the street called Straight and ask at the house of Judas for a man from Tarsus named Saul. He is there praying, [12]and in a vision he has seen a man named Ananias come in and lay his hands on him, that he may regain his sight." [13]But Ananias replied, "Lord, I have heard from many sources about this man, what evil things he has done to your holy ones in Jerusalem. [14]And here he has authority from the chief priests to imprison all who call upon your name." [15]But the Lord said to him, "Go, for this man is a chosen instrument of mine to carry my name before Gentiles, kings, and children of Israel, [16]and I will show him what he will have to suffer for my name." [17]So Ananias went and entered the house; laying his hands on him, he said, "Saul, my brother, the Lord has sent me, Jesus who appeared to you on the way by which you came, that you may regain your sight and be filled with the Holy Spirit." [18]Immediately things like scales fell from his eyes and he regained his sight. He got up and was baptized, [19]and when he had eaten, he recovered his strength.

He stayed some days with the disciples in Damascus, [20]and he began at once to proclaim Jesus in the synagogues, that he is the Son of God. [21]All who heard him were astounded and said, "Is not this the man who in Jerusalem ravaged those who call upon this name, and came here expressly to take them back in chains to the chief priests?" [22]But Saul grew all the stronger and confounded the Jews who lived in Damascus, proving that this is the Christ.

Responsorial Psalm: Psalms 117:1BC, 2

R. *(Mark 16:15)* **Go out to all the world and tell the Good News. Or R. Alleluia, alleluia.**

[1BC]Praise the LORD, all you nations;
    glorify him, all you peoples!

R. Go out to all the world, and tell the Good News. Or R. Alleluia, alleluia.

[2] For steadfast is his kindness toward us,
    and the fidelity of the LORD endures
        forever.

R. Go out to all the world, and tell the Good News. Or R. Alleluia, alleluia.

Alleluia: cf. John 15:16

R. Alleluia, alleluia.
[16]I chose you from the world,
to go and bear fruit that will last, says the
        Lord.
R. Alleluia, alleluia.

Gospel: Mark 16:15-18

[15]Jesus appeared to the Eleven and said to them: "Go into the whole world and proclaim the Gospel to every creature. [16]Whoever believes and is baptized will be saved; whoever does not believe will be condemned. [17]These signs will accompany those who believe: in my name they will drive out demons, they will speak new languages. [18]They will pick up serpents with their hands, and if they drink any deadly thing, it will not harm them. They will lay hands on the sick, and they will recover."

Friday January 26, 2024

Memorial of Saints Timothy and Titus - Bps

First Reading: 2 Timothy 1:1-8

[1]Paul, an Apostle of Christ Jesus by the will of God for the promise of life in Christ Jesus, [2]to Timothy, my dear child: grace, mercy, and peace from God the Father and Christ Jesus our Lord.

[3]I am grateful to God, whom I worship with a clear conscience as my ancestors did, as I remember you constantly in my prayers, night and day. [4]I yearn to see you again, recalling your tears, so that I may be filled with joy, [5]as I recall your sincere faith that first

lived in your grandmother Lois and in your mother Eunice and that I am confident lives also in you.

⁶For this reason, I remind you to stir into flame the gift of God that you have through the imposition of my hands. ⁷For God did not give us a spirit of cowardice but rather of power and love and self-control. ⁸So do not be ashamed of your testimony to our Lord, nor of me, a prisoner for his sake; but bear your share of hardship for the Gospel with the strength that comes from God.

Or Titus 1:1-5

¹Paul, a slave of God and Apostle of Jesus Christ for the sake of the faith of God's chosen ones and the recognition of religious truth, ²in the hope of eternal life that God, who does not lie, promised before time began, ³who indeed at the proper time revealed his word in the proclamation with which I was entrusted by the command of God our savior, ⁴to Titus, my true child in our common faith: grace and peace from God the Father and Christ Jesus our savior.

⁵For this reason I left you in Crete so that you might set right what remains to be done and appoint presbyters in every town, as I directed you.

Responsorial Psalm: Psalms 96:1-2A, 2B-3, 7-8A, 10

R. ⁽³⁾ *Proclaim God's marvelous deeds to all the*
        nations.
¹Sing to the LORD a new song;
        sing to the LORD, all you lands.
²ᴬSing to the LORD; bless his name.
R. *Proclaim God's marvelous deeds to all the*
        nations.

²ᴮ Announce his salvation, day after day.
³Tell his glory among the nations;
        among all peoples, his wondrous deeds.
R. *Proclaim God's marvelous deeds to all the*
        nations.

⁷Give to the LORD, you families of nations,
        give to the LORD glory and praise;
        ⁸ᴬgive to the LORD the glory due his name!
R. *Proclaim God's marvelous deeds to all the*
        nations.

¹⁰Say among the nations: The LORD is king.
He has made the world firm, not to be moved;
        he governs the peoples with equity.
R. *Proclaim God's marvelous deeds to all the*

nations.

Alleluia: cf Matthew 11:25

R. Alleluia, alleluia.

[25] Blessed are you, Father, Lord of heaven and
          earth;
you have revealed to little ones the
          mysteries of the Kingdom.

R. Alleluia, alleluia.

Gospel: Mark 4:26-34

[26]Jesus said to the crowds: "This is how it is with the Kingdom of God; it is as if a man were to scatter seed on the land [27]and would sleep and rise night and day and the seed would sprout and grow, he knows not how.[28]Of its own accord the land yields fruit, first the blade, then the ear, then the full grain in the ear.[29]And when the grain is ripe, he wields the sickle at once, for the harvest has come."

[30]He said, "To what shall we compare the Kingdom of God, or what parable can we use for it? [31]It is like a mustard seed that, when it is sown in the ground, is the smallest of all the seeds on the earth. [32]But once it is sown, it springs up and becomes the largest of plants and puts forth large branches, so that the birds of the sky can dwell in its shade." [33]With many such parables he spoke the word to them as they were able to understand it. [34]Without parables he did not speak to them, but to his own disciples he explained everything in private.

Saturday January 27, 2024

Saturday of the Third Week in Ordinary Time
First Reading: 2 Samuel 12:1-7A, 10-17

[1]The LORD sent Nathan to David, and when he came to him, Nathan said: "Judge this case for me! In a certain town there were two men, one rich, the other poor. [2]The rich man had flocks and herds in great numbers. [3]But the poor man had nothing at all except one little ewe lamb that he had bought. He nourished her, and she grew up with him and his children. She shared the little food he had and drank from his cup and slept in his bosom. She was like a daughter to him. [4]Now, the rich man received a visitor, but he would not take from his own flocks and herds to prepare a meal for the wayfarer who had come to him. Instead he took the poor man's ewe lamb and made a meal of it for his visitor." [5]David grew very angry with that man and said to him: "As the LORD lives, the man who has done this merits death! [6]He shall restore the ewe lamb fourfold because he has done this and has had no pity."

[7]Then Nathan said to David: "You are the man! Thus says the LORD God of Israel: [10]'The sword shall never depart from your house, because you have despised me and have

taken the wife of Uriah to be your wife.' [11]Thus says the LORD: 'I will bring evil upon you out of your own house. I will take your wives while you live to see it, and will give them to your neighbor. He shall lie with your wives in broad daylight. [12]You have done this deed in secret, but I will bring it about in the presence of all Israel, and with the sun looking down.'"

[13]Then David said to Nathan, "I have sinned against the LORD." Nathan answered David: "The LORD on his part has forgiven your sin: you shall not die. [14]But since you have utterly spurned the LORD by this deed, the child born to you must surely die." [15]Then Nathan returned to his house.

The LORD struck the child that the wife of Uriah had borne to David, and it became desperately ill. [16]David besought God for the child. He kept a fast, retiring for the night to lie on the ground clothed in sackcloth. [17]The elders of his house stood beside him urging him to rise from the ground; but he would not, nor would he take food with them.

Responsorial Psalm: Psalms 51:12-13, 14-15, 16-17
R. [(12a)] *Create a clean heart in me, O God.*
[12]A clean heart create for me, O God,
    and a steadfast spirit renew within me.
[13]Cast me not out from your presence,
    and your Holy Spirit take not from me.
R. *Create a clean heart in me, O God.*

[14]Give me back the joy of your salvation,
    and a willing spirit sustain in me.
[15]I will teach transgressors your ways,
    and sinners shall return to you.
R. *Create a clean heart in me, O God.*

[16]Free me from blood guilt, O God, my saving
        God;
    then my tongue shall revel in your
        justice.
[17]O Lord, open my lips,
    and my mouth shall proclaim your
        praise.
R. *Create a clean heart in me, O God.*

Alleluia: John 3:16
R. Alleluia, alleluia.
[16]God so loved the world that he gave his only-
        begotten Son,
so that everyone who believes in him might

have eternal life.
R. Alleluia, alleluia.

Gospel: Mark 4:35-41

[35]On that day, as evening drew on, Jesus said to his disciples: "Let us cross to the other side." [36]Leaving the crowd, they took Jesus with them in the boat just as he was. And other boats were with him. [37]A violent squall came up and waves were breaking over the boat, so that it was already filling up. [38]Jesus was in the stern, asleep on a cushion. They woke him and said to him, "Teacher, do you not care that we are perishing?" [39]He woke up, rebuked the wind, and said to the sea, "Quiet! Be still!" The wind ceased and there was great calm. [40]Then he asked them, "Why are you terrified? Do you not yet have faith?" [41]They were filled with great awe and said to one another, "Who then is this whom even wind and sea obey?"

Sunday January 28, 2024

Fourth Sunday in Ordinary Time Year B
First Reading: Deuteronomy 18:15-20

Moses spoke to all the people, saying: [15]"A prophet like me will the LORD, your God, raise up for you from among your own kin; to him you shall listen.[16]This is exactly what you requested of the LORD, your God, at Horeb on the day of the assembly, when you said, 'Let us not again hear the voice of the LORD, our God, nor see this great fire any more, lest we die.' [17]And the LORD said to me, 'This was well said. [18]I will raise up for them a prophet like you from among their kin, and will put my words into his mouth; he shall tell them all that I command him.[19]Whoever will not listen to my words which he speaks in my name, I myself will make him answer for it.[20]But if a prophet presumes to speak in my name an oracle that I have not commanded him to speak, or speaks in the name of other gods, he shall die.'"

Responsorial Psalm: Psalms 95:1-2, 6-7, 7-9

R. [(8)] *If today you hear his voice, harden not your*
hearts.
[1] Come, let us sing joyfully to the LORD;
    let us acclaim the rock of our salvation.
[2] Let us come into his presence with
      thanksgiving;
    let us joyfully sing psalms to him.
R. If today you hear his voice, harden not your
hearts.

[6] Come, let us bow down in worship;
    let us kneel before the LORD who made us.
[7ABC] For he is our God,

and we are the people he shepherds, the
flock he guides.
**R. If today you hear his voice, harden not your
hearts.**

[7D] Oh, that today you would hear his voice:
[8] "Harden not your hearts as at Meribah,
as in the day of Massah in the desert,
[9] Where your fathers tempted me;
they tested me though they had seen my
works."
**R. If today you hear his voice, harden not your
hearts.**

Second Reading: 1 Corinthians 7:32-35

Brothers and sisters: [32]I should like you to be free of anxieties. An unmarried man is anxious about the things of the Lord, how he may please the Lord. [33]But a married man is anxious about the things of the world, how he may please his wife,[34]and he is divided. An unmarried woman or a virgin is anxious about the things of the Lord, so that she may be holy in both body and spirit. A married woman, on the other hand, is anxious about the things of the world, how she may please her husband.[5]I am telling you this for your own benefit, not to impose a restraint upon you, but for the sake of propriety and adherence to the Lord without distraction.

Alleluia: Matthew 4:16

R. Alleluia, alleluia.
[16]The people who sit in darkness have seen a
great light;
on those dwelling in a land overshadowed
by death,
light has arisen.
R. Alleluia, alleluia.

Gospel: Mark 1:21-28

[21]Then they came to Capernaum, and on the sabbath Jesus entered the synagogue and taught. [22]The people were astonished at his teaching, for he taught them as one having authority and not as the scribes. [23]In their synagogue was a man with an unclean spirit; [24]he cried out, "What have you to do with us, Jesus of Nazareth? Have you come to destroy us? I know who you are—the Holy One of God!" [25]Jesus rebuked him and said, "Quiet! Come out of him!" [26]The unclean spirit convulsed him and with a loud cry came out of him. [27]All were amazed and asked one another, "What is this? A new teaching with authority. He commands even the unclean spirits and they obey him." [28]His fame spread everywhere throughout the whole region of Galilee.

Monday of Fourth Week in Ordinary Time
First Reading: 2 Samuel 15:13-14,30; 16:5-13

[13]An informant came to David with the report, "The children of Israel have transferred their loyalty to Absalom." [14]At this, David said to all his servants who were with him in Jerusalem: "Up! Let us take flight, or none of us will escape from Absalom. Leave quickly, lest he hurry and overtake us, then visit disaster upon us and put the city to the sword."

[30]As David went up the Mount of Olives, he wept without ceasing. His head was covered, and he was walking barefoot. All those who were with him also had their heads covered and were weeping as they went.

[5]As David was approaching Bahurim, a man named Shimei, the son of Gera of the same clan as Saul's family, was coming out of the place, cursing as he came. [6]He threw stones at David and at all the king's officers, even though all the soldiers, including the royal guard, were on David's right and on his left. [7]Shimei was saying as he cursed: "Away, away, you murderous and wicked man! [8]The LORD has requited you for all the bloodshed in the family of Saul, in whose stead you became king, and the LORD has given over the kingdom to your son Absalom. And now you suffer ruin because you are a murderer." [9]Abishai, son of Zeruiah, said to the king: "Why should this dead dog curse my lord the king? Let me go over, please, and lop off his head." [10]But the king replied: "What business is it of mine or of yours, sons of Zeruiah, that he curses? Suppose the LORD has told him to curse David; who then will dare to say, 'Why are you doing this?'" [11]Then the king said to Abishai and to all his servants: "If my own son, who came forth from my loins, is seeking my life, how much more might this Benjaminite do so? Let him alone and let him curse, for the LORD has told him to. [12]Perhaps the LORD will look upon my affliction and make it up to me with benefits for the curses he is uttering this day." [13]David and his men continued on the road, while Shimei kept abreast of them on the hillside, all the while cursing and throwing stones and dirt as he went.

Responsorial Psalm: Psalms 3:2-3, 4-5, 6-7

R. [8a] *Lord, rise up and save me.*

[2] O LORD, how many are my adversaries!
    Many rise up against me!
[3] Many are saying of me,
    "There is no salvation for him in God."

R. *Lord, rise up and save me.*

[4] But you, O LORD, are my shield;
    my glory, you lift up my head!
[5] When I call out to the LORD,
    he answers me from his holy mountain.

R. *Lord, rise up and save me.*

^{6} When I lie down in sleep,
>   I wake again, for the LORD sustains me.
^{7} I fear not the myriads of people
>   arrayed against me on every side.
R. Lord, rise up and save me.

Alleluia: Luke 7:16
R. Alleluia, alleluia.
^{16}A great prophet has arisen in our midst and God has visited his people.
R. Alleluia, alleluia.

Gospel: Mark 5:1-20
^{1}Jesus and his disciples came to the other side of the sea, to the territory of the Gerasenes. ^{2}When he got out of the boat, at once a man from the tombs who had an unclean spirit met him. ^{3}The man had been dwelling among the tombs, and no one could restrain him any longer, even with a chain. ^{4}In fact, he had frequently been bound with shackles and chains, but the chains had been pulled apart by him and the shackles smashed, and no one was strong enough to subdue him. ^{5}Night and day among the tombs and on the hillsides he was always crying out and bruising himself with stones. ^{6}Catching sight of Jesus from a distance, he ran up and prostrated himself before him, ^{7}crying out in a loud voice, "What have you to do with me, Jesus, Son of the Most High God? I adjure you by God, do not torment me!" ^{8}(He had been saying to him, "Unclean spirit, come out of the man!") ^{9}He asked him, "What is your name?" He replied, "Legion is my name. There are many of us." ^{10}And he pleaded earnestly with him not to drive them away from that territory.

^{11}Now a large herd of swine was feeding there on the hillside. ^{12}And they pleaded with him, "Send us into the swine. Let us enter them." ^{13}And he let them, and the unclean spirits came out and entered the swine. The herd of about two thousand rushed down a steep bank into the sea, where they were drowned. ^{14}The swineherds ran away and reported the incident in the town and throughout the countryside. And people came out to see what had happened. ^{15}As they approached Jesus, they caught sight of the man who had been possessed by Legion, sitting there clothed and in his right mind. And they were seized with fear. ^{16}Those who witnessed the incident explained to them what had happened to the possessed man and to the swine. ^{17}Then they began to beg him to leave their district. ^{18}As he was getting into the boat, the man who had been possessed pleaded to remain with him. ^{19}But Jesus would not permit him but told him instead, "Go home to your family and announce to them all that the Lord in his pity has done for you." ^{20}Then the man went off and began to proclaim in the Decapolis what Jesus had done for him; and all were amazed.

Tuesday of Fourth Week in Ordinary Time
First Reading: 2 Samuel 18:9-10, 14B, 24-25A, 30–19:3

[9]Absalom unexpectedly came up against David's servants. He was mounted on a mule, and, as the mule passed under the branches of a large terebinth, his hair caught fast in the tree. He hung between heaven and earth while the mule he had been riding ran off. [10]Someone saw this and reported to Joab that he had seen Absalom hanging from a terebinth. [14B]And taking three pikes in hand, he thrust for the heart of Absalom, still hanging from the tree alive.

[24]Now David was sitting between the two gates, and a lookout went up to the roof of the gate above the city wall, where he looked about and saw a man running all alone. [25A]The lookout shouted to inform the king, who said, "If he is alone, he has good news to report." [30]The king said, "Step aside and remain in attendance here." So he stepped aside and remained there. [31]When the Cushite messenger came in, he said, "Let my lord the king receive the good news that this day the LORD has taken your part, freeing you from the grasp of all who rebelled against you." [32]But the king asked the Cushite, "Is young Absalom safe?" The Cushite replied, "May the enemies of my lord the king and all who rebel against you with evil intent be as that young man!"

[1]The king was shaken, and went up to the room over the city gate to weep. He said as he wept, "My son Absalom! My son, my son Absalom! If only I had died instead of you, Absalom, my son, my son!"

[2]Joab was told that the king was weeping and mourning for Absalom; [3]and that day's victory was turned into mourning for the whole army when they heard that the king was grieving for his son.

Responsorial Psalm: Psalms 86:1-2, 3-4, 5-6

R. [(1a)] *Listen, Lord, and answer me.*

[1]Incline your ear, O LORD; answer me,
    for I am afflicted and poor.
[2]Keep my life, for I am devoted to you;
    save your servant who trusts in you.
    You are my God.

R. *Listen, Lord, and answer me.*

[3]Have mercy on me, O Lord,
    for to you I call all the day.
[4]Gladden the soul of your servant,
    for to you, O Lord, I lift up my soul.

R. *Listen, Lord, and answer me.*

[5]For you, O Lord, are good and forgiving,
    abounding in kindness to all who call

upon you.

[6]Hearken, O LORD, to my prayer
   and attend to the sound of my pleading.

R. Listen, Lord, and answer me.

Alleluia: Matthew 8:17

R. Alleluia, alleluia.

[17]Christ took away our infirmities
and bore our diseases.

R. Alleluia, alleluia.

Gospel: Mark 5:21-43

[21]When Jesus had crossed again in the boat to the other side, a large crowd gathered around him, and he stayed close to the sea. [22]One of the synagogue officials, named Jairus, came forward. Seeing him he fell at his feet [23]and pleaded earnestly with him, saying, "My daughter is at the point of death. Please, come lay your hands on her that she may get well and live." [24]He went off with him and a large crowd followed him.

[25]There was a woman afflicted with hemorrhages for twelve years. [26]She had suffered greatly at the hands of many doctors and had spent all that she had. Yet she was not helped but only grew worse. [27]She had heard about Jesus and came up behind him in the crowd and touched his cloak. [28]She said, "If I but touch his clothes, I shall be cured." [29]Immediately her flow of blood dried up. She felt in her body that she was healed of her affliction. [30]Jesus, aware at once that power had gone out from him, turned around in the crowd and asked, "Who has touched my clothes?" [31]But his disciples said to him, "You see how the crowd is pressing upon you, and yet you ask, Who touched me?" [32]And he looked around to see who had done it. [33]The woman, realizing what had happened to her, approached in fear and trembling. She fell down before Jesus and told him the whole truth. [34]He said to her, "Daughter, your faith has saved you. Go in peace and be cured of your affliction."

[35]While he was still speaking, people from the synagogue official's house arrived and said, "Your daughter has died; why trouble the teacher any longer?" [36]Disregarding the message that was reported, Jesus said to the synagogue official, "Do not be afraid; just have faith." [37]He did not allow anyone to accompany him inside except Peter, James, and John, the brother of James. [38]When they arrived at the house of the synagogue official, he caught sight of a commotion, people weeping and wailing loudly. [39]So he went in and said to them, "Why this commotion and weeping? The child is not dead but asleep." [40]And they ridiculed him. Then he put them all out. He took along the child's father and mother and those who were with him and entered the room where the child was. [41]He took the child by the hand and said to her, *"Talitha koum,"* which means, "Little girl, I say to you, arise!" [42]The girl, a child of twelve, arose immediately and walked around. At that they were utterly astounded. [43]He gave strict orders that no one should know this and said that she should be given something to eat.

Memorial of Saint John Bosco, Priest
First Reading: 2 Samuel 24:2, 9-17

[2] King David said to Joab and the leaders of the army who were with him, "Tour all the tribes in Israel from Dan to Beer-sheba and register the people, that I may know their number." [9]Joab then reported to the king the number of people registered: in Israel, eight hundred thousand men fit for military service; in Judah, five hundred thousand.

[10]Afterward, however, David regretted having numbered the people, and said to the LORD: "I have sinned grievously in what I have done. But now, LORD, forgive the guilt of your servant, for I have been very foolish." [11]When David rose in the morning, the LORD had spoken to the prophet Gad, David's seer, saying: [12]"Go and say to David, 'This is what the LORD says: I offer you three alternatives; choose one of them, and I will inflict it on you.'" [13]Gad then went to David to inform him. He asked: "Do you want a three years' famine to come upon your land, or to flee from your enemy three months while he pursues you, or to have a three days' pestilence in your land? Now consider and decide what I must reply to him who sent me." [14]David answered Gad: "I am in very serious difficulty. Let us fall by the hand of God, for he is most merciful; but let me not fall by the hand of man." [15]Thus David chose the pestilence. Now it was the time of the wheat harvest when the plague broke out among the people. The LORD then sent a pestilence over Israel from morning until the time appointed, and seventy thousand of the people from Dan to Beer-sheba died. [16]But when the angel stretched forth his hand toward Jerusalem to destroy it, the LORD regretted the calamity and said to the angel causing the destruction among the people, "Enough now! Stay your hand." The angel of the LORD was then standing at the threshing floor of Araunah the Jebusite. [17]When David saw the angel who was striking the people, he said to the LORD: "It is I who have sinned; it is I, the shepherd, who have done wrong. But these are sheep; what have they done? Punish me and my kindred."

Responsorial Psalm: Psalms 32:1-2, 5, 6, 7

R. (see 5c) **Lord, forgive the wrong I have done.**

[1] Blessed is he whose fault is taken away,
     whose sin is covered.
[2] Blessed the man to whom the LORD imputes
         not guilt,
     in whose spirit there is no guile.
R. **Lord, forgive the wrong I have done.**

[5] Then I acknowledged my sin to you,
     my guilt I covered not.
I said, "I confess my faults to the LORD,"
     and you took away the guilt of my sin.
R. **Lord, forgive the wrong I have done.**

⁶ For this shall every faithful man pray to you
    in time of stress.
Though deep waters overflow,
    they shall not reach him.
R. Lord, forgive the wrong I have done.

⁷You are my shelter; from distress you will
        preserve me;
        with glad cries of freedom you will ring
        me round.
R. Lord, forgive the wrong I have done.

Alleluia: John 10:27
R. Alleluia, alleluia.
²⁷My sheep hear my voice, says the Lord;
I know them, and they follow me.
R. Alleluia, alleluia.

Gospel: Mark 6:1-6
¹Jesus departed from there and came to his native place, accompanied by his disciples. ²When the sabbath came he began to teach in the synagogue, and many who heard him were astonished. They said, "Where did this man get all this? What kind of wisdom has been given him? What mighty deeds are wrought by his hands! ³Is he not the carpenter, the son of Mary, and the brother of James and Joseph and Judas and Simon? And are not his sisters here with us?" And they took offense at him. ⁴Jesus said to them, "A prophet is not without honor except in his native place and among his own kin and in his own house." ⁵So he was not able to perform any mighty deed there, apart from curing a few sick people by laying his hands on them. ⁶He was amazed at their lack of faith.

FEBRUARY 2024
Thursday February 1, 2024

Thursday of Fourth Week in Ordinary Time
First Reading: 1 Kings 2:1-4, 10-12
¹ When the time of David's death drew near, he gave these instructions to his son Solomon: ² "I am going the way of all flesh. Take courage and be a man. ³ Keep the mandate of the LORD, your God, following his ways and observing his statutes, commands, ordinances, and decrees as they are written in the law of Moses, that you may succeed in whatever you do, wherever you turn, ⁴ and the LORD may fulfill the promise he made on my behalf when he said, 'If your sons so conduct themselves that they remain faithful to me with their whole heart and with their whole soul, you shall always have someone of your line on the throne of Israel.'"

¹⁰ David rested with his ancestors and was buried in the City of David. ¹¹ The length of David's reign over Israel was forty years: he reigned seven years in Hebron and thirty-three years in Jerusalem.

[12] Solomon was seated on the throne of his father David, with his sovereignty firmly established.

Responsorial Psalm: 1 Chronicles 29:10, 11AB, 11D-12A, 12BCD

R. *(12b)* *Lord, you are exalted over all.*

[10] "Blessed may you be, O LORD,
  God of Israel our father,
  from eternity to eternity."

R. *Lord, you are exalted over all.*

[11AB] "Yours, O LORD, are grandeur and power,
  majesty, splendor, and glory."

R. *Lord, you are exalted over all.*

[11D] "LORD, you are exalted over all.
  Yours, O LORD, is the sovereignty;
  you are exalted as head over all.
[12A] Riches and honor are from you."

R. *Lord, you are exalted over all.*

[12BCD] "In your hand are power and might;
  it is yours to give grandeur and strength
   to all."

R. *Lord, you are exalted over all.*

Alleluia: Mark 1:15

R. Alleluia, alleluia.

[15] The Kingdom of God is at hand;
repent and believe in the Gospel.

R. Alleluia, alleluia.

Gospel: Mark 6:7-13

[7] Jesus summoned the Twelve and began to send them out two by two and gave them authority over unclean spirits. [8] He instructed them to take nothing for the journey but a walking stick –no food, no sack, no money in their belts. [9] They were, however, to wear sandals but not a second tunic. [10] He said to them, "Wherever you enter a house, stay there until you leave from there. [11] Whatever place does not welcome you or listen to you, leave there and shake the dust off your feet in testimony against them." [12] So they went off and preached repentance. [13] The Twelve drove out many demons, and they anointed with oil many who were sick and cured them.

Feast of the Presentation of the Lord
First Reading: Malachi 3:1-4

¹ Thus says the Lord GOD:
Lo, I am sending my messenger
    to prepare the way before me;
And suddenly there will come to the temple
    the LORD whom you seek,
And the messenger of the covenant whom
        you desire.
    Yes, he is coming, says the LORD of hosts.
² But who will endure the day of his coming?
    And who can stand when he appears?
For he is like the refiner's fire,
    or like the fuller's lye.
³ He will sit refining and purifying silver,
    and he will purify the sons of Levi,
Refining them like gold or like silver
    that they may offer due sacrifice to the
        LORD.
⁴ Then the sacrifice of Judah and Jerusalem
    will please the LORD,
    as in the days of old, as in years gone by.

Responsorial Psalm: Psalms 24:7, 8, 9, 10
R. (8) *Who is this king of glory? It is the Lord!*
⁷ Lift up, O gates, your lintels;
    reach up, you ancient portals,
    that the king of glory may come in!
R. *Who is this king of glory? It is the Lord!*

⁸ Who is this king of glory?
    The LORD, strong and mighty,
    the LORD, mighty in battle.
R. *Who is this king of glory? It is the Lord!*

⁹ Lift up, O gates, your lintels;
    reach up, you ancient portals,
    that the king of glory may come in!
R. *Who is this king of glory? It is the Lord!*

¹⁰ Who is this king of glory?

    The LORD of hosts; he is the king of glory.

R. Who is this king of glory? It is the Lord!

Second Reading: Hebrews 2:14-18

¹⁴ Since the children share in blood and flesh, Jesus likewise shared in them, that through death he might destroy the one who has the power of death, that is, the Devil, ¹⁵ and free those who through fear of death had been subject to slavery all their life. ¹⁶Surely he did not help angels but rather the descendants of Abraham; ¹⁷ therefore, he had to become like his brothers and sisters in every way, that he might be a merciful and faithful high priest before God to expiate the sins of the people. ¹⁸Because he himself was tested through what he suffered, he is able to help those who are being tested.

Alleluia: Luke 2:32

R. Alleluia, alleluia.

³² A light of revelation to the Gentiles,

and glory for your people Israel.

R. Alleluia, alleluia.

Gospel: Luke 2:22-40

²² When the days were completed for their purification according to the law of Moses, Mary and Joseph took Jesus up to Jerusalem to present him to the Lord, ²³ just as it is written in the law of the Lord, *Every male that opens the womb shall be consecrated to the Lord*, ²⁴ and to offer the sacrifice of *a pair of turtledoves or two young pigeons*, in accordance with the dictate in the law of the Lord.

    ²⁵ Now there was a man in Jerusalem whose name was Simeon. This man was righteous and devout, awaiting the consolation of Israel, and the Holy Spirit was upon him. ²⁶ It had been revealed to him by the Holy Spirit that he should not see death before he had seen the Christ of the Lord. ²⁷ He came in the Spirit into the temple; and when the parents brought in the child Jesus to perform the custom of the law in regard to him, ²⁸ he took him into his arms and blessed God, saying:

²⁹ "Now, Master, you may let your servant

      go

   in peace, according to your word,

³⁰ for my eyes have seen your salvation,

    ³¹ which you prepared in the sight of all

      the peoples:

³² a light for revelation to the Gentiles,

    and glory for your people Israel."

³³ The child's father and mother were amazed at what was said about him; ³⁴ and Simeon blessed them and said to Mary his mother, "Behold, this child is destined for the fall and

rise of many in Israel, and to be a sign that will be contradicted [35] —and you yourself a sword will pierce— so that the thoughts of many hearts may be revealed." [36] There was also a prophetess, Anna, the daughter of Phanuel, of the tribe of Asher. She was advanced in years, having lived seven years with her husband after her marriage, [37] and then as a widow until she was eighty-four. She never left the temple, but worshiped night and day with fasting and prayer. [38]And coming forward at that very time, she gave thanks to God and spoke about the child to all who were awaiting the redemption of Jerusalem.

[39] When they had fulfilled all the prescriptions of the law of the Lord, they returned to Galilee, to their own town of Nazareth. [40] The child grew and became strong, filled with wisdom; and the favor of God was upon him.

Or Luke 2:22-32

[22] When the days were completed for their purification according to the law of Moses, Mary and Joseph took Jesus up to Jerusalem to present him to the Lord, [23] just as it is written in the law of the Lord, *Every male that opens the womb shall be consecrated to the Lord,* [24] and to offer the sacrifice of *a pair of turtledoves or two young pigeons,* in accordance with the dictate in the law of the Lord.

[25] Now there was a man in Jerusalem whose name was Simeon. This man was righteous and devout, awaiting the consolation of Israel, and the Holy Spirit was upon him. [26]It had been revealed to him by the Holy Spirit that he should not see death before he had seen the Christ of the Lord. [27]He came in the Spirit into the temple; and when the parents brought in the child Jesus to perform the custom of the law in regard to him, [28]he took him into his arms and blessed God, saying:

[29] "Now, Master, you may let your servant

      go

    in peace, according to your word,

[30] for my eyes have seen your salvation,

    [31] which you prepared in the sight of all

      the peoples:

[32] a light for revelation to the Gentiles,

    and glory for your people Israel."

Saturday February 3, 2024

Saturday of Fourth Week in Ordinary Time
First Reading: 1 Kings 3:4-13

[4] Solomon went to Gibeon to sacrifice there, because that was the most renowned high place. Upon its altar Solomon offered a thousand burnt offerings. [5] In Gibeon the LORD appeared to Solomon in a dream at night. God said, "Ask something of me and I will give it to you." [6] Solomon answered: "You have shown great favor to your servant, my father David, because he behaved faithfully toward you, with justice and an upright heart; and you have continued this great favor toward him, even today, seating a son of his on his throne. [7] O LORD, my God, you have made me, your servant, king to succeed my father

David; but I am a mere youth, not knowing at all how to act. [8] I serve you in the midst of the people whom you have chosen, a people so vast that it cannot be numbered or counted. [9] Give your servant, therefore, an understanding heart to judge your people and to distinguish right from wrong. For who is able to govern this vast people of yours?"

[10] The LORD was pleased that Solomon made this request. [11] So God said to him: "Because you have asked for this —not for a long life for yourself, nor for riches, nor for the life of your enemies, but for understanding so that you may know what is right— [12] I do as you requested. I give you a heart so wise and understanding that there has never been anyone like you up to now, and after you there will come no one to equal you. [13] In addition, I give you what you have not asked for, such riches and glory that among kings there is not your like."

Responsorial Psalm: Psalms 119:9, 10, 11, 12, 13, 14

R. [12b] **Lord, teach me your statutes.**

[9] How shall a young man be faultless in his
        way?
    By keeping to your words.
R. **Lord, teach me your statutes.**

[10] With all my heart I seek you;
    let me not stray from your commands.
R. **Lord, teach me your statutes.**

[11] Within my heart I treasure your promise,
    that I may not sin against you.
R. **Lord, teach me your statutes.**

[12] Blessed are you, O LORD;
    teach me your statutes.
R. **Lord, teach me your statutes.**

[13] With my lips I declare
    all the ordinances of your mouth.
R. **Lord, teach me your statutes.**

[14] In the way of your decrees I rejoice,
    as much as in all riches.
R. **Lord, teach me your statutes.**

Alleluia: John 10:27

R. **Alleluia, alleluia.**
[27] My sheep hear my voice, says the Lord;
I know them, and they follow me.

R. Alleluia, alleluia.

Gospel: Mark 6:30-34

[30] The Apostles gathered together with Jesus and reported all they had done and taught. [31] He said to them, "Come away by yourselves to a deserted place and rest a while." People were coming and going in great numbers, and they had no opportunity even to eat. [32] So they went off in the boat by themselves to a deserted place. [33] People saw them leaving and many came to know about it. They hastened there on foot from all the towns and arrived at the place before them.

[34] When Jesus disembarked and saw the vast crowd, his heart was moved with pity for them, for they were like sheep without a shepherd; and he began to teach them many things.

Sunday February 4, 2024

Fifth Sunday in Ordinary Time Year B
First Reading: Job 7:1-4, 6-7

Job spoke, saying:

[1] Is not man's life on earth a drudgery?
    Are not his days those of hirelings?
[2] He is a slave who longs for the shade,
    a hireling who waits for his wages.
[3] So I have been assigned months of misery,
    and troubled nights have been allotted to
        me.
[4] If in bed I say, "When shall I arise?"
    then the night drags on;
    I am filled with restlessness until the
        dawn.
[6] My days are swifter than a weaver's shuttle;
    they come to an end without hope.
[7] Remember that my life is like the wind;
    I shall not see happiness again.

Responsorial Psalm: Psalms 147:1-2,3-4, 5-6

R. [(cf. 3a)] **Praise the Lord, who heals the brokenhearted** or: R. **Alleluia.**
[1] Praise the LORD, for he is good;
    sing praise to our God, for he is gracious;
    it is fitting to praise him.
[2] The LORD rebuilds Jerusalem;
    the dispersed of Israel he gathers.
R. **Praise the Lord, who heals the brokenhearted.** or: R. **Alleluia.**
[3] He heals the brokenhearted
    and binds up their wounds.

^{4} He tells the number of the stars;
  he calls each by name.
R. Praise the Lord, who heals the brokenhearted. *or:* **R. Alleluia.**

^{5} Great is our Lord and mighty in power;
  to his wisdom there is no limit.
^{6} The LORD sustains the lowly;
  the wicked he casts to the ground.
R. Praise the Lord, who heals the brokenhearted. *or:* **R. Alleluia.**

Second Reading: 1 Corinthians 9:16-19, 22-23

Brothers and sisters: ^{16} If I preach the gospel, this is no reason for me to boast, for an obligation has been imposed on me, and woe to me if I do not preach it! ^{17} If I do so willingly, I have a recompense, but if unwillingly, then I have been entrusted with a stewardship. ^{18} What then is my recompense? That, when I preach, I offer the gospel free of charge so as not to make full use of my right in the gospel.

^{19} Although I am free in regard to all, I have made myself a slave to all so as to win over as many as possible. ^{22} To the weak I became weak, to win over the weak. I have become all things to all, to save at least some. ^{23} All this I do for the sake of the gospel, so that I too may have a share in it.

Alleluia: Matthew 8:17

R. Alleluia, alleluia.
^{17} Christ took away our infirmities
and bore our diseases.
R. Alleluia, alleluia.

Gospel: Mark 1:29-39

^{29} On leaving the synagogue Jesus entered the house of Simon and Andrew with James and John. ^{30} Simon's mother-in-law lay sick with a fever. They immediately told him about her. ^{31} He approached, grasped her hand, and helped her up. Then the fever left her and she waited on them.

^{32} When it was evening, after sunset, they brought to him all who were ill or possessed by demons. ^{33} The whole town was gathered at the door. ^{34} He cured many who were sick with various diseases, and he drove out many demons, not permitting them to speak because they knew him.

^{35} Rising very early before dawn, he left and went off to a deserted place, where he prayed. ^{36} Simon and those who were with him pursued him ^{37} and on finding him said, "Everyone is looking for you." ^{38} He told them, "Let us go on to the nearby villages that I may preach there also. For this purpose have I come." ^{39} So he went into their synagogues, preaching and driving out demons throughout the whole of Galilee.

Memorial of Saint Agatha, Virgin & Martyr
First Reading: 1 Kings 8:1-7, 9-13

[1] The elders of Israel and all the leaders of the tribes, the princes in the ancestral houses of the children of Israel, came to King Solomon in Jerusalem, to bring up the ark of the LORD's covenant from the City of David, which is Zion. [2] All the people of Israel assembled before King Solomon during the festival in the month of Ethanim (the seventh month). [3] When all the elders of Israel had arrived, the priests took up the ark; [4] they carried the ark of the LORD and the meeting tent with all the sacred vessels that were in the tent. (The priests and Levites carried them.)

[5] King Solomon and the entire community of Israel present for the occasion sacrificed before the ark sheep and oxen too many to number or count. [6] The priests brought the ark of the covenant of the LORD to its place beneath the wings of the cherubim in the sanctuary, the holy of holies of the temple. [7] The cherubim had their wings spread out over the place of the ark, sheltering the ark and its poles from above. [9] There was nothing in the ark but the two stone tablets which Moses had put there at Horeb, when the LORD made a covenant with the children of Israel at their departure from the land of Egypt.

[10] When the priests left the holy place, the cloud filled the temple of the LORD [11] so that the priests could no longer minister because of the cloud, since the LORD's glory had filled the temple of the LORD. [12] Then Solomon said, "The LORD intends to dwell in the dark cloud; [13] I have truly built you a princely house, a dwelling where you may abide forever."

Responsorial Psalm: Psalms 132:6-7, 8-10

R. [8a] *Lord, go up to the place of your rest!*

[6] Behold, we heard of it in Ephrathah;
   we found it in the fields of Jaar.
[7] Let us enter into his dwelling,
   let us worship at his footstool.

R. *Lord, go up to the place of your rest!*

[8] Advance, O LORD, to your resting place,
   you and the ark of your majesty.
[9] May your priests be clothed with justice;
   let your faithful ones shout merrily for
      joy.
[10] For the sake of David your servant,
   reject not the plea of your anointed.

R. *Lord, go up to the place of your rest!*

Alleluia: Matthew 4:23

R. Alleluia, alleluia.

[23] Jesus preached the Gospel of the Kingdom and cured every disease among the people.

R. Alleluia, alleluia.

Gospel: Mark 6:53-56

53 After making the crossing to the other side of the sea, Jesus and his disciples came to land at Gennesaret and tied up there. 54 As they were leaving the boat, people immediately recognized him. 55 They scurried about the surrounding country and began to bring in the sick on mats to wherever they heard he was. 56 Whatever villages or towns or countryside he entered, they laid the sick in the marketplaces and begged him that they might touch only the tassel on his cloak; and as many as touched it were healed.

Tuesday February 6, 2024

Memorial of Saints Paul Miki and his Companions, Martyrs
First Reading: 1 Kings 8:22-23, 27-30

22 Solomon stood before the altar of the LORD in the presence of the whole community of Israel, and stretching forth his hands toward heaven, 23 he said, "LORD, God of Israel, there is no God like you in heaven above or on earth below; you keep your covenant of mercy with your servants who are faithful to you with their whole heart.

27 "Can it indeed be that God dwells on earth? If the heavens and the highest heavens cannot contain you, how much less this temple which I have built! 28 Look kindly on the prayer and petition of your servant, O LORD, my God, and listen to the cry of supplication which I, your servant, utter before you this day. 29 May your eyes watch night and day over this temple, the place where you have decreed you shall be honored; may you heed the prayer which I, your servant, offer in this place. 30 Listen to the petitions of your servant and of your people Israel which they offer in this place. Listen from your heavenly dwelling and grant pardon."

Responsorial Psalm: Psalms 84:3, 4, 5 AND 10, 11

R. (2) *How lovely is your dwelling place, Lord,*
mighty God!

3 My soul yearns and pines
for the courts of the LORD.
My heart and my flesh
cry out for the living God.
R. *How lovely is your dwelling place, Lord,*
mighty God!

4 Even the sparrow finds a home,
and the swallow a nest
in which she puts her young—
Your altars, O LORD of hosts,
my king and my God!
R. *How lovely is your dwelling place, Lord,*

mighty God!

⁵ Blessed they who dwell in your house!
    continually they praise you.
¹⁰ O God, behold our shield,
    and look upon the face of your anointed.
R. How lovely is your dwelling place, Lord,
    mighty God!

¹¹ I had rather one day in your courts
    than a thousand elsewhere;
I had rather lie at the threshold of the house
    of my God
    than dwell in the tents of the wicked.
R. How lovely is your dwelling place, Lord,
    mighty God!

Alleluia: Psalms 119:36, 29B

R. Alleluia, alleluia.
³⁶ Incline my heart, O God, to your decrees;
²⁹ᴮ and favor me with your law.
R. Alleluia, alleluia.

Gospel: Mark 7:1-13

¹ When the Pharisees with some scribes who had come from Jerusalem gathered around Jesus, ² they observed that some of his disciples ate their meals with unclean, that is, unwashed, hands. ³ (For the Pharisees and, in fact, all Jews, do not eat without carefully washing their hands, keeping the tradition of the elders. ⁴And on coming from the marketplace they do not eat without purifying themselves. And there are many other things that they have traditionally observed, the purification of cups and jugs and kettles and beds.) ⁵ So the Pharisees and scribes questioned him, "Why do your disciples not follow the tradition of the elders but instead eat a meal with unclean hands?" ⁶ He responded, "Well did Isaiah prophesy about you hypocrites, as it is written:

This people honors me with their lips,
    but their hearts are far from me;
⁷ *in vain do they worship me,*
    teaching as doctrines human precepts.

⁸ You disregard God's commandment but cling to human tradition." ⁹ He went on to say, "How well you have set aside the commandment of God in order to uphold your tradition! ¹⁰ For Moses said, *Honor your father and your mother,* and *Whoever curses father or mother shall die.* ¹¹ Yet you say, 'If someone says to father or mother, "Any support you

might have had from me is *qorban*"' (meaning, dedicated to God), [12] you allow him to do nothing more for his father or mother. [13] You nullify the word of God in favor of your tradition that you have handed on. And you do many such things."

Wednesday of Fifth Week in Ordinary Time
First Reading: 1 Kings 10:1-10

[1] The queen of Sheba, having heard of Solomon's fame, came to test him with subtle questions. [2] She arrived in Jerusalem with a very numerous retinue, and with camels bearing spices, a large amount of gold, and precious stones. She came to Solomon and questioned him on every subject in which she was interested. [3] King Solomon explained everything she asked about, and there remained nothing hidden from him that he could not explain to her.

[4] When the queen of Sheba witnessed Solomon's great wisdom, the palace he had built, [5] the food at his table, the seating of his ministers, the attendance and garb of his waiters, his banquet service, and the burnt offerings he offered in the temple of the LORD, she was breathless. [6] "The report I heard in my country about your deeds and your wisdom is true," she told the king. [7] "Though I did not believe the report until I came and saw with my own eyes, I have discovered that they were not telling me the half. Your wisdom and prosperity surpass the report I heard. [8] Blessed are your men, blessed these servants of yours, who stand before you always and listen to your wisdom. [9] Blessed be the LORD, your God, whom it has pleased to place you on the throne of Israel. In his enduring love for Israel, the LORD has made you king to carry out judgment and justice." [10] Then she gave the king one hundred and twenty gold talents, a very large quantity of spices, and precious stones.

Never again did anyone bring such an abundance of spices as the queen of Sheba gave to King Solomon.

Responsorial Psalm: Psalms 37:5-6, 30-31, 39-40

R. (30a) *The mouth of the just murmurs wisdom.*

[5] Commit to the LORD your way;
    trust in him, and he will act.
[6] He will make justice dawn for you like the
        light;
    bright as the noonday shall be your
        vindication.

R. *The mouth of the just murmurs wisdom.*

[30] The mouth of the just man tells of wisdom
    and his tongue utters what is right.
[31] The law of his God is in his heart,
    and his steps do not falter.

R. The mouth of the just murmurs wisdom.

[39] The salvation of the just is from the LORD;
>   he is their refuge in time of distress.
[40] And the LORD helps them and delivers them;
>   he delivers them from the wicked and
>   saves them,
>   because they take refuge in him.

R. The mouth of the just murmurs wisdom.

Alleluia: John 17:17B, 17A
R. Alleluia, alleluia.
[17B]Your word, O Lord, is truth:
[17A] consecrate us in the truth.
R. Alleluia, alleluia.

Gospel: Mark 7:14-23

[14] Jesus summoned the crowd again and said to them, "Hear me, all of you, and understand. [15] Nothing that enters one from outside can defile that person; but the things that come out from within are what defile."

[17] When he got home away from the crowd his disciples questioned him about the parable. [18] He said to them, "Are even you likewise without understanding? Do you not realize that everything that goes into a person from outside cannot defile, [19] since it enters not the heart but the stomach and passes out into the latrine?" (Thus he declared all foods clean.) [20] "But what comes out of the man, that is what defiles him. [21] From within the man, from his heart, come evil thoughts, unchastity, theft, murder, [22] adultery, greed, malice, deceit, licentiousness, envy, blasphemy, arrogance, folly. [23] All these evils come from within and they defile."

Thursday of Fifth Week in Ordinary Time
First Reading: 1 Kings 11:4-13

[4] When Solomon was old his wives had turned his heart to strange gods, and his heart was not entirely with the LORD, his God, as the heart of his father David had been. [5] By adoring Astarte, the goddess of the Sidonians, and Milcom, the idol of the Ammonites, [6] Solomon did evil in the sight of the LORD; he did not follow him unreservedly as his father David had done. [7]Solomon then built a high place to Chemosh, the idol of Moab, and to Molech, the idol of the Ammonites, on the hill opposite Jerusalem. [8] He did the same for all his foreign wives who burned incense and sacrificed to their gods. [9] The LORD, therefore, became angry with Solomon, because his heart was turned away from the LORD, the God of Israel, who had appeared to him twice [10] (for though the LORD had forbidden him this very act of following strange gods, Solomon had not obeyed him).

[11] So the LORD said to Solomon: "Since this is what you want, and you have not kept my covenant and my statutes which I enjoined on you, I will deprive you of the kingdom and give it to your servant. [12] I will not do this during your lifetime, however, for the sake of your father David; it is your son whom I will deprive. [13] Nor will I take away the whole kingdom. I will leave your son one tribe for the sake of my servant David and of Jerusalem, which I have chosen."

Responsorial Psalm: Psalms 106:3-4, 35-36, 37 AND 40

R. [(4a)]*Remember us, O Lord, as you favor your*
people.

[3] Blessed are they who observe what is right,
who do always what is just.
[4] Remember us, O LORD, as you favor your
people;
visit us with your saving help.

R. *Remember us, O Lord, as you favor your*
people.

[35] But they mingled with the nations
and learned their works.
[36] They served their idols,
which became a snare for them.

R. *Remember us, O Lord, as you favor your*
people.

[37] They sacrificed their sons
and their daughters to demons.
[40] And the LORD grew angry with his people,
and abhorred his inheritance.

R. *Remember us, O Lord, as you favor your*
people.

Alleluia: James 1:21BC

R. Alleluia, alleluia.
[21BC] Humbly welcome the word that has been
planted in you
and is able to save your souls.
R. Alleluia, alleluia.

Gospel: Mark 7:24-30

[24] Jesus went to the district of Tyre. He entered a house and wanted no one to know about it, but he could not escape notice. [25] Soon a woman whose daughter had an unclean

spirit heard about him. She came and fell at his feet. [26] The woman was a Greek, a Syrophoenician by birth, and she begged him to drive the demon out of her daughter. [27] He said to her, "Let the children be fed first. For it is not right to take the food of the children and throw it to the dogs." [28] She replied and said to him, "Lord, even the dogs under the table eat the children's scraps." [29] Then he said to her, "For saying this, you may go. The demon has gone out of your daughter." [30] When the woman went home, she found the child lying in bed and the demon gone.

Friday February 9, 2024

Friday of the Fifth Week in Ordinary Time
First Reading: 1 Kings 11:29-32; 12:19

[29] Jeroboam left Jerusalem, and the prophet Ahijah the Shilonite met him on the road. The two were alone in the area, and the prophet was wearing a new cloak. [30] Ahijah took off his new cloak, tore it into twelve pieces, [31] and said to Jeroboam:

"Take ten pieces for yourself; the LORD, the God of Israel, says: 'I will tear away the kingdom from Solomon's grasp and will give you ten of the tribes. [32] One tribe shall remain to him for the sake of David my servant, and of Jerusalem, the city I have chosen out of all the tribes of Israel.'" [19] Israel went into rebellion against David's house to this day.

Responsorial Psalm: Psalms 81:10-11AB, 12-13, 14-15
R. [11a and 9a] **I am the Lord, your God: hear my voice.**
[10] "There shall be no strange god among you
        nor shall you worship any alien god.
[11AB] I, the LORD, am your God
            who led you forth from the land of
                Egypt."
R. **I am the Lord, your God: hear my voice.**

[12] "My people heard not my voice,
        and Israel obeyed me not;
[13] So I gave them up to the hardness of their
                hearts;
            they walked according to their own
                counsels."
R. **I am the Lord, your God: hear my voice.**

[14] "If only my people would hear me,
        and Israel walk in my ways,
[15] Quickly would I humble their enemies;
        against their foes I would turn my hand."
R. **I am the Lord, your God: hear my voice.**

Alleluia: Acts 16:14B

R. Alleluia, alleluia.

[14B] Open our hearts, O Lord,
to listen to the words of your Son.

R. Alleluia, alleluia.

Gospel: Mark 7:31-37

[31] Jesus left the district of Tyre and went by way of Sidon to the Sea of Galilee, into the district of the Decapolis. [32] And people brought to him a deaf man who had a speech impediment and begged him to lay his hand on him. [33] He took him off by himself away from the crowd. He put his finger into the man's ears and, spitting, touched his tongue; [34] then he looked up to heaven and groaned, and said to him, "*Ephphatha!*" (that is, "Be opened!") [35] And immediately the man's ears were opened, his speech impediment was removed, and he spoke plainly. [36] He ordered them not to tell anyone. But the more he ordered them not to, the more they proclaimed it. [37] They were exceedingly astonished and they said, "He has done all things well. He makes the deaf hear and the mute speak."

Saturday February 10, 2024

Memorial of Saint Scholastica, Virgin
First Reading: 1 Kings 12:26-32; 13:33-34

[26] Jeroboam thought to himself: "The kingdom will return to David's house. [27] If now this people go up to offer sacrifices in the temple of the LORD in Jerusalem, the hearts of this people will return to their master, Rehoboam, king of Judah, and they will kill me." [28] After taking counsel, the king made two calves of gold and said to the people: "You have been going up to Jerusalem long enough. Here is your God, O Israel, who brought you up from the land of Egypt." [29] And he put one in Bethel, the other in Dan. [30] This led to sin, because the people frequented those calves in Bethel and in Dan. [31] He also built temples on the high places and made priests from among the people who were not Levites. [32] Jeroboam established a feast in the eighth month on the fifteenth day of the month to duplicate in Bethel the pilgrimage feast of Judah, with sacrifices to the calves he had made; and he stationed in Bethel priests of the high places he had built.

[33] Jeroboam did not give up his evil ways after this, but again made priests for the high places from among the common people. Whoever desired it was consecrated and became a priest of the high places. [34] This was a sin on the part of the house of Jeroboam for which it was to be cut off and destroyed from the earth.

Responsorial Psalm: Psalms 106:6-7AB, 19-20, 21-22

R. [4a] ***Remember us, O Lord, as you favor your
     people.***

[6] We have sinned, we and our fathers;
       we have committed crimes; we have done
          wrong.

7AB Our fathers in Egypt
      considered not your wonders.
R. Remember us, O Lord, as you favor your
        people.

19 They made a calf in Horeb
      and adored a molten image;
20 They exchanged their glory
      for the image of a grass-eating bullock.
R. Remember us, O Lord, as you favor your
        people.

21 They forgot the God who had saved them,
      who had done great deeds in Egypt,
22 Wondrous deeds in the land of Ham,
      terrible things at the Red Sea.
R. Remember us, O Lord, as you favor your
        people.

Alleluia: Matthew 4:4B

R. Alleluia, alleluia.
4B One does not live on bread alone,
but on every word that comes forth from the
        mouth of God.
R. Alleluia, alleluia.

Gospel: Mark 8:1-10

1 In those days when there again was a great crowd without anything to eat, Jesus summoned the disciples and said, 2 "My heart is moved with pity for the crowd, because they have been with me now for three days and have nothing to eat. 3 If I send them away hungry to their homes, they will collapse on the way, and some of them have come a great distance." 4 His disciples answered him, "Where can anyone get enough bread to satisfy them here in this deserted place?" 5 Still he asked them, "How many loaves do you have?" They replied, "Seven." 6 He ordered the crowd to sit down on the ground. Then, taking the seven loaves he gave thanks, broke them, and gave them to his disciples to distribute, and they distributed them to the crowd. 7 They also had a few fish. He said the blessing over them and ordered them distributed also. 8 They ate and were satisfied. They picked up the fragments left over— seven baskets. 9 There were about four thousand people.

      He dismissed the crowd 10 and got into the boat with his disciples and came to the region of Dalmanutha.

Sixth Sunday in ordinary Time Year B

First Reading: Leviticus 13:1-2, 44-46

[1] The LORD said to Moses and Aaron, [2] "If someone has on his skin a scab or pustule or blotch which appears to be the sore of leprosy, he shall be brought to Aaron, the priest, or to one of the priests among his descendants. [44] If the man is leprous and unclean, the priest shall declare him unclean by reason of the sore on his head.

[45] "The one who bears the sore of leprosy shall keep his garments rent and his head bare, and shall muffle his beard; he shall cry out, 'Unclean, unclean!' [46] As long as the sore is on him he shall declare himself unclean, since he is in fact unclean. He shall dwell apart, making his abode outside the camp."

Responsorial Psalm: Psalms 32:1-2, 5, 11

R. [7] *I turn to you, Lord, in time of trouble, and you fill me with the joy of salvation.*

[1] Blessed is he whose fault is taken away,
   whose sin is covered.
[2] Blessed the man to whom the LORD imputes
      not guilt,
   in whose spirit there is no guile.
R. *I turn to you, Lord, in time of trouble, and you fill me with the joy of salvation.*
[5] Then I acknowledged my sin to you,
   my guilt I covered not.
I said, "I confess my faults to the LORD,"
   and you took away the guilt of my sin.
R. *I turn to you, Lord, in time of trouble, and you fill me with the joy of salvation.*

[11] Be glad in the LORD and rejoice, you just;
   exult, all you upright of heart.
R. *I turn to you, Lord, in time of trouble, and you fill me with the joy of salvation.*

Second Reading: 1 Corinthians 10:31-11:1

Brothers and sisters, [31] Whether you eat or drink, or whatever you do, do everything for the glory of God. [32] Avoid giving offense, whether to the Jews or Greeks or the church of God, [33] just as I try to please everyone in every way, not seeking my own benefit but that of the many, that they may be saved. [1] Be imitators of me, as I am of Christ.

Alleluia: Luke 7:16

R. Alleluia, alleluia.

[16] A great prophet has arisen in our midst,
God has visited his people.

R. Alleluia, alleluia.

Gospel: Mark 1:40-45

[40] A leper came to Jesus and kneeling down begged him and said, "If you wish, you can make me clean." [41] Moved with pity, he stretched out his hand, touched him, and said to him, "I do will it. Be made clean." [42] The leprosy left him immediately, and he was made clean. [43] Then, warning him sternly, he dismissed him at once.

[44] He said to him, "See that you tell no one anything, but go, show yourself to the priest and offer for your cleansing what Moses prescribed; that will be proof for them."

[45] The man went away and began to publicize the whole matter. He spread the report abroad so that it was impossible for Jesus to enter a town openly. He remained outside in deserted places, and people kept coming to him from everywhere.

Monday February 12, 2024

Monday of the Sixth Week in Ordinary Time

First Reading: James 1:1-11

[1] James, a servant of God and of the Lord Jesus Christ, to the twelve tribes in the dispersion, greetings.

[2] Consider it all joy, my brothers and sisters, when you encounter various trials, [3] for you know that the testing of your faith produces perseverance. [4] And let perseverance be perfect, so that you may be perfect and complete, lacking in nothing. [5] But if any of you lacks wisdom, he should ask God who gives to all generously and ungrudgingly, and he will be given it. [6] But he should ask in faith, not doubting, for the one who doubts is like a wave of the sea that is driven and tossed about by the wind. [7] For that person must not suppose that he will receive anything from the Lord, [8] since he is a man of two minds, unstable in all his ways.

[9] The brother in lowly circumstances should take pride in high standing, [10] and the rich one in his lowliness, for he will pass away "like the flower of the field." [11] For the sun comes up with its scorching heat and dries up the grass, its flower droops, and the beauty of its appearance vanishes. So will the rich person fade away in the midst of his pursuits.

Responsorial Psalm: Psalms 119:67, 68, 71, 72, 75, 76

R. [(77a)] Be kind to me, Lord, and I shall live.

[67] Before I was afflicted I went astray,
    but now I hold to your promise.

R. Be kind to me, Lord, and I shall live.

[68] You are good and bountiful;
    teach me your statutes.

R. Be kind to me, Lord, and I shall live.

[71] It is good for me that I have been afflicted,
    that I may learn your statutes.
R. Be kind to me, Lord, and I shall live.

[72] The law of your mouth is to me more
      precious
    than thousands of gold and silver pieces.
R. Be kind to me, Lord, and I shall live.

[75] I know, O LORD, that your ordinances are just,
    and in your faithfulness you have
      afflicted me.
R. Be kind to me, Lord, and I shall live.

[76] Let your kindness comfort me
    according to your promise to your
      servants.
R. Be kind to me, Lord, and I shall live.

Alleluia: John 14:6
R. Alleluia, alleluia.
[6] I am the way and the truth and the life, says
    the Lord;
no one comes to the Father except through
    me.
R. Alleluia, alleluia.

Gospel: Mark 8:11-13
[11] The Pharisees came forward and began to argue with Jesus, seeking from him a sign from heaven to test him. [12] He sighed from the depth of his spirit and said, "Why does this generation seek a sign? Amen, I say to you, no sign will be given to this generation." [13] Then he left them, got into the boat again, and went off to the other shore.

Tuesday February 13, 2024

Tuesday of the Sixth Week in Ordinary Time
First Reading: James 1:12-18
[12] Blessed is he who perseveres in temptation, for when he has been proven he will receive the crown of life that he promised to those who love him. [13] No one experiencing temptation should say, "I am being tempted by God"; for God is not subject to temptation to evil, and he himself tempts no one. [14] Rather, each person is tempted when lured and enticed by his desire. [15] Then desire conceives and brings forth sin, and when sin reaches maturity it gives birth to death.

[16] Do not be deceived, my beloved brothers and sisters: [17] all good giving and every perfect gift is from above, coming down from the Father of lights, with whom there is no alteration or shadow caused by change. [18] He willed to give us birth by the word of truth that we may be a kind of firstfruits of his creatures.

Responsorial Psalm: Psalms 94:12-13A, 14-15, 18-19

R. [(12a)]**Blessed the man you instruct, O Lord.**

[12] Blessed the man whom you instruct, O LORD,
      whom by your law you teach,
[13A] Giving him rest from evil days.
R. **Blessed the man you instruct, O Lord.**

[14] For the LORD will not cast off his people,
      nor abandon his inheritance;
[15] But judgment shall again be with justice,
      and all the upright of heart shall follow it.
R. **Blessed the man you instruct, O Lord.**

[18] When I say, "My foot is slipping,"
      your mercy, O LORD, sustains me;
[19] When cares abound within me,
      your comfort gladdens my soul.
R. **Blessed the man you instruct, O Lord.**

Alleluia: John 14:23

R. **Alleluia, alleluia.**
[23] Whoever loves me will keep my word, says
         the Lord;
and my Father will love him
and we will come to him.
R. **Alleluia, alleluia.**

Gospel: Mark 8:14-21

[14] The disciples had forgotten to bring bread, and they had only one loaf with them in the boat. [15] Jesus enjoined them, "Watch out, guard against the leaven of the Pharisees and the leaven of Herod." [16] They concluded among themselves that it was because they had no bread. [17] When he became aware of this he said to them, "Why do you conclude that it is because you have no bread? Do you not yet understand or comprehend? Are your hearts hardened? [18] Do you have eyes and not see, ears and not hear? And do you not remember, [19] when I broke the five loaves for the five thousand, how many wicker baskets full of fragments you picked up?" They answered him, "Twelve." [20] "When I broke the seven loaves for the four thousand, how many full baskets of fragments did you pick up?" They answered him, "Seven." [21] He said to them, "Do you still not understand?"

Ash Wednesday

First Reading: Joel 2:12-18

[12] Even now, says the LORD,
     return to me with your whole heart,
     with fasting, and weeping, and mourning;
[13] Rend your hearts, not your garments,
     and return to the LORD, your God.
For gracious and merciful is he,
     slow to anger, rich in kindness,
     and relenting in punishment.
[14] Perhaps he will again relent
     and leave behind him a blessing,
Offerings and libations
     for the LORD, your God.

[15] Blow the trumpet in Zion!
     proclaim a fast,
     call an assembly;
[16] Gather the people,
     notify the congregation;
Assemble the elders,
     gather the children
     and the infants at the breast;
Let the bridegroom quit his room
     and the bride her chamber.
[17] Between the porch and the altar
     let the priests, the ministers of the LORD,
          weep,
And say, "Spare, O LORD, your people,
     and make not your heritage a reproach,
     with the nations ruling over them!
Why should they say among the peoples,
     'Where is their God?'"

[18] Then the LORD was stirred to concern for his
          land
     and took pity on his people.

Responsorial Psalm: Psalms 51:3-4, 5-6AB, 12-13, 14 AND 17

R. [see 3a] *Be merciful, O Lord, for we have sinned.*

³ Have mercy on me, O God, in your goodness;
      in the greatness of your compassion wipe
        out my offense.
⁴ Thoroughly wash me from my guilt
      and of my sin cleanse me.

R. Be merciful, O Lord, for we have sinned.

⁵ For I acknowledge my offense,
      and my sin is before me always:
⁶ᴬᴮ "Against you only have I sinned,
      and done what is evil in your sight."

R. Be merciful, O Lord, for we have sinned.

¹² A clean heart create for me, O God,
      and a steadfast spirit renew within me.
¹³ Cast me not out from your presence,
      and your Holy Spirit take not from me.

R. Be merciful, O Lord, for we have sinned.

¹⁴ Give me back the joy of your salvation,
      and a willing spirit sustain in me.
¹⁷ O Lord, open my lips,
      and my mouth shall proclaim your
        praise.

R. Be merciful, O Lord, for we have sinned.

Second Reading: 2 Corinthians 5:20-6:2

²⁰ Brothers and sisters: We are ambassadors for Christ, as if God were appealing through us. We implore you on behalf of Christ, be reconciled to God. ²¹ For our sake he made him to be sin who did not know sin, so that we might become the righteousness of God in him.

      ¹ Working together, then, we appeal to you not to receive the grace of God in vain. ² For he says:

In an acceptable time I heard you,
      and on the day of salvation I helped you.

Behold, now is a very acceptable time; behold, now is the day of salvation.

Verse Before the Gospel: cf. Psalms 95:8

⁸ If today you hear his voice,
harden not your hearts.

Gospel: Matthew 6:1-6, 16-18

Jesus said to his disciples: ¹ "Take care not to perform righteous deeds in order that people may see them; otherwise, you will have no recompense from your heavenly

Father. [2] When you give alms, do not blow a trumpet before you, as the hypocrites do in the synagogues and in the streets to win the praise of others. Amen, I say to you, they have received their reward. [3] But when you give alms, do not let your left hand know what your right is doing, [4] so that your almsgiving may be secret. And your Father who sees in secret will repay you.

[5] "When you pray, do not be like the hypocrites, who love to stand and pray in the synagogues and on street corners so that others may see them. Amen, I say to you, they have received their reward. [6] But when you pray, go to your inner room, close the door, and pray to your Father in secret. And your Father who sees in secret will repay you.

[16] "When you fast, do not look gloomy like the hypocrites. They neglect their appearance, so that they may appear to others to be fasting. Amen, I say to you, they have received their reward. [17] But when you fast, anoint your head and wash your face, [18] so that you may not appear to be fasting, except to your Father who is hidden. And your Father who sees what is hidden will repay you."

Thursday February 15, 2024

Thursday after Ash Wednesday
First Reading: Deuteronomy 30:15-20

[15] Moses said to the people: "Today I have set before you life and prosperity, death and doom. [16] If you obey the commandments of the LORD, your God, which I enjoin on you today, loving him, and walking in his ways, and keeping his commandments, statutes and decrees, you will live and grow numerous, and the LORD, your God, will bless you in the land you are entering to occupy. [17] If, however, you turn away your hearts and will not listen, but are led astray and adore and serve other gods, [18] I tell you now that you will certainly perish; you will not have a long life on the land that you are crossing the Jordan to enter and occupy. [19] I call heaven and earth today to witness against you: I have set before you life and death, the blessing and the curse. Choose life, then, that you and your descendants may live, [20] by loving the LORD, your God, heeding his voice, and holding fast to him. For that will mean life for you, a long life for you to live on the land that the LORD swore he would give to your fathers Abraham, Isaac and Jacob."

Responsorial Psalm: Psalms 1:1-2,3,4AND 6

R. [(40:5a)] *Blessed are they who hope in the Lord.*
[1] Blessed the man who follows not
  the counsel of the wicked
Nor walks in the way of sinners,
  nor sits in the company of the insolent,
[2] But delights in the law of the LORD
  and meditates on his law day and night.
R. Blessed are they who hope in the Lord.

[3] He is like a tree

planted near running water,
That yields its fruit in due season,
and whose leaves never fade.
Whatever he does, prospers.
R. Blessed are they who hope in the Lord.

[4] Not so the wicked, not so;
they are like chaff which the wind drives
away.
[6] For the LORD watches over the way of the
just,
but the way of the wicked vanishes.
R. Blessed are they who hope in the Lord.

Verse Before The Gospel: Matthew 4:17

[17] Repent, says the Lord;
the Kingdom of heaven is at hand.

Gospel: Luke 9:22-25

[22] Jesus said to his disciples: "The Son of Man must suffer greatly and be rejected by the elders, the chief priests, and the scribes, and be killed and on the third day be raised."

[23] Then he said to all, "If anyone wishes to come after me, he must deny himself and take up his cross daily and follow me. [24] For whoever wishes to save his life will lose it, but whoever loses his life for my sake will save it. [25] What profit is there for one to gain the whole world yet lose or forfeit himself?"

Friday February 16, 2024

Friday after Ash Wednesday
First Reading: Isaiah 58:1-9A

[1] Thus says the Lord GOD:
Cry out full-throated and unsparingly,
lift up your voice like a trumpet blast;
Tell my people their wickedness,
and the house of Jacob their sins.
[2] They seek me day after day,
and desire to know my ways,
Like a nation that has done what is just
and not abandoned the law of their God;
They ask me to declare what is due them,
pleased to gain access to God.
[3] "Why do we fast, and you do not see it?
afflict ourselves, and you take no note of

it?"

Lo, on your fast day you carry out your own
        pursuits,
     and drive all your laborers.
[4] Yes, your fast ends in quarreling and
        fighting,
     striking with wicked claw.
Would that today you might fast
     so as to make your voice heard on high!
[5] Is this the manner of fasting I wish,
     of keeping a day of penance:
That a man bow his head like a reed
     and lie in sackcloth and ashes?
Do you call this a fast,
     a day acceptable to the LORD?
[6] This, rather, is the fasting that I wish:
     releasing those bound unjustly,
     untying the thongs of the yoke;
Setting free the oppressed,
     breaking every yoke;
[7] Sharing your bread with the hungry,
     sheltering the oppressed and the
        homeless;
Clothing the naked when you see them,
     and not turning your back on your own.
[8] Then your light shall break forth like the
        dawn,
     and your wound shall quickly be healed;
Your vindication shall go before you,
     and the glory of the LORD shall be your
        rear guard.
[9A] Then you shall call, and the LORD will answer,
     you shall cry for help, and he will say:
        Here I am!

Responsorial Psalm: Psalms 51:3-4, 5-6AB, 18-19
R. [(19b)] *A heart contrite and humbled, O God, you*
         will not spurn.
[3] Have mercy on me, O God, in your goodness;
     in the greatness of your compassion wipe
        out my offense.

⁴ Thoroughly wash me from my guilt
     and of my sin cleanse me.
R. A heart contrite and humbled, O God, you will
         not spurn.

⁵ For I acknowledge my offense,
     and my sin is before me always:
6AB "Against you only have I sinned,
     and done what is evil in your sight."
R. A heart contrite and humbled, O God, you will
         not spurn.

¹⁸ For you are not pleased with sacrifices;
     should I offer a burnt offering, you would
         not accept it.
¹⁹ My sacrifice, O God, is a contrite spirit;
     a heart contrite and humbled, O God, you
         will not spurn.
R. A heart contrite and humbled, O God, you will
         not spurn.

Verse Before the Gospel: cf. Amos 5:14

¹⁴ Seek good and not evil so that you may live,
and the Lord will be with you.

Gospel: Matthew 9:14-15

¹⁴ The disciples of John approached Jesus and said, "Why do we and the Pharisees fast much, but your disciples do not fast?" ¹⁵ Jesus answered them, "Can the wedding guests mourn as long as the bridegroom is with them? The days will come when the bridegroom is taken away from them, and then they will fast."

Saturday after Ash Wednesday
First Reading: Isaiah 58:9B-14

9B Thus says the LORD:
If you remove from your midst oppression,
     false accusation and malicious speech;
¹⁰ If you bestow your bread on the hungry
     and satisfy the afflicted;
Then light shall rise for you in the darkness,
     and the gloom shall become for you like
         midday;

[11] Then the LORD will guide you always
      and give you plenty even on the parched
            land.
He will renew your strength,
      and you shall be like a watered garden,
      like a spring whose water never fails.
[12] The ancient ruins shall be rebuilt for your
            sake,
      and the foundations from ages past you
            shall raise up;
"Repairer of the breach," they shall call you,
      "Restorer of ruined homesteads."

[13] If you hold back your foot on the sabbath
      from following your own pursuits on my
            holy day;
If you call the sabbath a delight,
      and the LORD's holy day honorable;
If you honor it by not following your ways,
      seeking your own interests, or speaking
            with malice—
[14] Then you shall delight in the LORD,
      and I will make you ride on the heights of
            the earth;
I will nourish you with the heritage of Jacob,
      your father,
      for the mouth of the LORD has spoken.

Responsorial Psalm: Psalms 86:1-2, 3-4, 5-6

R. [11ab] *Teach me your way, O Lord, that I may*
                  walk in your truth.
[1] Incline your ear, O LORD; answer me,
      for I am afflicted and poor.
[2] Keep my life, for I am devoted to you;
      save your servant who trusts in you.
      You are my God.
R. *Teach me your way, O Lord, that I may walk*
            in your truth.

[3] Have mercy on me, O Lord,
      for to you I call all the day.
[4] Gladden the soul of your servant,

for to you, O Lord, I lift up my soul.
**R. Teach me your way, O Lord, that I may walk
in your truth.**

[5] For you, O Lord, are good and forgiving,
abounding in kindness to all who call
upon you.
[6] Hearken, O LORD, to my prayer
and attend to the sound of my pleading.
**R. Teach me your way, O Lord, that I may walk
in your truth.**

Verse Before the Gospel: Ezekiel 33:11
[11] I take no pleasure in the death of the wicked
man, says the Lord,
but rather in his conversion, that he may
live.

Gospel: Luke 5:27-32
[27] Jesus saw a tax collector named Levi sitting at the customs post. He said to him, "Follow me." [28] And leaving everything behind, he got up and followed him. [29] Then Levi gave a great banquet for him in his house, and a large crowd of tax collectors and others were at table with them. [30] The Pharisees and their scribes complained to his disciples, saying, "Why do you eat and drink with tax collectors and sinners?" [31] Jesus said to them in reply, "Those who are healthy do not need a physician, but the sick do. [32] I have not come to call the righteous to repentance but sinners."

Sunday February 18, 2024

First Sunday of Lent, Year B
First Reading: Genesis 9:8-15
[8] God said to Noah and to his sons with him: [9] "See, I am now establishing my covenant with you and your descendants after you [10] and with every living creature that was with you: all the birds, and the various tame and wild animals that were with you and came out of the ark. [11] I will establish my covenant with you, that never again shall all bodily creatures be destroyed by the waters of a flood; there shall not be another flood to devastate the earth." [12] God added: "This is the sign that I am giving for all ages to come, of the covenant between me and you and every living creature with you: [13] I set my bow in the clouds to serve as a sign of the covenant between me and the earth. [14] When I bring clouds over the earth, and the bow appears in the clouds, [15] I will recall the covenant I have made between me and you and all living beings, so that the waters shall never again become a flood to destroy all mortal beings."

Responsorial Psalm: Psalms 25:4-5, 6-7, 8-9.

R. (cf. 10) Your ways, O Lord, are love and truth to those who keep your covenant.

4 Your ways, O LORD, make known to me;
　　teach me your paths.
5 Guide me in your truth and teach me,
　　for you are God my savior.

R. Your ways, O Lord, are love and truth to those who keep your covenant.

6 Remember that your compassion, O LORD,
　　and your love are from of old.
7 In your kindness remember me,
　　because of your goodness, O LORD.

R. Your ways, O Lord, are love and truth to those who keep your covenant.

8 Good and upright is the LORD,
　　thus he shows sinners the way.
9 He guides the humble to justice,
　　and he teaches the humble his way.

R. Your ways, O Lord, are love and truth to those who keep your covenant.

Second Reading: 1 Peter 3:18-22

Beloved: 18 Christ suffered for sins once, the righteous for the sake of the unrighteous, that he might lead you to God. Put to death in the flesh, he was brought to life in the Spirit. 19 In it he also went to preach to the spirits in prison, 20 who had once been disobedient while God patiently waited in the days of Noah during the building of the ark, in which a few persons, eight in all, were saved through water. 21 This prefigured baptism, which saves you now. It is not a removal of dirt from the body but an appeal to God for a clear conscience, through the resurrection of Jesus Christ, 22 who has gone into heaven and is at the right hand of God, with angels, authorities, and powers subject to him.

Verse Before the Gospel: Matthew 4:4B

4B One does not live on bread alone,
but on every word that comes forth from the
　　mouth of God.

Gospel: Mark 1:12-15

12 The Spirit drove Jesus out into the desert, 13 and he remained in the desert for forty days, tempted by Satan. He was among wild beasts, and the angels ministered to him.

[14] After John had been arrested, Jesus came to Galilee proclaiming the gospel of God: [15] "This is the time of fulfillment. The kingdom of God is at hand. Repent, and believe in the gospel."

Monday of the First Week of Lent
First Reading: Leviticus 19:1-2, 11-18

[1] The LORD said to Moses, [2] "Speak to the whole assembly of the children of Israel and tell them: Be holy, for I, the LORD, your God, am holy.

[11] "You shall not steal. You shall not lie or speak falsely to one another. [12] You shall not swear falsely by my name, thus profaning the name of your God. I am the LORD.

[13] "You shall not defraud or rob your neighbor. You shall not withhold overnight the wages of your day laborer. [14] You shall not curse the deaf, or put a stumbling block in front of the blind, but you shall fear your God. I am the LORD.

[15] "You shall not act dishonestly in rendering judgment. Show neither partiality to the weak nor deference to the mighty, but judge your fellow men justly. [16] You shall not go about spreading slander among your kin; nor shall you stand by idly when your neighbor's life is at stake. I am the LORD.

[17] "You shall not bear hatred for your brother in your heart. Though you may have to reprove him, do not incur sin because of him. [18] Take no revenge and cherish no grudge against your fellow countrymen. You shall love your neighbor as yourself. I am the LORD."

Responsorial Psalm: Psalms 19:8, 9, 10, 15
R. (John 6:63b) **Your words, Lord, are Spirit and life.**
[8] The law of the LORD is perfect,
　　refreshing the soul.
The decree of the LORD is trustworthy,
　　giving wisdom to the simple.
R. **Your words, Lord, are Spirit and life.**

[9] The precepts of the LORD are right,
　　rejoicing the heart.
The command of the LORD is clear,
　　enlightening the eye.
R. **Your words, Lord, are Spirit and life.**

[10] The fear of the LORD is pure,
　　enduring forever;
The ordinances of the LORD are true,
　　all of them just.
R. **Your words, Lord, are Spirit and life.**
[15] Let the words of my mouth and the thought

of my heart
find favor before you,
O LORD, my rock and my redeemer.
R. Your words, Lord, are Spirit and life.

Verse Before the Gospel: 2 Corinthians 6:2B

[2B] Behold, now is a very acceptable time;
behold, now is the day of salvation.

Gospel: Matthew 25:31-46

Jesus said to his disciples: [31] "When the Son of Man comes in his glory, and all the angels with him, he will sit upon his glorious throne, [32] and all the nations will be assembled before him. And he will separate them one from another, as a shepherd separates the sheep from the goats. [33] He will place the sheep on his right and the goats on his left. [34] Then the king will say to those on his right, 'Come, you who are blessed by my Father. Inherit the kingdom prepared for you from the foundation of the world. [35] For I was hungry and you gave me food, I was thirsty and you gave me drink, a stranger and you welcomed me, [36] naked and you clothed me, ill and you cared for me, in prison and you visited me.' [37] Then the righteous will answer him and say, 'Lord, when did we see you hungry and feed you, or thirsty and give you drink? [38] When did we see you a stranger and welcome you, or naked and clothe you? [39] When did we see you ill or in prison, and visit you?'
[40] And the king will say to them in reply, 'Amen, I say to you, whatever you did for one of these least brothers of mine, you did for me.' [41] Then he will say to those on his left, 'Depart from me, you accursed, into the eternal fire prepared for the Devil and his angels. [42] For I was hungry and you gave me no food, I was thirsty and you gave me no drink, [43] a stranger and you gave me no welcome, naked and you gave me no clothing, ill and in prison, and you did not care for me.' [44] Then they will answer and say, 'Lord, when did we see you hungry or thirsty or a stranger or naked or ill or in prison, and not minister to your needs?' [45] He will answer them, 'Amen, I say to you, what you did not do for one of these least ones, you did not do for me.' [46] And these will go off to eternal punishment, but the righteous to eternal life."

Tuesday February 20, 2024

Tuesday of the First Week of Lent
First Reading: Isaiah 55:10-11

[10] Thus says the LORD:
Just as from the heavens
the rain and snow come down
And do not return there
till they have watered the earth,
making it fertile and fruitful,

Giving seed to the one who sows
    and bread to the one who eats,
[11] So shall my word be
        that goes forth from my mouth;
It shall not return to me void,
        but shall do my will,
            achieving the end for which I sent it.

Responsorial Psalm: Psalms 34:4-5, 6-7, 16-17, 18-19

R. [18b]*From all their distress God rescues the just.*
[4] Glorify the LORD with me,
        let us together extol his name.
[5] I sought the LORD, and he answered me
        and delivered me from all my fears.
R. *From all their distress God rescues the just.*

[6] Look to him that you may be radiant with
                joy,
        and your faces may not blush with
                shame.
[7] When the poor one called out, the LORD
                heard,
        and from all his distress he saved him.
R. *From all their distress God rescues the just.*

[16] The LORD has eyes for the just,
        and ears for their cry.
[17] The LORD confronts the evildoers,
        to destroy remembrance of them from
                the earth.
R. *From all their distress God rescues the just.*

[18] When the just cry out, the LORD hears them,
        and from all their distress he rescues
                them.
[19] The LORD is close to the brokenhearted;
        and those who are crushed in spirit he
                saves.
R. *From all their distress God rescues the just.*

Verse Before the Gospel: Matthew 4:4B

[4B] One does not live on bread alone,

but on every word that comes forth from the
      mouth of God.

Gospel: Matthew 6:7-15

Jesus said to his disciples: [7] "In praying, do not babble like the pagans, who think that they will be heard because of their many words. [8] Do not be like them. Your Father knows what you need before you ask him.
[9] "This is how you are to pray:

Our Father who art in heaven,
    hallowed be thy name,
      [10] thy Kingdom come,
thy will be done,
    on earth as it is in heaven.
[11] Give us this day our daily bread;
      [12] and forgive us our trespasses,
    as we forgive those who trespass against
        us;
      [13] and lead us not into temptation,
    but deliver us from evil.

[14] "If you forgive men their transgressions, your heavenly Father will forgive you. [15] But if you do not forgive men, neither will your Father forgive your transgressions."

Wednesday February 21, 2024

Wednesday of the First Week of Lent
First Reading: Jonah 3:1-10

[1] The word of the LORD came to Jonah a second time: [2] "Set out for the great city of Nineveh, and announce to it the message that I will tell you." [3] So Jonah made ready and went to Nineveh, according to the LORD's bidding. Now Nineveh was an enormously large city; it took three days to go through it. [4] Jonah began his journey through the city, and had gone but a single day's walk announcing, "Forty days more and Nineveh shall be destroyed," [5] when the people of Nineveh believed God; they proclaimed a fast and all of them, great and small, put on sackcloth.

    [6] When the news reached the king of Nineveh, he rose from his throne, laid aside his robe, covered himself with sackcloth, and sat in the ashes. [7] Then he had this proclaimed throughout Nineveh, by decree of the king and his nobles: "Neither man nor beast, neither cattle nor sheep, shall taste anything; they shall not eat, nor shall they drink water. [8] Man and beast shall be covered with sackcloth and call loudly to God; every man shall turn from his evil way and from the violence he has in hand. [9] Who knows, God may relent and forgive, and withhold his blazing wrath, so that we shall not perish." [10] When

God saw by their actions how they turned from their evil way, he repented of the evil that he had threatened to do to them; he did not carry it out.

Responsorial Psalm: Psalms 51:3-4, 12-13, 18-19

R. [19b]*A heart contrite and humbled, O God, you will not spurn.*

[3] Have mercy on me, O God, in your goodness;
    in the greatness of your compassion wipe
      out my offense.
[4] Thoroughly wash me from my guilt
    and of my sin cleanse me.

R. *A heart contrite and humbled, O God, you will not spurn.*

[12] A clean heart create for me, O God,
    and a steadfast spirit renew within me.
[13] Cast me not out from your presence,
    and your Holy Spirit take not from me.

R. *A heart contrite and humbled, O God, you will not spurn.*

[18] For you are not pleased with sacrifices;
    should I offer a burnt offering, you would
      not accept it.
[19] My sacrifice, O God, is a contrite spirit;
    a heart contrite and humbled, O God, you
      will not spurn.

R. *A heart contrite and humbled, O God, you will not spurn.*

Verse Before the Gospel: Joel 2:12-13

[12] Even now, says the LORD,
[13] return to me with your whole heart
for I am gracious and merciful.

Gospel: Luke 11:29-32

[29] While still more people gathered in the crowd, Jesus said to them, "This generation is an evil generation; it seeks a sign, but no sign will be given it, except the sign of Jonah. [30] Just as Jonah became a sign to the Ninevites, so will the Son of Man be to this generation. [31] At the judgment the queen of the south will rise with the men of this generation and she will condemn them, because she came from the ends of the earth to hear the wisdom of Solomon, and there is something greater than Solomon here. [32] At the judgment the men of Nineveh will arise with this generation and condemn it, because at the preaching of Jonah they repented, and there is something greater than Jonah here."

Feast of the Chair of Saint Peter, Apostle

First Reading: 1 Peter 5:1-4

Beloved: [1] I exhort the presbyters among you, as a fellow presbyter and witness to the sufferings of Christ and one who has a share in the glory to be revealed. [2] Tend the flock of God in your midst, overseeing not by constraint but willingly, as God would have it, not for shameful profit but eagerly. [3] Do not lord it over those assigned to you, but be examples to the flock. [4] And when the chief Shepherd is revealed, you will receive the unfading crown of glory.

Responsorial Psalm: Psalms 23:1-3A, 4, 5, 6

R. [1] *The Lord is my shepherd; there is nothing I*
shall want.

[1] The LORD is my shepherd; I shall not want.
[2] In verdant pastures he gives me repose;
Beside restful waters he leads me;
[3A] he refreshes my soul.

R. *The Lord is my shepherd; there is nothing I*
shall want.

[4] Even though I walk in the dark valley
I fear no evil; for you are at my side
With your rod and your staff
that give me courage.

R. *The Lord is my shepherd; there is nothing I*
shall want.

[5] You spread the table before me
in the sight of my foes;
You anoint my head with oil;
my cup overflows.

R. *The Lord is my shepherd; there is nothing I*
shall want.

[6] Only goodness and kindness follow me
all the days of my life;
And I shall dwell in the house of the LORD
for years to come.

R. *The Lord is my shepherd; there is nothing I*
shall want.

Alleluia: Matthew 16:18

R. Alleluia, alleluia.

[18] You are Peter, and upon this rock I will build
    my Church;
the gates of the netherworld shall not prevail
    against it.

R. Alleluia, alleluia.

Gospel: Matthew 16:13-19

[13] When Jesus went into the region of Caesarea Philippi he asked his disciples, "Who do people say that the Son of Man is?" [14] They replied, "Some say John the Baptist, others Elijah, still others Jeremiah or one of the prophets." [15] He said to them, "But who do you say that I am?" [16] Simon Peter said in reply, "You are the Christ, the Son of the living God." [17] Jesus said to him in reply, "Blessed are you, Simon son of Jonah. For flesh and blood has not revealed this to you, but my heavenly Father. [18] And so I say to you, you are Peter, and upon this rock I will build my Church, and the gates of the netherworld shall not prevail against it. [19] I will give you the keys to the Kingdom of heaven. Whatever you bind on earth shall be bound in heaven; and whatever you loose on earth shall be loosed in heaven."

Friday February 23, 2024

Friday of the First Week of Lent
First Reading: Ezekiel 18:21-28

[21] Thus says the Lord GOD: If the wicked man turns away from all the sins he committed, if he keeps all my statutes and does what is right and just, he shall surely live, he shall not die. [22] None of the crimes he committed shall be remembered against him; he shall live because of the virtue he has practiced. [23] Do I indeed derive any pleasure from the death of the wicked? says the Lord GOD. Do I not rather rejoice when he turns from his evil way that he may live?

[24] And if the virtuous man turns from the path of virtue to do evil, the same kind of abominable things that the wicked man does, can he do this and still live? None of his virtuous deeds shall be remembered, because he has broken faith and committed sin; because of this, he shall die. [25] You say, "The LORD's way is not fair!" Hear now, house of Israel: Is it my way that is unfair, or rather, are not your ways unfair? [26] When someone virtuous turns away from virtue to commit iniquity, and dies, it is because of the iniquity he committed that he must die. [27] But if the wicked, turning from the wickedness he has committed, does what is right and just, he shall preserve his life; [28] since he has turned away from all the sins that he committed, he shall surely live, he shall not die.

Responsorial Psalm: Psalms 130:1-2, 3-4, 5-7A, 7BC-8

R. [3]**If you, O Lord, mark iniquities, who can
    stand?**

[1] Out of the depths I cry to you, O LORD;
    LORD, hear my voice!

² Let your ears be attentive
   to my voice in supplication.
**R. If you, O Lord, mark iniquities, who can
    stand?**

³ If you, O LORD, mark iniquities,
   LORD, who can stand?
⁴ But with you is forgiveness,
   that you may be revered.
**R. If you, O Lord, mark iniquities, who can
    stand?**

⁵ I trust in the LORD;
   my soul trusts in his word.
⁶ My soul waits for the LORD
   more than sentinels wait for the dawn.
    ^{7A} Let Israel wait for the LORD.
**R. If you, O Lord, mark iniquities, who can
    stand?**

^{7BC} For with the LORD is kindness
   and with him is plenteous redemption;
⁸ And he will redeem Israel
   from all their iniquities.
**R. If you, O Lord, mark iniquities, who can
    stand?**

Verse Before the Gospel: Ezekiel 18:31

³¹ Cast away from you all the crimes you have
    committed, says the Lord,
and make for yourselves a new heart and a
    new spirit.

Gospel: Matthew 5:20-26

Jesus said to his disciples: ²⁰ "I tell you, unless your righteousness surpasses that of the scribes and Pharisees, you will not enter into the Kingdom of heaven.

  ²¹ "You have heard that it was said to your ancestors, *You shall not kill; and whoever kills will be liable to judgment.* ²² But I say to you, whoever is angry with his brother will be liable to judgment, and whoever says to his brother, *Raqa*, will be answerable to the Sanhedrin, and whoever says, 'You fool,' will be liable to fiery Gehenna. ²³ Therefore, if you bring your gift to the altar, and there recall that your brother has anything against you, ²⁴ leave your gift there at the altar, go first and be reconciled with

your brother, and then come and offer your gift. ²⁵ Settle with your opponent quickly while on the way to court. Otherwise your opponent will hand you over to the judge, and the judge will hand you over to the guard, and you will be thrown into prison. ²⁶ Amen, I say to you, you will not be released until you have paid the last penny."

Saturday of the First Week of Lent
First Reading: Deuteronomy 26:16-19

¹⁶ Moses spoke to the people, saying: "This day the LORD, your God, commands you to observe these statutes and decrees. Be careful, then, to observe them with all your heart and with all your soul. ¹⁷ Today you are making this agreement with the LORD: he is to be your God and you are to walk in his ways and observe his statutes, commandments and decrees, and to hearken to his voice. ¹⁸ And today the LORD is making this agreement with you: you are to be a people peculiarly his own, as he promised you; and provided you keep all his commandments,¹⁹ he will then raise you high in praise and renown and glory above all other nations he has made, and you will be a people sacred to the LORD, your God, as he promised."

Responsorial Psalm: Psalms 119:1-2, 4-5,7-8

R. ⁽¹ᵇ⁾**Blessed are they who follow the law of the**
Lord!

¹ Blessed are they whose way is blameless,
who walk in the law of the LORD.
² Blessed are they who observe his decrees,
who seek him with all their heart.

R. **Blessed are they who follow the law of the**
Lord!

⁴ You have commanded that your precepts
be diligently kept.
⁵ Oh, that I might be firm in the ways
of keeping your statutes!

R. **Blessed are they who follow the law of the**
Lord!

⁷ I will give you thanks with an upright heart,
when I have learned your just
ordinances.
⁸ I will keep your statutes;
do not utterly forsake me.

R. **Blessed are they who follow the law of the**
Lord!

Verse Before the Gospel: 2 Corinthians 6:2B

[6B] Behold, now is a very acceptable time;
behold, now is the day of salvation.

Gospel: Matthew 5:43-48

Jesus said to his disciples: [43] "You have heard that it was said, You shall love your neighbor and hate your enemy. [44] But I say to you, love your enemies, and pray for those who persecute you, [45] that you may be children of your heavenly Father, for he makes his sun rise on the bad and the good, and causes rain to fall on the just and the unjust. [46] For if you love those who love you, what recompense will you have? Do not the tax collectors do the same? [47] And if you greet your brothers and sisters only, what is unusual about that? Do not the pagans do the same? [48] So be perfect, just as your heavenly Father is perfect."

Sunday February 25, 2024

Second Sunday of Lent, Year B
First Reading: Genesis 22:1-2, 9A, 10-13, 15-18

[1] God put Abraham to the test. He called to him, "Abraham!" "Here I am!" he replied. [2] Then God said: "Take your son Isaac, your only one, whom you love, and go to the land of Moriah. There you shall offer him up as a holocaust on a height that I will point out to you."

[9A] When they came to the place of which God had told him, Abraham built an altar there and arranged the wood on it. [10] Then he reached out and took the knife to slaughter his son. [11] But the LORD's messenger called to him from heaven, "Abraham, Abraham!" "Here I am!" he answered. [12] "Do not lay your hand on the boy," said the messenger. "Do not do the least thing to him. I know now how devoted you are to God, since you did not withhold from me your own beloved son." [13] As Abraham looked about, he spied a ram caught by its horns in the thicket. So he went and took the ram and offered it up as a holocaust in place of his son.

[15] Again the LORD's messenger called to Abraham from heaven [16] and said: "I swear by myself, declares the LORD, that because you acted as you did in not withholding from me your beloved son, [17] I will bless you abundantly and make your descendants as countless as the stars of the sky and the sands of the seashore; your descendants shall take possession of the gates of their enemies, [18] and in your descendants all the nations of the earth shall find blessing— all this because you obeyed my command."

Responsorial Psalm: Psalms 116:10, 15, 16-17, 18-19

R. [(116:9)] *I will walk before the Lord, in the land of the living.*

[10] I believed, even when I said,
  "I am greatly afflicted."

¹⁵ Precious in the eyes of the LORD
　　　is the death of his faithful ones.
R. I will walk before the Lord, in the land of the
　　　　　living.

¹⁶ O LORD, I am your servant;
　　　I am your servant, the son of your
　　　　　handmaid;
　　　you have loosed my bonds.
¹⁷ To you will I offer sacrifice of thanksgiving,
　　　and I will call upon the name of the LORD.
R. I will walk before the Lord, in the land of the
　　　　　living.

¹⁸ My vows to the LORD I will pay
　　　in the presence of all his people,
¹⁹ In the courts of the house of the LORD,
　　　in your midst, O Jerusalem.
R. I will walk before the Lord, in the land of the
　　　　　living.

Second Reading: Romans 8:31B-34

Brothers and sisters: ^{31B} If God is for us, who can be against us? ³² He who did not spare his own Son but handed him over for us all, how will he not also give us everything else along with him?

　　　³³ Who will bring a charge against God's chosen ones? It is God who acquits us. ³⁴ Who will condemn? Christ Jesus it is who died—or, rather, was raised—who also is at the right hand of God, who indeed intercedes for us.

Verse Before the Gospel: Matthew 17:5

⁵ From the shining cloud the Father's voice is
　　　heard:
This is my beloved Son, listen to him.

Gospel: Mark 9:2-10

² Jesus took Peter, James, and John and led them up a high mountain apart by themselves. And he was transfigured before them, ³ and his clothes became dazzling white, such as no fuller on earth could bleach them. ⁴ Then Elijah appeared to them along with Moses, and they were conversing with Jesus. ⁵ Then Peter said to Jesus in reply, "Rabbi, it is good that we are here! Let us make three tents: one for you, one for Moses, and one for Elijah." ⁶ He hardly knew what to say, they were so terrified. ⁷ Then a cloud came, casting a shadow over them; from the cloud came a voice, "This is my beloved Son. Listen to him." ⁸ Suddenly, looking around, they no longer saw anyone but Jesus alone with them.

⁹As they were coming down from the mountain, he charged them not to relate what they had seen to anyone, except when the Son of Man had risen from the dead. So they kept the matter to themselves, questioning what rising from the dead meant.

Monday of the Second Week of Lent
First Reading: Daniel 9:4B-10

^{4B} "Lord, great and awesome God, you who keep your merciful covenant toward those who love you and observe your commandments! ⁵ We have sinned, been wicked and done evil; we have rebelled and departed from your commandments and your laws. ⁶ We have not obeyed your servants the prophets, who spoke in your name to our kings, our princes, our fathers, and all the people of the land. ⁷ Justice, O Lord, is on your side; we are shamefaced even to this day: we, the men of Judah, the residents of Jerusalem, and all Israel, near and far, in all the countries to which you have scattered them because of their treachery toward you. ⁸ O LORD, we are shamefaced, like our kings, our princes, and our fathers, for having sinned against you. ⁹ But yours, O Lord, our God, are compassion and forgiveness! Yet we rebelled against you ¹⁰ and paid no heed to your command, O LORD, our God, to live by the law you gave us through your servants the prophets."

Responsorial Psalm: Psalms 79:8, 9,11 AND 13

R. *(see 103:10a)* **Lord, do not deal with us according**
                    to our sins.

⁸ Remember not against us the iniquities of
        the past;
        may your compassion quickly come to us,
        for we are brought very low.
R. **Lord, do not deal with us according to our**
                    sins.

⁹ Help us, O God our savior,
        because of the glory of your name;
Deliver us and pardon our sins
        for your name's sake.
R. **Lord, do not deal with us according to our**
                    sins.

¹¹ Let the prisoners' sighing come before you;
        with your great power free those doomed
                to death.
¹³ Then we, your people and the sheep of your
            pasture,
        will give thanks to you forever;

through all generations we will declare
     your praise.
R. Lord, do not deal with us according to our
     sins.

Verse Before the Gospel: cf John 6:63C, 68C

[63C] Your words, Lord, are Spirit and life;
[68C] you have the words of everlasting life.

Gospel: Luke 6:36-38

[36] Jesus said to his disciples: "Be merciful, just as your Father is merciful.

[37] "Stop judging and you will not be judged. Stop condemning and you will not be condemned. Forgive and you will be forgiven. [38] Give and gifts will be given to you; a good measure, packed together, shaken down, and overflowing, will be poured into your lap. For the measure with which you measure will in return be measured out to you."

Tuesday of the Second Week of Lent
First Reading: Isaiah 1:10, 16-20

[10] Hear the word of the LORD,
     princes of Sodom!
Listen to the instruction of our God,
     people of Gomorrah!

[16] Wash yourselves clean!
Put away your misdeeds from before my
     eyes;
     cease doing evil; [17] learn to do good.
Make justice your aim: redress the wronged,
     hear the orphan's plea, defend the widow.

[18] Come now, let us set things right,
     says the LORD:
Though your sins be like scarlet,
     they may become white as snow;
Though they be crimson red,
     they may become white as wool.
[19] If you are willing, and obey,
     you shall eat the good things of the land;
[20] But if you refuse and resist,
     the sword shall consume you:
     for the mouth of the LORD has spoken!

Responsorial Psalm: Psalms 50:8-9, 16BC-17, 21 AND 23

R. [23b] *To the upright I will show the saving
power of God.*

[8] "Not for your sacrifices do I rebuke you,
for your burnt offerings are before me
always.
[9] I take from your house no bullock,
no goats out of your fold."

R. *To the upright I will show the saving power of
God.*

[16BC] "Why do you recite my statutes,
and profess my covenant with your
mouth,
[17] Though you hate discipline
and cast my words behind you?"

R. *To the upright I will show the saving power of
God.*

[21] "When you do these things, shall I be deaf to
it?
Or do you think that I am like yourself?
I will correct you by drawing them up
before your eyes.
[23] He that offers praise as a sacrifice glorifies
me;
and to him that goes the right way I will
show the salvation of God."

R. *To the upright I will show the saving power of
God.*

Verse Before the Gospel: Ezekiel 18:31

[31] Cast away from you all the crimes you have
committed, says the Lord,
and make for yourselves a new heart and a
new spirit.

Gospel: Matthew 23:1-12

[1] Jesus spoke to the crowds and to his disciples, [2] saying, "The scribes and the Pharisees have taken their seat on the chair of Moses. [3] Therefore, do and observe all things whatsoever they tell you, but do not follow their example. For they preach but they do not practice. [4] They tie up heavy burdens hard to carry and lay them on people's shoulders, but they will not lift a finger to move them. [5] All their works are performed to

be seen. They widen their phylacteries and lengthen their tassels. [6] They love places of honor at banquets, seats of honor in synagogues, [7] greetings in marketplaces, and the salutation 'Rabbi.' [8] As for you, do not be called 'Rabbi.' You have but one teacher, and you are all brothers. [9] Call no one on earth your father; you have but one Father in heaven. [10] Do not be called 'Master'; you have but one master, the Christ. [11] The greatest among you must be your servant. [12] Whoever exalts himself will be humbled; but whoever humbles himself will be exalted."

Wednesday of the Second Week of Lent

First Reading: Jeremiah 18:18-20

[18] The people of Judah and the citizens of Jerusalem said, "Come, let us contrive a plot against Jeremiah. It will not mean the loss of instruction from the priests, nor of counsel from the wise, nor of messages from the prophets. And so, let us destroy him by his own tongue; let us carefully note his every word."

[19] Heed me, O LORD,
    and listen to what my adversaries say.
[20] Must good be repaid with evil
    that they should dig a pit to take my life?
Remember that I stood before you
        to speak in their behalf,
        to turn away your wrath from them.

Responsorial Psalm: Psalms 31:5-6,14, 15-16

R. [(17b)] *Save me, O Lord, in your kindness.*

[5] You will free me from the snare they set for
        me,
    for you are my refuge.
[6] Into your hands I commend my spirit;
    you will redeem me, O LORD, O faithful
        God.

R. *Save me, O Lord, in your kindness.*

[14] I hear the whispers of the crowd, that
        frighten me from every side,
    as they consult together against me,
        plotting to take my life.

R. *Save me, O Lord, in your kindness.*

[15] But my trust is in you, O LORD;
    I say, "You are my God."
[16] In your hands is my destiny; rescue me

  from the clutches of my enemies and my
    persecutors.
R. Save me, O Lord, in your kindness.

Verse Before the Gospel: John 8:12

[12] I am the light of the world, says the Lord;
whoever follows me will have the light of
  life.

Gospel: Matthew 20:17-28

[17] As Jesus was going up to Jerusalem, he took the Twelve disciples aside by themselves, and said to them on the way, [18] "Behold, we are going up to Jerusalem, and the Son of Man will be handed over to the chief priests and the scribes, and they will condemn him to death, [19] and hand him over to the Gentiles to be mocked and scourged and crucified, and he will be raised on the third day."

  [20] Then the mother of the sons of Zebedee approached Jesus with her sons and did him homage, wishing to ask him for something. [21] He said to her, "What do you wish?" She answered him, "Command that these two sons of mine sit, one at your right and the other at your left, in your kingdom." [22] Jesus said in reply, "You do not know what you are asking. Can you drink the chalice that I am going to drink?" They said to him, "We can." [23] He replied, "My chalice you will indeed drink, but to sit at my right and at my left, this is not mine to give but is for those for whom it has been prepared by my Father." [24] When the ten heard this, they became indignant at the two brothers. [25] But Jesus summoned them and said, "You know that the rulers of the Gentiles lord it over them, and the great ones make their authority over them felt. [26] But it shall not be so among you. Rather, whoever wishes to be great among you shall be your servant; [27] whoever wishes to be first among you shall be your slave. [28] Just so, the Son of Man did not come to be served but to serve and to give his life as a ransom for many."

Thursday February 29, 2024

Thursday of the Second Week of Lent
First Reading: Jeremiah 17:5-10

[5] Thus says the LORD:
Cursed is the man who trusts in human
  beings,
  who seeks his strength in flesh,
  whose heart turns away from the LORD.
[6] He is like a barren bush in the desert
  that enjoys no change of season,
But stands in a lava waste,
  a salt and empty earth.
[7] Blessed is the man who trusts in the LORD,
  whose hope is the LORD.

[8] He is like a tree planted beside the waters
    that stretches out its roots to the stream:
It fears not the heat when it comes,
    its leaves stay green;
In the year of drought it shows no distress,
    but still bears fruit.
[9] More tortuous than all else is the human
      heart,
    beyond remedy; who can understand it?
[10] I, the LORD, alone probe the mind
    and test the heart,
To reward everyone according to his ways,
    according to the merit of his deeds.

Responsorial Psalm: Psalms 1:1-2, 3,4 AND 6

R. [40:5a] *Blessed are they who hope in the Lord.*
[1] Blessed the man who follows not
    the counsel of the wicked
Nor walks in the way of sinners,
    nor sits in the company of the insolent,
[2] But delights in the law of the LORD
    and meditates on his law day and night.
R. *Blessed are they who hope in the Lord.*

[3] He is like a tree
    planted near running water,
That yields its fruit in due season,
    and whose leaves never fade.
    Whatever he does, prospers.
R. *Blessed are they who hope in the Lord.*

[4] Not so, the wicked, not so;
    they are like chaff which the wind drives
      away.
[6] For the LORD watches over the way of the
      just,
    but the way of the wicked vanishes.
R. *Blessed are they who hope in the Lord.*

Verse Before the Gospel: cf. Luke 8:15

[15] Blessed are they who have kept the word
      with a generous heart

and yield a harvest through perseverance.

Gospel: Luke 16:19-31

Jesus said to the Pharisees: [19] "There was a rich man who dressed in purple garments and fine linen and dined sumptuously each day. [20] And lying at his door was a poor man named Lazarus, covered with sores,[21]who would gladly have eaten his fill of the scraps that fell from the rich man's table. Dogs even used to come and lick his sores.

[22] When the poor man died, he was carried away by angels to the bosom of Abraham. The rich man also died and was buried, [23] and from the netherworld, where he was in torment, he raised his eyes and saw Abraham far off and Lazarus at his side. [24] And he cried out, 'Father Abraham, have pity on me. Send Lazarus to dip the tip of his finger in water and cool my tongue, for I am suffering torment in these flames.' [25] Abraham replied, 'My child, remember that you received what was good during your lifetime while Lazarus likewise received what was bad; but now he is comforted here, whereas you are tormented.

[26] Moreover, between us and you a great chasm is established to prevent anyone from crossing who might wish to go from our side to yours or from your side to ours.' [27] He said, 'Then I beg you, father, send him to my father's house, [28] for I have five brothers, so that he may warn them, lest they too come to this place of torment.' [29] But Abraham replied, 'They have Moses and the prophets. Let them listen to them.' [30] He said, 'Oh no, father Abraham, but if someone from the dead goes to them, they will repent.' [31] Then Abraham said, 'If they will not listen to Moses and the prophets, neither will they be persuaded if someone should rise from the dead.'"

MARCH 2024

Friday March 1, 2024

Friday of the Second Week of Lent
First Reading: Genesis 37:3-4, 12-13A, 17B-28A

[3] Israel loved Joseph best of all his sons, for he was the child of his old age; and he had made him a long tunic. [4] When his brothers saw that their father loved him best of all his sons, they hated him so much that they would not even greet him.

[12] One day, when his brothers had gone to pasture their father's flocks at Shechem, [13A] Israel said to Joseph, "Your brothers, you know, are tending our flocks at Shechem. Get ready; I will send you to them."

[17B] So Joseph went after his brothers and caught up with them in Dothan. [18] They noticed him from a distance, and before he came up to them, they plotted to kill him. [19] They said to one another: "Here comes that master dreamer! [20] Come on, let us kill him and throw him into one of the cisterns here; we could say that a wild beast devoured him. We shall then see what comes of his dreams."

[21] When Reuben heard this, he tried to save him from their hands, saying, "We must not take his life. [22] Instead of shedding blood," he continued, "just throw him into that cistern there in the desert; but do not kill him outright." His purpose was to rescue him from their hands and return him to his father. [23] So when Joseph came up to them,

106

they stripped him of the long tunic he had on; [24] then they took him and threw him into the cistern, which was empty and dry.

[25] They then sat down to their meal. Looking up, they saw a caravan of Ishmaelites coming from Gilead, their camels laden with gum, balm and resin to be taken down to Egypt. [26] Judah said to his brothers: "What is to be gained by killing our brother and concealing his blood? [27] Rather, let us sell him to these Ishmaelites, instead of doing away with him ourselves. After all, he is our brother, our own flesh." His brothers agreed. [28B] They sold Joseph to the Ishmaelites for twenty pieces of silver.

Responsorial Psalm: Psalms 105:16-17, 18-19, 20-21

R. [5a] *Remember the marvels the Lord has done.*

[16] When the LORD called down a famine on the
        land
       and ruined the crop that sustained them,
[17] He sent a man before them,
       Joseph, sold as a slave.
R. *Remember the marvels the Lord has done.*

[18] They had weighed him down with fetters,
       and he was bound with chains,
[19] Till his prediction came to pass
       and the word of the LORD proved him
         true.
R. *Remember the marvels the Lord has done.*

[20] The king sent and released him,
       the ruler of the peoples set him free.
[21] He made him lord of his house
       and ruler of all his possessions.
R. *Remember the marvels the Lord has done.*

Verse Before the Gospel: John 3:16

[16] God so loved the world that he gave his only-
       begotten Son;
so that everyone who believes in him might
       have eternal life.

Gospel: Matthew 21:33-43, 45-46

[33] Jesus said to the chief priests and the elders of the people: "Hear another parable. There was a landowner who planted a vineyard, put a hedge around it, dug a wine press in it, and built a tower. Then he leased it to tenants and went on a journey. [34] When vintage time drew near, he sent his servants to the tenants to obtain his produce. [35] But the tenants seized the servants and one they beat, another they killed, and a third they stoned. [36] Again he sent other servants, more numerous than the first ones, but they

treated them in the same way. ³⁷ Finally, he sent his son to them, thinking, 'They will respect my son.' ³⁸ But when the tenants saw the son, they said to one another, 'This is the heir. Come, let us kill him and acquire his inheritance.' ³⁹ They seized him, threw him out of the vineyard, and killed him. ⁴⁰ What will the owner of the vineyard do to those tenants when he comes?" ⁴¹They answered him, "He will put those wretched men to a wretched death and lease his vineyard to other tenants who will give him the produce at the proper times." ⁴² Jesus said to them, "Did you never read in the Scriptures:

The stone that the builders rejected
*   has become the cornerstone;*
by the Lord has this been done,
*   and it is wonderful in our eyes*?

⁴³ Therefore, I say to you, the Kingdom of God will be taken away from you and given to a people that will produce its fruit." ⁴⁵ When the chief priests and the Pharisees heard his parables, they knew that he was speaking about them. ⁴⁶ And although they were attempting to arrest him, they feared the crowds, for they regarded him as a prophet.

Saturday of the Second Week of Lent
First Reading: Micah 7:14-15, 18-20

¹⁴ Shepherd your people with your staff,
        the flock of your inheritance,
That dwells apart in a woodland,
        in the midst of Carmel.
Let them feed in Bashan and Gilead,
        as in the days of old;
¹⁵ As in the days when you came from the land
            of Egypt,
        show us wonderful signs.

¹⁸ Who is there like you, the God who removes
            guilt
        and pardons sin for the remnant of his
            inheritance;
Who does not persist in anger forever,
        but delights rather in clemency,
¹⁹ And will again have compassion on us,
        treading underfoot our guilt?
You will cast into the depths of the sea all
            our sins;
²⁰ You will show faithfulness to Jacob,

and grace to Abraham,
As you have sworn to our fathers
    from days of old.

Responsorial Psalm: Psalms 103:1-2, 3-4, 9-10, 11-12

R. *(8a)The Lord is kind and merciful.*
¹ Bless the LORD, O my soul;
    and all my being, bless his holy name.
² Bless the LORD, O my soul,
    and forget not all his benefits.
R. *The Lord is kind and merciful.*

³ He pardons all your iniquities,
    he heals all your ills.
⁴ He redeems your life from destruction,
    he crowns you with kindness and
        compassion.
R. *The Lord is kind and merciful.*

⁹ He will not always chide,
    nor does he keep his wrath forever.
¹⁰ Not according to our sins does he deal with us,
    nor does he requite us according to our
        crimes.
R. *The Lord is kind and merciful.*

¹¹ For as the heavens are high above the earth,
    so surpassing is his kindness toward
        those who fear him.
¹² As far as the east is from the west,
    so far has he put our transgressions from
        us.
R. *The Lord is kind and merciful.*

Verse Before the Gospel: Luke 15:18

¹⁸ I will get up and go to my father and shall
        say to him,
Father, I have sinned against heaven and
        against you.

Gospel: Luke 15:1-3, 11-32

[1] Tax collectors and sinners were all drawing near to listen to Jesus, [2] but the Pharisees and scribes began to complain, saying, "This man welcomes sinners and eats with them." [3] So to them Jesus addressed this parable. [11] "A man had two sons, [12] and the younger son said to his father, 'Father, give me the share of your estate that should come to me.' So the father divided the property between them. [13] After a few days, the younger son collected all his belongings and set off to a distant country where he squandered his inheritance on a life of dissipation. [14] When he had freely spent everything, a severe famine struck that country, and he found himself in dire need. [15] So he hired himself out to one of the local citizens who sent him to his farm to tend the swine. [16] And he longed to eat his fill of the pods on which the swine fed, but nobody gave him any. [17] Coming to his senses he thought, 'How many of my father's hired workers have more than enough food to eat, but here am I, dying from hunger. [18] I shall get up and go to my father and I shall say to him, "Father, I have sinned against heaven and against you. [19] I no longer deserve to be called your son; treat me as you would treat one of your hired workers."' [20] So he got up and went back to his father. While he was still a long way off, his father caught sight of him, and was filled with compassion. He ran to his son, embraced him and kissed him. [21] His son said to him, 'Father, I have sinned against heaven and against you; I no longer deserve to be called your son.' [22] But his father ordered his servants, 'Quickly, bring the finest robe and put it on him; put a ring on his finger and sandals on his feet. [23] Take the fattened calf and slaughter it. Then let us celebrate with a feast, [24] because this son of mine was dead, and has come to life again; he was lost, and has been found.' Then the celebration began. [25] Now the older son had been out in the field and, on his way back, as he neared the house, he heard the sound of music and dancing. [26] He called one of the servants and asked what this might mean. [27] The servant said to him, 'Your brother has returned and your father has slaughtered the fattened calf because he has him back safe and sound.' [28] He became angry, and when he refused to enter the house, his father came out and pleaded with him. [29] He said to his father in reply, 'Look, all these years I served you and not once did I disobey your orders; yet you never gave me even a young goat to feast on with my friends. [30] But when your son returns who swallowed up your property with prostitutes, for him you slaughter the fattened calf.' [31] He said to him, 'My son, you are here with me always; everything I have is yours. [32] But now we must celebrate and rejoice, because your brother was dead and has come to life again; he was lost and has been found.'"

Sunday March 3, 2024

Third Sunday of Lent, Year B
First Reading: Exodus 20:1-17

[1] In those days, God delivered all these commandments: [2] "I, the LORD, am your God, who brought you out of the land of Egypt, that place of slavery. [3] You shall not have other gods besides me. [4] You shall not carve idols for yourselves in the shape of anything in the sky above or on the earth below or in the waters beneath the earth; [5] you shall not bow down

before them or worship them. For I, the LORD, your God, am a jealous God, inflicting punishment for their fathers' wickedness on the children of those who hate me, down to the third and fourth generation; [6] but bestowing mercy down to the thousandth generation on the children of those who love me and keep my commandments.

[7] "You shall not take the name of the LORD, your God, in vain. For the LORD will not leave unpunished the one who takes his name in vain.

[8] "Remember to keep holy the sabbath day. [9] Six days you may labor and do all your work, [10] but the seventh day is the sabbath of the LORD, your God. No work may be done then either by you, or your son or daughter, or your male or female slave, or your beast, or by the alien who lives with you. [11] In six days the LORD made the heavens and the earth, the sea and all that is in them; but on the seventh day he rested. That is why the LORD has blessed the sabbath day and made it holy.

[12] "Honor your father and your mother, that you may have a long life in the land which the LORD, your God, is giving you. [13] You shall not kill. [14] You shall not commit adultery. [15] You shall not steal. [16] You shall not bear false witness against your neighbor. [17] You shall not covet your neighbor's house. You shall not covet your neighbor's wife, nor his male or female slave, nor his ox or ass, nor anything else that belongs to him."

Or Exodus 20:1-3, 7-8, 12-17

[1] In those days, God delivered all these commandments: [2] "I, the LORD, am your God, who brought you out of the land of Egypt, that place of slavery. [3] You shall not have other gods besides me.

[7] "You shall not take the name of the LORD, your God, in vain. For the LORD will not leave unpunished the one who takes his name in vain.

[8] "Remember to keep holy the sabbath day. [12] "Honor your father and your mother, that you may have a long life in the land which the LORD, your God, is giving you. [13] You shall not kill. [14] You shall not commit adultery. [15] You shall not steal.[16] You shall not bear false witness against your neighbor. [17] You shall not covet your neighbor's house. You shall not covet your neighbor's wife, nor his male or female slave, nor his ox or ass, nor anything else that belongs to him."

Responsorial Psalm: Psalms 19:8, 9, 10, 11.

R. *(John 6:68c)* **Lord, you have the words of everlasting life.**

[8] The law of the LORD is perfect,
    refreshing the soul;
The decree of the LORD is trustworthy,
    giving wisdom to the simple.

R. Lord, you have the words of everlasting life.

[9] The precepts of the LORD are right,
    rejoicing the heart;
the command of the LORD is clear,
    enlightening the eye.

R. Lord, you have the words of everlasting life.

[10] The fear of the LORD is pure,
      enduring forever;
the ordinances of the LORD are true,
      all of them just.
R. Lord, you have the words of everlasting life.

[11] They are more precious than gold,
      than a heap of purest gold;
sweeter also than syrup
      or honey from the comb.
R. Lord, you have the words of everlasting life.

Second Reading: 1 Corinthians 1:22-25

Brothers and sisters: [22] Jews demand signs and Greeks look for wisdom, [23] but we proclaim Christ crucified, a stumbling block to Jews and foolishness to Gentiles, [24] but to those who are called, Jews and Greeks alike, Christ the power of God and the wisdom of God. [25] For the foolishness of God is wiser than human wisdom, and the weakness of God is stronger than human strength.

Verse Before the Gospel: John 3:16

[16] God so loved the world that he gave his only
        Son,
so that everyone who believes in him might
        have eternal life.

Gospel: John 2:13-25

[13] Since the Passover of the Jews was near, Jesus went up to Jerusalem. [14] He found in the temple area those who sold oxen, sheep, and doves, as well as the money changers seated there. [15] He made a whip out of cords and drove them all out of the temple area, with the sheep and oxen, and spilled the coins of the money changers and overturned their tables, [16] and to those who sold doves he said, "Take these out of here, and stop making my Father's house a marketplace." [17] His disciples recalled the words of Scripture, *Zeal for your house will consume me*. [18] At this the Jews answered and said to him, "What sign can you show us for doing this?" [19] Jesus answered and said to them, "Destroy this temple and in three days I will raise it up." [20] The Jews said, "This temple has been under construction for forty-six years, and you will raise it up in three days?" [21] But he was speaking about the temple of his body. [22] Therefore, when he was raised from the dead, his disciples remembered that he had said this, and they came to believe the Scripture and the word Jesus had spoken.

    [23] While he was in Jerusalem for the feast of Passover, many began to believe in his name when they saw the signs he was doing. [24] But Jesus would not trust himself to them

because he knew them all, [25] and did not need anyone to testify about human nature. He himself understood it well.

Monday of the Third Week of Lent
First Reading: 2 Kings 5:1-15AB

[1] Naaman, the army commander of the king of Aram, was highly esteemed and respected by his master, for through him the LORD had brought victory to Aram. But valiant as he was, the man was a leper. [2] Now the Arameans had captured in a raid on the land of Israel a little girl, who became the servant of Naaman's wife. "If only my master would present himself to the prophet in Samaria," [3] she said to her mistress, "he would cure him of his leprosy." [4] Naaman went and told his lord just what the slave girl from the land of Israel had said. [5] "Go," said the king of Aram. "I will send along a letter to the king of Israel." So Naaman set out, taking along ten silver talents, six thousand gold pieces, and ten festal garments. [6] To the king of Israel he brought the letter, which read: "With this letter I am sending my servant Naaman to you, that you may cure him of his leprosy."

[7] When he read the letter, the king of Israel tore his garments and exclaimed: "Am I a god with power over life and death, that this man should send someone to me to be cured of leprosy? Take note! You can see he is only looking for a quarrel with me!" [8] When Elisha, the man of God, heard that the king of Israel had torn his garments, he sent word to the king: "Why have you torn your garments? Let him come to me and find out that there is a prophet in Israel."

[9] Naaman came with his horses and chariots and stopped at the door of Elisha's house. [10] The prophet sent him the message: "Go and wash seven times in the Jordan, and your flesh will heal, and you will be clean." [11] But Naaman went away angry, saying, "I thought that he would surely come out and stand there to invoke the LORD his God, and would move his hand over the spot, and thus cure the leprosy. [12] Are not the rivers of Damascus, the Abana and the Pharpar, better than all the waters of Israel? Could I not wash in them and be cleansed?" With this, he turned about in anger and left.

[13] But his servants came up and reasoned with him. "My father," they said, "if the prophet had told you to do something extraordinary, would you not have done it? All the more now, since he said to you, 'Wash and be clean,' should you do as he said." [14] So Naaman went down and plunged into the Jordan seven times at the word of the man of God. His flesh became again like the flesh of a little child, and he was clean.

[15] He returned with his whole retinue to the man of God. On his arrival he stood before him and said, "Now I know that there is no God in all the earth, except in Israel."

Responsorial Psalm: Psalms 42:2, 3; 43:3, 4
R. *(see 42:3)***Athirst is my soul for the living God.**
   When shall I go and behold the face of God?
[2] As the hind longs for the running waters,
   so my soul longs for you, O God.

***R. Athirst is my soul for the living God. When
shall I go and behold the face of God?***

³ Athirst is my soul for God, the living God.
   When shall I go and behold the face of
      God?
***R. Athirst is my soul for the living God. When
shall I go and behold the face of God?***

³ Send forth your light and your fidelity;
   they shall lead me on
And bring me to your holy mountain,
   to your dwelling-place.
***R. Athirst is my soul for the living God. When
shall I go and behold the face of God?***

⁴ Then will I go in to the altar of God,
   the God of my gladness and joy;
Then will I give you thanks upon the harp,
   O God, my God!
***R. Athirst is my soul for the living God. When
shall I go and behold the face of God?***

Verse Before the Gospel: cf. Psalms 130:5, 7
⁵ I hope in the LORD, I trust in his word;
⁷ with him there is kindness and plenteous
         redemption.

Gospel: Luke 4:24-30
²⁴ Jesus said to the people in the synagogue at Nazareth: "Amen, I say to you, no prophet is accepted in his own native place. ²⁵ Indeed, I tell you, there were many widows in Israel in the days of Elijah when the sky was closed for three and a half years and a severe famine spread over the entire land. ²⁶ It was to none of these that Elijah was sent, but only to a widow in Zarephath in the land of Sidon. ²⁷Again, there were many lepers in Israel during the time of Elisha the prophet; yet not one of them was cleansed, but only Naaman the Syrian." ²⁸ When the people in the synagogue heard this, they were all filled with fury. ²⁹ They rose up, drove him out of the town, and led him to the brow of the hill on which their town had been built, to hurl him down headlong. ³⁰ But he passed through the midst of them and went away.

Tuesday of the Third Week of Lent
First Reading: Daniel 3:25, 34-43

25 Azariah stood up in the fire and prayed aloud:
34 "For your name's sake, O Lord, do not deliver
          us up forever,
      or make void your covenant.
35 Do not take away your mercy from us,
      for the sake of Abraham, your beloved,
      Isaac your servant, and Israel your holy
          one,
36 To whom you promised to multiply their
          offspring
      like the stars of heaven,
      or the sand on the shore of the sea.
37 For we are reduced, O Lord, beyond any
          other nation,
      brought low everywhere in the world this
          day
      because of our sins.
38 We have in our day no prince, prophet, or
          leader,
      no burnt offering, sacrifice, oblation, or
          incense,
      no place to offer first fruits, to find favor
          with you.
39 But with a contrite heart and humble spirit
      let us be received;
As though it were burnt offerings of rams
          and bullocks
      or thousands of fat lambs,
40 So let our sacrifice be in your presence today
      as we follow you unreservedly;
      for those who trust in you cannot be put
          to shame.
41 And now we follow you with our whole
          heart,
      we fear you and we pray to you.
Do not let us be put to shame,
      42 but deal with us in your kindness and
          great mercy.

115

⁴³ Deliver us by your wonders,
and bring glory to your name, O Lord."

Responsorial Psalm: Psalms 25:4-5AB, 6 AND 7BC, 8-9
R. ^(6a) *Remember your mercies, O Lord.*
⁴ Your ways, O LORD, make known to me;
teach me your paths,
^{5AB} Guide me in your truth and teach me,
for you are God my savior.
R. *Remember your mercies, O Lord.*

⁶ Remember that your compassion, O LORD,
and your kindness are from of old.
^{7BC} In your kindness remember me,
because of your goodness, O LORD.
R. *Remember your mercies, O Lord.*

⁸ Good and upright is the LORD;
thus he shows sinners the way.
⁹ He guides the humble to justice,
he teaches the humble his way.
R. *Remember your mercies, O Lord.*

Verse Before the Gospel: Joel 2:12-13
¹² Even now, says the LORD,
return to me with your whole heart;
¹³ for I am gracious and merciful.

Gospel: Matthew 18:21-35
²¹ Peter approached Jesus and asked him, "Lord, if my brother sins against me, how often must I forgive him? As many as seven times?" ²² Jesus answered, "I say to you, not seven times but seventy-seven times. ²³ That is why the Kingdom of heaven may be likened to a king who decided to settle accounts with his servants. ²⁴ When he began the accounting, a debtor was brought before him who owed him a huge amount. ²⁵ Since he had no way of paying it back, his master ordered him to be sold, along with his wife, his children, and all his property, in payment of the debt. ²⁶ At that, the servant fell down, did him homage, and said, 'Be patient with me, and I will pay you back in full.' ²⁷ Moved with compassion the master of that servant let him go and forgave him the loan. ²⁸ When that servant had left, he found one of his fellow servants who owed him a much smaller amount. He seized him and started to choke him, demanding, 'Pay back what you owe.' ²⁹ Falling to his knees, his fellow servant begged him, 'Be patient with me, and I will pay you back.' ³⁰ But

he refused. Instead, he had him put in prison until he paid back the debt. [31] Now when his fellow servants saw what had happened, they were deeply disturbed, and went to their master and reported the whole affair. [32] His master summoned him and said to him, 'You wicked servant! I forgave you your entire debt because you begged me to. [33] Should you not have had pity on your fellow servant, as I had pity on you?' [34] Then in anger his master handed him over to the torturers until he should pay back the whole debt. [35] So will my heavenly Father do to you, unless each of you forgives your brother from your heart."

Wednesday of the Third Week of Lent

First Reading: Deuteronomy 4:1, 5-9

[1] Moses spoke to the people and said: "Now, Israel, hear the statutes and decrees which I am teaching you to observe, that you may live, and may enter in and take possession of the land which the LORD, the God of your fathers, is giving you. [5] Therefore, I teach you the statutes and decrees as the LORD, my God, has commanded me, that you may observe them in the land you are entering to occupy. [6] Observe them carefully, for thus will you give evidence of your wisdom and intelligence to the nations, who will hear of all these statutes and say, 'This great nation is truly a wise and intelligent people.' [7] For what great nation is there that has gods so close to it as the LORD, our God, is to us whenever we call upon him? [8] Or what great nation has statutes and decrees that are as just as this whole law which I am setting before you today?

[9] "However, take care and be earnestly on your guard not to forget the things which your own eyes have seen, nor let them slip from your memory as long as you live, but teach them to your children and to your children's children."

Responsorial Psalm: Psalms 147:12-13, 15-16, 19-20

R. [12a] *Praise the Lord, Jerusalem.*

[12] Glorify the LORD, O Jerusalem;
      praise your God, O Zion.
[13] For he has strengthened the bars of your
        gates;
      he has blessed your children within you.
R. *Praise the Lord, Jerusalem.*

[15] He sends forth his command to the earth;
      swiftly runs his word!
[16] He spreads snow like wool;
      frost he strews like ashes.
R. *Praise the Lord, Jerusalem.*

[19] He has proclaimed his word to Jacob,
      his statutes and his ordinances to Israel.

20 He has not done thus for any other nation;
    his ordinances he has not made known to
      them.
R. Praise the Lord, Jerusalem.

Verse Before the Gospel: John 6:63C, 68C
63C Your words, Lord, are Spirit and life;
68C you have the words of everlasting life.

Gospel: Matthew 5:17-19
Jesus said to his disciples: 17 "Do not think that I have come to abolish the law or the prophets. I have come not to abolish but to fulfill. 18 Amen, I say to you, until heaven and earth pass away, not the smallest letter or the smallest part of a letter will pass from the law, until all things have taken place. 19 Therefore, whoever breaks one of the least of these commandments and teaches others to do so will be called least in the Kingdom of heaven. But whoever obeys and teaches these commandments will be called greatest in the Kingdom of heaven."

Thursday of the Third Week of Lent
First Reading: Jeremiah 7:23-28
Thus says the LORD:

23 This is what I commanded my people:
    Listen to my voice;
    then I will be your God and you shall be
      my people.
Walk in all the ways that I command you,
    so that you may prosper.

24 But they obeyed not, nor did they pay heed.
They walked in the hardness of their evil
      hearts
    and turned their backs, not their faces, to
      me.
25 From the day that your fathers left the land
      of Egypt even to this day,
    I have sent you untiringly all my servants
      the prophets.
26 Yet they have not obeyed me nor paid heed;
    they have stiffened their necks and done
      worse than their fathers.

^{27} When you speak all these words to them,
>   they will not listen to you either;
>   when you call to them, they will not
>   answer you.
^{28} Say to them:
>   This is the nation that does not listen
>   to the voice of the LORD, its God,
>   or take correction.
Faithfulness has disappeared;
>   the word itself is banished from their
>   speech.

Responsorial Psalm: Psalms 95:1-2, 6-7, 8-9

R. $^{(8)}$ *If today you hear his voice, harden not your*
>   *hearts.*
^{1} Come, let us sing joyfully to the LORD;
>   let us acclaim the Rock of our salvation.
^{2} Let us come into his presence with
>   thanksgiving;
>   let us joyfully sing psalms to him.
R. *If today you hear his voice, harden not your*
>   *hearts.*

^{6} Come, let us bow down in worship;
>   let us kneel before the LORD who made us.
^{7ABC} For he is our God,
>   and we are the people he shepherds, the
>   flock he guides.
R. *If today you hear his voice, harden not your*
>   *hearts.*

^{7D} Oh, that today you would hear his voice:
> ^{8} "Harden not your hearts as at Meribah,
>   as in the day of Massah in the desert,
^{9} Where your fathers tempted me;
>   they tested me though they had seen my
>   works."
R. *If today you hear his voice, harden not your*
>   *hearts.*

Verse Before the Gospel: Joel 2:12-13

^{12} Even now, says the LORD,
return to me with your whole heart,
^{13} for I am gracious and merciful.

Gospel: Luke 11:14-23

[14] Jesus was driving out a demon that was mute, and when the demon had gone out, the mute man spoke and the crowds were amazed. [15] Some of them said, "By the power of Beelzebul, the prince of demons, he drives out demons." [16] Others, to test him, asked him for a sign from heaven. [17] But he knew their thoughts and said to them, "Every kingdom divided against itself will be laid waste and house will fall against house.

[18] And if Satan is divided against himself, how will his kingdom stand? For you say that it is by Beelzebul that I drive out demons. [19] If I, then, drive out demons by Beelzebul, by whom do your own people drive them out? Therefore they will be your judges. [20] But if it is by the finger of God that I drive out demons, then the Kingdom of God has come upon you. [21] When a strong man fully armed guards his palace, his possessions are safe. [22] But when one stronger than he attacks and overcomes him, he takes away the armour on which he relied and distributes the spoils. [23] Whoever is not with me is against me, and whoever does not gather with me scatters."

Friday of the Third Week of Lent
First Reading: Hosea 14:2-10

[2] Thus says the LORD:

Return, O Israel, to the LORD, your God;
    you have collapsed through your guilt.
[3] Take with you words,
    and return to the LORD;
Say to him, "Forgive all iniquity,
    and receive what is good, that we may
        render
    as offerings the bullocks from our stalls.
[4] Assyria will not save us,
    nor shall we have horses to mount;
We shall say no more, 'Our god,'
    to the work of our hands;
    for in you the orphan finds compassion."

[5] I will heal their defection, says the LORD,
    I will love them freely;
    for my wrath is turned away from them.
[6] I will be like the dew for Israel:
    he shall blossom like the lily;
He shall strike root like the Lebanon cedar,
    [7] and put forth his shoots.
His splendor shall be like the olive tree

and his fragrance like the Lebanon cedar.
8 Again they shall dwell in his shade
    and raise grain;
They shall blossom like the vine,
    and his fame shall be like the wine of
        Lebanon.

9 Ephraim! What more has he to do with
        idols?
    I have humbled him, but I will prosper
        him.
"I am like a verdant cypress tree" -
    Because of me you bear fruit!

10 Let him who is wise understand these
        things;
    let him who is prudent know them.
Straight are the paths of the LORD,
    in them the just walk,
    but sinners stumble in them.

Responsorial Psalm: Psalms 81:6C-8A, 8BC-9,10-11AB,14 AND 17

R. (see 11 and 9a) *I am the Lord your God: hear my voice.*
7 An unfamiliar speech I hear:
    "I relieved his shoulder of the burden;
    his hands were freed from the basket.
8A In distress you called, and I rescued you."
R. I am the Lord your God: hear my voice.

8BC "Unseen, I answered you in thunder;
    I tested you at the waters of Meribah.
9 Hear, my people, and I will admonish you;
    O Israel, will you not hear me?"
R. I am the Lord your God: hear my voice.

10 "There shall be no strange god among you
    nor shall you worship any alien god.
11AB I, the LORD, am your God
    who led you forth from the land of
        Egypt."
R. I am the Lord your God: hear my voice.

14 "If only my people would hear me,

and Israel walk in my ways,
17 I would feed them with the best of wheat,
and with honey from the rock I would fill
them."
R. I am the Lord your God: hear my voice.

Verse Before the Gospel: Matthew 4:17
17 Repent, says the Lord;
the Kingdom of heaven is at hand.

Gospel: Mark 12:28-34
28 One of the scribes came to Jesus and asked him, "Which is the first of all the commandments?" 29 Jesus replied, "The first is this: *Hear, O Israel! The Lord our God is Lord alone! 30 You shall love the Lord your God with all your heart, with all your soul, with all your mind, and with all your strength.* 31 The second is this: *You shall love your neighbor as yourself.* There is no other commandment greater than these." 32 The scribe said to him, "Well said, teacher. You are right in saying, *He is One and there is no other than he.* 33 And *to love him with all your heart, with all your understanding, with all your strength, and to love your neighbor as yourself* is worth more than all burnt offerings and sacrifices." 34 And when Jesus saw that he answered with understanding, he said to him, "You are not far from the Kingdom of God." And no one dared to ask him any more questions.

Saturday March 9, 2024

Saturday of the Third Week of Lent
First Reading: Hosea 6:1-6
1 "Come, let us return to the LORD,
it is he who has rent, but he will heal us;
he has struck us, but he will bind our
wounds.
2 He will revive us after two days;
on the third day he will raise us up,
to live in his presence.
3 Let us know, let us strive to know the LORD;
as certain as the dawn is his coming,
and his judgment shines forth like the
light of day!
He will come to us like the rain,
like spring rain that waters the earth."

4 What can I do with you, Ephraim?
What can I do with you, Judah?

Your piety is like a morning cloud,
    like the dew that early passes away.
⁵ For this reason I smote them through the
        prophets,
    I slew them by the words of my mouth;
⁶ For it is love that I desire, not sacrifice,
    and knowledge of God rather than burnt
        offerings.

Responsorial Psalm: Psalms 51:3-4, 18-19, 20-21AB

R. *(see Hosea 6:6)* **It is mercy I desire, and not sacrifice.**

³ Have mercy on me, O God, in your goodness;
    in the greatness of your compassion wipe
        out my offense.
⁴ Thoroughly wash me from my guilt
    and of my sin cleanse me.

R. It is mercy I desire, and not sacrifice.

¹⁸ For you are not pleased with sacrifices;
    should I offer a burnt offering, you would
        not accept it.
¹⁹ My sacrifice, O God, is a contrite spirit;
    a heart contrite and humbled, O God, you
        will not spurn.

R. It is mercy I desire, and not sacrifice.

²⁰ Be bountiful, O LORD, to Zion in your
        kindness
    by rebuilding the walls of Jerusalem;
²¹ᴬᴮ Then shall you be pleased with due
        sacrifices,
    burnt offerings and holocausts.

R. It is mercy I desire, and not sacrifice.

Verse Before the Gospel: Psalms 95:8

⁸ If today you hear his voice,
harden not your hearts.

Gospel: Luke 18:9-14

⁹ Jesus addressed this parable to those who were convinced of their own righteousness and despised everyone else. ¹⁰ "Two people went up to the temple area to pray; one was a Pharisee and the other was a tax collector. ¹¹ The Pharisee took up his position and spoke this prayer to himself, 'O God, I thank you that I am not like the rest of humanity — greedy, dishonest, adulterous— or even like this tax collector. ¹² I fast twice a week, and I

pay tithes on my whole income.' [13] But the tax collector stood off at a distance and would not even raise his eyes to heaven but beat his breast and prayed, 'O God, be merciful to me a sinner.' [14] I tell you, the latter went home justified, not the former; for everyone who exalts himself will be humbled, and the one who humbles himself will be exalted."

Fourth Sunday of Lent, Year B
First Reading: 2 Chronicles 36:14-16, 19-23

[14] In those days, all the princes of Judah, the priests, and the people added infidelity to infidelity, practicing all the abominations of the nations and polluting the LORD's temple which he had consecrated in Jerusalem.

[15] Early and often did the LORD, the God of their fathers, send his messengers to them, for he had compassion on his people and his dwelling place. [16] But they mocked the messengers of God, despised his warnings, and scoffed at his prophets, until the anger of the LORD against his people was so inflamed that there was no remedy. [19] Their enemies burnt the house of God, tore down the walls of Jerusalem, set all its palaces afire, and destroyed all its precious objects. [20] Those who escaped the sword were carried captive to Babylon, where they became servants of the king of the Chaldeans and his sons until the kingdom of the Persians came to power. [21] All this was to fulfill the word of the LORD spoken by Jeremiah: "Until the land has retrieved its lost sabbaths, during all the time it lies waste it shall have rest while seventy years are fulfilled."

[22] In the first year of Cyrus, king of Persia, in order to fulfill the word of the LORD spoken by Jeremiah, the LORD inspired King Cyrus of Persia to issue this proclamation throughout his kingdom, both by word of mouth and in writing: [23] "Thus says Cyrus, king of Persia: All the kingdoms of the earth the LORD, the God of heaven, has given to me, and he has also charged me to build him a house in Jerusalem, which is in Judah. Whoever, therefore, among you belongs to any part of his people, let him go up, and may his God be with him!"

Responsorial Psalm: Psalms 137:1-2,3,4-5,6.

R. (6ab) *Let my tongue be silenced, if I ever forget you!*

[1] By the streams of Babylon
    we sat and wept when we remembered
        Zion.
[2] On the aspens of that land
    we hung up our harps.

R. *Let my tongue be silenced, if I ever forget you!*

[3] For there our captors asked of us
    the lyrics of our songs,
And our despoilers urged us to be joyous:
    "Sing for us the songs of Zion!"

R. *Let my tongue be silenced, if I ever forget you!*

⁴ How could we sing a song of the LORD
      in a foreign land?
⁵ If I forget you, Jerusalem,
      may my right hand be forgotten!
R. Let my tongue be silenced, if I ever forget you!

⁶ May my tongue cleave to my palate
      if I remember you not,
If I place not Jerusalem
      ahead of my joy.
R. Let my tongue be silenced, if I ever forget you!

Second Reading: Ephesians 2:4-10

Brothers and sisters: ⁴ God, who is rich in mercy, because of the great love he had for us, ⁵ even when we were dead in our transgressions, brought us to life with Christ— by grace you have been saved—, ⁶ raised us up with him, and seated us with him in the heavens in Christ Jesus, ⁷ that in the ages to come he might show the immeasurable riches of his grace in his kindness to us in Christ Jesus. ⁸ For by grace you have been saved through faith, and this is not from you; it is the gift of God; ⁹ it is not from works, so no one may boast. ¹⁰ For we are his handiwork, created in Christ Jesus for the good works that God has prepared in advance, that we should live in them.

Verse Before the Gospel: John 3:16

¹⁶ God so loved the world that he gave his only
            Son,
so everyone who believes in him might have
            eternal life.

Gospel: John 3:14-21

Jesus said to Nicodemus: ¹⁴ "Just as Moses lifted up the serpent in the desert, so must the Son of Man be lifted up, ¹⁵ so that everyone who believes in him may have eternal life."

¹⁶ For God so loved the world that he gave his only Son, so that everyone who believes in him might not perish but might have eternal life. ¹⁷ For God did not send his Son into the world to condemn the world, but that the world might be saved through him. ¹⁸ Whoever believes in him will not be condemned, but whoever does not believe has already been condemned, because he has not believed in the name of the only Son of God.

¹⁹ And this is the verdict, that the light came into the world, but people preferred darkness to light, because their works were evil. ²⁰ For everyone who does wicked things hates the light and does not come toward the light, so that his works might not be exposed. ²¹ But whoever lives the truth comes to the light, so that his works may be clearly seen as done in God.

Monday of the Fourth Week of Lent
First Reading: Isaiah 65:17-21

[17] Thus says the LORD:

Lo, I am about to create new heavens
    and a new earth;
The things of the past shall not be
        remembered
    or come to mind.
[18] Instead, there shall always be rejoicing and
        happiness
    in what I create;
For I create Jerusalem to be a joy
    and its people to be a delight;
[19] I will rejoice in Jerusalem
    and exult in my people.
[20] No longer shall the sound of weeping be
        heard there,
    or the sound of crying;
No longer shall there be in it
    an infant who lives but a few days,
    or an old man who does not round out
        his full lifetime;
He dies a mere youth who reaches but a
        hundred years,
    and he who fails of a hundred shall be
        thought accursed.
[21] They shall live in the houses they build,
    and eat the fruit of the vineyards they
        plant.

Responsorial Psalm: Psalms 30:2 AND 4, 5-6, 11-12A AND 13B

R. [(2a)] *I will praise you, Lord, for you have*
                rescued me.

[2] I will extol you, O LORD, for you drew me
        clear
    and did not let my enemies rejoice over
        me.
[4] O LORD, you brought me up from the nether
        world;
    you preserved me from among those

126

going down into the pit.
R. I will praise you, Lord, for you have rescued
me.

[5] Sing praise to the LORD, you his faithful ones,
   and give thanks to his holy name.
[6] For his anger lasts but a moment;
   a lifetime, his good will.
At nightfall, weeping enters in,
   but with the dawn, rejoicing.
R. I will praise you, Lord, for you have rescued
me.

[11] "Hear, O LORD, and have pity on me;
   O LORD, be my helper."
[12A] You changed my mourning into dancing;
      [13B] O LORD, my God, forever will I give you
      thanks.
R. I will praise you, Lord, for you have rescued
me.

Verse Before the Gospel: Amos 5:14

[14] Seek good and not evil so that you may live,
and the LORD will be with you.

Gospel: John 4:43-54

[43] At that time Jesus left [Samaria] for Galilee. [44] For Jesus himself testified that a prophet has no honor in his native place. [45] When he came into Galilee, the Galileans welcomed him, since they had seen all he had done in Jerusalem at the feast; for they themselves had gone to the feast.

[46] Then he returned to Cana in Galilee, where he had made the water wine. Now there was a royal official whose son was ill in Capernaum. [47] When he heard that Jesus had arrived in Galilee from Judea, he went to him and asked him to come down and heal his son, who was near death. [48] Jesus said to him, "Unless you people see signs and wonders, you will not believe." [49] The royal official said to him, "Sir, come down before my child dies." [50] Jesus said to him, "You may go; your son will live." The man believed what Jesus said to him and left. [51] While the man was on his way back, his slaves met him and told him that his boy would live. [52] He asked them when he began to recover. They told him, "The fever left him yesterday, about one in the afternoon." [53] The father realized that just at that time Jesus had said to him, "Your son will live," and he and his whole household came to believe. [54] Now this was the second sign Jesus did when he came to Galilee from Judea.

Tuesday of the Fourth Week of Lent
First Reading: Ezekiel 47:1-9, 12

[1] The angel brought me, Ezekiel, back to the entrance of the temple of the LORD, and I saw water flowing out from beneath the threshold of the temple toward the east, for the façade of the temple was toward the east; the water flowed down from the right side of the temple, south of the altar. [2] He led me outside by the north gate, and around to the outer gate facing the east, where I saw water trickling from the right side. [3] Then when he had walked off to the east with a measuring cord in his hand, he measured off a thousand cubits and had me wade through the water, which was ankle-deep. [4] He measured off another thousand and once more had me wade through the water, which was now knee-deep. Again he measured off a thousand and had me wade; the water was up to my waist. [5] Once more he measured off a thousand, but there was now a river through which I could not wade; for the water had risen so high it had become a river that could not be crossed except by swimming. [6] He asked me, "Have you seen this, son of man?" Then he brought me to the bank of the river, where he had me sit. [7] Along the bank of the river I saw very many trees on both sides. [8] He said to me, "This water flows into the eastern district down upon the Arabah, and empties into the sea, the salt waters, which it makes fresh. [9] Wherever the river flows, every sort of living creature that can multiply shall live, and there shall be abundant fish, for wherever this water comes the sea shall be made fresh. [12] Along both banks of the river, fruit trees of every kind shall grow; their leaves shall not fade, nor their fruit fail. Every month they shall bear fresh fruit, for they shall be watered by the flow from the sanctuary. Their fruit shall serve for food, and their leaves for medicine."

Responsorial Psalm: Psalms 46:2-3, 5-6, 8-9

R. [8] *The Lord of hosts is with us; our stronghold*
is the God of Jacob.

[2] God is our refuge and our strength,
     an ever-present help in distress.
[3] Therefore we fear not, though the earth be
          shaken
     and mountains plunge into the depths of
          the sea.

R. *The Lord of hosts is with us; our stronghold is*
     the God of Jacob.

[5] There is a stream whose runlets gladden the
          city of God,
     the holy dwelling of the Most High.
[6] God is in its midst; it shall not be disturbed;

God will help it at the break of dawn.

R. The Lord of hosts is with us; our stronghold is the God of Jacob.

[8] The LORD of hosts is with us;
  our stronghold is the God of Jacob.
[9] Come! behold the deeds of the LORD,
  the astounding things he has wrought on
    earth.

R. The Lord of hosts is with us; our stronghold is the God of Jacob.

Verse Before the Gospel: Psalms 51:12A, 14A

[12A] A clean heart create for me, O God;
[14A] give me back the joy of your salvation.

Gospel: John 5:1-16

[1] There was a feast of the Jews, and Jesus went up to Jerusalem. [2] Now there is in Jerusalem at the Sheep Gate a pool called in Hebrew Bethesda, with five porticoes. [3] In these lay a large number of ill, blind, lame, and crippled. [5] One man was there who had been ill for thirty-eight years. [6] When Jesus saw him lying there and knew that he had been ill for a long time, he said to him, "Do you want to be well?" [7] The sick man answered him, "Sir, I have no one to put me into the pool when the water is stirred up; while I am on my way, someone else gets down there before me." [8] Jesus said to him, "Rise, take up your mat, and walk." [9] Immediately the man became well, took up his mat, and walked.

Now that day was a sabbath. [10] So the Jews said to the man who was cured, "It is the sabbath, and it is not lawful for you to carry your mat." [11] He answered them, "The man who made me well told me, 'Take up your mat and walk.'" [12] They asked him, "Who is the man who told you, 'Take it up and walk'?" [13] The man who was healed did not know who it was, for Jesus had slipped away, since there was a crowd there. [14] After this Jesus found him in the temple area and said to him, "Look, you are well; do not sin anymore, so that nothing worse may happen to you." [15] The man went and told the Jews that Jesus was the one who had made him well. [16] Therefore, the Jews began to persecute Jesus because he did this on a sabbath.

Wednesday March 13, 2024

Wednesday of the Fourth Week of Lent
First Reading: Isaiah 49:8-15

[8] Thus says the LORD:
In a time of favor I answer you,
  on the day of salvation I help you;
  and I have kept you and given you as a
    covenant to the people,
To restore the land

and allot the desolate heritages,
9 Saying to the prisoners: Come out!
To those in darkness: Show yourselves!
Along the ways they shall find pasture,
　　on every bare height shall their pastures
　　　　be.
10 They shall not hunger or thirst,
　　nor shall the scorching wind or the sun
　　　　strike them;
For he who pities them leads them
　　and guides them beside springs of water.
11 I will cut a road through all my mountains,
　　and make my highways level.
12 See, some shall come from afar,
　　others from the north and the west,
　　and some from the land of Syene.
13 Sing out, O heavens, and rejoice, O earth,
　　break forth into song, you mountains.
For the LORD comforts his people
　　and shows mercy to his afflicted.
14 But Zion said, "The LORD has forsaken me;
　　my Lord has forgotten me."
15 Can a mother forget her infant,
　　be without tenderness for the child of her
　　　　womb?
Even should she forget,
　　I will never forget you.

Responsorial Psalm: Psalms 145:8-9, 13CD-14, 17-18

R. (8a) *The Lord is gracious and merciful.*
8 The LORD is gracious and merciful,
　　slow to anger and of great kindness.
9 The LORD is good to all
　　and compassionate toward all his works.
R. *The Lord is gracious and merciful.*

13CD The LORD is faithful in all his words
　　and holy in all his works.
14 The LORD lifts up all who are falling
　　and raises up all who are bowed down.
R. *The Lord is gracious and merciful.*

¹⁷The LORD is just in all his ways
    and holy in all his works.
¹⁸The LORD is near to all who call upon him,
    to all who call upon him in truth.
R. The Lord is gracious and merciful.

Verse Before the Gospel: John 11:25A, 26

²⁵ᴬ I am the resurrection and the life, says the
       Lord;
²⁶ whoever believes in me will never die.

Gospel: John 5:17-30

¹⁷ Jesus answered the Jews: "My Father is at work until now, so I am at work." ¹⁸ For this reason they tried all the more to kill him, because he not only broke the sabbath but he also called God his own father, making himself equal to God.

¹⁹ Jesus answered and said to them, "Amen, amen, I say to you, the Son cannot do anything on his own, but only what he sees the Father doing; for what he does, the Son will do also. ²⁰ For the Father loves the Son and shows him everything that he himself does, and he will show him greater works than these, so that you may be amazed. ²¹ For just as the Father raises the dead and gives life, so also does the Son give life to whomever he wishes. ²² Nor does the Father judge anyone, but he has given all judgment to the Son, ²³ so that all may honor the Son just as they honor the Father. Whoever does not honor the Son does not honor the Father who sent him. ²⁴ Amen, amen, I say to you, whoever hears my word and believes in the one who sent me has eternal life and will not come to condemnation, but has passed from death to life. ²⁵ Amen, amen, I say to you, the hour is coming and is now here when the dead will hear the voice of the Son of God, and those who hear will live. ²⁶ For just as the Father has life in himself, so also he gave to the Son the possession of life in himself. ²⁷ And he gave him power to exercise judgment, because he is the Son of Man. ²⁸ Do not be amazed at this, because the hour is coming in which all who are in the tombs will hear his voice ²⁹ and will come out, those who have done good deeds to the resurrection of life, but those who have done wicked deeds to the resurrection of condemnation.

³⁰ "I cannot do anything on my own; I judge as I hear, and my judgment is just, because I do not seek my own will but the will of the one who sent me."

Thursday March 14, 2024

Thursday of the Fourth Week of Lent
First Reading: Exodus 32:7-14

⁷ The LORD said to Moses, "Go down at once to your people whom you brought out of the land of Egypt, for they have become depraved. ⁸ They have soon turned aside from the way I pointed out to them, making for themselves a molten calf and worshiping it, sacrificing to it and crying out, 'This is your God, O Israel, who brought you out of the land of Egypt!' ⁹ The LORD said to Moses, "I see how stiff-necked this people is. ¹⁰ Let me alone, then, that my wrath may blaze up against them to consume them. Then I will make of you a great nation."

¹¹ But Moses implored the LORD, his God, saying, "Why, O LORD, should your wrath blaze up against your own people, whom you brought out of the land of Egypt with such great power and with so strong a hand? ¹² Why should the Egyptians say, 'With evil intent he brought them out, that he might kill them in the mountains and exterminate them from the face of the earth'? Let your blazing wrath die down; relent in punishing your people. ¹³ Remember your servants Abraham, Isaac and Israel, and how you swore to them by your own self, saying, 'I will make your descendants as numerous as the stars in the sky; and all this land that I promised, I will give your descendants as their perpetual heritage.'" ¹⁴ So the LORD relented in the punishment he had threatened to inflict on his people.

Responsorial Psalm: Psalms 106:19-20, 21-22, 23

R. *(4a)* **Remember us, O Lord, as you favor your people.**

¹⁹ Our fathers made a calf in Horeb
and adored a molten image;
²⁰ They exchanged their glory
for the image of a grass-eating bullock.

R. **Remember us, O Lord, as you favor your people.**

²¹ They forgot the God who had saved them,
who had done great deeds in Egypt,
²² Wondrous deeds in the land of Ham,
terrible things at the Red Sea.

R. **Remember us, O Lord, as you favor your people.**

²³ Then he spoke of exterminating them,
but Moses, his chosen one,
Withstood him in the breach
to turn back his destructive wrath.

R. **Remember us, O Lord, as you favor your people.**

Verse Before the Gospel: John 3:16

¹⁶ God so loved the world that he gave his only-
begotten Son,
so that everyone who believes in him might have
eternal life.

Gospel: John 5:31-47

³¹Jesus said to the Jews: "If I testify on my own behalf, my testimony is not true. ³² But there is another who testifies on my behalf, and I know that the testimony he gives on my

behalf is true. [33] You sent emissaries to John, and he testified to the truth. [34] I do not accept human testimony, but I say this so that you may be saved. [35] He was a burning and shining lamp, and for a while you were content to rejoice in his light. [36] But I have testimony greater than John's. The works that the Father gave me to accomplish, these works that I perform testify on my behalf that the Father has sent me. [37] Moreover, the Father who sent me has testified on my behalf. But you have never heard his voice nor seen his form, [38] and you do not have his word remaining in you, because you do not believe in the one whom he has sent. [39] You search the Scriptures, because you think you have eternal life through them; even they testify on my behalf. [40] But you do not want to come to me to have life.

[41] "I do not accept human praise; [42] moreover, I know that you do not have the love of God in you. [43] I came in the name of my Father, but you do not accept me; yet if another comes in his own name, you will accept him. [44] How can you believe, when you accept praise from one another and do not seek the praise that comes from the only God? [45] Do not think that I will accuse you before the Father: the one who will accuse you is Moses, in whom you have placed your hope. [46] For if you had believed Moses, you would have believed me, because he wrote about me. [47] But if you do not believe his writings, how will you believe my words?"

Friday of the Fourth Week of Lent
First Reading: Wisdom 2:1A, 12-22

[1A] The wicked said among themselves,
     thinking not aright:
[12] "Let us beset the just one, because he is
          obnoxious to us;
     he sets himself against our doings,
Reproaches us for transgressions of the law
     and charges us with violations of our
          training.
[13] He professes to have knowledge of God
     and styles himself a child of the LORD.
[14] To us he is the censure of our thoughts;
     merely to see him is a hardship for us,
[15] Because his life is not like that of others,
     and different are his ways.
[16] He judges us debased;
     he holds aloof from our paths as from
          things impure.
He calls blest the destiny of the just
     and boasts that God is his Father.
[17] Let us see whether his words be true;

let us find out what will happen to him.

[18] For if the just one be the son of God, he will
defend him
and deliver him from the hand of his
foes.

[19] With revilement and torture let us put him
to the test
that we may have proof of his gentleness
and try his patience.

[20] Let us condemn him to a shameful death;
for according to his own words, God will
take care of him."

[21] These were their thoughts, but they erred;
for their wickedness blinded them,

[22] and they knew not the hidden counsels of
God;
neither did they count on a recompense
of holiness
nor discern the innocent souls' reward.

Responsorial Psalm: Psalms 34:17-18, 19-20, 21 AND 23

R. [19a] *The Lord is close to the brokenhearted.*

[17] The LORD confronts the evildoers,
to destroy remembrance of them from
the earth.

[18] When the just cry out, the LORD hears them,
and from all their distress he rescues
them.

R. *The Lord is close to the brokenhearted.*

[19] The LORD is close to the brokenhearted;
and those who are crushed in spirit he
saves.

[20] Many are the troubles of the just man,
but out of them all the LORD delivers him.

R. *The Lord is close to the brokenhearted.*

[21] He watches over all his bones;
not one of them shall be broken.

[23] The LORD redeems the lives of his servants;
no one incurs guilt who takes refuge in
him.

R. The Lord is close to the brokenhearted.

Verse Before the Gospel: Matthew 4:4B

4B One does not live on bread alone,
but on every word that comes forth from the
mouth of God.

Gospel: John 7:1-2, 10, 25-30

1 Jesus moved about within Galilee; he did not wish to travel in Judea, because the Jews were trying to kill him. 2 But the Jewish feast of Tabernacles was near.

10 But when his brothers had gone up to the feast, he himself also went up, not openly but as it were in secret.

25 Some of the inhabitants of Jerusalem said, "Is he not the one they are trying to kill? 26 And look, he is speaking openly and they say nothing to him. Could the authorities have realized that he is the Christ? 27 But we know where he is from. When the Christ comes, no one will know where he is from." 28 So Jesus cried out in the temple area as he was teaching and said, "You know me and also know where I am from. Yet I did not come on my own, but the one who sent me, whom you do not know, is true. 29 I know him, because I am from him, and he sent me." 30 So they tried to arrest him, but no one laid a hand upon him, because his hour had not yet come.

Saturday March 16, 2024

Saturday of the Fourth Week of Lent
First Reading: Jeremiah 11:18-20

18 I knew their plot because the LORD informed me; at that time you, O LORD, showed me their doings.

19 Yet I, like a trusting lamb led to slaughter, had not realized that they were hatching plots against me: "Let us destroy the tree in its vigor; let us cut him off from the land of the living, so that his name will be spoken no more."
20 But, you, O LORD of hosts, O just Judge,
searcher of mind and heart,
Let me witness the vengeance you take on
them,
for to you I have entrusted my cause!

Responsorial Psalm: Psalms 7:2-3, 9BC-10, 11-12

R. (2a)O Lord, my God, in you I take refuge.
2 O LORD, my God, in you I take refuge;
save me from all my pursuers and rescue
me,
3 Lest I become like the lion's prey,
to be torn to pieces, with no one to rescue
me.

R. O Lord, my God, in you I take refuge.

[9BC] Do me justice, O LORD, because I am just,
 and because of the innocence that is
  mine.
[10] Let the malice of the wicked come to an end,
 but sustain the just,
  O searcher of heart and soul, O just God.
R. O Lord, my God, in you I take refuge.

[11] A shield before me is God,
 who saves the upright of heart;
[12] A just judge is God,
 a God who punishes day by day.
R. O Lord, my God, in you I take refuge.

Verse Before the Gospel: Luke 8:15
[15] Blessed are they who have kept the word
  with a generous heart
and yield a harvest through perseverance.

Gospel: John 7:40-53
[40] Some in the crowd who heard these words of Jesus said, "This is truly the Prophet." [41] Others said, "This is the Christ." But others said, "The Christ will not come from Galilee, will he? [42] Does not Scripture say that the Christ will be of David's family and come from Bethlehem, the village where David lived?" [43] So a division occurred in the crowd because of him. [44] Some of them even wanted to arrest him, but no one laid hands on him.

[45] So the guards went to the chief priests and Pharisees, who asked them, "Why did you not bring him?" [46] The guards answered, "Never before has anyone spoken like this man." [47] So the Pharisees answered them, "Have you also been deceived? [48] Have any of the authorities or the Pharisees believed in him? [49] But this crowd, which does not know the law, is accursed." [50] Nicodemus, one of their members who had come to him earlier, said to them, [51] "Does our law condemn a man before it first hears him and finds out what he is doing?" [52] They answered and said to him, "You are not from Galilee also, are you? Look and see that no prophet arises from Galilee".

Then each went to his own house.

Sunday March 17, 2024

Fifth Sunday of Lent, Year B
First Reading: Jeremiah 31:31-34
[31] The days are coming, says the LORD,
 when I will make a new covenant with

the house of Israel
and the house of Judah.
[32] It will not be like the covenant I made with
their fathers
the day I took them by the hand
to lead them forth from the land of Egypt;
for they broke my covenant,
and I had to show myself their master,
says the LORD.
[33] But this is the covenant that I will make
with the house of Israel after those days,
says the LORD.
I will place my law within them and write it
upon their hearts;
I will be their God, and they shall be my
people.
[34] No longer will they have need to teach their
friends and relatives
how to know the LORD.
All, from least to greatest, shall know me,
says the LORD,
for I will forgive their evildoing and
remember their sin no more.

Responsorial Psalm: Psalms 51:3-4, 12-13, 14-15.

R. [(12a)] *Create a clean heart in me, O God.*
[3] Have mercy on me, O God, in your goodness;
in the greatness of your compassion wipe
out my offense.
[4] Thoroughly wash me from my guilt
and of my sin cleanse me.
R. Create a clean heart in me, O God.

[12] A clean heart create for me, O God,
and a steadfast spirit renew within me.
[13] Cast me not out from your presence,
and your Holy Spirit take not from me.
R. Create a clean heart in me, O God.

[14] Give me back the joy of your salvation,
and a willing spirit sustain in me.
[15] I will teach transgressors your ways,

and sinners shall return to you.
R. *Create a clean heart in me, O God.*

Second Reading: Hebrews 5:7-9

[7] In the days when Christ Jesus was in the flesh, he offered prayers and supplications with loud cries and tears to the one who was able to save him from death, and he was heard because of his reverence. [8] Son though he was, he learned obedience from what he suffered; [9] and when he was made perfect, he became the source of eternal salvation for all who obey him.

Verse Before the Gospel: John 12:26

[26] Whoever serves me must follow me, says the
 Lord;
and where I am, there also will my servant
 be.

Gospel: John 12:20-33

[20] Some Greeks who had come to worship at the Passover Feast [21] came to Philip, who was from Bethsaida in Galilee, and asked him, "Sir, we would like to see Jesus." [22] Philip went and told Andrew; then Andrew and Philip went and told Jesus. [23] Jesus answered them, "The hour has come for the Son of Man to be glorified. [24] Amen, amen, I say to you, unless a grain of wheat falls to the ground and dies, it remains just a grain of wheat; but if it dies, it produces much fruit. [25] Whoever loves his life loses it, and whoever hates his life in this world will preserve it for eternal life. [26] Whoever serves me must follow me, and where I am, there also will my servant be. The Father will honor whoever serves me.

[27] "I am troubled now. Yet what should I say, 'Father, save me from this hour'? But it was for this purpose that I came to this hour. [28] Father, glorify your name." Then a voice came from heaven, "I have glorified it and will glorify it again." [29] The crowd there heard it and said it was thunder; but others said, "An angel has spoken to him." [30] Jesus answered and said, "This voice did not come for my sake but for yours. [31] Now is the time of judgment on this world; now the ruler of this world will be driven out. [32] And when I am lifted up from the earth, I will draw everyone to myself." He said this indicating the kind of death he would die.

Monday March 18, 2024

Monday of the Fifth Week of Lent
First Reading: Daniel 13:1-9,15-17, 19-30, 33-62

[1] In Babylon there lived a man named Joakim, [2] who married a very beautiful and God-fearing woman, Susanna, the daughter of Hilkiah; [3] her pious parents had trained their daughter according to the law of Moses. [4] Joakim was very rich; he had a garden near his house, and the Jews had recourse to him often because he was the most respected of them all.

[5] That year, two elders of the people were appointed judges, of whom the Lord said, "Wickedness has come out of Babylon: from the elders who were to govern the

people as judges." ⁶ These men, to whom all brought their cases, frequented the house of Joakim. ⁷When the people left at noon, Susanna used to enter her husband's garden for a walk. ⁸ When the old men saw her enter every day for her walk, they began to lust for her. ⁹ They suppressed their consciences; they would not allow their eyes to look to heaven, and did not keep in mind just judgments.

¹⁵ One day, while they were waiting for the right moment, she entered the garden as usual, with two maids only. She decided to bathe, for the weather was warm. ¹⁶ Nobody else was there except the two elders, who had hidden themselves and were watching her. ¹⁷ "Bring me oil and soap," she said to the maids, "and shut the garden doors while I bathe."

¹⁹ As soon as the maids had left, the two old men got up and hurried to her. ²⁰ "Look," they said, "the garden doors are shut, and no one can see us; give in to our desire, and lie with us. ²¹ If you refuse, we will testify against you that you dismissed your maids because a young man was here with you."

²² "I am completely trapped," Susanna groaned. "If I yield, it will be my death; if I refuse, I cannot escape your power. ²³ Yet it is better for me to fall into your power without guilt than to sin before the Lord." ²⁴ Then Susanna shrieked, and the old men also shouted at her, ²⁵ as one of them ran to open the garden doors. ²⁶ When the people in the house heard the cries from the garden, they rushed in by the side gate to see what had happened to her. ²⁷ At the accusations by the old men, the servants felt very much ashamed, for never had any such thing been said about Susanna.

²⁸ When the people came to her husband Joakim the next day, the two wicked elders also came, fully determined to put Susanna to death. ²⁹ Before all the people they ordered: "Send for Susanna, the daughter of Hilkiah, the wife of Joakim." When she was sent for, ³⁰ she came with her parents, children and all her relatives. ³³ All her relatives and the onlookers were weeping.

³⁴ In the midst of the people the two elders rose up and laid their hands on her head. ³⁵ Through tears she looked up to heaven, for she trusted in the Lord wholeheartedly. ³⁶ The elders made this accusation: "As we were walking in the garden alone, this woman entered with two girls and shut the doors of the garden, dismissing the girls. ³⁷ A young man, who was hidden there, came and lay with her. ³⁸ When we, in a corner of the garden, saw this crime, we ran toward them. ³⁹ We saw them lying together, but the man we could not hold, because he was stronger than we; he opened the doors and ran off. ⁴⁰ Then we seized her and asked who the young man was, ⁴¹ but she refused to tell us. We testify to this." The assembly believed them, since they were elders and judges of the people, and they condemned her to death.

⁴² But Susanna cried aloud: "O eternal God, you know what is hidden and are aware of all things before they come to be: ⁴³ you know that they have testified falsely against me. Here I am about to die, though I have done none of the things with which these wicked men have charged me."

⁴⁴ The Lord heard her prayer. ⁴⁵ As she was being led to execution, God stirred up the holy spirit of a young boy named Daniel, ⁴⁶ and he cried aloud: "I will have no part in the death of this woman." ⁴⁷ All the people turned and asked him, "What is this you are saying?" ⁴⁸ He stood in their midst and continued, "Are you such fools, O children of Israel!

To condemn a woman of Israel without examination and without clear evidence? [49] Return to court, for they have testified falsely against her."

[50] Then all the people returned in haste. To Daniel the elders said, "Come, sit with us and inform us, since God has given you the prestige of old age." [51] But he replied, "Separate these two far from each other that I may examine them."

[52] After they were separated one from the other, he called one of them and said: "How you have grown evil with age! Now have your past sins come to term: [53] passing unjust sentences, condemning the innocent, and freeing the guilty, although the Lord says, 'The innocent and the just you shall not put to death.' [54] Now, then, if you were a witness, tell me under what tree you saw them together." [55] "Under a mastic tree," he answered. Daniel replied, "Your fine lie has cost you your head, for the angel of God shall receive the sentence from him and split you in two." [56] Putting him to one side, he ordered the other one to be brought. Daniel said to him, "Offspring of Canaan, not of Judah, beauty has seduced you, lust has subverted your conscience. [57] This is how you acted with the daughters of Israel, and in their fear they yielded to you; but a daughter of Judah did not tolerate your wickedness. [58] Now, then, tell me under what tree you surprised them together." [59] "Under an oak," he said. Daniel replied, "Your fine lie has cost you also your head, for the angel of God waits with a sword to cut you in two so as to make an end of you both."

[60] The whole assembly cried aloud, blessing God who saves those who hope in him. [61] They rose up against the two elders, for by their own words Daniel had convicted them of perjury. [62] According to the law of Moses, they inflicted on them the penalty they had plotted to impose on their neighbor: they put them to death. Thus was innocent blood spared that day.

or Daniel 13:41c-62

[41c] The assembly believed them, since they were elders and judges of the people, and they condemned her to death.

[42] But Susanna cried aloud: "Eternal God, you know what is hidden and are aware of all things before they come to be: [43] you know that they have testified falsely against me. Here I am about to die, though I have done none of the things for which these men have condemned me."

[44] The Lord heard her prayer. [45] As she was being led to execution, God stirred up the holy spirit of a young boy named Daniel, [46] and he cried aloud: "I am innocent of this woman's blood." [47] All the people turned and asked him, "What are you saying?" [48] He stood in their midst and said, "Are you such fools, you Israelites, to condemn a daughter of Israel without investigation and without clear evidence? [49] Return to court, for they have testified falsely against her."

[50] Then all the people returned in haste. To Daniel the elders said, "Come, sit with us and inform us, since God has given you the prestige of old age." [51] But he replied, "Separate these two far from one another, and I will examine them."

[52] After they were separated from each other, he called one of them and said: "How you have grown evil with age! Now have your past sins come to term: [53] passing unjust sentences, condemning the innocent, and freeing the guilty, although the Lord says, 'The innocent and the just you shall not put to death.' [54] Now, then, if you were a witness, tell me under what tree you saw them together." [55] "Under a mastic tree," he answered. "Your fine lie has cost you your head," said Daniel; "for the angel of God has already received the sentence from God and shall split you in two." [56] Putting him to one side, he ordered the other one to be brought. "Offspring of Canaan, not of Judah," Daniel said to him, "beauty has seduced you, lust has perverted your heart. [57] This is how you acted with the daughters of Israel, and in their fear they yielded to you; but a daughter of Judah did not tolerate your lawlessness. [58] Now, then, tell me under what tree you surprised them together." [59] "Under an oak," he said. "Your fine lie has cost you also your head," said Daniel; "for the angel of God waits with a sword to cut you in two so as to destroy you both."

[60] The whole assembly cried aloud, blessing God who saves those who hope in him. [61] They rose up against the two old men, for by their own words Daniel had convicted them of bearing false witness. They condemned them to the fate they had planned for their neighbor: [62] in accordance with the law of Moses they put them to death. Thus was innocent blood spared that day.

Responsorial Psalm: Psalms 23:1-3A, 3B-4, 5, 6

R. [4ab] *Even though I walk in the dark valley I fear*
no evil; for you are at my side.

[1] The LORD is my shepherd; I shall not want.
[2] In verdant pastures he gives me repose;
Beside restful waters he leads me;
[3A] he refreshes my soul.

R. *Even though I walk in the dark valley I fear no*
evil; for you are at my side.

[3BC] He guides me in right paths
for his name's sake.
[4] Even though I walk in the dark valley
I fear no evil; for you are at my side
With your rod and your staff
that give me courage.

R. *Even though I walk in the dark valley I fear no*
evil; for you are at my side.

[5] You spread the table before me
in the sight of my foes;
You anoint my head with oil;
my cup overflows.

R. *Even though I walk in the dark valley I fear no*
evil; for you are at my side.

⁶Only goodness and kindness follow me
     all the days of my life;
And I shall dwell in the house of the LORD
     for years to come.

R. Even though I walk in the dark valley I fear no evil; for you are at my side.

Verse Before the Gospel: Ezekiel 33:11

¹¹ I take no pleasure in the death of the wicked
     man, says the Lord,
but rather in his conversion, that he may
     live.

Gospel: John 8:1-11

¹ Jesus went to the Mount of Olives. ² But early in the morning he arrived again in the temple area, and all the people started coming to him, and he sat down and taught them. ³ Then the scribes and the Pharisees brought a woman who had been caught in adultery and made her stand in the middle. ⁴ They said to him, "Teacher, this woman was caught in the very act of committing adultery. ⁵ Now in the law, Moses commanded us to stone such women. So what do you say?" ⁶ They said this to test him, so that they could have some charge to bring against him. Jesus bent down and began to write on the ground with his finger. ⁷ But when they continued asking him, he straightened up and said to them, "Let the one among you who is without sin be the first to throw a stone at her." ⁸ Again he bent down and wrote on the ground. ⁹ And in response, they went away one by one, beginning with the elders. So he was left alone with the woman before him. ¹⁰ Then Jesus straightened up and said to her, "Woman, where are they? Has no one condemned you?" ¹¹ She replied, "No one, sir." Then Jesus said, "Neither do I condemn you. Go, and from now on do not sin anymore."

Tuesday March 19, 2024

Solemnity of Saint Joseph, Husband of the Blessed Virgin Mary

First Reading: 2 Samuel 7:4-5A, 12-14A, 16

⁴ The LORD spoke to Nathan and said: ^{5A} "Go, tell my servant David, ¹² 'When your time comes and you rest with your ancestors, I will raise up your heir after you, sprung from your loins, and I will make his kingdom firm. ¹³ It is he who shall build a house for my name. And I will make his royal throne firm forever. ^{14A} I will be a father to him, and he shall be a son to me. ¹⁶ Your house and your kingdom shall endure forever before me; your throne shall stand firm forever.'"

Responsorial Psalm: Psalms 89:2-3, 4-5, 27 and 29

R. ⁽³⁷⁾ **The son of David will live for ever.**

² The promises of the LORD I will sing forever;
     through all generations my mouth shall
       proclaim your faithfulness,

³ For you have said, "My kindness is
        established for ever";
    in heaven you have confirmed your
        faithfulness.
R. The son of David will live for ever.
⁴ "I have made a covenant with my chosen
        one,
    I have sworn to David my servant:
⁵ Forever will I confirm your posterity
    and establish your throne for all
        generations."
R. The son of David will live for ever.

²⁷ "He shall say of me, 'You are my father,
    my God, the Rock, my savior.'
²⁹ Forever I will maintain my kindness toward
        him,
    and my covenant with him stands firm."
R. The son of David will live for ever.

Second Reading: Romans 4:13, 16-18, 22

Brothers and sisters: ¹³ It was not through the law that the promise was made to Abraham and his descendants that he would inherit the world, but through the righteousness that comes from faith. ¹⁶ For this reason, it depends on faith, so that it may be a gift, and the promise may be guaranteed to all his descendants, not to those who only adhere to the law but to those who follow the faith of Abraham, who is the father of all of us, ¹⁷ as it is written, *I have made you father of many nations*. He is our father in the sight of God, in whom he believed, who gives life to the dead and calls into being what does not exist. ¹⁸ He believed, hoping against hope, that he would become *the father of many nations*, according to what was said, *Thus shall your descendants be*. ²² That is why *it was credited to him as righteousness*.

Verse Before the Gospel: Psalms 84:5

⁵ Blessed are those who dwell in your house, O
        Lord;
they never cease to praise you.

Gospel: Matthew 1:16, 18-21, 24A

¹⁶ Jacob was the father of Joseph, the husband of Mary. Of her was born Jesus who is called the Christ.

    ¹⁸ Now this is how the birth of Jesus Christ came about. When his mother Mary was betrothed to Joseph, but before they lived together, she was found with child

through the Holy Spirit. ¹⁹ Joseph her husband, since he was a righteous man, yet unwilling to expose her to shame, decided to divorce her quietly. ²⁰ Such was his intention when, behold, the angel of the Lord appeared to him in a dream and said, "Joseph, son of David, do not be afraid to take Mary your wife into your home. For it is through the Holy Spirit that this child has been conceived in her. ²¹ She will bear a son and you are to name him Jesus, because he will save his people from their sins." ²⁴ When Joseph awoke, he did as the angel of the Lord had commanded him and took his wife into his home.

Or Luke 2:41-51A

⁴¹ Each year Jesus' parents went to Jerusalem for the feast of Passover, ⁴² and when he was twelve years old, they went up according to festival custom. ⁴³ After they had completed its days, as they were returning, the boy Jesus remained behind in Jerusalem, but his parents did not know it. ⁴⁴ Thinking that he was in the caravan, they journeyed for a day and looked for him among their relatives and acquaintances, ⁴⁵ but not finding him, they returned to Jerusalem to look for him. ⁴⁶ After three days they found him in the temple, sitting in the midst of the teachers, listening to them and asking them questions, ⁴⁷ and all who heard him were astounded at his understanding and his answers. ⁴⁸ When his parents saw him, they were astonished, and his mother said to him, "Son, why have you done this to us? Your father and I have been looking for you with great anxiety." ⁴⁹ And he said to them, "Why were you looking for me? Did you not know that I must be in my Father's house?" ⁵⁰ But they did not understand what he said to them. ⁵¹ᴬ He went down with them and came to Nazareth, and was obedient to them.

Wednesday March 20, 2024

Wednesday of the Fifth Week of Lent
First Reading: Daniel 3:14-20, 91-92, 95

¹⁴ King Nebuchadnezzar said: "Is it true, Shadrach, Meshach, and Abednego, that you will not serve my god, or worship the golden statue that I set up? ¹⁵ Be ready now to fall down and worship the statue I had made, whenever you hear the sound of the trumpet, flute, lyre, harp, psaltery, bagpipe, and all the other musical instruments; otherwise, you shall be instantly cast into the white-hot furnace; and who is the God who can deliver you out of my hands?" ¹⁶ Shadrach, Meshach, and Abednego answered King Nebuchadnezzar, "There is no need for us to defend ourselves before you in this matter. ¹⁷ If our God, whom we serve, can save us from the white-hot furnace and from your hands, O king, may he save us! ¹⁸ But even if he will not, know, O king, that we will not serve your god or worship the golden statue that you set up."

¹⁹ King Nebuchadnezzar's face became livid with utter rage against Shadrach, Meshach, and Abednego. He ordered the furnace to be heated seven times more than usual ²⁰ and had some of the strongest men in his army bind Shadrach, Meshach, and Abednego and cast them into the white-hot furnace.

⁹¹ Nebuchadnezzar rose in haste and asked his nobles, "Did we not cast three men bound into the fire?" "Assuredly, O king," they answered. ⁹² "But," he replied, "I see four

men unfettered and unhurt, walking in the fire, and the fourth looks like a son of God." [95] Nebuchadnezzar exclaimed, "Blessed be the God of Shadrach, Meshach, and Abednego, who sent his angel to deliver the servants who trusted in him; they disobeyed the royal command and yielded their bodies rather than serve or worship any god except their own God."

Responsorial Psalm: Daniel 3:52, 53, 54, 55, 56

R. [(52b)] **Glory and praise for ever!**

[52] "Blessed are you, O Lord, the God of our
              fathers,
         praiseworthy and exalted above all
              forever;
And blessed is your holy and glorious name,
         praiseworthy and exalted above all for all
              ages."

R. **Glory and praise for ever!**

[53] "Blessed are you in the temple of your holy
              glory,
         praiseworthy and exalted above all
              forever."

R. **Glory and praise for ever!**

[54] "Blessed are you on the throne of your
              Kingdom,
         praiseworthy and exalted above all
              forever."

R. **Glory and praise for ever!**

[55] "Blessed are you who look into the depths
         from your throne upon the cherubim;
         praiseworthy and exalted above all
              forever."

R. **Glory and praise for ever!**

[56] "Blessed are you in the firmament of heaven,
         praiseworthy and glorious forever."

R. **Glory and praise for ever!**

Verse Before the Gospel: Luke 8:15

[15] Blessed are they who have kept the word
         with a generous heart
and yield a harvest through perseverance.

Gospel: John 8:31-42

Jesus said to those Jews who believed in him, [31] "If you remain in my word, you will truly be my disciples, [32] and you will know the truth, and the truth will set you free." [33] They answered him, "We are descendants of Abraham and have never been enslaved to anyone. How can you say, 'You will become free'?" [34] Jesus answered them, "Amen, amen, I say to you, everyone who commits sin is a slave of sin. [35] A slave does not remain in a household forever, but a son always remains. [36] So if the Son frees you, then you will truly be free. [37] I know that you are descendants of Abraham. But you are trying to kill me, because my word has no room among you. [38] I tell you what I have seen in the Father's presence; then do what you have heard from the Father."

[39] They answered and said to him, "Our father is Abraham." Jesus said to them, "If you were Abraham's children, you would be doing the works of Abraham. [40] But now you are trying to kill me, a man who has told you the truth that I heard from God; Abraham did not do this. [41] You are doing the works of your father!" So they said to him, "We were not born of fornication. We have one Father, God." [42] Jesus said to them, "If God were your Father, you would love me, for I came from God and am here; I did not come on my own, but he sent me."

Thursday March 21, 2024

Thursday of the Fifth Week of Lent

First Reading: Genesis 17:3-9

[3] When Abram prostrated himself, God spoke to him: [4] "My covenant with you is this: you are to become the father of a host of nations. [5] No longer shall you be called Abram; your name shall be Abraham, for I am making you the father of a host of nations. [6] I will render you exceedingly fertile; I will make nations of you; kings shall stem from you. [7] I will maintain my covenant with you and your descendants after you throughout the ages as an everlasting pact, to be your God and the God of your descendants after you. [8] I will give to you and to your descendants after you the land in which you are now staying, the whole land of Canaan, as a permanent possession; and I will be their God."

[9] God also said to Abraham: "On your part, you and your descendants after you must keep my covenant throughout the ages."

Responsorial Psalm: Psalms 105:4-5, 6-7, 8-9

R. [8a] *The Lord remembers his covenant for ever.*
[4] Look to the LORD in his strength;
    seek to serve him constantly.
[5] Recall the wondrous deeds that he has
       wrought,
    his portents, and the judgments he has
       uttered.
R. *The Lord remembers his covenant for ever.*

⁶ You descendants of Abraham, his servants,
    sons of Jacob, his chosen ones!
⁷ He, the LORD, is our God;
    throughout the earth his judgments
        prevail.
R. The Lord remembers his covenant for ever.

⁸ He remembers forever his covenant
    which he made binding for a thousand
        generations–
⁹ Which he entered into with Abraham
    and by his oath to Isaac.
R. The Lord remembers his covenant for ever.

Verse Before the Gospel: Psalms 95:8

⁸ If today you hear his voice,
harden not your hearts.

Gospel: John 8:51-59

⁵¹ Jesus said to the Jews: "Amen, amen, I say to you, whoever keeps my word will never see death." ⁵² So the Jews said to him, "Now we are sure that you are possessed. Abraham died, as did the prophets, yet you say, 'Whoever keeps my word will never taste death.' ⁵³ Are you greater than our father Abraham, who died? Or the prophets, who died? Who do you make yourself out to be?" ⁵⁴ Jesus answered, "If I glorify myself, my glory is worth nothing; but it is my Father who glorifies me, of whom you say, 'He is our God.' ⁵⁵ You do not know him, but I know him. And if I should say that I do not know him, I would be like you a liar. But I do know him and I keep his word. ⁵⁶ Abraham your father rejoiced to see my day; he saw it and was glad." ⁵⁷ So the Jews said to him, "You are not yet fifty years old and you have seen Abraham?" ⁵⁸ Jesus said to them, "Amen, amen, I say to you, before Abraham came to be, I AM." ⁵⁹ So they picked up stones to throw at him; but Jesus hid and went out of the temple area.

Friday March 22, 2024

Friday of the Fifth Week of Lent
First Reading: Jeremiah 20:10-13

¹⁰ I hear the whisperings of many:
    "Terror on every side!
    Denounce! let us denounce him!"
All those who were my friends
    are on the watch for any misstep of mine.
"Perhaps he will be trapped; then we can
        prevail,
    and take our vengeance on him."

¹¹ But the LORD is with me, like a mighty
       champion:
         my persecutors will stumble, they will
          not triumph.
In their failure they will be put to utter
       shame,
         to lasting, unforgettable confusion.
¹² O LORD of hosts, you who test the just,
       who probe mind and heart,
Let me witness the vengeance you take on
       them,
        for to you I have entrusted my cause.
¹³ Sing to the LORD,
       praise the LORD,
For he has rescued the life of the poor
       from the power of the wicked!

Responsorial Psalm: Psalms 18:2-3A, 3BC-4, 5-6, 7

R. *(see 7)* ***In my distress I called upon the Lord,***
      and he heard my voice.
² I love you, O LORD, my strength,
   ^{3A} O LORD, my rock, my fortress, my
      deliverer.
R. In my distress I called upon the Lord, and he
      heard my voice.

^{3BC} My God, my rock of refuge,
      my shield, the horn of my salvation, my
       stronghold!
⁴ Praised be the LORD, I exclaim,
    and I am safe from my enemies.
R. In my distress I called upon the Lord, and he
      heard my voice.

⁵ The breakers of death surged round about
      me,
      the destroying floods overwhelmed me;
⁶ The cords of the nether world enmeshed me,
      the snares of death overtook me.
R. In my distress I called upon the Lord, and he
      heard my voice.

[7] In my distress I called upon the LORD
and cried out to my God;
From his temple he heard my voice,
and my cry to him reached his ears.
**R. In my distress I called upon the Lord, and he
heard my voice.**

Verse Before the Gospel: John 6:63C, 68C

[63C] Your words, Lord, are Spirit and life;
[68C] you have the words of everlasting life.

Gospel: John 10:31-42

[31] The Jews picked up rocks to stone Jesus. [32] Jesus answered them, "I have shown you many good works from my Father. For which of these are you trying to stone me?" [33] The Jews answered him, "We are not stoning you for a good work but for blasphemy. You, a man, are making yourself God." [34] Jesus answered them, "Is it not written in your law, 'I said, 'You are gods''? [35] If it calls them gods to whom the word of God came, and Scripture cannot be set aside, [36] can you say that the one whom the Father has consecrated and sent into the world blasphemes because I said, 'I am the Son of God'? [37] If I do not perform my Father's works, do not believe me; [38] but if I perform them, even if you do not believe me, believe the works, so that you may realize and understand that the Father is in me and I am in the Father." [39] Then they tried again to arrest him; but he escaped from their power.

[40] He went back across the Jordan to the place where John first baptized, and there he remained. [41] Many came to him and said, "John performed no sign, but everything John said about this man was true." [42] And many there began to believe in him.

Saturday March 23, 2024

Saturday of the Fifth Week of Lent
First Reading: Ezekiel 37:21-28

[21] Thus says the Lord GOD: I will take the children of Israel from among the nations to which they have come, and gather them from all sides to bring them back to their land. [22] I will make them one nation upon the land, in the mountains of Israel, and there shall be one prince for them all. Never again shall they be two nations, and never again shall they be divided into two kingdoms.

[23] No longer shall they defile themselves with their idols, their abominations, and all their transgressions. I will deliver them from all their sins of apostasy, and cleanse them so that they may be my people and I may be their God. [24] My servant David shall be prince over them, and there shall be one shepherd for them all; they shall live by my statutes and carefully observe my decrees. [25] They shall live on the land that I gave to my servant Jacob, the land where their fathers lived; they shall live on it forever, they, and their children, and their children's children, with my servant David their prince forever. [26] I will make with them a covenant of peace; it shall be an everlasting covenant with them, and I will

multiply them, and put my sanctuary among them forever. [27] My dwelling shall be with them; I will be their God, and they shall be my people. [28] Thus the nations shall know that it is I, the LORD, who make Israel holy, when my sanctuary shall be set up among them forever.

Responsorial Psalm: Jeremiah 31:10, 11-12ABCD, 13

R. [(see 10d)] *The Lord will guard us, as a shepherd guards his flock.*

[10] Hear the word of the LORD, O nations,
    proclaim it on distant isles, and say:
He who scattered Israel, now gathers them
        together,
    he guards them as a shepherd his flock.

R. *The Lord will guard us, as a shepherd guards his flock.*

[11] The LORD shall ransom Jacob,
        he shall redeem him from the hand of his
        conqueror.
[12] Shouting, they shall mount the heights of
        Zion,
    they shall come streaming to the LORD's
        blessings:
The grain, the wine, and the oil,
    the sheep and the oxen.

R. *The Lord will guard us, as a shepherd guards his flock.*

[13] Then the virgins shall make merry and
        dance,
    and young men and old as well.
I will turn their mourning into joy,
    I will console and gladden them after
        their sorrows.

R. *The Lord will guard us, as a shepherd guards his flock.*

Verse Before the Gospel: Ezekiel 18:31

[31] Cast away from you all the crimes you have
        committed, says the Lord,
and make for yourselves a new heart and a
        new spirit.

Gospel: John 11:45-56

[45] Many of the Jews who had come to Mary and seen what Jesus had done began to believe in him. [46] But some of them went to the Pharisees and told them what Jesus had done. [47] So the chief priests and the Pharisees convened the Sanhedrin and said, "What are we going to do? This man is performing many signs. [48] If we leave him alone, all will believe in him, and the Romans will come and take away both our land and our nation." [49] But one of them, Caiaphas, who was high priest that year, said to them, "You know nothing, [50] nor do you consider that it is better for you that one man should die instead of the people, so that the whole nation may not perish." [51] He did not say this on his own, but since he was high priest for that year, he prophesied that Jesus was going to die for the nation, [52] and not only for the nation, but also to gather into one the dispersed children of God. [53] So from that day on they planned to kill him.

[54] So Jesus no longer walked about in public among the Jews, but he left for the region near the desert, to a town called Ephraim, and there he remained with his disciples.

[55] Now the Passover of the Jews was near, and many went up from the country to Jerusalem before Passover to purify themselves. [56] They looked for Jesus and said to one another as they were in the temple area, "What do you think? That he will not come to the feast?"

Sunday March 24, 2024
Palm Sunday, Year B

At The Procession with Palms – Gospel – Mark 11: 1-10

[1] When Jesus and his disciples drew near to Jerusalem, to Bethphage and Bethany at the Mount of Olives, he sent two of his disciples [2] and said to them, "Go into the village opposite you, and immediately on entering it, you will find a colt tethered on which no one has ever sat. Untie it and bring it here. [3] If anyone should say to you, 'Why are you doing this?' reply, 'The Master has need of it and will send it back here at once.'" [4] So they went off and found a colt tethered at a gate outside on the street, and they untied it. [5] Some of the bystanders said to them, "What are you doing, untying the colt?" [6] They answered them just as Jesus had told them to, and they permitted them to do it. [7] So they brought the colt to Jesus and put their cloaks over it. And he sat on it. [8] Many people spread their cloaks on the road, and others spread leafy branches that they had cut from the fields. [9] Those preceding him as well as those following kept crying out:

"Hosanna!
   Blessed is he who comes in the name
      of the Lord!
[10] Blessed is the kingdom of our father
      David that is to come!
Hosanna in the highest!"

Or John 12: 12-16

[12] When the great crowd that had come to the feast heard that Jesus was coming to Jerusalem, [13] they took palm branches and went out to meet him, and cried out:

"Hosanna!
Blessed is he who comes in the name of
      the Lord, the king of Israel."

[14] Jesus found an ass and sat upon it, as is written:

[15] *"Fear no more, O daughter Zion;*
see, your king comes, seated upon an
      ass's colt."

[16] His disciples did not understand this at first, but when Jesus had been glorified they remembered that these things were written about him and that they had done this for him.

At The Mass – First Reading: Isaiah 50:4-7

[4] The Lord GOD has given me
      a well-trained tongue,
that I might know how to speak to the weary
      a word that will rouse them.
Morning after morning
      he opens my ear that I may hear;
[5] and I have not rebelled,
      have not turned back.
      [6] I gave my back to those who beat me,
      my cheeks to those who plucked my
         beard;
my face I did not shield
      from buffets and spitting.

[7] The Lord GOD is my help,
      therefore I am not disgraced;
I have set my face like flint,
      knowing that I shall not be put to shame.

Responsorial Psalm: Psalms 22:8-9, 17-18, 19-20, 23-24

R. *(2a)* **My God, my God, why have you**
             abandoned me?
[8] All who see me scoff at me;
      they mock me with parted lips, they wag

their heads:

[9] "He relied on the LORD; let him deliver him,
  let him rescue him, if he loves him."

**R. My God, my God, why have you abandoned
    me?**

[17] Indeed, many dogs surround me,
  a pack of evildoers closes in upon me;
[18] They have pierced my hands and my feet;
  I can count all my bones.

**R. My God, my God, why have you abandoned
    me?**

[19] They divide my garments among them,
  and for my vesture they cast lots.
[20] But you, O LORD, be not far from me;
  O my help, hasten to aid me.

**R. My God, my God, why have you abandoned
    me?**

[23] I will proclaim your name to my brethren;
  in the midst of the assembly I will praise
    you:
[24] "You who fear the LORD, praise him;
  all you descendants of Jacob, give glory to
    him;
  revere him, all you descendants of
    Israel!"

**R. My God, my God, why have you abandoned
    me?**

Second Reading: Philippians 2:6-11

[6] Christ Jesus, though he was in the form of
    God,
  did not regard equality with God
  something to be grasped.
[7] Rather, he emptied himself,
  taking the form of a slave,
  coming in human likeness;
  and found human in appearance,
[8] he humbled himself,
  becoming obedient to the point of death,
  even death on a cross.

[9] Because of this, God greatly exalted him
and bestowed on him the name
which is above every name,
[10] that at the name of Jesus
every knee should bend,
of those in heaven and on earth and
under the earth,
[11] and every tongue confess that
Jesus Christ is Lord,
to the glory of God the Father.

Verse Before the Gospel: Philippians 2:8-9

[8] Christ became obedient to the point of death,
even death on a cross.
[9] Because of this, God greatly exalted him
and bestowed on him the name which is
above every name.

Gospel: Mark 14: 1 – 15: 47

[14:1] The Passover and the Feast of Unleavened Bread were to take place in two days' time. So the chief priests and the scribes were seeking a way to arrest him by treachery and put him to death. [2] They said, "Not during the festival, for fear that there may be a riot among the people."

[3] When he was in Bethany reclining at table in the house of Simon the leper, a woman came with an alabaster jar of perfumed oil, costly genuine spikenard. She broke the alabaster jar and poured it on his head. [4] There were some who were indignant. "Why has there been this waste of perfumed oil? [5] It could have been sold for more than three hundred days' wages and the money given to the poor." They were infuriated with her. [6] Jesus said, "Let her alone. Why do you make trouble for her? She has done a good thing for me. [7] The poor you will always have with you, and whenever you wish you can do good to them, but you will not always have me. [8] She has done what she could. She has anticipated anointing my body for burial. [9] Amen, I say to you, wherever the gospel is proclaimed to the whole world, what she has done will be told in memory of her."

[10] Then Judas Iscariot, one of the Twelve, went off to the chief priests to hand him over to them. [11] When they heard him they were pleased and promised to pay him money. Then he looked for an opportunity to hand him over.

[12] On the first day of the Feast of Unleavened Bread, when they sacrificed the Passover lamb, his disciples said to him, "Where do you want us to go and prepare for you to eat the Passover?" [13] He sent two of his disciples and said to them, "Go into the city and a man will meet you, carrying a jar of water. Follow him. [14] Wherever he enters, say to the master of the house, 'The Teacher says, "Where is my guest room where I may eat the Passover with my disciples?"' [15] Then he will show you a large upper room furnished and

ready. Make the preparations for us there." ¹⁶ The disciples then went off, entered the city, and found it just as he had told them; and they prepared the Passover.

¹⁷ When it was evening, he came with the Twelve. ¹⁸ And as they reclined at table and were eating, Jesus said, "Amen, I say to you, one of you will betray me, one who is eating with me." ¹⁹ They began to be distressed and to say to him, one by one, "Surely it is not I?" ²⁰ He said to them, "One of the Twelve, the one who dips with me into the dish. ²¹ For the Son of Man indeed goes, as it is written of him, but woe to that man by whom the Son of Man is betrayed. It would be better for that man if he had never been born."

²² While they were eating, he took bread, said the blessing, broke it, and gave it to them, and said, "Take it; this is my body." ²³ Then he took a cup, gave thanks, and gave it to them, and they all drank from it. ²⁴ He said to them, "This is my blood of the covenant, which will be shed for many. ²⁵ Amen, I say to you, I shall not drink again the fruit of the vine until the day when I drink it new in the kingdom of God." ²⁶ Then, after singing a hymn, they went out to the Mount of Olives.

²⁷ Then Jesus said to them, "All of you will have your faith shaken, for it is written:

'I will strike the shepherd,
    and the sheep will be dispersed.'

²⁸ But after I have been raised up, I shall go before you to Galilee." ²⁹ Peter said to him, "Even though all should have their faith shaken, mine will not be." ³⁰ Then Jesus said to him, "Amen, I say to you, this very night before the cock crows twice you will deny me three times." ³¹ But he vehemently replied, "Even though I should have to die with you, I will not deny you." And they all spoke similarly.

³² Then they came to a place named Gethsemane, and he said to his disciples, "Sit here while I pray." ³³ He took with him Peter, James, and John, and began to be troubled and distressed. ³⁴ Then he said to them, "My soul is sorrowful even to death. Remain here and keep watch." ³⁵ He advanced a little and fell to the ground and prayed that if it were possible the hour might pass by him; ³⁶ he said, "Abba, Father, all things are possible to you. Take this cup away from me, but not what I will but what you will." ³⁷ When he returned he found them asleep. He said to Peter, "Simon, are you asleep? Could you not keep watch for one hour? ³⁸ Watch and pray that you may not undergo the test. The spirit is willing but the flesh is weak." ³⁹ Withdrawing again, he prayed, saying the same thing. ⁴⁰ Then he returned once more and found them asleep, for they could not keep their eyes open and did not know what to answer him. ⁴¹ He returned a third time and said to them, "Are you still sleeping and taking your rest? It is enough. The hour has come. Behold, the Son of Man is to be handed over to sinners. ⁴² Get up, let us go. See, my betrayer is at hand."

⁴³ Then, while he was still speaking, Judas, one of the Twelve, arrived, accompanied by a crowd with swords and clubs who had come from the chief priests, the scribes, and the elders. ⁴⁴ His betrayer had arranged a signal with them, saying, "The man I shall kiss is the one; arrest him and lead him away securely." ⁴⁵ He came and immediately went over to him and said, "Rabbi." And he kissed him. ⁴⁶ At this they laid hands on him

and arrested him. ⁴⁷ One of the bystanders drew his sword, struck the high priest's servant, and cut off his ear. ⁴⁸ Jesus said to them in reply, "Have you come out as against a robber, with swords and clubs, to seize me? ⁴⁹ Day after day I was with you teaching in the temple area, yet you did not arrest me; but that the scriptures may be fulfilled." ⁵⁰ And they all left him and fled. ⁵¹ Now a young man followed him wearing nothing but a linen cloth about his body. They seized him, ⁵² but he left the cloth behind and ran off naked.

⁵³ They led Jesus away to the high priest, and all the chief priests and the elders and the scribes came together. ⁵⁴ Peter followed him at a distance into the high priest's courtyard and was seated with the guards, warming himself at the fire. ⁵⁵ The chief priests and the entire Sanhedrin kept trying to obtain testimony against Jesus in order to put him to death, but they found none. ⁵⁶ Many gave false witness against him, but their testimony did not agree. ⁵⁷ Some took the stand and testified falsely against him, alleging, ⁵⁸ "We heard him say, 'I will destroy this temple made with hands and within three days I will build another not made with hands.'" ⁵⁹ Even so their testimony did not agree. ⁶⁰ The high priest rose before the assembly and questioned Jesus, saying, "Have you no answer? What are these men testifying against you?" ⁶¹ But he was silent and answered nothing. Again the high priest asked him and said to him, "Are you the Messiah, the son of the Blessed One?" ⁶² Then Jesus answered, "I am;

and 'you will see the Son of Man
    seated at the right hand of the Power
    and coming with the clouds of
        heaven.'"

⁶³ At that the high priest tore his garments and said, "What further need have we of witnesses? ⁶⁴ You have heard the blasphemy. What do you think?" They all condemned him as deserving to die. ⁶⁵ Some began to spit on him. They blindfolded him and struck him and said to him, "Prophesy!" And the guards greeted him with blows.

⁶⁶ While Peter was below in the courtyard, one of the high priest's maids came along. ⁶⁷ Seeing Peter warming himself, she looked intently at him and said, "You too were with the Nazarene, Jesus." ⁶⁸ But he denied it saying, "I neither know nor understand what you are talking about." So he went out into the outer court. Then the cock crowed. ⁶⁹ The maid saw him and began again to say to the bystanders, "This man is one of them." ⁷⁰ Once again he denied it. A little later the bystanders said to Peter once more, "Surely you are one of them; for you too are a Galilean." ⁷¹ He began to curse and to swear, "I do not know this man about whom you are talking." ⁷² And immediately a cock crowed a second time. Then Peter remembered the word that Jesus had said to him, "Before the cock crows twice you will deny me three times." He broke down and wept.

¹⁵:¹ As soon as morning came, the chief priests with the elders and the scribes, that is, the whole Sanhedrin, held a council. They bound Jesus, led him away, and handed him over to Pilate. ² Pilate questioned him, "Are you the king of the Jews?" He said to him in reply, "You say so." ³ The chief priests accused him of many things. ⁴ Again Pilate

questioned him, "Have you no answer? See how many things they accuse you of." ⁵ Jesus gave him no further answer, so that Pilate was amazed.

⁶ Now on the occasion of the feast he used to release to them one prisoner whom they requested. ⁷ A man called Barabbas was then in prison along with the rebels who had committed murder in a rebellion. ⁸ The crowd came forward and began to ask him to do for them as he was accustomed. ⁹ Pilate answered, "Do you want me to release to you the king of the Jews?" ¹⁰ For he knew that it was out of envy that the chief priests had handed him over. ¹¹ But the chief priests stirred up the crowd to have him release Barabbas for them instead. ¹² Pilate again said to them in reply, "Then what do you want me to do with the man you call the king of the Jews?" ¹³ They shouted again, "Crucify him." ¹⁴ Pilate said to them, "Why? What evil has he done?" They only shouted the louder, "Crucify him." ¹⁵ So Pilate, wishing to satisfy the crowd, released Barabbas to them and, after he had Jesus scourged, handed him over to be crucified.

¹⁶ The soldiers led him away inside the palace, that is, the praetorium, and assembled the whole cohort. ¹⁷ They clothed him in purple and, weaving a crown of thorns, placed it on him. ¹⁸ They began to salute him with, "Hail, King of the Jews!" ¹⁹ and kept striking his head with a reed and spitting upon him. They knelt before him in homage. ²⁰ And when they had mocked him, they stripped him of the purple cloak, dressed him in his own clothes, and led him out to crucify him.

²¹ They pressed into service a passer-by, Simon, a Cyrenian, who was coming in from the country, the father of Alexander and Rufus, to carry his cross.

²² They brought him to the place of Golgotha—which is translated Place of the Skull—. ²³ They gave him wine drugged with myrrh, but he did not take it. ²⁴ Then they crucified him and divided his garments by casting lots for them to see what each should take. ²⁵ It was nine o'clock in the morning when they crucified him. ²⁶ The inscription of the charge against him read, "The King of the Jews." ²⁷ With him they crucified two revolutionaries, one on his right and one on his left. [28] ²⁹ Those passing by reviled him, shaking their heads and saying, "Aha! You who would destroy the temple and rebuild it in three days, ³⁰ save yourself by coming down from the cross." ³¹ Likewise the chief priests, with the scribes, mocked him among themselves and said, "He saved others; he cannot save himself. ³² Let the Christ, the King of Israel, come down now from the cross that we may see and believe." Those who were crucified with him also kept abusing him.

³³ At noon darkness came over the whole land until three in the afternoon. ³⁴ And at three o'clock Jesus cried out in a loud voice, *Eloi, Eloi, lema sabachthani?* which is translated, "My God, my God, why have you forsaken me?" ³⁵ Some of the bystanders who heard it said, "Look, he is calling Elijah." ³⁶ One of them ran, soaked a sponge with wine, put it on a reed, and gave it to him to drink, saying, "Wait, let us see if Elijah comes to take him down." ³⁷ Jesus gave a loud cry and breathed his last.

(Here all kneel and pause for a short time)

³⁸ The veil of the sanctuary was torn in two from top to bottom. ³⁹ When the centurion who stood facing him saw how he breathed his last he said, "Truly this man was the Son of God!" ⁴⁰ There were also women looking on from a distance. Among them

were Mary Magdalene, Mary the mother of the younger James and of Joses, and Salome. [41] These women had followed him when he was in Galilee and ministered to him. There were also many other women who had come up with him to Jerusalem.

[42] When it was already evening, since it was the day of preparation, the day before the sabbath, [43] Joseph of Arimathea, a distinguished member of the council, who was himself awaiting the kingdom of God, came and courageously went to Pilate and asked for the body of Jesus. [44] Pilate was amazed that he was already dead. He summoned the centurion and asked him if Jesus had already died. [45] And when he learned of it from the centurion, he gave the body to Joseph. [46] Having bought a linen cloth, he took him down, wrapped him in the linen cloth and laid him in a tomb that had been hewn out of the rock. Then he rolled a stone against the entrance to the tomb. [47] Mary Magdalene and Mary the mother of Joses watched where he was laid.

OR Mark 15:1-39

[15:1] As soon as morning came, the chief priests with the elders and the scribes, that is, the whole Sanhedrin, held a council. They bound Jesus, led him away, and handed him over to Pilate. [2] Pilate questioned him, "Are you the king of the Jews?" He said to him in reply, "You say so." [3] The chief priests accused him of many things. [4] Again Pilate questioned him, "Have you no answer? See how many things they accuse you of." [5] Jesus gave him no further answer, so that Pilate was amazed.

[6] Now on the occasion of the feast he used to release to them one prisoner whom they requested. [7] A man called Barabbas was then in prison along with the rebels who had committed murder in a rebellion. [8] The crowd came forward and began to ask him to do for them as he was accustomed. [9] Pilate answered, "Do you want me to release to you the king of the Jews?" [10] For he knew that it was out of envy that the chief priests had handed him over. [11] But the chief priests stirred up the crowd to have him release Barabbas for them instead. [12] Pilate again said to them in reply, "Then what do you want me to do with the man you call the king of the Jews?" [13] They shouted again, "Crucify him." [14] Pilate said to them, "Why? What evil has he done?" They only shouted the louder, "Crucify him." [15] So Pilate, wishing to satisfy the crowd, released Barabbas to them and, after he had Jesus scourged, handed him over to be crucified.

[16] The soldiers led him away inside the palace, that is, the praetorium, and assembled the whole cohort. [17] They clothed him in purple and, weaving a crown of thorns, placed it on him. [18] They began to salute him with, "Hail, King of the Jews!" [19] and kept striking his head with a reed and spitting upon him. They knelt before him in homage. [20] And when they had mocked him, they stripped him of the purple cloak, dressed him in his own clothes, and led him out to crucify him.

[21] They pressed into service a passer-by, Simon, a Cyrenian, who was coming in from the country, the father of Alexander and Rufus, to carry his cross.

[22] They brought him to the place of Golgotha—which is translated Place of the Skull—. [23] They gave him wine drugged with myrrh, but he did not take it. [24] Then they crucified him and divided his garments by casting lots for them to see what each should

take. ²⁵ It was nine o'clock in the morning when they crucified him. ²⁶ The inscription of the charge against him read, "The King of the Jews." ²⁷ With him they crucified two revolutionaries, one on his right and one on his left. [28] ²⁹ Those passing by reviled him, shaking their heads and saying, "Aha! You who would destroy the temple and rebuild it in three days, ³⁰ save yourself by coming down from the cross." ³¹ Likewise the chief priests, with the scribes, mocked him among themselves and said, "He saved others; he cannot save himself. ³² Let the Christ, the King of Israel, come down now from the cross that we may see and believe." Those who were crucified with him also kept abusing him.

³³ At noon darkness came over the whole land until three in the afternoon. ³⁴ And at three o'clock Jesus cried out in a loud voice, "*Eloi, Eloi, lema sabachthani*?" which is translated, "My God, my God, why have you forsaken me?" ³⁵ Some of the bystanders who heard it said, "Look, he is calling Elijah." ³⁶ One of them ran, soaked a sponge with wine, put it on a reed, and gave it to him to drink, saying, "Wait, let us see if Elijah comes to take him down." ³⁷ Jesus gave a loud cry and breathed his last.

(Here all kneel and pause for a short time)

³⁸ The veil of the sanctuary was torn in two from top to bottom. ³⁹ When the centurion who stood facing him saw how he breathed his last he said, "Truly this man was the Son of God!"

Monday of Holy Week
First Reading: Isaiah 42:1-7

¹ Here is my servant whom I uphold,
    my chosen one with whom I am pleased,
Upon whom I have put my Spirit;
    he shall bring forth justice to the nations,
² Not crying out, not shouting,
    not making his voice heard in the street.
³ A bruised reed he shall not break,
    and a smoldering wick he shall not
        quench,
⁴ Until he establishes justice on the earth;
    the coastlands will wait for his teaching.

⁵ Thus says God, the LORD,
    who created the heavens and stretched
        them out,
    who spreads out the earth with its crops,
Who gives breath to its people
    and spirit to those who walk on it:
⁶ I, the LORD, have called you for the victory of
        justice,
    I have grasped you by the hand;

I formed you, and set you
>> as a covenant of the people,
>> a light for the nations,
[7] To open the eyes of the blind,
>> to bring out prisoners from confinement,
>> and from the dungeon, those who live in
>>> darkness.

Responsorial Psalm: Psalms 27:1, 2, 3, 13-14

R. [1a] *The Lord is my light and my salvation.*

[1] The LORD is my light and my salvation;
>> whom should I fear?
The LORD is my life's refuge;
>> of whom should I be afraid?
R. *The Lord is my light and my salvation.*

[2] When evildoers come at me
>> to devour my flesh,
My foes and my enemies
>> themselves stumble and fall.
R. *The Lord is my light and my salvation.*

[3] Though an army encamp against me,
>> my heart will not fear;
Though war be waged upon me,
>> even then will I trust.
R. *The Lord is my light and my salvation.*

[13] I believe that I shall see the bounty of the
>>> LORD
>> in the land of the living.
[14] Wait for the LORD with courage;
>> be stouthearted, and wait for the LORD.
R. *The Lord is my light and my salvation.*

Verse Before the Gospel

Hail to you, our King;
you alone are compassionate with our faults.

Gospel: John 12:1-11

[1] Six days before Passover Jesus came to Bethany, where Lazarus was, whom Jesus had raised from the dead. [2] They gave a dinner for him there, and Martha served, while Lazarus was one of those reclining at table with him. [3] Mary took a liter of costly perfumed

oil made from genuine aromatic nard and anointed the feet of Jesus and dried them with her hair; the house was filled with the fragrance of the oil. [4] Then Judas the Iscariot, one of his disciples, and the one who would betray him, said, [5] "Why was this oil not sold for three hundred days' wages and given to the poor?" [6] He said this not because he cared about the poor but because he was a thief and held the money bag and used to steal the contributions. [7] So Jesus said, "Leave her alone. Let her keep this for the day of my burial. [8] You always have the poor with you, but you do not always have me."

[9] The large crowd of the Jews found out that he was there and came, not only because of him, but also to see Lazarus, whom he had raised from the dead. [10] And the chief priests plotted to kill Lazarus too, [11] because many of the Jews were turning away and believing in Jesus because of him.

Tuesday March 26, 2024

Tuesday of Holy Week
First Reading: Isaiah 49:1-6

[1] Hear me, O islands,
> listen, O distant peoples.
The LORD called me from birth,
> from my mother's womb he gave me my
> > name.
[2] He made of me a sharp-edged sword
> and concealed me in the shadow of his
> > arm.
He made me a polished arrow,
> in his quiver he hid me.
[3] You are my servant, he said to me,
> Israel, through whom I show my glory.

[4] Though I thought I had toiled in vain,
> and for nothing, uselessly, spent my
> > strength,
Yet my reward is with the LORD,
> my recompense is with my God.
[5] For now the LORD has spoken
> who formed me as his servant from the
> > womb,
That Jacob may be brought back to him
> and Israel gathered to him;
And I am made glorious in the sight of the
> > LORD,
> and my God is now my strength!
[6] It is too little, he says, for you to be my

servant,
>to raise up the tribes of Jacob,
>and restore the survivors of Israel;
I will make you a light to the nations,
>that my salvation may reach to the ends
>>of the earth.

Responsorial Psalm: Psalms 71:1-2, 3-4A,5AB-6AB,15and 17

R. *(see 15ab)* **I will sing of your salvation.**

[1] In you, O LORD, I take refuge;
>let me never be put to shame.
[2] In your justice rescue me, and deliver me;
>incline your ear to me, and save me.

R. *I will sing of your salvation.*

[3] Be my rock of refuge,
>a stronghold to give me safety,
>for you are my rock and my fortress.
[4A] O my God, rescue me from the hand of the
>>wicked.

R. *I will sing of your salvation.*

[5AB] For you are my hope, O Lord;
>my trust, O God, from my youth.
[6AB] On you I depend from birth;
>from my mother's womb you are my
>>strength.

R. *I will sing of your salvation.*

[15] My mouth shall declare your justice,
>day by day your salvation.
[17] O God, you have taught me from my youth,
>and till the present I proclaim your
>>wondrous deeds.

R. *I will sing of your salvation.*

Verse Before the Gospel

Hail to you, our King, obedient to the Father;
you were led to your crucifixion like a gentle
>>lamb to the slaughter.

Gospel: John 13:21-33, 36-38

[21] Reclining at table with his disciples, Jesus was deeply troubled and testified, "Amen, amen, I say to you, one of you will betray me." [22] The disciples looked at one another, at a loss as to whom he meant. [23] One of his disciples, the one whom Jesus loved, was reclining at Jesus' side. [24] So Simon Peter nodded to him to find out whom he meant. [25] He leaned back against Jesus' chest and said to him, "Master, who is it?" [26] Jesus answered, "It is the one to whom I hand the morsel after I have dipped it." So he dipped the morsel and took it and handed it to Judas, son of Simon the Iscariot. [27] After Judas took the morsel, Satan entered him. So Jesus said to him, "What you are going to do, do quickly." [28] Now none of those reclining at table realized why he said this to him. [29] Some thought that since Judas kept the money bag, Jesus had told him, "Buy what we need for the feast," or to give something to the poor. [30] So Judas took the morsel and left at once. And it was night.

[31] When he had left, Jesus said, "Now is the Son of Man glorified, and God is glorified in him. [32] If God is glorified in him, God will also glorify him In himself, and he will glorify him at once. [33] My children, I will be with you only a little while longer. You will look for me, and as I told the Jews, 'Where I go you cannot come,' so now I say it to you."

[36] Simon Peter said to him, "Master, where are you going?" Jesus answered him, "Where I am going, you cannot follow me now, though you will follow later." [37] Peter said to him, "Master, why can I not follow you now? I will lay down my life for you." [38] Jesus answered, "Will you lay down your life for me? Amen, amen, I say to you, the cock will not crow before you deny me three times."

Wednesday of Holy Week
First Reading: Isaiah 50:4-9A

[4] The Lord GOD has given me
    a well-trained tongue,
That I might know how to speak to the
      weary
    a word that will rouse them.
Morning after morning
    he opens my ear that I may hear;
[5] And I have not rebelled,
    have not turned back.
[6] I gave my back to those who beat me,
    my cheeks to those who plucked my
      beard;
My face I did not shield
    from buffets and spitting.

[7] The Lord GOD is my help,
    therefore I am not disgraced;

I have set my face like flint,
    knowing that I shall not be put to shame.
[8] He is near who upholds my right;
    if anyone wishes to oppose me,
    let us appear together.
Who disputes my right?
    Let him confront me.
[9] See, the Lord GOD is my help;
    who will prove me wrong?

Responsorial Psalm: Psalms 69:8-10, 21-22, 31 and 33-34

R. [(14c)] *Lord, in your great love, answer me.*
[8] For your sake I bear insult,
    and shame covers my face.
[9] I have become an outcast to my brothers,
    a stranger to my mother's sons,
[10] because zeal for your house consumes me,
        and the insults of those who blaspheme
            you fall upon me.
R. Lord, in your great love, answer me.

[21] Insult has broken my heart, and I am weak,
        I looked for sympathy, but there was
            none;
        for consolers, not one could I find.
[22] Rather they put gall in my food,
        and in my thirst they gave me vinegar to
            drink.
R. Lord, in your great love, answer me.

[31] I will praise the name of God in song,
        and I will glorify him with thanksgiving:
[33] "See, you lowly ones, and be glad;
        you who seek God, may your hearts
            revive!
[34] For the LORD hears the poor,
        and his own who are in bonds he spurns
            not."
R. Lord, in your great love, answer me.

Verse Before the Gospel

Hail to you, our King;

you alone are compassionate with our
errors.

Or

Hail to you, our King, obedient to the Father;
you were led to your crucifixion like a gentle
lamb to the slaughter.

Gospel: Matthew 26:14-25

14 One of the Twelve, who was called Judas Iscariot, went to the chief priests 15 and said, "What are you willing to give me if I hand him over to you?" They paid him thirty pieces of silver, 16 and from that time on he looked for an opportunity to hand him over.

17 On the first day of the Feast of Unleavened Bread, the disciples approached Jesus and said, "Where do you want us to prepare for you to eat the Passover?" 18 He said, "Go into the city to a certain man and tell him, 'The teacher says, "My appointed time draws near; in your house I shall celebrate the Passover with my disciples."'" 19 The disciples then did as Jesus had ordered, and prepared the Passover.

20 When it was evening, he reclined at table with the Twelve. 21 And while they were eating, he said, "Amen, I say to you, one of you will betray me." 22 Deeply distressed at this, they began to say to him one after another, "Surely it is not I, Lord?" 23 He said in reply, "He who has dipped his hand into the dish with me is the one who will betray me. 24 The Son of Man indeed goes, as it is written of him, but woe to that man by whom the Son of Man is betrayed. It would be better for that man if he had never been born." 25 Then Judas, his betrayer, said in reply, "Surely it is not I, Rabbi?" He answered, "You have said so."

Thursday March 28, 2024

Holy Thursday of the Lord's Supper
First Reading: Exodus 12:1-8, 11-14

1 The LORD said to Moses and Aaron in the land of Egypt, 2 "This month shall stand at the head of your calendar; you shall reckon it the first month of the year. 3 Tell the whole community of Israel: On the tenth of this month every one of your families must procure for itself a lamb, one apiece for each household. 4 If a family is too small for a whole lamb, it shall join the nearest household in procuring one and shall share in the lamb in proportion to the number of persons who partake of it. 5 The lamb must be a year-old male and without blemish. You may take it from either the sheep or the goats. 6 You shall keep it until the fourteenth day of this month, and then, with the whole assembly of Israel present, it shall be slaughtered during the evening twilight. 7 They shall take some of its blood and apply it to the two doorposts and the lintel of every house in which they partake of the lamb. 8 That same night they shall eat its roasted flesh with unleavened bread and bitter herbs.

11 "This is how you are to eat it: with your loins girt, sandals on your feet and your staff in hand, you shall eat like those who are in flight. It is the Passover of the LORD. 12 For on this same night I will go through Egypt, striking down every firstborn of the land, both man and beast, and executing judgment on all the gods of Egypt—I, the LORD! 13 But the

blood will mark the houses where you are. Seeing the blood, I will pass over you; thus, when I strike the land of Egypt, no destructive blow will come upon you.

14 "This day shall be a memorial feast for you, which all your generations shall celebrate with pilgrimage to the LORD, as a perpetual institution."

Responsorial Psalm: Psalms 116:12-13, 15-16BC, 17-18

R. (cf. 1 Cor 10:16) *Our blessing-cup is a communion*
                                     with the Blood of Christ.

12 How shall I make a return to the LORD
         for all the good he has done for me?
13 The cup of salvation I will take up,
         and I will call upon the name of the LORD.
R. *Our blessing-cup is a communion with the*
         Blood of Christ.

15 Precious in the eyes of the LORD
         is the death of his faithful ones.
16BC I am your servant, the son of your
               handmaid;
         you have loosed my bonds.
R. *Our blessing-cup is a communion with the*
         Blood of Christ.

17 To you will I offer sacrifice of thanksgiving,
         and I will call upon the name of the LORD.
18 My vows to the LORD I will pay
         in the presence of all his people.
R. *Our blessing-cup is a communion with the*
         Blood of Christ.

Second Reading: 1 Corinthians 11:23-26

Brothers and sisters: 23 I received from the Lord what I also handed on to you, that the Lord Jesus, on the night he was handed over, took bread, 24 and, after he had given thanks, broke it and said, "This is my body that is for you. Do this in remembrance of me." 25 In the same way also the cup, after supper, saying, "This cup is the new covenant in my blood. Do this, as often as you drink it, in remembrance of me." 26 For as often as you eat this bread and drink the cup, you proclaim the death of the Lord until he comes.

Verse Before the Gospel: John 13:34

34 I give you a new commandment, says the Lord:
love one another as I have loved you.

Gospel: John 13:1-15

[1] Before the feast of Passover, Jesus knew that his hour had come to pass from this world to the Father. He loved his own in the world and he loved them to the end. [2] The devil had already induced Judas, son of Simon the Iscariot, to hand him over. So, during supper, [3] fully aware that the Father had put everything into his power and that he had come from God and was returning to God, [4] he rose from supper and took off his outer garments. He took a towel and tied it around his waist. [5] Then he poured water into a basin and began to wash the disciples' feet and dry them with the towel around his waist. [6] He came to Simon Peter, who said to him, "Master, are you going to wash my feet?" [7] Jesus answered and said to him, "What I am doing, you do not understand now, but you will understand later." [8] Peter said to him, "You will never wash my feet." Jesus answered him, "Unless I wash you, you will have no inheritance with me." [9] Simon Peter said to him, "Master, then not only my feet, but my hands and head as well." [10] Jesus said to him, "Whoever has bathed has no need except to have his feet washed, for he is clean all over; so you are clean, but not all." [11] For he knew who would betray him; for this reason, he said, "Not all of you are clean."

[12] So when he had washed their feet and put his garments back on and reclined at table again, he said to them, "Do you realize what I have done for you? [13] You call me 'teacher' and 'master,' and rightly so, for indeed I am. [14] If I, therefore, the master and teacher, have washed your feet, you ought to wash one another's feet. [15] I have given you a model to follow, so that as I have done for you, you should also do."

Friday March 29, 2024

Good Friday of the Lord's Passion
First Reading: Isaiah 52:13-53:12

[13] See, my servant shall prosper,
  he shall be raised high and greatly
   exalted.
[14] Even as many were amazed at him—
  so marred was his look beyond human
   semblance
  and his appearance beyond that of the
   sons of man—
[15] so shall he startle many nations,
  because of him kings shall stand
   speechless;
for those who have not been told shall see,
  those who have not heard shall ponder it.

[1] Who would believe what we have heard?
  To whom has the arm of the LORD been
   revealed?
[2] He grew up like a sapling before him,

like a shoot from the parched earth;
there was in him no stately bearing to make
            us look at him,
            nor appearance that would attract us to
            him.
³ He was spurned and avoided by people,
            a man of suffering, accustomed to
            infirmity,
one of those from whom people hide their
            faces,
            spurned, and we held him in no esteem.
⁴ Yet it was our infirmities that he bore,
            our sufferings that he endured,
while we thought of him as stricken,
            as one smitten by God and afflicted.
⁵ But he was pierced for our offenses,
            crushed for our sins;
upon him was the chastisement that makes
            us whole,
            by his stripes we were healed.
            ⁶ We had all gone astray like sheep,
            each following his own way;
but the LORD laid upon him
            the guilt of us all.

⁷ Though he was harshly treated, he
            submitted
            and opened not his mouth;
like a lamb led to the slaughter
            or a sheep before the shearers,
            he was silent and opened not his mouth.
            ⁸ Oppressed and condemned, he was taken
            away,
            and who would have thought any more of
            his destiny?
When he was cut off from the land of the
            living,
            and smitten for the sin of his people,
⁹ a grave was assigned him among the wicked
            and a burial place with evildoers,
though he had done no wrong
            nor spoken any falsehood.

[10] But the LORD was pleased
  to crush him in infirmity.

If he gives his life as an offering for sin,
  he shall see his descendants in a long life,
  and the will of the LORD shall be
    accomplished through him.

[11] Because of his affliction
  he shall see the light
  in fullness of days;
through his suffering, my servant shall
    justify many,
  and their guilt he shall bear.
    [12] Therefore I will give him his portion
      among the great,
and he shall divide the spoils with the
    mighty,
because he surrendered himself to death
  and was counted among the wicked;
and he shall take away the sins of many,
  and win pardon for their offenses.

Responsorial Psalm: Psalms 31:2, 6, 12-13, 15-16, 17, 25

R. *(Luke 23:46)* **Father, into your hands I commend my spirit.**
[2] In you, O LORD, I take refuge;
  let me never be put to shame.
In your justice rescue me.
  [6] Into your hands I commend my spirit;
you will redeem me, O LORD, O faithful God.
R. Father, into your hands I commend my spirit.

[12] For all my foes I am an object of reproach,
  a laughingstock to my neighbors, and a dread
    to my friends;
  they who see me abroad flee from me.
[13] I am forgotten like the unremembered dead;
  I am like a dish that is broken.
R. Father, into your hands I commend my spirit.

[15] But my trust is in you, O LORD;
  I say, "You are my God.

[16] In your hands is my destiny; rescue me
      from the clutches of my enemies and my
        persecutors."
R. Father, into your hands I commend my spirit.

[17] Let your face shine upon your servant;
      save me in your kindness.
[25] Take courage and be stouthearted,
      all you who hope in the LORD.
R. Father, into your hands I commend my spirit.

Second Reading: Hebrews 4:14-16; 5:7-9

[14] Brothers and sisters: Since we have a great high priest who has passed through the heavens, Jesus, the Son of God, let us hold fast to our confession. [15] For we do not have a high priest who is unable to sympathize with our weaknesses, but one who has similarly been tested in every way, yet without sin. [16] So let us confidently approach the throne of grace to receive mercy and to find grace for timely help.

    [7] In the days when Christ was in the flesh, he offered prayers and supplications with loud cries and tears to the one who was able to save him from death, and he was heard because of his reverence. [8] Son though he was, he learned obedience from what he suffered; [9] and when he was made perfect, he became the source of eternal salvation for all who obey him.

Verse Before the Gospel: Philippians 2:8-9

[8] Christ became obedient to the point of death,
even death on a cross.
[9] Because of this, God greatly exalted him
and bestowed on him the name which is
      above every other name.

(**Please Note:** The passion narratives are proclaimed in full so that all see vividly the love of Christ for each person. In light of this, the crimes during the Passion of Christ cannot be attributed, in either preaching or catechesis, indiscriminately to all Jews of that time, nor to Jews today. The Jewish people should not be referred to as though rejected or cursed, as if this view followed from Scripture. The Church ever keeps in mind that Jesus, his mother Mary, and the apostles all were Jewish. As the Church has always held, Christ freely suffered his passion and death because of the sins of all, that all might be saved).

Gospel: John 18:1-19:42

[1] Jesus went out with his disciples across the Kidron valley to where there was a garden, into which he and his disciples entered. [2] Judas his betrayer also knew the place, because Jesus had often met there with his disciples. [3] So Judas got a band of soldiers and guards

from the chief priests and the Pharisees and went there with lanterns, torches, and weapons. [4] Jesus, knowing everything that was going to happen to him, went out and said to them, "Whom are you looking for?" [5] They answered him, "Jesus the Nazorean." He said to them, "I AM." Judas his betrayer was also with them. [6] When he said to them, "I AM," they turned away and fell to the ground. [7] So he again asked them, "Whom are you looking for?" They said, "Jesus the Nazorean." [8] Jesus answered, "I told you that I AM. So if you are looking for me, let these men go." [9] This was to fulfill what he had said, "I have not lost any of those you gave me." [10] Then Simon Peter, who had a sword, drew it, struck the high priest's slave, and cut off his right ear. The slave's name was Malchus. [11] Jesus said to Peter, "Put your sword into its scabbard. Shall I not drink the cup that the Father gave me?"

[12] So the band of soldiers, the tribune, and the Jewish guards seized Jesus, bound him, [13] and brought him to Annas first. He was the father-in-law of Caiaphas, who was high priest that year. [14] It was Caiaphas who had counseled the Jews that it was better that one man should die rather than the people.

[15] Simon Peter and another disciple followed Jesus. Now the other disciple was known to the high priest, and he entered the courtyard of the high priest with Jesus. [16] But Peter stood at the gate outside. So the other disciple, the acquaintance of the high priest, went out and spoke to the gatekeeper and brought Peter in. [17] Then the maid who was the gatekeeper said to Peter, "You are not one of this man's disciples, are you?" He said, "I am not." [18] Now the slaves and the guards were standing around a charcoal fire that they had made, because it was cold, and were warming themselves. Peter was also standing there keeping warm.

[19] The high priest questioned Jesus about his disciples and about his doctrine. [20] Jesus answered him, "I have spoken publicly to the world. I have always taught in a synagogue or in the temple area where all the Jews gather, and in secret I have said nothing. [21] Why ask me? Ask those who heard me what I said to them. They know what I said." [22] When he had said this, one of the temple guards standing there struck Jesus and said, "Is this the way you answer the high priest?" [23] Jesus answered him, "If I have spoken wrongly, testify to the wrong; but if I have spoken rightly, why do you strike me?" [24] Then Annas sent him bound to Caiaphas the high priest.

[25] Now Simon Peter was standing there keeping warm. And they said to him, "You are not one of his disciples, are you?" He denied it and said, "I am not." [26] One of the slaves of the high priest, a relative of the one whose ear Peter had cut off, said, "Didn't I see you in the garden with him?" [27] Again Peter denied it. And immediately the cock crowed.

[28] Then they brought Jesus from Caiaphas to the praetorium. It was morning. And they themselves did not enter the praetorium, in order not to be defiled so that they could eat the Passover. [29] So Pilate came out to them and said, "What charge do you bring against this man?" [30] They answered and said to him, "If he were not a criminal, we would not have handed him over to you." [31] At this, Pilate said to them, "Take him yourselves, and judge him according to your law." The Jews answered him, "We do not have the right to execute anyone, " [32] in order that the word of Jesus might be fulfilled that he said indicating the kind of death he would die. [33] So Pilate went back into the praetorium and

summoned Jesus and said to him, "Are you the King of the Jews?" [34] Jesus answered, "Do you say this on your own or have others told you about me?" [35] Pilate answered, "I am not a Jew, am I? Your own nation and the chief priests handed you over to me. What have you done?" [36] Jesus answered, "My kingdom does not belong to this world. If my kingdom did belong to this world, my attendants would be fighting to keep me from being handed over to the Jews. But as it is, my kingdom is not here." [37] So Pilate said to him, "Then you are a king?" Jesus answered, "You say I am a king. For this I was born and for this I came into the world, to testify to the truth. Everyone who belongs to the truth listens to my voice." [38] Pilate said to him, "What is truth?"

When he had said this, he again went out to the Jews and said to them, "I find no guilt in him. [39] But you have a custom that I release one prisoner to you at Passover. Do you want me to release to you the King of the Jews?" [40] They cried out again, "Not this one but Barabbas!" Now Barabbas was a revolutionary.

[1] Then Pilate took Jesus and had him scourged. [2] And the soldiers wove a crown out of thorns and placed it on his head, and clothed him in a purple cloak, [3] and they came to him and said, "Hail, King of the Jews!" And they struck him repeatedly. [4] Once more Pilate went out and said to them, "Look, I am bringing him out to you, so that you may know that I find no guilt in him." [5] So Jesus came out, wearing the crown of thorns and the purple cloak. And he said to them, "Behold, the man!" [6] When the chief priests and the guards saw him they cried out, "Crucify him, crucify him!" Pilate said to them, "Take him yourselves and crucify him. I find no guilt in him." [7] The Jews answered, "We have a law, and according to that law he ought to die, because he made himself the Son of God." [8] Now when Pilate heard this statement, he became even more afraid, [9] and went back into the praetorium and said to Jesus, "Where are you from?" Jesus did not answer him. [10] So Pilate said to him, "Do you not speak to me? Do you not know that I have power to release you and I have power to crucify you?" [11] Jesus answered him, "You would have no power over me if it had not been given to you from above. For this reason the one who handed me over to you has the greater sin." [12] Consequently, Pilate tried to release him; but the Jews cried out, "If you release him, you are not a Friend of Caesar. Everyone who makes himself a king opposes Caesar."

[13] When Pilate heard these words he brought Jesus out and seated him on the judge's bench in the place called Stone Pavement, in Hebrew, Gabbatha. [14] It was preparation day for Passover, and it was about noon. And he said to the Jews, "Behold, your king!" [15] They cried out, "Take him away, take him away! Crucify him!" Pilate said to them, "Shall I crucify your king?" The chief priests answered, "We have no king but Caesar." [16] Then he handed him over to them to be crucified.

So they took Jesus, [17] and, carrying the cross himself, he went out to what is called the Place of the Skull, in Hebrew, Golgotha. [18] There they crucified him, and with him two others, one on either side, with Jesus in the middle. [19] Pilate also had an inscription written and put on the cross. It read, "Jesus the Nazorean, the King of the Jews." [20] Now many of the Jews read this inscription, because the place where Jesus was crucified was near the city; and it was written in Hebrew, Latin, and Greek. [21] So the chief priests of the

Jews said to Pilate, "Do not write 'The King of the Jews,' but that he said, 'I am the King of the Jews'." ²² Pilate answered, "What I have written, I have written."

²³ When the soldiers had crucified Jesus, they took his clothes and divided them into four shares, a share for each soldier. They also took his tunic, but the tunic was seamless, woven in one piece from the top down. ²⁴ So they said to one another, "Let's not tear it, but cast lots for it to see whose it will be, " in order that the passage of Scripture might be fulfilled that says:

They divided my garments among them,
    and for my vesture they cast lots.

This is what the soldiers did. ²⁵ Standing by the cross of Jesus were his mother and his mother's sister, Mary the wife of Clopas, and Mary of Magdala. ²⁶ When Jesus saw his mother and the disciple there whom he loved he said to his mother, "Woman, behold, your son." ²⁷ Then he said to the disciple, "Behold, your mother." And from that hour the disciple took her into his home.

²⁸ After this, aware that everything was now finished, in order that the Scripture might be fulfilled, Jesus said, "I thirst." ²⁹ There was a vessel filled with common wine. So they put a sponge soaked in wine on a sprig of hyssop and put it up to his mouth. ³⁰ When Jesus had taken the wine, he said, "It is finished." And bowing his head, he handed over the spirit.

(Here all kneel and pause for a short time)

³¹ Now since it was preparation day, in order that the bodies might not remain on the cross on the sabbath, for the sabbath day of that week was a solemn one, the Jews asked Pilate that their legs be broken and that they be taken down. ³² So the soldiers came and broke the legs of the first and then of the other one who was crucified with Jesus. ³³ But when they came to Jesus and saw that he was already dead, they did not break his legs, ³⁴ but one soldier thrust his lance into his side, and immediately blood and water flowed out. ³⁵ An eyewitness has testified, and his testimony is true; he knows that he is speaking the truth, so that you also may come to believe. ³⁶ For this happened so that the Scripture passage might be fulfilled:

Not a bone of it will be broken.

³⁷ And again another passage says:

They will look upon him whom they have
    pierced.

³⁸ After this, Joseph of Arimathea, secretly a disciple of Jesus for fear of the Jews, asked Pilate if he could remove the body of Jesus. And Pilate permitted it. So he came and took his body. ³⁹ Nicodemus, the one who had first come to him at night, also came bringing a mixture of myrrh and aloes weighing about one hundred pounds. ⁴⁰ They took the body of Jesus and bound it with burial cloths along with the spices, according to the Jewish burial custom. ⁴¹ Now in the place where he had been crucified there was a garden, and in the garden a new tomb, in which no one had yet been buried. ⁴² So they laid Jesus there because of the Jewish preparation day; for the tomb was close by.

Holy Saturday Night of Easter – Easter Vigil
First Reading: Genesis 1:1-2:2

[1] In the beginning, when God created the heavens and the earth, [2] the earth was a formless wasteland, and darkness covered the abyss, while a mighty wind swept over the waters.

[3] Then God said, "Let there be light," and there was light. [4] God saw how good the light was. God then separated the light from the darkness. [5] God called the light "day," and the darkness he called "night." Thus evening came, and morning followed—the first day.

[6] Then God said, "Let there be a dome in the middle of the waters, to separate one body of water from the other." And so it happened: [7] God made the dome, and it separated the water above the dome from the water below it. [8] God called the dome "the sky." Evening came, and morning followed—the second day.

[9] Then God said, "Let the water under the sky be gathered into a single basin, so that the dry land may appear." And so it happened: the water under the sky was gathered into its basin, and the dry land appeared. [10] God called the dry land "the earth, " and the basin of the water he called "the sea." God saw how good it was. [11] Then God said, "Let the earth bring forth vegetation: every kind of plant that bears seed and every kind of fruit tree on earth that bears fruit with its seed in it." And so it happened: [12] the earth brought forth every kind of plant that bears seed and every kind of fruit tree on earth that bears fruit with its seed in it. God saw how good it was. [13] Evening came, and morning followed—the third day.

[14] Then God said: "Let there be lights in the dome of the sky, to separate day from night. Let them mark the fixed times, the days and the years, [15] and serve as luminaries in the dome of the sky, to shed light upon the earth." And so it happened: [16] God made the two great lights, the greater one to govern the day, and the lesser one to govern the night; and he made the stars. [17] God set them in the dome of the sky, to shed light upon the earth, [18] to govern the day and the night, and to separate the light from the darkness. God saw how good it was. [19] Evening came, and morning followed—the fourth day.

[20] Then God said, "Let the water teem with an abundance of living creatures, and on the earth let birds fly beneath the dome of the sky." And so it happened: [21] God created the great sea monsters and all kinds of swimming creatures with which the water teems, and all kinds of winged birds. God saw how good it was, [22] and God blessed them, saying, "Be fertile, multiply, and fill the water of the seas; and let the birds multiply on the earth." [23] Evening came, and morning followed—the fifth day.

[24] Then God said, "Let the earth bring forth all kinds of living creatures: cattle, creeping things, and wild animals of all kinds." And so it happened: [25] God made all kinds of wild animals, all kinds of cattle, and all kinds of creeping things of the earth. God saw how good it was. [26] Then God said: "Let us make man in our image, after our likeness. Let

them have dominion over the fish of the sea, the birds of the air, and the cattle, and over all the wild animals and all the creatures that crawl on the ground."

[27] God created man in his image;

> in the image of God he created him;
>
> male and female he created them.

[28] God blessed them, saying: "Be fertile and multiply; fill the earth and subdue it. Have dominion over the fish of the sea, the birds of the air, and all the living things that move on the earth." [29] God also said: "See, I give you every seed-bearing plant all over the earth and every tree that has seed-bearing fruit on it to be your food; [30] and to all the animals of the land, all the birds of the air, and all the living creatures that crawl on the ground, I give all the green plants for food." And so it happened. [31] God looked at everything he had made, and he found it very good. Evening came, and morning followed—the sixth day.

> [1] Thus the heavens and the earth and all their array were completed. [2] Since on the seventh day God was finished with the work he had been doing, he rested on the seventh day from all the work he had undertaken.

Or Genesis 1:1, 26-31A

[1] In the beginning, when God created the heavens and the earth, [26] God said: "Let us make man in our image, after our likeness. Let them have dominion over the fish of the sea, the birds of the air, and the cattle, and over all the wild animals and all the creatures that crawl on the ground."

[27] God created man in his image;

> in the image of God he created him;
>
> male and female he created them.

[28] God blessed them, saying: "Be fertile and multiply; fill the earth and subdue it. Have dominion over the fish of the sea, the birds of the air, and all the living things that move on the earth." [29] God also said: "See, I give you every seed-bearing plant all over the earth and every tree that has seed-bearing fruit on it to be your food; [30] and to all the animals of the land, all the birds of the air, and all the living creatures that crawl on the ground, I give all the green plants for food." And so it happened. [31] God looked at everything he had made, and he found it very good.

Responsorial Psalm: Psalms 104:1-2, 5-6, 10,12,13-14, 24, 35

R. [(30)] *Lord, send out your Spirit, and renew the*
> *face of the earth.*

[1] Bless the LORD, O my soul!

> O LORD, my God, you are great indeed!

[2] You are clothed with majesty and glory,

> robed in light as with a cloak.

R. *Lord, send out your Spirit, and renew the*
> *face of the earth.*

⁵ You fixed the earth upon its foundation,
    not to be moved forever;
⁶ with the ocean, as with a garment, you
        covered it;
    above the mountains the waters
        stood.
**R. Lord, send out your Spirit, and renew the
        face of the earth.**

¹⁰ You send forth springs into the
        watercourses
    that wind among the mountains.
¹² Beside them the birds of heaven dwell;
    from among the branches they send
        forth their song.
**R. Lord, send out your Spirit, and renew the
        face of the earth.**

¹³ You water the mountains from your
        palace;
    the earth is replete with the fruit of
        your works.
¹⁴ You raise grass for the cattle,
    and vegetation for man's use,
producing bread from the earth.
**R. Lord, send out your Spirit, and renew the
        face of the earth.**

²⁴ How manifold are your works, O LORD!
    In wisdom you have wrought them
        all—
the earth is full of your creatures.
        ³⁵ Bless the LORD, O my soul!
**R. Lord, send out your Spirit, and renew the
        face of the earth.**

Or Psalms 33:4-5, 6-7, 12-13, 20 and 22
**R. ⁽⁵ᵇ⁾ The earth is full of the goodness of the
        Lord.**
⁴ Upright is the word of the LORD,
    and all his works are trustworthy.

[5] He loves justice and right;
>   of the kindness of the LORD the earth
>   is full.
R. The earth is full of the goodness of the Lord.

[6] By the word of the LORD the heavens
>   were made;
>   by the breath of his mouth all their
>   host.
[7] He gathers the waters of the sea as in a
>   flask;
>   in cellars he confines the deep.
R. The earth is full of the goodness of the Lord.

[12] Blessed the nation whose God is the
>   LORD,
>   the people he has chosen for his own
>   inheritance.
[13] From heaven the LORD looks down;
>   he sees all mankind.
R. The earth is full of the goodness of the Lord.

[20] Our soul waits for the LORD,
>   who is our help and our shield.
[22] May your kindness, O LORD, be upon us
>   who have put our hope in you.
R. The earth is full of the goodness of the Lord.

Second Reading: Genesis 22:1-18

[1] God put Abraham to the test. He called to him, "Abraham!" "Here I am, " he replied. [2] Then God said: "Take your son Isaac, your only one, whom you love, and go to the land of Moriah. There you shall offer him up as a holocaust on a height that I will point out to you." [3] Early the next morning Abraham saddled his donkey, took with him his son Isaac and two of his servants as well, and with the wood that he had cut for the holocaust, set out for the place of which God had told him.

[4] On the third day Abraham got sight of the place from afar. [5] Then he said to his servants: "Both of you stay here with the donkey, while the boy and I go on over yonder. We will worship and then come back to you." [6] Thereupon Abraham took the wood for the holocaust and laid it on his son Isaac's shoulders, while he himself carried the fire and the

knife. As the two walked on together, [7]Isaac spoke to his father Abraham: "Father!" Isaac said. "Yes, son," he replied. Isaac continued, "Here are the fire and the wood, but where is the sheep for the holocaust?" [8] "Son," Abraham answered, "God himself will provide the sheep for the holocaust." Then the two continued going forward.

[9] When they came to the place of which God had told him, Abraham built an altar there and arranged the wood on it. Next he tied up his son Isaac, and put him on top of the wood on the altar. [10] Then he reached out and took the knife to slaughter his son. [11] But the LORD's messenger called to him from heaven, "Abraham, Abraham!" "Here I am!" he answered. [12] "Do not lay your hand on the boy," said the messenger. "Do not do the least thing to him. I know now how devoted you are to God, since you did not withhold from me your own beloved son." [13] As Abraham looked about, he spied a ram caught by its horns in the thicket. So he went and took the ram and offered it up as a holocaust in place of his son. [14] Abraham named the site Yahweh-yireh; hence people now say, "On the mountain the LORD will see."

[15] Again the LORD's messenger called to Abraham from heaven [16] and said: "I swear by myself, declares the LORD, that because you acted as you did in not withholding from me your beloved son, [17] I will bless you abundantly and make your descendants as countless as the stars of the sky and the sands of the seashore; [18] your descendants shall take possession of the gates of their enemies, and in your descendants all the nations of the earth shall find blessings— all this because you obeyed my command."

Or Genesis 22:1-2, 9A, 10-13, 15-18

[1] God put Abraham to the test. He called to him, "Abraham!" "Here I am, " he replied. [2] Then God said: "Take your son Isaac, your only one, whom you love, and go to the land of Moriah. There you shall offer him up as a holocaust on a height that I will point out to you."

[9A] When they came to the place of which God had told him, Abraham built an altar there and arranged the wood on it. [10] Then he reached out and took the knife to slaughter his son. [11] But the LORD's messenger called to him from heaven, "Abraham, Abraham!" "Here I am," he answered. [12] "Do not lay your hand on the boy, " said the messenger. "Do not do the least thing to him. I know now how devoted you are to God, since you did not withhold from me your own beloved son." [13] As Abraham looked about, he spied a ram caught by its horns in the thicket. So he went and took the ram and offered it up as a holocaust in place of his son.

[15] Again the LORD's messenger called to Abraham from heaven [16] and said: "I swear by myself, declares the LORD, that because you acted as you did in not withholding from me your beloved son, [17] I will bless you abundantly and make your descendants as countless as the stars of the sky and the sands of the seashore; [18] your descendants shall take possession of the gates of their enemies, and in your descendants all the nations of the earth shall find blessing— all this because you obeyed my command."

Responsorial Psalm: Psalms 16:5, 8, 9-10, 11

R. (1) *You are my inheritance, O Lord.*

[5] O LORD, my allotted portion and my cup,
   you it is who hold fast my lot.
[8] I set the LORD ever before me;
   with him at my right hand I shall not be
      disturbed.

R. *You are my inheritance, O Lord.*

[9] Therefore my heart is glad and my soul
      rejoices,
   my body, too, abides in confidence;
[10] because you will not abandon my soul to the
      netherworld,
   nor will you suffer your faithful one to
      undergo corruption.

R. *You are my inheritance, O Lord.*

[11] You will show me the path to life,
   fullness of joys in your presence,
   the delights at your right hand forever.

R. *You are my inheritance, O Lord.*

Third Reading: Exodus 14:15-15:1

[15] The LORD said to Moses, "Why are you crying out to me? Tell the Israelites to go forward. [16] And you, lift up your staff and, with hand outstretched over the sea, split the sea in two, that the Israelites may pass through it on dry land. [17] But I will make the Egyptians so obstinate that they will go in after them. Then I will receive glory through Pharaoh and all his army, his chariots and charioteers. [18] The Egyptians shall know that I am the LORD, when I receive glory through Pharaoh and his chariots and charioteers."

[19] The angel of God, who had been leading Israel's camp, now moved and went around behind them. The column of cloud also, leaving the front, took up its place behind them, [20] so that it came between the camp of the Egyptians and that of Israel. But the cloud now became dark, and thus the night passed without the rival camps coming any closer together all night long. [21] Then Moses stretched out his hand over the sea, and the LORD swept the sea with a strong east wind throughout the night and so turned it into dry land. [22] When the water was thus divided, the Israelites marched into the midst of the sea on dry land, with the water like a wall to their right and to their left.

[23] The Egyptians followed in pursuit; all Pharaoh's horses and chariots and charioteers went after them right into the midst of the sea. [24] In the night watch just before dawn the LORD cast through the column of the fiery cloud upon the Egyptian force a glance that threw it into a panic; [25] and he so clogged their chariot wheels that they

could hardly drive. With that the Egyptians sounded the retreat before Israel, because the LORD was fighting for them against the Egyptians.

[26] Then the LORD told Moses, stretch out your hand over the sea, that the water may flow back upon the Egyptians, upon their chariots and their charioteers." [27] So Moses stretched out his hand over the sea, and at dawn the sea flowed back to its normal depth. The Egyptians were fleeing head on toward the sea, when the LORD hurled them into its midst. [28] As the water flowed back, it covered the chariots and the charioteers of Pharaoh's whole army which had followed the Israelites into the sea. Not a single one of them escaped. [29] But the Israelites had marched on dry land through the midst of the sea, with the water like a wall to their right and to their left. [30] Thus the LORD saved Israel on that day from the power of the Egyptians. When Israel saw the Egyptians lying dead on the seashore [31] and beheld the great power that the LORD had shown against the Egyptians, they feared the LORD and believed in him and in his servant Moses.

[1] Then Moses and the Israelites sang this song to the LORD:

I will sing to the LORD, for he is gloriously
    triumphant;
    horse and chariot he has cast into the sea.

Responsorial Psalm: Exodus 15:1-2, 3-4, 5-6, 17-18

R. [1b] *Let us sing to the Lord; he has covered*
          himself in glory.

[1] I will sing to the LORD, for he is gloriously
    triumphant;
    horse and chariot he has cast into the sea.
[2] My strength and my courage is the LORD,
    and he has been my savior.
He is my God, I praise him;
    the God of my father, I extol him.
R. *Let us sing to the Lord; he has covered himself*
          in glory.

[3] The LORD is a warrior,
    LORD is his name!
[4] Pharaoh's chariots and army he hurled into
        the sea;
the elite of his officers were submerged in
        the Red Sea.
R. *Let us sing to the Lord; he has covered himself*
          in glory.

[5] The flood waters covered them,

they sank into the depths like a stone.

[6] Your right hand, O LORD, magnificent in
power,
your right hand, O LORD, has shattered the
enemy.

*R. Let us sing to the Lord; he has covered himself
in glory.*

[17] You brought in the people you redeemed
and planted them on the mountain of
your inheritance—
the place where you made your seat, O LORD,
the sanctuary, LORD, which your hands
established.

[18] The LORD shall reign forever and ever.

*R. Let us sing to the Lord; he has covered himself
in glory.*

Fourth Reading: Isaiah 54:5-14

[5] The One who has become your husband is
your Maker;
his name is the LORD of hosts;
your redeemer is the Holy One of Israel,
called God of all the earth.

[6] The LORD calls you back,
like a wife forsaken and grieved in spirit,
a wife married in youth and then cast off,
says your God.

[7] For a brief moment I abandoned you,
but with great tenderness I will take you
back.

[8] In an outburst of wrath, for a moment
I hid my face from you;
but with enduring love I take pity on you,
says the LORD, your redeemer.

[9] This is for me like the days of Noah,
when I swore that the waters of Noah
should never again deluge the earth;
so I have sworn not to be angry with you,
or to rebuke you.

[10] Though the mountains leave their place
and the hills be shaken,
my love shall never leave you

nor my covenant of peace be shaken,
	says the LORD, who has mercy on you.
[11] O afflicted one, storm-battered and
		unconsoled,
	I lay your pavements in carnelians,
	and your foundations in sapphires;
[12] I will make your battlements of rubies,
	your gates of carbuncles,
	and all your walls of precious stones.
[13] All your children shall be taught by the LORD,
	and great shall be the peace of your
		children.
[14] In justice shall you be established,
	far from the fear of oppression,
	where destruction cannot come near you.

Responsorial Psalm: Psalms 30:2, 4, 5-6, 11-12, 13

R. [2a] *I will praise you, Lord, for you have*
		rescued me.
[2] I will extol you, O LORD, for you drew me
		clear
	and did not let my enemies rejoice over
		me.
[4] O LORD, you brought me up from the
		netherworld;
	you preserved me from among those
		going down into the pit.
R. *I will praise you, Lord, for you have rescued*
		me.

[5] Sing praise to the LORD, you his faithful ones,
	and give thanks to his holy name.
[6] For his anger lasts but a moment;
	a lifetime, his good will.
At nightfall, weeping enters in,
	but with the dawn, rejoicing.
R. *I will praise you, Lord, for you have rescued*
		me.

[11] Hear, O LORD, and have pity on me;
	O LORD, be my helper.
[12] You changed my mourning into dancing;

[13] O LORD, my God, forever will I give you thanks.

R. I will praise you, Lord, for you have rescued me.

Fifth Reading: Isaiah 55:1-11

[1] Thus says the LORD:

All you who are thirsty,
    come to the water!
You who have no money,
    come, receive grain and eat;
come, without paying and without cost,
    drink wine and milk!
[2] Why spend your money for what is not bread,
    your wages for what fails to satisfy?
Heed me, and you shall eat well,
    you shall delight in rich fare.
[3] Come to me heedfully,
    listen, that you may have life.
I will renew with you the everlasting covenant,
    the benefits assured to David.
[4] As I made him a witness to the peoples,
    a leader and commander of nations,
[5] so shall you summon a nation you knew not,
    and nations that knew you not shall run to you,
because of the LORD, your God,
    the Holy One of Israel, who has glorified you.

[6] Seek the LORD while he may be found,
    call him while he is near.
[7] Let the scoundrel forsake his way,
    and the wicked man his thoughts;
let him turn to the LORD for mercy;
    to our God, who is generous in forgiving.
[8] For my thoughts are not your thoughts,
    nor are your ways my ways, says the LORD.
[9] As high as the heavens are above the earth,

so high are my ways above your ways
and my thoughts above your thoughts.

[10] For just as from the heavens
the rain and snow come down
and do not return there
till they have watered the earth,
making it fertile and fruitful,
giving seed to the one who sows
and bread to the one who eats,
[11] so shall my word be
that goes forth from my mouth;
my word shall not return to me void,
but shall do my will,
achieving the end for which I sent it.

Responsorial Psalm: Isaiah 12:2-3, 4, 5-6

R. [(3)] *You will draw water joyfully from the*
springs of salvation.

[2] God indeed is my savior;
I am confident and unafraid.
My strength and my courage is the LORD,
and he has been my savior.
[3] With joy you will draw water
at the fountain of salvation.

R. *You will draw water joyfully from the springs*
of salvation.

[4] Give thanks to the LORD, acclaim his name;
among the nations make known his
deeds,
proclaim how exalted is his name.

R. *You will draw water joyfully from the springs*
of salvation.

[5] Sing praise to the LORD for his glorious
achievement;
let this be known throughout all the
earth.
[6] Shout with exultation, O city of Zion,
for great in your midst
is the Holy One of Israel!

R. *You will draw water joyfully from the springs*

of salvation.

Sixth Reading: Baruch 3:9-15, 32C4:4

[9] Hear, O Israel, the commandments of life:
   listen, and know prudence!
[10] How is it, Israel,
   that you are in the land of your foes,
   grown old in a foreign land,
[11] defiled with the dead,
   accounted with those destined for the
      netherworld?
[12] You have forsaken the fountain of wisdom!
   [13] Had you walked in the way of God,
   you would have dwelt in enduring peace.
   [14] Learn where prudence is,
   where strength, where understanding;
that you may know also
   where are length of days, and life,
   where light of the eyes, and peace.
[15] Who has found the place of wisdom,
   who has entered into her treasuries?

[32] The One who knows all things knows her;
   he has probed her by his knowledge—
the One who established the earth for all
      time,
   and filled it with four-footed beasts;
   [33] he who dismisses the light, and it departs,
   calls it, and it obeys him trembling;
[34] before whom the stars at their posts
   shine and rejoice;
[35] when he calls them, they answer, "Here we
      are!"
   shining with joy for their Maker.
   [36] Such is our God;
   no other is to be compared to him:
[37] he has traced out the whole way of
      understanding,
   and has given her to Jacob, his servant,
   to Israel, his beloved son.

[38] Since then she has appeared on earth,

and moved among people.
¹ She is the book of the precepts of God,
    the law that endures forever;
all who cling to her will live,
    but those will die who forsake her.
² Turn, O Jacob, and receive her:
    walk by her light toward splendor.
³ Give not your glory to another,
    your privileges to an alien race.
⁴ Blessed are we, O Israel;
    for what pleases God is known to us!

Responsorial Psalm: Psalms 19:8, 9, 10, 11

R. *(John 6:68c)* **Lord, you have the words of everlasting life.**
⁸ The law of the LORD is perfect,
    refreshing the soul;
the decree of the LORD is trustworthy,
    giving wisdom to the simple.
R. Lord, you have the words of everlasting life.

⁹ The precepts of the LORD are right,
    rejoicing the heart;
the command of the LORD is clear,
    enlightening the eye.
R. Lord, you have the words of everlasting life.

¹⁰ The fear of the LORD is pure,
    enduring forever;
the ordinances of the LORD are true,
    all of them just.
R. Lord, you have the words of everlasting life.

¹¹ They are more precious than gold,
    than a heap of purest gold;
sweeter also than syrup
    or honey from the comb.
R. Lord, you have the words of everlasting life.

Seventh Reading: Ezekiel 36:16-17A, 18-28

¹⁶ The word of the LORD came to me, saying: ¹⁷Son of man, when the house of Israel lived in their land, they defiled it by their conduct and deeds. ¹⁸ Therefore I poured out my fury upon them because of the blood that they poured out on the ground, and because they

defiled it with idols. [19] I scattered them among the nations, dispersing them over foreign lands; according to their conduct and deeds I judged them. [20] But when they came among the nations wherever they came, they served to profane my holy name, because it was said of them: "These are the people of the LORD, yet they had to leave their land." [21] So I have relented because of my holy name which the house of Israel profaned among the nations where they came. [22] Therefore say to the house of Israel: Thus says the Lord GOD: Not for your sakes do I act, house of Israel, but for the sake of my holy name, which you profaned among the nations to which you came.

[23] I will prove the holiness of my great name, profaned among the nations, in whose midst you have profaned it. Thus the nations shall know that I am the LORD, says the Lord GOD, when in their sight I prove my holiness through you. [24] For I will take you away from among the nations, gather you from all the foreign lands, and bring you back to your own land. [25] I will sprinkle clean water upon you to cleanse you from all your impurities, and from all your idols I will cleanse you. [26] I will give you a new heart and place a new spirit within you, taking from your bodies your stony hearts and giving you natural hearts. [27] I will put my spirit within you and make you live by my statutes, careful to observe my decrees. [28] You shall live in the land I gave your fathers; you shall be my people, and I will be your God.

Responsorial Psalm: Psalms 42:3, 5; 43:3, 4
When baptism is celebrated on Easter Vigil
R. [42:2] *Like a deer that longs for running*
                streams, my soul longs for you, my
                God.
[3] Athirst is my soul for God, the living
            God.
        When shall I go and behold the face
            of God?
R. *Like a deer that longs for running*
                streams, my soul longs for you, my
                God.
[5] I went with the throng
        and led them in procession to the
            house of God,
Amid loud cries of joy and thanksgiving,
        with the multitude keeping festival.
R. *Like a deer that longs for running*
                streams, my soul longs for you, my
                God.

[3] Send forth your light and your fidelity;
        they shall lead me on
And bring me to your holy mountain,

to your dwelling-place.
**R. Like a deer that longs for running
streams, my soul longs for you, my
God.**

[4] Then will I go in to the altar of God,
the God of my gladness and joy;
then will I give you thanks upon the
harp,
O God, my God!
**R. Like a deer that longs for running
streams, my soul longs for you, my
God.**

Or Psalms 51:12-13, 14-15, 18-19
When baptism is not celebrated During Easter Vigil
R. (12a) Create a clean heart in me, O God.
[12] A clean heart create for me, O God,
and a steadfast spirit renew within
me.
[13] Cast me not out from your presence,
and your Holy Spirit take not from
me.
R. Create a clean heart in me, O God.

[14] Give me back the joy of your salvation,
and a willing spirit sustain in me.
[15] I will teach transgressors your ways,
and sinners shall return to you.
R. Create a clean heart in me, O God.

[18] For you are not pleased with sacrifices;
should I offer a holocaust, you would
not accept it.
[19] My sacrifice, O God, is a contrite spirit;
a heart contrite and humbled, O God,
you will not spurn.
R. Create a clean heart in me, O God.

Epistle: Romans 6:3-11
Brothers and sisters: [3] Are you unaware that we who were baptized into Christ Jesus were baptized into his death? [4] We were indeed buried with him through baptism into death, so

that, just as Christ was raised from the dead by the glory of the Father, we too might live in newness of life.

[5] For if we have grown into union with him through a death like his, we shall also be united with him in the resurrection. [6] We know that our old self was crucified with him, so that our sinful body might be done away with, that we might no longer be in slavery to sin. [7] For a dead person has been absolved from sin. [8] If, then, we have died with Christ, we believe that we shall also live with him. [9] We know that Christ, raised from the dead, dies no more; death no longer has power over him. [10] As to his death, he died to sin once and for all; as to his life, he lives for God. [11] Consequently, you too must think of yourselves as being dead to sin and living for God in Christ Jesus.

Responsorial Psalm: Psalms 118:1-2, 16-17, 22-23

R. Alleluia, alleluia, alleluia.

[1] Give thanks to the LORD, for he is good,
    for his mercy endures forever.
[2] Let the house of Israel say,
    "His mercy endures forever."

R. Alleluia, alleluia, alleluia.

[16] The right hand of the LORD has struck with
      power;
    the right hand of the LORD is exalted.
[17] I shall not die, but live,
    and declare the works of the LORD.

R. Alleluia, alleluia, alleluia.

[22] The stone the builders rejected
    has become the cornerstone.
[23] By the LORD has this been done;
    it is wonderful in our eyes.

R. Alleluia, alleluia, alleluia.

Gospel: Mark 16: 1-7

[1] When the sabbath was over, Mary Magdalene, Mary, the mother of James, and Salome bought spices so that they might go and anoint him. [2] Very early when the sun had risen, on the first day of the week, they came to the tomb. [3] They were saying to one another, "Who will roll back the stone for us from the entrance to the tomb?" [4] When they looked up, they saw that the stone had been rolled back; it was very large. [5] On entering the tomb they saw a young man sitting on the right side, clothed in a white robe, and they were utterly amazed. [6] He said to them, "Do not be amazed! You seek Jesus of Nazareth, the crucified. He has been raised; he is not here. Behold, the place where they laid him. [7] But go and tell his disciples and Peter, 'He is going before you to Galilee; there you will see him, as he told you.'"

Easter Sunday

First Reading: Acts 10:34A, 37-43

[34A] Peter proceeded to speak and said: [37] "You know what has happened all over Judea, beginning in Galilee after the baptism that John preached, [38] how God anointed Jesus of Nazareth with the Holy Spirit and power. He went about doing good and healing all those oppressed by the devil, for God was with him. [39] We are witnesses of all that he did both in the country of the Jews and in Jerusalem. They put him to death by hanging him on a tree. [40] This man God raised on the third day and granted that he be visible, [41] not to all the people, but to us, the witnesses chosen by God in advance, who ate and drank with him after he rose from the dead. [42] He commissioned us to preach to the people and testify that he is the one appointed by God as judge of the living and the dead. [43] To him all the prophets bear witness, that everyone who believes in him will receive forgiveness of sins through his name."

Responsorial Psalm: Psalms 118:1-2, 16-17, 22-23.

R. [(24)] *This is the day the Lord has made; let us
rejoice and be glad.* or: *R. Alleluia.*

[1] Give thanks to the LORD, for he is good,
for his mercy endures forever.
[2] Let the house of Israel say,
"His mercy endures forever."

*R. This is the day the Lord has made; let us
rejoice and be glad.* or: **R. Alleluia.**

[16] The right hand of the LORD has struck with
power;
the right hand of the LORD is exalted.
[17] I shall not die, but live,
and declare the works of the LORD.

*R. This is the day the Lord has made; let us
rejoice and be glad.* or: **R. Alleluia.**

[22] The stone which the builders rejected
has become the cornerstone.
[23] By the LORD has this been done;
it is wonderful in our eyes.

*R. This is the day the Lord has made; let us
rejoice and be glad.* or: **R. Alleluia.**

Second Reading: Colossians 3:1-4

Brothers and sisters: [1] If then you were raised with Christ, seek what is above, where Christ is seated at the right hand of God. [2] Think of what is above, not of what is on earth.

[3] For you have died, and your life is hidden with Christ in God. [4] When Christ your life appears, then you too will appear with him in glory.

Or 1 Corinthians 5:6B-8

Brothers and sisters: [6B] Do you not know that a little yeast leavens all the dough? [7] Clear out the old yeast, so that you may become a fresh batch of dough, inasmuch as you are unleavened. For our paschal lamb, Christ, has been sacrificed. [8] Therefore, let us celebrate the feast, not with the old yeast, the yeast of malice and wickedness, but with the unleavened bread of sincerity and truth.

Sequence - *Victimae Paschali Laudes*

Christians, to the Paschal Victim
Offer your thankful praises!
A Lamb the sheep redeems;
Christ, who only is sinless,
Reconciles sinners to the Father.
Death and life have contended in that combat stupendous:
The Prince of life, who died, reigns immortal.
Speak, Mary, declaring
What you saw, wayfaring.
"The tomb of Christ, who is living,
The glory of Jesus' resurrection;
Bright angels attesting,
The shroud and napkin resting.
Yes, Christ my hope is arisen;
To Galilee he goes before you."
Christ indeed from death is risen, our new life obtaining.
Have mercy, victor King, ever reigning!
Amen. Alleluia.

Alleluia: cf. 1 Corinthians 5:7B-8A

R. Alleluia, alleluia.
[7B] Christ, our paschal lamb, has been
            sacrificed;
[8A] let us then feast with joy in the Lord.
R. Alleluia, alleluia.

Gospel: John 20:1-9

[1] On the first day of the week, Mary of Magdala came to the tomb early in the morning, while it was still dark, and saw the stone removed from the tomb. [2] So she ran and went to Simon Peter and to the other disciple whom Jesus loved, and told them, "They have

taken the Lord from the tomb, and we don't know where they put him." [3] So Peter and the other disciple went out and came to the tomb. [4] They both ran, but the other disciple ran faster than Peter and arrived at the tomb first; [5] he bent down and saw the burial cloths there, but did not go in. [6] When Simon Peter arrived after him, he went into the tomb and saw the burial cloths there, [7] and the cloth that had covered his head, not with the burial cloths but rolled up in a separate place. [8] Then the other disciple also went in, the one who had arrived at the tomb first, and he saw and believed. [9] For they did not yet understand the Scripture that he had to rise from the dead.

Or Mark 16:1-7

[1] When the sabbath was over, Mary Magdalene, Mary, the mother of James, and Salome bought spices so that they might go and anoint him. [2] Very early when the sun had risen, on the first day of the week, they came to the tomb. [3] They were saying to one another, "Who will roll back the stone for us from the entrance to the tomb?" [4] When they looked up, they saw that the stone had been rolled back; it was very large. [5] On entering the tomb they saw a young man sitting on the right side, clothed in a white robe, and they were utterly amazed. [6] He said to them, "Do not be amazed! You seek Jesus of Nazareth, the crucified. He has been raised; he is not here. Behold the place where they laid him. [7] But go and tell his disciples and Peter, 'He is going before you to Galilee; there you will see him, as he told you.'"

Or Luke: 24:13-35

At an afternoon or evening Mass.

[13] That very day, the first day of the week, two of Jesus' disciples were going to a village seven miles from Jerusalem called Emmaus, [14] and they were conversing about all the things that had occurred. [15] And it happened that while they were conversing and debating, Jesus himself drew near and walked with them, [16] but their eyes were prevented from recognizing him. [17] He asked them, "What are you discussing as you walk along?" They stopped, looking downcast. [18] One of them, named Cleopas, said to him in reply, "Are you the only visitor to Jerusalem who does not know of the things that have taken place there in these days?" [19] And he replied to them, "What sort of things?" They said to him, "The things that happened to Jesus the Nazarene, who was a prophet mighty in deed and word before God and all the people, [20] how our chief priests and rulers both handed him over to a sentence of death and crucified him. [21] But we were hoping that he would be the one to redeem Israel; and besides all this, it is now the third day since this took place. [22] Some women from our group, however, have astounded us: they were at the tomb early in the morning [23] and did not find his body; they came back and reported that they had indeed seen a vision of angels who announced that he was alive. [24] Then some of those with us went to the tomb and found things just as the women had described, but him they did not see." [25] And he said to them, "Oh, how foolish you are! How slow of heart to believe all that the prophets spoke! [26] Was it not necessary that the Christ should suffer these things and enter into his glory?" [27] Then beginning with Moses and all the prophets, he interpreted to them what referred to him in all the Scriptures. [28] As they

approached the village to which they were going, he gave the impression that he was going on farther. [29] But they urged him, "Stay with us, for it is nearly evening and the day is almost over." So he went in to stay with them. [30] And it happened that, while he was with them at table, he took bread, said the blessing, broke it, and gave it to them. [31] With that their eyes were opened and they recognized him, but he vanished from their sight.

[32] Then they said to each other, "Were not our hearts burning within us while he spoke to us on the way and opened the Scriptures to us?" [33] So they set out at once and returned to Jerusalem where they found gathered together the eleven and those with them [34] who were saying, "The Lord has truly been raised and has appeared to Simon!" [35] Then the two recounted what had taken place on the way and how he was made known to them in the breaking of bread.

APRIL 2024
Monday April 1, 2024

Monday in the Octave of Easter
First Reading: Acts 2:14, 22-33

[14] On the day of Pentecost, Peter stood up with the Eleven, raised his voice, and proclaimed: "You who are Jews, indeed all of you staying in Jerusalem. Let this be known to you, and listen to my words.

[22] "You who are children of Israel, hear these words. Jesus the Nazorean was a man commended to you by God with mighty deeds, wonders, and signs, which God worked through him in your midst, as you yourselves know. [23] This man, delivered up by the set plan and foreknowledge of God, you killed, using lawless men to crucify him. [24] But God raised him up, releasing him from the throes of death, because it was impossible for him to be held by it. [25] For David says of him:

I saw the Lord ever before me,
with him at my right hand I shall not be
disturbed.
[26] *Therefore my heart has been glad and my*
tongue has exulted;
my flesh, too, will dwell in hope,
[27] *because you will not abandon my soul to the*
nether world,
nor will you suffer your holy one to see
corruption.
[28] *You have made known to me the paths of life;*
you will fill me with joy in your presence.

[29] My brothers, one can confidently say to you about the patriarch David that he died and was buried, and his tomb is in our midst to this day. [30] But since he was a prophet and knew that God had sworn an oath to him that he would set one of his descendants upon

his throne, [31] he foresaw and spoke of the resurrection of the Christ, that neither was he abandoned to the netherworld nor did his flesh see corruption. [32] God raised this Jesus; of this we are all witnesses. [33] Exalted at the right hand of God, he poured forth the promise of the Holy Spirit that he received from the Father, as you both see and hear."

Responsorial Psalm: Psalms 16:1-2A AND 5, 7-8, 9-10, 11

R. [(1)]*Keep me safe, O God; you are my hope.* or: *Alleluia.*

[1] Keep me, O God, for in you I take refuge;
> [2A] I say to the LORD, "My Lord are you."
[5] O LORD, my allotted portion and my cup,
> you it is who hold fast my lot.

R. *Keep me safe, O God; you are my hope.* or: *Alleluia.*

[7] I bless the LORD who counsels me;
> even in the night my heart exhorts me.
[8] I set the LORD ever before me;
> with him at my right hand I shall not be
> > disturbed.

R. *Keep me safe, O God; you are my hope.* or: *Alleluia.*

[9] Therefore my heart is glad and my soul
> > rejoices,
> my body, too, abides in confidence;
[10] Because you will not abandon my soul to the
> > nether world,
> nor will you suffer your faithful one to
> > undergo corruption.

R. *Keep me safe, O God; you are my hope.* or: *Alleluia.*

[11] You will show me the path to life,
> fullness of joys in your presence,
> the delights at your right hand forever.

R. *Keep me safe, O God; you are my hope.* or: *Alleluia.*

Alleluia: Psalms 118:24

R. Alleluia, alleluia.
[24] This is the day the LORD has made;
let us be glad and rejoice in it.
R. Alleluia, alleluia.

Gospel: Matthew 28:8-15

[8] Mary Magdalene and the other Mary went away quickly from the tomb, fearful yet overjoyed, and ran to announce the news to his disciples. [9] And behold, Jesus met them on their way and greeted them. They approached, embraced his feet, and did him homage. [10] Then Jesus said to them, "Do not be afraid. Go tell my brothers to go to Galilee, and there they will see me."

[11] While they were going, some of the guard went into the city and told the chief priests all that had happened. [12] The chief priests assembled with the elders and took counsel; then they gave a large sum of money to the soldiers, [13] telling them, "You are to say, 'His disciples came by night and stole him while we were asleep.' [14] And if this gets to the ears of the governor, we will satisfy him and keep you out of trouble." [15] The soldiers took the money and did as they were instructed. And this story has circulated among the Jews to the present day.

Tuesday April 2, 2024

Tuesday in the Octave of Easter
First Reading: Acts 2:36-41

[36] On the day of Pentecost, Peter said to the Jewish people, "Let the whole house of Israel know for certain that God has made him both Lord and Christ, this Jesus whom you crucified."

[37] Now when they heard this, they were cut to the heart, and they asked Peter and the other Apostles, "What are we to do, my brothers?" [38] Peter said to them, "Repent and be baptized, every one of you, in the name of Jesus Christ, for the forgiveness of your sins; and you will receive the gift of the Holy Spirit. [39] For the promise is made to you and to your children and to all those far off, whomever the Lord our God will call." [40] He testified with many other arguments, and was exhorting them, "Save yourselves from this corrupt generation." [41] Those who accepted his message were baptized, and about three thousand persons were added that day.

Responsorial Psalm: Psalms 33:4-5, 18-19, 20 AND 22

R. [5b] *The earth is full of the goodness of the Lord. or: Alleluia.*
[4] Upright is the word of the LORD,
　　and all his works are trustworthy.
[5] He loves justice and right;
　　of the kindness of the LORD the earth is
　　　full.
R. *The earth is full of the goodness of the Lord. or: Alleluia.*

[18] See, the eyes of the LORD are upon those who
　　fear him,
　　upon those who hope for his kindness,
[19] To deliver them from death
　　and preserve them in spite of famine.
R. *The earth is full of the goodness of the Lord. or: Alleluia.*

²⁰ Our soul waits for the LORD,
    who is our help and our shield.
²² May your kindness, O LORD, be upon us
    who have put our hope in you.
R. The earth is full of the goodness of the Lord. *or: Alleluia.*

Alleluia: Psalms 118:24
R. Alleluia, alleluia.
²⁴ This is the day the LORD has made;
let us be glad and rejoice in it.
R. Alleluia, alleluia.

Gospel: John 20:11-18
¹¹ Mary Magdalene stayed outside the tomb weeping. And as she wept, she bent over into the tomb ¹² and saw two angels in white sitting there, one at the head and one at the feet where the Body of Jesus had been. ¹³ And they said to her, "Woman, why are you weeping?" She said to them, "They have taken my Lord, and I don't know where they laid him." ¹⁴ When she had said this, she turned around and saw Jesus there, but did not know it was Jesus. ¹⁵ Jesus said to her, "Woman, why are you weeping? Whom are you looking for?" She thought it was the gardener and said to him, "Sir, if you carried him away, tell me where you laid him, and I will take him." ¹⁶ Jesus said to her, "Mary!" She turned and said to him in Hebrew, "Rabbouni," which means Teacher. ¹⁷ Jesus said to her, "Stop holding on to me, for I have not yet ascended to the Father. But go to my brothers and tell them, 'I am going to my Father and your Father, to my God and your God.'" ¹⁸ Mary went and announced to the disciples, "I have seen the Lord," and then reported what he had told her.

Wednesday April 3, 2024

Wednesday in the Octave of Easter
First Reading: Acts 3:1-10
¹ Peter and John were going up to the temple area for the three o'clock hour of prayer. ² And a man crippled from birth was carried and placed at the gate of the temple called "the Beautiful Gate" every day to beg for alms from the people who entered the temple. ³ When he saw Peter and John about to go into the temple, he asked for alms. ⁴ But Peter looked intently at him, as did John, and said, "Look at us." ⁵ He paid attention to them, expecting to receive something from them. ⁶ Peter said, "I have neither silver nor gold, but what I do have I give you: in the name of Jesus Christ the Nazorean, rise and walk." ⁷ Then Peter took him by the right hand and raised him up, and immediately his feet and ankles grew strong. ⁸ He leaped up, stood, and walked around, and went into the temple with them, walking and jumping and praising God. ⁹ When all the people saw him walking and praising God, ¹⁰ they recognized him as the one who used to sit begging at the Beautiful

Gate of the temple, and they were filled with amazement and astonishment at what had happened to him.

Responsorial Psalm: Psalms 105:1-2, 3-4, 6-7, 8-9

R. *(3b)Rejoice, O hearts that seek the Lord. or: Alleluia.*

[1] Give thanks to the LORD, invoke his name;
>   make known among the nations his
>   deeds.
[2] Sing to him, sing his praise,
>   proclaim all his wondrous deeds.

R. *Rejoice, O hearts that seek the Lord. or: Alleluia.*

[3] Glory in his holy name;
>   rejoice, O hearts that seek the LORD!
[4] Look to the LORD in his strength;
>   seek to serve him constantly.

R. *Rejoice, O hearts that seek the Lord. or: Alleluia.*

[6] You descendants of Abraham, his servants,
>   sons of Jacob, his chosen ones!
[7] He, the LORD, is our God;
>   throughout the earth his judgments
>   prevail.

R. *Rejoice, O hearts that seek the Lord. or: Alleluia.*

[8] He remembers forever his covenant
>   which he made binding for a thousand
>   generations—
[9] Which he entered into with Abraham
>   and by his oath to Isaac.

R. *Rejoice, O hearts that seek the Lord. or: Alleluia.*

Alleluia: Psalms 118:24

R. Alleluia, alleluia.
[24] This is the day the LORD has made;
let us be glad and rejoice in it.
R. Alleluia, alleluia.

Gospel: Luke 24:13-35

[13] That very day, the first day of the week, two of Jesus' disciples were going to a village seven miles from Jerusalem called Emmaus, [14] and they were conversing about all the things that had occurred. [15] And it happened that while they were conversing and debating, Jesus himself drew near and walked with them, [16] but their eyes were prevented

from recognizing him. ¹⁷ He asked them, "What are you discussing as you walk along?" They stopped, looking downcast. ¹⁸ One of them, named Cleopas, said to him in reply, "Are you the only visitor to Jerusalem who does not know of the things that have taken place there in these days?" ¹⁹ And he replied to them, "What sort of things?" They said to him, "The things that happened to Jesus the Nazarene, who was a prophet mighty in deed and word before God and all the people, ²⁰ how our chief priests and rulers both handed him over to a sentence of death and crucified him. ²¹ But we were hoping that he would be the one to redeem Israel; and besides all this, it is now the third day since this took place. ²² Some women from our group, however, have astounded us: they were at the tomb early in the morning ²³ and did not find his Body; they came back and reported that they had indeed seen a vision of angels who announced that he was alive. ²⁴ Then some of those with us went to the tomb and found things just as the women had described, but him they did not see." ²⁵ And he said to them, "Oh, how foolish you are! How slow of heart to believe all that the prophets spoke! ²⁶ Was it not necessary that the Christ should suffer these things and enter into his glory?" ²⁷ Then beginning with Moses and all the prophets, he interpreted to them what referred to him in all the Scriptures. ²⁸ As they approached the village to which they were going, he gave the impression that he was going on farther. ²⁹ But they urged him, "Stay with us, for it is nearly evening and the day is almost over." So he went in to stay with them. ³⁰ And it happened that, while he was with them at table, he took bread, said the blessing, broke it, and gave it to them. ³¹ With that their eyes were opened and they recognized him, but he vanished from their sight. ³² Then they said to each other, "Were not our hearts burning within us while he spoke to us on the way and opened the Scriptures to us?"

³³ So they set out at once and returned to Jerusalem where they found gathered together the Eleven and those with them ³⁴ who were saying, "The Lord has truly been raised and has appeared to Simon!" ³⁵ Then the two recounted what had taken place on the way and how he was made known to them in the breaking of the bread.

Thursday in the Octave of Easter
First Reading: Acts 3:11-26

¹¹As the crippled man who had been cured clung to Peter and John, all the people hurried in amazement toward them in the portico called "Solomon's Portico." ¹² When Peter saw this, he addressed the people, "You children of Israel, why are you amazed at this, and why do you look so intently at us as if we had made him walk by our own power or piety? ¹³ The God of Abraham, the God of Isaac, and the God of Jacob, the God of our fathers, has glorified his servant Jesus whom you handed over and denied in Pilate's presence, when he had decided to release him. ¹⁴ You denied the Holy and Righteous One and asked that a murderer be released to you. ¹⁵ The author of life you put to death, but God raised him from the dead; of this we are witnesses. ¹⁶ And by faith in his name, this man, whom you see and know, his name has made strong, and the faith that comes through it has given him this perfect health, in the presence of all of you. ¹⁷ Now I know, brothers and

sisters, that you acted out of ignorance, just as your leaders did; [18] but God has thus brought to fulfillment what he had announced beforehand through the mouth of all the prophets, that his Christ would suffer. [19] Repent, therefore, and be converted, that your sins may be wiped away, [20] and that the Lord may grant you times of refreshment and send you the Christ already appointed for you, Jesus, [21] whom heaven must receive until the times of universal restoration of which God spoke through the mouth of his holy prophets from of old. [22] For Moses said:

A prophet like me will the Lord, your God,
raise up for you
from among your own kin;
to him you shall listen in all that he may
say to you.
[23] *Everyone who does not listen to that prophet*
will be cut off from the people.

[24] "Moreover, all the prophets who spoke, from Samuel and those afterwards, also announced these days. [25] You are the children of the prophets and of the covenant that God made with your ancestors when he said to Abraham,

In your offspring all the families of the earth
shall be blessed.

[26] For you first, God raised up his servant and sent him to bless you by turning each of you from your evil ways."

Responsorial Psalm: Psalms 8:2AB and 5, 6-7, 8-9

R. *(2ab)O Lord, our God, how wonderful your*
name in all the earth! or: *Alleluia.*
[2AB] O LORD, our Lord,
how glorious is your name over all the
earth!
[5] What is man that you should be mindful of
him,
or the son of man that you should care
for him?
R. *O Lord, our God, how wonderful your name in*
all the earth! or: *Alleluia.*

[6] You have made him little less than the
angels,
and crowned him with glory and honor.

[7] You have given him rule over the works of
        your hands,
        putting all things under his feet.
**R. O Lord, our God, how wonderful your name in
        all the earth! or: Alleluia.**

[8] All sheep and oxen,
        yes, and the beasts of the field,
[9] The birds of the air, the fishes of the sea,
        and whatever swims the paths of the
        seas.
**R. O Lord, our God, how wonderful your name in
        all the earth! or: Alleluia.**

Alleluia: Psalms 118:24
R. Alleluia, alleluia.
[24] This is the day the LORD has made;
let us be glad and rejoice in it.
R. Alleluia, alleluia.

Gospel: Luke 24:35-48
[35] The disciples of Jesus recounted what had taken place along the way, and how they had come to recognize him in the breaking of bread.

[36] While they were still speaking about this, he stood in their midst and said to them, "Peace be with you." [37] But they were startled and terrified and thought that they were seeing a ghost. [38] Then he said to them, "Why are you troubled? And why do questions arise in your hearts? [39] Look at my hands and my feet, that it is I myself. Touch me and see, because a ghost does not have flesh and bones as you can see I have." [40] And as he said this, he showed them his hands and his feet. [41] While they were still incredulous for joy and were amazed, he asked them, "Have you anything here to eat?" [42] They gave him a piece of baked fish; [43] he took it and ate it in front of them.

[44] He said to them, "These are my words that I spoke to you while I was still with you, that everything written about me in the law of Moses and in the prophets and psalms must be fulfilled." [45] Then he opened their minds to understand the Scriptures. [46] And he said to them, "Thus it is written that the Christ would suffer and rise from the dead on the third day [47] and that repentance, for the forgiveness of sins, would be preached in his name to all the nations, beginning from Jerusalem. [48] You are witnesses of these things."

Friday in the Octave of Easter
First Reading: Acts 4:1-12

¹ After the crippled man had been cured, while Peter and John were still speaking to the people, the priests, the captain of the temple guard, and the Sadducees confronted them, ² disturbed that they were teaching the people and proclaiming in Jesus the resurrection of the dead. ³ They laid hands on Peter and John and put them in custody until the next day, since it was already evening. ⁴ But many of those who heard the word came to believe and the number of men grew to about five thousand.

⁵ On the next day, their leaders, elders, and scribes were assembled in Jerusalem, ⁶ with Annas the high priest, Caiaphas, John, Alexander, and all who were of the high-priestly class. ⁷ They brought them into their presence and questioned them, "By what power or by what name have you done this?" ⁸ Then Peter, filled with the Holy Spirit, answered them, "Leaders of the people and elders: ⁹ If we are being examined today about a good deed done to a cripple, namely, by what means he was saved, ¹⁰ then all of you and all the people of Israel should know that it was in the name of Jesus Christ the Nazorean whom you crucified, whom God raised from the dead; in his name this man stands before you healed. ¹¹ He is *the stone rejected by you, the builders, which has become the cornerstone.* ¹² There is no salvation through anyone else, nor is there any other name under heaven given to the human race by which we are to be saved."

Responsorial Psalm: Psalms 118:1-2 and 4, 22-24, 25-27A

R. (22) **The stone rejected by the builders has become the cornerstone. or: Alleluia.**

¹ Give thanks to the LORD, for he is good,
    for his mercy endures forever.
² Let the house of Israel say,
    "His mercy endures forever."
⁴ Let those who fear the LORD say,
    "His mercy endures forever."

R. **The stone rejected by the builders has become the cornerstone. or: Alleluia.**

²² The stone which the builders rejected
    has become the cornerstone.
²³ By the LORD has this been done;
    it is wonderful in our eyes.
²⁴ This is the day the LORD has made;
    let us be glad and rejoice in it.

R. **The stone rejected by the builders has become the cornerstone. or: Alleluia.**

²⁵ O LORD, grant salvation!
O LORD, grant prosperity!
²⁶ Blessed is he who comes in the name of the
LORD;
we bless you from the house of the LORD.
²⁷ᴬ The LORD is God, and he has given us light.
R. The stone rejected by the builders has become the cornerstone. or: **Alleluia.**

Alleluia: Psalms 118:24
R. Alleluia, alleluia.
²⁴ This is the day the LORD has made;
let us be glad and rejoice in it.
R. Alleluia, alleluia.

Gospel: John 21:1-14
¹ Jesus revealed himself again to his disciples at the Sea of Tiberias. He revealed himself in this way. ² Together were Simon Peter, Thomas called Didymus, Nathanael from Cana in Galilee, Zebedee's sons, and two others of his disciples. ³ Simon Peter said to them, "I am going fishing." They said to him, "We also will come with you." So they went out and got into the boat, but that night they caught nothing. ⁴ When it was already dawn, Jesus was standing on the shore; but the disciples did not realize that it was Jesus. ⁵ Jesus said to them, "Children, have you caught anything to eat?" They answered him, "No." ⁶ So he said to them, "Cast the net over the right side of the boat and you will find something." So they cast it, and were not able to pull it in because of the number of fish. ⁷ So the disciple whom Jesus loved said to Peter, "It is the Lord." When Simon Peter heard that it was the Lord, he tucked in his garment, for he was lightly clad, and jumped into the sea. ⁸ The other disciples came in the boat, for they were not far from shore, only about a hundred yards, dragging the net with the fish. ⁹ When they climbed out on shore, they saw a charcoal fire with fish on it and bread. ¹⁰ Jesus said to them, "Bring some of the fish you just caught." ¹¹ So Simon Peter went over and dragged the net ashore full of one hundred fifty-three large fish. Even though there were so many, the net was not torn. ¹² Jesus said to them, "Come, have breakfast." And none of the disciples dared to ask him, "Who are you?" because they realized it was the Lord. ¹³ Jesus came over and took the bread and gave it to them, and in like manner the fish. ¹⁴ This was now the third time Jesus was revealed to his disciples after being raised from the dead.

Saturday April 6, 2024

Saturday in the Octave of Easter
First Reading: Acts 4:13-21
¹³ Observing the boldness of Peter and John and perceiving them to be uneducated, ordinary men, the leaders, elders, and scribes were amazed, and they recognized them as the companions of Jesus. ¹⁴ Then when they saw the man who had been cured standing

there with them, they could say nothing in reply. [15] So they ordered them to leave the Sanhedrin, and conferred with one another, saying, [16] "What are we to do with these men? Everyone living in Jerusalem knows that a remarkable sign was done through them, and we cannot deny it. [17] But so that it may not be spread any further among the people, let us give them a stern warning never again to speak to anyone in this name."

[18] So they called them back and ordered them not to speak or teach at all in the name of Jesus. [19] Peter and John, however, said to them in reply, "Whether it is right in the sight of God for us to obey you rather than God, you be the judges. [20]It is impossible for us not to speak about what we have seen and heard." [21] After threatening them further, they released them, finding no way to punish them, on account of the people who were all praising God for what had happened.

Responsorial Psalm: Psalms 118:1 and 14-15AB,16-18,19-21

R. [(21a)] *I will give thanks to you, for you have*
                  answered me. or: *Alleluia.*

[1] Give thanks to the LORD, for he is good,
     for his mercy endures forever.
[14] My strength and my courage is the LORD,
     and he has been my savior.
[15AB] The joyful shout of victory
     in the tents of the just.

R. *I will give thanks to you, for you have*
                  answered me. or: *Alleluia.*

[16] "The right hand of the LORD is exalted;
     the right hand of the LORD has struck with
          power."
[17] I shall not die, but live,
     and declare the works of the LORD.
[18] Though the LORD has indeed chastised me,
     yet he has not delivered me to death.

R. *I will give thanks to you, for you have*
                  answered me. or: *Alleluia.*

[19] Open to me the gates of justice;
     I will enter them and give thanks to the
          LORD.
[20] This is the gate of the LORD;
     the just shall enter it.
[21] I will give thanks to you, for you have
          answered me
     and have been my savior.

R. *I will give thanks to you, for you have*

answered me. or: *Alleluia.*

Alleluia: Psalms 118:24
R. Alleluia, alleluia.
²⁴ This is the day the LORD has made;
let us be glad and rejoice in it.
R. Alleluia, alleluia.

Gospel: Mark 16:9-15
⁹ When Jesus had risen, early on the first day of the week, he appeared first to Mary Magdalene, out of whom he had driven seven demons. ¹⁰ She went and told his companions who were mourning and weeping. ¹¹ When they heard that he was alive and had been seen by her, they did not believe.

¹² After this he appeared in another form to two of them walking along on their way to the country. ¹³ They returned and told the others; but they did not believe them either.

¹⁴ But later, as the Eleven were at table, he appeared to them and rebuked them for their unbelief and hardness of heart because they had not believed those who saw him after he had been raised. ¹⁵ He said to them, "Go into the whole world and proclaim the Gospel to every creature."

Sunday April 7, 2024

Second Sunday of Easter – Divine Mercy Sunday Year B
First Reading: Acts 4:32-35
³² The community of believers was of one heart and mind, and no one claimed that any of his possessions was his own, but they had everything in common. ³³ With great power the apostles bore witness to the resurrection of the Lord Jesus, and great favor was accorded them all. ³⁴ There was no needy person among them, for those who owned property or houses would sell them, bring the proceeds of the sale, ³⁵ and put them at the feet of the apostles, and they were distributed to each according to need.

Responsorial Psalm: Psalms 118:2-4, 13-15, 22-24
R. *⁽¹⁾ Give thanks to the Lord for he is good,*
his love is everlasting. or: *Alleluia.*
² Let the house of Israel say,
"His mercy endures forever."
³ Let the house of Aaron say,
"His mercy endures forever."
⁴ Let those who fear the LORD say,
"His mercy endures forever."
R. *Give thanks to the Lord for he is good, his*
love is everlasting. or: *Alleluia.*

[13] I was hard pressed and was falling,
   but the LORD helped me.
[14] My strength and my courage is the LORD,
   and he has been my savior.
[15] The joyful shout of victory
   in the tents of the just:
**R. Give thanks to the Lord for he is good, his
        love is everlasting.** or: **Alleluia.**

[22] The stone which the builders rejected
   has become the cornerstone.
[23] By the LORD has this been done;
   it is wonderful in our eyes.
[24] This is the day the LORD has made;
   let us be glad and rejoice in it.
**R. Give thanks to the Lord for he is good, his
        love is everlasting.** or: **Alleluia.**

Second Reading: 1 John 5:1-6

Beloved: [1] Everyone who believes that Jesus is the Christ is begotten by God, and everyone who loves the Father loves also the one begotten by him. [2] In this way we know that we love the children of God when we love God and obey his commandments. [3] For the love of God is this, that we keep his commandments. And his commandments are not burdensome, [4] for whoever is begotten by God conquers the world. And the victory that conquers the world is our faith.[5] Who indeed is the victor over the world but the one who believes that Jesus is the Son of God?

   [6] This is the one who came through water and blood, Jesus Christ, not by water alone, but by water and blood. The Spirit is the one that testifies, and the Spirit is truth.

Alleluia: John 20:29

R. Alleluia, alleluia.
[29] You believe in me, Thomas, because you
        have seen me, says the Lord;
Blessed are those who have not seen me, but
        still believe!
R. Alleluia, alleluia.

Gospel: John 20:19-31

[19] On the evening of that first day of the week, when the doors were locked, where the disciples were, for fear of the Jews, Jesus came and stood in their midst and said to them, "Peace be with you." [20] When he had said this, he showed them his hands and his side.

The disciples rejoiced when they saw the Lord. [21] Jesus said to them again, "Peace be with you. As the Father has sent me, so I send you." [22] And when he had said this, he breathed on them and said to them, "Receive the Holy Spirit. [23] Whose sins you forgive are forgiven them, and whose sins you retain are retained."

[24] Thomas, called Didymus, one of the Twelve, was not with them when Jesus came. [25] So the other disciples said to him, "We have seen the Lord." But he said to them, "Unless I see the mark of the nails in his hands and put my finger into the nailmarks and put my hand into his side, I will not believe."

[26] Now a week later his disciples were again inside and Thomas was with them. Jesus came, although the doors were locked, and stood in their midst and said, "Peace be with you." [27] Then he said to Thomas, "Put your finger here and see my hands, and bring your hand and put it into my side, and do not be unbelieving, but believe." [28] Thomas answered and said to him, "My Lord and my God!" [29] Jesus said to him, "Have you come to believe because you have seen me? Blessed are those who have not seen and have believed."

[30] Now Jesus did many other signs in the presence of his disciples that are not written in this book. [31] But these are written that you may come to believe that Jesus is the Christ, the Son of God, and that through this belief you may have life in his name.

Monday April 8, 2024

Solemnity of the Annunciation of the Lord
First Reading: Isaiah 7:10-14; 8:10

[10] The LORD spoke to Ahaz, saying: [11] Ask for a sign from the LORD, your God; let it be deep as the nether world, or high as the sky! [12] But Ahaz answered, "I will not ask! I will not tempt the LORD!" [13] Then Isaiah said: Listen, O house of David! Is it not enough for you to weary people, must you also weary my God? [14] Therefore the Lord himself will give you this sign: the virgin shall be with child, and bear a son, and shall name him Emmanuel, which means "God is with us!"

Responsorial Psalm: Psalms 40:7-8A, 8B-9, 10, 11

R. (8a and 9a) **Here I am, Lord; I come to do your will.**

[7] Sacrifice or oblation you wished not,
    but ears open to obedience you gave me.
[8A] Holocausts or sin-offerings you sought not;
    then said I, "Behold I come."
R. **Here I am, Lord; I come to do your will.**

[8B] "In the written scroll it is prescribed for me,
[9] To do your will, O my God, is my delight,
    and your law is within my heart!"
R. **Here I am, Lord; I come to do your will.**

[10] I announced your justice in the vast

206

assembly;
> I did not restrain my lips, as you, O LORD,
> know.

R. Here I am, Lord; I come to do your will.

11 Your justice I kept not hid within my heart;
> your faithfulness and your salvation I
> > have spoken of;

I have made no secret of your kindness and
> your truth
> > in the vast assembly.

R. Here I am, Lord; I come to do your will.

Second Reading: Hebrews 10:4-10

Brothers and sisters: 4 It is impossible that the blood of bulls and goats take away sins. 5 For this reason, when Christ came into the world, he said:

"Sacrifice and offering you did not desire,
> but a body you prepared for me;
> > 6 in holocausts and sin offerings you took
> > > no delight.

7 Then I said, 'As is written of me in the scroll,
> behold, I come to do your will, O God.'"

8 First, he says, "Sacrifices and offerings, holocausts and sin offerings, you neither desired nor delighted in." These are offered according to the law. 9 Then he says, "Behold, I come to do your will." He takes away the first to establish the second. 10 By this "will," we have been consecrated through the offering of the Body of Jesus Christ once for all.

Verse Before the Gospel: John 1:14AB

14AB The Word of God became flesh and made his
> dwelling among us;

and we saw his glory.

Gospel: Luke 1:26-38

26 The angel Gabriel was sent from God to a town of Galilee called Nazareth, 27 to a virgin betrothed to a man named Joseph, of the house of David, and the virgin's name was Mary. 28 And coming to her, he said, "Hail, full of grace! The Lord is with you." 29 But she was greatly troubled at what was said and pondered what sort of greeting this might be. 30 Then the angel said to her, "Do not be afraid, Mary, for you have found favor with God. 31Behold, you will conceive in your womb and bear a son, and you shall name him

Jesus. [32] He will be great and will be called Son of the Most High, and the Lord God will give him the throne of David his father, [33] and he will rule over the house of Jacob forever, and of his Kingdom there will be no end." [34] But Mary said to the angel, "How can this be, since I have no relations with a man?" [35] And the angel said to her in reply, "The Holy Spirit will come upon you, and the power of the Most High will overshadow you. Therefore the child to be born will be called holy, the Son of God. [36] And behold, Elizabeth, your relative, has also conceived a son in her old age, and this is the sixth month for her who was called barren; [37] for nothing will be impossible for God." [38] Mary said, "Behold, I am the handmaid of the Lord. May it be done to me according to your word." Then the angel departed from her.

Tuesday April 9, 2024

Tuesday of the Second Week of Easter
First Reading: Acts 4:32-37

[32] The community of believers was of one heart and mind, and no one claimed that any of his possessions was his own, but they had everything in common. [33] With great power the Apostles bore witness to the resurrection of the Lord Jesus, and great favor was accorded them all. [34] There was no needy person among them, for those who owned property or houses would sell them, bring the proceeds of the sale, [35] and put them at the feet of the Apostles, and they were distributed to each according to need.

[36] Thus Joseph, also named by the Apostles Barnabas (which is translated "son of encouragement"), a Levite, a Cypriot by birth, [37]sold a piece of property that he owned, then brought the money and put it at the feet of the Apostles.

Responsorial Psalm: Psalms 93:1AB, 1CD-2, 5

R. [1a]*The Lord is king; he is robed in majesty.* or: *Alleluia.*

[1AB] The LORD is king, in splendor robed;
      robed is the LORD and girt about with
         strength.

R. *The Lord is king; he is robed in majesty.* or: *Alleluia.*

[1CD] And he has made the world firm,
      not to be moved.
[2] Your throne stands firm from of old;
      from everlasting you are, O LORD.

R. *The Lord is king; he is robed in majesty.* or: *Alleluia.*

[5] Your decrees are worthy of trust indeed:
      holiness befits your house,
      O LORD, for length of days.

R. *The Lord is king; he is robed in majesty.* or: *Alleluia.*

Alleluia: John 3:14-15

R. Alleluia, alleluia.

14 The Son of Man must be lifted up,

15 so that everyone who believes in him
may have eternal life.

R. Alleluia, alleluia.

Gospel: John 3:7B-15

7B Jesus said to Nicodemus: "'You must be born from above.' 8 The wind blows where it wills, and you can hear the sound it makes, but you do not know where it comes from or where it goes; so it is with everyone who is born of the Spirit." 9 Nicodemus answered and said to him, 'How can this happen?" 10 Jesus answered and said to him, "You are the teacher of Israel and you do not understand this? 11 Amen, amen, I say to you, we speak of what we know and we testify to what we have seen, but you people do not accept our testimony. 12 If I tell you about earthly things and you do not believe, how will you believe if I tell you about heavenly things? 13 No one has gone up to heaven except the one who has come down from heaven, the Son of Man. 14 And just as Moses lifted up the serpent in the desert, so must the Son of Man be lifted up, so that everyone who believes in him may have eternal life."

Wednesday of the Second Week of Easter

First Reading: Acts 5:17-26

17 The high priest rose up and all his companions, that is, the party of the Sadducees, and, filled with jealousy, 18 laid hands upon the Apostles and put them in the public jail. 19 But during the night, the angel of the Lord opened the doors of the prison, led them out, and said, 20 "Go and take your place in the temple area, and tell the people everything about this life." 21 When they heard this, they went to the temple early in the morning and taught. When the high priest and his companions arrived, they convened the Sanhedrin, the full senate of the children of Israel, and sent to the jail to have them brought in. 22 But the court officers who went did not find them in the prison, so they came back and reported, 23 "We found the jail securely locked and the guards stationed outside the doors, but when we opened them, we found no one inside." 24 When the captain of the temple guard and the chief priests heard this report, they were at a loss about them, as to what this would come to. 25 Then someone came in and reported to them, "The men whom you put in prison are in the temple area and are teaching the people." 26 Then the captain and the court officers went and brought them, but without force, because they were afraid of being stoned by the people.

Responsorial Psalm: Psalms 34:2-3, 4-5, 6-7, 8-9

R. *(7a)* **The Lord hears the cry of the poor.** Or: *Alleluia.*

2 I will bless the LORD at all times;
> his praise shall be ever in my mouth.

3 Let my soul glory in the LORD;

the lowly will hear me and be glad.
R. The Lord hears the cry of the poor. or: **Alleluia.**

[4] Glorify the LORD with me,
let us together extol his name.
[5] I sought the LORD, and he answered me
and delivered me from all my fears.
R. The Lord hears the cry of the poor. or: **Alleluia.**

[6] Look to him that you may be radiant with
joy,
and your faces may not blush with
shame.
[7] When the poor one called out, the LORD
heard,
and from all his distress he saved him.
R. The Lord hears the cry of the poor. or: **Alleluia.**

[8] The angel of the LORD encamps
around those who fear him, and delivers
them.
[9] Taste and see how good the LORD is;
blessed the man who takes refuge in him.
R. The Lord hears the cry of the poor. or: **Alleluia.**

Alleluia: John 3:16
R. Alleluia, alleluia.
[16] God so love the world that he gave his only-
begotten Son,
so that everyone who believes in him might
have eternal life.
R. Alleluia, alleluia.

Gospel: John 3:16-21
[16] God so loved the world that he gave his only-begotten Son, so that everyone who believes in him might not perish but might have eternal life. [17] For God did not send his Son into the world to condemn the world, but that the world might be saved through him. [18] Whoever believes in him will not be condemned, but whoever does not believe has already been condemned, because he has not believed in the name of the only-begotten Son of God. [19] And this is the verdict, that the light came into the world, but people preferred darkness to light, because their works were evil. [20] For everyone who does wicked things hates the light and does not come toward the light, so that his works might not be exposed. [21] But whoever lives the truth comes to the light, so that his works may be clearly seen as done in God.

Memorial of Saint Stanislaus, Bp & Martyr
First Reading: Acts 5:27-33

27 When the court officers had brought the Apostles in and made them stand before the Sanhedrin, the high priest questioned them, 28 "We gave you strict orders did we not, to stop teaching in that name. Yet you have filled Jerusalem with your teaching and want to bring this man's blood upon us." 29 But Peter and the Apostles said in reply, "We must obey God rather than men. 30 The God of our ancestors raised Jesus, though you had him killed by hanging him on a tree. 31 God exalted him at his right hand as leader and savior to grant Israel repentance and forgiveness of sins. 32 We are witnesses of these things, as is the Holy Spirit whom God has given to those who obey him."

33 When they heard this, they became infuriated and wanted to put them to death.

Responsorial Psalm: Psalms 34:2 and 9, 17-18, 19-20

R. *(7a)* *The Lord hears the cry of the poor.* or: *Alleluia.*

2 I will bless the LORD at all times;
    his praise shall be ever in my mouth.
9 Taste and see how good the LORD is;
    blessed the man who takes refuge in him.
R. *The Lord hears the cry of the poor.* or: *Alleluia.*

17 The LORD confronts the evildoers,
    to destroy remembrance of them from
        the earth.
18 When the just cry out, the LORD hears them,
    and from all their distress he rescues
        them.
R. *The Lord hears the cry of the poor.* or: *Alleluia.*

19 The LORD is close to the brokenhearted;
    and those who are crushed in spirit he
        saves.
20 Many are the troubles of the just man,
    but out of them all the LORD delivers him.
R. *The Lord hears the cry of the poor.* or: *Alleluia.*

Alleluia: John 20:29

R. Alleluia, alleluia.

29 You believe in me, Thomas, because you
        have seen me, says the Lord;
blessed are those who have not seen, but still
        believe!

R. Alleluia, alleluia.

Gospel: John 3:31-36

[31] The one who comes from above is above all. The one who is of the earth is earthly and speaks of earthly things. But the one who comes from heaven is above all. [32] He testifies to what he has seen and heard, but no one accepts his testimony. [33] Whoever does accept his testimony certifies that God is trustworthy. [34] For the one whom God sent speaks the words of God. He does not ration his gift of the Spirit. [35] The Father loves the Son and has given everything over to him. [36] Whoever believes in the Son has eternal life, but whoever disobeys the Son will not see life, but the wrath of God remains upon him.

Friday April 12, 2024

Friday of the Second Week of Easter
First Reading: Acts 5:34-42

[34] A Pharisee in the Sanhedrin named Gamaliel, a teacher of the law, respected by all the people, stood up, ordered the Apostles to be put outside for a short time, [35] and said to the Sanhedrin, "Fellow children of Israel, be careful what you are about to do to these men. [36] Some time ago, Theudas appeared, claiming to be someone important, and about four hundred men joined him, but he was killed, and all those who were loyal to him were disbanded and came to nothing. [37] After him came Judas the Galilean at the time of the census. He also drew people after him, but he too perished and all who were loyal to him were scattered. [38] So now I tell you, have nothing to do with these men, and let them go. For if this endeavor or this activity is of human origin, it will destroy itself. [39] But if it comes from God, you will not be able to destroy them; you may even find yourselves fighting against God." They were persuaded by him. [40] After recalling the Apostles, they had them flogged, ordered them to stop speaking in the name of Jesus, and dismissed them. [41] So they left the presence of the Sanhedrin, rejoicing that they had been found worthy to suffer dishonor for the sake of the name. [42] And all day long, both at the temple and in their homes, they did not stop teaching and proclaiming the Christ, Jesus.

Responsorial Psalm: Psalms 27:1, 4, 13-14

R. [(see 4abc)] **One thing I seek: to dwell in the house
of the Lord.** or: *Alleluia.*

[1] The LORD is my light and my salvation;
     whom should I fear?
The LORD is my life's refuge;
     of whom should I be afraid?
R. *One thing I seek: to dwell in the house of the
     Lord.* Or: *Alleluia.*

[4] One thing I ask of the LORD;
     this I seek:
To dwell in the house of the LORD
     all the days of my life,

That I may gaze on the loveliness of the LORD
     and contemplate his temple.
R. One thing I seek: to dwell in the house of the
              Lord. Or: **Alleluia.**
[13] I believe that I shall see the bounty of the
         LORD
     in the land of the living.
[14] Wait for the LORD with courage;
     be stouthearted, and wait for the LORD.
R. One thing I seek: to dwell in the house of the
              Lord. Or: **Alleluia.**

Alleluia: Matthew 4:4B

R. Alleluia, alleluia.
[4B] One does not live on bread alone,
but on every word that comes forth from the
        mouth of God.
R. Alleluia, alleluia.

Gospel: John 6:1-15

[1] Jesus went across the Sea of Galilee. [2] A large crowd followed him, because they saw the signs he was performing on the sick. [3] Jesus went up on the mountain, and there he sat down with his disciples. [4] The Jewish feast of Passover was near. [5] When Jesus raised his eyes and saw that a large crowd was coming to him, he said to Philip, "Where can we buy enough food for them to eat?" [6] He said this to test him, because he himself knew what he was going to do. Philip answered him, [7] "Two hundred days' wages worth of food would not be enough for each of them to have a little." [8] One of his disciples, Andrew, the brother of Simon Peter, said to him, [9] "There is a boy here who has five barley loaves and two fish; but what good are these for so many?" [10] Jesus said, "Have the people recline." Now there was a great deal of grass in that place. So the men reclined, about five thousand in number. [11] Then Jesus took the loaves, gave thanks, and distributed them to those who were reclining, and also as much of the fish as they wanted. [12] When they had had their fill, he said to his disciples, "Gather the fragments left over, so that nothing will be wasted." [13] So they collected them, and filled twelve wicker baskets with fragments from the five barley loaves that had been more than they could eat. [14] When the people saw the sign he had done, they said, "This is truly the Prophet, the one who is to come into the world." [15] Since Jesus knew that they were going to come and carry him off to make him king, he withdrew again to the mountain alone.

Saturday of the Second Week of Easter
First Reading: Acts 6:1-7

[1] As the number of disciples continued to grow, the Hellenists complained against the Hebrews because their widows were being neglected in the daily distribution. [2] So the Twelve called together the community of the disciples and said, "It is not right for us to neglect the word of God to serve at table. [3] Brothers, select from among you seven reputable men, filled with the Spirit and wisdom, whom we shall appoint to this task, [4] whereas we shall devote ourselves to prayer and to the ministry of the word." [5] The proposal was acceptable to the whole community, so they chose Stephen, a man filled with faith and the Holy Spirit, also Philip, Prochorus, Nicanor, Timon, Parmenas, and Nicholas of Antioch, a convert to Judaism. [6] They presented these men to the Apostles who prayed and laid hands on them. [7] The word of God continued to spread, and the number of the disciples in Jerusalem increased greatly; even a large group of priests were becoming obedient to the faith.

Responsorial Psalm: Psalms 33:1-2, 4-5, 18-19

R. [22]*Lord, let your mercy be on us, as we place*
our trust in you. or: *Alleluia.*

[1] Exult, you just, in the LORD;
praise from the upright is fitting.
[2] Give thanks to the LORD on the harp;
with the ten-stringed lyre chant his
praises.

R. Lord, let your mercy be on us, as we place our trust in you. Or: Alleluia.

[4] Upright is the word of the LORD,
and all his works are trustworthy.
[5] He loves justice and right;
of the kindness of the LORD the earth is
full.

R. Lord, let your mercy be on us, as we place our trust in you. Or: Alleluia.

[18] See, the eyes of the LORD are upon those who
fear him,
upon those who hope for his kindness,
[19] To deliver them from death
and preserve them in spite of famine.

R. Lord, let your mercy be on us, as we place our trust in you. Or: Alleluia.

Alleluia
R. Alleluia, alleluia.
Christ is risen, who made all things;
he has shown mercy on all people.
R. Alleluia, alleluia.

Gospel: John 6:16-21
16 When it was evening, the disciples of Jesus went down to the sea, 17 embarked in a boat, and went across the sea to Capernaum. It had already grown dark, and Jesus had not yet come to them. 18 The sea was stirred up because a strong wind was blowing. 19 When they had rowed about three or four miles, they saw Jesus walking on the sea and coming near the boat, and they began to be afraid. 20 But he said to them, "It is I. Do not be afraid." 21 They wanted to take him into the boat, but the boat immediately arrived at the shore to which they were heading.

Sunday April 14, 2024

Third Sunday of Easter Year B
First Reading: Acts 3:13-15, 17-19
Peter said to the people: 13 "The God of Abraham, the God of Isaac, and the God of Jacob, the God of our fathers, has glorified his servant Jesus, whom you handed over and denied in Pilate's presence when he had decided to release him. 14 You denied the Holy and Righteous One and asked that a murderer be released to you. 15 The author of life you put to death, but God raised him from the dead; of this we are witnesses. 17 Now I know, brothers, that you acted out of ignorance, just as your leaders did; 18 but God has thus brought to fulfillment what he had announced beforehand through the mouth of all the prophets, that his Christ would suffer. 19 Repent, therefore, and be converted, that your sins may be wiped away."

Responsorial Psalm: Psalms 4:2, 4, 7-8, 9
*R. (7a) **Lord, let your face shine on us.** or: **Alleluia.***
2 When I call, answer me, O my just God,
    you who relieve me when I am in
        distress;
    have pity on me, and hear my prayer!
R. Lord, let your face shine on us.** or: **Alleluia.

4 Know that the LORD does wonders for his
        faithful one;
    the LORD will hear me when I call upon him.
R. Lord, let your face shine on us.** or: **Alleluia.

7 O LORD, let the light of your countenance
        shine upon us!

⁸ You put gladness into my heart.
R. Lord, let your face shine on us. or: **Alleluia.**

⁹ As soon as I lie down, I fall peacefully asleep,
    for you alone, O LORD,
    bring security to my dwelling.
R. Lord, let your face shine on us. or: **Alleluia.**

Second Reading: 1 John 2:1-5A

¹ My children, I am writing this to you so that you may not commit sin. But if anyone does sin, we have an Advocate with the Father, Jesus Christ the righteous one. ² He is expiation for our sins, and not for our sins only but for those of the whole world. ³ The way we may be sure that we know him is to keep his commandments. ⁴ Those who say, "I know him," but do not keep his commandments are liars, and the truth is not in them. ^{5A} But whoever keeps his word, the love of God is truly perfected in him.

Alleluia: cf. Luke 24:32

R. Alleluia, alleluia.
³² Lord Jesus, open the Scriptures to us;
make our hearts burn while you speak to us.
R. Alleluia, alleluia.

Gospel: Luke 24:35-48

³⁵ The two disciples recounted what had taken place on the way, and how Jesus was made known to them in the breaking of bread.

³⁶ While they were still speaking about this, he stood in their midst and said to them, "Peace be with you." ³⁷ But they were startled and terrified and thought that they were seeing a ghost. ³⁸ Then he said to them, "Why are you troubled? And why do questions arise in your hearts? ³⁹ Look at my hands and my feet, that it is I myself. Touch me and see, because a ghost does not have flesh and bones as you can see I have." ⁴⁰ And as he said this, he showed them his hands and his feet. ⁴¹ While they were still incredulous for joy and were amazed, he asked them, "Have you anything here to eat?" ⁴² They gave him a piece of baked fish; ⁴³ he took it and ate it in front of them.

⁴⁴ He said to them, "These are my words that I spoke to you while I was still with you, that everything written about me in the law of Moses and in the prophets and psalms must be fulfilled." ⁴⁵ Then he opened their minds to understand the Scriptures. ⁴⁶ And he said to them, "Thus it is written that the Christ would suffer and rise from the dead on the third day ⁴⁷ and that repentance, for the forgiveness of sins, would be preached in his name to all the nations, beginning from Jerusalem. ⁴⁸ You are witnesses of these things."

Monday of the Third Week of Easter
First Reading: Acts 6:8-15

[8] Stephen, filled with grace and power, was working great wonders and signs among the people. [9] Certain members of the so-called Synagogue of Freedmen, Cyreneans, and Alexandrians, and people from Cilicia and Asia, came forward and debated with Stephen, [10]but they could not withstand the wisdom and the Spirit with which he spoke. [11] Then they instigated some men to say, "We have heard him speaking blasphemous words against Moses and God." [12] They stirred up the people, the elders, and the scribes, accosted him, seized him, and brought him before the Sanhedrin. [13] They presented false witnesses who testified, "This man never stops saying things against this holy place and the law. [14] For we have heard him claim that this Jesus the Nazorean will destroy this place and change the customs that Moses handed down to us." [15] All those who sat in the Sanhedrin looked intently at him and saw that his face was like the face of an angel.

Responsorial Psalm: Psalms 119:23-24, 26-27, 29-30

R. [1ab] *Blessed are they who follow the law of the*
Lord! or: *Alleluia.*

[23] Though princes meet and talk against me,
your servant meditates on your statutes.
[24] Yes, your decrees are my delight;
they are my counselors.
R. *Blessed are they who follow the law of the*
Lord! or: *Alleluia.*

[26] I declared my ways, and you answered me;
teach me your statutes.
[27] Make me understand the way of your
precepts,
and I will meditate on your wondrous
deeds.
R. *Blessed are they who follow the law of the*
Lord! or: *Alleluia.*
[29] Remove from me the way of falsehood,
and favor me with your law.
[30] The way of truth I have chosen;
I have set your ordinances before me.
R. *Blessed are they who follow the law of the*
Lord! or: *Alleluia.*

Alleluia: Matthew 4:4B

R. Alleluia, alleluia.

[4B] One does not live on bread alone
but on every word that comes forth from the
    mouth of God.

R. Alleluia, alleluia.

Gospel: John 6:22-29

[After Jesus had fed the five thousand men, his disciples saw him walking on the sea.] [22] The next day, the crowd that remained across the sea saw that there had been only one boat there, and that Jesus had not gone along with his disciples in the boat, but only his disciples had left. [23] Other boats came from Tiberias near the place where they had eaten the bread when the Lord gave thanks. [24] When the crowd saw that neither Jesus nor his disciples were there, they themselves got into boats and came to Capernaum looking for Jesus. [25] And when they found him across the sea they said to him, "Rabbi, when did you get here?" [26] Jesus answered them and said, "Amen, amen, I say to you, you are looking for me not because you saw signs but because you ate the loaves and were filled. [27] Do not work for food that perishes but for the food that endures for eternal life, which the Son of Man will give you. For on him the Father, God, has set his seal." [28] So they said to him, "What can we do to accomplish the works of God?" [29] Jesus answered and said to them, "This is the work of God, that you believe in the one he sent."

Tuesday of the Third Week of Easter

First Reading: Acts 7:51-8:1A

[51] Stephen said to the people, the elders, and the scribes: "You stiff-necked people, uncircumcised in heart and ears, you always oppose the Holy Spirit; you are just like your ancestors. [52] Which of the prophets did your ancestors not persecute? They put to death those who foretold the coming of the righteous one, whose betrayers and murderers you have now become. [53] You received the law as transmitted by angels, but you did not observe it."

[54] When they heard this, they were infuriated, and they ground their teeth at him. [55] But Stephen, filled with the Holy Spirit, looked up intently to heaven and saw the glory of God and Jesus standing at the right hand of God, [56] and Stephen said, "Behold, I see the heavens opened and the Son of Man standing at the right hand of God." [57] But they cried out in a loud voice, covered their ears, and rushed upon him together. [58] They threw him out of the city, and began to stone him. The witnesses laid down their cloaks at the feet of a young man named Saul. [59] As they were stoning Stephen, he called out, "Lord Jesus, receive my spirit." [60] Then he fell to his knees and cried out in a loud voice, "Lord, do not hold this sin against them"; and when he said this, he fell asleep.

[1A] Now Saul was consenting to his execution.

Responsorial Psalm: Psalms 31:3CD-4, 6 AND 7B AND 8A, 17 AND 21AB

R. [6a] *Into your hands, O Lord, I commend my*
spirit. or: *Alleluia.*

3CD Be my rock of refuge,
a stronghold to give me safety.
4 You are my rock and my fortress;
for your name's sake you will lead and
guide me.

R. *Into your hands, O Lord, I commend my*
spirit. or: *Alleluia.*

6 Into your hands I commend my spirit;
you will redeem me, O LORD, O faithful
God.
7B My trust is in the LORD;
8A I will rejoice and be glad of your mercy.

R. *Into your hands, O Lord, I commend my*
spirit. or: *Alleluia.*

17 Let your face shine upon your servant;
save me in your kindness.
21AB You hide them in the shelter of your
presence
from the plottings of men.

R. *Into your hands, O Lord, I commend my*
spirit. or: *Alleluia.*

Alleluia: John 6:35AB

R. Alleluia, alleluia.
35AB I am the bread of life, says the Lord;
whoever comes to me will never hunger.
R. Alleluia, alleluia.

Gospel: John 6:30-35

30 The crowd said to Jesus: "What sign can you do, that we may see and believe in you? What can you do? 31 Our ancestors ate manna in the desert, as it is written:

He gave them bread from heaven to eat."

32So Jesus said to them, "Amen, amen, I say to you, it was not Moses who gave the bread from heaven; my Father gives you the true bread from heaven. 33 For the bread of God is that which comes down from heaven and gives life to the world."

[34] So they said to Jesus, "Sir, give us this bread always." [35] Jesus said to them, "I am the bread of life; whoever comes to me will never hunger, and whoever believes in me will never thirst."

Wednesday of the Third Week of Easter
First Reading: Acts 8:1B-8

[1B] There broke out a severe persecution of the Church in Jerusalem, and all were scattered throughout the countryside of Judea and Samaria, except the Apostles. [2] Devout men buried Stephen and made a loud lament over him. [3] Saul, meanwhile, was trying to destroy the Church; entering house after house and dragging out men and women, he handed them over for imprisonment.

[4] Now those who had been scattered went about preaching the word. [5] Thus Philip went down to the city of Samaria and proclaimed the Christ to them. [6] With one accord, the crowds paid attention to what was said by Philip when they heard it and saw the signs he was doing. [7] For unclean spirits, crying out in a loud voice, came out of many possessed people, and many paralyzed and crippled people were cured. [8] There was great joy in that city.

Responsorial Psalm: Psalms 66:1-3A, 4-5, 6-7A

R. [1] *Let all the earth cry out to God with joy.* or: *Alleluia.*

[2] Shout joyfully to God, all the earth,
      sing praise to the glory of his name;
      proclaim his glorious praise.
[3A] Say to God, "How tremendous are your
            deeds!"
R. *Let all the earth cry out to God with joy.* or: *Alleluia.*

[4] "Let all on earth worship and sing praise to
            you,
      sing praise to your name!"
[5] Come and see the works of God,
      his tremendous deeds among the
            children of Adam.
R. *Let all the earth cry out to God with joy.* or: *Alleluia.*

[6] He has changed the sea into dry land;
      through the river they passed on foot;
      therefore let us rejoice in him.
[7A] He rules by his might forever.
R. *Let all the earth cry out to God with joy.* or: *Alleluia.*

Alleluia: cf. John 6:40

R. Alleluia, alleluia.

[40] Everyone who believes in the Son has
eternal life,
and I shall raise him on the last day, says the
Lord.

R. Alleluia, alleluia.

Gospel: John 6:35-40

[35] Jesus said to the crowds, "I am the bread of life; whoever comes to me will never hunger, and whoever believes in me will never thirst. [36] But I told you that although you have seen me, you do not believe. [37] Everything that the Father gives me will come to me, and I will not reject anyone who comes to me, [38] because I came down from heaven not to do my own will but the will of the one who sent me. [39] And this is the will of the one who sent me, that I should not lose anything of what he gave me, but that I should raise it on the last day. [40] For this is the will of my Father, that everyone who sees the Son and believes in him may have eternal life, and I shall raise him on the last day."

Thursday April 18, 2024

Thursday of the Third Week of Easter
First Reading: Acts 8:26-40

[26] The angel of the Lord spoke to Philip, "Get up and head south on the road that goes down from Jerusalem to Gaza, the desert route." [27] So he got up and set out. Now there was an Ethiopian eunuch, a court official of the Candace, that is, the queen of the Ethiopians, in charge of her entire treasury, who had come to Jerusalem to worship, [28] and was returning home. Seated in his chariot, he was reading the prophet Isaiah. [29] The Spirit said to Philip, "Go and join up with that chariot." [30] Philip ran up and heard him reading Isaiah the prophet and said, "Do you understand what you are reading?" [31] He replied, "How can I, unless someone instructs me?" So he invited Philip to get in and sit with him. [32] This was the Scripture passage he was reading:

Like a sheep he was led to the slaughter,
and as a lamb before its shearer is silent,
so he opened not his mouth.
[33] In his humiliation justice was denied him.
Who will tell of his posterity?
For his life is taken from the earth.

[34] Then the eunuch said to Philip in reply, "I beg you, about whom is the prophet saying this? About himself, or about someone else?" [35] Then Philip opened his mouth and, beginning with this Scripture passage, he proclaimed Jesus to him. [36] As they traveled along the road they came to some water, and the eunuch said, "Look, there is water.

What is to prevent my being baptized?" [38] Then he ordered the chariot to stop, and Philip and the eunuch both went down into the water, and he baptized him. [39] When they came out of the water, the Spirit of the Lord snatched Philip away, and the eunuch saw him no more, but continued on his way rejoicing. [40] Philip came to Azotus, and went about proclaiming the good news to all the towns until he reached Caesarea.

Responsorial Psalm: Psalms 66:8-9, 16-17, 20

R. [1] *Let all the earth cry out to God with joy.* or: *Alleluia.*

[8] Bless our God, you peoples,
    loudly sound his praise;
[9] He has given life to our souls,
    and has not let our feet slip.

R. *Let all the earth cry out to God with joy.* or: *Alleluia.*

[16] Hear now, all you who fear God, while I
        declare
    what he has done for me.
[17] When I appealed to him in words,
    praise was on the tip of my tongue.

R. *Let all the earth cry out to God with joy.* or: *Alleluia.*

[20] Blessed be God who refused me not
    my prayer or his kindness!

R. *Let all the earth cry out to God with joy.* or: *Alleluia.*

Alleluia: John 6:51

R. Alleluia, alleluia.

[51] I am the living bread that came down from
        heaven,
says the Lord;
whoever eats this bread will live forever.

R. Alleluia, alleluia.

Gospel: John 6:44-51

[44] Jesus said to the crowds: "No one can come to me unless the Father who sent me draw him, and I will raise him on the last day. [45] It is written in the prophets:

They shall all be taught by God.

Everyone who listens to my Father and learns from him comes to me. [46] Not that anyone has seen the Father except the one who is from God; he has seen the Father. [47] Amen, amen, I say to you, whoever believes has eternal life. [48] I am the bread of life. [49] Your ancestors ate the manna in the desert, but they died; [50] this is the bread that comes down from heaven so that one may eat it and not die. [51] I am the living bread that came down from heaven; whoever eats this bread will live forever; and the bread that I will give is my Flesh for the life of the world."

Friday of the Third Week of Easter
First Reading: Acts 9:1-20

[1] Saul, still breathing murderous threats against the disciples of the Lord, went to the high priest [2] and asked him for letters to the synagogues in Damascus, that, if he should find any men or women who belonged to the Way, he might bring them back to Jerusalem in chains. [3] On his journey, as he was nearing Damascus, a light from the sky suddenly flashed around him. [4] He fell to the ground and heard a voice saying to him, "Saul, Saul, why are you persecuting me?" [5] He said, "Who are you, sir?" The reply came, "I am Jesus, whom you are persecuting. [6] Now get up and go into the city and you will be told what you must do." [7] The men who were traveling with him stood speechless, for they heard the voice but could see no one. [8] Saul got up from the ground, but when he opened his eyes he could see nothing; so they led him by the hand and brought him to Damascus. [9] For three days he was unable to see, and he neither ate nor drank.

[10] There was a disciple in Damascus named Ananias, and the Lord said to him in a vision, "Ananias." He answered, "Here I am, Lord." [11] The Lord said to him, "Get up and go to the street called Straight and ask at the house of Judas for a man from Tarsus named Saul. He is there praying, [12] and in a vision he has seen a man named Ananias come in and lay his hands on him, that he may regain his sight." [13] But Ananias replied, "Lord, I have heard from many sources about this man, what evil things he has done to your holy ones in Jerusalem. [14] And here he has authority from the chief priests to imprison all who call upon your name." [15] But the Lord said to him, "Go, for this man is a chosen instrument of mine to carry my name before Gentiles, kings, and children of Israel, [16] and I will show him what he will have to suffer for my name." [17] So Ananias went and entered the house; laying his hands on him, he said, "Saul, my brother, the Lord has sent me, Jesus who appeared to you on the way by which you came, that you may regain your sight and be filled with the Holy Spirit." [18] Immediately things like scales fell from his eyes and he regained his sight. He got up and was baptized, [19] and when he had eaten, he recovered his strength.

He stayed some days with the disciples in Damascus, [20] and he began at once to proclaim Jesus in the synagogues, that he is the Son of God.

Responsorial Psalm: Psalms 117:1BC, 2
R. (Mark 16:15) **Go out to all the world and tell the**
                    Good News. or: **Alleluia.**
[1BC] Praise the LORD, all you nations;
        glorify him, all you peoples!
R. **Go out to all the world and tell the Good**

News. or: *Alleluia.*

² For steadfast is his kindness toward us,
>   and the fidelity of the LORD endures
>   forever.
**R. Go out to all the world and tell the Good
>   News.** or: *Alleluia.*

Alleluia: John 6:56
R. Alleluia, alleluia.
⁵⁶ Whoever eats my Flesh and drinks my
>   Blood,
remains in me and I in him, says the Lord.
R. Alleluia, alleluia.

Gospel: John 6:52-59
⁵² The Jews quarreled among themselves, saying, "How can this man give us his Flesh to eat?" ⁵³ Jesus said to them, "Amen, amen, I say to you, unless you eat the Flesh of the Son of Man and drink his Blood, you do not have life within you. ⁵⁴ Whoever eats my Flesh and drinks my Blood has eternal life, and I will raise him on the last day. ⁵⁵ For my Flesh is true food, and my Blood is true drink. ⁵⁶ Whoever eats my Flesh and drinks my Blood remains in me and I in him. ⁵⁷ Just as the living Father sent me and I have life because of the Father, so also the one who feeds on me will have life because of me. ⁵⁸ This is the bread that came down from heaven.
Unlike your ancestors who ate and still died, whoever eats this bread will live forever." ⁵⁹ These things he said while teaching in the synagogue in Capernaum.

Saturday April 20, 2024

Saturday of the Third Week of Easter
First Reading: Acts 9:31-42
³¹ The Church throughout all Judea, Galilee, and Samaria was at peace. She was being built up and walked in the fear of the Lord, and with the consolation of the Holy Spirit she grew in numbers.

³² As Peter was passing through every region, he went down to the holy ones living in Lydda. ³³ There he found a man named Aeneas, who had been confined to bed for eight years, for he was paralyzed. ³⁴ Peter said to him, "Aeneas, Jesus Christ heals you. Get up and make your bed." He got up at once. ³⁵ And all the inhabitants of Lydda and Sharon saw him, and they turned to the Lord.

³⁶ Now in Joppa there was a disciple named Tabitha (which translated is Dorcas). She was completely occupied with good deeds and almsgiving. ³⁷ Now during those days she fell sick and died, so after washing her, they laid her out in a room upstairs. ³⁸ Since Lydda was near Joppa, the disciples, hearing that Peter was there, sent two men to him

with the request, "Please come to us without delay." [39] So Peter got up and went with them. When he arrived, they took him to the room upstairs where all the widows came to him weeping and showing him the tunics and cloaks that Dorcas had made while she was with them. [40] Peter sent them all out and knelt down and prayed. Then he turned to her body and said, "Tabitha, rise up." She opened her eyes, saw Peter, and sat up. [41] He gave her his hand and raised her up, and when he had called the holy ones and the widows, he presented her alive. [42] This became known all over Joppa, and many came to believe in the Lord.

Responsorial Psalm: Psalms 116:12-13, 14-15, 16-17

R. [12] *How shall I make a return to the Lord for all*
    the good he has done for me? or: *Alleluia.*

[12] How shall I make a return to the LORD
    for all the good he has done for me?
[13] The cup of salvation I will take up,
    and I will call upon the name of the LORD.

R. *How shall I make a return to the Lord for all*
    the good he has done for me? or: *Alleluia.*

[14] My vows to the LORD I will pay
    in the presence of all his people.
[15] Precious in the eyes of the LORD
    is the death of his faithful ones.

R. *How shall I make a return to the Lord for all*
    the good he has done for me? or: *Alleluia.*

[16] O LORD, I am your servant;
    I am your servant, the son of your
        handmaid;
    you have loosed my bonds.
[17] To you will I offer sacrifice of thanksgiving,
    and I will call upon the name of the LORD.

R. *How shall I make a return to the Lord for all*
    the good he has done for me? or: *Alleluia.*

Alleluia: cf. John 6:63C, 68C

R. Alleluia, alleluia.
[63C] Your words, Lord, are Spirit and life;
[68C] you have the words of everlasting life.
R. Alleluia, alleluia.

Gospel: John 6:60-69

[60] Many of the disciples of Jesus who were listening said, "This saying is hard; who can accept it?" [61] Since Jesus knew that his disciples were murmuring about this, he said to them, "Does this shock you? [62] What if you were to see the Son of Man ascending to where he was before? [63] It is the Spirit that gives life, while the flesh is of no avail. The words I have spoken to you are Spirit and life. [64] But there are some of you who do not believe." Jesus knew from the beginning the ones who would not believe and the one who would betray him. [65] And he said, "For this reason I have told you that no one can come to me unless it is granted him by my Father."

[66] As a result of this, many of his disciples returned to their former way of life and no longer walked with him. [67] Jesus then said to the Twelve, "Do you also want to leave?" [68] Simon Peter answered him, "Master, to whom shall we go? You have the words of eternal life. [69] We have come to believe and are convinced that you are the Holy One of God."

Sunday April 21, 2024

Fourth Sunday of Easter, Year B
First Reading: Acts 4:8-12

[8] Peter, filled with the Holy Spirit, said: "Leaders of the people and elders: [9] If we are being examined today about a good deed done to a cripple, namely, by what means he was saved, [10] then all of you and all the people of Israel should know that it was in the name of Jesus Christ the Nazorean whom you crucified, whom God raised from the dead; in his name this man stands before you healed. [11] *He is the stone rejected by you, the builders, which has become the cornerstone*. [12] There is no salvation through anyone else, nor is there any other name under heaven given to the human race by which we are to be saved."

Responsorial Psalm: Psalms 118:1, 8-9, 21-23, 26, 28, 29

R. [22] ***The stone rejected by the builders has become the cornerstone.*** or: ***Alleluia.***

[1] Give thanks to the LORD, for he is good,
    for his mercy endures forever.
[8] It is better to take refuge in the LORD
    than to trust in man.
[9] It is better to take refuge in the LORD
    than to trust in princes.

R. ***The stone rejected by the builders has become the cornerstone.*** or: ***Alleluia.***

[21] I will give thanks to you, for you have
    answered me
    and have been my savior.
[22] The stone which the builders rejected

has become the cornerstone.
^{23} By the LORD has this been done;
  it is wonderful in our eyes.
R. The stone rejected by the builders has become the cornerstone. or: *Alleluia.*

^{26} Blessed is he who comes in the name of the
    LORD;
  we bless you from the house of the LORD.
^{28} I will give thanks to you, for you have
    answered me
  and have been my savior.
^{29} Give thanks to the LORD, for he is good;
  for his kindness endures forever.
R. The stone rejected by the builders has become the cornerstone. or: *Alleluia.*

Second Reading: 1 John 3:1-2

Beloved: ^{1} See what love the Father has bestowed on us that we may be called the children of God. Yet so we are. The reason the world does not know us is that it did not know him. ^{2} Beloved, we are God's children now; what we shall be has not yet been revealed. We do know that when it is revealed we shall be like him, for we shall see him as he is.

Alleluia: John 10:14

R. Alleluia, alleluia.
^{14} I am the good shepherd, says the Lord;
I know my sheep, and mine know me.
R. Alleluia, alleluia.

Gospel: John 10:11-18

Jesus said: ^{11} "I am the good shepherd. A good shepherd lays down his life for the sheep. ^{12} A hired man, who is not a shepherd and whose sheep are not his own, sees a wolf coming and leaves the sheep and runs away, and the wolf catches and scatters them. ^{13} This is because he works for pay and has no concern for the sheep. ^{14} I am the good shepherd, and I know mine and mine know me, ^{15} just as the Father knows me and I know the Father; and I will lay down my life for the sheep. ^{16} I have other sheep that do not belong to this fold. These also I must lead, and they will hear my voice, and there will be one flock, one shepherd. ^{17} This is why the Father loves me, because I lay down my life in order to take it up again. ^{18} No one takes it from me, but I lay it down on my own. I have power to lay it down, and power to take it up again. This command I have received from my Father."

Monday of the Fourth Week of Easter
First Reading: Acts 11:1-18

[1] The Apostles and the brothers who were in Judea heard that the Gentiles too had accepted the word of God. [2] So when Peter went up to Jerusalem the circumcised believers confronted him, [3] saying, "You entered the house of uncircumcised people and ate with them." [4] Peter began and explained it to them step by step, saying, [5] "I was at prayer in the city of Joppa when in a trance I had a vision, something resembling a large sheet coming down, lowered from the sky by its four corners, and it came to me. [6] Looking intently into it, I observed and saw the four-legged animals of the earth, the wild beasts, the reptiles, and the birds of the sky. [7] I also heard a voice say to me, 'Get up, Peter. Slaughter and eat.' [8] But I said, 'Certainly not, sir, because nothing profane or unclean has ever entered my mouth.' [9] But a second time a voice from heaven answered, 'What God has made clean, you are not to call profane.' [10] This happened three times, and then everything was drawn up again into the sky. [11] Just then three men appeared at the house where we were, who had been sent to me from Caesarea. [12] The Spirit told me to accompany them without discriminating. These six brothers also went with me, and we entered the man's house. [13] He related to us how he had seen the angel standing in his house, saying, 'Send someone to Joppa and summon Simon, who is called Peter, [14] who will speak words to you by which you and all your household will be saved.' [15] As I began to speak, the Holy Spirit fell upon them as it had upon us at the beginning, [16] and I remembered the word of the Lord, how he had said, 'John baptized with water but you will be baptized with the Holy Spirit.' [17] If then God gave them the same gift he gave to us when we came to believe in the Lord Jesus Christ, who was I to be able to hinder God?" [18] When they heard this, they stopped objecting and glorified God, saying, "God has then granted life-giving repentance to the Gentiles too."

Responsorial Psalm: Psalms 42:2-3; 43:3, 4

R. *(see 3a)* **Athirst is my soul for the living God.** or: **Alleluia.**

[2] As the hind longs for the running waters,
    so my soul longs for you, O God.
[3] Athirst is my soul for God, the living God.
    When shall I go and behold the face of
        God?
R. **Athirst is my soul for the living God.** or: **Alleluia.**

[3] Send forth your light and your fidelity;
    they shall lead me on
And bring me to your holy mountain,
    to your dwelling-place.
R. **Athirst is my soul for the living God.** or: **Alleluia.**

⁴ Then will I go in to the altar of God,
>   the God of my gladness and joy;
Then will I give you thanks upon the harp,
>   O God, my God!
R. Athirst is my soul for the living God. or: **Alleluia.**

Alleluia: John 10:14
R. Alleluia, alleluia.
¹⁴ I am the good shepherd, says the Lord;
I know my sheep, and mine know me.
R. Alleluia, alleluia.

Gospel: John 10:1-10
¹ Jesus said: "Amen, amen, I say to you, whoever does not enter a sheepfold through the gate but climbs over elsewhere is a thief and a robber. ² But whoever enters through the gate is the shepherd of the sheep. ³ The gatekeeper opens it for him, and the sheep hear his voice, as the shepherd calls his own sheep by name and leads them out. ⁴ When he has driven out all his own, he walks ahead of them, and the sheep follow him, because they recognize his voice. ⁵ But they will not follow a stranger; they will run away from him, because they do not recognize the voice of strangers." ⁶ Although Jesus used this figure of speech, they did not realize what he was trying to tell them.

⁷ So Jesus said again, "Amen, amen, I say to you, I am the gate for the sheep. ⁸ All who came before me are thieves and robbers, but the sheep did not listen to them. ⁹ I am the gate. Whoever enters through me will be saved, and will come in and go out and find pasture. ¹⁰ A thief comes only to steal and slaughter and destroy; I came so that they might have life and have it more abundantly."

Tuesday April 23, 2024

Tuesday of the Fourth Week of Easter
First Reading: Acts 11:19-26
¹⁹ Those who had been scattered by the persecution that arose because of Stephen went as far as Phoenicia, Cyprus, and Antioch, preaching the word to no one but Jews. ²⁰ There were some Cypriots and Cyrenians among them, however, who came to Antioch and began to speak to the Greeks as well, proclaiming the Lord Jesus. ²¹ The hand of the Lord was with them and a great number who believed turned to the Lord. ²² The news about them reached the ears of the Church in Jerusalem, and they sent Barnabas to go to Antioch. ²⁴ When he arrived and saw the grace of God, he rejoiced and encouraged them all to remain faithful to the Lord in firmness of heart, for he was a good man, filled with the Holy Spirit and faith. And a large number of people was added to the Lord. ²⁵ Then he went to Tarsus to look for Saul, ²⁶ and when he had found him he brought him to Antioch. For a whole year they met with the Church and taught a large number of people, and it was in Antioch that the disciples were first called Christians.

Responsorial Psalm: Psalms 87:1B-3,4-5,6-7

R. *(117:1a)* **All you nations, praise the Lord.** or: **Alleluia.**

[1B] His foundation upon the holy mountains
>   the LORD loves:
[2] The gates of Zion,
>   more than any dwelling of Jacob.
[3] Glorious things are said of you,
>   O city of God!

R. All you nations, praise the Lord. or: **Alleluia.**

[4] I tell of Egypt and Babylon
>   among those who know the LORD;
Of Philistia, Tyre, Ethiopia:
>   "This man was born there."
[5] And of Zion they shall say:
>   "One and all were born in her;
And he who has established her
>   is the Most High LORD."

R. All you nations, praise the Lord. or: **Alleluia.**

[6] They shall note, when the peoples are
>   enrolled:
>   "This man was born there."
[7] And all shall sing, in their festive dance:
>   "My home is within you."

R. All you nations, praise the Lord. or: **Alleluia.**

Alleluia: John 10:27

R. Alleluia, alleluia.

[27] My sheep hear my voice, says the Lord;
I know them, and they follow me.

R. Alleluia, alleluia.

Gospel: John 10:22-30

[22] The feast of the Dedication was taking place in Jerusalem. It was winter. [23] And Jesus walked about in the temple area on the Portico of Solomon. [24] So the Jews gathered around him and said to him, "How long are you going to keep us in suspense? If you are the Christ, tell us plainly." [25] Jesus answered them, "I told you and you do not believe. The works I do in my Father's name testify to me. [26] But you do not believe, because you are not among my sheep. [27] My sheep hear my voice; I know them, and they follow me. [28] I give them eternal life, and they shall never perish. No one can take them out of my hand.

[29] My Father, who has given them to me, is greater than all, and no one can take them out of the Father's hand. [30] The Father and I are one."

Wednesday of the Fourth Week of Easter
First Reading: Acts 12:24-13:5a

[24] The word of God continued to spread and grow.

[25] After Barnabas and Saul completed their relief mission, they returned to Jerusalem, taking with them John, who is called Mark.

[1] Now there were in the Church at Antioch prophets and teachers: Barnabas, Symeon who was called Niger, Lucius of Cyrene, Manaen who was a close friend of Herod the tetrarch, and Saul. [2] While they were worshiping the Lord and fasting, the Holy Spirit said, "Set apart for me Barnabas and Saul for the work to which I have called them." [3] Then, completing their fasting and prayer, they laid hands on them and sent them off.

[4] So they, sent forth by the Holy Spirit, went down to Seleucia and from there sailed to Cyprus. [5A] When they arrived in Salamis, they proclaimed the word of God in the Jewish synagogues.

Responsorial Psalm: Psalms 67:2-3,5,6 & 8

R. [(4)] *O God, let all the nations praise you!* or: *Alleluia.*

[2] May God have pity on us and bless us;
     may he let his face shine upon us.
[3] So may your way be known upon earth;
     among all nations, your salvation.
R. *O God, let all the nations praise you!* or: *Alleluia.*

[5] May the nations be glad and exult
     because you rule the peoples in equity;
     the nations on the earth you guide.
R. *O God, let all the nations praise you!* or: *Alleluia.*

[6] May the peoples praise you, O God;
     may all the peoples praise you!
[8] May God bless us,
     and may all the ends of the earth fear
          him!
R. *O God, let all the nations praise you!* or: *Alleluia.*

Alleluia: John 8:12

R. Alleluia, alleluia.
[12] I am the light of the world, says the Lord;
whoever follows me will have the light of
          life.
R. Alleluia, alleluia.

Gospel: John 12:44-50

[44] Jesus cried out and said, "Whoever believes in me believes not only in me but also in the one who sent me, [45] and whoever sees me sees the one who sent me. [46] I came into the world as light, so that everyone who believes in me might not remain in darkness. [47] And if anyone hears my words and does not observe them, I do not condemn him, for I did not come to condemn the world but to save the world. [48] Whoever rejects me and does not accept my words has something to judge him: the word that I spoke, it will condemn him on the last day, [49] because I did not speak on my own, but the Father who sent me commanded me what to say and speak. [50] And I know that his commandment is eternal life. So what I say, I say as the Father told me."

Thursday April 25, 2024

Feast of Saint Mark the Evangelist

First Reading: 1 Peter 5:5B-14

[5B] Beloved: Clothe yourselves with humility in your dealings with one another, for:

God opposes the proud
but bestows favor on the humble.

[6] So humble yourselves under the mighty hand of God, that he may exalt you in due time. [7] Cast all your worries upon him because he cares for you.

[8] Be sober and vigilant. Your opponent the Devil is prowling around like a roaring lion looking for someone to devour. [9] Resist him, steadfast in faith, knowing that your brothers and sisters throughout the world undergo the same sufferings. [10] The God of all grace who called you to his eternal glory through Christ Jesus will himself restore, confirm, strengthen, and establish you after you have suffered a little. [11] To him be dominion forever. Amen.

[12] I write you this briefly through Silvanus, whom I consider a faithful brother, exhorting you and testifying that this is the true grace of God. Remain firm in it. [13] The chosen one at Babylon sends you greeting, as does Mark, my son. [14] Greet one another with a loving kiss. Peace to all of you who are in Christ.

Responsorial Psalm: Psalms 89:2-3,6-7,16-17

R. [(2)]*For ever I will sing the goodness of the Lord.* or: *Alleluia.*
[2] The favors of the LORD I will sing forever;
    through all generations my mouth shall
        proclaim your faithfulness.
[3] For you have said, "My kindness is
        established forever";
    in heaven you have confirmed your
        faithfulness.
R. *For ever I will sing the goodness of the Lord.* or: *Alleluia.*

⁶ The heavens proclaim your wonders, O LORD,
    and your faithfulness, in the assembly of
        the holy ones.
⁷ For who in the skies can rank with the LORD?
    Who is like the LORD among the sons of
        God?
R. For ever I will sing the goodness of the Lord. or: *Alleluia.*

¹⁶ Blessed the people who know the joyful
        shout;
    in the light of your countenance, O LORD,
        they walk.
¹⁷ At your name they rejoice all the day,
    and through your justice they are exalted.
R. For ever I will sing the goodness of the Lord. or: *Alleluia.*

Alleluia: 1 Corinthians 1:23A-24B

R. Alleluia, alleluia.
²³ᴬ We proclaim Christ crucified;
²⁴ᴮ he is the power of God and the wisdom of
        God.
R. Alleluia, alleluia.

Gospel: Mark 16:15-20

¹⁵ Jesus appeared to the Eleven and said to them: "Go into the whole world and proclaim the Gospel to every creature. ¹⁶ Whoever believes and is baptized will be saved; whoever does not believe will be condemned. ¹⁷ These signs will accompany those who believe: in my name they will drive out demons, they will speak new languages. ¹⁸ They will pick up serpents with their hands, and if they drink any deadly thing, it will not harm them. They will lay hands on the sick, and they will recover."

¹⁹ Then the Lord Jesus, after he spoke to them, was taken up into heaven and took his seat at the right hand of God. ²⁰ But they went forth and preached everywhere, while the Lord worked with them and confirmed the word through accompanying signs.

Friday April 26, 2024

Friday of the Fourth Week of Easter
First Reading: Acts 13:26-33

²⁶ When Paul came to Antioch in Pisidia, he said in the synagogue: "My brothers, children of the family of Abraham, and those others among you who are God-fearing, to us this word of salvation has been sent. ²⁷ The inhabitants of Jerusalem and their leaders failed to recognize him, and by condemning him they fulfilled the oracles of the prophets that are read sabbath after sabbath. ²⁸ For even though they found no grounds for a death

sentence, they asked Pilate to have him put to death, [29] and when they had accomplished all that was written about him, they took him down from the tree and placed him in a tomb. [30] But God raised him from the dead, [31] and for many days he appeared to those who had come up with him from Galilee to Jerusalem. These are now his witnesses before the people. [32] We ourselves are proclaiming this good news to you that what God promised our fathers [33] he has brought to fulfillment for us, their children, by raising up Jesus, as it is written in the second psalm, *You are my Son; this day I have begotten you.*"

Responsorial Psalm: Psalms 2:6-7, 8-9, 10-11AB

R. [7bc] *You are my Son; this day I have begotten you.* or: *Alleluia.*

[6] "I myself have set up my king
    on Zion, my holy mountain."
[7] I will proclaim the decree of the LORD:
    The LORD said to me, "You are my Son;
    this day I have begotten you."

R. *You are my Son; this day I have begotten you.* or: *Alleluia.*

[8] "Ask of me and I will give you
    the nations for an inheritance
    and the ends of the earth for your
        possession.
[9] You shall rule them with an iron rod;
    you shall shatter them like an earthen
        dish."

R. *You are my Son; this day I have begotten you.* or: *Alleluia.*

[10] And now, O kings, give heed;
    take warning, you rulers of the earth.
[11AB] Serve the LORD with fear, and rejoice before
        him;
    with trembling rejoice.

R. *You are my Son; this day I have begotten you.* or: *Alleluia.*

Alleluia: John 14:6

R. Alleluia, alleluia.

[6] I am the way and the truth and the life, says
        the Lord;
no one comes to the Father except through
        me.

R. Alleluia, alleluia.

Gospel: John 14:1-6

[1] Jesus said to his disciples: "Do not let your hearts be troubled. You have faith in God; have faith also in me. [2] In my Father's house there are many dwelling places. If there were

not, would I have told you that I am going to prepare a place for you? ³ And if I go and prepare a place for you, I will come back again and take you to myself, so that where I am you also may be. ⁴ Where I am going you know the way." ⁵ Thomas said to him, "Master, we do not know where you are going; how can we know the way?" ⁶ Jesus said to him, "I am the way and the truth and the life. No one comes to the Father except through me."

Saturday of the Fourth Week of Easter
First Reading: Acts 13:44-52

⁴⁴ On the following sabbath almost the whole city gathered to hear the word of the Lord. ⁴⁵ When the Jews saw the crowds, they were filled with jealousy and with violent abuse contradicted what Paul said. ⁴⁶ Both Paul and Barnabas spoke out boldly and said, "It was necessary that the word of God be spoken to you first, but since you reject it and condemn yourselves as unworthy of eternal life, we now turn to the Gentiles. ⁴⁷ For so the Lord has commanded us, *I have made you a light to the Gentiles, that you may be an instrument of salvation to the ends of the earth."*

⁴⁸ The Gentiles were delighted when they heard this and glorified the word of the Lord. All who were destined for eternal life came to believe, ⁴⁹ and the word of the Lord continued to spread through the whole region. ⁵⁰ The Jews, however, incited the women of prominence who were worshipers and the leading men of the city, stirred up a persecution against Paul and Barnabas, and expelled them from their territory. ⁵¹ So they shook the dust from their feet in protest against them and went to Iconium. ⁵² The disciples were filled with joy and the Holy Spirit.

Responsorial Psalm: Psalms 98:1, 2-3AB, 3CD-4

R. *(3cd)All the ends of the earth have seen the saving power of God.* or: *Alleluia.*

¹ Sing to the LORD a new song,
for he has done wondrous deeds;
His right hand has won victory for him,
his holy arm.

R. *All the ends of the earth have seen the saving power of God.* or: *Alleluia.*

² The LORD has made his salvation known:
in the sight of the nations he has revealed
his justice.
³ᴬᴮ He has remembered his kindness and his
faithfulness
toward the house of Israel.

R. *All the ends of the earth have seen the saving power of God.* or: *Alleluia.*

³ᶜᴰ All the ends of the earth have seen
the salvation by our God.
⁴ Sing joyfully to the LORD, all you lands;

break into song; sing praise.
R. All the ends of the earth have seen the saving power of God. or: *Alleluia.*

Alleluia: John 8:31B-32
R. Alleluia, alleluia.
[31B] If you remain in my word, you will truly be
      my disciples,
[32] and you will know the truth, says the Lord.
R. Alleluia, alleluia.

Gospel: John 14:7-14
[7] Jesus said to his disciples: "If you know me, then you will also know my Father. From now on you do know him and have seen him." [8] Philip said to Jesus, "Master, show us the Father, and that will be enough for us." [9] Jesus said to him, "Have I been with you for so long a time and you still do not know me, Philip? Whoever has seen me has seen the Father. How can you say, 'Show us the Father'? [10] Do you not believe that I am in the Father and the Father is in me? The words that I speak to you I do not speak on my own. The Father who dwells in me is doing his works. [11] Believe me that I am in the Father and the Father is in me, or else, believe because of the works themselves. [12] Amen, amen, I say to you, whoever believes in me will do the works that I do, and will do greater ones than these, because I am going to the Father. [13] And whatever you ask in my name, I will do, so that the Father may be glorified in the Son. [14] If you ask anything of me in my name, I will do it."

Sunday April 28, 2024

Fifth Sunday of Easter, Year B
First Reading: Acts 9:26-31
[26] When Saul arrived in Jerusalem he tried to join the disciples, but they were all afraid of him, not believing that he was a disciple. [27] Then Barnabas took charge of him and brought him to the apostles, and he reported to them how he had seen the Lord, and that he had spoken to him, and how in Damascus he had spoken out boldly in the name of Jesus. [28] He moved about freely with them in Jerusalem, and spoke out boldly in the name of the Lord. [29] He also spoke and debated with the Hellenists, but they tried to kill him. [30] And when the brothers learned of this, they took him down to Caesarea and sent him on his way to Tarsus.

[31] The church throughout all Judea, Galilee, and Samaria was at peace. It was being built up and walked in the fear of the Lord, and with the consolation of the Holy Spirit it grew in numbers.

Responsorial Psalm: Psalms 22:26-27, 28, 30, 31-32
R. [26a] **I will praise you, Lord, in the assembly of**
      your people. or: *Alleluia.*
[26] I will fulfill my vows before those who fear

the LORD.
²⁷ The lowly shall eat their fill;
they who seek the LORD shall praise him:
"May your hearts live forever!"
*R. I will praise you, Lord, in the assembly of your
people. or: Alleluia.*

²⁸ All the ends of the earth
    shall remember and turn to the LORD;
all the families of the nations
    shall bow down before him.
*R. I will praise you, Lord, in the assembly of your
people. or: Alleluia.*

³⁰ To him alone shall bow down
    all who sleep in the earth;
before him shall bend
    all who go down into the dust.
*R. I will praise you, Lord, in the assembly of your
people. or: Alleluia.*

³¹ And to him my soul shall live;
    my descendants shall serve him.
³² Let the coming generation be told of the LORD
        that they may proclaim to a people yet to
            be born
        the justice he has shown.
*R. I will praise you, Lord, in the assembly of your
people. or: Alleluia.*

Second Reading: 1 John 3:18-24

¹⁸ Children, let us love not in word or speech but in deed and truth. ¹⁹ Now this is how we shall know that we belong to the truth and reassure our hearts before him ²⁰ in whatever our hearts condemn, for God is greater than our hearts and knows everything. ²¹ Beloved, if our hearts do not condemn us, we have confidence in God ²² and receive from him whatever we ask, because we keep his commandments and do what pleases him. ²³ And his commandment is this: we should believe in the name of his Son, Jesus Christ, and love one another just as he commanded us. ²⁴ Those who keep his commandments remain in him, and he in them, and the way we know that he remains in us is from the Spirit he gave us.

Alleluia: John 15:4A, 5B

R. Alleluia, alleluia.

⁴ᴬ Remain in me as I remain in you, says the
        Lord.

5B Whoever remains in me will bear much
fruit.
R. Alleluia, alleluia.

Gospel: John 15:1-8

Jesus said to his disciples: ¹ "I am the true vine, and my Father is the vine grower. ² He takes away every branch in me that does not bear fruit, and every one that does he prunes so that it bears more fruit. ³ You are already pruned because of the word that I spoke to you. ⁴ Remain in me, as I remain in you. Just as a branch cannot bear fruit on its own unless it remains on the vine, so neither can you unless you remain in me. ⁵ I am the vine, you are the branches. Whoever remains in me and I in him will bear much fruit, because without me you can do nothing. ⁶ Anyone who does not remain in me will be thrown out like a branch and wither; people will gather them and throw them into a fire and they will be burned. ⁷ If you remain in me and my words remain in you, ask for whatever you want and it will be done for you. ⁸ By this is my Father glorified, that you bear much fruit and become my disciples."

Saint Catherine of Siena, Virgin and Doctor
First Reading: Acts 14:5-18

⁵ There was an attempt in Iconium by both the Gentiles and the Jews, together with their leaders, to attack and stone Paul and Barnabas. ⁶ They realized it, and fled to the Lycaonian cities of Lystra and Derbe and to the surrounding countryside, ⁷ where they continued to proclaim the Good News.

⁸ At Lystra there was a crippled man, lame from birth, who had never walked. ⁹ He listened to Paul speaking, who looked intently at him, saw that he had the faith to be healed, ¹⁰ and called out in a loud voice, "Stand up straight on your feet." He jumped up and began to walk about. ¹¹ When the crowds saw what Paul had done, they cried out in Lycaonian, "The gods have come down to us in human form." ¹² They called Barnabas "Zeus" and Paul "Hermes," because he was the chief speaker. ¹³ And the priest of Zeus, whose temple was at the entrance to the city, brought oxen and garlands to the gates, for he together with the people intended to offer sacrifice.

¹⁴ The Apostles Barnabas and Paul tore their garments when they heard this and rushed out into the crowd, shouting, ¹⁵ "Men, why are you doing this? We are of the same nature as you, human beings. We proclaim to you good news that you should turn from these idols to the living God, *who made heaven and earth and sea and all that is in them.* ¹⁶ In past generations he allowed all Gentiles to go their own ways; ¹⁷ yet, in bestowing his goodness, he did not leave himself without witness, for he gave you rains from heaven and fruitful seasons, and filled you with nourishment and gladness for your hearts." ¹⁸ Even with these words, they scarcely restrained the crowds from offering sacrifice to them.

Responsorial Psalm: Psalms 115:1-2, 3-4, 15-16

R. *(1ab)Not to us, O Lord, but to your name give the glory.* or: *Alleluia.*

[1] Not to us, O LORD, not to us
> but to your name give glory
> because of your mercy, because of your
>> truth.

[2] Why should the pagans say,
> "Where is their God?"

R. *Not to us, O Lord, but to your name give the glory.* or: *Alleluia.*

[3] Our God is in heaven;
> whatever he wills, he does.

[4] Their idols are silver and gold,
> the handiwork of men.

R. *Not to us, O Lord, but to your name give the glory.* or: *Alleluia.*

[15] May you be blessed by the LORD,
> who made heaven and earth.

[16] Heaven is the heaven of the LORD,
> but the earth he has given to the children
>> of men.

R. *Not to us, O Lord, but to your name give the glory.* or: *Alleluia.*

Alleluia: John 14:26

R. Alleluia, alleluia.

[26] The Holy Spirit will teach you everything and remind you of all I told you.

R. Alleluia, alleluia.

Gospel: John 14:21-26

[21] Jesus said to his disciples: "Whoever has my commandments and observes them is the one who loves me. Whoever loves me will be loved by my Father, and I will love him and reveal myself to him." [22] Judas, not the Iscariot, said to him, "Master, then what happened that you will reveal yourself to us and not to the world?" [23] Jesus answered and said to him, "Whoever loves me will keep my word, and my Father will love him, and we will come to him and make our dwelling with him. [24] Whoever does not love me does not keep my words; yet the word you hear is not mine but that of the Father who sent me.

[25] "I have told you this while I am with you. [26] The Advocate, the Holy Spirit whom the Father will send in my name— he will teach you everything and remind you of all that I told you."

Tuesday April 30, 2024

Tuesday of the Fifth Week of Easter

First Reading: Acts 14:19-28

[19] In those days, some Jews from Antioch and Iconium arrived and won over the crowds. They stoned Paul and dragged him out of the city, supposing that he was dead. [20] But when the disciples gathered around him, he got up and entered the city. On the following day he left with Barnabas for Derbe.

[21] After they had proclaimed the good news to that city and made a considerable number of disciples, they returned to Lystra and to Iconium and to Antioch. [22] They strengthened the spirits of the disciples and exhorted them to persevere in the faith, saying, "It is necessary for us to undergo many hardships to enter the Kingdom of God." [23] They appointed presbyters for them in each Church and, with prayer and fasting, commended them to the Lord in whom they had put their faith. [24] Then they traveled through Pisidia and reached Pamphylia. [25] After proclaiming the word at Perga they went down to Attalia. [26] From there they sailed to Antioch, where they had been commended to the grace of God for the work they had now accomplished. [27] And when they arrived, they called the Church together and reported what God had done with them and how he had opened the door of faith to the Gentiles. [28] Then they spent no little time with the disciples.

Responsial Psalm: Psalms 145:10-11, 12-13AB, 21

R. (see 12) *Your friends make known, O Lord, the*
glorious splendor of your kingdom.

or: *Alleluia.*

[10] Let all your works give you thanks, O LORD,
and let your faithful ones bless you.
[11] Let them discourse of the glory of your
kingdom
and speak of your might.

R. *Your friends make known, O Lord, the*
glorious splendor of your kingdom.

or: *Alleluia.*

[12] Making known to men your might
and the glorious splendor of your
kingdom.
[13AB] Your kingdom is a kingdom for all ages,
and your dominion endures through all
generations.

R. Your friends make known, O Lord, the
        glorious splendor of your kingdom.
or: *Alleluia.*

[21] May my mouth speak the praise of the LORD,
        and may all flesh bless his holy name
                forever and ever.
R. Your friends make known, O Lord, the
        glorious splendor of your kingdom.
or: *Alleluia.*

Alleluia: cf. Luke 24:46, 26
R. Alleluia, alleluia.
[46] Christ had to suffer and to rise from the
        dead,
[26] and so enter into his glory.
R. Alleluia, alleluia.

Gospel: John 14:27-31A
[27] Jesus said to his disciples: "Peace I leave with you; my peace I give to you. Not as the world gives do I give it to you. Do not let your hearts be troubled or afraid. [28] You heard me tell you, 'I am going away and I will come back to you.' If you loved me, you would rejoice that I am going to the Father; for the Father is greater than I. [29] And now I have told you this before it happens, so that when it happens you may believe. [30] I will no longer speak much with you, for the ruler of the world is coming. He has no power over me, [31A] but the world must know that I love the Father and that I do just as the Father has commanded me."

Wednesday of the Fifth Week of Easter
First Reading: Acts 15:1-6
[1] Some who had come down from Judea were instructing the brothers, "Unless you are circumcised according to the Mosaic practice, you cannot be saved." [2] Because there arose no little dissension and debate by Paul and Barnabas with them, it was decided that Paul, Barnabas, and some of the others should go up to Jerusalem to the Apostles and presbyters about this question. [3] They were sent on their journey by the Church, and passed through Phoenicia and Samaria telling of the conversion of the Gentiles, and brought great joy to all the brethren. [4] When they arrived in Jerusalem, they were welcomed by the Church, as well as by the Apostles and the presbyters, and they reported what God had done with them. [5] But some from the party of the Pharisees who had become believers stood up and said, "It is necessary to circumcise them and direct them to observe the Mosaic law."
        [6] The Apostles and the presbyters met together to see about this matter.

Responsorial Psalm: Psalms 122:1-2, 3-4AB, 4CD-5

R. *(see 1)***Let us go rejoicing to the house of the Lord.** or: *Alleluia*.

[1] I rejoiced because they said to me,
  "We will go up to the house of the LORD."
[2] And now we have set foot
  within your gates, O Jerusalem.

R. Let us go rejoicing to the house of the Lord. or: *Alleluia.*

[3] Jerusalem, built as a city
  with compact unity.
[4AB] To it the tribes go up,
  the tribes of the LORD.

R. Let us go rejoicing to the house of the Lord. or: *Alleluia.*

[4CD] According to the decree for Israel,
  to give thanks to the name of the LORD.
[5] In it are set up judgment seats,
  seats for the house of David.

R. Let us go rejoicing to the house of the Lord. or: *Alleluia.*

Alleluia: John 15:4A, 5B

R. Alleluia, alleluia.

[4A] Remain in me, as I remain in you, says the
    Lord;
[5B] whoever remains in me will bear much fruit.

R. Alleluia, alleluia.

Gospel: John 15:1-8

[1] Jesus said to his disciples: "I am the true vine, and my Father is the vine grower. [2] He takes away every branch in me that does not bear fruit, and everyone that does he prunes so that it bears more fruit. [3] You are already pruned because of the word that I spoke to you. [4] Remain in me, as I remain in you. Just as a branch cannot bear fruit on its own unless it remains on the vine, so neither can you unless you remain in me. [5] I am the vine, you are the branches. Whoever remains in me and I in him will bear much fruit, because without me you can do nothing. [6] Anyone who does not remain in me will be thrown out like a branch and wither; people will gather them and throw them into a fire and they will be burned. [7] If you remain in me and my words remain in you, ask for whatever you want and it will be done for you. [8] By this is my Father glorified, that you bear much fruit and become my disciples."

Memorial of Saint Athanasius – Bp and Doc

First Reading: Acts 15:7-21

[7] After much debate had taken place, Peter got up and said to the Apostles and the presbyters, "My brothers, you are well aware that from early days God made his choice among you that through my mouth the Gentiles would hear the word of the Gospel and believe. [8] And God, who knows the heart, bore witness by granting them the Holy Spirit just as he did us. [9] He made no distinction between us and them, for by faith he purified their hearts. [10] Why, then, are you now putting God to the test by placing on the shoulders of the disciples a yoke that neither our ancestors nor we have been able to bear? [11] On the contrary, we believe that we are saved through the grace of the Lord Jesus, in the same way as they." [12] The whole assembly fell silent, and they listened while Paul and Barnabas described the signs and wonders God had worked among the Gentiles through them.

[13] After they had fallen silent, James responded, "My brothers, listen to me. [14] Symeon has described how God first concerned himself with acquiring from among the Gentiles a people for his name. [15] The words of the prophets agree with this, as is written:

[16] *After this I shall return*
and rebuild the fallen hut of David;
from its ruins I shall rebuild it
and raise it up again,
[17] *so that the rest of humanity may seek out the*
Lord,
even all the Gentiles on whom my name is
invoked.
Thus says the Lord who accomplishes these
things,
[18] *known from of old.*

[19] It is my judgment, therefore, that we ought to stop troubling the Gentiles who turn to God, [20] but tell them by letter to avoid pollution from idols, unlawful marriage, the meat of strangled animals, and blood. [21] For Moses, for generations now, has had those who proclaim him in every town, as he has been read in the synagogues every sabbath."

Responsorial Psalm: Psalms 96:1-2A,2B-3,10

R. [(3)]*Proclaim God's marvelous deeds to all the*
nations. or: *Alleluia.*

[1] Sing to the LORD a new song;
sing to the LORD, all you lands.
[2A] Sing to the LORD; bless his name.

R. *Proclaim God's marvelous deeds to all the*
nations. or: *Alleluia.*

2B Announce his salvation, day after day.
3Tell his glory among the nations;
    among all peoples, his wondrous deeds.
R. Proclaim God's marvelous deeds to all the
    nations. or: **Alleluia.**

10Say among the nations: The LORD is king.
He has made the world firm, not to be
        moved;
    he governs the peoples with equity.
R. Proclaim God's marvelous deeds to all the
    nations. or: **Alleluia.**

Alleluia: John 10:27

R. Alleluia, alleluia.
[27] My sheep hear my voice, says the Lord;
I know them, and they follow me.
R. Alleluia, alleluia.

Gospel: John 15:9-11

[9] Jesus said to his disciples: "As the Father loves me, so I also love you. Remain in my love. [10] If you keep my commandments, you will remain in my love, just as I have kept my Father's commandments and remain in his love.

[11] "I have told you this so that my joy might be in you and your joy might be complete."

Friday May 3, 2024

Feast of Saints Philip and James, Apostles
First Reading: 1 Corinthians 15:1-8

[1] I am reminding you, brothers and sisters, of the Gospel I preached to you, which you indeed received and in which you also stand. [2] Through it you are also being saved, if you hold fast to the word I preached to you, unless you believed in vain. [3] For I handed on to you as of first importance what I also received: that Christ died for our sins in accordance with the Scriptures; [4] that he was buried; that he was raised on the third day in accordance with the Scriptures; [5] that he appeared to Cephas, then to the Twelve. [6] After that, he appeared to more than five hundred brothers and sisters at once, most of whom are still living, though some have fallen asleep. [7] After that he appeared to James, then to all the Apostles. [8] Last of all, as to one born abnormally, he appeared to me.

Responsorial Psalm: Psalms 19:2-3, 4-5

R. [5] **Their message goes out through all the earth.** or: **Alleluia.**
[2] The heavens declare the glory of God;

and the firmament proclaims his
      handiwork.
³ Day pours out the word to day;
      and night to night imparts knowledge.
R. Their message goes out through all the earth. or: **Alleluia.**

⁴ Not a word nor a discourse
      whose voice is not heard;
⁵ Through all the earth their voice resounds,
      and to the ends of the world, their
            message.
R. Their message goes out through all the earth. or: **Alleluia.**

Alleluia: John 14:6B, 9C
R. Alleluia, alleluia.
⁶ᴮ I am the way, the truth, and the life, says the
      Lord;
⁹ᶜ Philip, whoever has seen me has seen the
      Father.
R. Alleluia, alleluia.

Gospel: John 14:6-14
⁶ Jesus said to Thomas, "I am the way and the truth and the life. No one comes to the Father except through me. ⁷ If you know me, then you will also know my Father. From now on you do know him and have seen him." ⁸ Philip said to him, "Master, show us the Father, and that will be enough for us." ⁹ Jesus said to him, "Have I been with you for so long a time and you still do not know me, Philip? Whoever has seen me has seen the Father. How can you say, 'Show us the Father'? ¹⁰ Do you not believe that I am in the Father and the Father is in me? The words that I speak to you I do not speak on my own. The Father who dwells in me is doing his works. ¹¹ Believe me that I am in the Father and the Father is in me, or else, believe because of the works themselves. ¹² Amen, amen, I say to you, whoever believes in me will do the works that I do, and will do greater ones than these, because I am going to the Father. ¹³ And whatever you ask in my name, I will do, so that the Father may be glorified in the Son. ¹⁴ If you ask anything of me in my name, I will do it."

Saturday May 4, 2024

Saturday of the Fifth Week of Easter
First Reading: Acts 16:1-10
¹ Paul reached also Derbe and Lystra where there was a disciple named Timothy, the son of a Jewish woman who was a believer, but his father was a Greek. ² The brothers in Lystra and Iconium spoke highly of him, ³ and Paul wanted him to come along with him. On account of the Jews of that region, Paul had him circumcised, for they all knew that his

father was a Greek. [4] As they traveled from city to city, they handed on to the people for observance the decisions reached by the Apostles and presbyters in Jerusalem. [5] Day after day the churches grew stronger in faith and increased in number.

[6] They travelled through the Phrygian and Galatian territory because they had been prevented by the Holy Spirit from preaching the message in the province of Asia. [7] When they came to Mysia, they tried to go on into Bithynia, but the Spirit of Jesus did not allow them, [8] so they crossed through Mysia and came down to Troas. [9] During the night Paul had a vision. A Macedonian stood before him and implored him with these words, "Come over to Macedonia and help us." [10] When he had seen the vision, we sought passage to Macedonia at once, concluding that God had called us to proclaim the Good News to them.

Responsorial Psalm: Psalms 100:1B-2, 3, 5

R. [2a]*Let all the earth cry out to God with joy.* or: *Alleluia.*

[1B] Sing joyfully to the LORD, all you lands;
> [2] serve the LORD with gladness;
> come before him with joyful song.

R. *Let all the earth cry out to God with joy.* or: *Alleluia.*

[3] Know that the LORD is God;
> he made us, his we are;
> his people, the flock he tends.

R. *Let all the earth cry out to God with joy.* or: *Alleluia.*

[5] The LORD is good:
> his kindness endures forever,
> and his faithfulness, to all generations.

R. *Let all the earth cry out to God with joy.* or: *Alleluia.*

Alleluia: Colossians 3:1

R. Alleluia, alleluia.

[1] If then you were raised with Christ,
seek what is above,
where Christ is seated at the right hand of
> God.

R. Alleluia, alleluia.

Gospel: John 15:18-21

[18] Jesus said to his disciples: "If the world hates you, realize that it hated me first. [19] If you belonged to the world, the world would love its own; but because you do not belong to the world, and I have chosen you out of the world, the world hates you. [20] Remember the word I spoke to you, 'No slave is greater than his master.' If they persecuted me, they will

also persecute you. If they kept my word, they will also keep yours. [21] And they will do all these things to you on account of my name, because they do not know the one who sent me."

Sixth Sunday of Easter, Year B
First Reading: Acts 10:25-26, 34-35, 44-48

[25] When Peter entered, Cornelius met him and, falling at his feet, paid him homage. [26] Peter, however, raised him up, saying, "Get up. I myself am also a human being."

[34] Then Peter proceeded to speak and said, "In truth, I see that God shows no partiality. [35] Rather, in every nation whoever fears him and acts uprightly is acceptable to him."

[44] While Peter was still speaking these things, the Holy Spirit fell upon all who were listening to the word. [45] The circumcised believers who had accompanied Peter were astounded that the gift of the Holy Spirit should have been poured out on the Gentiles also, [46] for they could hear them speaking in tongues and glorifying God. Then Peter responded, [47] "Can anyone withhold the water for baptizing these people, who have received the Holy Spirit even as we have?" [48] He ordered them to be baptized in the name of Jesus Christ.

Responsorial Psalm: Psalms 98:1, 2-3, 3-4

R. (cf. 2b) **The Lord has revealed to the nations his saving power.** or: *Alleluia.*

[1] Sing to the LORD a new song,
    for he has done wondrous deeds;
His right hand has won victory for him,
    his holy arm.
R. **The Lord has revealed to the nations his saving power.** or: *Alleluia.*

[2] The LORD has made his salvation known:
    in the sight of the nations he has revealed
        his justice.
[3AB] He has remembered his kindness and his
        faithfulness
    toward the house of Israel.
R. **The Lord has revealed to the nations his saving power.** or: *Alleluia.*

[3BC] All the ends of the earth have seen
    the salvation by our God.
[4] Sing joyfully to the LORD, all you lands;
    break into song; sing praise.
R. **The Lord has revealed to the nations his**

saving power. or: *Alleluia.*

Second Reading: 1 John 4:7-10

[7] Beloved, let us love one another, because love is of God; everyone who loves is begotten by God and knows God. [8] Whoever is without love does not know God, for God is love. [9] In this way the love of God was revealed to us: God sent his only Son into the world so that we might have life through him. [10] In this is love: not that we have loved God, but that he loved us and sent his Son as expiation for our sins.

Alleluia: John 14:23

R. Alleluia, alleluia.

[23] Whoever loves me will keep my word,
        says the Lord,
and my Father will love him and we will
        come to him.

R. Alleluia, alleluia.

Gospel: John 15:9-17

Jesus said to his disciples: [9] "As the Father loves me, so I also love you. Remain in my love. [10] If you keep my commandments, you will remain in my love, just as I have kept my Father's commandments and remain in his love.

[11] "I have told you this so that my joy may be in you and your joy might be complete. [12] This is my commandment: love one another as I love you. [13] No one has greater love than this, to lay down one's life for one's friends. [14] You are my friends if you do what I command you. [15] I no longer call you slaves, because a slave does not know what his master is doing. I have called you friends, because I have told you everything I have heard from my Father. [16] It was not you who chose me, but I who chose you and appointed you to go and bear fruit that will remain, so that whatever you ask the Father in my name he may give you. [17] This I command you: love one another."

Monday May 6, 2024

Monday of the Sixth Week of Easter

First Reading: Acts 16:11-15

[11] We set sail from Troas, making a straight run for Samothrace, and on the next day to Neapolis, [12] and from there to Philippi, a leading city in that district of Macedonia and a Roman colony. We spent some time in that city. [13] On the sabbath we went outside the city gate along the river where we thought there would be a place of prayer. We sat and spoke with the women who had gathered there. [14] One of them, a woman named Lydia, a dealer in purple cloth, from the city of Thyatira, a worshiper of God, listened, and the Lord opened her heart to pay attention to what Paul was saying. [15] After she and her household had been baptized, she offered us an invitation, "If you consider me a believer in the Lord, come and stay at my home," and she prevailed on us.

Responsorial Psalm: Psalms 149:1B-2, 3-4, 5-6A AND 9B

R. *(see 4a)* **The Lord takes delight in his people.** or: *Alleluia.*

1B Sing to the LORD a new song
of praise in the assembly of the faithful.
2 Let Israel be glad in their maker,
let the children of Zion rejoice in their
king.

R. **The Lord takes delight in his people.** or: *Alleluia.*

3 Let them praise his name in the festive
dance,
let them sing praise to him with timbrel
and harp.
4 For the LORD loves his people,
and he adorns the lowly with victory.

R. **The Lord takes delight in his people.** or: *Alleluia.*

5 Let the faithful exult in glory;
let them sing for joy upon their couches.
6A Let the high praises of God be in their
throats.
9B This is the glory of all his faithful.
Alleluia.

R. **The Lord takes delight in his people.** or: *Alleluia.*

Alleluia: John 15:26B, 27A

R. Alleluia, alleluia.

26B The Spirit of truth will testify to me, says the
Lord,
27A and you also will testify.

R. Alleluia, alleluia.

Gospel: John 15:26-16:4A

26 Jesus said to his disciples: "When the Advocate comes whom I will send you from the Father, the Spirit of truth who proceeds from the Father, he will testify to me. 27 And you also testify, because you have been with me from the beginning.

1 "I have told you this so that you may not fall away. 2 They will expel you from the synagogues; in fact, the hour is coming when everyone who kills you will think he is offering worship to God. 3 They will do this because they have not known either the Father or me. 4A I have told you this so that when their hour comes you may remember that I told you."

Tuesday of the Sixth Week of Easter
First Reading: Acts 16:22-34

22 The crowd in Philippi joined in the attack on Paul and Silas, and the magistrates had them stripped and ordered them to be beaten with rods. 23 After inflicting many blows on them, they threw them into prison and instructed the jailer to guard them securely. 24 When he received these instructions, he put them in the innermost cell and secured their feet to a stake.

25 About midnight, while Paul and Silas were praying and singing hymns to God as the prisoners listened, 26 there was suddenly such a severe earthquake that the foundations of the jail shook; all the doors flew open, and the chains of all were pulled loose. 27 When the jailer woke up and saw the prison doors wide open, he drew his sword and was about to kill himself, thinking that the prisoners had escaped. 28 But Paul shouted out in a loud voice, "Do no harm to yourself; we are all here."

29 He asked for a light and rushed in and, trembling with fear, he fell down before Paul and Silas. 30 Then he brought them out and said, "Sirs, what must I do to be saved?" 31 And they said, "Believe in the Lord Jesus and you and your household will be saved." 32 So they spoke the word of the Lord to him and to everyone in his house. 33 He took them in at that hour of the night and bathed their wounds; then he and all his family were baptized at once. 34 He brought them up into his house and provided a meal and with his household rejoiced at having come to faith in God.

Responsorial Psalm: Psalms 138:1-2AB, 2CDE-3, 7C-8

R. (7c)*Your right hand saves me, O Lord.* or: *Alleluia.*

1 I will give thanks to you, O LORD, with all my
	heart,
	for you have heard the words of my
	mouth;
	in the presence of the angels I will sing
	your praise;
2AB I will worship at your holy temple,
	and give thanks to your name.

R. *Your right hand saves me, O Lord.* or: *Alleluia.*

2CDE Because of your kindness and your truth,
	you have made great above all things
	your name and your promise.
3 When I called, you answered me;
	you built up strength within me.

R. *Your right hand saves me, O Lord.* or: *Alleluia.*

7C Your right hand saves me.

⁸ The LORD will complete what he has done for
            me;
      your kindness, O LORD, endures forever;
      forsake not the work of your hands.
R. Your right hand saves me, O Lord. or: *Alleluia.*

Alleluia: cf. John 16:7, 13
R. Alleluia, alleluia.
⁷ I will send to you the Spirit of truth, says the
            Lord;
¹³ he will guide you to all truth.
R. Alleluia, alleluia.

Gospel: John 16:5-11
⁵ Jesus said to his disciples: "Now I am going to the one who sent me, and not one of you asks me, 'Where are you going?' ⁶ But because I told you this, grief has filled your hearts. ⁷ But I tell you the truth, it is better for you that I go. For if I do not go, the Advocate will not come to you. But if I go, I will send him to you. ⁸ And when he comes he will convict the world in regard to sin and righteousness and condemnation: ⁹ sin, because they do not believe in me; ¹⁰ righteousness, because I am going to the Father and you will no longer see me; ¹¹ condemnation, because the ruler of this world has been condemned."

Wednesday of the Sixth Week of Easter
First Reading: Acts 17:15, 22-18:1
¹⁵ After Paul's escorts had taken him to Athens, they came away with instructions for Silas and Timothy to join him as soon as possible.

    ²² Then Paul stood up at the Areopagus and said: "You Athenians, I see that in every respect you are very religious. ²³ For as I walked around looking carefully at your shrines, I even discovered an altar inscribed, 'To an Unknown God.' What therefore you unknowingly worship, I proclaim to you. ²⁴ The God who made the world and all that is in it, the Lord of heaven and earth, does not dwell in sanctuaries made by human hands, ²⁵ nor is he served by human hands because he needs anything. Rather it is he who gives to everyone life and breath and everything. ²⁶ He made from one the whole human race to dwell on the entire surface of the earth, and he fixed the ordered seasons and the boundaries of their regions, ²⁷ so that people might seek God, even perhaps grope for him and find him, though indeed he is not far from any one of us. ²⁸ For 'In him, we live and move and have our being,' as even some of your poets have said, 'For we too are his offspring.'

²⁹ Since therefore we are the offspring of God, we ought not to think that the divinity is like an image fashioned from gold, silver, or stone by human art and imagination. ³⁰ God has overlooked the times of ignorance, but now he demands that all people everywhere repent ³¹ because he has established a day on which he will 'judge the world with justice'

through a man, he has appointed, and he has provided confirmation for all by raising him from the dead."

³² When they heard about resurrection of the dead, some began to scoff, but others said, "We should like to hear you on this some other time." ³³ And so Paul left them. ³⁴ But some did join him, and became believers. Among them were Dionysius, a member of the Court of the Areopagus, a woman named Damaris, and others with them.

¹ After this he left Athens and went to Corinth.

Responsorial Psalm: Psalms 148:1-2, 11-12, 13, 14

R. Heaven and earth are full of your glory. or: *Alleluia.*

¹ Praise the LORD from the heavens;
   praise him in the heights.
² Praise him, all you his angels;
   praise him, all you his hosts.

R. Heaven and earth are full of your glory. or: *Alleluia.*

¹¹ Let the kings of the earth and all peoples,
   the princes and all the judges of the
      earth,
¹² Young men too, and maidens,
   old men and boys.

R. Heaven and earth are full of your glory. or: *Alleluia.*

¹³ Praise the name of the LORD,
   for his name alone is exalted;
His majesty is above earth and heaven.

R. Heaven and earth are full of your glory. or: *Alleluia.*

¹⁴ He has lifted up the horn of his people;
Be this his praise from all his faithful ones,
   from the children of Israel, the people
      close to him.
Alleluia.

R. Heaven and earth are full of your glory. or: *Alleluia.'*

Alleluia: John 14:16

R. Alleluia, alleluia.
¹⁶ I will ask the Father
and he will give you another Advocate
to be with you always.
R. Alleluia, alleluia.

Gospel: John 16:12-15

Jesus said to his disciples: [12] "I have much more to tell you, but you cannot bear it now. [13] But when he comes, the Spirit of truth, he will guide you to all truth. He will not speak on his own, but he will speak what he hears, and will declare to you the things that are coming. [14] He will glorify me, because he will take from what is mine and declare it to you. [15] Everything that the Father has is mine; for this reason, I told you that he will take from what is mine and declare it to you."

Thursday May 9, 2024

Thursday before Ascension Sunday
First Reading: Acts 18:1-8

[1] Paul left Athens and went to Corinth. [2] There he met a Jew named Aquila, a native of Pontus, who had recently come from Italy with his wife Priscilla because Claudius had ordered all the Jews to leave Rome. He went to visit them [3] and, because he practised the same trade, stayed with them and worked, for they were tentmakers by trade. [4] Every sabbath, he entered into discussions in the synagogue, attempting to convince both Jews and Greeks.

[5] When Silas and Timothy came down from Macedonia, Paul began to occupy himself totally with preaching the word, testifying to the Jews that the Christ was Jesus. [6] When they opposed him and reviled him, he shook out his garments and said to them, "Your blood be on your heads! I am clear of responsibility. From now on I will go to the Gentiles." [7] So he left there and went to a house belonging to a man named Titus Justus, a worshiper of God; his house was next to a synagogue. [8] Crispus, the synagogue official, came to believe in the Lord along with his entire household, and many of the Corinthians who heard believed and were baptized.

Responsorial Psalm: Psalms 98:1, 2-3AB, 3CD-4

R. (see 2b) *The Lord has revealed to the nations his*
saving power. or: *Alleluia.*

[1] Sing to the LORD a new song,
for he has done wondrous deeds;
His right hand has won victory for him,
his holy arm.
R. *The Lord has revealed to the nations his*
saving power. or: *Alleluia.*

[2] The LORD has made his salvation known:
in the sight of the nations he has revealed
his justice.
[3AB] He has remembered his kindness and his
faithfulness
toward the house of Israel.
R. *The Lord has revealed to the nations his*
saving power. or: *Alleluia.*

^{3CD} All the ends of the earth have seen
     the salvation by our God.
⁴ Sing joyfully to the LORD, all you lands;
     break into song; sing praise.
R. The Lord has revealed to the nations his
       saving power. or: *Alleluia.*

Alleluia: John 14:18

R. Alleluia, alleluia.
¹⁵ I will not leave you orphans, says the Lord;
I will come back to you, and your hearts will
     rejoice.
R. Alleluia, alleluia.

Gospel: John 16:16-20

¹⁶ Jesus said to his disciples: "A little while and you will no longer see me, and again a little while later and you will see me." ¹⁷ So some of his disciples said to one another, "What does this mean that he is saying to us, 'A little while and you will not see me, and again a little while and you will see me,' and 'Because I am going to the Father'?" ¹⁸ So they said, "What is this 'little while' of which he speaks? We do not know what he means." ¹⁹ Jesus knew that they wanted to ask him, so he said to them, "Are you discussing with one another what I said, 'A little while and you will not see me, and again a little while and you will see me'? ²⁰ Amen, amen, I say to you, you will weep and mourn, while the world rejoices; you will grieve, but your grief will become joy."

Friday May 10, 2024

Friday before Ascension Sunday
First Reading: Acts 18:9-18

⁹ One night while Paul was in Corinth, the Lord said to him in a vision, "Do not be afraid. Go on speaking, and do not be silent, ¹⁰ for I am with you. No one will attack and harm you, for I have many people in this city." ¹¹He settled there for a year and a half and taught the word of God among them.

    ¹² But when Gallio was proconsul of Achaia, the Jews rose up together against Paul and brought him to the tribunal, ¹³ saying, "This man is inducing people to worship God contrary to the law." ¹⁴ When Paul was about to reply, Gallio spoke to the Jews, "If it were a matter of some crime or malicious fraud, I should with reason hear the complaint of you Jews; ¹⁵ but since it is a question of arguments over doctrine and titles and your own law, see to it yourselves. I do not wish to be a judge of such matters." ¹⁶ And he drove them away from the tribunal. ¹⁷ They all seized Sosthenes, the synagogue official, and beat him in full view of the tribunal. But none of this was of concern to Gallio.

[18] Paul remained for quite some time, and after saying farewell to the brothers he sailed for Syria, together with Priscilla and Aquila. At Cenchreae he had shaved his head because he had taken a vow.

Responsorial Psalm: Psalms 47:2-3, 4-5, 6-7

R. *(8a)* **God is king of all the earth.** or: ***Alleluia.***

[2] All you peoples, clap your hands,
  shout to God with cries of gladness,
[3] For the LORD, the Most High, the awesome,
  is the great king over all the earth.

R. *God is king of all the earth.* or: *Alleluia.*

[4] He brings people under us;
  nations under our feet.
[5] He chooses for us our inheritance,
  the glory of Jacob, whom he loves.

R. *God is king of all the earth.* or: *Alleluia.*

[6] God mounts his throne amid shouts of joy;
  the LORD, amid trumpet blasts.
[7] Sing praise to God, sing praise;
  sing praise to our king, sing praise.

R. *God is king of all the earth.* or: *Alleluia.*

Alleluia: cf. Luke 24:46, 26

R. Alleluia, alleluia.

[46] Christ had to suffer and to rise from the
  dead,
[26] and so enter into his glory.

R. Alleluia, alleluia.

Gospel: John 16:20-23

[20] Jesus said to his disciples: "Amen, amen, I say to you, you will weep and mourn, while the world rejoices; you will grieve, but your grief will become joy. [21] When a woman is in labor, she is in anguish because her hour has arrived; but when she has given birth to a child, she no longer remembers the pain because of her joy that a child has been born into the world. [22] So you also are now in anguish. But I will see you again, and your hearts will rejoice, and no one will take your joy away from you. [23] On that day you will not question me about anything. Amen, amen, I say to you, whatever you ask the Father in my name he will give you."

Saturday before Ascension Sunday
First Reading: Acts 18:23-28

23 After staying in Antioch some time, Paul left and travelled in orderly sequence through the Galatian country and Phrygia, bringing strength to all the disciples.

24 A Jew named Apollos, a native of Alexandria, an eloquent speaker, arrived in Ephesus. He was an authority on the Scriptures. 25 He had been instructed in the Way of the Lord and, with ardent spirit, spoke and taught accurately about Jesus, although he knew only the baptism of John. 26 He began to speak boldly in the synagogue; but when Priscilla and Aquila heard him, they took him aside and explained to him the Way of God more accurately. 27 And when he wanted to cross to Achaia, the brothers encouraged him and wrote to the disciples there to welcome him. After his arrival, he gave great assistance to those who had come to believe through grace. 28 He vigorously refuted the Jews in public, establishing from the Scriptures that the Christ is Jesus.

Responsorial Psalm: Psalms 47:2-3, 8-9, 10
R.(8a) *God is king of all the earth.* or: *Alleluia.*
2 All you peoples, clap your hands;
    shout to God with cries of gladness.
3 For the LORD, the Most High, the awesome,
    is the great king over all the earth.
R. *God is king of all the earth.* or: *Alleluia.*

8 For king of all the earth is God;
    sing hymns of praise.
9 God reigns over the nations,
    God sits upon his holy throne.
R. *God is king of all the earth.* or: *Alleluia.*

10 The princes of the peoples are gathered
        together
    with the people of the God of Abraham.
For God's are the guardians of the earth;
    he is supreme.
R. *God is king of all the earth.* or: *Alleluia.*

Alleluia: John 16:28
R. Alleluia, alleluia.
28 I came from the Father and have come into
        the world;
now I am leaving the world and going back

to the Father.
R. Alleluia, alleluia.

Gospel: John 16:23B-28

Jesus said to his disciples: [23B] "Amen, amen, I say to you, whatever you ask the Father in my name he will give you. [24] Until now you have not asked anything in my name; ask and you will receive, so that your joy may be complete.

[25] "I have told you this in figures of speech. The hour is coming when I will no longer speak to you in figures but I will tell you clearly about the Father. [26] On that day you will ask in my name, and I do not tell you that I will ask the Father for you. [27] For the Father himself loves you because you have loved me and have come to believe that I came from God. [28] I came from the Father and have come into the world. Now I am leaving the world and going back to the Father."

Sunday May 12, 2024

Solemnity of Ascension of the Lord
First Reading: Acts 1:1-11

[1] In the first book, Theophilus, I dealt with all that Jesus did and taught [2] until the day he was taken up, after giving instructions through the Holy Spirit to the apostles whom he had chosen. [3] He presented himself alive to them by many proofs after he had suffered, appearing to them during forty days and speaking about the kingdom of God. [4] While meeting with them, he enjoined them not to depart from Jerusalem, but to wait for "the promise of the Father about which you have heard me speak; [5] for John baptized with water, but in a few days you will be baptized with the Holy Spirit."

[6] When they had gathered together they asked him, "Lord, are you at this time going to restore the kingdom to Israel?" [7] He answered them, "It is not for you to know the times or seasons that the Father has established by his own authority. [8] But you will receive power when the Holy Spirit comes upon you, and you will be my witnesses in Jerusalem, throughout Judea and Samaria, and to the ends of the earth." [9] When he had said this, as they were looking on, he was lifted up, and a cloud took him from their sight. [10] While they were looking intently at the sky as he was going, suddenly two men dressed in white garments stood beside them. [11] They said, "Men of Galilee, why are you standing there looking at the sky? This Jesus who has been taken up from you into heaven will return in the same way as you have seen him going into heaven."

Responsorial Psalm: Psalms 47:2-3, 6-7, 8-9

R. [6] ***God mounts his throne to shouts of joy: a***
                blare of trumpets for the Lord.

or: ***Alleluia.***

[2] All you peoples, clap your hands,
    shout to God with cries of gladness,
[3] For the LORD, the Most High, the awesome,
    is the great king over all the earth.

**R. God mounts his throne to shouts of joy: a
blare of trumpets for the Lord.**
or: **Alleluia.**

[6] God mounts his throne amid shouts of joy;
    the LORD, amid trumpet blasts.
[7] Sing praise to God, sing praise;
    sing praise to our king, sing praise.
**R. God mounts his throne to shouts of joy: a
blare of trumpets for the Lord.**
or: **Alleluia.**

[8] For king of all the earth is God;
    sing hymns of praise.
[9] God reigns over the nations,
    God sits upon his holy throne.
**R. God mounts his throne to shouts of joy: a
blare of trumpets for the Lord.**
or: **Alleluia.**

Second Reading: Ephesians 1:17-23

Brothers and sisters: [17] May the God of our Lord Jesus Christ, the Father of glory, give you a Spirit of wisdom and revelation resulting in knowledge of him. [18] May the eyes of your hearts be enlightened, that you may know what is the hope that belongs to his call, what are the riches of glory in his inheritance among the holy ones, [19] and what is the surpassing greatness of his power for us who believe, in accord with the exercise of his great might, [20] which he worked in Christ, raising him from the dead and seating him at his right hand in the heavens, [21] far above every principality, authority, power, and dominion, and every name that is named not only in this age but also in the one to come. [22] And he put all things beneath his feet and gave him as head over all things to the church, which is his body, the fullness of the one who fills all things in every way.

OR Ephesians 4:1-13

[1] Brothers and sisters, I, a prisoner for the Lord, urge you to live in a manner worthy of the call you have received, [2] with all humility and gentleness, with patience, bearing with one another through love, [3] striving to preserve the unity of the Spirit through the bond of peace: [4] one body and one Spirit, as you were also called to the one hope of your call; [5] one Lord, one faith, one baptism; [6] one God and Father of all, who is over all and through all and in all.

[7] But grace was given to each of us according to the measure of Christ's gift. [8] Therefore, it says: *He ascended on high and took prisoners captive; he gave gifts to men.* [9] What does "he ascended" mean except that he also descended into the lower regions of

the earth? [10] The one who descended is also the one who ascended far above all the heavens, that he might fill all things.

[11] And he gave some as apostles, others as prophets, others as evangelists, others as pastors and teachers,[12] to equip the holy ones for the work of ministry, for building up the body of Christ, [13] until we all attain to the unity of faith and knowledge of the Son of God, to mature manhood, to the extent of the full stature of Christ.

OR Ephesians 4:1-7, 11-13

[1] Brothers and sisters, I, a prisoner for the Lord, urge you to live in a manner worthy of the calling you have received, [2] with all humility and gentleness, with patience, bearing with one another through love, [3] striving to preserve the unity of the Spirit through the bond of peace: [4] one body and one Spirit, as you were also called to the one hope of your calling; [5] one Lord, one faith, one baptism; [6] one God and Father of all, who is over all and through all and in all.

[7] But grace was given to each of us according to the measure of Christ's gift.

[11] And he gave some as apostles, others as prophets, others as evangelists, others as pastors and teachers, [12] to equip the holy ones for the work of ministry, for building up the body of Christ, [13] until we all attain to the unity of faith and knowledge of the Son of God, to mature manhood, to the extent of the full stature of Christ.

Alleluia: Matthew 28:19A, 20B

R. Alleluia, alleluia.
[19A] Go and teach all nations, says the Lord;
[20B] I am with you always, until the end of the
       world.
R. Alleluia, alleluia.

Gospel: Mark 16: 15-20

[15] Jesus said to his disciples: "Go into the whole world and proclaim the gospel to every creature. [16] Whoever believes and is baptized will be saved; whoever does not believe will be condemned. [17] These signs will accompany those who believe: in my name they will drive out demons, they will speak new languages. [18] They will pick up serpents with their hands, and if they drink any deadly thing, it will not harm them. They will lay hands on the sick, and they will recover."

[19] So then the Lord Jesus, after he spoke to them, was taken up into heaven and took his seat at the right hand of God. [20] But they went forth and preached everywhere, while the Lord worked with them and confirmed the word through accompanying signs.

Monday May 13, 2024

Monday of the Seventh Week of Easter
First Reading: Acts 19:1-8

[1] While Apollos was in Corinth, Paul travelled through the interior of the country and down to Ephesus where he found some disciples. [2] He said to them, "Did you receive the

Holy Spirit when you became believers?" They answered him, "We have never even heard that there is a Holy Spirit." ³ He said, "How were you baptized?" They replied, "With the baptism of John." ⁴ Paul then said, "John baptized with a baptism of repentance, telling the people to believe in the one who was to come after him, that is, in Jesus." ⁵ When they heard this, they were baptized in the name of the Lord Jesus. ⁶ And when Paul laid his hands on them, the Holy Spirit came upon them, and they spoke in tongues and prophesied. ⁷ Altogether there were about twelve men.

⁸ He entered the synagogue, and for three months debated boldly with persuasive arguments about the Kingdom of God.

Responsorial Psalm: Psalms 68:2-3AB, 4-5ACD, 6-7AB

R.*(33a)* *Sing to God, O kingdoms of the earth.* or: *Alleluia.*

² God arises; his enemies are scattered,
     and those who hate him flee before him.
3AB As smoke is driven away, so are they driven;
     as wax melts before the fire.

R. *Sing to God, O kingdoms of the earth.* or: *Alleluia.*

⁴ But the just rejoice and exult before God;
     they are glad and rejoice.
5ACD Sing to God, chant praise to his name;
     whose name is the LORD.

R. *Sing to God, O kingdoms of the earth.* or: *Alleluia.*

⁶ The father of orphans and the defender of
          widows
     is God in his holy dwelling.
7AB God gives a home to the forsaken;
     he leads forth prisoners to prosperity.

R. *Sing to God, O kingdoms of the earth.* or: *Alleluia.*

Alleluia: Colossians 3:1

R. Alleluia, alleluia.

¹ If then you were raised with Christ,
seek what is above,
where Christ is seated at the right hand of
          God.

R. Alleluia, alleluia.

Gospel: John 16:29-33

²⁹ The disciples said to Jesus, "Now you are talking plainly, and not in any figure of speech. ³⁰ Now we realize that you know everything and that you do not need to have anyone

question you. Because of this, we believe that you came from God." [31] Jesus answered them, "Do you believe now? [32] Behold, the hour is coming and has arrived when each of you will be scattered to his own home and you will leave me alone. But I am not alone, because the Father is with me. [33] I have told you this so that you might have peace in me. In the world you will have trouble, but take courage, I have conquered the world."

Feast of Saint Matthias, Apostle
First Reading: Acts 1:15-17, 20-26

[15] Peter stood up in the midst of the brothers and sisters (there was a group of about one hundred and twenty persons in the one place). [16] He said, "My brothers and sisters, the Scripture had to be fulfilled which the Holy Spirit spoke beforehand through the mouth of David, concerning Judas, who was the guide for those who arrested Jesus. [17] Judas was numbered among us and was allotted a share in this ministry. [20] For it is written in the Book of Psalms:

Let his encampment become desolate,
*   and may no one dwell in it,*
and:
May another take his office.

[21] Therefore, it is necessary that one of the men who accompanied us the whole time the Lord Jesus came and went among us, [22] beginning from the baptism of John until the day on which he was taken up from us, become with us a witness to his resurrection." [23] So they proposed two, Joseph called Barsabbas, who was also known as Justus, and Matthias. [24] Then they prayed, "You, Lord, who know the hearts of all, show which one of these two you have chosen [25] to take the place in this apostolic ministry from which Judas turned away to go to his own place." [26] Then they gave lots to them, and the lot fell upon Matthias, and he was counted with the Eleven Apostles.

Responsorial Psalm: Psalms 113:1-2, 3-4, 5-6, 7-8

R. [8] ***The Lord will give him a seat with the***
              leaders of his people. or: ***Alleluia.***

[1] Praise, you servants of the LORD,
    praise the name of the LORD.
[2] Blessed be the name of the LORD
    both now and forever.
R. ***The Lord will give him a seat with the leaders***
        of his people. or: ***Alleluia.***

[3] From the rising to the setting of the sun
    is the name of the LORD to be praised.
[4] High above all nations is the LORD;

above the heavens is his glory.
**R. The Lord will give him a seat with the leaders
of his people.** or: *Alleluia.*

[5] Who is like the LORD, our God, who is
enthroned on high
[6] and looks upon the heavens and the earth
below?
**R. The Lord will give him a seat with the leaders
of his people.** or: *Alleluia.*

[7] He raises up the lowly from the dust;
from the dunghill he lifts up the poor
[8] To seat them with princes,
with the princes of his own people.
**R. The Lord will give him a seat with the leaders
of his people.** or: *Alleluia.*

Alleluia: cf. John 15:16
R. Alleluia, alleluia.
[16] I chose you from the world,
to go and bear fruit that will last, says the
Lord.
R. Alleluia, alleluia.

Gospel: John 15:9-17
[9] Jesus said to his disciples: "As the Father loves me, so I also love you. Remain in my love. [10] If you keep my commandments, you will remain in my love, just as I have kept my Father's commandments and remain in his love.
[11] "I have told you this so that my joy might be in you and your joy might be complete. [12] This is my commandment: love one another as I love you. [13] No one has greater love than this, to lay down one's life for one's friends. [14] You are my friends if you do what I command you. [15] I no longer call you slaves, because a slave does not know what his master is doing. I have called you friends, because I have told you everything I have heard from my Father. [16] It was not you who chose me, but I who chose you and appointed you to go and bear fruit that will remain, so that whatever you ask the Father in my name he may give you. [17] This I command you: love one another."

Wednesday of the Seventh Week of Easter

First Reading: Acts 20:28-38

[28] At Miletus, Paul spoke to the presbyters of the Church of Ephesus: "Keep watch over yourselves and over the whole flock of which the Holy Spirit has appointed you overseers, in which you tend the Church of God that he acquired with his own Blood. [29] I know that after my departure savage wolves will come among you, and they will not spare the flock. [30] And from your own group, men will come forward perverting the truth to draw the disciples away after them. [31] So be vigilant and remember that for three years, night and day, I unceasingly admonished each of you with tears. [32] And now I commend you to God and to that gracious word of his that can build you up and give you the inheritance among all who are consecrated. [33] I have never wanted anyone's silver or gold or clothing. [34] You know well that these very hands have served my needs and my companions. [35] In every way I have shown you that by hard work of that sort we must help the weak, and keep in mind the words of the Lord Jesus who himself said, 'It is more blessed to give than to receive.'"

[36] When he had finished speaking he knelt down and prayed with them all. [37] They were all weeping loudly as they threw their arms around Paul and kissed him, [38] for they were deeply distressed that he had said that they would never see his face again. Then they escorted him to the ship.

Responsorial Psalm: Psalms 68:29-30, 33-35A, 35BC-36AB

R. [33a] *Sing to God, O kingdoms of the earth*. or: *Alleluia.*

[29] Show forth, O God, your power,
    the power, O God, with which you took
        our part;
[30] For your temple in Jerusalem
    let the kings bring you gifts.

R. *Sing to God, O Kingdoms of the earth*. or: *Alleluia.*

[33] You kingdoms of the earth, sing to God,
    chant praise to the Lord
        [34] who rides on the heights of the ancient
            heavens.
Behold, his voice resounds, the voice of
        power:
    [35A] "Confess the power of God!"

R. *Sing to God, O Kingdoms of the earth*. or: *Alleluia.*

[35BC] Over Israel is his majesty;
    his power is in the skies.
[36AB] Awesome in his sanctuary is God, the God of
        Israel;

he gives power and strength to his
people.
R. Sing to God, O Kingdoms of the earth. or: *Alleluia.*

Alleluia: cf. John 17:17B, 17A
R. Alleluia, alleluia.
Your word, O Lord, is truth;
consecrate us in the truth.
R. Alleluia, alleluia.

Gospel: John 17:11B-19
Lifting up his eyes to heaven, Jesus prayed, saying: [11B] "Holy Father, keep them in your name that you have given me, so that they may be one just as we are one. [12] When I was with them I protected them in your name that you gave me, and I guarded them, and none of them was lost except the son of destruction, in order that the Scripture might be fulfilled. [13] But now I am coming to you. I speak this in the world so that they may share my joy completely. [14] I gave them your word, and the world hated them because they do not belong to the world any more than I belong to the world. [15] I do not ask that you take them out of the world but that you keep them from the Evil One. [16] They do not belong to the world any more than I belong to the world. [17] Consecrate them in the truth. Your word is truth. [18] As you sent me into the world, so I sent them into the world. [19] And I consecrate myself for them, so that they also may be consecrated in truth."

Thursday May 16, 2024

Thursday of the Seventh Week of Easter
First Reading: Acts 22:30; 23:6-11
[30] Wishing to determine the truth about why Paul was being accused by the Jews, the commander freed him and ordered the chief priests and the whole Sanhedrin to convene. Then he brought Paul down and made him stand before them.

[6] Paul was aware that some were Sadducees and some Pharisees, so he called out before the Sanhedrin, "My brothers, I am a Pharisee, the son of Pharisees; I am on trial for hope in the resurrection of the dead." [7] When he said this, a dispute broke out between the Pharisees and Sadducees, and the group became divided. [8] For the Sadducees say that there is no resurrection or angels or spirits, while the Pharisees acknowledge all three. [9] A great uproar occurred, and some scribes belonging to the Pharisee party stood up and sharply argued, "We find nothing wrong with this man. Suppose a spirit or an angel has spoken to him?" [10] The dispute was so serious that the commander, afraid that Paul would be torn to pieces by them, ordered his troops to go down and rescue Paul from their midst and take him into the compound. [11] The following night the Lord stood by him and said, "Take courage. For just as you have borne witness to my cause in Jerusalem, so you must also bear witness in Rome."

Responsorial Psalm: Psalms 16:1-2A AND 5, 7-8, 9-10, 11

R. *(1)* ***Keep me safe, O God; you are my hope.*** or: *Alleluia*.

[1] Keep me, O God, for in you I take refuge;
> [2A] I say to the LORD, "My Lord are you."

[5] O LORD, my allotted portion and my cup,
> you it is who hold fast my lot.

R. *Keep me safe, O God; you are my hope.* or: *Alleluia.*

[7] I bless the LORD who counsels me;
> even in the night, my heart exhorts me.

[8] I set the LORD ever before me;
> with him, at my right hand, I shall not be
>> disturbed.

R. *Keep me safe, O God; you are my hope.* or: *Alleluia.*

[9] Therefore my heart is glad and my soul
>> rejoices,
> my body, too, abides in confidence;

[10] Because you will not abandon my soul to the
>> nether world,
> nor will you suffer your faithful one to
>> undergo corruption.

R. *Keep me safe, O God; you are my hope.* or: *Alleluia.*

[11] You will show me the path to life,
> fullness of joys in your presence,
> the delights at your right hand forever.

R. *Keep me safe, O God; you are my hope.* or: *Alleluia.*

Alleluia: John 17:21

R. Alleluia, alleluia.

[21] May they all be one as you, Father, are in me
> and I in you,
that the world may believe that you sent me,
> says the Lord.

R. Alleluia, alleluia.

Gospel: John 17:20-26

Lifting up his eyes to heaven, Jesus prayed saying: [20] "I pray not only for these but also for those who will believe in me through their word, [21] so that they may all be one, as you, Father, are in me and I in you, that they also may be in us, that the world may believe that you sent me. ²² And I have given them the glory you gave me, so that they may be one, as we are one, ²³ I in them and you in me, that they may be brought to perfection as one, that the world may know that you sent me, and that you loved them even as you loved me. ²⁴ Father, they are your gift to me. I wish that where I am they also may be with me, that they may see my glory that you gave me because you loved me before the foundation of the world. ²⁵ Righteous Father, the world also does not know you, but I know you, and they know that you sent me. ²⁶ I made known to them your name and I will make it known, that the love with which you loved me may be in them and I in them."

Friday of the Seventh Week of Easter
First Reading: Acts 25:13B-21

¹³ᴮ King Agrippa and Bernice arrived in Caesarea on a visit to Festus. ¹⁴ Since they spent several days there, Festus referred Paul's case to the king, saying, "There is a man here left in custody by Felix. ¹⁵ When I was in Jerusalem the chief priests and the elders of the Jews brought charges against him and demanded his condemnation. ¹⁶ I answered them that it was not Roman practice to hand over an accused person before he has faced his accusers and had the opportunity to defend himself against their charge. ¹⁷ So when they came together here, I made no delay; the next day I took my seat on the tribunal and ordered the man to be brought in. ¹⁸ His accusers stood around him, but did not charge him with any of the crimes I suspected. ¹⁹ Instead they had some issues with him about their own religion and about a certain Jesus who had died but who Paul claimed was alive. ²⁰ Since I was at a loss on how to investigate this controversy, I asked if he were willing to go to Jerusalem and there stand trial on these charges. ²¹ And when Paul appealed that he be held in custody for the Emperor's decision, I ordered him held until I could send him to Caesar."

Responsorial Psalm: Psalms 103:1-2, 11-12, 19-20AB

R. ⁽¹⁹ᵃ⁾ *The Lord has established his throne in*
           heaven. or: *Alleluia.*

¹ Bless the LORD, O my soul;
        and all my being, bless his holy name.
² Bless the LORD, O my soul,
        and forget not all his benefits.
R. *The Lord has established his throne in*
           heaven. or: *Alleluia.*

¹¹ For as the heavens are high above the earth,
        so surpassing is his kindness toward
            those who fear him.
¹² As far as the east is from the west,
        so far has he put our transgressions from
            us.

R. The Lord has established his throne in
heaven. or: *Alleluia.*

[19] The LORD has established his throne in
heaven,
and his kingdom rules over all.
[20AB] Bless the LORD, all you his angels,
you mighty in strength, who do his
bidding.
R. The Lord has established his throne in
heaven. or: *Alleluia.*

Alleluia: John 14:26
R. Alleluia, alleluia.
[26] The Holy Spirit will teach you everything and remind you of all I told you.
R. Alleluia, alleluia.

Gospel: John 21:15-19
[15] After Jesus had revealed himself to his disciples and eaten breakfast with them, he said to Simon Peter, "Simon, son of John, do you love me more than these?" Simon Peter answered him, "Yes, Lord, you know that I love you." Jesus said to him, "Feed my lambs." [16] He then said to Simon Peter a second time, "Simon, son of John, do you love me?" Simon Peter answered him, "Yes, Lord, you know that I love you." He said to him, "Tend my sheep." [17] He said to him the third time, "Simon, son of John, do you love me?" Peter was distressed that he had said to him a third time, "Do you love me?" and he said to him, "Lord, you know everything; you know that I love you." Jesus said to him, "Feed my sheep. [18] Amen, amen, I say to you, when you were younger, you used to dress yourself and go where you wanted; but when you grow old, you will stretch out your hands, and someone else will dress you and lead you where you do not want to go." [19] He said this signifying by what kind of death he would glorify God. And when he had said this, he said to him, "Follow me."

Saturday May 18, 2024

Saturday of the Seventh Week of Easter
First Reading: Acts 28:16-20, 30-31
[16] When he entered Rome, Paul was allowed to live by himself, with the soldier who was guarding him.

[17] Three days later he called together the leaders of the Jews. When they had gathered he said to them, "My brothers, although I had done nothing against our people or our ancestral customs, I was handed over to the Romans as a prisoner from Jerusalem. [18] After trying my case the Romans wanted to release me, because they found nothing against me deserving the death penalty. [19] But when the Jews objected, I was obliged to

appeal to Caesar, even though I had no accusation to make against my own nation. [20] This is the reason, then, I have requested to see you and to speak with you, for it is on account of the hope of Israel that I wear these chains."

[30] He remained for two full years in his lodgings. He received all who came to him, [31] and with complete assurance and without hindrance he proclaimed the Kingdom of God and taught about the Lord Jesus Christ.

Responsorial Psalm: Psalms 11:4, 5 AND 7

R. [(see 7b)] *The just will gaze on your face, O Lord.* or: *Alleluia.*

[4] The LORD is in his holy temple;
    the LORD's throne is in heaven.
His eyes behold,
    his searching glance is on mankind.

R. *The just will gaze on your face, O Lord.* or: *Alleluia.*

[5] The LORD searches the just and the wicked;
    the lover of violence he hates.
[7] For the LORD is just, he loves just deeds;
    the upright shall see his face.

R. *The just will gaze on your face, O Lord.* or: *Alleluia.*

Alleluia: John 16:7, 13

R. Alleluia, alleluia.

[7] I will send to you the Spirit of truth, says the
        Lord;
[13] he will guide you to all truth.

R. Alleluia, alleluia.

Gospel: John 21:20-25

[20] Peter turned and saw the disciple following whom Jesus loved, the one who had also reclined upon his chest during the supper and had said, "Master, who is the one who will betray you?" [21] When Peter saw him, he said to Jesus, "Lord, what about him?" [22] Jesus said to him, "What if I want him to remain until I come? What concern is it of yours? You follow me." [23] So the word spread among the brothers that that disciple would not die. But Jesus had not told him that he would not die, just "What if I want him to remain until I come? What concern is it of yours?"

[24] It is this disciple who testifies to these things and has written them, and we know that his testimony is true. [25] There are also many other things that Jesus did, but if these were to be described individually, I do not think the whole world would contain the books that would be written.

Pentecost Vigil

First Reading: Genesis 11:1-9

[1] The whole world spoke the same language, using the same words. [2] While the people were migrating in the east, they came upon a valley in the land of Shinar and settled there. [3] They said to one another, "Come, let us mold bricks and harden them with fire." They used bricks for stone, and bitumen for mortar.

[4] Then they said, "Come, let us build ourselves a city and a tower with its top in the sky, and so make a name for ourselves; otherwise we shall be scattered all over the earth."

[5] The LORD came down to see the city and the tower that the people had built. [6] Then the LORD said: "If now, while they are one people, all speaking the same language, they have started to do this, nothing will later stop them from doing whatever they presume to do. [7] Let us then go down there and confuse their language, so that one will not understand what another says." [8] Thus the LORD scattered them from there all over the earth, and they stopped building the city. [9] That is why it was called Babel, because there the LORD confused the speech of all the world. It was from that place that he scattered them all over the earth.

OR Exodus 19:3-8A, 16-20B

[3] Moses went up the mountain to God. Then the LORD called to him and said, "Thus shall you say to the house of Jacob; tell the Israelites: [4] You have seen for yourselves how I treated the Egyptians and how I bore you up on eagle wings and brought you here to myself. [5] Therefore, if you hearken to my voice and keep my covenant, you shall be my special possession, dearer to me than all other people, though all the earth is mine. [6] You shall be to me a kingdom of priests, a holy nation. That is what you must tell the Israelites." [7] So Moses went and summoned the elders of the people. When he set before them all that the LORD had ordered him to tell them, [8A] the people all answered together, "Everything the LORD has said, we will do."

[16] On the morning of the third day there were peals of thunder and lightning, and a heavy cloud over the mountain, and a very loud trumpet blast, so that all the people in the camp trembled. [17] But Moses led the people out of the camp to meet God, and they stationed themselves at the foot of the mountain. [18] Mount Sinai was all wrapped in smoke, for the LORD came down upon it in fire. The smoke rose from it as though from a furnace, and the whole mountain trembled violently. [19] The trumpet blast grew louder and louder, while Moses was speaking, and God answering him with thunder.

[20] When the LORD came down to the top of Mount Sinai, he summoned Moses to the top of the mountain.

OR Ezekiel 37:1-14

[1] The hand of the LORD came upon me, and he led me out in the spirit of the LORD and set me in the center of the plain, which was now filled with bones. [2] He made me walk among the bones in every direction so that I saw how many they were on the surface of the plain.

How dry they were! [3] He asked me: Son of man, can these bones come to life? I answered, "Lord GOD, you alone know that." [4] Then he said to me: Prophesy over these bones, and say to them: Dry bones, hear the word of the LORD! [5] Thus says the Lord GOD to these bones: See! I will bring spirit into you, that you may come to life. [6] I will put sinews upon you, make flesh grow over you, cover you with skin, and put spirit in you so that you may come to life and know that I am the LORD. [7] I, Ezekiel, prophesied as I had been told, and even as I was prophesying I heard a noise; it was a rattling as the bones came together, bone joining bone. [8] I saw the sinews and the flesh come upon them, and the skin cover them, but there was no spirit in them. [9] Then the LORD said to me: Prophesy to the spirit, prophesy, son of man, and say to the spirit: Thus says the Lord GOD: From the four winds come, O spirit, and breathe into these slain that they may come to life. [10] I prophesied as he told me, and the spirit came into them; they came alive and stood upright, a vast army. [11] Then he said to me: Son of man, these bones are the whole house of Israel. They have been saying, "Our bones are dried up, our hope is lost, and we are cut off." [12] Therefore, prophesy and say to them: Thus says the Lord GOD: O my people, I will open your graves and have you rise from them, and bring you back to the land of Israel. [13] Then you shall know that I am the LORD, when I open your graves and have you rise from them, O my people! [14] I will put my spirit in you that you may live, and I will settle you upon your land; thus you shall know that I am the LORD. I have promised, and I will do it, says the LORD.

OR Joel 3:1-5

[1] Thus says the LORD:

I will pour out my spirit upon all flesh.
Your sons and daughters shall prophesy,
     your old men shall dream dreams,
     your young men shall see visions;
[2] even upon the servants and the
          handmaids,
     in those days, I will pour out my
          spirit.
[3] And I will work wonders in the heavens
          and on the earth,
     blood, fire, and columns of smoke;
[4] the sun will be turned to darkness,
     and the moon to blood,
at the coming of the day of the LORD,
     the great and terrible day.
[5] Then everyone shall be rescued
     who calls on the name of the LORD;
for on Mount Zion there shall be a

remnant,
as the LORD has said,
and in Jerusalem survivors
whom the LORD shall call.

Responsorial Psalm: Psalms 104:1-2,24 AND 35,27-28, 29-30

R. *(cf. 30)* **Lord, send out your Spirit, and renew the face of the earth.** or: *Alleluia.*

[1] Bless the LORD, O my soul!
O LORD, my God, you are great indeed!
[2] You are clothed with majesty and glory,
robed in light as with a cloak.

R. Lord, send out your Spirit, and renew the face of the earth. or: *Alleluia.*

[24] How manifold are your works, O LORD!
In wisdom you have wrought them all—
the earth is full of your creatures;
[35C] bless the LORD, O my soul! Alleluia.

R. Lord, send out your Spirit, and renew the face of the earth. or: *Alleluia.*

[27] Creatures all look to you
to give them food in due time.
[28] When you give it to them, they gather it;
when you open your hand, they are filled
with good things.

R. Lord, send out your Spirit, and renew the face of the earth. or: *Alleluia.*

[29] If you take away their breath, they perish
and return to their dust.
[30] When you send forth your spirit, they are
created,
and you renew the face of the earth.

R. Lord, send out your Spirit, and renew the face of the earth. or: *Alleluia.*

Second Reading: Romans 8:22-27

Brothers and sisters: [22] We know that all creation is groaning in labor pains even until now; [23] and not only that, but we ourselves, who have the first fruits of the Spirit, we also groan within ourselves as we wait for adoption, the redemption of our bodies. [24] For in hope we were saved. Now hope that sees is not hope. For who hopes for what one sees? [25] But if we hope for what we do not see, we wait with endurance.

[26] In the same way, the Spirit too comes to the aid of our weakness; for we do not know how to pray as we ought, but the Spirit himself intercedes with inexpressible groanings. [27] And the one who searches hearts knows what is the intention of the Spirit, because he intercedes for the holy ones according to God's will.

Alleluia
R. Alleluia, alleluia.
Come, Holy Spirit, fill the hearts of your
    faithful
and kindle in them the fire of your love.
R. Alleluia, alleluia.

Gospel: John 7:37-39
On the last and greatest day of the feast, [37] Jesus stood up and exclaimed, "Let anyone who thirsts come to me and drink. [38] As Scripture says: *Rivers of living water will flow from within him* who believes in me." [39] He said this in reference to the Spirit that those who came to believe in him were to receive. There was, of course, no Spirit yet, because Jesus had not yet been glorified.

Sunday May 19, 2024
Pentecost Sunday

First Reading: Acts 2:1-11
[1] When the time for Pentecost was fulfilled, they were all in one place together. [2] And suddenly there came from the sky a noise like a strong driving wind, and it filled the entire house in which they were. [3] Then there appeared to them tongues as of fire, which parted and came to rest on each one of them. [4] And they were all filled with the Holy Spirit and began to speak in different tongues, as the Spirit enabled them to proclaim.

[5] Now there were devout Jews from every nation under heaven staying in Jerusalem. [6] At this sound, they gathered in a large crowd, but they were confused because each one heard them speaking in his own language. [7] They were astounded, and in amazement, they asked, "Are not all these people who are speaking Galileans? [8] Then how does each of us hear them in his native language? [9] We are Parthians, Medes, and Elamites, inhabitants of Mesopotamia, Judea and Cappadocia, Pontus and Asia, [10] Phrygia and Pamphylia, Egypt and the districts of Libya near Cyrene, as well as travellers from Rome, [11] both Jews and converts to Judaism, Cretans and Arabs, yet we hear them speaking in our own tongues of the mighty acts of God."

Responsorial Psalm: Psalms 104:1, 24, 29-30, 31, 34
R. [(cf. 30)] ***Lord, send out your Spirit, and renew the face of the earth.*** or: ***Alleluia.***

[1] Bless the LORD, O my soul!
    O LORD, my God, you are great indeed!
[24] How manifold are your works, O LORD!
    The earth is full of your creatures;
R. *Lord, send out your Spirit, and renew the face*
    of the earth. or: *Alleluia.*

[29] If you take away their breath, they perish
    and return to their dust.
[30] When you send forth your spirit, they are
        created,
    and you renew the face of the earth.
R. *Lord, send out your Spirit, and renew the face*
    of the earth. or: *Alleluia.*

[31] May the glory of the LORD endure forever;
    may the LORD be glad in his works!
[34] Pleasing to him be my theme;
    I will be glad in the LORD.
R. *Lord, send out your Spirit, and renew the face*
    of the earth. or: *Alleluia.*

Second Reading: 1 Corinthians 12:3B-7, 12-13

Brothers and sisters: [3B] No one can say, "Jesus is Lord," except by the Holy Spirit. [4] There are different kinds of spiritual gifts but the same Spirit; [5] there are different forms of service but the same Lord; [6] there are different workings but the same God who produces all of them in everyone. [7] To each individual the manifestation of the Spirit is given for some benefit.

[12] As a body is one though it has many parts, and all the parts of the body, though many, are one body, so also Christ. [13] For in one Spirit we were all baptized into one body, whether Jews or Greeks, slaves or free persons, and we were all given to drink of one Spirit.

OR Galatians 5:16-25

[16] Brothers and sisters, live by the Spirit and you will certainly not gratify the desire of the flesh. [17] For the flesh has desires against the Spirit, and the Spirit against the flesh; these are opposed to each other, so that you may not do what you want. [18] But if you are guided by the Spirit, you are not under the law. [19] Now the works of the flesh are obvious: immorality, impurity, lust, [20] idolatry, sorcery, hatreds, rivalry, jealousy, outbursts of fury, acts of selfishness, dissensions, factions, [21] occasions of envy, drinking bouts, orgies, and the like. I warn you, as I warned you before, that those who do such things will not inherit the kingdom of God. [22] In contrast, the fruit of the Spirit is love, joy, peace, patience, kindness, generosity, faithfulness, [23] gentleness, self-control. Against such there is no law. [24] Now those who belong to Christ Jesus have crucified their flesh with its passions and desires. [25] If we live in the Spirit, let us also follow the Spirit.

Sequence - *Veni, Sancte Spiritus*

Come, Holy Spirit, come!
And from your celestial home
Shed a ray of light divine!
Come, Father of the poor!
Come, source of all our store!
Come, within our bosoms shine.
You, of comforters the best;
You, the soul's most welcome guest;
Sweet refreshment here below;
In our labor, rest most sweet;
Grateful coolness in the heat;
Solace in the midst of woe.
O most blessed Light divine,
Shine within these hearts of yours,
And our inmost being fill!
Where you are not, we have naught,
Nothing good in deed or thought,
Nothing free from taint of ill.
Heal our wounds, our strength renew;
On our dryness pour your dew;
Wash the stains of guilt away:
Bend the stubborn heart and will;
Melt the frozen, warm the chill;
Guide the steps that go astray.
On the faithful, who adore
And confess you, evermore
In your sevenfold gift descend;
Give them virtue's sure reward;
Give them your salvation, Lord;
Give them joys that never end. Amen.
Alleluia.

Alleluia

R. Alleluia, alleluia.
Come, Holy Spirit, fill the hearts of your
        faithful
and kindle in them the fire of your love.
R. Alleluia, alleluia.

Gospel: John 20:19-23

[19] On the evening of that first day of the week, when the doors were locked, where the disciples were, for fear of the Jews, Jesus came and stood in their midst and said to them, "Peace be with you." [20] When he had said this, he showed them his hands and his side. The disciples rejoiced when they saw the Lord. [21] Jesus said to them again, "Peace be with you. As the Father has sent me, so I send you." [22] And when he had said this, he breathed on them and said to them, "Receive the Holy Spirit. [23] Whose sins you forgive are forgiven them, and whose sins you retain are retained."

Or: John 15:26-27; 16:12-15

Jesus said to his disciples: [26] "When the Advocate comes whom I will send you from the Father, the Spirit of truth that proceeds from the Father, he will testify to me. [27] And you also testify, because you have been with me from the beginning.

[12] "I have much more to tell you, but you cannot bear it now. [13] But when he comes, the Spirit of truth, he will guide you to all truth. He will not speak on his own, but he will speak what he hears, and will declare to you the things that are coming. [14] He will glorify me, because he will take from what is mine and declare it to you. [15] Everything that the Father has is mine; for this reason I told you that he will take from what is mine and declare it to you."

Monday May 20, 2024

Monday of Seventh Week in Ordinary Time
First Reading: James 3:13-18

Beloved: [13]Who among you is wise and understanding? Let him show his works by a good life in the humility that comes from wisdom.[14] But if you have bitter jealousy and selfish ambition in your hearts, do not boast and be false to the truth.[15] Wisdom of this kind does not come down from above but is earthly, unspiritual, demonic.[16] For where jealousy and selfish ambition exist, there is disorder and every foul practice.[17] But the wisdom from above is first of all pure, then peaceable, gentle, compliant, full of mercy and good fruits, without inconstancy or insincerity.[18] And the fruit of righteousness is sown in peace for those who cultivate peace.

Responsorial Psalm: Psalms 19:8, 9, 10, 15

R. [9a] *The precepts of the Lord give joy to the heart.*

[8] The law of the LORD is perfect,
      refreshing the soul;
The decree of the LORD is trustworthy,
      giving wisdom to the simple.

R. *The precepts of the Lord give joy to the heart.*

[9] The precepts of the LORD are right,
      rejoicing the heart;
The command of the LORD is clear,
      enlightening the eye.

R. *The precepts of the Lord give joy to the heart.*

[10] The fear of the LORD is pure,
      enduring forever;
The ordinances of the LORD are true,
      all of them just.
R. The precepts of the Lord give joy to the heart.

[15] Let the words of my mouth and the thought
            of my heart
      find favor before you,
            O LORD, my rock and my redeemer.
R. The precepts of the Lord give joy to the heart.

Alleluia: 2 Timothy 1:10
R. Alleluia, alleluia.
[10] Our Savior Jesus Christ has destroyed death and brought life to light through the Gospel.
R. Alleluia, alleluia.

Gospel: Mark 9:14-29
[14] As Jesus came down from the mountain with Peter, James, John and approached the other disciples, they saw a large crowd around them and scribes arguing with them. [15] Immediately on seeing him, the whole crowd was utterly amazed. They ran up to him and greeted him. [16] He asked them, "What are you arguing about with them?" [17] Someone from the crowd answered him, "Teacher, I have brought to you my son possessed by a mute spirit. [18] Wherever it seizes him, it throws him down; he foams at the mouth, grinds his teeth, and becomes rigid. I asked your disciples to drive it out, but they were unable to do so." [19] He said to them in reply, "O faithless generation, how long will I be with you? How long will I endure you? Bring him to me." [20] They brought the boy to him. And when he saw him, the spirit immediately threw the boy into convulsions. As he fell to the ground, he began to roll around and foam at the mouth. [21] Then he questioned his father, "How long has this been happening to him?" He replied, "Since childhood. [22] It has often thrown him into fire and into water to kill him. But if you can do anything, have compassion on us and help us." [23] Jesus said to him, "'If you can!' Everything is possible to one who has faith." [24] Then the boy's father cried out, "I do believe, help my unbelief!" [25] Jesus, on seeing a crowd rapidly gathering, rebuked the unclean spirit and said to it, "Mute and deaf spirit, I command you: come out of him and never enter him again!" [26] Shouting and throwing the boy into convulsions, it came out. He became like a corpse, which caused many to say, "He is dead!" [27] But Jesus took him by the hand, raised him, and he stood up. [28] When he entered the house, his disciples asked him in private, "Why could we not drive the spirit out?" [29] He said to them, "This kind can only come out through prayer."

Tuesday of Seventh Week in Ordinary Time
First Reading: James 4:1-10

Beloved: [1] Where do the wars and where do the conflicts among you come from? Is it not from your passions that make war within your members? [2] You covet but do not possess. You kill and envy but you cannot obtain; you fight and wage war. You do not possess because you do not ask. [3] You ask but do not receive, because you ask wrongly, to spend it on your passions. [4] Adulterers! Do you not know that to be a lover of the world means enmity with God? Therefore, whoever wants to be a lover of the world makes himself an enemy of God. [5] Or do you suppose that the Scripture speaks without meaning when it says,

*The spirit that he has made to dwell in us
        tends toward jealousy?*

[6] But he bestows a greater grace; therefore, it says:

*God resists the proud,
        but gives grace to the humble.*

[7] So submit yourselves to God. Resist the Devil, and he will flee from you. [8] Draw near to God, and he will draw near to you. Cleanse your hands, you sinners, and purify your hearts, you of two minds. [9] Begin to lament, to mourn, to weep. Let your laughter be turned into mourning and your joy into dejection. [10] Humble yourselves before the Lord and he will exalt you.

Responsorial Psalm: Psalms 55:7-8, 9-10A, 10B-11A, 23

R. [23a] *Throw your cares on the Lord, and he will
                    support you.*

[7] And I say, "Had I but wings like a dove,
        I would fly away and be at rest.
[8] Far away I would flee;
        I would lodge in the wilderness."
R. *Throw your cares on the Lord, and he will
                support you.*

[9] "I would wait for him who saves me
        from the violent storm and the tempest."
[10A] Engulf them, O Lord; divide their counsels.
R. *Throw your cares on the Lord, and he will
                support you.*

[10B] In the city I see violence and strife,
        [11A] day and night they prowl about upon its

277

walls.
R. Throw your cares on the Lord, and he will support you.

23 Cast your care upon the LORD,
    and he will support you;
      never will he permit the just man to be
        disturbed.
R. Throw your cares on the Lord, and he will support you.

Alleluia: Galatians 6:14
R. Alleluia, alleluia.
14 May I never boast except in the Cross of our
    Lord Jesus Christ,
through which the world has been crucified
    to me and I to the world.
R. Alleluia, alleluia.

Gospel: Mark 9:30-37
30 Jesus and his disciples left from there and began a journey through Galilee, but he did not wish anyone to know about it. 31 He was teaching his disciples and telling them, "The Son of Man is to be handed over to men and they will kill him, and three days after his death the Son of Man will rise." 32 But they did not understand the saying, and they were afraid to question him.

33 They came to Capernaum and, once inside the house, he began to ask them, "What were you arguing about on the way?" 34 But they remained silent. For they had been discussing among themselves on the way who was the greatest. 35 Then he sat down, called the Twelve, and said to them, "If anyone wishes to be first, he shall be the last of all and the servant of all." 36 Taking a child, he placed it in their midst, and putting his arms around it, he said to them, 37 "Whoever receives one child such as this in my name, receives me; and whoever receives me, receives not me but the One who sent me."

Wednesday May 22, 2024

Wednesday of Seventh Week in Ordinary Time
First Reading: James 4:13-17
Beloved: 13 Come now, you who say, "Today or tomorrow we shall go into such and such a town, spend a year there doing business, and make a profit" 14—you have no idea what your life will be like tomorrow. You are a puff of smoke that appears briefly and then disappears. 15 Instead you should say, "If the Lord wills it, we shall live to do this or that." 16 But now you are boasting in your arrogance. All such boasting is evil. 17 So for one who knows the right thing to do and does not do it, it is a sin.

Responsorial Psalm: Psalms 49:2-3, 6-7, 8-10, 11

R. *(Matthew 5:3)* **Blessed are the poor in spirit; the Kingdom of heaven is theirs!**

[2] Hear this, all you peoples;
 hearken, all who dwell in the world,
[3] Of lowly birth or high degree,
 rich and poor alike.

R. *Blessed are the poor in spirit; the Kingdom of heaven is theirs!*

[6] Why should I fear in evil days
 when my wicked ensnarers ring me
 round?
[7] They trust in their wealth;
 the abundance of their riches is their
 boast.

R. *Blessed are the poor in spirit; the Kingdom of heaven is theirs!*

[8] Yet in no way can a man redeem himself,
 or pay his own ransom to God;
[9] Too high is the price to redeem one's life; [10] he
 would never have enough
 to remain alive always and not see
 destruction.

R. *Blessed are the poor in spirit; the Kingdom of heaven is theirs!*

[11] For he can see that wise men die,
 and likewise the senseless and the stupid
 pass away,
 leaving to others their wealth.

R. *Blessed are the poor in spirit; the Kingdom of heaven is theirs!*

Alleluia: John 14:6

R. Alleluia, alleluia.
[6] I am the way and the truth and the life, says
 the Lord;
no one comes to the Father except through
 me.
R. Alleluia, alleluia.

Gospel: Mark 9:38-40

[38] John said to Jesus, "Teacher, we saw someone driving out demons in your name, and we tried to prevent him because he does not follow us." [39] Jesus replied, "Do not prevent him. There is no one who performs a mighty deed in my name who can at the same time speak ill of me. [40] For whoever is not against us is for us."

Thursday of Seventh Week in Ordinary Time

First Reading: James 5:1-6

[1] Come now, you rich, weep and wail over your impending miseries. [2] Your wealth has rotted away, your clothes have become moth-eaten,[3] your gold and silver have corroded, and that corrosion will be a testimony against you; it will devour your flesh like a fire. You have stored up treasure for the last days. [4] Behold, the wages you withheld from the workers who harvested your fields are crying aloud; and the cries of the harvesters have reached the ears of the Lord of hosts. [5] You have lived on earth in luxury and pleasure; you have fattened your hearts for the day of slaughter. [6] You have condemned; you have murdered the righteous one; he offers you no resistance.

Responsorial Psalm: Psalms 49:14-15AB, 15CD-16, 17-18, 19-20

R. (Matthew 5:3) *Blessed are the poor in spirit; the Kingdom of heaven is theirs!*

[14] This is the way of those whose trust is folly,
    the end of those contented with their lot:
[15AB] Like sheep they are herded into the nether
      world;
    death is their shepherd and the upright
      rule over them.

R. *Blessed are the poor in spirit; the Kingdom of heaven is theirs!*

[15CD] Quickly their form is consumed;
    the nether world is their palace.
[16] But God will redeem me
    from the power of the nether world by
      receiving me.

R. *Blessed are the poor in spirit; the Kingdom of heaven is theirs!*

[17] Fear not when a man grows rich,
    when the wealth of his house becomes
        great,
[18] For when he dies, he shall take none of it;

his wealth shall not follow him down.

R. Blessed are the poor in spirit; the Kingdom of heaven is theirs!

19 Though in his lifetime he counted himself
blessed,
"They will praise you for doing well for
yourself,"
20 He shall join the circle of his forebears
who shall never more see light.

R. Blessed are the poor in spirit; the Kingdom of heaven is theirs!

Alleluia: cf.1 Thessalonians 2:13
R. Alleluia, alleluia.
13 Receive the word of God, not as the word of
men,
but as it truly is, the word of God.
R. Alleluia, alleluia.

Gospel: Mark 9:41-50
41 Jesus said to his disciples: "Anyone who gives you a cup of water to drink because you belong to Christ, amen, I say to you, will surely not lose his reward.

42 "Whoever causes one of these little ones who believe in me to sin, it would be better for him if a great millstone were put around his neck and he were thrown into the sea. 43 If your hand causes you to sin, cut it off. It is better for you to enter into life maimed than with two hands to go into Gehenna, into the unquenchable fire. 45 And if your foot causes you to sin, cut if off. It is better for you to enter into life crippled than with two feet to be thrown into Gehenna. 47 And if your eye causes you to sin, pluck it out. Better for you to enter into the Kingdom of God with one eye than with two eyes to be thrown into Gehenna, 48 where *their worm does not die, and the fire is not quenched.*

49 "Everyone will be salted with fire. 50 Salt is good, but if salt becomes insipid, with what will you restore its flavor? Keep salt in yourselves and you will have peace with one another."

Friday May 24, 2024
Friday of Seventh Week in Ordinary Time
First Reading: James 5:9-12
9 Do not complain, brothers and sisters, about one another, that you may not be judged. Behold, the Judge is standing before the gates. 10 Take as an example of hardship and patience, brothers and sisters, the prophets who spoke in the name of the Lord. 11 Indeed we call blessed those who have persevered. You have heard of the perseverance of Job,

and you have seen the purpose of the Lord, because *the Lord is compassionate and merciful.*

[12] But above all, my brothers and sisters, do not swear, either by heaven or by earth or with any other oath, but let your "Yes" mean "Yes" and your "No" mean "No," that you may not incur condemnation.

Responsorial Psalm: Psalms 103:1-2, 3-4, 8-9, 11-12

R. *(8a)* **The Lord is kind and merciful.**

[1] Bless the LORD, O my soul;
    and all my being, bless his holy name.
[2] Bless the LORD, O my soul,
    and forget not all his benefits.
R. The Lord is kind and merciful.

[3] He pardons all your iniquities,
    he heals all your ills.
[4] He redeems your life from destruction,
    he crowns you with kindness and
        compassion.
R. The Lord is kind and merciful.

[8] Merciful and gracious is the LORD,
    slow to anger and abounding in kindness.
[9] He will not always chide,
    nor does he keep his wrath forever.
R. The Lord is kind and merciful.

[11] For as the heavens are high above the earth,
    so surpassing is his kindness toward
        those who fear him.
[12] As far as the east is from the west,
    so far has he put our transgressions from
        us.
R. The Lord is kind and merciful.

Alleluia: cf. John 17:17B, 17A

R. Alleluia, alleluia.

[17B] Your word, O Lord, is truth;
[17A] consecrate us in the truth.

R. Alleluia, alleluia.

Gospel: Mark 10:1-12

[1] Jesus came into the district of Judea and across the Jordan. Again crowds gathered around him and, as was his custom, he again taught them. [2] The Pharisees approached

him and asked, "Is it lawful for a husband to divorce his wife?" They were testing him. [3] He said to them in reply, "What did Moses command you?" [4] They replied, "Moses permitted a husband to write a bill of divorce and dismiss her." [5] But Jesus told them, "Because of the hardness of your hearts he wrote you this commandment. [6] But from the beginning of creation, *God made them male and female.* [7] *For this reason a man shall leave his father and mother and be joined to his wife,* [8] *and the two shall become one flesh.* So they are no longer two but one flesh.[9]Therefore what God has joined together, no human being must separate." [10] In the house the disciples again questioned Jesus about this. [11] He said to them, "Whoever divorces his wife and marries another commits adultery against her; [12] and if she divorces her husband and marries another, she commits adultery."

Saturday May 25, 2024

Saturday of Seventh Week in Ordinary Time
First Reading: James 5:13-20

[13] Beloved: Is anyone among you suffering? He should pray. Is anyone in good spirits? He should sing a song of praise. [14] Is anyone among you sick? He should summon the presbyters of the Church, and they should pray over him and anoint him with oil in the name of the Lord. [15] The prayer of faith will save the sick person, and the Lord will raise him up. If he has committed any sins, he will be forgiven.

[16] Therefore, confess your sins to one another and pray for one another, that you may be healed. The fervent prayer of a righteous person is very powerful. [17] Elijah was a man like us; yet he prayed earnestly that it might not rain, and for three years and six months it did not rain upon the land. [18] Then Elijah prayed again, and the sky gave rain and the earth produced its fruit.

[19] My brothers and sisters, if anyone among you should stray from the truth and someone bring him back, [20] he should know that whoever brings back a sinner from the error of his way will save his soul from death and will cover a multitude of sins.

Responsorial Psalm: Psalms 141:1-2,3 & 8
R. [2a] *Let my prayer come like incense before you.*
[1] O LORD, to you I call; hasten to me;
>> hearken to my voice when I call upon
>>> you.
[2] Let my prayer come like incense before you;
>> the lifting up of my hands, like the
>>> evening sacrifice.
R. *Let my prayer come like incense before you.*

[3] O LORD, set a watch before my mouth,
>> a guard at the door of my lips.
[8] For toward you, O God, my LORD, my eyes are
>> turned;

in you I take refuge; strip me not of life.
R. *Let my prayer come like incense before you.*

Alleluia: cf. Matthew 11:25
R. Alleluia, alleluia.
[25] Blessed are you, Father, Lord of heaven and
      earth;
you have revealed to little ones the
      mysteries of the Kingdom.
R. Alleluia, alleluia.

Gospel: Mark 10:13-16
[13] People were bringing children to Jesus that he might touch them, but the disciples rebuked them. [14] When Jesus saw this he became indignant and said to them, "Let the children come to me; do not prevent them, for the Kingdom of God belongs to such as these. [15] Amen, I say to you, whoever does not accept the Kingdom of God like a child will not enter it." [16] Then he embraced the children and blessed them, placing his hands on them.

Sunday May 26, 2024
Solemnity of the Most Holy Trinity
First Reading: Deuteronomy 4:32-34, 39-40
[32] Moses said to the people: "Ask now of the days of old, before your time, ever since God created man upon the earth; ask from one end of the sky to the other: Did anything so great ever happen before? Was it ever heard of? [33] Did a people ever hear the voice of God speaking from the midst of fire, as you did, and live? [34] Or did any god venture to go and take a nation for himself from the midst of another nation, by testings, by signs and wonders, by war, with strong hand and outstretched arm, and by great terrors, all of which the LORD, your God, did for you in Egypt before your very eyes? [39] This is why you must now know, and fix in your heart, that the LORD is God in the heavens above and on earth below, and that there is no other. [40] You must keep his statutes and commandments that I enjoin on you today, that you and your children after you may prosper, and that you may have long life on the land which the LORD, your God, is giving you forever."

Responsorial Psalm: Psalms 33:4-5, 6, 9, 18-19, 20, 22
R. [12b] *Blessed the people the Lord has chosen*
               to be his own.
[4] Upright is the word of the LORD,
    and all his works are trustworthy.
[5] He loves justice and right;
      of the kindness of the LORD the earth is
        full.

***R. Blessed the people the Lord has chosen to be
his own.***

[6] By the word of the LORD the heavens were
made;
   by the breath of his mouth all their host.
[9] For he spoke, and it was made;
   he commanded, and it stood forth.
***R. Blessed the people the Lord has chosen to be
his own.***

[18] See, the eyes of the LORD are upon those who
fear him,
   upon those who hope for his kindness,
[19] to deliver them from death
   and preserve them in spite of famine.
***R. Blessed the people the Lord has chosen to be
his own.***

[20] Our soul waits for the LORD,
   who is our help and our shield.
[22] May your kindness, O LORD, be upon us
   who have put our hope in you.
***R. Blessed the people the Lord has chosen to be
his own.***

Second Reading: Romans 8:14-17

Brothers and sisters: [14] Those who are led by the Spirit of God are sons of God. [15] For you did not receive a spirit of slavery to fall back into fear, but you received a Spirit of adoption, through whom we cry, "Abba, Father!" [16] The Spirit himself bears witness with our spirit that we are children of God, [17] and if children, then heirs, heirs of God and joint heirs with Christ, if only we suffer with him so that we may also be glorified with him.

Alleluia: Revelation 1:8

R. Alleluia, alleluia.
[8] Glory to the Father, the Son, and the Holy
Spirit;
to God who is, who was, and who is to come.
R. Alleluia, alleluia.

Gospel: Matthew 28:16-20

[16] The eleven disciples went to Galilee, to the mountain to which Jesus had ordered them. [17] When they all saw him, they worshiped, but they doubted. [18] Then Jesus approached and said to them, "All power in heaven and on earth has been given to me. [19] Go, therefore, and make disciples of all nations, baptizing them in the name of the Father, and of the Son, and of the Holy Spirit, [20] teaching them to observe all that I have commanded you. And behold, I am with you always, until the end of the age."

Monday May 27, 2024
Monday of Eighth Week in ordinary Time

First Reading: 1 Peter 1:3-9

[3] Blessed be the God and Father of our Lord Jesus Christ, who in his great mercy gave us a new birth to a living hope through the resurrection of Jesus Christ from the dead, [4] to an inheritance that is imperishable, undefiled, and unfading, kept in heaven for you [5] who by the power of God are safeguarded through faith, to a salvation that is ready to be revealed in the final time. [6] In this you rejoice, although now for a little while you may have to suffer through various trials, [7] so that the genuineness of your faith, more precious than gold that is perishable even though tested by fire, may prove to be for praise, glory, and honor at the revelation of Jesus Christ. [8] Although you have not seen him you love him; even though you do not see him now yet you believe in him, you rejoice with an indescribable and glorious joy, [9] as you attain the goal of faith, the salvation of your souls.

Responsorial Psalm: Psalms 111:1-2, 5-6, 9 AND 10C

R. [5] *The Lord will remember his covenant for ever.* or: *Alleluia.*

[1] I will give thanks to the LORD with all my
    heart
    in the company and assembly of the just.
[2] Great are the works of the LORD,
    exquisite in all their delights.

R. *The Lord will remember his covenant for ever.* or: *Alleluia.*

[5] He has given food to those who fear him;
    he will forever be mindful of his
        covenant.
[6] He has made known to his people the power
        of his works,
    giving them the inheritance of the
        nations.

R. *The Lord will remember his covenant for ever.* or: *Alleluia.*

[9] He has sent deliverance to his people;
    he has ratified his covenant forever;

holy and awesome is his name.
^{10c} His praise endures forever.
R. The Lord will remember his covenant for ever. or: *Alleluia.*

Alleluia: 2 Corinthians 8:9
R. Alleluia, alleluia.
⁹ Jesus Christ became poor although he was
            rich,
so that by his poverty you might become
            rich.
R. Alleluia, alleluia.

Gospel: Mark 10:17-27
¹⁷ As Jesus was setting out on a journey, a man ran up, knelt down before him, and asked him, "Good teacher, what must I do to inherit eternal life?" ¹⁸ Jesus answered him, "Why do you call me good? No one is good but God alone. ¹⁹ You know the commandments: *You shall not kill; you shall not commit adultery; you shall not steal; you shall not bear false witness; you shall not defraud; honor your father and your mother."* ²⁰ He replied and said to him, "Teacher, all of these I have observed from my youth." ²¹ Jesus, looking at him, loved him and said to him, "You are lacking in one thing. Go, sell what you have, and give to the poor and you will have treasure in heaven; then come, follow me." ²² At that statement, his face fell, and he went away sad, for he had many possessions.

²³ Jesus looked around and said to his disciples, "How hard it is for those who have wealth to enter the Kingdom of God!" ²⁴ The disciples were amazed at his words. So Jesus again said to them in reply, "Children, how hard it is to enter the Kingdom of God! ²⁵ It is easier for a camel to pass through the eye of a needle than for one who is rich to enter the Kingdom of God." ²⁶ They were exceedingly astonished and said among themselves, "Then who can be saved?" ²⁷ Jesus looked at them and said, "For men it is impossible, but not for God. All things are possible for God."

Tuesday May 28, 2024
Tuesday of Eighth Week in ordinary Time
First Reading: 1 Peter 1:10-16
Beloved: ¹⁰ Concerning the salvation of your souls the prophets who prophesied about the grace that was to be yours searched and investigated it ¹¹ investigating the time and circumstances that the Spirit of Christ within them indicated when it testified in advance to the sufferings destined for Christ and the glories to follow them. ¹² It was revealed to them that they were serving not themselves but you with regard to the things that have now been announced to you by those who preached the Good News to you through the Holy Spirit sent from heaven, things into which angels longed to look.

¹³ Therefore, gird up the loins of your mind, live soberly, and set your hopes completely on the grace to be brought to you at the revelation of Jesus Christ. ¹⁴ Like

obedient children, do not act in compliance with the desires of your former ignorance [15] but, as he who called you is holy, be holy yourselves in every aspect of your conduct, [16] for it is written, *Be holy because I am holy.*

Responsorial Psalm: Psalms 98:1, 2-3AB, 3CD-4

R. *(2a)* **The Lord has made known his salvation.**

[1] Sing to the LORD a new song,
    for he has done wondrous deeds;
His right hand has won victory for him,
    his holy arm.
R. *The Lord has made known his salvation.*

[2] The LORD has made his salvation known:
    in the sight of the nations he has revealed
        his justice.
[3AB] He has remembered his kindness and his
        faithfulness
    toward the house of Israel.
R. *The Lord has made known his salvation.*

[3CD] All the ends of the earth have seen
    the salvation by our God.
[4] Sing joyfully to the LORD, all you lands;
    break into song; sing praise.
R. *The Lord has made known his salvation.*

Alleluia: cf. Matthew 11:25

R. Alleluia, alleluia.
[25] Blessed are you, Father, Lord of heaven and
        earth;
you have revealed to little ones the
        mysteries of the Kingdom.
R. Alleluia, alleluia.

Gospel: Mark 10:28-31

[28] Peter began to say to Jesus, "We have given up everything and followed you." [29] Jesus said, "Amen, I say to you, there is no one who has given up house or brothers or sisters or mother or father or children or lands for my sake and for the sake of the Gospel [30] who will not receive a hundred times more now in this present age: houses and brothers and sisters and mothers and children and lands, with persecutions, and eternal life in the age to come. [31] But many that are first will be last, and the last will be first."

Wednesday of Eighth Week in ordinary Time

First Reading: 1 Peter 1:18-25

Beloved: [18] realize that you were ransomed from your futile conduct, handed on by your ancestors, not with perishable things like silver or gold [19] but with the precious Blood of Christ as of a spotless unblemished Lamb. [20] He was known before the foundation of the world but revealed in the final time for you, [21] who through him believe in God who raised him from the dead and gave him glory, so that your faith and hope are in God.

[22] Since you have purified yourselves by obedience to the truth for sincere brotherly love, love one another intensely from a pure heart. [23] You have been born anew, not from perishable but from imperishable seed, through the living and abiding word of God, [24] for:
"All flesh is like grass,
    and all its glory like the flower of the field;
the grass withers,
    and the flower wilts;
[25] but the word of the Lord remains forever."
This is the word that has been proclaimed to you.

Responsorial Psalm: Psalms 147:12-13, 14-15, 19-20

R. *(12a) Praise the Lord, Jerusalem.* or: *Alleluia.*

[12] Glorify the LORD, O Jerusalem;
    praise your God, O Zion.
[13] For he has strengthened the bars of your
        gates;
    he has blessed your children within you.
R. *Praise the Lord, Jerusalem.* or: *Alleluia.*

[14] He has granted peace in your borders;
    with the best of wheat he fills you.
[15] He sends forth his command to the earth;
    swiftly runs his word!
R. *Praise the Lord, Jerusalem.* or: *Alleluia.*

[19] He has proclaimed his word to Jacob,
    his statutes and his ordinances to Israel.
[20] He has not done thus for any other nation;
    his ordinances he has not made known to
        them. Alleluia.
R. *Praise the Lord, Jerusalem.* or: *Alleluia.*

Alleluia: Mark 10:45

R. Alleluia, alleluia.
[45] The Son of Man came to serve,

and to give his life as a ransom for many.
R. Alleluia, alleluia.

Gospel: Mark 10:32-45

[32] The disciples were on the way, going up to Jerusalem, and Jesus went ahead of them. They were amazed, and those who followed were afraid. Taking the Twelve aside again, he began to tell them what was going to happen to him. [33] "Behold, we are going up to Jerusalem, and the Son of Man will be handed over to the chief priests and the scribes, and they will condemn him to death and hand him over to the Gentiles [34] who will mock him, spit upon him, scourge him, and put him to death, but after three days he will rise."

[35] Then James and John, the sons of Zebedee, came to Jesus and said to him, "Teacher, we want you to do for us whatever we ask of you." [36] He replied, "What do you wish me to do for you?" [37] They answered him, "Grant that in your glory we may sit one at your right and the other at your left." [38] Jesus said to them, "You do not know what you are asking. Can you drink the cup that I drink or be baptized with the baptism with which I am baptized?" [39] They said to him, "We can." Jesus said to them, "The cup that I drink, you will drink, and with the baptism with which I am baptized, you will be baptized; [40] but to sit at my right or at my left is not mine to give but is for those for whom it has been prepared." [41] When the ten heard this, they became indignant at James and John. [42] Jesus summoned them and said to them, "You know that those who are recognized as rulers over the Gentiles lord it over them, and their great ones make their authority over them felt. [43] But it shall not be so among you. Rather, whoever wishes to be great among you will be your servant; [44] whoever wishes to be first among you will be the slave of all. [45] For the Son of Man did not come to be served but to serve and to give his life as a ransom for many."

Thursday May 30, 2024
Thursday of Eighth Week in ordinary Time
First Reading: 1 Peter 2:2-5, 9-12

Beloved: [2] Like newborn infants, long for pure spiritual milk so that through it you may grow into salvation, [3] for you have tasted that the Lord is good. [4] Come to him, a living stone, rejected by human beings but chosen and precious in the sight of God, [5] and, like living stones, let yourselves be built into a spiritual house to be a holy priesthood to offer spiritual sacrifices acceptable to God through Jesus Christ.

[9] You are *"a chosen race, a royal priesthood, a holy nation, a people of his own, so that you may announce the praises"* of him who called you out of darkness into his wonderful light.

[10] Once you were *"no people"*
   but now you are God's people;
you *"had not received mercy"*
   but now you have received mercy.

[11] Beloved, I urge you as aliens and sojourners to keep away from worldly desires that wage war against the soul. [12] Maintain good conduct among the Gentiles, so that if they speak of you as evildoers, they may observe your good works and glorify God on the day of visitation.

Responsorial Psalm: Psalms 100:2, 3, 4, 5

R. [2c] *Come with joy into the presence of the Lord.*

[2] Sing joyfully to the LORD, all you lands;
    serve the LORD with gladness;
    come before him with joyful song.

R. *Come with joy into the presence of the Lord.*

[3] Know that the LORD is God;
    he made us, his we are;
    his people, the flock he tends.

R. *Come with joy into the presence of the Lord.*

[4] Enter his gates with thanksgiving,
    his courts with praise;
Give thanks to him;
    bless his name.

R. *Come with joy into the presence of the Lord.*

[5] The LORD is good:
    his kindness endures forever,
    and his faithfulness, to all generations.

R. *Come with joy into the presence of the Lord.*

Alleluia: John 8:12

R. Alleluia, alleluia.

[12] I am the light of the world, says the Lord;
whoever follows me will have the light of life.

R. Alleluia, alleluia.

Gospel: Mark 10:46-52

[46] As Jesus was leaving Jericho with his disciples and a sizable crowd, Bartimaeus, a blind man, the son of Timaeus, sat by the roadside begging. [47] On hearing that it was Jesus of Nazareth, he began to cry out and say, "Jesus, son of David, have pity on me." [48] And many rebuked him, telling him to be silent. But he kept calling out all the more, "Son of David, have pity on me." [49] Jesus stopped and said, "Call him." So they called the blind man, saying to him, "Take courage; get up, he is calling you." [50] He threw aside his cloak, sprang up, and came to Jesus. [51] Jesus said to him in reply, "What do you want me to do for you?" The blind man replied to him, "Master, I want to see." [52] Jesus told him, "Go your way; your faith has saved you." Immediately he received his sight and followed him on the way.

Feast of Visitation of Blessed Virgin Mary
First Reading: Zephaniah 3:14-18A

14 Shout for joy, O daughter Zion!
    Sing joyfully, O Israel!
Be glad and exult with all your heart,
    O daughter Jerusalem!
15 The LORD has removed the judgment
        against you,
    he has turned away your enemies;
The King of Israel, the LORD, is in your
        midst,
    you have no further misfortune to
        fear.
16 On that day, it shall be said to Jerusalem:
    Fear not, O Zion, be not discouraged!
17 The LORD, your God, is in your midst,
    a mighty savior;
He will rejoice over you with gladness,
    and renew you in his love,
He will sing joyfully because of you,
    18A as one sings at festivals.

Or Romans 12:9-16

9 Brothers and sisters: Let love be sincere; hate what is evil, hold on to what is good; 10 love one another with mutual affection; anticipate one another in showing honor. 11 Do not grow slack in zeal, be fervent in spirit, serve the Lord. 12 Rejoice in hope, endure in affliction, persevere in prayer. 13 Contribute to the needs of the holy ones, exercise hospitality. 14 Bless those who persecute you, bless and do not curse them. 15 Rejoice with those who rejoice, weep with those who weep. 16 Have the same regard for one another; do not be haughty but associate with the lowly; do not be wise in your own estimation.

Responsorial Psalm: Isaiah 12:2-3, 4BCD, 5-6
R. (6) *Among you is the great and Holy One of*
        Israel.
2 God indeed is my savior;
    I am confident and unafraid.
My strength and my courage is the LORD,
    and he has been my savior.
3 With joy you will draw water
    at the fountain of salvation.

R. Among you is the great and Holy One of Israel.

4BCD Give thanks to the LORD, acclaim his name;
>   among the nations make known his
>   deeds,
>   proclaim how exalted is his name.

R. Among you is the great and Holy One of Israel.

5 Sing praise to the LORD for his glorious
>   achievement;
>   let this be known throughout all the
>   earth.
6 Shout with exultation, O city of Zion,
>   for great in your midst
>   is the Holy One of Israel!

R. Among you is the great and Holy One of Israel.

Alleluia: cf. Luke 1:45
R. Alleluia, alleluia.
45 Blessed are you, O Virgin Mary, who believed
that what was spoken to you by the Lord
>   would be fulfilled.
R. Alleluia, alleluia.

Gospel: Luke 1:39-56
39 Mary set out and travelled to the hill country in haste to a town of Judah, 40 where she entered the house of Zechariah and greeted Elizabeth. 41 When Elizabeth heard Mary's greeting, the infant leaped in her womb, and Elizabeth, filled with the Holy Spirit, 42 cried out in a loud voice and said, "Most blessed are you among women, and blessed is the fruit of your womb. 43 And how does this happen to me, that the mother of my Lord should come to me? 44 For at the moment the sound of your greeting reached my ears, the infant in my womb leaped for joy. 45 Blessed are you who believed that what was spoken to you by the Lord would be fulfilled."
46 And Mary said:

"My soul proclaims the greatness of the
>   Lord;
>   47 my spirit rejoices in God my Savior,
>   48 for he has looked with favor on his lowly

293

servant.
From this day all generations will call me
  blessed:
   49 the Almighty has done great things for
   me,
  and holy is his Name.
50 He has mercy on those who fear him
  in every generation.
51 He has shown the strength of his arm,
  he has scattered the proud in their
   conceit.
52 He has cast down the mighty from their
   thrones,
  and has lifted up the lowly.
53 He has filled the hungry with good things,
  and the rich he has sent away empty.
54 He has come to the help of his servant Israel
  for he has remembered his promise of
   mercy,
   55 the promise he made to our fathers,
  to Abraham and his children forever."

56 Mary remained with her about three months and then returned to her home.

JUNE 2024
Saturday June 1, 2024

Memorial of Saint Justin, Martyr
First Reading: Jude 1:17,20B-25
17 Beloved, remember the words spoken beforehand by the Apostles of our Lord Jesus Christ, 20 But you, beloved, build yourselves up in your most holy faith; pray in the Holy Spirit. 21 Keep yourselves in the love of God and wait for the mercy of our Lord Jesus Christ that leads to eternal life. 22 On those who waver, have mercy; 23 save others by snatching them out of the fire; on others have mercy with fear, abhorring even the outer garment stained by the flesh.

  24 To the one who is able to keep you from stumbling and to present you unblemished and exultant, in the presence of his glory, 25 to the only God, our savior, through Jesus Christ our Lord be glory, majesty, power, and authority from ages past, now, and for ages to come. Amen.

Responsorial Psalm: Psalms 63:2, 3-4, 5-6
R. (2b) *My soul is thirsting for you, O Lord my God.*
2 O God, you are my God whom I seek;

for you my flesh pines and my soul thirsts
like the earth, parched, lifeless and
without water.
R. My soul is thirsting for you, O Lord my God.

3 Thus have I gazed toward you in the
sanctuary
to see your power and your glory,
4 For your kindness is a greater good than life;
my lips shall glorify you.
R. My soul is thirsting for you, O Lord my God.

5 Thus will I bless you while I live;
lifting up my hands, I will call upon your
name.
6 As with the riches of a banquet shall my soul
be satisfied,
and with exultant lips my mouth shall
praise you.
R. My soul is thirsting for you, O Lord my God.

Alleluia: Colossians 3:16A, 17C
R. Alleluia, alleluia.
16A Let the word of Christ dwell in you richly;
17A giving thanks to God the Father through him.
R. Alleluia, alleluia.

Gospel: Mark 11:27-33
27 Jesus and his disciples returned once more to Jerusalem. As he was walking in the temple area, the chief priests, the scribes, and the elders approached him 28 and said to him, "By what authority are you doing these things? Or who gave you this authority to do them?" 29 Jesus said to them, "I shall ask you one question. Answer me, and I will tell you by what authority I do these things. 30 Was John's baptism of heavenly or of human origin? Answer me." 31 They discussed this among themselves and said, "If we say, 'Of heavenly origin,' he will say, 'Then why did you not believe him?' 32 But shall we say, 'Of human origin'?"—they feared the crowd, for they all thought John really was a prophet. 33 So they said to Jesus in reply, "We do not know." Then Jesus said to them, "Neither shall I tell you by what authority I do these things."

Solemnity of Body and Blood of Christ (*Corpus Christi*)

First Reading: Exodus 24:3-8

3 When Moses came to the people and related all the words and ordinances of the LORD, they all answered with one voice, "We will do everything that the LORD has told us." 4 Moses then wrote down all the words of the LORD and, rising early the next day, he erected at the foot of the mountain an altar and twelve pillars for the twelve tribes of Israel. 5 Then, having sent certain young men of the Israelites to offer holocausts and sacrifice young bulls as peace offerings to the LORD, 6 Moses took half of the blood and put it in large bowls; the other half he splashed on the altar. 7 Taking the book of the covenant, he read it aloud to the people, who answered, "All that the LORD has said, we will heed and do." 8 Then he took the blood and sprinkled it on the people, saying, "This is the blood of the covenant that the LORD has made with you in accordance with all these words of his."

Responsorial Psalm: Psalms 116:12-13, 15-16, 17-18

R. (13) *I will take the cup of salvation, and call on
the name of the Lord.* or: *Alleluia.*

12 How shall I make a return to the LORD
for all the good he has done for me?
13 The cup of salvation I will take up,
and I will call upon the name of the LORD.

R. *I will take the cup of salvation, and call on the
name of the Lord.* or: *Alleluia.*

15 Precious in the eyes of the LORD
is the death of his faithful ones.
16 I am your servant, the son of your
handmaid;
you have loosed my bonds.

R. *I will take the cup of salvation, and call on the
name of the Lord.* or: *Alleluia.*

17 To you will I offer sacrifice of thanksgiving,
and I will call upon the name of the LORD.
18 My vows to the LORD I will pay
in the presence of all his people.

R. *I will take the cup of salvation, and call on the
name of the Lord.* or: *Alleluia.*

Second Reading: Hebrews 9:11-15

[11] Brothers and sisters: When Christ came as high priest of the good things that have come to be, passing through the greater and more perfect tabernacle not made by hands, that is, not belonging to this creation, [12] he entered once for all into the sanctuary, not with the blood of goats and calves but with his own blood, thus obtaining eternal redemption. [13] For if the blood of goats and bulls and the sprinkling of a heifer's ashes can sanctify those who are defiled so that their flesh is cleansed, [14] how much more will the blood of Christ, who through the eternal Spirit offered himself unblemished to God, cleanse our consciences from dead works to worship the living God.

[15] For this reason he is mediator of a new covenant: since a death has taken place for deliverance from transgressions under the first covenant, those who are called may receive the promised eternal inheritance.

Sequence - *Lauda Sion*

Laud, O Zion, your salvation,
Laud with hymns of exultation,
Christ, your king and shepherd true:

Bring him all the praise you know,
He is more than you bestow.
Never can you reach his due.

Special theme for glad thanksgiving
Is the quick'ning and the living
Bread today before you set:

From his hands of old partaken,
As we know, by faith unshaken,
Where the Twelve at supper met.

Full and clear ring out your chanting,
Joy nor sweetest grace be wanting,
From your heart let praises burst:

For today the feast is holden,
When the institution olden
Of that supper was rehearsed.

Here the new law's new oblation,
By the new king's revelation,
Ends the form of ancient rite:

Now the new the old effaces,
Truth away the shadow chases,
Light dispels the gloom of night.

What he did at supper seated,
Christ ordained to be repeated,
His memorial ne'er to cease:

And his rule for guidance taking,
Bread and wine we hallow, making
Thus our sacrifice of peace.

This the truth each Christian learns,
Bread into his flesh he turns,
To his precious blood the wine:

Sight has fail'd, nor thought conceives,
But a dauntless faith believes,
Resting on a pow'r divine.

Here beneath these signs are hidden
Priceless things to sense forbidden;
Signs, not things are all we see:

Blood is poured and flesh is broken,
Yet in either wondrous token
Christ entire we know to be.

Whoso of this food partakes,
Does not rend the Lord nor breaks;
Christ is whole to all that taste:

Thousands are, as one, receivers,
One, as thousands of believers,
Eats of him who cannot waste.

Bad and good the feast are sharing,
Of what divers dooms preparing,
Endless death, or endless life.

Life to these, to those damnation,
See how like participation

Is with unlike issues rife.

When the sacrament is broken,
Doubt not, but believe 'tis spoken,
That each sever'd outward token
doth the very whole contain.

Nought the precious gift divides,
Breaking but the sign betides
Jesus still the same abides,
still unbroken does remain.

The shorter form of the sequence begins here.

Lo! the angel's food is given
To the pilgrim who has striven;
See the children's bread from heaven,
which on dogs may not be spent.

Truth the ancient types fulfilling,
Isaac bound, a victim willing,
Paschal lamb, its lifeblood spilling,
manna to the fathers sent.

Very bread, good shepherd, tend us,
Jesu, of your love befriend us,
You refresh us, you defend us,
Your eternal goodness send us
In the land of life to see.

You who all things can and know,
Who on earth such food bestow,
Grant us with your saints, though lowest,
Where the heav'nly feast you show,
Fellow heirs and guests to be. Amen.
 Alleluia.

Alleluia: John 6:51
R. Alleluia, alleluia.
[51] I am the living bread that came down from
        heaven, says the Lord;
whoever eats this bread will live forever.

R. Alleluia, alleluia.

Gospel: Mark 14:12-16, 22-26

[12] On the first day of the Feast of Unleavened Bread, when they sacrificed the Passover lamb, Jesus' disciples said to him, "Where do you want us to go and prepare for you to eat the Passover?" [13] He sent two of his disciples and said to them, "Go into the city and a man will meet you, carrying a jar of water. Follow him. [14] Wherever he enters, say to the master of the house, 'The Teacher says, "Where is my guest room where I may eat the Passover with my disciples?"' [15] Then he will show you a large upper room furnished and ready. Make the preparations for us there." [16] The disciples then went off, entered the city, and found it just as he had told them; and they prepared the Passover.

[22] While they were eating, he took bread, said the blessing, broke it, gave it to them, and said, "Take it; this is my body." [23] Then he took a cup, gave thanks, and gave it to them, and they all drank from it. [24] He said to them, "This is my blood of the covenant, which will be shed for many. [25] Amen, I say to you, I shall not drink again the fruit of the vine until the day when I drink it new in the kingdom of God." [26] Then, after singing a hymn, they went out to the Mount of Olives.

Monday June 3, 2024

Memorial of Saints Charles Lwanga and Companions, Martyrs
First Reading: 2 Peter 1:2-7

[2] Beloved: May grace and peace be yours in abundance through knowledge of God and of Jesus our Lord.

[3] His divine power has bestowed on us everything that makes for life and devotion, through the knowledge of him who called us by his own glory and power. [4] Through these, he has bestowed on us the precious and very great promises, so that through them you may come to share in the divine nature, after escaping from the corruption that is in the world because of evil desire. [5] For this very reason, make every effort to supplement your faith with virtue, virtue with knowledge, [6] knowledge with self-control, self-control with endurance, endurance with devotion, [7] devotion with mutual affection, mutual affection with love.

Responsorial Psalm: Psalms 91:1-2, 14-15B, 15C-16

R. (see 2b) *In you, my God, I place my trust.*

[1] You who dwell in the shelter of the Most
          High,
     who abide in the shadow of the Almighty,
[2] Say to the LORD, "My refuge and my fortress,
     my God, in whom I trust."
R. *In you, my God, I place my trust.*

[14] Because he clings to me, I will deliver him;
     I will set him on high because he

acknowledges my name.
^{15B} He shall call upon me, and I will answer
      him;
    I will be with him in distress.
R. In you, my God, I place my trust.

^{15C} I will deliver him and glorify him;
    ¹⁶ with length of days I will gratify him
    and will show him my salvation.
R. In you, my God, I place my trust.

Alleluia: cf. Revelation 1:5AB
R. Alleluia, alleluia.
^{5AB} Jesus Christ, you are the faithful witness,
the firstborn of the dead;
you have loved us and freed us from our sins
      by your Blood.
R. Alleluia, alleluia.

Gospel: Mark 12:1-12
¹ Jesus began to speak to the chief priests, the scribes, and the elders in parables. "A man planted a vineyard, put a hedge around it, dug a wine press, and built a tower. Then he leased it to tenant farmers and left on a journey. ² At the proper time he sent a servant to the tenants to obtain from them some of the produce of the vineyard. ³ But they seized him, beat him, and sent him away empty-handed. ⁴ Again he sent them another servant. And that one they beat over the head and treated shamefully. ⁵ He sent yet another whom they killed. So, too, many others; some they beat, others they killed. ⁶ He had one other to send, a beloved son. He sent him to them last of all, thinking, 'They will respect my son.' ⁷ But those tenants said to one another, 'This is the heir. Come, let us kill him, and the inheritance will be ours.' ⁸ So they seized him and killed him, and threw him out of the vineyard. ⁹ What then will the owner of the vineyard do? He will come, put the tenants to death, and give the vineyard to others. ¹⁰ Have you not read this Scripture passage:
'The stone that the builders rejected has become the cornerstone; ¹¹ *by the Lord has this been done, and it is wonderful in our eyes'*?"

    ¹² They were seeking to arrest him, but they feared the crowd, for they realized that he had addressed the parable to them. So they left him and went away.

Tuesday of the Ninth Week in Ordinary Time
First Reading: 2 Peter 3:12-15A, 17-18

Beloved: [12] Wait for and hasten the coming of the day of God, because of which the heavens will be dissolved in flames and the elements melted by fire. [13] But according to his promise we await new heavens and a new earth in which righteousness dwells.

[14] Therefore, beloved, since you await these things, be eager to be found without spot or blemish before him, at peace. [15] And consider the patience of our Lord as salvation.

[17] Therefore, beloved, since you are forewarned, be on your guard not to be led into the error of the unprincipled and to fall from your own stability. [18] But grow in grace and in the knowledge of our Lord and savior Jesus Christ. To him be glory now and to the day of eternity. Amen.

Responsorial Psalm: Psalms 90:2, 3-4, 10, 14 AND 16

R. [1] *In every age, O Lord, you have been our*
refuge.

[2] Before the mountains were begotten
and the earth and the world were
brought forth,
from everlasting to everlasting you are
God.
R. In every age, O Lord, you have been our
refuge.

[3] You turn man back to dust,
saying, "Return, O children of men."
[4] For a thousand years in your sight
are as yesterday, now that it is past,
or as a watch of the night.
R. In every age, O Lord, you have been our
refuge.

[10] Seventy is the sum of our years,
or eighty, if we are strong,
And most of them are fruitless toil,
for they pass quickly and we drift away.
R. In every age, O Lord, you have been our
refuge.

[14] Fill us at daybreak with your kindness,
that we may shout for joy and gladness

all our days.
¹⁶ Let your work be seen by your servants
    and your glory by their children.
**R. In every age, O Lord, you have been our
    refuge.**

Alleluia: cf. Ephesians 1:17-18
R. Alleluia, alleluia.
¹⁷ᴬ May the Father of our Lord Jesus Christ
¹⁸ᴬᴮ enlighten the eyes of our hearts,
that we may know what is the hope
that belongs to his call.
R. Alleluia, alleluia.

Gospel: Mark 12:13-17
¹³ Some Pharisees and Herodians were sent to Jesus to ensnare him in his speech. ¹⁴ They came and said to him, "Teacher, we know that you are a truthful man and that you are not concerned with anyone's opinion. You do not regard a person's status but teach the way of God in accordance with the truth. Is it lawful to pay the census tax to Caesar or not? Should we pay or should we not pay?" ¹⁵ Knowing their hypocrisy he said to them, "Why are you testing me? Bring me a denarius to look at." ¹⁶ They brought one to him and he said to them, "Whose image and inscription is this?" They replied to him, "Caesar's." ¹⁷ So Jesus said to them, "Repay to Caesar what belongs to Caesar and to God what belongs to God." They were utterly amazed at him.

Wednesday June 5, 2024
Memorial of Saint Boniface, Bishop & Martyr
First Reading: 2 Timothy 1:1-3, 6-12
¹ Paul, an Apostle of Christ Jesus by the will of God for the promise of life in Christ Jesus, ² to Timothy, my dear child: grace, mercy, and peace from God the Father and Christ Jesus our Lord.

³ I am grateful to God, whom I worship with a clear conscience as my ancestors did, as I remember you constantly in my prayers, night and day.

⁶ For this reason, I remind you to stir into flame the gift of God that you have through the imposition of my hands. ⁷ For God did not give us a spirit of cowardice but rather of power and love and self-control. ⁸ So do not be ashamed of your testimony to our Lord, nor of me, a prisoner for his sake; but bear your share of hardship for the Gospel with the strength that comes from God.

⁹ He saved us and called us to a holy life, not according to our works but according to his own design and the grace bestowed on us in Christ Jesus before time began, ¹⁰ but now made manifest through the appearance of our savior Christ Jesus, who destroyed death and brought life and immortality to light through the Gospel, ¹¹ for which I was

appointed preacher and Apostle and teacher. [12] On this account I am suffering these things; but I am not ashamed, for I know him in whom I have believed and am confident that he is able to guard what has been entrusted to me until that day.

Responsorial Psalm: Psalms 123:1B-2AB, 2CDEF

R. [1b] *To you, O Lord, I lift up my eyes.*

[1B] To you I lift up my eyes
> who are enthroned in heaven.

[2AB] Behold, as the eyes of servants
> are on the hands of their masters.

R. *To you, O Lord, I lift up my eyes.*

[2CDEF] As the eyes of a maid
> are on the hands of her mistress,

So are our eyes on the LORD, our God,
> till he have pity on us.

R. *To you, O Lord, I lift up my eyes.*

Alleluia: John 11:25A, 26

R. Alleluia, alleluia.

[25A] I am the resurrection and the life, says the
> Lord;

[26] whoever believes in me will never die.

R. Alleluia, alleluia.

Gospel: Mark 12:18-27

[18] Some Sadducees, who say there is no resurrection, came to Jesus and put this question to him, [19] saying, "Teacher, Moses wrote for us, '*If someone's brother dies, leaving a wife but no child, his brother must take the wife and raise up descendants for his brother.*' [20] Now there were seven brothers. The first married a woman and died, leaving no descendants. [21] So the second married her and died, leaving no descendants, and the third likewise. [22] And the seven left no descendants. Last of all the woman also died. [23] At the resurrection when they arise whose wife will she be? For all seven had been married to her." [24] Jesus said to them, "Are you not misled because you do not know the Scriptures or the power of God? [25] When they rise from the dead, they neither marry nor are given in marriage, but they are like the angels in heaven. [26] As for the dead being raised, have you not read in the Book of Moses, in the passage about the bush, how God told him, '*I am the God of Abraham, the God of Isaac, and the God of Jacob*'? [27] He is not God of the dead but of the living. You are greatly misled."

Thursday June 6, 2024

Thursday of Ninth Week in ordinary Time
First Reading: 2 Timothy 2:8-15

Beloved: [8] Remember Jesus Christ, raised from the dead, a descendant of David: such is my Gospel, [9] for which I am suffering, even to the point of chains, like a criminal. But the word of God is not chained. [10] Therefore, I bear with everything for the sake of those who are chosen, so that they too may obtain the salvation that is in Christ Jesus, together with eternal glory. [11] This saying is trustworthy:

If we have died with him
we shall also live with him;
[12] if we persevere
we shall also reign with him.
But if we deny him
he will deny us.
[13] If we are unfaithful
he remains faithful,
for he cannot deny himself.

[14] Remind people of these things and charge them before God to stop disputing about words. This serves no useful purpose since it harms those who listen. [15] Be eager to present yourself as acceptable to God, a workman who causes no disgrace, imparting the word of truth without deviation.

Responsorial Psalm: Psalms 25:4-5AB, 8-9, 10 AND 14

R. [4] *Teach me your ways, O Lord.*
[4] Your ways, O LORD, make known to me;
teach me your paths,
[5AB] Guide me in your truth and teach me,
for you are God my savior.
R. *Teach me your ways, O Lord.*

[8] Good and upright is the LORD;
thus he shows sinners the way.
[9] He guides the humble to justice,
he teaches the humble his way.
R. *Teach me your ways, O Lord.*

[10] All the paths of the LORD are kindness and constancy
toward those who keep his covenant and
his decrees.

305

¹⁴ The friendship of the LORD is with those who
        fear him,
        and his covenant, for their instruction.
R. Teach me your ways, O Lord.

Alleluia: cf. 2 Timothy 1:10
R. Alleluia, alleluia.
¹⁰ Our Savior Jesus Christ has destroyed death
and brought life to light through the Gospel.
R. Alleluia, alleluia.

Gospel: Mark 12:28-34
²⁸ One of the scribes came to Jesus and asked him, "Which is the first of all the commandments?" ²⁹ Jesus replied, "The first is this: *'Hear, O Israel! The Lord our God is Lord alone!* ³⁰ *You shall love the Lord your God with all your heart, with all your soul, with all your mind, and with all your strength.'* ³¹ The second is this: *'You shall love your neighbor as yourself.'* There is no other commandment greater than these." ³² The scribe said to him, "Well said, teacher. You are right in saying, *'He is One and there is no other than he.'* ³³ And *'to love him with all your heart, with all your understanding, with all your strength,* and *to love your neighbor as yourself'* is worth more than all burnt offerings and sacrifices." ³⁴ And when Jesus saw that he answered with understanding, he said to him, "You are not far from the Kingdom of God." And no one dared to ask him any more questions.

Friday June 7, 2024

Solemnity of Sacred Heart of Jesus
First Reading: Hosea 11:1, 3-4, 8c-9
Thus says the LORD:

¹ When Israel was a child I loved him,
    out of Egypt I called my son.
³ Yet it was I who taught Ephraim to walk,
    who took them in my arms;
        but they did not know that I cared for them.
⁴ I drew them with human cords,
    with bands of love;
I fostered them like those
    who raise an infant to their cheeks;
yet, though I stooped to feed my child,
    they did not know that I was their healer.

^{8c} My heart is overwhelmed,

my pity is stirred.
⁹ I will not give vent to my blazing anger,
   I will not destroy Ephraim again;
For I am God and not a man,
   the Holy One present among you;
   I will not let the flames consume you.

Responsorial Psalm: Is 12:2-3, 4, 5-6.
R. *(3) You will draw water joyfully from the*
       springs of salvation.

² God indeed is my savior;
     I am confident and unafraid.
My strength and my courage is the LORD,
     and he has been my savior.
³ With joy you will draw water
     at the fountain of salvation.
R. *You will draw water joyfully from the springs*
     of salvation.
⁴ Give thanks to the LORD, acclaim his name;
     among the nations make known his
       deeds,
     proclaim how exalted is his name.
R. *You will draw water joyfully from the springs*
     of salvation.

⁵ Sing praise to the LORD for his glorious
       achievement;
     let this be known throughout all the
       earth.
⁶ Shout with exultation, O city of Zion,
     for great in your midst
     is the Holy One of Israel!
R. *You will draw water joyfully from the springs*
     of salvation.

Second Reading: Ephesians 3:8-12, 14-19
Brothers and sisters: ⁸ To me, the very least of all the holy ones, this grace was given, to preach to the Gentiles the inscrutable riches of Christ, ⁹ and to bring to light for all what is the plan of the mystery hidden from ages past in God who created all things, ¹⁰ so that the manifold wisdom of God might now be made known through the church to the principalities and authorities in the heavens. ¹¹ This was according to the eternal purpose

that he accomplished in Christ Jesus our Lord, [12] in whom we have boldness of speech and confidence of access through faith in him.

[14] For this reason I kneel before the Father, [15] from whom every family in heaven and on earth is named, [16] that he may grant you in accord with the riches of his glory to be strengthened with power through his Spirit in the inner self, [17] and that Christ may dwell in your hearts through faith; that you, rooted and grounded in love, [18] may have strength to comprehend with all the holy ones what is the breadth and length and height and depth, [19] and to know the love of Christ that surpasses knowledge, so that you may be filled with all the fullness of God.

Alleluia: Matthew 11:29ab
R. Alleluia, alleluia.
[29ab] Take my yoke upon you, says the Lord;
and learn from me, for I am meek and
      humble of heart.
R. Alleluia, alleluia.

Or: 1 John 4:10b
R. Alleluia, alleluia.
[10b] God first loved us
and sent his Son as expiation for our sins.
R. Alleluia, alleluia.

Gospel: John 19:31-37
[31] Since it was preparation day, in order that the bodies might not remain on the cross on the sabbath, for the sabbath day of that week was a solemn one, the Jews asked Pilate that their legs be broken and they be taken down. [32] So the soldiers came and broke the legs of the first and then of the other one who was crucified with Jesus. [33] But when they came to Jesus and saw that he was already dead, they did not break his legs, [34] but one soldier thrust his lance into his side, and immediately blood and water flowed out. [35] An eyewitness has testified, and his testimony is true; he knows that he is speaking the truth, so that you also may come to believe. [36] For this happened so that the Scripture passage might be fulfilled:

"Not a bone of it will be broken."

[37] And again another passage says:

*"They will look upon him whom they have
      pierced."*

Memorial of The Immaculate Heart of Mary
First Reading: 2 Timothy 4:1-8

Beloved: [1] I charge you in the presence of God and of Christ Jesus, who will judge the living and the dead, and by his appearing and his kingly power: [2] proclaim the word; be persistent whether it is convenient or inconvenient; convince, reprimand, encourage through all patience and teaching. [3] For the time will come when people will not tolerate sound doctrine but, following their own desires and insatiable curiosity, will accumulate teachers [4] and will stop listening to the truth and will be diverted to myths. [5] But you, be self-possessed in all circumstances; put up with hardship; perform the work of an evangelist; fulfill your ministry.

[6] For I am already being poured out like a libation, and the time of my departure is at hand. [7] I have competed well; I have finished the race; I have kept the faith. [8] From now on the crown of righteousness awaits me, which the Lord, the just judge, will award to me on that day, and not only to me, but to all who have longed for his appearance.

Responsorial Psalm: Psalms 71:8-9, 14-15AB, 16-17, 22

R. (see 15ab) *I will sing of your salvation.*

[8] My mouth shall be filled with your praise,
    with your glory day by day.
[9] Cast me not off in my old age;
    as my strength fails, forsake me not.
R. *I will sing of your salvation.*

[14] But I will always hope
    and praise you ever more and more.
[15AB] My mouth shall declare your justice,
    day by day your salvation.
R. *I will sing of your salvation.*

[16] I will treat of the mighty works of the Lord;
    O GOD, I will tell of your singular justice.
[17] O God, you have taught me from my youth,
    and till the present I proclaim your
        wondrous deeds.
R. *I will sing of your salvation.*
[22] So will I give you thanks with music on the
        lyre,
    for your faithfulness, O my God!
I will sing your praises with the harp,
    O Holy One of Israel!
R. *I will sing of your salvation.*

Alleluia: Matthew 5:3
R. Alleluia, alleluia.
[3] Blessed are the poor in spirit;
for theirs is the Kingdom of heaven.
R. Alleluia, alleluia.

Gospel: Luke 2:41-51
[41] Each year Jesus' parents went to Jerusalem for the feast of Passover, [42] and when he was twelve years old, they went up according to festival custom. [43] After they had completed its days, as they were returning, the boy Jesus remained behind in Jerusalem, but his parents did not know it. [44] Thinking that he was in the caravan, they journeyed for a day and looked for him among their relatives and acquaintances, [45] but not finding him, they returned to Jerusalem to look for him. [46] After three days they found him in the temple, sitting in the midst of the teachers, listening to them and asking them questions, [47] and all who heard him were astounded at his understanding and his answers. [48] When his parents saw him, they were astonished, and his mother said to him, "Son, why have you done this to us? Your father and I have been looking for you with great anxiety." [49] And he said to them, "Why were you looking for me? Did you not know that I must be in my Father's house?" [50] But they did not understand what he said to them. [51] He went down with them and came to Nazareth, and was obedient to them; and his mother kept all these things in her heart.

Sunday June 9, 2024

Tenth Sunday in Ordinary Time, Year B
First Reading: Genesis 3:9-15
[9] After the man, Adam, had eaten of the tree, the LORD God called to the man and asked him, "Where are you?" [10] He answered, "I heard you in the garden; but I was afraid, because I was naked, so I hid myself." [11] Then he asked, "Who told you that you were naked? You have eaten, then, from the tree of which I had forbidden you to eat!" [12] The man replied, "The woman whom you put here with me— she gave me fruit from the tree, and so I ate it." [13] The LORD God then asked the woman, "Why did you do such a thing?" The woman answered, "The serpent tricked me into it, so I ate it."
   [14] Then the LORD God said to the serpent:

"Because you have done this, you shall be
      banned
    from all the animals
    and from all the wild creatures;
on your belly shall you crawl,
      and dirt shall you eat
      all the days of your life.
[15] I will put enmity between you and the

310

woman,
      and between your offspring and hers;
he will strike at your head,
      while you strike at his heel."

Responsorial Psalm: Psalms 130:1-2, 3-4, 5-6, 7-8

R. *(7bc) With the Lord there is mercy, and fullness
            of redemption.*
¹ Out of the depths I cry to you, O LORD;
      LORD, hear my voice!
² Let your ears be attentive
      to my voice in supplication.
R. *With the Lord there is mercy, and fullness of
      redemption.*

³ If you, O LORD, mark iniquities,
      LORD, who can stand?
⁴ But with you is forgiveness,
      that you may be revered.
R. *With the Lord there is mercy, and fullness of
      redemption.*

⁵ I trust in the LORD;
      my soul trusts in his word.
⁶ More than sentinels wait for the dawn,
      let Israel wait for the LORD.
R. *With the Lord there is mercy, and fullness of
      redemption.*

⁷ For with the LORD is kindness
      and with him is plenteous redemption
⁸ and he will redeem Israel
      from all their iniquities.
R. *With the Lord there is mercy, and fullness of
      redemption.*

Second Reading: 2 Corinthians 4:13-5:1

¹³ Brothers and sisters: Since we have the same spirit of faith, according to what is written, *I believed, therefore I spoke*, we too believe and therefore we speak,¹⁴ knowing that the one who raised the Lord Jesus will raise us also with Jesus and place us with you in his presence. ¹⁵ Everything indeed is for you, so that the grace bestowed in abundance on more and more people may cause the thanksgiving to overflow for the glory of God. ¹⁶ Therefore, we are not discouraged; rather, although our outer self is wasting away, our

inner self is being renewed day by day. [17] For this momentary light affliction is producing for us an eternal weight of glory beyond all comparison, [18] as we look not to what is seen but to what is unseen; for what is seen is transitory, but what is unseen is eternal. [1] For we know that if our earthly dwelling, a tent, should be destroyed, we have a building from God, a dwelling not made with hands, eternal in heaven.

Alleluia: John 12:31B-32

R. Alleluia, alleluia.

[31B] Now the ruler of the world will be driven
        out, says the Lord;
[32] and when I am lifted up from the earth, I
        will draw everyone to myself.

R. Alleluia, alleluia.

Gospel: Mark 3:20-35

[20] Jesus came home with his disciples. Again the crowd gathered, making it impossible for them even to eat. [21] When his relatives heard of this they set out to seize him, for they said, "He is out of his mind." [22] The scribes who had come from Jerusalem said, "He is possessed by Beelzebul," and "By the prince of demons he drives out demons."

[23] Summoning them, he began to speak to them in parables, "How can Satan drive out Satan? [24] If a kingdom is divided against itself, that kingdom cannot stand. [25] And if a house is divided against itself, that house will not be able to stand. [26] And if Satan has risen up against himself and is divided, he cannot stand; that is the end of him. [27] But no one can enter a strong man's house to plunder his property unless he first ties up the strong man. Then he can plunder the house. [28] Amen, I say to you, all sins and all blasphemies that people utter will be forgiven them. [29] But whoever blasphemes against the Holy Spirit will never have forgiveness, but is guilty of an everlasting sin." [30] For they had said, "He has an unclean spirit."

[31] His mother and his brothers arrived. Standing outside they sent word to him and called him. [32] A crowd seated around him told him, "Your mother and your brothers and your sisters are outside asking for you." [33] But he said to them in reply, "Who are my mother and my brothers?" [34] And looking around at those seated in the circle he said, "Here are my mother and my brothers. [35] For whoever does the will of God is my brother and sister and mother."

Monday June 10, 2024

Monday of the Tenth Week in Ordinary Time

First Reading: 1 Kings 17:1-6

[1] Elijah the Tishbite, from Tishbe in Gilead, said to Ahab: "As the LORD, the God of Israel, lives, whom I serve, during these years there shall be no dew or rain except at my word." [2] The LORD then said to Elijah: [3] "Leave here, go east and hide in the Wadi Cherith, east of the Jordan. [4] You shall drink of the stream, and I have commanded ravens to feed you

there." [5] So he left and did as the LORD had commanded. He went and remained by the Wadi Cherith, east of the Jordan. [6] Ravens brought him bread and meat in the morning, and bread and meat in the evening, and he drank from the stream.

Responsorial Psalm: Psalms 121:1BC-2, 3-4, 5-6, 7-8

R. (see 2) **Our help is from the Lord, who made heaven and earth.**

[1BC] I lift up my eyes toward the mountains;
    whence shall help come to me?
[2] My help is from the LORD,
    who made heaven and earth.

R. Our help is from the Lord, who made heaven and earth.

[3] May he not suffer your foot to slip;
    may he slumber not who guards you:
[4] Indeed he neither slumbers nor sleeps,
    the guardian of Israel.

R. Our help is from the Lord, who made heaven and earth.

[5] The LORD is your guardian; the LORD is your shade;
    he is beside you at your right hand.
[6] The sun shall not harm you by day,
    nor the moon by night.

R. Our help is from the Lord, who made heaven and earth.

[7] The LORD will guard you from all evil;
    he will guard your life.
[8] The LORD will guard your coming and your going,
    both now and forever.

R. Our help is from the Lord, who made heaven and earth.

Alleluia: Matthew 5:12A

R. Alleluia, alleluia.
[12A] Rejoice and be glad;
for your reward will be great in heaven.
R. Alleluia, alleluia.

Gospel: Matthew 5:1-12

[1] When Jesus saw the crowds, he went up the mountain, and after he had sat down, his disciples came to him. [2] He began to teach them, saying:

[3] "Blessed are the poor in spirit,
  for theirs is the Kingdom of heaven.
[4] Blessed are they who mourn,
  for they will be comforted.
[5] Blessed are the meek,
  for they will inherit the land.
[6] Blessed are they who hunger and thirst for
    righteousness,
  for they will be satisfied.
[7] Blessed are the merciful,
  for they will be shown mercy.
[8] Blessed are the clean of heart,
  for they will see God.
[9] Blessed are the peacemakers,
  for they will be called children of God.
[10] Blessed are they who are persecuted for the
    sake of righteousness,
  for theirs is the Kingdom of heaven.
[11] Blessed are you when they insult you and
    persecute you
  and utter every kind of evil against you
    falsely because of me.
[12] Rejoice and be glad,
  for your reward will be great in heaven.
Thus they persecuted the prophets who were
    before you."

Tuesday June 11, 2024

Feast of Saint Barnabas, Apostle
First Reading: Acts 11:21B-26; 13:1-3

[21B] In those days a great number who believed turned to the Lord. [22] The news about them reached the ears of the Church in Jerusalem, and they sent Barnabas to go to Antioch. [23] When he arrived and saw the grace of God, he rejoiced and encouraged them all to remain faithful to the Lord in firmness of heart, [24] for he was a good man, filled with the Holy Spirit and faith. And a large number of people was added to the Lord. [25] Then he went to Tarsus to look for Saul, [26] and when he had found him he brought him to Antioch. For a whole year they met with the Church and taught a large number of people, and it was in Antioch that the disciples were first called Christians.

[1] Now there were in the Church at Antioch prophets and teachers: Barnabas, Symeon who was called Niger, Lucius of Cyrene, Manaen who was a close friend of Herod the tetrarch, and Saul. [2] While they were worshiping the Lord and fasting, the Holy Spirit said, "Set apart for me Barnabas and Saul for the work to which I have called them." [3] Then, completing their fasting and prayer, they laid hands on them and sent them off.

Responsorial Psalm: Psalms 98:1, 2-3AB, 3CD-4, 5-6

R. (see 2b) **The Lord has revealed to the nations his
saving power.**

[1] Sing to the LORD a new song,
for he has done wondrous deeds;
His right hand has won victory for him,
his holy arm.
**R. The Lord has revealed to the nations his
saving power.**

[2] The LORD has made his salvation known:
in the sight of the nations he has revealed
his justice.
[3AB] He has remembered his kindness and his
faithfulness
toward the house of Israel.
**R. The Lord has revealed to the nations his
saving power.**

[3CD] All the ends of the earth have seen
the salvation by our God.
[4] Sing joyfully to the LORD, all you lands;
break into song; sing praise.
**R. The Lord has revealed to the nations his
saving power.**

[5] Sing praise to the LORD with the harp,
with the harp and melodious song.
[6] With trumpets and the sound of the horn
sing joyfully before the King, the LORD.
**R. The Lord has revealed to the nations his
saving power.**

Alleluia: Matthew 5:16

R. Alleluia, alleluia.
[16] Let your light shine before others
that they may see your good deeds and

glorify your heavenly Father.
R. Alleluia, alleluia.

Gospel: Matthew 5:13-16

Jesus said to his disciples: [13] "You are the salt of the earth. But if salt loses its taste, with what can it be seasoned? It is no longer good for anything but to be thrown out and trampled underfoot. [14] You are the light of the world. A city set on a mountain cannot be hidden. [15] Nor do they light a lamp and then put it under a bushel basket; it is set on a lampstand, where it gives light to all in the house. [16] Just so, your light must shine before others, that they may see your good deeds and glorify your heavenly Father."

Wednesday of Tenth Week in Ordinary Time
First Reading: 1 Kings 18:20-39

[20] Ahab sent to all the children of Israel and had the prophets assemble on Mount Carmel.

[21] Elijah appealed to all the people and said, "How long will you straddle the issue? If the LORD is God, follow him; if Baal, follow him." The people, however, did not answer him. [22] So Elijah said to the people, "I am the only surviving prophet of the LORD, and there are four hundred and fifty prophets of Baal. [23] Give us two young bulls. Let them choose one, cut it into pieces, and place it on the wood, but start no fire. I shall prepare the other and place it on the wood, but shall start no fire. [24] You shall call on your gods, and I will call on the LORD. The God who answers with fire is God." All the people answered, "Agreed!"

[25] Elijah then said to the prophets of Baal, "Choose one young bull and prepare it first, for there are more of you. Call upon your gods, but do not start the fire." [26] Taking the young bull that was turned over to them, they prepared it and called on Baal from morning to noon, saying, "Answer us, Baal!" But there was no sound, and no one answering. And they hopped around the altar they had prepared. [27] When it was noon, Elijah taunted them: "Call louder, for he is a god and may be meditating, or may have retired, or may be on a journey. Perhaps he is asleep and must be awakened." [28] They called out louder and slashed themselves with swords and spears, as was their custom, until blood gushed over them. [29] Noon passed and they remained in a prophetic state until the time for offering sacrifice. But there was not a sound; no one answered, and no one was listening.

[30] Then Elijah said to all the people, "Come here to me." When the people had done so, he repaired the altar of the LORD that had been destroyed. [31] He took twelve stones, for the number of tribes of the sons of Jacob, to whom the LORD had said, "Your name shall be Israel." [32] He built an altar in honor of the LORD with the stones, and made a trench around the altar large enough for two measures of grain.

[33] When he had arranged the wood, he cut up the young bull and laid it on the wood. [34] "Fill four jars with water," he said, "and pour it over the burnt offering and over the wood." "Do it again," he said, and they did it again. "Do it a third time," he said, and they

did it a third time. [35] The water flowed around the altar, and the trench was filled with the water.

[36] At the time for offering sacrifice, the prophet Elijah came forward and said, "LORD, God of Abraham, Isaac, and Israel, let it be known this day that you are God in Israel and that I am your servant and have done all these things by your command. [37] Answer me, LORD! Answer me, that this people may know that you, LORD, are God and that you have brought them back to their senses." [38] The LORD's fire came down and consumed the burnt offering, wood, stones, and dust, and it lapped up the water in the trench. [39] Seeing this, all the people fell prostrate and said, "The LORD is God! The LORD is God!"

Responsorial Psalm: Psalms 16:1B-2AB, 4, 5AB AND 8, 11

R. [(1b)] *Keep me safe, O God; you are my hope.*
[1B] Keep me, O God, for in you I take refuge;
[2AB] I say to the LORD, "My Lord are you."
R. *Keep me safe, O God; you are my hope.*

[4] They multiply their sorrows
who court other gods.
Blood libations to them I will not pour out,
nor will I take their names upon my lips.
R. *Keep me safe, O God; you are my hope.*

[5AB] O LORD, my allotted portion and cup,
you it is who hold fast my lot.
[8] I set the LORD ever before me;
with him at my right hand I shall not be
disturbed.
R. *Keep me safe, O God; you are my hope.*

[11] You will show me the path to life,
fullness of joys in your presence,
the delights at your right hand forever.
R. *Keep me safe, O God; you are my hope.*

Alleluia: Psalms 25:4B, 5A

R. Alleluia, alleluia.
[4B] Teach me your paths, my God,
[5A] and guide me in your truth.
R. Alleluia, alleluia.

Gospel: Matthew 5:17-19

[17] Jesus said to his disciples: "Do not think that I have come to abolish the law or the prophets. I have come not to abolish but to fulfill. [18] Amen, I say to you, until heaven and earth pass away, not the smallest letter or the smallest part of a letter will pass from the law, until all things have taken place. [19] Therefore, whoever breaks one of the least of these commandments and teaches others to do so will be called least in the Kingdom of heaven. But whoever obeys and teaches these commandments will be called greatest in the Kingdom of heaven."

Thursday June 13, 2024

Memorial of Saint Anthony of Padua, Priest & Doctor
First Reading: 1 Kings 18:41-46

[41] Elijah said to Ahab, "Go up, eat and drink, for there is the sound of a heavy rain." [42] So Ahab went up to eat and drink, while Elijah climbed to the top of Carmel, crouched down to the earth, and put his head between his knees. [43] "Climb up and look out to sea," he directed his servant, who went up and looked, but reported, "There is nothing." Seven times he said, "Go, look again!" [44] And the seventh time the youth reported, "There is a cloud as small as a man's hand rising from the sea." Elijah said, "Go and say to Ahab, 'Harness up and leave the mountain before the rain stops you.'" [45] In a trice the sky grew dark with clouds and wind, and a heavy rain fell. Ahab mounted his chariot and made for Jezreel. [46] But the hand of the LORD was on Elijah, who girded up his clothing and ran before Ahab as far as the approaches to Jezreel.

Responsorial Psalm: Psalms 65:10, 11, 12-13

R. [2a] *It is right to praise you in Zion, O God.*

[10] You have visited the land and watered it;
    greatly have you enriched it.
God's watercourses are filled;
    you have prepared the grain.
R. *It is right to praise you in Zion, O God.*

[11] Thus have you prepared the land:
    drenching its furrows, breaking up its
        clods,
Softening it with showers,
    blessing its yield.
R. *It is right to praise you in Zion, O God.*

[12] You have crowned the year with your
        bounty,
    and your paths overflow with a rich
        harvest;

¹³ The untilled meadows overflow with it,
   and rejoicing clothes the hills.
R. It is right to praise you in Zion, O God.

Alleluia: John 13:34
R. Alleluia, alleluia.
³⁴ I give you a new commandment:
love one another as I have loved you.
R. Alleluia, alleluia.

Gospel: Matthew 5:20-26
²⁰ Jesus said to his disciples: "I tell you, unless your righteousness surpasses that of the scribes and Pharisees, you will not enter into the Kingdom of heaven.

²¹ "You have heard that it was said to your ancestors, *You shall not kill; and whoever kills will be liable to judgment.* ²² But I say to you, whoever is angry with his brother will be liable to judgment, and whoever says to his brother, *Raqa*, will be answerable to the Sanhedrin, and whoever says, 'You fool,' will be liable to fiery Gehenna. ²³ Therefore, if you bring your gift to the altar, and there recall that your brother has anything against you, ²⁴ leave your gift there at the altar, go first and be reconciled with your brother, and then come and offer your gift. ²⁵ Settle with your opponent quickly while on the way to court with him. Otherwise your opponent will hand you over to the judge, and the judge will hand you over to the guard, and you will be thrown into prison. ²⁶ Amen, I say to you, you will not be released until you have paid the last penny."

Friday June 14, 2024

Friday of the Tenth Week in Ordinary Time
First Reading: 1 Kings 19:9A, 11-16
⁹ᴬ At the mountain of God, Horeb, Elijah came to a cave, where he took shelter. ¹¹ But the word of the LORD came to him, "Go outside and stand on the mountain before the LORD; the LORD will be passing by." A strong and heavy wind was rending the mountains and crushing rocks before the LORD —but the LORD was not in the wind. After the wind there was an earthquake— but the LORD was not in the earthquake. ¹² After the earthquake there was fire— but the LORD was not in the fire. After the fire there was a tiny whispering sound. ¹³ When he heard this, Elijah hid his face in his cloak and went and stood at the entrance of the cave. A voice said to him, "Elijah, why are you here?" ¹⁴ He replied, "I have been most zealous for the LORD, the God of hosts. But the children of Israel have forsaken your covenant, torn down your altars, and put your prophets to the sword. I alone am left, and they seek to take my life." ¹⁵ The LORD said to him, "Go, take the road back to the desert near Damascus. When you arrive, you shall anoint Hazael as king of Aram. ¹⁶ Then you shall anoint Jehu, son of Nimshi, as king of Israel, and Elisha, son of Shaphat of Abel-meholah, as prophet to succeed you."

Responsorial Psalm: Psalms 27:7-8A, 8B-9ABC, 13-14

R. *(8b)* *I long to see your face, O Lord.*

[7] Hear, O LORD, the sound of my call;
    have pity on me, and answer me.
[8A] Of you my heart speaks; you my glance
      seeks.

R. *I long to see your face, O Lord.*

[8B] Your presence, O LORD, I seek.
[9ABC] Hide not your face from me;
    do not in anger repel your servant.
You are my helper: cast me not off.

R. *I long to see your face, O Lord.*

[13] I believe that I shall see the bounty of the
      LORD
    in the land of the living.
[14] Wait for the LORD with courage;
    be stouthearted, and wait for the LORD.

R. *I long to see your face, O Lord.*

Alleluia: Philippians 2:15D, 16A

R. Alleluia, alleluia.
[15D] Shine like lights in the world,
[16A] as you hold on to the word of life.

R. Alleluia, alleluia.

Gospel: Matthew 5:27-32

[27] Jesus said to his disciples: "You have heard that it was said, *You shall not commit adultery.* [28] But I say to you, everyone who looks at a woman with lust has already committed adultery with her in his heart. [29] If your right eye causes you to sin, tear it out and throw it away. It is better for you to lose one of your members than to have your whole body thrown into Gehenna. [30] And if your right hand causes you to sin, cut it off and throw it away. It is better for you to lose one of your members than to have your whole body go into Gehenna.

    [31] "It was also said, *Whoever divorces his wife must give her a bill of divorce.* [32] But I say to you, whoever divorces his wife (unless the marriage is unlawful) causes her to commit adultery, and whoever marries a divorced woman commits adultery."

Saturday of Tenth Week in Ordinary Time
First Reading: 1 Kings 19:19-21

[19] Elijah set out, and came upon Elisha, son of Shaphat, as he was plowing with twelve yoke of oxen; he was following the twelfth. Elijah went over to him and threw his cloak over him. [20] Elisha left the oxen, ran after Elijah, and said, "Please, let me kiss my father and mother goodbye, and I will follow you." Elijah answered, "Go back! Have I done anything to you?" [21] Elisha left him and, taking the yoke of oxen, slaughtered them; he used the plowing equipment for fuel to boil their flesh, and gave it to his people to eat. Then he left and followed Elijah as his attendant.

Responsorial Psalm: Psalms 16:1B-2A AND 5, 7-8, 9-10

R. (see 5a) *You are my inheritance, O Lord.*

[1B] Keep me, O God, for in you I take refuge;
   [5] I say to the LORD, "My Lord are you."
O LORD, my allotted portion and my cup,
   you it is who hold fast my lot.

R. *You are my inheritance, O Lord.*

[7] I bless the LORD who counsels me;
   even in the night my heart exhorts me.
[8] I set the LORD ever before me;
   with him at my right hand I shall not be
      disturbed.

R. *You are my inheritance, O Lord.*

[9] Therefore my heart is glad and my soul
      rejoices,
   my body, too, abides in confidence;
[10] Because you will not abandon my soul to the
      nether world,
   nor will you suffer your faithful one to
      undergo corruption.

R. *You are my inheritance, O Lord.*

Alleluia: Psalms 119:36A, 29B

R. Alleluia, alleluia.

[36A] Incline my heart, O God, to your decrees;
[29B] and favor me with your law.

R. Alleluia, alleluia.

Gospel: Matthew 5:33-37

[33] Jesus said to his disciples: "You have heard that it was said to your ancestors, *Do not take a false oath, but make good to the Lord all that you vow.* [34] But I say to you, do not swear at all; not by heaven, for it is God's throne; [35] nor by the earth, for it is his footstool; nor by Jerusalem, for it is the city of the great King. [36] Do not swear by your head, for you cannot make a single hair white or black. [37] Let your 'Yes' mean 'Yes,' and your 'No' mean 'No.' Anything more is from the Evil One."

Sunday June 16, 2024

Eleventh Sunday in Ordinary Time, Year B
First Reading: Ezekiel 17:22-24

[22] Thus says the Lord GOD:

I, too, will take from the crest of the cedar,
from its topmost branches tear off a
tender shoot,
and plant it on a high and lofty mountain;
[23] on the mountain heights of Israel I will
plant it.
It shall put forth branches and bear fruit,
and become a majestic cedar.
Birds of every kind shall dwell beneath it,
every winged thing in the shade of its
boughs.
[24] And all the trees of the field shall know
that I, the LORD,
bring low the high tree,
lift high the lowly tree,
wither up the green tree,
and make the withered tree bloom.
As I, the LORD, have spoken, so will I do.

Responsorial Psalm: Psalms 92:2-3, 13-14, 15-16

R. (cf. 2a) **Lord, it is good to give thanks to you.**
[2] It is good to give thanks to the LORD,
to sing praise to your name, Most High,
[3] To proclaim your kindness at dawn
and your faithfulness throughout the
night.
R. **Lord, it is good to give thanks to you.**

[13] The just one shall flourish like the palm tree,

322

like a cedar of Lebanon shall he grow.
14 They that are planted in the house of the
LORD
shall flourish in the courts of our God.
R. Lord, it is good to give thanks to you.

15 They shall bear fruit even in old age;
vigorous and sturdy shall they be,
16 Declaring how just is the LORD,
my rock, in whom there is no wrong.
R. Lord, it is good to give thanks to you.

Second Reading: 2 Corinthians 5:6-10

6 Brothers and sisters: We are always courageous, although we know that while we are at home in the body we are away from the Lord, 7 for we walk by faith, not by sight. 8 Yet we are courageous, and we would rather leave the body and go home to the Lord. 9 Therefore, we aspire to please him, whether we are at home or away. 10 For we must all appear before the judgment seat of Christ, so that each may receive recompense, according to what he did in the body, whether good or evil.

Alleluia

R. Alleluia, alleluia.
The seed is the word of God, Christ is the
sower.
All who come to him will live for ever.
R. Alleluia, alleluia.

Gospel: Mark 4:26-34

26 Jesus said to the crowds: "This is how it is with the kingdom of God; it is as if a man were to scatter seed on the land 27 and would sleep and rise night and day and through it all the seed would sprout and grow, he knows not how. 28 Of its own accord the land yields fruit, first the blade, then the ear, then the full grain in the ear. 29 And when the grain is ripe, he wields the sickle at once, for the harvest has come."

30 He said, "To what shall we compare the kingdom of God, or what parable can we use for it? 31 It is like a mustard seed that, when it is sown in the ground, is the smallest of all the seeds on the earth. 32 But once it is sown, it springs up and becomes the largest of plants and puts forth large branches, so that the birds of the sky can dwell in its shade." 33 With many such parables he spoke the word to them as they were able to understand it. 34 Without parables he did not speak to them, but to his own disciples he explained everything in private.

Monday of Eleventh Week in Ordinary Time
First Reading: 1 Kings 21:1-16

[1] Naboth the Jezreelite had a vineyard in Jezreel next to the palace of Ahab, king of Samaria. [2] Ahab said to Naboth, "Give me your vineyard to be my vegetable garden, since it is close by, next to my house. I will give you a better vineyard in exchange, or, if you prefer, I will give you its value in money." [3] Naboth answered him, "The LORD forbid that I should give you my ancestral heritage." [4] Ahab went home disturbed and angry at the answer Naboth the Jezreelite had made to him: "I will not give you my ancestral heritage." Lying down on his bed, he turned away from food and would not eat.

[5] His wife Jezebel came to him and said to him, "Why are you so angry that you will not eat?" [6] He answered her, "Because I spoke to Naboth the Jezreelite and said to him, 'Sell me your vineyard, or, if you prefer, I will give you a vineyard in exchange.' But he refused to let me have his vineyard." [7] His wife Jezebel said to him, "A fine ruler over Israel you are indeed! Get up. Eat and be cheerful. I will obtain the vineyard of Naboth the Jezreelite for you."

[8] So she wrote letters in Ahab's name and, having sealed them with his seal, sent them to the elders and to the nobles who lived in the same city with Naboth. [9] This is what she wrote in the letters: "Proclaim a fast and set Naboth at the head of the people. [10] Next, get two scoundrels to face him and accuse him of having cursed God and king. Then take him out and stone him to death." [11] His fellow citizens (the elders and nobles who dwelt in his city) did as Jezebel had ordered them in writing, through the letters she had sent them. [12] They proclaimed a fast and placed Naboth at the head of the people. [13] Two scoundrels came in and confronted him with the accusation, "Naboth has cursed God and king." And they led him out of the city and stoned him to death. [14] Then they sent the information to Jezebel that Naboth had been stoned to death.

[15] When Jezebel learned that Naboth had been stoned to death, she said to Ahab, "Go on, take possession of the vineyard of Naboth the Jezreelite that he refused to sell you, because Naboth is not alive, but dead." [16] On hearing that Naboth was dead, Ahab started off on his way down to the vineyard of Naboth the Jezreelite, to take possession of it.

Responsorial Psalm: Psalms 5:2-3AB, 4B-6A, 6B-7

R. [2b] *Lord, listen to my groaning.*
[2] Hearken to my words, O LORD,
    attend to my sighing.
[3AB] Heed my call for help,
    my king and my God!
R. *Lord, listen to my groaning.*

[4B] At dawn I bring my plea expectantly before
       you.

[5] For you, O God, delight not in wickedness;
    no evil man remains with you;
[6A] the arrogant may not stand in your sight.
R. Lord, listen to my groaning.

[6B] You hate all evildoers.
    [7] You destroy all who speak falsehood;
The bloodthirsty and the deceitful
    the LORD abhors.
R. Lord, listen to my groaning.

Alleluia: Psalms 119:105
R. Alleluia, alleluia.
[105] A lamp to my feet is your word,
a light to my path.
R. Alleluia, alleluia.

Gospel: Matthew 5:38-42
[38] Jesus said to his disciples: "You have heard that it was said, *An eye for an eye and a tooth for a tooth*. [39] But I say to you, offer no resistance to one who is evil. When someone strikes you on your right cheek, turn the other one to him as well. [40] If anyone wants to go to law with you over your tunic, hand him your cloak as well. [41] Should anyone press you into service for one mile, go with him for two miles. [42] Give to the one who asks of you, and do not turn your back on one who wants to borrow."

Tuesday of Eleventh Week in Ordinary Time
First Reading: 1 Kings 21:17-29
[17] After the death of Naboth the LORD said to Elijah the Tishbite: [18] "Start down to meet Ahab, king of Israel, who rules in Samaria. He will be in the vineyard of Naboth, of which he has come to take possession. [19] This is what you shall tell him, 'The LORD says: After murdering, do you also take possession? For this, the LORD says: In the place where the dogs licked up the blood of Naboth, the dogs shall lick up your blood, too.'" [20] Ahab said to Elijah, "Have you found me out, my enemy?" "Yes," he answered. "Because you have given yourself up to doing evil in the LORD's sight, [21] I am bringing evil upon you: I will destroy you and will cut off every male in Ahab's line, whether slave or freeman, in Israel. [22] I will make your house like that of Jeroboam, son of Nebat, and like that of Baasha, son of Ahijah, because of how you have provoked me by leading Israel into sin." [23] (Against Jezebel, too, the LORD declared, "The dogs shall devour Jezebel in the district of Jezreel.") [24] "When one of Ahab's line dies in the city, dogs will devour him; when one of them dies in the field, the birds of the sky will devour him." [25] Indeed, no one gave himself up to the doing of evil in the sight of the LORD as did Ahab, urged on by his wife Jezebel. [26] He became completely abominable by following idols, just as the Amorites had done, whom the LORD drove out before the children of Israel.

[27] When Ahab heard these words, he tore his garments and put on sackcloth over his bare flesh. He fasted, slept in the sackcloth, and went about subdued. [28] Then the LORD said to Elijah the Tishbite, [29] "Have you seen that Ahab has humbled himself before me? Since he has humbled himself before me, I will not bring the evil in his time. I will bring the evil upon his house during the reign of his son."

Responsorial Psalm: Psalms 51:3-4, 5-6AB, 11 AND 16

R. [(see 3a)] *Be merciful, O Lord, for we have sinned.*

[3] Have mercy on me, O God, in your goodness;
    in the greatness of your compassion wipe
      out my offense.
[4] Thoroughly wash me from my guilt
    and of my sin cleanse me.

R. *Be merciful, O Lord, for we have sinned.*

[5] For I acknowledge my offense,
    and my sin is before me always:
[6AB] "Against you only have I sinned,
    and done what is evil in your sight."

R. *Be merciful, O Lord, for we have sinned.*

[11] Turn away your face from my sins,
    and blot out all my guilt.
[16] Free me from blood guilt, O God, my saving
      God;
    then my tongue shall revel in your
      justice.

R. *Be merciful, O Lord, for we have sinned.*

Alleluia: John 13:34

R. Alleluia, alleluia.
[34] I give you a new commandment;
love one another as I have loved you.
R. Alleluia, alleluia.

Gospel: Matthew 5:43-48

[43] Jesus said to his disciples: "You have heard that it was said, *You shall love your neighbor and hate your enemy.* [44] But I say to you, love your enemies and pray for those who persecute you, [45] that you may be children of your heavenly Father, for he makes his sun rise on the bad and the good, and causes rain to fall on the just and the unjust. [46] For if you love those who love you, what recompense will you have? Do not the tax collectors do the same? [47] And if you greet your brothers only, what is unusual about that? Do not the pagans do the same? [48] So be perfect, just as your heavenly Father is perfect."

Wednesday of the Eleventh Week in Ordinary Time
First Reading: 2 Kings 2:1, 6-14

[1] When the LORD was about to take Elijah up to heaven in a whirlwind, he and Elisha were on their way from Gilgal. [6] Elijah said to Elisha, "Please stay here; the LORD has sent me on to the Jordan." "As the LORD lives, and as you yourself live, I will not leave you," Elisha replied. And so the two went on together. [7] Fifty of the guild prophets followed and when the two stopped at the Jordan, they stood facing them at a distance. [8] Elijah took his mantle, rolled it up and struck the water, which divided, and both crossed over on dry ground.

[9] When they had crossed over, Elijah said to Elisha, "Ask for whatever I may do for you, before I am taken from you." [10] Elisha answered, "May I receive a double portion of your spirit." "You have asked something that is not easy," Elijah replied. "Still, if you see me taken up from you, your wish will be granted; otherwise not." [11] As they walked on conversing, a flaming chariot and flaming horses came between them, and Elijah went up to heaven in a whirlwind. [12] When Elisha saw it happen he cried out, "My father! my father! Israel's chariots and drivers!" But when he could no longer see him, Elisha gripped his own garment and tore it in two.

[13] Then he picked up Elijah's mantle that had fallen from him, and went back and stood at the bank of the Jordan. [14] Wielding the mantle that had fallen from Elijah, Elisha struck the water in his turn and said, "Where is the LORD, the God of Elijah?" When Elisha struck the water it divided and he crossed over.

Responsorial Psalm: Psalms 31:20, 21, 24

R. [25]*Let your hearts take comfort, all who hope in the Lord.*

[20] How great is the goodness, O LORD,
　　　　which you have in store for those who
　　　　　　fear you,
And which, toward those who take refuge in
　　　　you,
　　　　you show in the sight of the children of
　　　　men.
R. *Let your hearts take comfort, all who hope in the Lord.*

[21] You hide them in the shelter of your
　　　　presence
　　　from the plottings of men;
You screen them within your abode
　　　from the strife of tongues.
R. *Let your hearts take comfort, all who hope in the Lord.*

²⁴ Love the LORD, all you his faithful ones!
>The LORD keeps those who are constant,
>but more than requites those who act
>proudly.

R. Let your hearts take comfort, all who hope in the Lord.

Alleluia: John 14:23
R. Alleluia, alleluia.
²³ Whoever loves me will keep my word,
and my Father will love him
and we will come to him.
R. Alleluia, alleluia.

Gospel: Matthew 6:1-6, 16-18

¹ Jesus said to his disciples: "Take care not to perform righteous deeds in order that people may see them; otherwise, you will have no recompense from your heavenly Father. ² When you give alms, do not blow a trumpet before you, as the hypocrites do in the synagogues and in the streets to win the praise of others. Amen, I say to you, they have received their reward. ³ But when you give alms, do not let your left hand know what your right is doing, ⁴ so that your almsgiving may be secret. And your Father who sees in secret will repay you.

⁵ "When you pray, do not be like the hypocrites, who love to stand and pray in the synagogues and on street corners so that others may see them. Amen, I say to you, they have received their reward. ⁶ But when you pray, go to your inner room, close the door, and pray to your Father in secret. And your Father who sees in secret will repay you.

¹⁶ "When you fast, do not look gloomy like the hypocrites. They neglect their appearance, so that they may appear to others to be fasting. Amen, I say to you, they have received their reward. ¹⁷ But when you fast, anoint your head and wash your face, ¹⁸ so that you may not appear to others to be fasting, except to your Father who is hidden. And your Father who sees what is hidden will repay you."

Thursday June 20, 2024

Thursday of the Eleventh Week in Ordinary Time
First Reading: Sirach 48:1-14

¹ Like a fire there appeared the prophet Elijah
>whose words were as a flaming furnace.
² Their staff of bread he shattered,
>in his zeal he reduced them to straits;
³ By the Lord's word he shut up the heavens
>and three times brought down fire.
⁴ How awesome are you, Elijah, in your

wondrous deeds!
Whose glory is equal to yours?
⁵ You brought a dead man back to life
from the nether world, by the will of the
LORD.
⁶ You sent kings down to destruction,
and easily broke their power into pieces.
You brought down nobles, from their beds of
sickness.
⁷ You heard threats at Sinai,
at Horeb avenging judgments.
⁸ You anointed kings who should inflict
vengeance,
and a prophet as your successor.
⁹ You were taken aloft in a whirlwind of fire,
in a chariot with fiery horses.
¹⁰ You were destined, it is written, in time to
come
to put an end to wrath before the day of
the LORD,
To turn back the hearts of fathers toward
their sons,
and to re-establish the tribes of Jacob.
¹¹ Blessed is he who shall have seen you
And who falls asleep in your friendship.
For we live only in our life,
but after death our name will not be
such.
¹² O Elijah, enveloped in the whirlwind!

Then Elisha, filled with the twofold portion
of his spirit,
wrought many marvels by his mere
word.
During his lifetime he feared no one,
nor was any man able to intimidate his
will.
¹³ Nothing was beyond his power;
beneath him flesh was brought back into
life.
¹⁴ In life he performed wonders,
and after death, marvelous deeds.

Responsorial Psalm: Psalms 97:1-2,3-4,5-6, 7

R. (12a) *Rejoice in the Lord, you just!*

[1] The LORD is king; let the earth rejoice;
    let the many isles be glad.
[2] Clouds and darkness are round about him,
        justice and judgment are the foundation
            of his throne.

R. *Rejoice in the Lord, you just!*

[3] Fire goes before him
        and consumes his foes round about.
[4] His lightnings illumine the world;
        the earth sees and trembles.

R. *Rejoice in the Lord, you just!*

[51] The mountains melt like wax before the
            LORD,
        before the Lord of all the earth.
[6] The heavens proclaim his justice,
        and all peoples see his glory.

R. *Rejoice in the Lord, you just!*

[7] All who worship graven things are put to
            shame,
        who glory in the things of nought;
        all gods are prostrate before him.

R. *Rejoice in the Lord, you just!*

Alleluia: Romans 8:15BC

R. Alleluia, alleluia.

[15BC] You have received a spirit of adoption as
                sons
through which we cry: Abba! Father!

R. Alleluia, alleluia.

Gospel: Matthew 6:7-15

[7] Jesus said to his disciples: "In praying, do not babble like the pagans, who think that they will be heard because of their many words. [8] Do not be like them. Your Father knows what you need before you ask him.
[9] "This is how you are to pray:

'Our Father who art in heaven,

hallowed be thy name,
   [10] thy Kingdom come,
thy will be done,
   on earth as it is in heaven.
[11] Give us this day our daily bread;
   [12] and forgive us our trespasses,
   as we forgive those who trespass against
      us;
   [13] and lead us not into temptation,
   but deliver us from evil.'

[14] "If you forgive others their transgressions, your heavenly Father will forgive you. [15] But if you do not forgive others, neither will your Father forgive your transgressions."

Friday June 21, 2024

Memorial of Saint Aloysius Gonzaga, Religious
First Reading: 2 Kings 11:1-4, 9-18, 20

[1] When Athaliah, the mother of Ahaziah, saw that her son was dead, she began to kill off the whole royal family. [2] But Jehosheba, daughter of King Jehoram and sister of Ahaziah, took Joash, his son, and spirited him away, along with his nurse, from the bedroom where the princes were about to be slain. She concealed him from Athaliah, and so he did not die. [3] For six years he remained hidden in the temple of the LORD, while Athaliah ruled the land.

[4] But in the seventh year, Jehoiada summoned the captains of the Carians and of the guards. He had them come to him in the temple of the LORD, exacted from them a sworn commitment, and then showed them the king's son.

[9] The captains did just as Jehoiada the priest commanded. Each one with his men, both those going on duty for the sabbath and those going off duty that week, came to Jehoiada the priest. [10] He gave the captains King David's spears and shields, which were in the temple of the LORD. [11] And the guards, with drawn weapons, lined up from the southern to the northern limit of the enclosure, surrounding the altar and the temple on the king's behalf. [12] Then Jehoiada led out the king's son and put the crown and the insignia upon him. They proclaimed him king and anointed him, clapping their hands and shouting, "Long live the king!"

[13] Athaliah heard the noise made by the people, and appeared before them in the temple of the LORD. [14] When she saw the king standing by the pillar, as was the custom, and the captains and trumpeters near him, with all the people of the land rejoicing and blowing trumpets, she tore her garments and cried out, "Treason, treason!" [15] Then Jehoiada the priest instructed the captains in command of the force: "Bring her outside through the ranks. If anyone follows her," he added, "let him die by the sword." He had given orders that she should not be slain in the temple of the LORD. [16] She was led out forcibly to the horse gate of the royal palace, where she was put to death.

[17] Then Jehoiada made a covenant between the LORD as one party and the king and the people as the other, by which they would be the LORD's people; and another

covenant, between the king and the people. [18] Thereupon all the people of the land went to the temple of Baal and demolished it. They shattered its altars and images completely, and slew Mattan, the priest of Baal, before the altars. Jehoiada appointed a detachment for the temple of the LORD. [20] All the people of the land rejoiced and the city was quiet, now that Athaliah had been slain with the sword at the royal palace.

Responsorial Psalm: Psalms 132:11, 12, 13-14, 17-18

R. [(13)]*The Lord has chosen Zion for his dwelling.*

[11] The LORD swore to David
>   a firm promise from which he will not
>   withdraw:
"Your own offspring
>   I will set upon your throne."

R. *The Lord has chosen Zion for his dwelling.*

[12] "If your sons keep my covenant
>   and the decrees which I shall teach them,
Their sons, too, forever
>   shall sit upon your throne."

R. *The Lord has chosen Zion for his dwelling.*

[13] For the LORD has chosen Zion;
>   he prefers her for his dwelling.
[14] "Zion is my resting place forever;
>   in her will I dwell, for I prefer her."

R. *The Lord has chosen Zion for his dwelling.*

[17] "In her will I make a horn to sprout forth for
>   David;
>   I will place a lamp for my anointed.
[18] His enemies I will clothe with shame,
>   but upon him my crown shall shine."

R. *The Lord has chosen Zion for his dwelling.*

Alleluia: Matthew 5:3

R. Alleluia, alleluia.

[3] Blessed are the poor in spirit;
for theirs is the Kingdom of heaven.

R. Alleluia, alleluia.

Gospel: Matthew 6:19-23

[19] Jesus said to his disciples: "Do not store up for yourselves treasures on earth, where moth and decay destroy, and thieves break in and steal. [20] But store up treasures in heaven, where neither moth nor decay destroys, nor thieves break in and steal. [21] For where your treasure is, there also will your heart be.

[22] "The lamp of the body is the eye. If your eye is sound, your whole body will be filled with light; [23] but if your eye is bad, your whole body will be in darkness. And if the light in you is darkness, how great will the darkness be."

Saturday June 22, 2024

Saturday of Eleventh Week in Ordinary Time
First Reading: 2 Chronicles 24:17-25

[17] After the death of Jehoiada, the princes of Judah came and paid homage to King Joash, and the king then listened to them. [18] They forsook the temple of the LORD, the God of their fathers, and began to serve the sacred poles and the idols; and because of this crime of theirs, wrath came upon Judah and Jerusalem. [19] Although prophets were sent to them to convert them to the LORD, the people would not listen to their warnings. [20] Then the Spirit of God possessed Zechariah, son of Jehoiada the priest. He took his stand above the people and said to them: "God says, 'Why are you transgressing the LORD's commands, so that you cannot prosper? Because you have abandoned the LORD, he has abandoned you.'" [21] But they conspired against him, and at the king's order they stoned him to death in the court of the LORD's temple. [22] Thus King Joash was unmindful of the devotion shown him by Jehoiada, Zechariah's father, and slew his son. And as Zechariah was dying, he said, "May the LORD see and avenge."

[23] At the turn of the year a force of Arameans came up against Joash. They invaded Judah and Jerusalem, did away with all the princes of the people, and sent all their spoil to the king of Damascus. [24] Though the Aramean force came with few men, the Lord surrendered a very large force into their power, because Judah had abandoned the LORD, the God of their fathers. So punishment was meted out to Joash. [25] After the Arameans had departed from him, leaving him in grievous suffering, his servants conspired against him because of the murder of the son of Jehoiada the priest. He was buried in the City of David, but not in the tombs of the kings.

Responsorial Psalm: Psalms 89:4-5, 29-30, 31-32, 33-34

R. [29a] *For ever I will maintain my love for my*
servant.

[4] "I have made a covenant with my chosen
one,
I have sworn to David my servant:
[5] Forever will I confirm your posterity
and establish your throne for all
generations."

R. *For ever I will maintain my love for my*

servant.

29 "Forever I will maintain my kindness toward
        him,
    and my covenant with him stands firm.
30 I will make his posterity endure forever
    and his throne as the days of heaven."
**R. For ever I will maintain my love for my
        servant.**

31 "If his sons forsake my law
    and walk not according to my
        ordinances,
32 If they violate my statutes
    and keep not my commands."
**R. For ever I will maintain my love for my
        servant.**

33 "I will punish their crime with a rod
    and their guilt with stripes.
34 Yet my mercy I will not take from him,
    nor will I belie my faithfulness."
**R. For ever I will maintain my love for my
        servant.**

Alleluia: 2 Corinthians 8:9
R. Alleluia, alleluia.
9 Jesus Christ became poor although he was
        rich,
so that by his poverty you might become
        rich.
R. Alleluia, alleluia.

Gospel: Matthew 6:24-34
24 Jesus said to his disciples: "No one can serve two masters. He will either hate one and love the other, or be devoted to one and despise the other. You cannot serve God and mammon.

25 "Therefore I tell you, do not worry about your life, what you will eat or drink, or about your body, what you will wear. Is not life more than food and the body more than clothing? 26 Look at the birds in the sky; they do not sow or reap, they gather nothing into barns, yet your heavenly Father feeds them. Are not you more important than they? 27 Can any of you by worrying add a single moment to your life-span? 28 Why are you anxious

about clothes? Learn from the way the wild flowers grow. They do not work or spin. [29] But I tell you that not even Solomon in all his splendor was clothed like one of them. [30] If God so clothes the grass of the field, which grows today and is thrown into the oven tomorrow, will he not much more provide for you, O you of little faith? [31] So do not worry and say, 'What are we to eat?' or 'What are we to drink?' or 'What are we to wear?' [32] All these things the pagans seek. Your heavenly Father knows that you need them all. [33] But seek first the Kingdom of God and his righteousness, and all these things will be given you besides. [34] Do not worry about tomorrow; tomorrow will take care of itself. Sufficient for a day is its own evil."

Sunday June 23, 2024

Twelfth Sunday in Ordinary Time, Year B
First Reading: Job 38:1, 8-11

[1] The Lord addressed Job out of the storm and said:

[8] Who shut within doors the sea,
    when it burst forth from the womb;
[9] when I made the clouds its garment
    and thick darkness its swaddling bands?
[10] When I set limits for it
    and fastened the bar of its door,
[11] and said: Thus far shall you come but no
       farther,
    and here shall your proud waves be
       stilled!

Responsorial Psalm: Psalms 107:23-24, 25-26, 28-29, 30-31

R. [1b] **Give thanks to the Lord, his love is**
        everlasting. or: **Alleluia.**

[23] They who sailed the sea in ships,
    trading on the deep waters,
[24] These saw the works of the LORD
    and his wonders in the abyss.
R. Give thanks to the Lord, his love is
        everlasting. or: **Alleluia.**

[25] His command raised up a storm wind
    which tossed its waves on high.
[26] They mounted up to heaven; they sank to the
       depths;
    their hearts melted away in their plight.
R. Give thanks to the Lord, his love is
        everlasting. or: **Alleluia.**

^{28} They cried to the LORD in their distress;
>   from their straits he rescued them,
^{29} He hushed the storm to a gentle breeze,
>   and the billows of the sea were stilled.
R. Give thanks to the Lord, his love is
>   **everlasting.** or: **Alleluia.**

^{30}They rejoiced that they were calmed,
>   and he brought them to their desired
>   haven.
^{31}Let them give thanks to the LORD for his
>   kindness
>   and his wondrous deeds to the children
>   of men.
R. Give thanks to the Lord, his love is
>   **everlasting.** or: **Alleluia.**

Second Reading: 2 Corinthians 5:14-17

Brothers and sisters: ^{14} The love of Christ impels us, once we have come to the conviction that one died for all; therefore, all have died. ^{15} He indeed died for all, so that those who live might no longer live for themselves but for him who for their sake died and was raised.

^{16} Consequently, from now on we regard no one according to the flesh; even if we once knew Christ according to the flesh, yet now we know him so no longer. ^{17} So whoever is in Christ is a new creation: the old things have passed away; behold, new things have come.

Alleluia: Luke 7:16

R. Alleluia, alleluia.
^{16}A great prophet has risen in our midst,
God has visited his people.
R. Alleluia, alleluia.

Gospel: Mark 4:35-41

^{35} On that day, as evening drew on, Jesus said to his disciples: "Let us cross to the other side." ^{36} Leaving the crowd, they took Jesus with them in the boat just as he was. And other boats were with him. ^{37} A violent squall came up and waves were breaking over the boat, so that it was already filling up. ^{38} Jesus was in the stern, asleep on a cushion. They woke him and said to him, "Teacher, do you not care that we are perishing?" ^{39} He woke up, rebuked the wind, and said to the sea, "Quiet! Be still!" The wind ceased and there was great calm. ^{40} Then he asked them, "Why are you terrified? Do you not yet have faith?" ⁴¹ They were filled with great awe and said to one another, "Who then is this whom even wind and sea obey?"

Solemnity of the Birthday of Saint John the Baptist

First Reading: Isaiah 49:1-6

[1] Hear me, O coastlands,
    listen, O distant peoples.
The LORD called me from birth,
        from my mother's womb, he gave me my
            name.
[2] He made of me a sharp-edged sword
        and concealed me in the shadow of his
            arm.
He made me a polished arrow,
        in his quiver he hid me.
[3] You are my servant, he said to me,
        Israel, through whom I show my glory.

[4] Though I thought I had toiled in vain,
        and for nothing, uselessly, spent my
            strength,
yet my reward is with the LORD,
        my recompense is with my God.
[5] For now, the LORD has spoken
        who formed me as his servant from the
            womb,
that Jacob may be brought back to him
        and Israel gathered to him;
and I am made glorious in the sight of the
            LORD,
        and my God is now my strength!
[6] It is too little, he says, for you to be my
            servant,
        to raise up the tribes of Jacob,
        and restore the survivors of Israel;
I will make you a light to the nations,
        that my salvation may reach to the ends
            of the earth.

Responsorial Psalm: Psalms 139:1B-3, 13-14AB, 14C-15

R. [14] *I praise you, for I am wonderfully made.*

[1B] O LORD, you have probed me, you know me:

337

2 you know when I sit and when I stand;
    you understand my thoughts from afar.
3 My journeys and my rest you scrutinize,
    with all my ways you are familiar.
R. I praise you for I am wonderfully made.

13 Truly you have formed my inmost being;
    you knit me in my mother's womb.
14AB I give you thanks that I am fearfully, wonderfully
        made;
    wonderful are your works.
R. I praise you, for I am wonderfully made.

14C My soul also you knew full well;
        15 nor was my frame unknown to you
When I was made in secret,
        when I was fashioned in the depths of the
            earth.
R. I praise you, for I am wonderfully made.

Second Reading: Acts 13:22-26

In those days, Paul said: 22 "God raised up David as king; of him God testified, *I have found David, son of Jesse, a man after my own heart; he will carry out my every wish.* 23 From this man's descendants God, according to his promise, has brought to Israel a savior, Jesus. 24 John heralded his coming by proclaiming a baptism of repentance to all the people of Israel; 25 and as John was completing his course, he would say, 'What do you suppose that I am? I am not he. Behold, one is coming after me; I am not worthy to unfasten the sandals of his feet.'

26 "My brothers, sons of the family of Abraham, and those others among you who are God-fearing, to us this word of salvation has been sent."

Alleluia: Luke 1:76

R. Alleluia, alleluia.
76You, child, will be called prophet of the Most
        High,
for you will go before the Lord to prepare his
        way.
R. Alleluia, alleluia.

Gospel: Luke 1:57-66, 80

⁵⁷ When the time arrived for Elizabeth to have her child she gave birth to a son. ⁵⁸ Her neighbors and relatives heard that the Lord had shown his great mercy toward her, and they rejoiced with her. ⁵⁹ When they came on the eighth day to circumcise the child, they were going to call him Zechariah after his father, ⁶⁰ but his mother said in reply, "No. He will be called John." ⁶¹ But they answered her, "There is no one among your relatives who has this name." ⁶² So they made signs, asking his father what he wished him to be called. ⁶³ He asked for a tablet and wrote, "John is his name," and all were amazed. ⁶⁴ Immediately his mouth was opened, his tongue freed, and he spoke blessing God. ⁶⁵ Then fear came upon all their neighbours, and all these matters were discussed throughout the hill country of Judea. ⁶⁶ All who heard these things took them to heart, saying, "What, then, will this child be?" For surely the hand of the Lord was with him. ⁸⁰ The child grew and became strong in spirit, and he was in the desert until the day of his manifestation to Israel.

Tuesday June 25, 2024

Tuesday of Twelfth Week in ordinary Time
First Reading: 2 Kings 19:9B-11, 14-21, 31-35A, 36

⁹ᴮ Sennacherib, king of Assyria, sent envoys to Hezekiah with this message: ¹⁰ "Thus shall you say to Hezekiah, king of Judah: 'Do not let your God on whom you rely deceive you by saying that Jerusalem will not be handed over to the king of Assyria. ¹¹ You have heard what the kings of Assyria have done to all other countries: they doomed them! Will you, then, be saved?'"

¹⁴ Hezekiah took the letter from the hand of the messengers and read it; then he went up to the temple of the LORD, and spreading it out before him, ¹⁵ he prayed in the LORD's presence: "O LORD, God of Israel, enthroned upon the cherubim! You alone are God over all the kingdoms of the earth. You have made the heavens and the earth. ¹⁶ Incline your ear, O LORD, and listen! Open your eyes, O LORD, and see! Hear the words of Sennacherib which he sent to taunt the living God. ¹⁷ Truly, O LORD, the kings of Assyria have laid waste the nations and their lands, ¹⁸ and cast their gods into the fire; they destroyed them because they were not gods, but the work of human hands, wood and stone. ¹⁹ Therefore, O LORD, our God, save us from the power of this man, that all the kingdoms of the earth may know that you alone, O LORD, are God."

²⁰ Then Isaiah, son of Amoz, sent this message to Hezekiah: "Thus says the LORD, the God of Israel, in answer to your prayer for help against Sennacherib, king of Assyria: I have listened! ²¹ This is the word the LORD has spoken concerning him:

"'She despises you, laughs you to scorn,
   the virgin daughter Zion!
Behind you she wags her head,
   daughter Jerusalem.

³¹ "'For out of Jerusalem shall come a remnant,
   and from Mount Zion, survivors.

The zeal of the LORD of hosts shall do this.'

32 "Therefore, thus says the LORD concerning the king of Assyria: 'He shall not reach this city, nor shoot an arrow at it, nor come before it with a shield, nor cast up siege-works against it. 33 He shall return by the same way he came, without entering the city, says the LORD. 34 I will shield and save this city for my own sake, and for the sake of my servant David.'"

35A That night the angel of the LORD went forth and struck down one hundred and eighty-five thousand men in the Assyrian camp. 36 So Sennacherib, the king of Assyria, broke camp, and went back home to Nineveh.

Responsorial Psalm: Psalms 48:2-3AB, 3CD-4, 10-11

R. *(see 9d)* **God upholds his city for ever.**
2 Great is the LORD and wholly to be praised
    in the city of our God.
3AB His holy mountain, fairest of heights,
    is the joy of all the earth.
R. **God upholds his city for ever.**

3CD Mount Zion, "the recesses of the North,"
    is the city of the great King.
4 God is with her castles;
    renowned is he as a stronghold.
R. **God upholds his city for ever.**

10 O God, we ponder your mercy
    within your temple.
11 As your name, O God, so also your praise
    reaches to the ends of the earth.
Of justice your right hand is full.
R. **God upholds his city for ever.**

Alleluia: John 8:12

R. **Alleluia, alleluia.**
12 I am the light of the world, says the Lord;
whoever follows me will have the light of
    life.
R. **Alleluia, alleluia.**

Gospel: Matthew 7:6, 12-14

6 Jesus said to his disciples: "Do not give what is holy to dogs, or throw your pearls before swine, lest they trample them underfoot, and turn and tear you to pieces.

12 "Do to others whatever you would have them do to you. This is the Law and the Prophets.

[13] "Enter through the narrow gate; for the gate is wide and the road broad that leads to destruction, and those who enter through it are many. [14] How narrow the gate and constricted the road that leads to life. And those who find it are few."

Wednesday of Twelfth Week in Ordinary Time
First Reading: 2 Kings 22:8-13; 23:1-3

[8] The high priest Hilkiah informed the scribe Shaphan, "I have found the book of the law in the temple of the LORD." Hilkiah gave the book to Shaphan, who read it. [9] Then the scribe Shaphan went to the king and reported, "Your servants have smelted down the metals available in the temple and have consigned them to the master workmen in the temple of the LORD." [10] The scribe Shaphan also informed the king that the priest Hilkiah had given him a book, and then read it aloud to the king. [11] When the king heard the contents of the book of the law, he tore his garments [12] and Issued this command to Hilkiah the priest, Ahikam, son of Shaphan, Achbor, son of Micaiah, the scribe Shaphan, and the king's servant Asaiah: [13] "Go, consult the LORD for me, for the people, for all Judah, about the stipulations of this book that has been found, for the anger of the LORD has been set furiously ablaze against us, because our fathers did not obey the stipulations of this book, nor fulfill our written obligations."

[1] The king then had all the elders of Judah and of Jerusalem summoned together before him. [2] The king went up to the temple of the LORD with all the men of Judah and all the inhabitants of Jerusalem: priests, prophets, and all the people, small and great. He had the entire contents of the book of the covenant that had been found in the temple of the LORD, read out to them. [3] Standing by the column, the king made a covenant before the LORD that they would follow him and observe his ordinances, statutes and decrees with their whole hearts and souls, thus reviving the terms of the covenant which were written in this book. And all the people stood as participants in the covenant.

Responsorial Psalm: Psalms 119:33, 34, 35, 36, 37, 40

R. [(33a)] *Teach me the way of your decrees, O Lord.*

[33] Instruct me, O LORD, in the way of your
     statutes,
    that I may exactly observe them.
R. *Teach me the way of your decrees, O Lord.*

[34] Give me discernment, that I may observe
     your law
    and keep it with all my heart.
R. *Teach me the way of your decrees, O Lord.*

[35] Lead me in the path of your commands,
     for in it I delight.
R. *Teach me the way of your decrees, O Lord.*

³⁶ Incline my heart to your decrees
>> and not to gain.
R. Teach me the way of your decrees, O Lord.

³⁷ Turn away my eyes from seeing what is
>> vain:
>> by your way give me life.
R. Teach me the way of your decrees, O Lord.

⁴⁰ Behold, I long for your precepts;
>> in your justice give me life.
R. Teach me the way of your decrees, O Lord.

Alleluia: John 15:4A, 5B
R. Alleluia, alleluia.
^{4A} Remain in me, as I remain in you, says the
>> Lord;
^{5B} whoever remains in me will bear much fruit.
R. Alleluia, alleluia.

Gospel: Matthew 7:15-20

¹⁵ Jesus said to his disciples: "Beware of false prophets, who come to you in sheep's clothing, but underneath are ravenous wolves. ¹⁶ By their fruits you will know them. Do people pick grapes from thorn bushes, or figs from thistles? ¹⁷ Just so, every good tree bears good fruit, and a rotten tree bears bad fruit. ¹⁸ A good tree cannot bear bad fruit, nor can a rotten tree bear good fruit. ¹⁹ Every tree that does not bear good fruit will be cut down and thrown into the fire. ²⁰ So by their fruits you will know them."

Thursday June 27, 2024

Thursday of Twelfth Week in Ordinary Time
First Reading: 2 Kings 24:8-17

⁸ Jehoiachin was eighteen years old when he began to reign, and he reigned three months in Jerusalem. His mother's name was Nehushta, daughter of Elnathan of Jerusalem. ⁹ He did evil in the sight of the LORD, just as his forebears had done.

>> ¹⁰At that time the officials of Nebuchadnezzar, king of Babylon, attacked Jerusalem, and the city came under siege. ¹¹ Nebuchadnezzar, king of Babylon, himself arrived at the city while his servants were besieging it. ¹² Then Jehoiachin, king of Judah, together with his mother, his ministers, officers, and functionaries, surrendered to the king of Babylon, who, in the eighth year of his reign, took him captive. ¹³ And he carried off all the treasures of the temple of the LORD and those of the palace, and broke up all the gold utensils that Solomon, king of Israel, had provided in the temple of the LORD, as the LORD had foretold. ¹⁴ He deported all Jerusalem: all the officers and men of the army, ten

thousand in number, and all the craftsmen and smiths. None were left among the people of the land except the poor. [15] He deported Jehoiachin to Babylon, and also led captive from Jerusalem to Babylon the king's mother and wives, his functionaries, and the chief men of the land. The king of Babylon also led captive to Babylon [16] all seven thousand men of the army, and a thousand craftsmen and smiths, all of them trained soldiers. [17] In place of Jehoiachin, the king of Babylon appointed his uncle Mattaniah king, and changed his name to Zedekiah.

Responsorial Psalm: Psalms 79:1B-2,3-5, 8, 9

R. [9] *For the glory of your name, O Lord, deliver us.*

[1B] O God, the nations have come into your
      inheritance;
    they have defiled your holy temple,
    they have laid Jerusalem in ruins.
[2] They have given the corpses of your servants
    as food to the birds of heaven,
    the flesh of your faithful ones to the
      beasts of the earth.

R. *For the glory of your name, O Lord, deliver us.*

[3] They have poured out their blood like water
    round about Jerusalem,
    and there is no one to bury them.
[4] We have become the reproach of our
      neighbors,
    the scorn and derision of those around
      us.
[5] O LORD, how long? Will you be angry
      forever?
    Will your jealousy burn like fire?

R. *For the glory of your name, O Lord, deliver us.*

[8] Remember not against us the iniquities of
      the past;
    may your compassion quickly come to us,
    for we are brought very low.

R. *For the glory of your name, O Lord, deliver us.*

[9] Help us, O God our savior,
      because of the glory of your name;
Deliver us and pardon our sins
    for your name's sake.

R. *For the glory of your name, O Lord, deliver us.*

Alleluia: John 14:23

R. Alleluia, alleluia.

[23] Whoever loves me will keep my word,
and my Father will love him
and we will come to him.

R. Alleluia, alleluia.

Gospel: Matthew 7:21-29

[21] Jesus said to his disciples: "Not everyone who says to me, 'Lord, Lord,' will enter the Kingdom of heaven, but only the one who does the will of my Father in heaven. [22] Many will say to me on that day, 'Lord, Lord, did we not prophesy in your name? Did we not drive out demons in your name? Did we not do mighty deeds in your name?' [23] Then I will declare to them solemnly, 'I never knew you. Depart from me, you evildoers.'

[24] "Everyone who listens to these words of mine and acts on them will be like a wise man who built his house on rock. [25] The rain fell, the floods came, and the winds blew and buffeted the house. But it did not collapse; it had been set solidly on rock. [26] And everyone who listens to these words of mine but does not act on them will be like a fool who built his house on sand. [27] The rain fell, the floods came, and the winds blew and buffeted the house. And it collapsed and was completely ruined."

[28] When Jesus finished these words, the crowds were astonished at his teaching, [29] for he taught them as one having authority, and not as their scribes.

Friday June 28, 2024

Memorial of Saint Irenaeus, Bishop & Martyr
First Reading: 2 Kings 25:1-12

[1] In the tenth month of the ninth year of Zedekiah's reign, on the tenth day of the month, Nebuchadnezzar, king of Babylon, and his whole army advanced against Jerusalem, encamped around it, and built siege walls on every side. [2] The siege of the city continued until the eleventh year of Zedekiah. [3] On the ninth day of the fourth month, when famine had gripped the city, and the people had no more bread, [4] the city walls were breached. Then the king and all the soldiers left the city by night through the gate between the two walls that was near the king's garden. Since the Chaldeans had the city surrounded, they went in the direction of the Arabah. [5] But the Chaldean army pursued the king and overtook him in the desert near Jericho, abandoned by his whole army.

[6] The king was therefore arrested and brought to Riblah to the king of Babylon, who pronounced sentence on him. [7] He had Zedekiah's sons slain before his eyes. Then he blinded Zedekiah, bound him with fetters, and had him brought to Babylon.

[8] On the seventh day of the fifth month (this was in the nineteenth year of Nebuchadnezzar, king of Babylon), Nebuzaradan, captain of the bodyguard, came to Jerusalem as the representative of the king of Babylon. [9] He burned the house of the LORD, the palace of the king, and all the houses of Jerusalem; every large building was

destroyed by fire. [10] Then the Chaldean troops who were with the captain of the guard tore down the walls that surrounded Jerusalem.

[11] Then Nebuzaradan, captain of the guard, led into exile the last of the people remaining in the city, and those who had deserted to the king of Babylon, and the last of the artisans. [12] But some of the country's poor, Nebuzaradan, captain of the guard, left behind as vinedressers and farmers.

Responsorial Psalm: Psalms 137:1-2, 3, 4-5, 6

R. *(6ab)* **Let my tongue be silenced, if I ever forget you!**

[1] By the streams of Babylon
    we sat and wept
    when we remembered Zion.
[2] On the aspens of that land
    we hung up our harps.
R. Let my tongue be silenced, if I ever forget you!

[3] Though there our captors asked of us
    the lyrics of our songs,
And our despoilers urged us to be joyous:
    "Sing for us the songs of Zion!"
R. Let my tongue be silenced, if I ever forget you!

[4] How could we sing a song of the LORD
    in a foreign land?
[5] If I forget you, Jerusalem,
    may my right hand be forgotten!
R. Let my tongue be silenced, if I ever forget you!

[6] May my tongue cleave to my palate
    if I remember you not,
If I place not Jerusalem
    ahead of my joy.
R. Let my tongue be silenced, if I ever forget you!

Alleluia: Matthew 8:17

R. Alleluia, alleluia.
[17] Christ took away our infirmities
and bore our diseases.
R. Alleluia, alleluia.

Gospel: Matthew 8:1-4

[1] When Jesus came down from the mountain, great crowds followed him. [2] And then a leper approached, did him homage, and said, "Lord, if you wish, you can make me clean."

³ He stretched out his hand, touched him, and said, "I will do it. Be made clean." His leprosy was cleansed immediately. ⁴ Then Jesus said to him, "See that you tell no one, but go show yourself to the priest, and offer the gift that Moses prescribed; that will be proof for them."

Solemnity of Saints Peter and Paul, Apostles
First Reading: Acts 12:1-11

¹ In those days, King Herod laid hands upon some members of the Church to harm them. ² He had James, the brother of John, killed by the sword, ³ and when he saw that this was pleasing to the Jews he proceeded to arrest Peter also. —It was the feast of Unleavened Bread.— ⁴ He had him taken into custody and put in prison under the guard of four squads of four soldiers each. He intended to bring him before the people after Passover. ⁵ Peter thus was being kept in prison, but prayer by the Church was fervently being made to God on his behalf.

⁶ On the very night before Herod was to bring him to trial, Peter, secured by double chains, was sleeping between two soldiers, while outside the door guards kept watch on the prison. ⁷ Suddenly the angel of the Lord stood by him and a light shone in the cell. He tapped Peter on the side and awakened him, saying, "Get up quickly." The chains fell from his wrists. ⁸ The angel said to him, "Put on your belt and your sandals." He did so. Then he said to him, "Put on your cloak and follow me." ⁹ So he followed him out, not realizing that what was happening through the angel was real; he thought he was seeing a vision. ¹⁰ They passed the first guard, then the second, and came to the iron gate leading out to the city, which opened for them by itself. They emerged and made their way down an alley, and suddenly the angel left him. ¹¹ Then Peter recovered his senses and said, "Now I know for certain that the Lord sent his angel and rescued me from the hand of Herod and from all that the Jewish people had been expecting."

Responsorial Psalm: Psalms 34:2-3, 4-5, 6-7, 8-9

R. ⁽⁵⁾ *The angel of the Lord will rescue those who*
fear him.

² I will bless the LORD at all times;
      his praise shall be ever in my mouth.
³ Let my soul glory in the LORD;
      the lowly will hear me and be glad.
R. *The angel of the Lord will rescue those who*
fear him.

⁴ Glorify the LORD with me,
      let us together extol his name.
⁵ I sought the LORD, and he answered me
      and delivered me from all my fears.

R. The angel of the Lord will rescue those who fear him.

6 Look to him that you may be radiant with
  joy,
    and your faces may not blush with
      shame.
7 When the poor one called out, the LORD
  heard,
    and from all his distress he saved him.

R. The angel of the Lord will rescue those who fear him.

8 The angel of the LORD encamps
  around those who fear him and delivers
    them.
9 Taste and see how good the LORD is;
  blessed the man who takes refuge in him.

R. The angel of the Lord will rescue those who fear him.

Second Reading: 2 Timothy 4:6-8, 17-18

6 I, Paul, am already being poured out like a libation, and the time of my departure is at hand. 7 I have competed well; I have finished the race; I have kept the faith. 8 From now on the crown of righteousness awaits me, which the Lord, the just judge, will award to me on that day, and not only to me, but to all who have longed for his appearance.

17 The Lord stood by me and gave me strength so that through me the proclamation might be completed and all the Gentiles might hear it. And I was rescued from the lion's mouth. 18 The Lord will rescue me from every evil threat and will bring me safe to his heavenly Kingdom. To him be glory forever and ever. Amen.

Alleluia: Matthew 16:18

R. Alleluia, alleluia.

18 You are Peter and upon this rock I will build
  my Church,
and the gates of the netherworld shall not
  prevail against it.

R. Alleluia, alleluia.

Gospel: Matthew 16:13-19

13 When Jesus went into the region of Caesarea Philippi he asked his disciples, "Who do people say that the Son of Man is?" 14 They replied, "Some say John the Baptist, others Elijah, still others Jeremiah or one of the prophets." 15 He said to them, "But who do you

say that I am?" [16] Simon Peter said in reply, "You are the Christ, the Son of the living God." [17]Jesus said to him in reply, "Blessed are you, Simon son of Jonah. For flesh and blood has not revealed this to you, but my heavenly Father. [18] And so I say to you, you are Peter, and upon this rock, I will build my Church, and the gates of the netherworld shall not prevail against it. [19] I will give you the keys to the Kingdom of heaven. Whatever you bind on earth shall be bound in heaven, and whatever you loose on earth shall be loosed in heaven."

Sunday June 30, 2024

Thirteenth Sunday in Ordinary Time, Year B
First Reading: Wisdom 1:13-15; 2:23-24

[13] God did not make death,
    nor does he rejoice in the destruction of
      the living.
[14] For he fashioned all things that they might
      have being;
    and the creatures of the world are
      wholesome,
and there is not a destructive drug among
      them
    nor any domain of the netherworld on
      earth,
    [15] for justice is undying.
[23] For God formed man to be imperishable;
    the image of his own nature he made
      him.
[24] But by the envy of the devil, death entered
      the world,
    and they who belong to his company
      experience it.

Responsorial Psalm: Psalms 30:2, 4, 5-6, 11, 12, 13

R. [(2a)] *I will praise you, Lord, for you have*
      rescued me.
[2] I will extol you, O LORD, for you drew me
      clear
    and did not let my enemies rejoice over
      me.
[4] O LORD, you brought me up from the
      netherworld;
    you preserved me from among those
      going down into the pit.

R. I will praise you, Lord, for you have rescued
        me.

[5] Sing praise to the LORD, you his faithful ones,
        and give thanks to his holy name.
[6] For his anger lasts but a moment;
        a lifetime, his good will.
At nightfall, weeping enters in,
        but with the dawn, rejoicing.
R. I will praise you, Lord, for you have rescued
        me.

[11] Hear, O LORD, and have pity on me;
        O LORD, be my helper.
[12] You changed my mourning into dancing;
        [13] O LORD, my God, forever will I give you
            thanks.
R. I will praise you, Lord, for you have rescued
        me.

Second Reading: 2 Corinthians 8:7, 9, 13-15

[7] Brothers and sisters: As you excel in every respect, in faith, discourse, knowledge, all earnestness, and in the love we have for you, may you excel in this gracious act also.

[9] For you know the gracious act of our Lord Jesus Christ, that though he was rich, for your sake he became poor, so that by his poverty you might become rich. [13] Not that others should have relief while you are burdened, but that as a matter of equality [14] your abundance at the present time should supply their needs, so that their abundance may also supply your needs, that there may be equality. [15] As it is written:

Whoever had much did not have more,
    and whoever had little did not have less.

Alleluia: cf. 2 Timothy 1:10
R. Alleluia, alleluia.
[10] Our Savior Jesus Christ destroyed death
and brought life to light through the Gospel.
R. Alleluia, alleluia.

Gospel: Mark 5:21-43

[21] When Jesus had crossed again in the boat to the other side, a large crowd gathered around him, and he stayed close to the sea. [22] One of the synagogue officials, named

Jairus, came forward. Seeing him he fell at his feet [23] and pleaded earnestly with him, saying, "My daughter is at the point of death. Please, come lay your hands on her that she may get well and live." [24] He went off with him, and a large crowd followed him and pressed upon him.

[25] There was a woman afflicted with hemorrhages for twelve years. [26] She had suffered greatly at the hands of many doctors and had spent all that she had. Yet she was not helped but only grew worse. [27] She had heard about Jesus and came up behind him in the crowd and touched his cloak. [28] She said, "If I but touch his clothes, I shall be cured." [29] Immediately her flow of blood dried up. She felt in her body that she was healed of her affliction. [30] Jesus, aware at once that power had gone out from him, turned around in the crowd and asked, "Who has touched my clothes?" [31] But his disciples said to Jesus, "You see how the crowd is pressing upon you, and yet you ask, 'Who touched me?'" [32] And he looked around to see who had done it. [33] The woman, realizing what had happened to her, approached in fear and trembling. She fell down before Jesus and told him the whole truth. [34] He said to her, "Daughter, your faith has saved you. Go in peace and be cured of your affliction."

[35] While he was still speaking, people from the synagogue official's house arrived and said, "Your daughter has died; why trouble the teacher any longer?" [36] Disregarding the message that was reported, Jesus said to the synagogue official, "Do not be afraid; just have faith." [37] He did not allow anyone to accompany him inside except Peter, James, and John, the brother of James. [38] When they arrived at the house of the synagogue official, he caught sight of a commotion, people weeping and wailing loudly. [39] So he went in and said to them, "Why this commotion and weeping? The child is not dead but asleep." [40] And they ridiculed him. Then he put them all out. He took along the child's father and mother and those who were with him and entered the room where the child was. [41] He took the child by the hand and said to her, *Talitha koum,*" which means, "Little girl, I say to you, arise!" [42] The girl, a child of twelve, arose immediately and walked around. At that they were utterly astounded. [43] He gave strict orders that no one should know this and said that she should be given something to eat.

OR Mark 5:21-24, 35B-43

[21] When Jesus had crossed again in the boat to the other side, a large crowd gathered around him, and he stayed close to the sea. [22] One of the synagogue officials, named Jairus, came forward. Seeing him he fell at his feet [23] and pleaded earnestly with him, saying, "My daughter is at the point of death. Please, come lay your hands on her that she may get well and live." [24] He went off with him, and a large crowd followed him and pressed upon him.

[35B] While he was still speaking, people from the synagogue official's house arrived and said, "Your daughter has died; why trouble the teacher any longer?" [36] Disregarding the message that was reported, Jesus said to the synagogue official, "Do not be afraid; just have faith." [37] He did not allow anyone to accompany him inside except Peter, James, and John, the brother of James. [38] When they arrived at the house of the synagogue official, he caught sight of a commotion, people weeping and wailing loudly. [39] So he went in and said to them, "Why this commotion and weeping? The child is not dead but asleep." [40] And they ridiculed him. Then he put them all out. He took along the child's father and mother and those who were with him and entered the room where the child was. [41] He took the child by the hand and said to her, "*Talitha koum*," which means, "Little girl, I say to you, arise!"

[42] The girl, a child of twelve, arose immediately and walked around. At that they were utterly astounded. [43] He gave strict orders that no one should know this and said that she should be given something to eat.

JULY 2024
Monday July 1, 2024

Monday of the Thirteenth Week in Ordinary Time
First Reading: Amos 2:6-10, 13-16

[6] Thus says the LORD:

For three crimes of Israel, and for four,
    I will not revoke my word;
Because they sell the just man for silver,
    and the poor man for a pair of sandals.
[7] They trample the heads of the weak
    into the dust of the earth,
    and force the lowly out of the way.
Son and father go to the same prostitute,
    profaning my holy name.
[8] Upon garments taken in pledge
    they recline beside any altar;
And the wine of those who have been fined
    they drink in the house of their god.

[9] Yet it was I who destroyed the Amorites
    before them,
    who were as tall as the cedars,
    and as strong as the oak trees.
I destroyed their fruit above,
    and their roots beneath.
[10] It was I who brought you up from the land of
    Egypt,
    and who led you through the desert for
    forty years,
    to occupy the land of the Amorites.

¹³ Beware, I will crush you into the ground
     as a wagon crushes when laden with
        sheaves.
¹⁴ Flight shall perish from the swift,
     and the strong man shall not retain his
        strength;
The warrior shall not save his life,
     ¹⁵ nor the bowman stand his ground;
The swift of foot shall not escape,
     nor the horseman save his life.
¹⁶ And the most stouthearted of warriors
     shall flee naked on that day, says the LORD.

Responsorial Psalm: Psalms 50:16BC-17, 18-19, 20-21, 22-23

R. *(22a)* **Remember this, you who never think of God.**

^{16BC} "Why do you recite my statutes,
     and profess my covenant with your
        mouth,
¹⁷ Though you hate discipline
     and cast my words behind you?"

R. Remember this, you who never think of God.

¹⁸ "When you see a thief, you keep pace with
        him,
     and with adulterers you throw in your
        lot.
¹⁹ To your mouth you give free rein for evil,
     you harness your tongue to deceit."

R. Remember this, you who never think of God.

²⁰ "You sit speaking against your brother;
     against your mother's son you spread
        rumors.
²¹ When you do these things, shall I be deaf to
        it?
     Or do you think that I am like yourself?
     I will correct you by drawing them up
        before your eyes."

R. Remember this, you who never think of God.

²² "Consider this, you who forget God,
     lest I rend you and there be no one to

rescue you.
[23] He that offers praise as a sacrifice glorifies
		me;
	and to him that goes the right way I will
		show the salvation of God."
R. Remember this, you who never think of God.

Alleluia: Psalms 95:8
R. Alleluia, alleluia.
[8] If today you hear his voice,
harden not your hearts.
R. Alleluia, alleluia.

Gospel: Matthew 8:18-22
[18] When Jesus saw a crowd around him, he gave orders to cross to the other shore. [19] A scribe approached and said to him, "Teacher, I will follow you wherever you go." [20] Jesus answered him, "Foxes have dens and birds of the sky have nests, but the Son of Man has nowhere to rest his head." [21] Another of his disciples said to him, "Lord, let me go first and bury my father." [22] But Jesus answered him, "Follow me, and let the dead bury their dead."

Tuesday July 2, 2024

Tuesday of the Thirteenth Week in Ordinary Time
First Reading: Amos 3:1-8; 4:11-12
[1] Hear this word, O children of Israel, that the LORD pronounces over you, over the whole family that I brought up from the land of Egypt:

[2] You alone have I favored,
	more than all the families of the earth;
Therefore I will punish you
	for all your crimes.

[3] Do two walk together
	unless they have agreed?
[4] Does a lion roar in the forest
	when it has no prey?
Does a young lion cry out from its den
	unless it has seized something?
[5] Is a bird brought to earth by a snare
	when there is no lure for it?
Does a snare spring up from the ground
	without catching anything?
[6] If the trumpet sounds in a city,

will the people not be frightened?
If evil befalls a city,
> has not the LORD caused it?

[7] Indeed, the Lord GOD does nothing
> without revealing his plan
> to his servants, the prophets.

[8] The lion roars—
> who will not be afraid!
The Lord GOD speaks—
> who will not prophesy!

[11] I brought upon you such upheaval
> as when God overthrew Sodom and
> > Gomorrah:
> you were like a brand plucked from the
> > fire;
Yet you returned not to me,
> says the LORD.

[12] So now I will deal with you in my own way,
> > O Israel!
> and since I will deal thus with you,
> prepare to meet your God, O Israel.

Responsorial Psalm: Psalms 5:4B-6A,6B-7, 8

R. *(9a)* **Lead me in your justice, Lord.**

[4B] At dawn I bring my plea expectantly before
> > you.
[5] For you, O God, delight not in wickedness;
> no evil man remains with you;
> > [6A] the arrogant may not stand in your sight.
R. *Lead me in your justice, Lord.*

[6B] You hate all evildoers;
> [7] you destroy all who speak falsehood;
The bloodthirsty and the deceitful
> the LORD abhors.
R. *Lead me in your justice, Lord.*

[8] But I, because of your abundant mercy,
> will enter your house;

I will worship at your holy temple
>   in fear of you, O LORD.
R. Lead me in your justice, Lord.

Alleluia: Psalms 130:5
R. Alleluia, alleluia.
[5] I trust in the LORD;
my soul trusts in his word.
R. Alleluia, alleluia.

Gospel: Matthew 8:23-27
[23] As Jesus got into a boat, his disciples followed him. [24] Suddenly a violent storm came up on the sea, so that the boat was being swamped by waves; but he was asleep. [25] They came and woke him, saying, "Lord, save us! We are perishing!" [26] He said to them, "Why are you terrified, O you of little faith?" Then he got up, rebuked the winds and the sea, and there was great calm. [27] The men were amazed and said, "What sort of man is this, whom even the winds and the sea obey?"

Wednesday July 3, 2024

Feast of Saint Thomas, Apostle
First Reading: Ephesians 2:19-22
Brothers and sisters: [19] You are no longer strangers and sojourners, but you are fellow citizens with the holy ones and members of the household of God, [20] built upon the foundation of the Apostles and prophets, with Christ Jesus himself as the capstone. [21] Through him, the whole structure is held together and grows into a temple sacred in the Lord; [22] in him, you also are being built together into a dwelling place of God in the Spirit.

Responsorial Psalm: Psalms 117:1BC, 2
R. [(Mark 16:15)]**Go out to all the world and tell the Good News.**
[1BC] Praise the LORD, all you nations;
>   glorify him, all you peoples!
R. Go out to all the world and tell the Good News.

[2] For steadfast is his kindness for us,
>   and the fidelity of the LORD endures
>   forever.
R. Go out to all the world and tell the Good News.

Alleluia: John 20:29
R. Alleluia, alleluia.
²⁹ You believe in me, Thomas, because you
> have seen me, says the Lord;
blessed are those who have not seen, but still
> believe!
R. Alleluia, alleluia.

Gospel: John 20:24-29
²⁴ Thomas, called Didymus, one of the Twelve, was not with them when Jesus came. ²⁵ So the other disciples said to him, "We have seen the Lord." But Thomas said to them, "Unless I see the mark of the nails in his hands and put my finger into the nailmarks and put my hand into his side, I will not believe." ²⁶ Now a week later his disciples were again inside and Thomas was with them. Jesus came, although the doors were locked, and stood in their midst and said, "Peace be with you." ²⁷ Then he said to Thomas, "Put your finger here and see my hands, and bring your hand and put it into my side, and do not be unbelieving, but believe." ²⁸ Thomas answered and said to him, "My Lord and my God!" ²⁹ Jesus said to him, "Have you come to believe because you have seen me? Blessed are those who have not seen and have believed."

Thursday of the Thirteenth Week in Ordinary Time
First Reading: Amos 7:10-17
¹⁰ Amaziah, the priest of Bethel, sent word to Jeroboam, king of Israel: "Amos has conspired against you here within Israel; the country cannot endure all his words. ¹¹ For this is what Amos says:

Jeroboam shall die by the sword,
> and Israel shall surely be exiled from its
> > land."

¹² To Amos, Amaziah said: "Off with you, visionary, flee to the land of Judah! There earn your bread by prophesying, ¹³ but never again prophesy in Bethel; for it is the king's sanctuary and a royal temple." ¹⁴ Amos answered Amaziah, "I was no prophet, nor have I belonged to a company of prophets; I was a shepherd and a dresser of sycamores.¹⁵ The LORD took me from following the flock, and said to me, 'Go, prophesy to my people Israel.' ¹⁶ Now hear the word of the LORD!"

You say: prophesy not against Israel,
> preach not against the house of Isaac.
¹⁷ Now thus says the LORD:
> Your wife shall be made a harlot in the

city,
   and your sons and daughters shall fall by
      the sword;
Your land shall be divided by measuring
      line,
   and you yourself shall die in an unclean
      land;
   Israel shall be exiled far from its land.

Responsorial Psalm: Psalms 19:8, 9, 10, 11

R. *(10cd)The judgments of the Lord are true, and
            all of them are just.*

[8] The law of the LORD is perfect,
      refreshing the soul;
The decree of the LORD is trustworthy,
      giving wisdom to the simple.
R. *The judgments of the Lord are true, and all of
            them are just.*

[9] The precepts of the LORD are right,
      rejoicing the heart;
The command of the LORD is clear,
      enlightening the eye.
R. *The judgments of the Lord are true, and all of
            them are just.*

[10] The fear of the LORD is pure,
      enduring forever;
The ordinances of the LORD are true,
      all of them just.
R. *The judgments of the Lord are true, and all of
            them are just.*

[11] They are more precious than gold,
      than a heap of purest gold;
Sweeter also than syrup
      or honey from the comb.
R. *The judgments of the Lord are true, and all of
            them are just.*

Alleluia: 2 Corinthians 5:19

R. Alleluia, alleluia.

[19] God was reconciling the world to himself in
Christ
and entrusting to us the message of
reconciliation.

R. Alleluia, alleluia.

Gospel: Matthew 9:1-8

[1] After entering a boat, Jesus made the crossing, and came into his own town. [2] And there people brought to him a paralytic lying on a stretcher. When Jesus saw their faith, he said to the paralytic, "Courage, child, your sins are forgiven." [3] At that, some of the scribes said to themselves, "This man is blaspheming." [4] Jesus knew what they were thinking, and said, "Why do you harbor evil thoughts? [5] Which is easier, to say, 'Your sins are forgiven,' or to say, 'Rise and walk'? [6] But that you may know that the Son of Man has authority on earth to forgive sins" he then said to the paralytic, "Rise, pick up your stretcher, and go home." [7] He rose and went home. [8] When the crowds saw this they were struck with awe and glorified God who had given such authority to men.

Friday of Thirteenth Week in Ordinary Time
First Reading: Amos 8:4-6, 9-12

[4] Hear this, you who trample upon the needy
and destroy the poor of the land!
[5] "When will the new moon be over," you ask,
"that we may sell our grain,
and the sabbath, that we may display the
wheat?"
We will diminish the containers for
measuring,
add to the weights,
and fix our scales for cheating!
[6] We will buy the lowly man for silver,
and the poor man for a pair of sandals;
even the refuse of the wheat we will sell!"

[9] On that day, says the Lord GOD,
I will make the sun set at midday
and cover the earth with darkness in
broad daylight.
[10] I will turn your feasts into mourning
and all your songs into lamentations.

I will cover the loins of all with sackcloth
   and make every head bald.
I will make them mourn as for an only son,
   and bring their day to a bitter end.

[11] Yes, days are coming, says the Lord GOD,
   when I will send famine upon the land:
Not a famine of bread, or thirst for water,
   but for hearing the word of the LORD.
[12] Then shall they wander from sea to sea
   and rove from the north to the east
In search of the word of the LORD,
   but they shall not find it.

Responsorial Psalm: Psalms 119:2, 10, 20, 30, 40, 131

R. [(Matthew 4:4)] *One does not live by bread alone,*
   but by every word that comes from the
   mouth of God.
[2] Blessed are they who observe his decrees,
   who seek him with all their heart.
R. One does not live by bread alone, but by every word that comes from the mouth of
God.

[10] With all my heart I seek you;
   let me not stray from your commands.
R. *One does not live by bread alone, but by every*
   word that comes from the mouth of
   God.

[20] My soul is consumed with longing
   for your ordinances at all times.
R. *One does not live by bread alone, but by every*
   word that comes from the mouth of
   God.

[30] The way of truth I have chosen;
   I have set your ordinances before me.
R. *One does not live by bread alone, but by every*
   word that comes from the mouth of
   God.
[40] Behold, I long for your precepts;
   in your justice give me life.

R. One does not live by bread alone, but by every word that comes from the mouth of God.

¹³¹ I gasp with open mouth
  in my yearning for your commands.
R. One does not live by bread alone, but by every word that comes from the mouth of God.

Alleluia: Matthew 11:28
R. Alleluia, alleluia.
²⁸ Come to me, all you who labor and are
   burdened,
and I will give you rest, says the Lord.
R. Alleluia, alleluia.

Gospel: Matthew 9:9-13
⁹ As Jesus passed by, he saw a man named Matthew sitting at the customs post. He said to him, "Follow me." And he got up and followed him. ¹⁰ While he was at table in his house, many tax collectors and sinners came and sat with Jesus and his disciples. ¹¹ The Pharisees saw this and said to his disciples, "Why does your teacher eat with tax collectors and sinners?" ¹² He heard this and said, "Those who are well do not need a physician, but the sick do. ¹³ Go and learn the meaning of the words, *I desire mercy, not sacrifice.* I did not come to call the righteous but sinners."

Saturday July 6, 2024
Saturday of the Thirteenth Week in Ordinary Time
First Reading: Amos 9:11-15
¹¹ Thus says the LORD:

On that day I will raise up
  the fallen hut of David;
I will wall up its breaches,
  raise up its ruins,
  and rebuild it as in the days of old,
¹² That they may conquer what is left of Edom
  and all the nations that shall bear my
   name,
  say I, the LORD, who will do this.
¹³ Yes, days are coming,
  says the LORD,

When the plowman shall overtake the
        reaper,
        and the vintager, him who sows the seed;
The juice of grapes shall drip down the
        mountains,
        and all the hills shall run with it.
[14] I will bring about the restoration of my
        people Israel;
        they shall rebuild and inhabit their
        ruined cities,
Plant vineyards and drink the wine,
        set out gardens and eat the fruits.
[15] I will plant them upon their own ground;
        never again shall they be plucked
From the land I have given them,
        say I, the LORD, your God.

Responsorial Psalm: Psalms 85:9AB AND 10, 11-12, 13-14

R. [(see 9b)] *The Lord speaks of peace to his people.*

[9AB] I will hear what God proclaims;
        the LORD—for he proclaims peace to his
        people.
[10] Near indeed is his salvation to those who
        fear him,
        glory dwelling in our land.
R. *The Lord speaks of peace to his people.*

[11] Kindness and truth shall meet;
        justice and peace shall kiss.
[12] Truth shall spring out of the earth,
        and justice shall look down from heaven.
R. *The Lord speaks of peace to his people.*

[13] The LORD himself will give his benefits;
        our land shall yield its increase.
[14] Justice shall walk before him,
        and salvation, along the way of his steps.
R. *The Lord speaks of peace to his people.*

Alleluia: John 10:27

R. Alleluia, alleluia.
[27] My sheep hear my voice, says the Lord;

I know them, and they follow me.
R. Alleluia, alleluia.

Gospel: Matthew 9:14-17

[14] The disciples of John approached Jesus and said, "Why do we and the Pharisees fast much, but your disciples do not fast?" [15] Jesus answered them, "Can the wedding guests mourn as long as the bridegroom is with them? The days will come when the bridegroom is taken away from them, and then they will fast. [16] No one patches an old cloak with a piece of unshrunken cloth, for its fullness pulls away from the cloak and the tear gets worse. [17] People do not put new wine into old wineskins. Otherwise the skins burst, the wine spills out, and the skins are ruined. Rather, they pour new wine into fresh wineskins, and both are preserved."

Sunday July 7, 2024

Fourteenth Sunday in Ordinary Time, Year B
First Reading: Ezekiel 2:2-5

[2] As the LORD spoke to me, the spirit entered into me and set me on my feet, and I heard the one who was speaking [3] say to me: Son of man, I am sending you to the Israelites, rebels who have rebelled against me; they and their ancestors have revolted against me to this very day. [4] Hard of face and obstinate of heart are they to whom I am sending you. But you shall say to them: Thus says the Lord GOD! [5] And whether they heed or resist—for they are a rebellious house—they shall know that a prophet has been among them.

Responsorial Psalm: Psalms 123:1-2, 2, 3-4

R. [2cd] **Our eyes are fixed on the Lord, pleading**
for his mercy.

[1] To you I lift up my eyes
who are enthroned in heaven—
[2AB] As the eyes of servants
are on the hands of their masters.
R. Our eyes are fixed on the Lord, pleading for
his mercy.

[2BC] As the eyes of a maid
are on the hands of her mistress,
So are our eyes on the LORD, our God,
till he have pity on us.
R. Our eyes are fixed on the Lord, pleading for
his mercy.

[3] Have pity on us, O LORD, have pity on us,
for we are more than sated with

contempt;

4 our souls are more than sated
   with the mockery of the arrogant,
   with the contempt of the proud.
R. Our eyes are fixed on the Lord, pleading for
              his mercy.

Second Reading: 2 Corinthians 12:7-10

7 Brothers and sisters: That I, Paul, might not become too elated, because of the abundance of the revelations, a thorn in the flesh was given to me, an angel of Satan, to beat me, to keep me from being too elated. 8 Three times I begged the Lord about this, that it might leave me, 9 but he said to me, "My grace is sufficient for you, for power is made perfect in weakness." I will rather boast most gladly of my weaknesses, in order that the power of Christ may dwell with me. 10 Therefore, I am content with weaknesses, insults, hardships, persecutions, and constraints, for the sake of Christ; for when I am weak, then I am strong.

Alleluia: cf. Luke 4:18

R. Alleluia, alleluia.
18 The Spirit of the Lord is upon me
for he sent me to bring glad tidings to the
         poor.
R. Alleluia, alleluia.

Gospel: Mark 6:1-6

1 Jesus departed from there and came to his native place, accompanied by his disciples. 2 When the sabbath came he began to teach in the synagogue, and many who heard him were astonished. They said, "Where did this man get all this? What kind of wisdom has been given him? What mighty deeds are wrought by his hands! 3 Is he not the carpenter, the son of Mary, and the brother of James and Joses and Judas and Simon? And are not his sisters here with us?" And they took offense at him. 4 Jesus said to them, "A prophet is not without honor except in his native place and among his own kin and in his own house." 5 So he was not able to perform any mighty deed there, apart from curing a few sick people by laying his hands on them. 6 He was amazed at their lack of faith.

Monday July 8, 2024

Monday of Fourteenth Week in Ordinary Time
First Reading: Hosea 2:16, 17C-18, 21-22

16 Thus says the LORD:

I will allure her;
   I will lead her into the desert
   and speak to her heart.

17c She shall respond there as in the days of her
        youth,
    when she came up from the land of
        Egypt.
18 On that day, says the LORD,
She shall call me "My husband,"
    and never again "My baal."

21 I will espouse you to me forever:
    I will espouse you in right and in justice,
    in love and in mercy;
22 I will espouse you in fidelity,
    and you shall know the LORD.

Responsorial Psalm: Psalms 145:2-3, 4-5, 6-7, 8-9

R. *(8a)* **The Lord is gracious and merciful.**
2 Every day will I bless you,
    and I will praise your name forever and
        ever.
3 Great is the LORD and highly to be praised;
    his greatness is unsearchable.
R. The Lord is gracious and merciful.

4 Generation after generation praises your
        works
    and proclaims your might.
5 They speak of the splendor of your glorious
        majesty
    and tell of your wondrous works.
R. The Lord is gracious and merciful.

6 They discourse of the power of your terrible
        deeds
    and declare your greatness.
7 They publish the fame of your abundant
        goodness
    and joyfully sing of your justice.
R. The Lord is gracious and merciful.

8 The LORD is gracious and merciful,
    slow to anger and of great kindness.
9 The LORD is good to all

and compassionate toward all his works.
R. The Lord is gracious and merciful.

Alleluia: cf. 2 Timothy 1:10
R. Alleluia, alleluia.
[10] Our Savior Jesus Christ has destroyed death and brought life to light through the Gospel.
R. Alleluia, alleluia.

Gospel: Matthew 9:18-26
[18] While Jesus was speaking, an official came forward, knelt down before him, and said, "My daughter has just died. But come, lay your hand on her, and she will live." [19] Jesus rose and followed him, and so did his disciples. [20] A woman suffering hemorrhages for twelve years came up behind him and touched the tassel on his cloak. [21] She said to herself, "If only I can touch his cloak, I shall be cured." [22] Jesus turned around and saw her, and said, "Courage, daughter! Your faith has saved you." And from that hour the woman was cured.

[23] When Jesus arrived at the official's house and saw the flute players and the crowd who were making a commotion, [24] he said, "Go away! The girl is not dead but sleeping." And they ridiculed him. [25] When the crowd was put out, he came and took her by the hand, and the little girl arose. [26] And news of this spread throughout all that land.

Tuesday July 9, 2024
Tuesday of the Fourteenth Week in Ordinary Time
First Reading: Hosea 8:4-7, 11-13
[4] Thus says the LORD:

They made kings in Israel, but not by my
        authority;
    they established princes, but without my
        approval.
With their silver and gold they made
    idols for themselves, to their own
        destruction.
[5] Cast away your calf, O Samaria!
    my wrath is kindled against them;
How long will they be unable to attain
    innocence in Israel?
[6] The work of an artisan,
    no god at all,
Destined for the flames—
    such is the calf of Samaria!

[7] When they sow the wind,

they shall reap the whirlwind;
The stalk of grain that forms no ear
    can yield no flour;
Even if it could,
    strangers would swallow it.

[11] When Ephraim made many altars to expiate
         sin,
    his altars became occasions of sin.
[12] Though I write for him my many ordinances,
    they are considered as a stranger's.
[13] Though they offer sacrifice,
    immolate flesh and eat it,
    the LORD is not pleased with them.
He shall still remember their guilt
    and punish their sins;
    they shall return to Egypt.

Responsorial Psalm: Psalms 115:3-4, 5-6, 7AB-8, 9-10

R. [9a] *The house of Israel trusts in the Lord. or: Alleluia.*
[3] Our God is in heaven;
    whatever he wills, he does.
[4] Their idols are silver and gold,
    the handiwork of men.
R. *The house of Israel trusts in the Lord. or: Alleluia.*

[5] They have mouths but speak not;
    they have eyes but see not;
[6] They have ears but hear not;
    they have noses but smell not.
R. *The house of Israel trusts in the Lord. or: Alleluia.*

[7AB] They have hands but feel not;
    they have feet but walk not.
[8] Their makers shall be like them,
    everyone that trusts in them.
R. *The house of Israel trusts in the Lord. or: Alleluia.*

Alleluia: John 10:14

R. Alleluia, alleluia.
[14] I am the good shepherd, says the Lord;
I know my sheep, and mine know me.

R. Alleluia, alleluia.

Gospel: Matthew 9:32-38

[32] A demoniac who could not speak was brought to Jesus, [33] and when the demon was driven out the mute man spoke. The crowds were amazed and said, "Nothing like this has ever been seen in Israel." [34] But the Pharisees said, "He drives out demons by the prince of demons."

[35] Jesus went around to all the towns and villages, teaching in their synagogues, proclaiming the Gospel of the Kingdom, and curing every disease and illness. [36] At the sight of the crowds, his heart was moved with pity for them because they were troubled and abandoned, like sheep without a shepherd. [37] Then he said to his disciples, "The harvest is abundant but the laborers are few; [38] so ask the master of the harvest to send out laborers for his harvest."

Wednesday of the Fourteenth Week in Ordinary Time
First Reading: Hosea 10:1-3, 7-8, 12

[1] Israel is a luxuriant vine
     whose fruit matches its growth.
The more abundant his fruit,
     the more altars he built;
The more productive his land,
     the more sacred pillars he set up.
[2] Their heart is false,
     now they pay for their guilt;
God shall break down their altars
     and destroy their sacred pillars.
[3] If they would say,
     "We have no king"—
Since they do not fear the LORD,
     what can the king do for them?

[7] The king of Samaria shall disappear,
     like foam upon the waters.
[8] The high places of Aven shall be destroyed,
     the sin of Israel;
     thorns and thistles shall overgrow their
          altars.
Then they shall cry out to the mountains,
        "Cover us!"
     and to the hills, "Fall upon us!"

[12] "Sow for yourselves justice,

reap the fruit of piety;
break up for yourselves a new field,
>for it is time to seek the LORD,
>till he come and rain down justice upon
>>you."

Responsorial Psalm: Psalms 105:2-3, 4-5, 6-7

R. [4b] *Seek always the face of the Lord.* or: *Alleluia.*

[2] Sing to him, sing his praise,
>proclaim all his wondrous deeds.
[3] Glory in his holy name;
>rejoice, O hearts that seek the LORD!

R. *Seek always the face of the Lord.* or: *Alleluia.*

[4] Look to the LORD in his strength;
>seek to serve him constantly.
[5] Recall the wondrous deeds that he has
>>wrought,
>his portents, and the judgments he has
>>uttered.

R. *Seek always the face of the Lord.* or: *Alleluia.*

[6] You descendants of Abraham, his servants,
>sons of Jacob, his chosen ones!
[7] He, the LORD, is our God;
>throughout the earth his judgments
>>prevail.

R. *Seek always the face of the Lord.* or: *Alleluia.*

Alleluia: Mark 1:15

R. Alleluia, alleluia.

[15] The Kingdom of God is at hand:
repent and believe in the Gospel.

R. Alleluia, alleluia.

Gospel: Matthew 10:1-7

[1] Jesus summoned his Twelve disciples and gave them authority over unclean spirits to drive them out and to cure every disease and every illness. [2] The names of the Twelve Apostles are these: first, Simon called Peter, and his brother Andrew; James, the son of Zebedee, and his brother John; [3] Philip and Bartholomew, Thomas and Matthew the tax collector; James, the son of Alphaeus, and Thaddeus; [4] Simon the Cananean, and Judas Iscariot who betrayed Jesus.

[5] Jesus sent out these Twelve after instructing them thus, "Do not go into pagan territory or enter a Samaritan town. [6] Go rather to the lost sheep of the house of Israel. [7] As you go, make this proclamation: 'The Kingdom of heaven is at hand.'"

Memorial of Saint Benedict, Abbot
First Reading: Hosea 11:1-4, 8E-9

[1] Thus says the LORD:

When Israel was a child I loved him,
    out of Egypt I called my son.
[2] The more I called them,
    the farther they went from me,
Sacrificing to the Baals
    and burning incense to idols.
[3] Yet it was I who taught Ephraim to walk,
    who took them in my arms;
[4] I drew them with human cords,
    with bands of love;
I fostered them like one
    who raises an infant to his cheeks;
Yet, though I stooped to feed my child,
    they did not know that I was their healer.

[8E] My heart is overwhelmed,
    my pity is stirred.
[9] I will not give vent to my blazing anger,
    I will not destroy Ephraim again;
For I am God and not man,
    the Holy One present among you;
I will not let the flames consume you.

Responsorial Psalm: Psalms 80:2AC AND 3B, 15-16

R. [(4b)]*Let us see your face, Lord, and we shall be*
saved.
[2AC] O shepherd of Israel, hearken.
From your throne upon the cherubim, shine
    forth.
[3B] Rouse your power.
R. Let us see your face, Lord, and we shall be
saved.

¹⁵ Once again, O LORD of hosts,
  look down from heaven, and see:
Take care of this vine,
  ¹⁶ and protect what your right hand has
    planted,
  the son of man whom you yourself made
    strong.
**R. Let us see your face, Lord, and we shall be
    saved.**

Alleluia: Mark 1:15
R. Alleluia, alleluia.
¹⁵The Kingdom of God is at hand:
repent and believe in the Gospel.
R. Alleluia, alleluia.

Gospel: Matthew 10:7-15
⁷ Jesus said to his Apostles: "As you go, make this proclamation: 'The Kingdom of heaven is at hand.' ⁸ Cure the sick, raise the dead, cleanse the lepers, drive out demons. Without cost you have received; without cost you are to give. ⁹ Do not take gold or silver or copper for your belts; ¹⁰ no sack for the journey, or a second tunic, or sandals, or walking stick. The laborer deserves his keep. ¹¹ Whatever town or village you enter, look for a worthy person in it, and stay there until you leave. ¹² As you enter a house, wish it peace. ¹³ If the house is worthy, let your peace come upon it; if not, let your peace return to you. ¹⁴ Whoever will not receive you or listen to your words go outside that house or town and shake the dust from your feet. ¹⁵ Amen, I say to you, it will be more tolerable for the land of Sodom and Gomorrah on the day of judgment than for that town."

Friday July 12, 2024
Friday of Fourteenth Week in Ordinary Time
First Reading: Hosea 14:2-10
² Thus says the LORD:

Return, O Israel, to the LORD, your God;
  you have collapsed through your guilt.
³ Take with you words,
  and return to the LORD;
Say to him, "Forgive all iniquity,
  and receive what is good, that we may
    render
   as offerings the bullocks from our stalls.
⁴ Assyria will not save us,

nor shall we have horses to mount;
We shall say no more, 'Our god,'
　　to the work of our hands;
　　for in you the orphan finds compassion."
[5] I will heal their defection, says the LORD,
　　I will love them freely;
　　for my wrath is turned away from them.
[6] I will be like the dew for Israel:
　　he shall blossom like the lily;
He shall strike root like the Lebanon cedar,
　　[7] and put forth his shoots.
His splendor shall be like the olive tree
　　and his fragrance like the Lebanon cedar.
[8] Again they shall dwell in his shade
　　and raise grain;
They shall blossom like the vine,
　　and his fame shall be like the wine of
　　　　Lebanon.

[9] Ephraim! What more has he to do with
　　idols?
　　I have humbled him, but I will prosper
　　him.
"I am like a verdant cypress tree"—
　　because of me you bear fruit!

[10] Let him who is wise understand these
　　things;
　　let him who is prudent know them.
Straight are the paths of the LORD,
　　in them the just walk,
　　but sinners stumble in them.

Responsorial Psalm: Psalms 51:3-4, 8-9, 12-13, 14 AND 17

R. [(17b)] *My mouth will declare your praise.*
[3] Have mercy on me, O God, in your goodness;
　　in the greatness of your compassion wipe
　　　　out my offense.
[4] Thoroughly wash me from my guilt
　　and of my sin cleanse me.
R. *My mouth will declare your praise.*

[8] Behold, you are pleased with sincerity of
       heart,
      and in my inmost being you teach me wisdom.
[9] Cleanse me of sin with hyssop, that I may be
       purified;
      wash me, and I shall be whiter than
      snow.
R. My mouth will declare your praise.

[12] A clean heart create for me, O God,
      and a steadfast spirit renew within me.
[13] Cast me not out from your presence,
      and your Holy Spirit take not from me.
R. My mouth will declare your praise.

[14] Give me back the joy of your salvation,
      and a willing spirit sustain in me.
[17] O Lord, open my lips,
      and my mouth shall proclaim your
      praise.
R. My mouth will declare your praise.

Alleluia: John 16:13A; 14:26D
R. Alleluia, alleluia.
[13A] When the Spirit of truth comes,
he will guide you to all truth
[26D] and remind you of all I told you.
R. Alleluia, alleluia.

Gospel: Matthew 10:16-23
[16] Jesus said to his Apostles: "Behold, I am sending you like sheep in the midst of wolves; so be shrewd as serpents and simple as doves. [17] But beware of men, for they will hand you over to courts and scourge you in their synagogues, [18] and you will be led before governors and kings for my sake as a witness before them and the pagans. [19] When they hand you over, do not worry about how you are to speak or what you are to say. You will be given at that moment what you are to say. [20] For it will not be you who speak but the Spirit of your Father speaking through you. [21] Brother will hand over brother to death, and the father his child; children will rise up against parents and have them put to death. [22] You will be hated by all because of my name, but whoever endures to the end will be saved. [23] When they persecute you in one town, flee to another. Amen, I say to you, you will not finish the towns of Israel before the Son of Man comes."

Saturday of the Fourteenth Week in Ordinary Time
First Reading: Isaiah 6:1-8

[1] In the year King Uzziah died, I saw the Lord seated on a high and lofty throne, with the train of his garment filling the temple. [2] Seraphim were stationed above; each of them had six wings: with two they veiled their faces, with two they veiled their feet, and with two they hovered aloft.

[3] They cried one to the other, "Holy, holy, holy is the LORD of hosts! All the earth is filled with his glory!" [4] At the sound of that cry, the frame of the door shook and the house was filled with smoke.

[5] Then I said, "Woe is me, I am doomed! For I am a man of unclean lips, living among a people of unclean lips; yet my eyes have seen the King, the LORD of hosts!" [6] Then one of the seraphim flew to me, holding an ember that he had taken with tongs from the altar.

[7] He touched my mouth with it and said, "See, now that this has touched your lips, your wickedness is removed, your sin purged."

[8] Then I heard the voice of the Lord saying, "Whom shall I send? Who will go for us?" "Here I am," I said; "send me!"

Responsorial Psalm: Psalms 93:1AB,1CD-2, 5
R. *(1a)The Lord is king; he is robed in majesty.*
[1AB] The LORD is king, in splendor robed;
　　　robed is the LORD and girt about with
　　　　　strength.
R. *The Lord is king; he is robed in majesty.*

[1CD] And he has made the world firm,
　　　not to be moved.
[2] Your throne stands firm from of old;
　　　from everlasting you are, O LORD.
R. *The Lord is king; he is robed in majesty.*

[5] Your decrees are worthy of trust indeed:
　　　holiness befits your house,
　　　O LORD, for length of days.
R. *The Lord is king; he is robed in majesty.*

Alleluia: 1 Peter 4:14
R. Alleluia, alleluia.
[14] If you are insulted for the name of Christ,
　　　blessed are you,
for the Spirit of God rests upon you.

R. Alleluia, alleluia.

Gospel: Matthew 10:24-33

[24] Jesus said to his Apostles: "No disciple is above his teacher, no slave above his master. [25] It is enough for the disciple that he become like his teacher, for the slave that he become like his master. If they have called the master of the house Beelzebul, how much more those of his household! [26] "Therefore do not be afraid of them. Nothing is concealed that will not be revealed, nor secret that will not be known. [27] What I say to you in the darkness, speak in the light; what you hear whispered, proclaim on the housetops. [28] And do not be afraid of those who kill the body but cannot kill the soul; rather, be afraid of the one who can destroy both soul and body in Gehenna. [29] Are not two sparrows sold for a small coin? Yet not one of them falls to the ground without your Father's knowledge. [30] Even all the hairs of your head are counted. [31] So do not be afraid; you are worth more than many sparrows. [32] Everyone who acknowledges me before others I will acknowledge before my heavenly Father. [33] But whoever denies me before others, I will deny before my heavenly Father."

Sunday July 14, 2024

Fifteenth Sunday in Ordinary Time, Year B

First Reading: Amos 7:12-15

[12] Amaziah, priest of Bethel, said to Amos, "Off with you, visionary, flee to the land of Judah! There earn your bread by prophesying, [13] but never again prophesy in Bethel; for it is the king's sanctuary and a royal temple."

[14] Amos answered Amaziah, "I was no prophet, nor have I belonged to a company of prophets; I was a shepherd and a dresser of sycamores. [15] The LORD took me from following the flock, and said to me, Go, prophesy to my people Israel."

Responsorial Psalm: Psalms 85:9-10, 11-12, 13-14

R. [8] *Lord, let us see your kindness, and grant*
us your salvation.

[9] I will hear what God proclaims;
    the LORD—for he proclaims peace.
[10] Near indeed is his salvation to those who
        fear him,
    glory dwelling in our land.

R. *Lord, let us see your kindness, and grant us*
your salvation.

[11] Kindness and truth shall meet;
    justice and peace shall kiss.
[12] Truth shall spring out of the earth,
    and justice shall look down from heaven.

R. *Lord, let us see your kindness, and grant us*

your salvation.

[13] The LORD himself will give his benefits;
  our land shall yield its increase.
[14] Justice shall walk before him,
  and prepare the way of his steps.
R. Lord, let us see your kindness, and grant us
  your salvation.

Second Reading: Ephesians 1:3-14

[3] Blessed be the God and Father of our Lord Jesus Christ, who has blessed us in Christ with every spiritual blessing in the heavens, [4] as he chose us in him, before the foundation of the world, to be holy and without blemish before him. In love [5] he destined us for adoption to himself through Jesus Christ, in accord with the favor of his will, [6] for the praise of the glory of his grace that he granted us in the beloved. [7] In him we have redemption by his blood, the forgiveness of transgressions, in accord with the riches of his grace [8] that he lavished upon us. In all wisdom and insight, [9] he has made known to us the mystery of his will in accord with his favor that he set forth in him [10] as a plan for the fullness of times, to sum up all things in Christ, in heaven and on earth.

[11] In him we were also chosen, destined in accord with the purpose of the One who accomplishes all things according to the intention of his will, [12] so that we might exist for the praise of his glory, we who first hoped in Christ. [13] In him you also, who have heard the word of truth, the gospel of your salvation, and have believed in him, were sealed with the promised Holy Spirit, [14] which is the first installment of our inheritance toward redemption as God's possession, to the praise of his glory.

Or Ephesians 1:3-10

[3] Blessed be the God and Father of our Lord Jesus Christ, who has blessed us in Christ with every spiritual blessing in the heavens, [4] as he chose us in him, before the foundation of the world, to be holy and without blemish before him. In love [5] he destined us for adoption to himself through Jesus Christ, in accord with the favor of his will, [6] for the praise of the glory of his grace that he granted us in the beloved.

[7] In him we have redemption by his blood, the forgiveness of transgressions, in accord with the riches of his grace [8] that he lavished upon us. In all wisdom and insight, [9] he has made known to us the mystery of his will in accord with his favor that he set forth in him [10] as a plan for the fullness of times, to sum up all things in Christ, in heaven and on earth.

Alleluia: cf. Ephesians 1:17-18
R. Alleluia, alleluia.
[17] May the Father of our Lord Jesus Christ
enlighten the eyes of our hearts,

¹⁸ that we may know what is the hope
that belongs to our call.
R. Alleluia, alleluia.

Gospel: Mark 6:7-13

⁷ Jesus summoned the Twelve and began to send them out two by two and gave them authority over unclean spirits. ⁸ He instructed them to take nothing for the journey but a walking stick—no food, no sack, no money in their belts. ⁹ They were, however, to wear sandals but not a second tunic. ¹⁰ He said to them, "Wherever you enter a house, stay there until you leave. ¹¹ Whatever place does not welcome you or listen to you, leave there and shake the dust off your feet in testimony against them." ¹² So they went off and preached repentance. ¹³ The Twelve drove out many demons, and they anointed with oil many who were sick and cured them.

Monday July 15, 2024

Memorial of Saint Bonaventure, Bishop & Doctor
First Reading: Isaiah 1:10-17

¹⁰ Hear the word of the LORD,
        princes of Sodom!
Listen to the instruction of our God,
        people of Gomorrah!
¹¹ What care I for the number of your
            sacrifices?
        says the LORD.
I have had enough of whole-burnt rams
        and fat of fatlings;
In the blood of calves, lambs and goats
        I find no pleasure.

¹² When you come in to visit me,
        who asks these things of you?
¹³ Trample my courts no more!
        Bring no more worthless offerings;
        your incense is loathsome to me.
New moon and sabbath, calling of
            assemblies,
        octaves with wickedness: these I cannot
            bear.
¹⁴ Your new moons and festivals I detest;
        they weigh me down, I tire of the load.
¹⁵ When you spread out your hands,
        I close my eyes to you;

376

Though you pray the more,
        I will not listen.
Your hands are full of blood!
        [16] Wash yourselves clean!
Put away your misdeeds from before my
            eyes;
        cease doing evil; [17] learn to do good.
Make justice your aim: redress the wronged,
        hear the orphan's plea, defend the widow.

Responsorial Psalm: Psalms 50:8-9, 16BC-17, 21 AND 23

R. [23b]**To the upright I will show the saving
                power of God.**

[8] "Not for your sacrifices do I rebuke you,
        for your burnt offerings are before me
            always.
[9] I take from your house no bullock,
        no goats out of your fold."
R. **To the upright I will show the saving power of
            God.**

[16BC] "Why do you recite my statutes,
        and profess my covenant with your
            mouth,
[17] Though you hate discipline
        and cast my words behind you?"
R. **To the upright I will show the saving power of
            God.**

[21] "When you do these things, shall I be deaf to
            it?
        Or do you think you that I am like
            yourself?
        I will correct you by drawing them up
            before your eyes.
[23] He that offers praise as a sacrifice glorifies
            me;
        and to him that goes the right way I will
            show the salvation of God."
R. **To the upright I will show the saving power of
            God.**

Alleluia: Matthew 5:10
R. Alleluia, alleluia.
¹⁰ Blessed are they who are persecuted for the
 sake of righteousness,
for theirs is the Kingdom of heaven.
R. Alleluia, alleluia.

Gospel: Matthew 10:34-11:1
³⁴ Jesus said to his Apostles: "Do not think that I have come to bring peace upon the earth. I have come to bring not peace but the sword. ³⁵ For I have come to set

a man against his father,
 a daughter against her mother,
and a daughter-in-law against her mother-
 in-law;
³⁶ and one's enemies will be those of his
 household.

³⁷ "Whoever loves father or mother more than me is not worthy of me, and whoever loves son or daughter more than me is not worthy of me; ³⁸ and whoever does not take up his cross and follow after me is not worthy of me. ³⁹ Whoever finds his life will lose it, and whoever loses his life for my sake will find it.
 ⁴⁰ "Whoever receives you receives me, and whoever receives me receives the one who sent me. ⁴¹ Whoever receives a prophet because he is a prophet will receive a prophet's reward, and whoever receives a righteous man because he is righteous will receive a righteous man's reward. ⁴² And whoever gives only a cup of cold water to one of these little ones to drink because he is a disciple— amen, I say to you, he will surely not lose his reward."
 ¹ When Jesus finished giving these commands to his Twelve disciples, he went away from that place to teach and to preach in their towns.

Tuesday July 16, 2024
Tuesday of Fifteenth Week in Ordinary Time
First Reading: Isaiah 7:1-9
¹ In the days of Ahaz, king of Judah, son of Jotham, son of Uzziah, Rezin, king of Aram, and Pekah, king of Israel, son of Remaliah, went up to attack Jerusalem, but they were not able to conquer it. ² When word came to the house of David that Aram was encamped in Ephraim, the heart of the king and the heart of the people trembled, as the trees of the forest tremble in the wind.
 ³ Then the LORD said to Isaiah: Go out to meet Ahaz, you and your son Shear-jashub, at the end of the conduit of the upper pool, on the highway of the fuller's field, ⁴ and say to him: Take care you remain tranquil and do not fear; let not your courage fail

before these two stumps of smoldering brands the blazing anger of Rezin and the Arameans, and of the son Remaliah, because of the mischief that [5] Aram, Ephraim and the son of Remaliah, plots against you, [6] saying, "Let us go up and tear Judah asunder, make it our own by force, and appoint the son of Tabeel king there."

[7] Thus says the LORD:

This shall not stand, it shall not be!
[8] Damascus is the capital of Aram,
    and Rezin is the head of Damascus;
[9] Samaria is the capital of Ephraim,
    and Remaliah's son the head of Samaria.

But within sixty years and five,
    Ephraim shall be crushed, no longer a
        nation.
Unless your faith is firm
    you shall not be firm!

Responsorial Psalm: Psalms 48:2-3A, 3B-4, 5-6, 7-8
R. [(see 9d)] **God upholds his city for ever.**
[2] Great is the LORD and wholly to be praised
    in the city of our God.
[3A] His holy mountain, fairest of heights,
    is the joy of all the earth.
R. God upholds his city for ever.

[3B] Mount Zion, "the recesses of the North,"
    is the city of the great King.
[4] God is with her castles;
    renowned is he as a stronghold.
R. God upholds his city for ever.

[5] For lo! the kings assemble,
    they come on together;
[6] They also see, and at once are stunned,
    terrified, routed.
R. God upholds his city for ever.

[7] Quaking seizes them there;
    anguish, like a woman's in labor,
[8] As though a wind from the east
    were shattering ships of Tarshish.

R. God upholds his city for ever.

Alleluia: Psalms 95:8
R. Alleluia, alleluia.
[8] If today you hear his voice,
harden not your hearts.
R. Alleluia, alleluia.

Gospel: Matthew 11:20-24
[20] Jesus began to reproach the towns where most of his mighty deeds had been done, since they had not repented. [22] "Woe to you, Chorazin! Woe to you, Bethsaida! For if the mighty deeds done in your midst had been done in Tyre and Sidon, they would long ago have repented in sackcloth and ashes. But I tell you, it will be more tolerable for Tyre and Sidon on the day of judgment than for you. [23] And as for you, Capernaum:

Will you be exalted to heaven?
You will go down to the netherworld.

For if the mighty deeds done in your midst had been done in Sodom, it would have remained until this day. [24] But I tell you, it will be more tolerable for the land of Sodom on the day of judgment than for you."

Wednesday July 17, 2024

Wednesday of the Fifteenth Week in Ordinary Time
First Reading: Isaiah 10:5-7, 13B-16
[5] Thus says the LORD:

Woe to Assyria! My rod in anger,
    my staff in wrath.
[6] Against an impious nation I send him,
        and against a people under my wrath I
            order him
To seize plunder, carry off loot,
        and tread them down like the mud of the
            streets.
[7] But this is not what he intends,
        nor does he have this in mind;
Rather, it is in his heart to destroy,
        to make an end of nations not a few.

    [13B] For he says:
"By my own power I have done it,

and by my wisdom, for I am shrewd.
I have moved the boundaries of peoples,
    their treasures I have pillaged,
      and, like a giant, I have put down the
        enthroned.
[14] My hand has seized like a nest
    the riches of nations;
As one takes eggs left alone,
    so I took in all the earth;
No one fluttered a wing,
    or opened a mouth, or chirped!"

[15] Will the axe boast against him who hews
      with it?
    Will the saw exalt itself above him who
      wields it?
As if a rod could sway him who lifts it,
    or a staff him who is not wood!
[16] Therefore the Lord, the LORD of hosts,
    will send among his fat ones leanness,
And instead of his glory there will be
      kindling
    like the kindling of fire.

Responsorial Psalm: Psalms 94:5-6, 7-8, 9-10, 14-15

R. [14a] *The Lord will not abandon his people.*
[5] Your people, O LORD, they trample down,
    your inheritance they afflict.
[6] Widow and stranger they slay,
    the fatherless they murder.
R. *The Lord will not abandon his people.*

[7] And they say, "The LORD sees not;
    the God of Jacob perceives not."
[8] Understand, you senseless ones among the
      people;
    and, you fools, when will you be wise?
R. *The Lord will not abandon his people.*

[9] Shall he who shaped the ear not hear?
    or he who formed the eye not see?
[10] Shall he who instructs nations not chastise,

he who teaches men knowledge?
R. The Lord will not abandon his people.

¹⁴ For the LORD will not cast off his people,
  nor abandon his inheritance;
¹⁵ But judgment shall again be with justice,
  and all the upright of heart shall follow it.
R. The Lord will not abandon his people.

Alleluia: Matthew 11:25
R. Alleluia, alleluia.
²⁵ Blessed are you, Father, Lord of heaven and
   earth,
you have revealed to little ones the
   mysteries of the Kingdom.
R. Alleluia, alleluia.

Gospel: Matthew 11:25-27
²⁵ At that time Jesus exclaimed: "I give praise to you, Father, Lord of heaven and earth, for although you have hidden these things from the wise and the learned you have revealed them to the childlike. ²⁶ Yes, Father, such has been your gracious will. ²⁷ All things have been handed over to me by my Father. No one knows the Son except the Father, and no one knows the Father except the Son and anyone to whom the Son wishes to reveal him."

Thursday July 18, 2024
Thursday of the Fifteenth Week in Ordinary Time
First Reading: Isaiah 26:7-9, 12, 16-19
⁷ The way of the just is smooth;
  the path of the just you make level.
⁸ Yes, for your way and your judgments, O
   LORD,
  we look to you;
Your name and your title
  are the desire of our souls.
⁹ My soul yearns for you in the night,
  yes, my spirit within me keeps vigil for
   you;
When your judgment dawns upon the earth,
  the world's inhabitants learn justice.
¹² O LORD, you mete out peace to us,
  for it is you who have accomplished all
   we have done.

[16] O LORD, oppressed by your punishment,
we cried out in anguish under your
chastising.
[17] As a woman about to give birth
writhes and cries out in her pains,
so were we in your presence, O LORD.
[18] We conceived and writhed in pain,
giving birth to wind;
Salvation we have not achieved for the
earth,
the inhabitants of the world cannot bring
it forth.
[19] But your dead shall live, their corpses shall
rise;
awake and sing, you who lie in the dust.
For your dew is a dew of light,
and the land of shades gives birth.

Responsorial Psalm: Psalms 102:13-14AB AND 15, 16-18, 19-21

R. [20b] *From heaven the Lord looks down on the
earth.*

[13] You, O LORD, abide forever,
and your name through all generations.
[14AB] You will arise and have mercy on Zion,
for it is time to pity her.
[15] For her stones are dear to your servants,
and her dust moves them to pity.

R. *From heaven the Lord looks down on the
earth.*

[16] The nations shall revere your name, O LORD,
and all the kings of the earth your glory,
[17] When the LORD has rebuilt Zion
and appeared in his glory;
[18] When he has regarded the prayer of the
destitute,
and not despised their prayer.

R. *From heaven the Lord looks down on the
earth.*

[19] Let this be written for the generation to
come,

and let his future creatures praise the
        LORD:
[20] "The LORD looked down from his holy height,
        from heaven he beheld the earth,
[21] To hear the groaning of the prisoners,
        to release those doomed to die."

R. From heaven the Lord looks down on the earth.

Alleluia: Matthew 11:28

R. Alleluia, alleluia.
[28]Come to me, all you who labor and are
        burdened,
and I will give you rest, says the Lord.
R. Alleluia, alleluia.

Gospel: Matthew 11:28-30

[28] Jesus said: "Come to me, all you who labor and are burdened, and I will give you rest. [29] Take my yoke upon you and learn from me, for I am meek and humble of heart; and you will find rest for yourselves. [30] For my yoke is easy, and my burden light."

Friday of Fifteenth Week in Ordinary Time

First Reading: Isaiah 38:1-6, 21-22, 7-8

[1] When Hezekiah was mortally ill, the prophet Isaiah, son of Amoz, came and said to him: "Thus says the LORD: Put your house in order, for you are about to die; you shall not recover." [2] Then Hezekiah turned his face to the wall and prayed to the LORD:

[3] "O LORD, remember how faithfully and wholeheartedly I conducted myself in your presence, doing what was pleasing to you!" And Hezekiah wept bitterly.

[4] Then the word of the LORD came to Isaiah: [5] "Go, tell Hezekiah: Thus says the LORD, the God of your father David: I have heard your prayer and seen your tears. I will heal you: in three days you shall go up to the LORD's temple; I will add fifteen years to your life. [6] I will rescue you and this city from the hand of the king of Assyria; I will be a shield to this city."

[21] Isaiah then ordered a poultice of figs to be taken and applied to the boil, that he might recover. [22] Then Hezekiah asked, "What is the sign that I shall go up to the temple of the LORD?"

[7] Isaiah answered: "This will be the sign for you from the LORD that he will do what he has promised: [8] See, I will make the shadow cast by the sun on the stairway to the terrace of Ahaz go back the ten steps it has advanced." So the sun came back the ten steps it had advanced.

Responsorial Psalm: Isaiah 38:10, 11, 12ABCD, 16

R. (see 17b)You saved my life, O Lord; I shall not die.

[10] Once I said,
>   "In the noontime of life I must depart!
> To the gates of the nether world I shall be
>   consigned
>   for the rest of my years."

R. You saved my life, O Lord; I shall not die.

[11] I said, "I shall see the LORD no more
>   in the land of the living.
> No longer shall I behold my fellow men
>   among those who dwell in the world."

R. You saved my life, O Lord; I shall not die.

[12ABCD] My dwelling, like a shepherd's tent,
>   is struck down and borne away from me;
> You have folded up my life, like a weaver
>   who severs the last thread.

R. You saved my life, O Lord; I shall not die.

[16] Those live whom the LORD protects;
>   yours is the life of my spirit.
> You have given me health and life.

R. You saved my life, O Lord; I shall not die.

Alleluia: John 10:27

R. Alleluia, alleluia.

[27] My sheep hear my voice, says the Lord;
I know them, and they follow me.

R. Alleluia, alleluia.

Gospel: Matthew 12:1-8

[1] Jesus was going through a field of grain on the sabbath. His disciples were hungry and began to pick the heads of grain and eat them. [2] When the Pharisees saw this, they said to him, "See, your disciples are doing what is unlawful to do on the sabbath." [3] He said to the them, "Have you not read what David did when he and his companions were hungry, [4] how he went into the house of God and ate the bread of offering, which neither he nor his companions but only the priests could lawfully eat? [5] Or have you not read in the law that on the sabbath the priests serving in the temple violate the sabbath and are innocent? [6] I say to you, something greater than the temple is here. [7] If you knew what this meant, *I desire mercy, not sacrifice*, you would not have condemned these innocent men. [8] For the Son of Man is Lord of the sabbath."

Saturday of Fifteenth Week in Ordinary Time
First Reading: Micah 2:1-5

¹ Woe to those who plan iniquity,
and work out evil on their couches;
In the morning light they accomplish it
when it lies within their power.
² They covet fields, and seize them;
houses, and they take them;
They cheat an owner of his house,
a man of his inheritance.

³ Therefore thus says the LORD:
Behold, I am planning against this race an
evil
from which you shall not withdraw your
necks;
Nor shall you walk with head high,
for it will be a time of evil.

⁴ On that day a satire shall be sung over you,
and there shall be a plaintive chant:
"Our ruin is complete,
our fields are portioned out among our
captors,
The fields of my people are measured out,
and no one can get them back!"
⁵ Thus you shall have no one
to mark out boundaries by lot
in the assembly of the LORD.

Responsorial Psalm: Psalms 10:1-2, 3-4, 7-8, 14
R. ⁽¹²ᵇ⁾*Do not forget the poor, O Lord!*
¹ Why, O LORD, do you stand aloof?
Why hide in times of distress?
² Proudly the wicked harass the afflicted,
who are caught in the devices the wicked
have contrived.
R. *Do not forget the poor, O Lord!*

³ For the wicked man glories in his greed,

and the covetous blasphemes, sets the
        LORD at nought.
[4] The wicked man boasts, "He will not avenge
        it";
    "There is no God," sums up his thoughts.
R. Do not forget the poor, O Lord!

[7] His mouth is full of cursing, guile and deceit;
        under his tongue are mischief and
        iniquity.
[8] He lurks in ambush near the villages;
        in hiding he murders the innocent;
        his eyes spy upon the unfortunate.
R. Do not forget the poor, O Lord!

[14] You do see, for you behold misery and
        sorrow,
        taking them in your hands.
On you the unfortunate man depends;
        of the fatherless you are the helper.
R. Do not forget the poor, O Lord!

Alleluia: 2 Corinthians 5:19
R. Alleluia, alleluia.
[19] God was reconciling the world to himself in
        Christ,
and entrusting to us the message of
        reconciliation.
R. Alleluia, alleluia.

Gospel: Matthew 12:14-21
[14] The Pharisees went out and took counsel against Jesus to put him to death.
  [15] When Jesus realized this, he withdrew from that place. Many people followed him, and he cured them all, [16] but he warned them not to make him known. [17] This was to fulfill what had been spoken through Isaiah the prophet:

[18] *Behold, my servant whom I have chosen,*
        my beloved in whom I delight;
I shall place my Spirit upon him,
        and he will proclaim justice to the
           Gentiles.
[19] *He will not contend or cry out,*

nor will anyone hear his voice in the
streets.
[20] *A bruised reed he will not break,*
a smoldering wick he will not quench,
until he brings justice to victory.
[21] *And in his name the Gentiles will hope.*

Sunday July 21, 2024

Sixteenth Sunday in Ordinary Time, Year B
First Reading: Jeremiah 23:1-6

[1] Woe to the shepherds
who mislead and scatter the flock of my
pasture,
says the LORD.
[2] Therefore, thus says the LORD, the God of
Israel,
against the shepherds who shepherd my
people:
You have scattered my sheep and driven
them away.
You have not cared for them,
but I will take care to punish your evil
deeds.
[3] I myself will gather the remnant of my flock
from all the lands to which I have driven
them
and bring them back to their meadow;
there they shall increase and multiply.
[4] I will appoint shepherds for them who will
shepherd them
so that they need no longer fear and
tremble;
and none shall be missing, says the LORD.

[5] Behold, the days are coming, says the
LORD,
when I will raise up a righteous shoot to
David;
as king he shall reign and govern wisely,
he shall do what is just and right in the
land.
[6] In his days Judah shall be saved,

388

Israel shall dwell in security.
This is the name they give him:
"The LORD our justice."

Responsorial Psalm: Psalms 23:1-3, 3-4, 5, 6

R. [1] *The Lord is my shepherd; there is nothing I
shall want.*

[1] The LORD is my shepherd; I shall not want.
[2] In verdant pastures he gives me repose;
beside restful waters he leads me;
[3A] he refreshes my soul.

R. *The Lord is my shepherd; there is nothing I
shall want.*

[3B] He guides me in right paths
for his name's sake.
[4] Even though I walk in the dark valley
I fear no evil; for you are at my side
with your rod and your staff
that give me courage.

R. *The Lord is my shepherd; there is nothing I
shall want.*

[5] You spread the table before me
in the sight of my foes;
you anoint my head with oil;
my cup overflows.

R. *The Lord is my shepherd; there is nothing I
shall want.*

[6] Only goodness and kindness follow me
all the days of my life;
and I shall dwell in the house of the LORD
for years to come.

R. *The Lord is my shepherd; there is nothing I
shall want.*

Second Reading: Ephesians 2:13-18

[13] Brothers and sisters: In Christ Jesus you who once were far off have become near by the blood of Christ.

[14] For he is our peace, he who made both one and broke down the dividing wall of enmity, through his flesh, [15] abolishing the law with its commandments and legal claims,

that he might create in himself one new person in place of the two, thus establishing peace, [16] and might reconcile both with God, in one body, through the cross, putting that enmity to death by it. [17] He came and preached peace to you who were far off and peace to those who were near, [18] for through him we both have access in one Spirit to the Father.

Alleluia: John 10:27
R. Alleluia, alleluia.
[27] My sheep hear my voice, says the Lord;
I know them, and they follow me.
R. Alleluia, alleluia.

Gospel: Mark 6:30-34
[30] The apostles gathered together with Jesus and reported all they had done and taught. [31] He said to them, "Come away by yourselves to a deserted place and rest a while." People were coming and going in great numbers, and they had no opportunity even to eat. [32] So they went off in the boat by themselves to a deserted place. [33] People saw them leaving and many came to know about it. They hastened there on foot from all the towns and arrived at the place before them.

[34] When he disembarked and saw the vast crowd, his heart was moved with pity for them, for they were like sheep without a shepherd; and he began to teach them many things.

Feast of Saint Mary Magdalene
First Reading: Songs of Solomon 3:1-4B
The Bride says:

[1] On my bed at night I sought him
    whom my heart loves—
    I sought him but I did not find him.
[2] I will rise then and go about the city;
    in the streets and crossings I will seek
Him whom my heart loves.
    I sought him but I did not find him.
[3] The watchmen came upon me,
    as they made their rounds of the city:
    Have you seen him whom my heart
        loves?
[4] I had hardly left them
    when I found him whom my heart
        loves.

OR 2 Corinthians 5:14-17

Brothers and sisters: [14] The love of Christ impels us, once we have come to the conviction that one died for all; therefore, all have died. [15] He indeed died for all, so that those who live might no longer live for themselves but for him who for their sake died and was raised.

[16] Consequently, from now on we regard no one according to the flesh; even if we once knew Christ according to the flesh, yet now we know him so no longer. [17] So whoever is in Christ is a new creation: the old things have passed away; behold, new things have come.

Responsorial Psalm: Psalms 63:2,3-4,5-6, 8-9

R. *(2)* *My soul is thirsting for you, O Lord my God.*

[2] O God, you are my God whom I seek;
   for you my flesh pines and my soul thirsts
   like the earth, parched, lifeless and
      without water.

R. *My soul is thirsting for you, O Lord my God.*

[3] Thus have I gazed toward you in the
      sanctuary
   to see your power and your glory,
[4] For your kindness is a greater good than life;
   my lips shall glorify you.

R. *My soul is thirsting for you, O Lord my God.*

[5] Thus will I bless you while I live;
   lifting up my hands, I will call upon your
      name.
[6] As with the riches of a banquet shall my soul
      be satisfied,
   and with exultant lips my mouth shall
      praise you.

R. *My soul is thirsting for you, O Lord my God.*

[8] You are my help,
   and in the shadow of your wings I shout
      for joy.
[9] My soul clings fast to you;
   your right hand upholds me.

R. *My soul is thirsting for you, O Lord my God.*

Alleluia

R. Alleluia, alleluia.

Tell us, Mary, what did you see on the way?
I saw the glory of the risen Christ, I saw his
     empty tomb.

R. Alleluia, alleluia.

Gospel: John 20:1-2, 11-18

[1] On the first day of the week, Mary Magdalene came to the tomb early in the morning, while it was still dark, and saw the stone removed from the tomb. [2] So she ran and went to Simon Peter and to the other disciple whom Jesus loved, and told them, "They have taken the Lord from the tomb, and we don't know where they put him."

[11] Mary stayed outside the tomb weeping. And as she wept, she bent over into the tomb [12] and saw two angels in white sitting there, one at the head and one at the feet where the Body of Jesus had been. [13] And they said to her, "Woman, why are you weeping?" She said to them, "They have taken my Lord, and I don't know where they laid him." [14] When she had said this, she turned around and saw Jesus there, but did not know it was Jesus. [15] Jesus said to her, "Woman, why are you weeping? Whom are you looking for?" She thought it was the gardener and said to him, "Sir, if you carried him away, tell me where you laid him, and I will take him." [16] Jesus said to her, "Mary!" She turned and said to him in Hebrew, "*Rabbouni*," which means Teacher. [17] Jesus said to her, "Stop holding on to me, for I have not yet ascended to the Father. But go to my brothers and tell them, 'I am going to my Father and your Father, to my God and your God.'" [18] Mary Magdalene went and announced to the disciples, "I have seen the Lord," and then reported what he told her.

Tuesday of Sixteenth Week in Ordinary Time
First Reading: Micah 7:14-15, 18-20

[14] Shepherd your people with your staff,
     the flock of your inheritance,
That dwells apart in a woodland,
     in the midst of Carmel.
Let them feed in Bashan and Gilead,
     as in the days of old;
[15] As in the days when you came from the land
          of Egypt,
     show us wonderful signs.

[18] Who is there like you, the God who removes
          guilt
     and pardons sin for the remnant of his

392

inheritance;
Who does not persist in anger forever,
    but delights rather in clemency,
[19] And will again have compassion on us,
    treading underfoot our guilt?
You will cast into the depths of the sea
    all our sins;
[20] You will show faithfulness to Jacob,
    and grace to Abraham,
As you have sworn to our fathers
    from days of old.

Responsorial Psalm: Psalms 85:2-4, 5-6, 7-8

R. [8a] *Lord, show us your mercy and love.*
[2] You have favored, O LORD, your land;
    you have brought back the captives of
      Jacob.
[3] You have forgiven the guilt of your people;
    you have covered all their sins.
[4] You have withdrawn all your wrath;
    you have revoked your burning anger.
R. Lord, show us your mercy and love.

[5] Restore us, O God our savior,
    and abandon your displeasure against us.
[6] Will you be ever angry with us,
    prolonging your anger to all generations?
R. Lord, show us your mercy and love.

[7] Will you not instead give us life;
    and shall not your people rejoice in you?
[8] Show us, O LORD, your kindness,
    and grant us your salvation.
R. Lord, show us your mercy and love.

Alleluia: John 14:23

R. Alleluia, alleluia.
[23] Whoever loves me will keep my word,
and my Father will love him
and we will come to him.
R. Alleluia, alleluia.

Gospel: Matthew 12:46-50

[46] While Jesus was speaking to the crowds, his mother and his brothers appeared outside, wishing to speak with him. [47] Someone told him, "Your mother and your brothers are standing outside, asking to speak with you." [48] But he said in reply to the one who told him, "Who is my mother? Who are my brothers?" [49] And stretching out his hand toward his disciples, he said, "Here are my mother and my brothers. [50] For whoever does the will of my heavenly Father is my brother, and sister, and mother."

Wednesday of the Sixteenth Week in Ordinary Time
First Reading: Jeremiah 1:1, 4-10

[1] The words of Jeremiah, son of Hilkiah, of a priestly family in Anathoth, in the land of Benjamin.

[4] The word of the LORD came to me thus:

[5] Before I formed you in the womb I knew
you,
before you were born I dedicated you,
a prophet to the nations I appointed you.
[6] "Ah, Lord GOD!" I said,
"I know not how to speak; I am too
young."

[7] But the LORD answered me,

Say not, "I am too young."
To whomever I send you, you shall go;
whatever I command you, you shall
speak.
[8] Have no fear before them,
because I am with you to deliver you,
says the LORD.

[9] Then the LORD extended his hand and touched my mouth, saying,

See, I place my words in your mouth!
[10] This day I set you
over nations and over kingdoms,
To root up and to tear down,
to destroy and to demolish,
to build and to plant.

Responsorial Psalm: Psalms 71:1-2, 3-4A, 5-6AB, 15 AND 17

R. *(see 15ab)I will sing of your salvation.*

[1] In you, O LORD, I take refuge;
    let me never be put to shame.
[2] In your justice rescue me, and deliver me;
    incline your ear to me, and save me.

R. *I will sing of your salvation.*

[3] Be my rock of refuge,
    a stronghold to give me safety,
    for you are my rock and my fortress.
[4A] O my God, rescue me from the hand of the
    wicked.

R. *I will sing of your salvation.*

[5] For you are my hope, O Lord;
    my trust, O God, from my youth.
[6AB] On you I depend from birth;
    from my mother's womb you are my
    strength.

R. *I will sing of your salvation.*

[15] My mouth shall declare your justice,
    day by day your salvation.
[17] O God, you have taught me from my youth,
    and till the present I proclaim your
    wondrous deeds.

R. *I will sing of your salvation.*

Alleluia

R. Alleluia, alleluia.
The seed is the word of God, Christ is the
    sower;
all who come to him will live for ever.
R. Alleluia, alleluia.

Gospel: Matthew 13:1-9

[1] On that day, Jesus went out of the house and sat down by the sea. [2] Such large crowds gathered around him that he got into a boat and sat down, and the whole crowd stood along the shore. [3] And he spoke to them at length in parables, saying: "A sower went out to sow. [4] And as he sowed, some seed fell on the path, and birds came and ate it up. [5] Some fell on rocky ground, where it had little soil. It sprang up at once because the soil

was not deep, [6] and when the sun rose it was scorched, and it withered for lack of roots.[7]Some seed fell among thorns, and the thorns grew up and choked it. [8] But some seed fell on rich soil, and produced fruit, a hundred or sixty or thirtyfold. [9] Whoever has ears ought to hear."

Thursday July 25, 2024

Feast of Saint James, Apostle

First Reading: 2 Corinthians 4:7-15

Brothers and sisters: [7] We hold this treasure in earthen vessels, that the surpassing power may be of God and not from us. [8] We are afflicted in every way, but not constrained; perplexed, but not driven to despair; [9] persecuted, but not abandoned; struck down, but not destroyed; [10] always carrying about in the body the dying of Jesus, so that the life of Jesus may also be manifested in our body. [11] For we who live are constantly being given up to death for the sake of Jesus, so that the life of Jesus may be manifested in our mortal flesh.

[12] So death is at work in us, but life in you. [13] Since, then, we have the same spirit of faith, according to what is written, *I believed, therefore I spoke*, we too believe and therefore speak, [14] knowing that the one who raised the Lord Jesus will raise us also with Jesus and place us with you in his presence. [15] Everything indeed is for you, so that the grace bestowed in abundance on more and more people may cause the thanksgiving to overflow for the glory of God.

Responsorial Psalm: Psalms 126:1BC-2AB, 2CD-3, 4-5, 6

R. *(5) Those who sow in tears shall reap rejoicing.*

[1BC] When the LORD brought back the captives of
      Zion,
      we were like men dreaming.
[2AB] Then our mouth was filled with laughter,
      and our tongue with rejoicing.

R. *Those who sow in tears shall reap rejoicing.*

[2CD] Then they said among the nations,
      "The LORD has done great things for
        them."
[3] The LORD has done great things for us;
      we are glad indeed.

R. *Those who sow in tears shall reap rejoicing.*

[4] Restore our fortunes, O LORD,
      like the torrents in the southern desert.
[5] Those that sow in tears
      shall reap rejoicing.

R. *Those who sow in tears shall reap rejoicing.*

[6] Although they go forth weeping,
  carrying the seed to be sown,
They shall come back rejoicing,
  carrying their sheaves.
R. Those who sow in tears shall reap rejoicing.

Alleluia: cf. John 15:16
R. Alleluia, alleluia.
[16] I chose you from the world,
to go and bear fruit that will last, says the
  Lord.
R. Alleluia, alleluia.

Gospel: Matthew 20:20-28
[20] The mother of the sons of Zebedee approached Jesus with her sons and did him homage, wishing to ask him for something. [21] He said to her, "What do you wish?" She answered him, "Command that these two sons of mine sit, one at your right and the other at your left, in your Kingdom." [22] Jesus said in reply, "You do not know what you are asking. Can you drink the chalice that I am going to drink?" They said to him, "We can." [23] He replied, "My chalice you will indeed drink, but to sit at my right and at my left, this is not mine to give but is for those for whom it has been prepared by my Father." [24] When the ten heard this, they became indignant at the two brothers. [25] But Jesus summoned them and said, "You know that the rulers of the Gentiles lord it over them, and the great ones make their authority over them felt. [26] But it shall not be so among you. Rather, whoever wishes to be great among you shall be your servant; [27] whoever wishes to be first among you shall be your slave. [28] Just so, the Son of Man did not come to be served but to serve and to give his life as a ransom for many."

Friday July 26, 2024

Memorial of Saints Joachim and Anne
First Reading: Jeremiah 3:14-17
[14] Return, rebellious children, says the LORD,
  for I am your Master;
I will take you, one from a city, two from a
  clan,
  and bring you to Zion.
[15] I will appoint over you shepherds after my
  own heart,
  who will shepherd you wisely and
  prudently.
[16] When you multiply and become fruitful in
  the land,
  says the LORD,
They will in those days no longer say,

"The ark of the covenant of the LORD!"
They will no longer think of it, or remember
         it,
      or miss it, or make another.

[17] At that time they will call Jerusalem the
         LORD's throne;
      there all nations will be gathered
         together
      to honor the name of the LORD at
         Jerusalem,
      and they will walk no longer in their
         hardhearted wickedness.

Responsorial Psalm: Jeremiah 31:10, 11-12ABCD, 13

R. *(see 10d)* **The Lord will guard us as a shepherd
            guards his flock.**

[10] Hear the word of the LORD, O nations,
         proclaim it on distant isles, and say:
He who scattered Israel, now gathers them
            together,
      he guards them as a shepherd his flock.
R. **The Lord will guard us as a shepherd guards
            his flock.**

[11] The LORD shall ransom Jacob,
         he shall redeem him from the hand of his
            conqueror.
[12ABCD] Shouting, they shall mount the heights of
            Zion,
         they shall come streaming to the LORD's
            blessings:
The grain, the wine, and the oil,
         the sheep and the oxen.
R. **The Lord will guard us as a shepherd guards
            his flock.**

[13] Then the virgins shall make merry and
            dance,
         and young men and old as well.
I will turn their mourning into joy,
         I will console and gladden them after

their sorrows.
**R. The Lord will guard us as a shepherd guards
his flock.**

Alleluia: cf. Luke 8:15
R. Alleluia, alleluia.
[15] Blessed are they who have kept the word
with a generous heart
and yield a harvest through perseverance.
R. Alleluia, alleluia.

Gospel: Matthew 13:18-23
[18] Jesus said to his disciples: "Hear the parable of the sower. [19] The seed sown on the path is the one who hears the word of the Kingdom without understanding it, and the Evil One comes and steals away what was sown in his heart. [20] The seed sown on rocky ground is the one who hears the word and receives it at once with joy. [21] But he has no root and lasts only for a time. When some tribulation or persecution comes because of the word, he immediately falls away. [22] The seed sown among thorns is the one who hears the word, but then worldly anxiety and the lure of riches choke the word and it bears no fruit. [23] But the seed sown on rich soil is the one who hears the word and understands it, who indeed bears fruit and yields a hundred or sixty or thirtyfold."

Saturday July 27, 2024
Saturday of the Sixteenth Week in Ordinary Time
First Reading: Jeremiah 7:1-11
[1] The following message came to Jeremiah from the LORD: [2] Stand at the gate of the house of the LORD, and there proclaim this message: Hear the word of the LORD, all you of Judah who enter these gates to worship the LORD! [3] Thus says the LORD of hosts, the God of Israel: Reform your ways and your deeds, so that I may remain with you in this place. [4] Put not your trust in the deceitful words: "This is the temple of the LORD! The temple of the LORD! The temple of the LORD!" [5] Only if you thoroughly reform your ways and your deeds; if each of you deals justly with his neighbor; [6] if you no longer oppress the resident alien, the orphan, and the widow; if you no longer shed innocent blood in this place, or follow strange gods to your own harm, [7] will I remain with you in this place, in the land I gave your fathers long ago and forever.

[8] But here you are, putting your trust in deceitful words to your own loss! [9] Are you to steal and murder, commit adultery and perjury, burn incense to Baal, go after strange gods that you know not, [10] and yet come to stand before me in this house which bears my name, and say: "We are safe; we can commit all these abominations again"? [11] Has this house which bears my name become in your eyes a den of thieves? I too see what is being done, says the LORD.

Responsorial Psalm: Psalms 84:3, 4, 5-6A AND 8A, 11

R. [2] *How lovely is your dwelling place, Lord,*
            mighty God!

[3] My soul yearns and pines
            for the courts of the LORD.
My heart and my flesh
            cry out for the living God.
R. *How lovely is your dwelling place, Lord,*
            mighty God!

[4] Even the sparrow finds a home,
            and the swallow a nest
            in which she puts her young—
Your altars, O LORD of hosts,
            my king and my God!
R. *How lovely is your dwelling place, Lord,*
            mighty God!

[5] Blessed they who dwell in your house!
            continually they praise you.
[6A] Blessed the men whose strength you are!
[8A] They go from strength to strength.
R. *How lovely is your dwelling place, Lord,*
            mighty God!

[11] I had rather one day in your courts
            than a thousand elsewhere;
I had rather lie at the threshold of the house
            of my God
            than dwell in the tents of the wicked.
R. *How lovely is your dwelling place, Lord,*
            mighty God!

Alleluia: James 1:21BC

R. Alleluia, alleluia.
[21BC] Humbly welcome the word that has been
            planted in you
and is able to save your souls.
R. Alleluia, alleluia.

Gospel: Matthew 13:24-30

24 Jesus proposed a parable to the crowds. "The Kingdom of heaven may be likened to a man who sowed good seed in his field. 25 While everyone was asleep his enemy came and sowed weeds all through the wheat, and then went off. 26 When the crop grew and bore fruit, the weeds appeared as well. 27 The slaves of the householder came to him and said, 'Master, did you not sow good seed in your field? Where have the weeds come from?' 28 He answered, 'An enemy has done this.' His slaves said to him, 'Do you want us to go and pull them up?' 29 He replied, 'No, if you pull up the weeds you might uproot the wheat along with them. 30 Let them grow together until harvest; then at harvest time I will say to the harvesters, "First collect the weeds and tie them in bundles for burning; but gather the wheat into my barn."'"

Sunday July 28, 2024

Seventeenth Sunday in Ordinary Time Year B

First Reading: 2 Kings 4:42-44

42 A man came from Baal-shalishah bringing to Elisha, the man of God, twenty barley loaves made from the firstfruits, and fresh grain in the ear. Elisha said, "Give it to the people to eat." 43 But his servant objected, "How can I set this before a hundred people?" Elisha insisted, "Give it to the people to eat." "For thus says the LORD, 'They shall eat and there shall be some left over.'" 44 And when they had eaten, there was some left over, as the LORD had said.

Responsorial Psalm: Psalms 145:10-11, 15-16, 17-18

R. (cf. 16) **The hand of the Lord feeds us; he answers all our needs.**

10 Let all your works give you thanks, O LORD,
and let your faithful ones bless you.
11 Let them discourse of the glory of your
kingdom
and speak of your might.

R. **The hand of the Lord feeds us; he answers all our needs.**

15 The eyes of all look hopefully to you,
and you give them their food in due
season;
16 you open your hand
and satisfy the desire of every living
thing.

R. **The hand of the Lord feeds us; he answers all our needs.**

17 The LORD is just in all his ways
and holy in all his works.

¹⁶ The LORD is near to all who call upon him,
to all who call upon him in truth.
**R. The hand of the Lord feeds us; he answers all
our needs.**

Second Reading: Ephesians 4:1-6

Brothers and sisters: ¹ I, a prisoner for the Lord, urge you to live in a manner worthy of the call you have received, ² with all humility and gentleness, with patience, bearing with one another through love, ³ striving to preserve the unity of the spirit through the bond of peace: ⁴ one body and one Spirit, as you were also called to the one hope of your call; ⁵ one Lord, one faith, one baptism; ⁶ one God and Father of all, who is over all and through all and in all.

Alleluia: Luke 7:16

R. Alleluia, alleluia.
¹⁶ A great prophet has risen in our midst.
God has visited his people.
R. Alleluia, alleluia.

Gospel: John 6:1-15

¹ Jesus went across the Sea of Galilee. ² A large crowd followed him, because they saw the signs he was performing on the sick. ³ Jesus went up on the mountain, and there he sat down with his disciples. ⁴ The Jewish feast of Passover was near. ⁵ When Jesus raised his eyes and saw that a large crowd was coming to him, he said to Philip, "Where can we buy enough food for them to eat?" ⁶ He said this to test him, because he himself knew what he was going to do. ⁷ Philip answered him, "Two hundred days' wages worth of food would not be enough for each of them to have a little." ⁸ One of his disciples, Andrew, the brother of Simon Peter, said to him, ⁹ "There is a boy here who has five barley loaves and two fish; but what good are these for so many?" ¹⁰ Jesus said, "Have the people recline." Now there was a great deal of grass in that place. So the men reclined, about five thousand in number. ¹¹ Then Jesus took the loaves, gave thanks, and distributed them to those who were reclining, and also as much of the fish as they wanted. ¹² When they had had their fill, he said to his disciples, "Gather the fragments left over, so that nothing will be wasted." ¹³ So they collected them, and filled twelve wicker baskets with fragments from the five barley loaves that had been more than they could eat. ¹⁴ When the people saw the sign he had done, they said, "This is truly the Prophet, the one who is to come into the world." ¹⁵ Since Jesus knew that they were going to come and carry him off to make him king, he withdrew again to the mountain alone.

Monday July 29, 2024
Memorial of Saint Martha

First Reading: Jeremiah 13:1-11

¹ The LORD said to me: Go buy yourself a linen loincloth; wear it on your loins, but do not put it in water. ² I bought the loincloth, as the LORD commanded, and put it on. ³ A second

time the word of the LORD came to me thus: [4] Take the loincloth which you bought and are wearing, and go now to the Parath; there hide it in a cleft of the rock. [5] Obedient to the LORD's command, I went to the Parath and buried the loincloth. [6] After a long interval, the LORD said to me: Go now to the Parath and fetch the loincloth which I told you to hide there. [7] Again I went to the Parath, sought out and took the loincloth from the place where I had hid it. But it was rotted, good for nothing! [8] Then the message came to me from the LORD: [9] Thus says the LORD: So also I will allow the pride of Judah to rot, the great pride of Jerusalem. [10] This wicked people who refuse to obey my words, who walk in the stubbornness of their hearts, and follow strange gods to serve and adore them, shall be like this loincloth which is good for nothing. [11] For, as close as the loincloth clings to a man's loins, so had I made the whole house of Israel and the whole house of Judah cling to me, says the LORD; to be my people, my renown, my praise, my beauty. But they did not listen.

Responsorial Psalm: Deuteronomy 32:18-19, 20, 21

R. *(see 18a)* **You have forgotten God who gave you birth.**

[18] You were unmindful of the Rock that begot
> you,
> You forgot the God who gave you birth.
[19] When the LORD saw this, he was filled with
> loathing
> and anger toward his sons and daughters.

R. **You have forgotten God who gave you birth.**

[20] "I will hide my face from them," he said,
> "and see what will then become of them.
What a fickle race they are,
> sons with no loyalty in them!"

R. **You have forgotten God who gave you birth.**

[21] "Since they have provoked me with their 'no-
> god'
> and angered me with their vain idols,
I will provoke them with a 'no-people';
> with a foolish nation I will anger them."

R. **You have forgotten God who gave you birth.**

Alleluia: James 1:18

R. Alleluia, alleluia.

[18] The Father willed to give us birth by the
> word of truth
that we may be a kind of firstfruits of his
> creatures.

R. Alleluia, alleluia.

Gospel: John 11:19-27

[19] Many of the Jews had come to Martha and Mary to comfort them about their brother Lazarus, who had died. [20] When Martha heard that Jesus was coming, she went to meet him; but Mary sat at home. [21] Martha said to Jesus, "Lord, if you had been here, my brother would not have died. [22] But even now I know that whatever you ask of God, God will give you." [23] Jesus said to her, "Your brother will rise." [24] Martha said to him, "I know he will rise, in the resurrection on the last day." [25] Jesus told her, "I am the resurrection and the life; whoever believes in me, even if he dies, will live, [26] and everyone who lives and believes in me will never die. Do you believe this?" [27] She said to him, "Yes, Lord. I have come to believe that you are the Christ, the Son of God, the one who is coming into the world."

OR Luke 10:38-42

[38] Jesus entered a village where a woman whose name was Martha welcomed him. [39] She had a sister named Mary who sat beside the Lord at his feet listening to him speak. [40] Martha, burdened with much serving, came to him and said, "Lord, do you not care that my sister has left me by myself to do the serving? Tell her to help me." [41] The Lord said to her in reply, "Martha, Martha, you are anxious and worried about many things. [42] There is need of only one thing. Mary has chosen the better part and it will not be taken from her."

Tuesday July 30, 2024

Tuesday of the Seventeenth Week in Ordinary Time
First Reading: Jeremiah 14:17-22

[17] Let my eyes stream with tears
     day and night, without rest,
Over the great destruction which
       overwhelms
     the virgin daughter of my people,
     over her incurable wound.
[18] If I walk out into the field,
     look! those slain by the sword;
If I enter the city,
     look! those consumed by hunger.
Even the prophet and the priest
     forage in a land they know not.

[19] Have you cast Judah off completely?
     Is Zion loathsome to you?
Why have you struck us a blow
     that cannot be healed?

We wait for peace, to no avail;
> for a time of healing, but terror comes
>> instead.
[20] We recognize, O LORD, our wickedness,
> the guilt of our fathers;
> that we have sinned against you.
[21] For your name's sake spurn us not,
> disgrace not the throne of your glory;
> remember your covenant with us, and
>> break it not.
[22] Among the nations' idols is there any that
>> gives rain?
> Or can the mere heavens send showers?
Is it not you alone, O LORD,
> our God, to whom we look?
> You alone have done all these things.

Responsorial Psalm: Psalms 79:8, 9, 11 AND 13

R. [(9)] *For the glory of your name, O Lord, deliver us.*

[8] Remember not against us the iniquities of
> the past;
>> may your compassion quickly come to us,
>> for we are brought very low.

R. *For the glory of your name, O Lord, deliver us.*

[9] Help us, O God our savior,
> because of the glory of your name;
Deliver us and pardon our sins
> for your name's sake.

R. *For the glory of your name, O Lord, deliver us.*

[11] Let the prisoners' sighing come before you;
> with your great power free those doomed
>> to death.
[13] Then we, your people and the sheep of your
>> pasture,
> will give thanks to you forever;
> through all generations we will declare
>> your praise.

R. *For the glory of your name, O Lord, deliver us.*

Alleluia

R. Alleluia, alleluia.

The seed is the word of God, Christ is the
       sower;
all who come to him will live for ever.

R. Alleluia, alleluia.

Gospel: Matthew 13:36-43

[36] Jesus dismissed the crowds and went into the house. His disciples approached him and said, "Explain to us the parable of the weeds in the field." [37] He said in reply, "He who sows good seed is the Son of Man, [38] the field is the world, the good seed the children of the Kingdom. The weeds are the children of the Evil One, [39] and the enemy who sows them is the Devil. The harvest is the end of the age, and the harvesters are angels. [40] Just as weeds are collected and burned up with fire, so will it be at the end of the age. [41] The Son of Man will send his angels, and they will collect out of his Kingdom all who cause others to sin and all evildoers. [42] They will throw them into the fiery furnace, where there will be wailing and grinding of teeth. [43] Then the righteous will shine like the sun in the Kingdom of their Father. Whoever has ears ought to hear."

Wednesday July 31, 2024

Memorial of Saint Ignatius Loyola, Priest
First Reading: Jeremiah 15:10, 16-21

[10] Woe to me, mother, that you gave me birth!
       a man of strife and contention to all the
          land!
I neither borrow nor lend,
       yet all curse me.
[16] When I found your words, I devoured them;
       they became my joy and the happiness of
          my heart,
Because I bore your name,
       O LORD, God of hosts.
[17] I did not sit celebrating
       in the circle of merrymakers;
Under the weight of your hand I sat alone
       because you filled me with indignation.
[18] Why is my pain continuous,
       my wound incurable, refusing to be
          healed?
You have indeed become for me a
       treacherous brook,
       whose waters do not abide!

[19] Thus the LORD answered me:

If you repent, so that I restore you,
        in my presence you shall stand;
If you bring forth the precious without the
                vile,
        you shall be my mouthpiece.
Then it shall be they who turn to you,
        and you shall not turn to them;
[20] And I will make you toward this people
        a solid wall of brass.
Though they fight against you,
        they shall not prevail,
For I am with you,
        to deliver and rescue you, says the LORD.
[21] I will free you from the hand of the wicked,
        and rescue you from the grasp of the
                violent.

Responsorial Psalm: Psalms 59:2-3, 4, 10-11, 17, 18

R. [(17d)]*God is my refuge on the day of distress.*
[2] Rescue me from my enemies, O my God;
        from my adversaries defend me.
[3] Rescue me from evildoers;
        from bloodthirsty men save me.
R. God is my refuge on the day of distress.

[4] For behold, they lie in wait for my life;
        mighty men come together against me,
Not for any offense or sin of mine, O LORD.
R. God is my refuge on the day of distress.

[10] O my strength! for you I watch;
        for you, O God, are my stronghold,
[11] As for my God, may his mercy go before me;
        may he show me the fall of my foes.
R. God is my refuge on the day of distress.

[17] But I will sing of your strength
        and revel at dawn in your mercy;
You have been my stronghold,
        my refuge in the day of distress.

R. *God is my refuge on the day of distress.*

¹⁸ O my strength! your praise will I sing;
     for you, O God, are my stronghold,
     my merciful God!
R. *God is my refuge on the day of distress.*

Alleluia: John 15:15B
R. **Alleluia, alleluia.**
¹⁵ᴮ I call you my friends, says the Lord,
for I have made known to you all that the
     Father has told me.
R. **Alleluia, alleluia.**

Gospel: Matthew 13:44-46
Jesus said to his disciples: ⁴⁴ "The Kingdom of heaven is like a treasure buried in a field, which a person finds and hides again, and out of joy goes and sells all that he has and buys that field. ⁴⁵ Again, the Kingdom of heaven is like a merchant searching for fine pearls. ⁴⁶ When he finds a pearl of great price, he goes and sells all that he has and buys it."

AUGUST 2024
Thursday August 1, 2024

Memorial of Saint Alphonsus Mary de Liguori, Bishop & Doctor

First Reading: Jeremiah 18:1-6
¹ This word came to Jeremiah from the LORD: ² Rise up, be off to the potter's house; there I will give you my message. ³ I went down to the potter's house and there he was, working at the wheel. ⁴ Whenever the object of clay which he was making turned out badly in his hand, he tried again, making of the clay another object of whatever sort he pleased. ⁵ Then the word of the LORD came to me: ⁶ Can I not do to you, house of Israel, as this potter has done? says the LORD. Indeed, like clay in the hand of the potter, so are you in my hand, house of Israel.

Responsorial Psalm: Psalms 146:1B-2, 3-4, 5-6AB
R. *(5a)* **Blessed is he whose help is the God of Jacob.** or: *Alleluia.*
¹ᴮ Praise the LORD, O my soul;
     ² I will praise the LORD all my life;
     I will sing praise to my God while I live.
R. **Blessed is he whose help is the God of Jacob.** or: *Alleluia.*

³ Put not your trust in princes,
     in the sons of men, in whom there is no

salvation.
[4] When his spirit departs he returns to his
earth;
on that day his plans perish.
R. Blessed is he whose help is the God of Jacob. or: **Alleluia.**

[5] Blessed he whose help is the God of Jacob,
whose hope is in the LORD, his God.
[6A] Who made heaven and earth,
the sea and all that is in them.
R. Blessed is he whose help is the God of Jacob. or: **Alleluia.**

Alleluia: cf. Acts 16:14B
R. Alleluia, alleluia.
[14B] Open our heart, O Lord,
to listen to the words of your Son.
R. Alleluia, alleluia.

Gospel: Matthew 13:47-53
Jesus said to the disciples: [47] "The Kingdom of heaven is like a net thrown into the sea, which collects fish of every kind. [48] When it is full they haul it ashore and sit down to put what is good into buckets. What is bad they throw away. [49] Thus it will be at the end of the age. The angels will go out and separate the wicked from the righteous [50] and throw them into the fiery furnace, where there will be wailing and grinding of teeth."

[51] "Do you understand all these things?" They answered, "Yes." [52] And he replied, "Then every scribe who has been instructed in the Kingdom of heaven is like the head of a household who brings from his storeroom both the new and the old." [53] When Jesus finished these parables, he went away from there.

Friday August 2, 2024

Friday of Seventeenth Week in Ordinary Time
First Reading: Jeremiah 26:1-9
[1] In the beginning of the reign of Jehoiakim, son of Josiah, king of Judah, this message came from the LORD: [2] Thus says the LORD: Stand in the court of the house of the LORD and speak to the people of all the cities of Judah who come to worship in the house of the LORD; whatever I command you, tell them, and omit nothing. [3] Perhaps they will listen and turn back, each from his evil way, so that I may repent of the evil I have planned to inflict upon them for their evil deeds. [4] Say to them: Thus says the LORD: If you disobey me, not living according to the law I placed before you [5] and not listening to the words of my servants the prophets, whom I send you constantly though you do not obey them, [6] I will treat this house like Shiloh, and make this the city to which all the nations of the earth shall refer when cursing another.

[7] Now the priests, the prophets, and all the people heard Jeremiah speak these words in the house of the LORD. [8] When Jeremiah finished speaking all that the LORD bade him speak to all the people, the priests and prophets laid hold of him, crying, [9] "You must be put to death! Why do you prophesy in the name of the LORD: 'This house shall be like Shiloh,' and 'This city shall be desolate and deserted'?" And all the people gathered about Jeremiah in the house of the LORD.

Responsorial Psalm: Psalms 69:5, 8-10, 14

R. [14c] *Lord, in your great love, answer me.*

[5] Those outnumber the hairs of my head
    who hate me without cause.
Too many for my strength
    are they who wrongfully are my enemies.
    Must I restore what I did not steal?

R. *Lord, in your great love, answer me.*

[8] Since for your sake I bear insult,
    and shame covers my face.
[9] I have become an outcast to my brothers,
    a stranger to my mother's sons,
[10] Because zeal for your house consumes me,
    and the insults of those who blaspheme
        you fall upon me.

R. *Lord, in your great love, answer me.*

[14] But I pray to you, O LORD,
    for the time of your favor, O God!
In your great kindness answer me
    with your constant help.

R. *Lord, in your great love, answer me.*

Alleluia: 1 Peter 1:25

R. Alleluia, alleluia.

[25] The word of the Lord remains forever;
this is the word that has been proclaimed to
    you.

R. Alleluia, alleluia.

Gospel: Matthew 13:54-58

[54] Jesus came to his native place and taught the people in their synagogue. They were astonished and said, "Where did this man get such wisdom and mighty deeds? [55] Is he not the carpenter's son? Is not his mother named Mary and his brothers James, Joseph,

Simon, and Judas? [56] Are not his sisters all with us? Where did this man get all this?" [57] And they took offense at him. But Jesus said to them, "A prophet is not without honor except in his native place and in his own house." [58] And he did not work many mighty deeds there because of their lack of faith.

Saturday of the Seventeenth Week in Ordinary Time
First Reading: Jeremiah 26:11-16, 24

[11] The priests and prophets said to the princes and to all the people, "This man deserves death; he has prophesied against this city, as you have heard with your own ears." [12] Jeremiah gave this answer to the princes and all the people: "It was the LORD who sent me to prophesy against this house and city all that you have heard. [13] Now, therefore, reform your ways and your deeds; listen to the voice of the LORD your God, so that the LORD will repent of the evil with which he threatens you. [14] As for me, I am in your hands; do with me what you think good and right. [15] But mark well: if you put me to death, it is innocent blood you bring on yourselves, on this city and its citizens. For in truth it was the LORD who sent me to you, to speak all these things for you to hear."

[16] Thereupon the princes and all the people said to the priests and the prophets, "This man does not deserve death; it is in the name of the LORD, our God, that he speaks to us."

[24] So Ahikam, son of Shaphan, protected Jeremiah, so that he was not handed over to the people to be put to death.

Responsorial Psalm: Psalms 69:15-16, 30-31, 33-34

R. [14c] *Lord, in your great love, answer me.*

[15] Rescue me out of the mire; may I not sink!
     may I be rescued from my foes,
     and from the watery depths.
[16] Let not the flood-waters overwhelm me,
     nor the abyss swallow me up,
     nor the pit close its mouth over me.
R. *Lord, in your great love, answer me.*

[30] But I am afflicted and in pain;
     let your saving help, O God, protect me.
[31] I will praise the name of God in song,
     and I will glorify him with thanksgiving.
R. *Lord, in your great love, answer me.*

[33] "See, you lowly ones, and be glad;
     you who seek God, may your hearts
          revive!

³⁴ For the LORD hears the poor,
>   and his own who are in bonds he spurns
>   not."

R. Lord, in your great love, answer me.

Alleluia: Matthew 5:10

R. Alleluia, alleluia.

¹⁰ Blessed are they who are persecuted for the
>   sake of righteousness

for theirs is the Kingdom of heaven.

R. Alleluia, alleluia.

Gospel: Matthew 14:1-12

¹ Herod the tetrarch heard of the reputation of Jesus ² and said to his servants, "This man is John the Baptist. He has been raised from the dead; that is why mighty powers are at work in him."

³ Now Herod had arrested John, bound him, and put him in prison on account of Herodias, the wife of his brother Philip, ⁴ for John had said to him, "It is not lawful for you to have her." ⁵ Although he wanted to kill him, he feared the people, for they regarded him as a prophet. ⁶ But at a birthday celebration for Herod, the daughter of Herodias performed a dance before the guests and delighted Herod ⁷ so much that he swore to give her whatever she might ask for. ⁸ Prompted by her mother, she said, "Give me here on a platter the head of John the Baptist." ⁹ The king was distressed, but because of his oaths and the guests who were present, he ordered that it be given, ¹⁰ and he had John beheaded in the prison. ¹¹ His head was brought in on a platter and given to the girl, who took it to her mother. ¹² His disciples came and took away the corpse and buried him; and they went and told Jesus.

Sunday August 4, 2024

Eighteenth Sunday in Ordinary Time, Year B

First Reading: Exodus 16:2-4, 12-15

² The whole Israelite community grumbled against Moses and Aaron. ³ The Israelites said to them, "Would that we had died at the LORD's hand in the land of Egypt, as we sat by our fleshpots and ate our fill of bread! But you had to lead us into this desert to make the whole community die of famine!"

⁴ Then the LORD said to Moses, "I will now rain down bread from heaven for you. Each day the people are to go out and gather their daily portion; thus will I test them, to see whether they follow my instructions or not.

¹² "I have heard the grumbling of the Israelites. Tell them: In the evening twilight you shall eat flesh, and in the morning you shall have your fill of bread, so that you may know that I, the LORD, am your God."

[13] In the evening quail came up and covered the camp. In the morning a dew lay all about the camp, [14] and when the dew evaporated, there on the surface of the desert were fine flakes like hoarfrost on the ground. [15] On seeing it, the Israelites asked one another, "What is this?" for they did not know what it was. But Moses told them, "This is the bread that the LORD has given you to eat."

Responsorial Psalm: Psalms 78:3-4, 23-24, 25, 54

R. [(24b)] *The Lord gave them bread from heaven.*

[3] What we have heard and know,
     and what our fathers have declared to us,
[4] We will declare to the generation to come
     the glorious deeds of the LORD and his
        strength
     and the wonders that he wrought.

R. *The Lord gave them bread from heaven.*

[23] He commanded the skies above
     and opened the doors of heaven;
[24] he rained manna upon them for food
     and gave them heavenly bread.

R. *The Lord gave them bread from heaven.*

[25] Man ate the bread of angels,
     food he sent them in abundance.
[54] And he brought them to his holy land,
     to the mountains his right hand had won.

R. *The Lord gave them bread from heaven.*

Second Reading: Ephesians 4:17, 20-24

Brothers and sisters: [17] I declare and testify in the Lord that you must no longer live as the Gentiles do, in the futility of their minds; [20] that is not how you learned Christ, [21] assuming that you have heard of him and were taught in him, as truth is in Jesus, [22] that you should put away the old self of your former way of life, corrupted through deceitful desires, [23] and be renewed in the spirit of your minds, [24] and put on the new self, created in God's way in righteousness and holiness of truth.

Alleluia: Matthew 4:4B

R. Alleluia, alleluia.

[4B] One does not live on bread alone, but on
     every
word that comes forth from the mouth of
     God.

R. Alleluia, alleluia.

Gospel: John 6:24-35

24 When the crowd saw that neither Jesus nor his disciples were there, they themselves got into boats and came to Capernaum looking for Jesus. 25 And when they found him across the sea they said to him, "Rabbi, when did you get here?" 26 Jesus answered them and said, "Amen, amen, I say to you, you are looking for me not because you saw signs but because you ate the loaves and were filled. 27 Do not work for food that perishes but for the food that endures for eternal life, which the Son of Man will give you. For on him the Father, God, has set his seal." 28 So they said to him, "What can we do to accomplish the works of God?" 29 Jesus answered and said to them, "This is the work of God, that you believe in the one he sent." 30 So they said to him, "What sign can you do, that we may see and believe in you? What can you do? 31 Our ancestors ate manna in the desert, as it is written: *He gave them bread from heaven to eat.*" 32 So Jesus said to them, "Amen, amen, I say to you, it was not Moses who gave the bread from heaven; my Father gives you the true bread from heaven. 33 For the bread of God is that which comes down from heaven and gives life to the world."

34 So they said to him, "Sir, give us this bread always." 35 Jesus said to them, "I am the bread of life; whoever comes to me will never hunger, and whoever believes in me will never thirst."

Monday August 5, 2024

Monday of Eighteenth Week in Ordinary Time
First Reading: Jeremiah 28:1-17

1 In the beginning of the reign of Zedekiah, king of Judah, in the fifth month of the fourth year, the prophet Hananiah, son of Azzur, from Gibeon, said to me in the house of the LORD in the presence of the priests and all the people: 2 "Thus says the LORD of hosts, the God of Israel: 'I will break the yoke of the king of Babylon. 3 Within two years I will restore to this place all the vessels of the temple of the LORD which Nebuchadnezzar, king of Babylon, took away from this place to Babylon. 4 And I will bring back to this place Jeconiah, son of Jehoiakim, king of Judah, and all the exiles of Judah who went to Babylon,' says the LORD, 'for I will break the yoke of the king of Babylon.'"

5 The prophet Jeremiah answered the prophet Hananiah in the presence of the priests and all the people assembled in the house of the LORD, 6 and said: Amen! thus may the LORD do! May he fulfill the things you have prophesied by bringing the vessels of the house of the LORD and all the exiles back from Babylon to this place! 7 But now, listen to what I am about to state in your hearing and the hearing of all the people. 8 From of old, the prophets who were before you and me prophesied war, woe, and pestilence against many lands and mighty kingdoms. 9 But the prophet who prophesies peace is recognized as truly sent by the LORD only when his prophetic prediction is fulfilled.

10 Thereupon the prophet Hananiah took the yoke from the neck of the prophet Jeremiah and broke it, 11 and said in the presence of all the people: "Thus says the LORD: 'Even so, within two years I will break the yoke of Nebuchadnezzar, king of Babylon, from off the neck of all the nations.'" At that, the prophet Jeremiah went away.

[12] Some time after the prophet Hananiah had broken the yoke from off the neck of the prophet Jeremiah, The word of the Lord came to Jeremiah: [13] Go tell Hananiah this: Thus says the LORD: By breaking a wooden yoke, you forge an iron yoke! [14] For thus says the LORD of hosts, the God of Israel: A yoke of iron I will place on the necks of all these nations serving Nebuchadnezzar, king of Babylon, and they shall serve him; even the beasts of the field I give him.

[15] To the prophet Hananiah the prophet Jeremiah said: Hear this, Hananiah! The LORD has not sent you, and you have raised false confidence in this people. [16] For this, says the LORD, I will dispatch you from the face of the earth; this very year you shall die, because you have preached rebellion against the LORD. [17] That same year, in the seventh month, Hananiah the prophet died.

Responsorial Psalm: Psalms 119:29, 43, 79, 80, 95, 102

R. [(68b)] *Lord, teach me your statutes.*

[29] Remove from me the way of falsehood,
　　and favor me with your law.
R. *Lord, teach me your statutes.*

[43] Take not the word of truth from my mouth,
　　for in your ordinances is my hope.
R. *Lord, teach me your statutes.*

[79] Let those turn to me who fear you
　　and acknowledge your decrees.
R. *Lord, teach me your statutes.*

[80] Let my heart be perfect in your statutes,
　　that I be not put to shame.
R. *Lord, teach me your statutes.*

[95] Sinners wait to destroy me,
　　but I pay heed to your decrees.
R. *Lord, teach me your statutes.*

[102] From your ordinances I turn not away,
　　for you have instructed me.
R. *Lord, teach me your statutes.*

Alleluia: Matthew 4:4

R. Alleluia, alleluia.
[4] One does not live on bread alone,
But on every word that comes forth from the
　　mouth of God.

R. Alleluia, alleluia.

Gospel: Matthew 14:13-21

[13] When Jesus heard of the death of John the Baptist, he withdrew in a boat to a deserted place by himself. The crowds heard of this and followed him on foot from their towns. [14] When he disembarked and saw the vast crowd, his heart was moved with pity for them, and he cured their sick. [15] When it was evening, the disciples approached him and said, "This is a deserted place and it is already late; dismiss the crowds so that they can go to the villages and buy food for themselves." [16] He said to them, "There is no need for them to go away; give them some food yourselves." [17] But they said to him, "Five loaves and two fish are all we have here." [18] Then he said, "Bring them here to me," [19] and he ordered the crowds to sit down on the grass. Taking the five loaves and the two fish, and looking up to heaven, he said the blessing, broke the loaves, and gave them to the disciples, who in turn gave them to the crowds. [20] They all ate and were satisfied, and they picked up the fragments left over–twelve wicker baskets full. [21] Those who ate were about five thousand men, not counting women and children.

Feast of the Transfiguration of the Lord
First Reading: Daniel 7:9-10, 13-14

As I watched:

[9] Thrones were set up
    and the Ancient One took his throne.
His clothing was bright as snow,
    and the hair on his head as white as
        wool;
his throne was flames of fire,
    with wheels of burning fire.
[10] A surging stream of fire
    flowed out from where he sat;
thousands upon thousands were ministering
        to him,
    and myriads upon myriads attended him.

The court was convened and the books were opened.
[13] As the visions during the night continued, I saw:

One like a Son of man coming,
    on the clouds of heaven;

when he reached the Ancient One
 and was presented before him,
[14] the one like a Son of man received dominion,
 glory, and kingship;
 all peoples, nations, and languages serve
 him.
His dominion is an everlasting dominion
 that shall not be taken away,
 his kingship shall not be destroyed.

Responsorial Psalm: Psalms 97:1-2, 5-6, 9

R. *(1a and 9a)* **The Lord is king, the Most High over all
 the earth.**

[1] The LORD is king; let the earth rejoice;
 let the many islands be glad.
[2] Clouds and darkness are round about him,
 justice and judgment are the foundation
 of his throne.

**R. The Lord is king, the Most High over all the
 earth.**

[5] The mountains melt like wax before the
 LORD,
 before the Lord of all the earth.
[6] The heavens proclaim his justice,
 and all peoples see his glory.

**R. The Lord is king, the Most High over all the
 earth.**

[9] Because you, O LORD, are the Most High over
 all the earth,
 exalted far above all gods.

**R. The Lord is king, the Most High over all the
 earth.**

Second Reading: 2 Peter 1:16-19

Beloved: [16] We did not follow cleverly devised myths when we made known to you the power and coming of our Lord Jesus Christ, but we had been eyewitnesses of his majesty. [17] For he received honor and glory from God the Father when that unique declaration came to him from the majestic glory, "This is my Son, my beloved, with whom I am well pleased." [18] We ourselves heard this voice come from heaven while we were with him on the holy mountain. [19] Moreover, we possess the prophetic message that is altogether reliable. You will do well to be attentive to it, as to a lamp shining in a dark place, until day dawns and the morning star rises in your hearts.

Alleluia: Matthew 17:5C
R. Alleluia, alleluia.

[5C] This is my beloved Son, with whom I am well
  pleased;
listen to him.

R. Alleluia, alleluia.

Gospel: Mark 9:2-10

[2] Jesus took Peter, James, and his brother John, and led them up a high mountain apart by themselves. And he was transfigured before them, [3] and his clothes became dazzling white, such as no fuller on earth could bleach them. [4] Then Elijah appeared to them along with Moses, and they were conversing with Jesus. [5] Then Peter said to Jesus in reply, "Rabbi, it is good that we are here! Let us make three tents: one for you, one for Moses, and one for Elijah." [6] He hardly knew what to say, they were so terrified. [7] Then a cloud came, casting a shadow over them; from the cloud came a voice, "This is my beloved Son. Listen to him." [8] Suddenly, looking around, they no longer saw anyone but Jesus alone with them.

[9] As they were coming down from the mountain, he charged them not to relate what they had seen to anyone, except when the Son of Man had risen from the dead. [10] So they kept the matter to themselves, questioning what rising from the dead meant.

Wednesday August 7, 2024

Wednesday of the Eighteenth Week in Ordinary Time
First Reading: Jeremiah 31:1-7

[1] At that time, says the LORD, I will be the God of all the tribes of Israel, and they shall be my people.

  [2] Thus says the LORD:
The people that escaped the sword
  have found favor in the desert.
As Israel comes forward to be given his rest,
  [3] the LORD appears to him from afar:
With age-old love I have loved you;
  so I have kept my mercy toward you.
[4] Again I will restore you, and you shall be
  rebuilt,

  O virgin Israel;
Carrying your festive tambourines,
  you shall go forth dancing with the
    merrymakers.
[5] Again you shall plant vineyards

on the mountains of Samaria;
   those who plant them shall enjoy the
      fruits.
⁶ Yes, a day will come when the watchmen
   will call out on Mount Ephraim:
"Rise up, let us go to Zion,
   to the LORD, our God."

⁷ For thus says the LORD:
Shout with joy for Jacob,
   exult at the head of the nations;
   proclaim your praise and say:
The LORD has delivered his people,
   the remnant of Israel.

Responsorial Psalm: Jeremiah 31:10, 11-12AB, 13

R. *(see 10d)* **The Lord will guard us as a shepherd**
                     guards his flock.
¹⁰ Hear the word of the LORD, O nations,
   proclaim it on distant isles, and say:
He who scattered Israel, now gathers them
      together,
   he guards them as a shepherd his flock.
R. **The Lord will guard us as a shepherd guards**
          his flock.

¹¹ The LORD shall ransom Jacob,
   he shall redeem him from the hand of his
      conqueror.
¹²ᴬᴮ Shouting, they shall mount the heights of
      Zion,
they shall come streaming to the LORD's
      blessings.
R. **The Lord will guard us as a shepherd guards**
          his flock.

¹³ Then the virgins shall make merry and
      dance,
   and young men and old as well.
I will turn their mourning into joy.
   I will console and gladden them after
      their sorrows.

*R. The Lord will guard us as a shepherd guards
         his flock.*

Alleluia: Luke 7:16
R. Alleluia, alleluia.
[16] A great prophet has arisen in our midst
and God has visited his people.
R. Alleluia, alleluia.

Gospel: Matthew 15:21-28
[21] At that time Jesus withdrew to the region of Tyre and Sidon. [22] And behold, a Canaanite woman of that district came and called out, "Have pity on me, Lord, Son of David! My daughter is tormented by a demon." [23] But he did not say a word in answer to her. His disciples came and asked him, "Send her away, for she keeps calling out after us." [24] He said in reply, "I was sent only to the lost sheep of the house of Israel." [25] But the woman came and did him homage, saying, "Lord, help me." [26] He said in reply, "It is not right to take the food of the children and throw it to the dogs." [27] She said, "Please, Lord, for even the dogs eat the scraps that fall from the table of their masters." [28] Then Jesus said to her in reply, "O woman, great is your faith! Let it be done for you as you wish." And her daughter was healed from that hour.

Thursday August 8, 2024

Memorial of Saint Dominic, Priest
First Reading: Jeremiah 31:31-34
[31] The days are coming, says the LORD, when I will make a new covenant with the house of Israel and the house of Judah. [32] It will not be like the covenant I made with their fathers: the day I took them by the hand to lead them forth from the land of Egypt; for they broke my covenant, and I had to show myself their master, says the LORD. [33] But this is the covenant that I will make with the house of Israel after those days, says the LORD. I will place my law within them, and write it upon their hearts; I will be their God, and they shall be my people. [34] No longer will they have need to teach their friends and relatives how to know the LORD. All, from least to greatest, shall know me, says the LORD, for I will forgive their evildoing and remember their sin no more.

Responsorial Psalm: Psalms 51:12-13, 14-15, 18-19
R. (12a) Create a clean heart in me, O God.
[12] A clean heart create for me, O God,
        and a steadfast spirit renew within me.
[13] Cast me not out from your presence,
        and your Holy Spirit take not from me.
R. Create a clean heart in me, O God.

[14] Give me back the joy of your salvation,

and a willing spirit sustain in me.
¹⁵ I will teach transgressors your ways,
and sinners shall return to you.
R. *Create a clean heart in me, O God.*

¹⁸ For you are not pleased with sacrifices;
should I offer a burnt offering, you would
not accept it.
¹⁹ My sacrifice, O God, is a contrite spirit;
a heart contrite and humbled, O God, you
will not spurn.
R. *Create a clean heart in me, O God.*

Alleluia: Matthew 16:18
R. Alleluia, alleluia.
¹⁸ You are Peter, and upon this rock I will build
my Church,
and the gates of the netherworld shall not
prevail against it.
R. Alleluia, alleluia.

Gospel: Matthew 16:13-23
¹³ Jesus went into the region of Caesarea Philippi and he asked his disciples, "Who do people say that the Son of Man is?" ¹⁴ They replied, "Some say John the Baptist, others Elijah, still others Jeremiah or one of the prophets." ¹⁵ He said to them, "But who do you say that I am?" ¹⁶ Simon Peter said in reply, "You are the Christ, the Son of the living God." ¹⁷ Jesus said to him in reply, "Blessed are you, Simon son of Jonah. For flesh and blood has not revealed this to you, but my heavenly Father. ¹⁸ And so I say to you, you are Peter, and upon this rock I will build my Church, and the gates of the netherworld shall not prevail against it. ¹⁹ I will give you the keys to the Kingdom of heaven. Whatever you bind on earth shall be bound in heaven; and whatever you loose on earth shall be loosed in heaven." ²⁰ Then he strictly ordered his disciples to tell no one that he was the Christ.

²¹ From that time on, Jesus began to show his disciples that he must go to Jerusalem and suffer greatly from the elders, the chief priests, and the scribes, and be killed and on the third day be raised. ²² Then Peter took Jesus aside and began to rebuke him, "God forbid, Lord! No such thing shall ever happen to you." ²³ He turned and said to Peter, "Get behind me, Satan! You are an obstacle to me. You are thinking not as God does, but as human beings do."

Friday August 9, 2024
Friday of Eighteenth Week in Ordinary Time
First Reading: Nahum 2:1, 3; 3:1-3, 6-7
¹ See, upon the mountains there advances

the bearer of good news,
    announcing peace!
Celebrate your feasts, O Judah,
    fulfill your vows!
For nevermore shall you be invaded
    by the scoundrel; he is completely
      destroyed.
3 The LORD will restore the vine of Jacob,
    the pride of Israel,
Though ravagers have ravaged them
    and ruined the tendrils.

1 Woe to the bloody city, all lies,
    full of plunder, whose looting never
      stops!
2 The crack of the whip, the rumbling sounds
    of wheels;
    horses a-gallop, chariots bounding,
3 Cavalry charging, the flame of the sword, the
    flash of the spear,
    the many slain, the heaping corpses,
    the endless bodies to stumble upon!
6 I will cast filth upon you,
    disgrace you and put you to shame;
7 Till everyone who sees you runs from you,
    saying,
    "Nineveh is destroyed; who can pity her?
    Where can one find any to console her?"

Responsorial Psalm: Deuteronomy 32:35-36, 39, 41

R. (39c) *It is I who deal death and give life.*
35 Close at hand is the day of their disaster,
    and their doom is rushing upon them!
36 Surely, the LORD shall do justice for his
    people;
    on his servants he shall have pity.
R. *It is I who deal death and give life.*

39 "Learn then that I, I alone, am God,
    and there is no god besides me.
It is I who bring both death and life,
    I who inflict wounds and heal them."

R. It is I who deal death and give life.

[41] I will sharpen my flashing sword,
      and my hand shall lay hold of my quiver,
"With vengeance I will repay my foes
      and requite those who hate me."
R. It is I who deal death and give life.

Alleluia: Matthew 16:18
R. Alleluia, alleluia.
[18] Blessed are they who are persecuted for the
        sake of righteousness;
for theirs is the Kingdom of heaven.
R. Alleluia, alleluia.

Gospel: Matthew 16:24-28
[24] Jesus said to his disciples, "Whoever wishes to come after me must deny himself, take up his cross, and follow me. [25] For whoever wishes to save his life will lose it, but whoever loses his life for my sake will find it. [26] What profit would there be for one to gain the whole world and forfeit his life? Or what can one give in exchange for his life? [27] For the Son of Man will come with his angels in his Father's glory, and then he will repay each according to his conduct. [28] Amen, I say to you, there are some standing here who will not taste death until they see the Son of Man coming in his Kingdom."

Saturday August 10, 2024

Feast of Saint Lawrence, Deacon and Martyr
First Reading: 2 Corinthians 9:6-10
Brothers and sisters: [6] Whoever sows sparingly will also reap sparingly, and whoever sows bountifully will also reap bountifully. [7] Each must do as already determined, without sadness or compulsion, for God loves a cheerful giver. [8] Moreover, God is able to make every grace abundant for you, so that in all things, always having all you need, you may have an abundance for every good work. [9] As it is written:

He scatters abroad, he gives to the poor;
    his righteousness endures forever.

[10] The one who supplies seed to the sower and bread for food will supply and multiply your seed and increase the harvest of your righteousness.

Responsorial Psalm: Psalms 112:1-2, 5-6, 7-8, 9
R. [(5)]Blessed the man who is gracious and lends
        to those in need.

¹ Blessed the man who fears the LORD,
     who greatly delights in his commands.
² His posterity shall be mighty upon the earth;
     the upright generation shall be blessed.
R. Blessed the man who is gracious and lends to those in need.

⁵ Well for the man who is gracious and lends,
     who conducts his affairs with justice;
⁶ He shall never be moved;
     the just one shall be in everlasting
     remembrance.
R. Blessed the man who is gracious and lends to those in need.

⁷ An evil report he shall not fear;
     his heart is firm, trusting in the LORD.
⁸ His heart is steadfast; he shall not fear
     till he looks down upon his foes.
R. Blessed the man who is gracious and lends to those in need.

⁹ Lavishly he gives to the poor,
     his generosity shall endure forever;
     his horn shall be exalted in glory.
R. Blessed the man who is gracious and lends to those in need.

Alleluia: John 8:12BC
R. Alleluia, alleluia.
[12BC] Whoever follows me will not walk in
     darkness
but will have the light of life, says the Lord.
R. Alleluia, alleluia.

Gospel: John 12:24-26
Jesus said to his disciples: ²⁴ "Amen, amen, I say to you, unless a grain of wheat falls to the ground and dies, it remains just a grain of wheat; but if it dies, it produces much fruit. ²⁵ Whoever loves his life loses it, and whoever hates his life in this world will preserve it for eternal life. ²⁶ Whoever serves me must follow me, and where I am, there also will my servant be. The Father will honor whoever serves me."

Nineteenth Sunday in Ordinary Time, Year B

First Reading: 1 Kings 19:4-8

[4] Elijah went a day's journey into the desert, until he came to a broom tree and sat beneath it. He prayed for death saying: "This is enough, O LORD! Take my life, for I am no better than my fathers." [5] He lay down and fell asleep under the broom tree, but then an angel touched him and ordered him to get up and eat. [6] Elijah looked and there at his head was a hearth cake and a jug of water. After he ate and drank, he lay down again, [7] but the angel of the LORD came back a second time, touched him, and ordered, "Get up and eat, else the journey will be too long for you!" [8] He got up, ate, and drank; then strengthened by that food, he walked forty days and forty nights to the mountain of God, Horeb.

Responsorial Psalm: Psalms 34:2-3, 4-5, 6-7, 8-9

R. [9a] *Taste and see the goodness of the Lord.*

[2] I will bless the LORD at all times;
   his praise shall be ever in my mouth.
[3] Let my soul glory in the LORD;
   the lowly will hear me and be glad.
R. *Taste and see the goodness of the Lord.*

[4] Glorify the LORD with me,
   let us together extol his name.
[5] I sought the LORD, and he answered me
   and delivered me from all my fears.
R. *Taste and see the goodness of the Lord.*

[6] Look to him that you may be radiant with
      joy,
   and your faces may not blush with
      shame.
[7] When the afflicted man called out, the LORD
      heard,
   and from all his distress he saved him.
R. *Taste and see the goodness of the Lord.*

[8] The angel of the LORD encamps
   around those who fear him and delivers
      them.
[9] Taste and see how good the LORD is;
   blessed the man who takes refuge in him.
R. *Taste and see the goodness of the Lord.*

Second Reading: Ephesians 4:30-5:2

Brothers and sisters: [30] Do not grieve the Holy Spirit of God, with which you were sealed for the day of redemption. [31] All bitterness, fury, anger, shouting, and reviling must be removed from you, along with all malice. [32] And be kind to one another, compassionate, forgiving one another as God has forgiven you in Christ.

[1] So be imitators of God, as beloved children, [2] and live in love, as Christ loved us and handed himself over for us as a sacrificial offering to God for a fragrant aroma.

Alleluia: John 6:51

R. Alleluia, alleluia.

[51] I am the living bread that came down from
      heaven, says the Lord;
whoever eats this bread will live forever.

R. Alleluia, alleluia.

Gospel: John 6:41-51

[41] The Jews murmured about Jesus because he said, "I am the bread that came down from heaven," [42] and they said, "Is this not Jesus, the son of Joseph? Do we not know his father and mother? Then how can he say, 'I have come down from heaven'?" [43] Jesus answered and said to them, "Stop murmuring among yourselves. [44] No one can come to me unless the Father who sent me draw him, and I will raise him on the last day. [45] It is written in the prophets:

They shall all be taught by God.

Everyone who listens to my Father and learns from him comes to me. [46] Not that anyone has seen the Father except the one who is from God; he has seen the Father. [47] Amen, amen, I say to you, whoever believes has eternal life. [48] I am the bread of life. [49] Your ancestors ate the manna in the desert, but they died; [50] this is the bread that comes down from heaven so that one may eat it and not die. [51] I am the living bread that came down from heaven; whoever eats this bread will live forever; and the bread that I will give is my flesh for the life of the world."

Monday August 12, 2024

Monday of Nineteenth Week in Ordinary Time
First Reading: Ezekiel 1:2-5, 24-28C

[2] On the fifth day of the fourth month of the fifth year, that is, of King Jehoiachin's exile, [3] The word of the LORD came to the priest Ezekiel, the son of Buzi, in the land of the Chaldeans by the river Chebar— There the hand of the LORD came upon me.

[4] As I looked, a stormwind came from the North, a huge cloud with flashing fire enveloped in brightness, from the midst of which (the midst of the fire) something

gleamed like electrum. ⁵ Within it were figures resembling four living creatures that looked like this: their form was human.

²⁴ Then I heard the sound of their wings, like the roaring of mighty waters, like the voice of the Almighty. When they moved, the sound of the tumult was like the din of an army. ²⁵ And when they stood still, they lowered their wings.

²⁶ Above the firmament over their heads something like a throne could be seen, looking like sapphire. ²⁷ Upon it was seated, up above, one who had the appearance of a man. Upward from what resembled his waist I saw what gleamed like electrum; downward from what resembled his waist I saw what looked like fire; he was surrounded with splendor. ²⁸ᶜ Like the bow which appears in the clouds on a rainy day was the splendor that surrounded him. Such was the vision of the likeness of the glory of the LORD.

Responsorial Psalm: Psalms 148:1-2, 11-12, 13, 14
R. Heaven and earth are filled with your glory. or: *Alleluia.*
¹ Praise the LORD from the heavens;
    praise him in the heights;
² Praise him, all you his angels;
    praise him, all you his hosts.
R. Heaven and earth are filled with your glory. or: *Alleluia.*

¹¹ Let the kings of the earth and all peoples,
    the princes and all the judges of the
        earth,
¹² Young men too, and maidens,
    old men and boys,
R. Heaven and earth are filled with your glory. or: *Alleluia.*

¹³ Praise the name of the LORD,
    for his name alone is exalted;
His majesty is above earth and heaven.
R. Heaven and earth are filled with your glory. or: *Alleluia.*

¹⁴ And he has lifted up the horn of his people.
Be this his praise from all his faithful ones,
    from the children of Israel, the people
        close to him.
    Alleluia.
R. Heaven and earth are filled with your glory. or: *Alleluia.*

Alleluia: cf. 2 Thessalonians 2:14
R. Alleluia, alleluia.
¹⁴ God has called you through the Gospel

to possess the glory of our Lord Jesus Christ.
R. Alleluia, alleluia.

Gospel: Matthew 17:22-27

[22] As Jesus and his disciples were gathering in Galilee, Jesus said to them, "The Son of Man is to be handed over to men, [23] and they will kill him, and he will be raised on the third day." And they were overwhelmed with grief.

[24] When they came to Capernaum, the collectors of the temple tax approached Peter and said, "Does not your teacher pay the temple tax?" [25] "Yes," he said. When he came into the house, before he had time to speak, Jesus asked him, "What is your opinion, Simon? From whom do the kings of the earth take tolls or census tax? From their subjects or from foreigners?" [26] When he said, "From foreigners," Jesus said to him, "Then the subjects are exempt. [27] But that we may not offend them, go to the sea, drop in a hook, and take the first fish that comes up. Open its mouth and you will find a coin worth twice the temple tax. Give that to them for me and for you."

Tuesday August 13, 2024

Tuesday of the Nineteenth Week in Ordinary Time
First Reading: Ezekiel 2:8-3:4

The Lord GOD said to me: [8] As for you, son of man, obey me when I speak to you: be not rebellious like this house of rebellion, but open your mouth and eat what I shall give you.

[9] It was then I saw a hand stretched out to me, in which was a written scroll which he unrolled before me. It was covered with writing front and back, and written on it was: Lamentation and wailing and woe!

[1] He said to me: Son of man, eat what is before you; eat this scroll, then go, speak to the house of Israel. [2] So I opened my mouth and he gave me the scroll to eat. [3] Son of man, he then said to me, feed your belly and fill your stomach with this scroll I am giving you. I ate it, and it was as sweet as honey in my mouth. [4] He said: Son of man, go now to the house of Israel, and speak my words to them.

Responsorial Psalm: Psalms 119:14, 24, 72, 103, 111, 131

R. [103a] *How sweet to my taste is your promise!*
[14] In the way of your decrees I rejoice,
    as much as in all riches.
R. How sweet to my taste is your promise!
[24] Yes, your decrees are my delight;
    they are my counselors.
R. How sweet to my taste is your promise!

[72] The law of your mouth is to me more
      precious
    than thousands of gold and silver pieces.

R. How sweet to my taste is your promise!

¹⁰³How sweet to my palate are your promises,
    sweeter than honey to my mouth!
R. How sweet to my taste is your promise!

¹¹¹Your decrees are my inheritance forever;
    the joy of my heart they are.
R. How sweet to my taste is your promise!

¹³¹I gasp with open mouth,
    in my yearning for your commands.
R. How sweet to my taste is your promise!

Alleluia: Matthew 11:29AB
R. Alleluia, alleluia.
²⁹ᴬᴮ Take my yoke upon you and learn from me,
for I am meek and humble of heart.
R. Alleluia, alleluia.

Gospel: Matthew 18:1-5, 10, 12-14
¹ The disciples approached Jesus and said, "Who is the greatest in the Kingdom of heaven?" ² He called a child over, placed it in their midst, ³ and said, "Amen, I say to you, unless you turn and become like children, you will not enter the Kingdom of heaven. ⁴ Whoever becomes humble like this child is the greatest in the Kingdom of heaven. ⁵ And whoever receives one child such as this in my name receives me.

    ¹⁰ "See that you do not despise one of these little ones, for I say to you that their angels in heaven always look upon the face of my heavenly Father. ¹² What is your opinion? If a man has a hundred sheep and one of them goes astray, will he not leave the ninety-nine in the hills and go in search of the stray? ¹³ And if he finds it, amen, I say to you, he rejoices more over it than over the ninety-nine that did not stray. ¹⁴ In just the same way, it is not the will of your heavenly Father that one of these little ones be lost."

Wednesday August 14, 2024

Memorial of Saint Maximilian Kolbe – Priest & Martyr
First Reading: Ezekiel 9:1-7; 10:18-22
¹ The LORD cried loud for me to hear: Come, you scourges of the city! ² With that I saw six men coming from the direction of the upper gate which faces the north, each with a destroying weapon in his hand. In their midst was a man dressed in linen, with a writer's case at his waist. They entered and stood beside the bronze altar. ³ Then he called to the man dressed in linen with the writer's case at his waist, ⁴ saying to him: Pass through the city, through Jerusalem, and mark a "Thau" on the foreheads of those who moan and

groan over all the abominations that are practiced within it. [5] To the others I heard the LORD say: Pass through the city after him and strike! Do not look on them with pity nor show any mercy! [6] Old men, youths and maidens, women and children-wipe them out! But do not touch any marked with the "Thau"; begin at my sanctuary. So they began with the men, the elders, who were in front of the temple. [7] Defile the temple, he said to them, and fill the courts with the slain; then go out and strike in the city.

[18] Then the glory of the LORD left the threshold of the temple and rested upon the cherubim. [19] These lifted their wings, and I saw them rise from the earth, the wheels rising along with them. They stood at the entrance of the eastern gate of the LORD's house, and the glory of the God of Israel was up above them. Then the cherubim lifted their wings, and the wheels went along with them, while up above them was the glory of the God of Israel.

Responsorial Psalm: Psalms 113:1-2, 3-4, 5-6

R. [(4b)] *The glory of the Lord is higher than the skies.* Or: *Alleluia.*

[1] Praise, you servants of the LORD,
    praise the name of the LORD.
[2] Blessed be the name of the LORD
    both now and forever.

R. *The glory of the Lord is higher than the skies.* or: *Alleluia.*

[3] From the rising to the setting of the sun
    is the name of the LORD to be praised.
[4] High above all nations is the LORD;
    above the heavens is his glory.

R. *The glory of the Lord is higher than the skies.* or: *Alleluia.*

[5] Who is like the LORD, our God, who is
        enthroned on high,
    [6] and looks upon the heavens and the earth
        below?

R. *The glory of the Lord is higher than the skies.* or: *Alleluia.*

Alleluia: 2 Corinthians 5:19

R. Alleluia, alleluia.

[19] God was reconciling the world to himself in
        Christ,
and entrusting to us the message of
        reconciliation.

R. Alleluia, alleluia.

Gospel: Matthew 18:15-20

Jesus said to his disciples: [15] "If your brother sins against you, go and tell him his fault between you and him alone. If he listens to you, you have won over your brother. [16] If he does not listen, take one or two others along with you, so that every fact may be established on the testimony of two or three witnesses. [17] If he refuses to listen to them, tell the Church. If he refuses to listen even to the Church, then treat him as you would a Gentile or a tax collector. [18] Amen, I say to you, whatever you bind on earth shall be bound in heaven, and whatever you loose on earth shall be loosed in heaven. [19] Again, amen, I say to you, if two of you agree on earth about anything for which they are to pray, it shall be granted to them by my heavenly Father. [20] For where two or three are gathered together in my name, there am I in the midst of them."

Wednesday August 14, 2024

Assumption of the Blessed Virgin Mary – Vigil Mass
First Reading: 1 Chronicles 15:3-4, 15-16; 16:1-2

[3] David assembled all Israel in Jerusalem to bring the ark of the LORD to the place which he had prepared for it. [4] David also called together the sons of Aaron and the Levites.

[15] The Levites bore the ark of God on their shoulders with poles, as Moses had ordained according to the word of the LORD.

[16] David commanded the chiefs of the Levites to appoint their kinsmen as chanters, to play on musical instruments, harps, lyres, and cymbals, to make a loud sound of rejoicing.

[1] They brought in the ark of God and set it within the tent which David had pitched for it. Then they offered up burnt offerings and peace offerings to God. [2] When David had finished offering up the burnt offerings and peace offerings, he blessed the people in the name of the LORD.

Responsorial Psalm: Psalms 132:6-7, 9-10, 13-14

R. [8] *Lord, go up to the place of your rest, you*
    and the ark of your holiness.

[6] Behold, we heard of it in Ephrathah;
    we found it in the fields of Jaar.
[7] Let us enter his dwelling,
    let us worship at his footstool.
R. *Lord, go up to the place of your rest, you and*
    the ark of your holiness.

[9] May your priests be clothed with justice;
    let your faithful ones shout merrily for
        joy.
[10] For the sake of David your servant,
    reject not the plea of your anointed.
R. *Lord, go up to the place of your rest, you and*
    the ark of your holiness.

[13] For the LORD has chosen Zion;
    he prefers her for his dwelling.

431

[14] "Zion is my resting place forever;
     in her will I dwell, for I prefer her."
**R. Lord, go up to the place of your rest, you and
              the ark of your holiness.**

Second Reading: 1 Corinthians 15:54B-57

Brothers and sisters: [54B] When that which is mortal clothes itself with immortality, then the word that is written shall come about:

[55] *Death is swallowed up in victory.*
Where, O death, is your victory?
Where, O death, is your sting?

[56] The sting of death is sin, and the power of sin is the law. [57] But thanks be to God who gives us the victory through our Lord Jesus Christ.

Alleluia: Luke 11:28

R. Alleluia, alleluia.
[28] Blessed are they who hear the word of God
and observe it.
R. Alleluia, alleluia.

Gospel: Luke 11:27-28

[27] While Jesus was speaking, a woman from the crowd called out and said to him, "Blessed is the womb that carried you and the breasts at which you nursed." [28] He replied, "Rather, blessed are those who hear the word of God and observe it."

Thursday August 15, 2024

Solemnity of the Assumption of the Blessed Virgin Mary (Mass during the Day)

First Reading: Revelation 11:19A; 12:1-6A, 10AB

[19A] God's temple in heaven was opened, and the ark of his covenant could be seen in the temple.

[1] A great sign appeared in the sky, a woman clothed with the sun, with the moon under her feet, and on her head a crown of twelve stars. [2] She was with child and wailed aloud in pain as she labored to give birth. [3] Then another sign appeared in the sky; it was a huge red dragon, with seven heads and ten horns, and on its heads were seven diadems. [4] Its tail swept away a third of the stars in the sky and hurled them down to the earth. Then the dragon stood before the woman about to give birth, to devour her child when she gave birth. [5] She gave birth to a son, a male child, destined to rule all the nations with an iron rod. Her child was caught up to God and his throne. [6A] The woman herself fled into the desert where she had a place prepared by God.

[10AB] Then I heard a loud voice in heaven say: "Now have salvation and power come, and the Kingdom of our God and the authority of his Anointed One."

Responsorial Psalm: Psalms 45:10, 11, 12, 16

R. [(10bc)] *The queen stands at your right hand,*
arrayed in gold.

[10] The queen takes her place at your right hand
in gold of Ophir.
R. *The queen stands at your right hand, arrayed*
in gold.

[11] Hear, O daughter, and see; turn your ear,
forget your people and your father's
house.
R. *The queen stands at your right hand, arrayed*
in gold.

[12] So shall the king desire your beauty;
for he is your lord.
R. *The queen stands at your right hand, arrayed*
in gold.

[16] They are borne in with gladness and joy;
they enter the palace of the king.
R. *The queen stands at your right hand, arrayed*
in gold.

Second Reading: 1 Corinthians 15:20-27

Brothers and sisters: [20] Christ has been raised from the dead, the firstfruits of those who have fallen asleep. [21] For since death came through man, the resurrection of the dead came also through man. [22] For just as in Adam all die, so too in Christ shall all be brought to life, [23] but each one in proper order: Christ the firstfruits; then, at his coming, those who belong to Christ; [24] then comes the end, when he hands over the Kingdom to his God and Father, when he has destroyed every sovereignty and every authority and power. [25] For he must reign until he has put all his enemies under his feet. [26] The last enemy to be destroyed is death, [27] for "he subjected everything under his feet."

Alleluia

R. Alleluia, alleluia.
Mary is taken up to heaven;
a chorus of angels exults.
R. Alleluia, alleluia.

Gospel: Luke 1:39-56

[39] Mary set out and traveled to the hill country in haste to a town of Judah, [40] where she entered the house of Zechariah and greeted Elizabeth. [41] When Elizabeth heard Mary's greeting, the infant leaped in her womb, and Elizabeth, filled with the Holy Spirit, [42] cried out in a loud voice and said, "Blessed are you among women, and blessed is the fruit of your womb. [43] And how does this happen to me that the mother of my Lord should come to me? [44] For at the moment the sound of your greeting reached my ears, the infant in my womb leaped for joy. [45] Blessed are you who believed that what was spoken to you by the Lord would be fulfilled."

[46] And Mary said:

"My soul proclaims the greatness of the
     Lord;
  [47] my spirit rejoices in God my Savior
  [48] for he has looked upon his lowly servant.
From this day all generations will call me
     blessed:
  [49] the Almighty has done great things for
     me
  and holy is his Name.
[50] He has mercy on those who fear him
     in every generation.
[51] He has shown the strength of his arm,
     and has scattered the proud in their
          conceit.
[52] He has cast down the mighty from their
          thrones,
     and has lifted up the lowly.
[53] He has filled the hungry with good things,
     and the rich he has sent away empty.
[54] He has come to the help of his servant Israel
     for he has remembered his promise of mercy,
  [55] the promise he made to our fathers,
     to Abraham and his children forever."

[56] Mary remained with her about three months and then returned to her home.

Friday August 16, 2024

Friday of Nineteenth Week in Ordinary Time
First Reading: Ezekiel 16:1-15, 60, 63

[1] The word of the LORD came to me: [2] Son of man, make known to Jerusalem her abominations. [3] Thus says the Lord GOD to Jerusalem: By origin and birth you are of the

land of Canaan; your father was an Amorite and your mother a Hittite. [4] As for your birth, the day you were born your navel cord was not cut; you were neither washed with water nor anointed, nor were you rubbed with salt, nor swathed in swaddling clothes. [5] No one looked on you with pity or compassion to do any of these things for you. Rather, you were thrown out on the ground as something loathsome, the day you were born.

[6] Then I passed by and saw you weltering in your blood. I said to you: Live in your blood [7] and grow like a plant in the field. You grew and developed, you came to the age of puberty; your breasts were formed, your hair had grown, but you were still stark naked. [8] Again I passed by you and saw that you were now old enough for love. So I spread the corner of my cloak over you to cover your nakedness; I swore an oath to you and entered into a covenant with you; you became mine, says the Lord GOD. [9] Then I bathed you with water, washed away your blood, and anointed you with oil. [10] I clothed you with an embroidered gown, put sandals of fine leather on your feet; I gave you a fine linen sash and silk robes to wear. [11] I adorned you with jewelry: I put bracelets on your arms, a necklace about your neck, [12] a ring in your nose, pendants in your ears, and a glorious diadem upon your head. [13] Thus you were adorned with gold and silver; your garments were of fine linen, silk, and embroidered cloth. Fine flour, honey, and oil were your food. You were exceedingly beautiful, with the dignity of a queen. [14] You were renowned among the nations for your beauty, perfect as it was, because of my splendor which I had bestowed on you, says the Lord GOD.

[15] But you were captivated by your own beauty, you used your renown to make yourself a harlot, and you lavished your harlotry on every passer-by, whose own you became.

[60] Yet I will remember the covenant I made with you when you were a girl, and I will set up an everlasting covenant with you, [63] that you may remember and be covered with confusion, and that you may be utterly silenced for shame when I pardon you for all you have done, says the Lord GOD.

Or: Ezekiel 16:59-63

[59] Thus says the LORD: I will deal with you according to what you have done, you who despised your oath, breaking a covenant. [60] Yet I will remember the covenant I made with you when you were a girl, and I will set up an everlasting covenant with you. [61] Then you shall remember your conduct and be ashamed when I take your sisters, those older and younger than you, and give them to you as daughters, even though I am not bound by my covenant with you. [62] For I will re-establish my covenant with you, that you may know that I am the LORD, [63] that you may remember and be covered with confusion, and that you may be utterly silenced for shame when I pardon you for all you have done, says the Lord GOD.

Responsorial Psalm: Isaiah 12:2-3, 4BCD, 5-6

R. [1c] *You have turned from your anger.*

[2] God indeed is my savior;
    I am confident and unafraid.
My strength and my courage is the LORD,
    and he has been my savior.

³ With joy you will draw water
    at the fountain of salvation.
R. You have turned from your anger.

⁴ᴮᶜᴰ Give thanks to the LORD, acclaim his name;
    among the nations make known his
        deeds,
    proclaim how exalted is his name.
R. You have turned from your anger.

⁵ Sing praise to the LORD for his glorious
        achievement;
    let this be known throughout all the
        earth.
⁶ Shout with exultation, O city of Zion,
    for great in your midst
    is the Holy One of Israel!
R. You have turned from your anger.

Alleluia: cf. 1 Thessalonians 2:13
R. Alleluia, alleluia.
¹³ Receive the word of God, not as the word of
        men,
but, as it truly is, the word of God.
R. Alleluia, alleluia.

Gospel: Matthew 19:3-12
³ Some Pharisees approached Jesus, and tested him, saying, "Is it lawful for a man to divorce his wife for any cause whatever?" ⁴ He said in reply, "Have you not read that from the beginning the Creator *made them male and female* ⁵ and said, *For this reason a man shall leave his father and mother and be joined to his wife, and the two shall become one flesh*? ⁶ So they are no longer two, but one flesh. Therefore, what God has joined together, man must not separate." ⁷ They said to him, "Then why did Moses command that the man give the woman a bill of divorce and dismiss her?" ⁸ He said to them, "Because of the hardness of your hearts Moses allowed you to divorce your wives, but from the beginning it was not so. ⁹ I say to you, whoever divorces his wife (unless the marriage is unlawful) and marries another commits adultery." ¹⁰ His disciples said to him, "If that is the case of a man with his wife, it is better not to marry." ¹¹ He answered, "Not all can accept this word, but only those to whom that is granted. ¹² Some are incapable of marriage because they were born so; some, because they were made so by others; some, because they have renounced marriage for the sake of the Kingdom of heaven. Whoever can accept this ought to accept it."

Saturday of the Nineteenth Week in Ordinary Time
First Reading: Ezekiel 18:1-10, 13B, 30-32

[1] The word of the LORD came to me: Son of man, [2] what is the meaning of this proverb that you recite in the land of Israel:

"Fathers have eaten green grapes,
    thus their children's teeth are on edge"?

[3] As I live, says the Lord GOD: I swear that there shall no longer be anyone among you who will repeat this proverb in Israel. [4] For all lives are mine; the life of the father is like the life of the son, both are mine; only the one who sins shall die.
    [5] If a man is virtuous—if he does what is right and just, if he does not eat on the mountains, nor raise his eyes to the idols of the house of Israel; if he does not defile his neighbor's wife, nor have relations with a woman in her menstrual period; [7] if he oppresses no one, gives back the pledge received for a debt, commits no robbery; if he gives food to the hungry and clothes the naked; [8] if he does not lend at interest nor exact usury; if he holds off from evildoing, judges fairly between a man and his opponent; [9] if he lives by my statutes and is careful to observe my ordinances, that man is virtuous—he shall surely live, says the Lord GOD.
    [10] But if he begets a son who is a thief, a murderer, or lends at interest and exacts usury— this son certainly shall not live. [13B] Because he practiced all these abominations, he shall surely die; his death shall be his own fault.
    [30] Therefore I will judge you, house of Israel, each one according to his ways, says the Lord GOD. Turn and be converted from all your crimes, that they may be no cause of guilt for you. [31] Cast away from you all the crimes you have committed, and make for yourselves a new heart and a new spirit. Why should you die, O house of Israel? [32] For I have no pleasure in the death of anyone who dies, says the Lord GOD. Return and live!

Responsorial Psalm: Psalms 51:12-13, 14-15, 18-19
R. [12a] ***Create a clean heart in me, O God.***
[12] A clean heart create for me, O God;
        and a steadfast spirit renew within me.
[13] Cast me not out from your presence,
        and your Holy Spirit take not from me.
R. ***Create a clean heart in me, O God.***

[14] Give me back the joy of your salvation,
        and a willing spirit sustain in me.
[15] I will teach transgressors your ways,
        and sinners shall return to you.

R. Create a clean heart in me, O God.

¹⁸ For you are not pleased with sacrifices;
> should I offer a burnt offering, you would
>> not accept it.

¹⁹ My sacrifice, O God, is a contrite spirit;
> a heart contrite and humbled, O God, you
>> will not spurn.

R. Create a clean heart in me, O God.

Alleluia: cf. Matthew 11:25
R. Alleluia, alleluia.

²⁵ Blessed are you, Father, Lord of heaven and
> earth;

you have revealed to little ones the
> mysteries of the Kingdom.

R. Alleluia, alleluia.

Gospel: Matthew 19:13-15

¹³ Children were brought to Jesus that he might lay his hands on them and pray. The disciples rebuked them, ¹⁴ but Jesus said, "Let the children come to me, and do not prevent them; for the Kingdom of heaven belongs to such as these." ¹⁵ After he placed his hands on them, he went away.

Sunday August 18, 2024

Twentieth Saturday in Ordinary Time, Year B
First Reading: Proverbs 9:1-6

¹ Wisdom has built her house,
> she has set up her seven columns;

² she has dressed her meat, mixed her wine,
> yes, she has spread her table.

³ She has sent out her maidens; she calls
> from the heights out over the city:

⁴ "Let whoever is simple turn in here";
> to the one who lacks understanding, she
>> says,

⁵ "Come, eat of my food,
> and drink of the wine I have mixed!

⁶ Forsake foolishness that you may live;
> advance in the way of understanding."

Responsorial Psalm: Psalms 34:2-3, 4-5, 6-7

R. *(9a)* *Taste and see the goodness of the Lord.*

[2] I will bless the LORD at all times;
> his praise shall be ever in my mouth.
[3] Let my soul glory in the LORD;
> the lowly will hear me and be glad.

R. *Taste and see the goodness of the Lord.*

[4] Glorify the LORD with me,
> let us together extol his name.
[5] I sought the LORD, and he answered me
> and delivered me from all my fears.

R. *Taste and see the goodness of the Lord.*

[6] Look to him that you may be radiant with
> joy,
> and your faces may not blush with
> shame.
[7] When the poor one called out, the LORD
> heard,
> and from all his distress he saved him.

R. *Taste and see the goodness of the Lord.*

Second Reading: Ephesians 5:15-20

Brothers and sisters: [15] Watch carefully how you live, not as foolish persons but as wise, [16] making the most of the opportunity, because the days are evil. [17] Therefore, do not continue in ignorance, but try to understand what is the will of the Lord. [18] And do not get drunk on wine, in which lies debauchery, but be filled with the Spirit, [19] addressing one another in psalms and hymns and spiritual songs, singing and playing to the Lord in your hearts, [20] giving thanks always and for everything in the name of our Lord Jesus Christ to God the Father.

Alleluia: John 6:56

R. Alleluia, alleluia.
[56] Whoever eats my flesh and drinks my blood remains in me and I in him, says the Lord.
R. Alleluia, alleluia.

Gospel: John 6:51-58

Jesus said to the crowds: [51] "I am the living bread that came down from heaven; whoever eats this bread will live forever; and the bread that I will give is my flesh for the life of the world."

[52] The Jews quarreled among themselves, saying, "How can this man give us his flesh to eat?" [53] Jesus said to them, "Amen, amen, I say to you, unless you eat the flesh of

the Son of Man and drink his blood, you do not have life within you. [54] Whoever eats my flesh and drinks my blood has eternal life, and I will raise him on the last day. [55] For my flesh is true food, and my blood is true drink. [56] Whoever eats my flesh and drinks my blood remains in me and I in him. [57] Just as the living Father sent me and I have life because of the Father, so also the one who feeds on me will have life because of me. [58] This is the bread that came down from heaven. Unlike your ancestors who ate and still died, whoever eats this bread will live forever."

Monday of Twentieth Week in Ordinary Time
First Reading: Ezekiel 24:15-23

[15] The word of the LORD came to me: [16] Son of man, by a sudden blow I am taking away from you the delight of your eyes, but do not mourn or weep or shed any tears. [17] Groan in silence, make no lament for the dead, bind on your turban, put your sandals on your feet, do not cover your beard, and do not eat the customary bread. [18] That evening my wife died, and the next morning I did as I had been commanded. [19] Then the people asked me, "Will you not tell us what all these things that you are doing mean for us?" I therefore spoke to the people that morning, saying to them: [20] Thus the word of the LORD came to me: [21] Say to the house of Israel: Thus says the Lord GOD: I will now desecrate my sanctuary, the stronghold of your pride, the delight of your eyes, the desire of your soul. The sons and daughters you left behind shall fall by the sword. [24] Ezekiel shall be a sign for you: all that he did you shall do when it happens. Thus you shall know that I am the LORD. [22] You shall do as I have done, not covering your beards nor eating the customary bread. [23] Your turbans shall remain on your heads, your sandals on your feet. You shall not mourn or weep, but you shall rot away because of your sins and groan one to another.

Responsorial Psalm: Deuteronomy 32:18-19, 20, 21

R. (see 18a) *You have forgotten God who gave you birth.*

[18] You were unmindful of the Rock that begot
        you.
    You forgot the God who gave you birth.
[19] When the LORD saw this, he was filled with
        loathing
    and anger toward his sons and daughters.
R. *You have forgotten God who gave you birth.*

[20] "I will hide my face from them," he said,
    "and see what will then become of them.
What a fickle race they are,
    sons with no loyalty in them!"
R. *You have forgotten God who gave you birth.*

²¹ "Since they have provoked me with their 'no-god'
   and angered me with their vain idols,
I will provoke them with a 'no-people';
   with a foolish nation I will anger them."
R. You have forgotten God who gave you birth.

Alleluia: Matthew 5:3
R. Alleluia, alleluia.
³ Blessed are the poor in spirit;
for theirs is the Kingdom of heaven.
R. Alleluia, alleluia.

Gospel: Matthew 19:16-22
¹⁶ A young man approached Jesus and said, "Teacher, what good must I do to gain eternal life?" ¹⁷ He answered him, "Why do you ask me about the good? There is only One who is good. If you wish to enter into life, keep the commandments." ¹⁸He asked him, "Which ones?" And Jesus replied, *"You shall not kill; you shall not commit adultery; you shall not steal; you shall not bear false witness;* ¹⁹ *honor your father and your mother*; and *you shall love your neighbor as yourself."* ²⁰ The young man said to him, "All of these I have observed. What do I still lack?" ²¹Jesus said to him, "If you wish to be perfect, go, sell what you have and give to the poor, and you will have treasure in heaven. Then come, follow me." ²² When the young man heard this statement, he went away sad, for he had many possessions.

Tuesday August 20, 2024

Memorial of Saint Bernard, Abbot & Doctor
First Reading: Ezekiel 28:1-10
¹ The word of the LORD came to me: ² Son of man, say to the prince of Tyre: Thus says the Lord GOD:

Because you are haughty of heart,
   you say, "A god am I!
I occupy a godly throne
   in the heart of the sea!"—
And yet you are a man, and not a god,
   however you may think yourself like a
      god.
³ Oh yes, you are wiser than Daniel,
   there is no secret that is beyond you.
⁴ By your wisdom and your intelligence
   you have made riches for yourself;
You have put gold and silver

into your treasuries.
⁵ By your great wisdom applied to your
        trading
        you have heaped up your riches;
        your heart has grown haughty from your
        riches—
        ⁶ therefore thus says the Lord GOD:
Because you have thought yourself
        to have the mind of a god,
⁷ Therefore I will bring against you
        foreigners, the most barbarous of
        nations.
They shall draw their swords
        against your beauteous wisdom,
        they shall run them through your
        splendid apparel.
⁸ They shall thrust you down to the pit, there
        to die
        a bloodied corpse, in the heart of the sea.
⁹ Will you then say, "I am a god!"
        when you face your murderers?
No, you are man, not a god,
        handed over to those who will slay you.
¹⁰ You shall die the death of the uncircumcised
        at the hands of foreigners,
        for I have spoken, says the Lord GOD.

Responsorial Psalm: Deuteronomy 32:26-27AB, 27CD-28, 30, 35CD-36AB

R. *(39c)* **It is I who deal death and give life.**
²⁶ "I would have said, 'I will make an end of
        them
        and blot out their name from men's
        memories,'
²⁷ᴬᴮ Had I not feared the insolence of their
        enemies,
        feared that these foes would mistakenly
        boast."
R. **It is I who deal death and give life.**

²⁷ᶜᴰ "'Our own hand won the victory;
        the LORD had nothing to do with it.'"
²⁸ For they are a people devoid of reason,

having no understanding.
R. It is I who deal death and give life.

[30] "How could one man rout a thousand,
        or two men put ten thousand to flight,
Unless it was because their Rock sold them
        and the LORD delivered them up?"
R. It is I who deal death and give life.

[35CD] Close at hand is the day of their disaster,
        and their doom is rushing upon them!
[36AB] Surely, the LORD shall do justice for his people;
        on his servants he shall have pity.
R. It is I who deal death and give life.

Alleluia: 2 Corinthians 8:9
R. Alleluia, alleluia.
[9] Jesus Christ became poor although he was
        rich
so that by his poverty you might become
        rich.
R. Alleluia, alleluia.

Gospel: Matthew 19:23-30
[23] Jesus said to his disciples: "Amen, I say to you, it will be hard for one who is rich to enter the Kingdom of heaven. [24] Again I say to you, it is easier for a camel to pass through the eye of a needle than for one who is rich to enter the Kingdom of God." [25] When the disciples heard this, they were greatly astonished and said, "Who then can be saved?" [26] Jesus looked at them and said, "For men this is impossible, but for God all things are possible." [27] Then Peter said to him in reply, "We have given up everything and followed you. What will there be for us?" [28] Jesus said to them, "Amen, I say to you that you who have followed me, in the new age, when the Son of Man is seated on his throne of glory, will yourselves sit on twelve thrones, judging the twelve tribes of Israel. [29] And everyone who has given up houses or brothers or sisters or father or mother or children or lands for the sake of my name will receive a hundred times more, and will inherit eternal life. [30] But many who are first will be last, and the last will be first."

Wednesday August 21, 2024

Wednesday of the Twentieth Week in Ordinary Time
First Reading: Ezekiel 34:1-11
[1] The word of the Lord came to me: [2] Son of man, prophesy against the shepherds of Israel, in these words prophesy to them to the shepherds: Thus says the Lord GOD: Woe

to the shepherds of Israel who have been pasturing themselves! Should not shepherds, rather, pasture sheep? [3] You have fed off their milk, worn their wool, and slaughtered the fatlings, but the sheep you have not pastured. [4] You did not strengthen the weak nor heal the sick nor bind up the injured. You did not bring back the strayed nor seek the lost, but you lorded it over them harshly and brutally. [5] So they were scattered for the lack of a shepherd, and became food for all the wild beasts. My sheep were scattered [6] and wandered over all the mountains and high hills; my sheep were scattered over the whole earth, with no one to look after them or to search for them.

[7] Therefore, shepherds, hear the word of the LORD: [8] As I live, says the Lord GOD, because my sheep have been given over to pillage, and because my sheep have become food for every wild beast, for lack of a shepherd; because my shepherds did not look after my sheep, but pastured themselves and did not pasture my sheep; [9] because of this, shepherds, hear the word of the LORD:

[10] Thus says the Lord GOD: I swear I am coming against these shepherds. I will claim my sheep from them and put a stop to their shepherding my sheep so that they may no longer pasture themselves. I will save my sheep, that they may no longer be food for their mouths.

[11] For thus says the Lord GOD: I myself will look after and tend my sheep.

Responsorial Psalm: Psalms 23:1-3A, 3B-4, 5, 6

R. [(1)]*The Lord is my shepherd; there is nothing I*
shall want.

[1] The LORD is my shepherd; I shall not want.
[2] In verdant pastures he gives me repose;
Beside restful waters he leads me;
[3A] he refreshes my soul.

R. *The Lord is my shepherd; there is nothing I*
shall want.

[3B] He guides me in right paths
for his name's sake.
[4] Even though I walk in the dark valley
I fear no evil; for you are at my side
With your rod and your staff
that give me courage.

R. *The Lord is my shepherd; there is nothing I*
shall want.

[5] You spread the table before me
in the sight of my foes;
You anoint my head with oil;
my cup overflows.

*R. The Lord is my shepherd; there is nothing I
shall want.*

⁶ Only goodness and kindness will follow me
 all the days of my life;
And I shall dwell in the house of the LORD
 for years to come.
*R. The Lord is my shepherd; there is nothing I
shall want.*

Alleluia: Hebrews 4:12

R. Alleluia, alleluia.
¹² The word of God is living and effective,
able to discern the reflections and thoughts
 of the heart.
R. Alleluia, alleluia.

Gospel: Matthew 20:1-16

Jesus told his disciples this parable: ¹ "The Kingdom of heaven is like a landowner who went out at dawn to hire laborers for his vineyard. ² After agreeing with them for the usual daily wage, he sent them into his vineyard. ³ Going out about nine o'clock, he saw others standing idle in the marketplace, ⁴ and he said to them, 'You too go into my vineyard, and I will give you what is just.' ⁵ So they went off. And he went out again around noon, and around three o'clock, and did likewise. ⁶ Going out about five o'clock, he found others standing around, and said to them, 'Why do you stand here idle all day?' ⁷ They answered, 'Because no one has hired us.' He said to them, 'You too go into my vineyard.' ⁸ When it was evening the owner of the vineyard said to his foreman, 'Summon the laborers and give them their pay, beginning with the last and ending with the first.' ⁹ When those who had started about five o'clock came, each received the usual daily wage. ¹⁰ So when the first came, they thought that they would receive more, but each of them also got the usual wage. ¹¹ And on receiving it they grumbled against the landowner, ¹² saying, 'These last ones worked only one hour, and you have made them equal to us, who bore the day's burden and the heat.' ¹³ He said to one of them in reply, 'My friend, I am not cheating you. Did you not agree with me for the usual daily wage? ¹⁴ Take what is yours and go. What if I wish to give this last one the same as you? ¹⁵ Or am I not free to do as I wish with my own money? Are you envious because I am generous?' ¹⁶ Thus, the last will be first, and the first will be last."

Thursday August 22, 2024

Thursday of the Twentieth Week in Ordinary Time
First Reading: Ezekiel 36:23-28

Thus says the LORD: ²³ I will prove the holiness of my great name, profaned among the nations, in whose midst you have profaned it. Thus the nations shall know that I am the LORD, says the Lord GOD, when in their sight I prove my holiness through you.

[24] For I will take you away from among the nations, gather you from all the foreign lands, and bring you back to your own land. [25] I will sprinkle clean water upon you to cleanse you from all your impurities, and from all your idols I will cleanse you. [26] I will give you a new heart and place a new spirit within you, taking from your bodies your stony hearts and giving you natural hearts. [27] I will put my spirit within you and make you live by my statutes, careful to observe my decrees. [28] You shall live in the land I gave your ancestors; you shall be my people, and I will be your God.

Responsorial Psalm: Psalms 51:12-13,14-15,18-19

R. *(Ezekiel 36:25)* **I will pour clean water on you and wash away all your sins.**

[12] A clean heart create for me, O God,
    and a steadfast spirit renew within me.
[13] Cast me not out from your presence,
    and your Holy Spirit take not from me.

R. I will pour clean water on you and wash away all your sins.

[14] Give me back the joy of your salvation,
    and a willing spirit sustain in me.
[15] I will teach transgressors your ways,
    and sinners shall return to you.

R. I will pour clean water on you and wash away all your sins.

[18] For you are not pleased with sacrifices;
    should I offer a burnt offering, you would
    not accept it.
[19] My sacrifice, O God, is a contrite spirit;
    a heart contrite and humbled, O God, you
    will not spurn.

R. I will pour clean water on you and wash away all your sins.

Alleluia: Psalms 95:8

R. Alleluia, alleluia.
[8] If today you hear his voice,
harden not your hearts.
R. Alleluia, alleluia.

Gospel: Matthew 22:1-14

[1] Jesus again in reply spoke to the chief priests and the elders of the people in parables saying, [2] "The Kingdom of heaven may be likened to a king who gave a wedding feast for

his son. ³ He dispatched his servants to summon the invited guests to the feast, but they refused to come. ⁴ A second time he sent other servants, saying, 'Tell those invited: "Behold, I have prepared my banquet, my calves and fattened cattle are killed, and everything is ready; come to the feast."' ⁵ Some ignored the invitation and went away, one to his farm, another to his business. ⁶ The rest laid hold of his servants, mistreated them, and killed them. ⁷ The king was enraged and sent his troops, destroyed those murderers, and burned their city. ⁸ Then the king said to his servants, 'The feast is ready, but those who were invited were not worthy to come. ⁹ Go out, therefore, into the main roads and invite to the feast whomever you find.' ¹⁰ The servants went out into the streets and gathered all they found, bad and good alike, and the hall was filled with guests. ¹¹ But when the king came in to meet the guests he saw a man there not dressed in a wedding garment. ¹² He said to him, 'My friend, how is it that you came in here without a wedding garment?' But he was reduced to silence. ¹³ Then the king said to his attendants, 'Bind his hands and feet, and cast him into the darkness outside, where there will be wailing and grinding of teeth.' ¹⁴ Many are invited, but few are chosen."

Friday August 23, 2024

Friday of Twentieth Week in Ordinary Time
First Reading: Ezekiel 37:1-14

¹ The hand of the LORD came upon me, and led me out in the Spirit of the LORD and set me in the center of the plain, which was now filled with bones. ² He made me walk among the bones in every direction so that I saw how many they were on the surface of the plain. How dry they were! ³ He asked me: Son of man, can these bones come to life? I answered, "Lord GOD, you alone know that." ⁴ Then he said to me: Prophesy over these bones, and say to them: Dry bones, hear the word of the LORD! ⁵ Thus says the Lord GOD to these bones: See! I will bring spirit into you, that you may come to life. ⁶ I will put sinews upon you, make flesh grow over you, cover you with skin, and put spirit in you so that you may come to life and know that I am the LORD. ⁷ I prophesied as I had been told, and even as I was prophesying I heard a noise; it was a rattling as the bones came together, bone joining bone. ⁸ I saw the sinews and the flesh come upon them, and the skin cover them, but there was no spirit in them. ⁹ Then the LORD said to me: Prophesy to the spirit, prophesy, son of man, and say to the spirit: Thus says the Lord GOD: From the four winds come, O spirit, and breathe into these slain that they may come to life. ¹⁰ I prophesied as he told me, and the spirit came into them; they came alive and stood upright, a vast army. ¹¹ Then he said to me: Son of man, these bones are the whole house of Israel. They have been saying, "Our bones are dried up, our hope is lost, and we are cut off." ¹² Therefore, prophesy and say to them: Thus says the Lord GOD: O my people, I will open your graves and have you rise from them, and bring you back to the land of Israel. ¹³ Then you shall know that I am the LORD, when I open your graves and have you rise from them, O my people! ¹⁴ I will put my spirit in you that you may live, and I will settle you upon your land; thus you shall know that I am the LORD. I have promised, and I will do it, says the LORD.

Responsorial Psalm: Psalms 107:2-3, 4-5, 6-7, 8-9

R. [1]*Give thanks to the Lord; his love is*
everlasting.

2 Let the redeemed of the LORD say,
those whom he has redeemed from the
hand of the foe
3 And gathered from the lands,
from the east and the west, from the
north and the south.

R. *Give thanks to the Lord; his love is*
everlasting.

4 They went astray in the desert wilderness;
the way to an inhabited city they did not
find.
5 Hungry and thirsty,
their life was wasting away within them.

R. *Give thanks to the Lord; his love is*
everlasting.

6 They cried to the LORD in their distress;
from their straits he rescued them.
7 And he led them by a direct way
to reach an inhabited city.

R. *Give thanks to the Lord; his love is*
everlasting.

8 Let them give thanks to the LORD for his
mercy
and his wondrous deeds to the children
of men,
9 Because he satisfied the longing soul
and filled the hungry soul with good
things.

R. *Give thanks to the Lord; his love is*
everlasting.

Alleluia: Psalms 25:4B, 5A

R. Alleluia, alleluia.
4B Teach me your paths, my God,
5A guide me in your truth.
R. Alleluia, alleluia.

Gospel: Matthew 22:34-40

³⁴ When the Pharisees heard that Jesus had silenced the Sadducees, they gathered together, ³⁵ and one of them, a scholar of the law, tested him by asking, ³⁶ "Teacher, which commandment in the law is the greatest?" ³⁷ He said to him, "You shall love the Lord, your God, with all your heart, with all your soul, and with all your mind. ³⁸ This is the greatest and the first commandment. ³⁹ The second is like it: You shall love your neighbor as yourself. ⁴⁰ The whole law and the prophets depend on these two commandments."

Saturday August 24, 2024

Feast of Saint Bartholomew, Apostle
First Reading: Revelation 21:9B-14

⁹ᴮ The angel spoke to me, saying, "Come here. I will show you the bride, the wife of the Lamb." ¹⁰ He took me in spirit to a great, high mountain and showed me the holy city Jerusalem coming down out of heaven from God. ¹¹ It gleamed with the splendor of God. Its radiance was like that of a precious stone, like jasper, clear as crystal. ¹² It had a massive, high wall, with twelve gates where twelve angels were stationed and on which names were inscribed, the names of the twelve tribes of the children of Israel. ¹³ There were three gates facing east, three north, three south, and three west. ¹⁴ The wall of the city had twelve courses of stones as its foundation, on which were inscribed the twelve names of the twelve Apostles of the Lamb.

Responsorial Psalm: Psalms 145:10-11, 12-13, 17-18

R. ⁽¹²⁾ *Your friends make known, O Lord, the*
   glorious splendor of your Kingdom.

¹⁰ Let all your works give you thanks, O LORD,
   and let your faithful ones bless you.
¹¹ Let them discourse of the glory of your
   Kingdom
   and speak of your might.
R. *Your friends make known, O Lord, the*
   glorious splendor of your Kingdom.

¹² Making known to men your might
   and the glorious splendor of your
   Kingdom.
¹³ Your Kingdom is a Kingdom for all ages,
   and your dominion endures through all
   generations.
R. *Your friends make known, O Lord, the*
   glorious splendor of your Kingdom.

¹⁷ The LORD is just in all his ways
   and holy in all his works.

¹⁸ The LORD is near to all who call upon him,
    to all who call upon him in truth.
R. Your friends make known, O Lord, the
      glorious splendor of your Kingdom.

Alleluia: John 1:49B
R. Alleluia, alleluia.
^{49B} Rabbi, you are the Son of God;
you are the King of Israel.
R. Alleluia, alleluia.

Gospel: John 1:45-51
⁴⁵ Philip found Nathanael and told him, "We have found the one about whom Moses wrote in the law, and also the prophets, Jesus son of Joseph, from Nazareth." ⁴⁶ But Nathanael said to him, "Can anything good come from Nazareth?" Philip said to him, "Come and see." ⁴⁷ Jesus saw Nathanael coming toward him and said of him, "Here is a true child of Israel. There is no duplicity in him." ⁴⁸ Nathanael said to him, "How do you know me?" Jesus answered and said to him, "Before Philip called you, I saw you under the fig tree." ⁴⁹ Nathanael answered him, "Rabbi, you are the Son of God; you are the King of Israel." ⁵⁰ Jesus answered and said to him, "Do you believe because I told you that I saw you under the fig tree? You will see greater things than this." ⁵¹ And he said to him, "Amen, amen, I say to you, you will see heaven opened and the angels of God ascending and descending on the Son of Man."

Sunday August 25, 2024

Twenty-first Sunday in Ordinary Time Year B
First Reading: Joshua 24:1-2A, 15-17, 18B
¹ Joshua gathered together all the tribes of Israel at Shechem, summoning their elders, their leaders, their judges, and their officers. When they stood in ranks before God, ^{2A} Joshua addressed all the people: ¹⁵ "If it does not please you to serve the LORD, decide today whom you will serve, the gods your fathers served beyond the River or the gods of the Amorites in whose country you are now dwelling. As for me and my household, we will serve the LORD."

¹⁶ But the people answered, "Far be it from us to forsake the LORD for the service of other gods. ¹⁷ For it was the LORD, our God, who brought us and our fathers up out of the land of Egypt, out of a state of slavery. He performed those great miracles before our very eyes and protected us along our entire journey and among the peoples through whom we passed. ^{18B} Therefore we also will serve the LORD, for he is our God."

Responsorial Psalm: Psalms 34:2-3, 16-17, 18-19, 20-21
R. ^(9a) Taste and see the goodness of the Lord.
² I will bless the LORD at all times;

450

his praise shall be ever in my mouth.
³ Let my soul glory in the LORD;
    the lowly will hear me and be glad.
R. Taste and see the goodness of the Lord.
¹⁶ The LORD has eyes for the just,
    and ears for their cry.
¹⁷ The LORD confronts the evildoers,
    to destroy remembrance of them from
        the earth.
R. Taste and see the goodness of the Lord.

¹⁸ When the just cry out, the LORD hears them,
    and from all their distress he rescues
        them.
¹⁹ The LORD is close to the brokenhearted;
    and those who are crushed in spirit he
        saves.
R. Taste and see the goodness of the Lord.

²⁰ Many are the troubles of the just one,
    but out of them all the LORD delivers him;
²¹ he watches over all his bones;
    not one of them shall be broken.
R. Taste and see the goodness of the Lord.

Second Reading: Ephesians 5:21-32

Brothers and sisters: ²¹ Be subordinate to one another out of reverence for Christ. ²² Wives should be subordinate to their husbands as to the Lord. ²³ For the husband is head of his wife just as Christ is head of the church, he himself the savior of the body. ²⁴ As the church is subordinate to Christ, so wives should be subordinate to their husbands in everything. ²⁵ Husbands, love your wives, even as Christ loved the church and handed himself over for her ²⁶ to sanctify her, cleansing her by the bath of water with the word, ²⁷ that he might present to himself the church in splendor, without spot or wrinkle or any such thing, that she might be holy and without blemish. ²⁸ So also husbands should love their wives as their own bodies. He who loves his wife loves himself. ²⁹ For no one hates his own flesh but rather nourishes and cherishes it, even as Christ does the church, ³⁰ because we are members of his body. ³¹ *For this reason a man shall leave his father and his mother and be joined to his wife, and the two shall become one flesh.* ³² This is a great mystery, but I speak in reference to Christ and the church.

OR Ephesians 5:2A, 25-32

Brothers and sisters: ²ᴬ Live in love, as Christ loved us. ²⁵ Husbands, love your wives, even as Christ loved the church and handed himself over for her ²⁶ to sanctify her, cleansing her by the bath of water with the word, [27] that he might present to himself the church in splendor, without spot or wrinkle or any such thing, that she might be holy and without blemish. [28] So also husbands should love their wives as their own bodies. He who loves his wife loves himself. [29] For no one hates his own flesh but rather nourishes and cherishes it, even as Christ does the church, [30] because we are members of his body. [31] *For this reason a man shall leave his father and his mother and be joined to his wife, and the two shall become one flesh.* [32] This is a great mystery, but I speak in reference to Christ and the church.

Alleluia: John 6:63C, 68C

R. Alleluia, alleluia.

[63C] Your words, Lord, are Spirit and life;

[68C] you have the words of everlasting life.

R. Alleluia, alleluia.

Gospel: John 6:60-69

[60] Many of Jesus' disciples who were listening said, "This saying is hard; who can accept it?" [61] Since Jesus knew that his disciples were murmuring about this, he said to them, "Does this shock you? [62] What if you were to see the Son of Man ascending to where he was before? [63] It is the spirit that gives life, while the flesh is of no avail. The words I have spoken to you are Spirit and life. [64] But there are some of you who do not believe." Jesus knew from the beginning the ones who would not believe and the one who would betray him. [65] And he said, "For this reason I have told you that no one can come to me unless it is granted him by my Father."

[66] As a result of this, many of his disciples returned to their former way of life and no longer accompanied him. [67] Jesus then said to the Twelve, "Do you also want to leave?" [68] Simon Peter answered him, "Master, to whom shall we go? You have the words of eternal life. [69] We have come to believe and are convinced that you are the Holy One of God."

Monday August 26, 2024

Monday of the Twenty-first Week in Ordinary Time
First Reading: 2 Thessalonians 1:1-5, 11-12

[1] Paul, Silvanus, and Timothy to the Church of the Thessalonians in God our Father and the Lord Jesus Christ: [2] grace to you and peace from God our Father and the Lord Jesus Christ.

[3] We ought to thank God always for you, brothers and sisters, as is fitting, because your faith flourishes ever more, and the love of every one of you for one another grows ever greater. [4] Accordingly, we ourselves boast of you in the churches of God regarding your endurance and faith in all your persecutions and the afflictions you endure.

[5] This is evidence of the just judgment of God, so that you may be considered worthy of the Kingdom of God for which you are suffering.

[11] We always pray for you, that our God may make you worthy of his calling and powerfully bring to fulfillment every good purpose and every effort of faith, [12] that the

name of our Lord Jesus may be glorified in you, and you in him, in accord with the grace of our God and Lord Jesus Christ.

Responsorial Psalm: Psalms 96:1-2A, 2B-3, 4-5

R. [3]*Proclaim God's marvelous deeds to all the nations.*

[1] Sing to the LORD a new song;
    sing to the LORD, all you lands.
[2A] Sing to the LORD; bless his name.

R. *Proclaim God's marvelous deeds to all the nations.*

[2B] Announce his salvation, day after day.
[3] Tell his glory among the nations;
    among all peoples, his wondrous deeds.

R. *Proclaim God's marvelous deeds to all the nations.*

[4] For great is the LORD and highly to be praised;
    awesome is he, beyond all gods.
[5] For all the gods of the nations are things of nought,
    but the LORD made the heavens.

R. *Proclaim God's marvelous deeds to all the nations.*

Alleluia: John 10:27

R. Alleluia, alleluia.
[27] My sheep hear my voice, says the Lord;
I know them, and they follow me.
R. Alleluia, alleluia.

Gospel: Matthew 23:13-22

Jesus said to the crowds and to his disciples: [13] "Woe to you, scribes and Pharisees, you hypocrites. You lock the Kingdom of heaven before men. You do not enter yourselves, nor do you allow entrance to those trying to enter.

[15] "Woe to you, scribes and Pharisees, you hypocrites. You traverse sea and land to make one convert, and when that happens you make him a child of Gehenna twice as much as yourselves.

[16] "Woe to you, blind guides, who say, 'If one swears by the temple, it means nothing, but if one swears by the gold of the temple, one is obligated.' [17] Blind fools, which is greater, the gold, or the temple that made the gold sacred? [18] And you say, 'If one

swears by the altar, it means nothing, but if one swears by the gift on the altar, one is obligated.' [19] You blind ones, which is greater, the gift, or the altar that makes the gift sacred? [20] One who swears by the altar swears by it and all that is upon it; [21] one who swears by the temple swears by it and by him who dwells in it; [22] one who swears by heaven swears by the throne of God and by him who is seated on it."

Memorial of Saint Monica

First Reading: 2 Thessalonians 2:1-3A,14-17

[1] We ask you, brothers and sisters, with regard to the coming of our Lord Jesus Christ and our assembling with him, [2] not to be shaken out of your minds suddenly, or to be alarmed either by a "spirit," or by an oral statement, or by a letter allegedly from us to the effect that the day of the Lord is at hand. [3A] Let no one deceive you in any way.

[14] To this end he has also called you through our Gospel to possess the glory of our Lord Jesus Christ. [15] Therefore, brothers and sisters, stand firm and hold fast to the traditions that you were taught, either by an oral statement or by a letter of ours.

[16] May our Lord Jesus Christ himself and God our Father, who has loved us and given us everlasting encouragement and good hope through his grace, [17] encourage your hearts and strengthen them in every good deed and word.

Responsorial Psalm: Psalms 96:10, 11-12, 13

R. [13b] *The Lord comes to judge the earth.*
[10] Say among the nations: The LORD is king.
He has made the world firm, not to be
     moved;
   he governs the peoples with equity.
R. *The Lord comes to judge the earth.*

[11] Let the heavens be glad and the earth
     rejoice;
   let the sea and what fills it resound;
    [12] let the plains be joyful and all that is in
     them!
Then shall all the trees of the forest exult.
R. *The Lord comes to judge the earth.*

[13] Before the LORD, for he comes;
   for he comes to rule the earth.
He shall rule the world with justice
   and the peoples with his constancy.
R. *The Lord comes to judge the earth.*

Alleluia: Hebrews 4:12

R. Alleluia, alleluia.

[12] The word of God is living and effective,
able to discern reflections and thoughts of
> the heart.

R. Alleluia, alleluia.

Gospel: Matthew 23:23-26

Jesus said: [23] "Woe to you, scribes and Pharisees, you hypocrites. You pay tithes of mint and dill and cummin, and have neglected the weightier things of the law: judgment and mercy and fidelity. But these you should have done, without neglecting the others. [24] Blind guides, who strain out the gnat and swallow the camel!

[25] "Woe to you, scribes and Pharisees, you hypocrites. You cleanse the outside of cup and dish, but inside they are full of plunder and self-indulgence. [26] Blind Pharisee, cleanse first the inside of the cup, so that the outside also may be clean."

Wednesday August 28, 2024

Memorial of Saint Augustine, Bishop & Doctor
First Reading: 2 Thessalonians 3:6-10, 16-18

[6] We instruct you, brothers and sisters, in the name of our Lord Jesus Christ, to shun any brother who walks in a disorderly way and not according to the tradition they received from us. [7] For you know how one must imitate us. For we did not act in a disorderly way among you, [8] nor did we eat food received free from anyone. On the contrary, in toil and drudgery, night and day we worked, so as not to burden any of you. [9] Not that we do not have the right. Rather, we wanted to present ourselves as a model for you, so that you might imitate us. [10] In fact, when we were with you, we instructed you that if anyone was unwilling to work, neither should that one eat.

[16] May the Lord of peace himself give you peace at all times and in every way. The Lord be with all of you.

[17] This greeting is in my own hand, Paul's. This is the sign in every letter; this is how I write. [18] The grace of our Lord Jesus Christ be with all of you.

Responsorial Psalm: Psalms 128:1-2, 4-5

R. [(1)] **Blessed are those who fear the Lord.**

[1] Blessed are you who fear the LORD,
> who walk in his ways!

[2] For you shall eat the fruit of your
> handiwork;
> blessed shall you be, and favored.

R. Blessed are those who fear the Lord.

[4] Behold, thus is the man blessed

who fears the LORD.
⁵ The LORD bless you from Zion:
> may you see the prosperity of Jerusalem
> all the days of your life.

R. Blessed are those who fear the Lord.

Alleluia: 1 John 2:5

R. Alleluia, alleluia.
⁵ Whoever keeps the word of Christ,
the love of God is truly perfected in him.
R. Alleluia, alleluia.

Gospel: Matthew 23:27-32

Jesus said, ²⁷ "Woe to you, scribes and Pharisees, you hypocrites. You are like whitewashed tombs, which appear beautiful on the outside, but inside are full of dead men's bones and every kind of filth. ²⁸ Even so, on the outside you appear righteous, but inside you are filled with hypocrisy and evildoing.

²⁹ "Woe to you, scribes and Pharisees, you hypocrites. You build the tombs of the prophets and adorn the memorials of the righteous, ³⁰ and you say, 'If we had lived in the days of our ancestors, we would not have joined them in shedding the prophets' blood.' ³¹ Thus you bear witness against yourselves that you are the children of those who murdered the prophets; ³² now fill up what your ancestors measured out!"

Thursday August 29, 2024

The Passion of Saint John the Baptist

First Reading: 1 Corinthians 1:1-9

¹ Paul, called to be an Apostle of Christ Jesus by the will of God, and Sosthenes our brother, ² to the Church of God that is in Corinth, to you who have been sanctified in Christ Jesus, called to be holy, with all those everywhere who call upon the name of our Lord Jesus Christ, their Lord and ours. ³ Grace to you and peace from God our Father and the Lord Jesus Christ.

⁴ I give thanks to my God always on your account for the grace of God bestowed on you in Christ Jesus, ⁵ that in him you were enriched in every way, with all discourse and all knowledge, ⁶ as the testimony to Christ was confirmed among you, ⁷ so that you are not lacking in any spiritual gift as you wait for the revelation of our Lord Jesus Christ. ⁸ He will keep you firm to the end, irreproachable on the day of our Lord Jesus Christ. ⁹ God is faithful, and by him you were called to fellowship with his Son, Jesus Christ our Lord.

Responsorial Psalm: Psalms 145:2-3,4-5, 6-7

R. ⁽¹⁾ I will praise your name for ever, Lord.
² Every day will I bless you,
> and I will praise your name forever and

ever.
³ Great is the LORD and highly to be praised;
      his greatness is unsearchable.
R. I will praise your name for ever, Lord.

⁴ Generation after generation praises your
         works
      and proclaims your might.
⁵ They speak of the splendor of your glorious
         majesty
      and tell of your wondrous works.
R. I will praise your name for ever, Lord.

⁶ They discourse of the power of your terrible
         deeds
      and declare your greatness.
⁷ They publish the fame of your abundant
         goodness
      and joyfully sing of your justice.
R. I will praise your name for ever, Lord.

Alleluia: Matthew 5:10
R. Alleluia, alleluia.
¹⁰ Blessed are those who are persecuted for the
         sake of righteousness,
for theirs is the Kingdom of heaven.
R. Alleluia, alleluia.

Gospel: Mark 6:17-29
¹⁷ Herod was the one who had John the Baptist arrested and bound in prison on account of Herodias, the wife of his brother Philip, whom he had married. ¹⁸ John had said to Herod, "It is not lawful for you to have your brother's wife." ¹⁹ Herodias harbored a grudge against him and wanted to kill him but was unable to do so. ²⁰ Herod feared John, knowing him to be a righteous and holy man, and kept him in custody. When he heard him speak he was very much perplexed, yet he liked to listen to him. ²¹ She had an opportunity one day when Herod, on his birthday, gave a banquet for his courtiers, his military officers, and the leading men of Galilee. ²² Herodias's own daughter came in and performed a dance that delighted Herod and his guests. The king said to the girl, "Ask of me whatever you wish and I will grant it to you." ²³ He even swore many things to her, "I will grant you whatever you ask of me, even to half of my kingdom." ²⁴ She went out and said to her mother, "What shall I ask for?" She replied, "The head of John the Baptist." ²⁵ The girl hurried back to the king's presence and made her request, "I want you to give me

at once on a platter the head of John the Baptist." [26] The king was deeply distressed, but because of his oaths and the guests he did not wish to break his word to her. [27] So he promptly dispatched an executioner with orders to bring back his head. He went off and beheaded him in the prison. [28] He brought in the head on a platter and gave it to the girl. The girl in turn gave it to her mother. [29] When his disciples heard about it, they came and took his body and laid it in a tomb.

Friday August 30, 2024

Friday of the Twenty-first Week in Ordinary Time

First Reading: 1 Corinthians 1:17-25

Brothers and sisters: [17] Christ did not send me to baptize but to preach the Gospel, and not with the wisdom of human eloquence, so that the cross of Christ might not be emptied of its meaning.

[18] The message of the cross is foolishness to those who are perishing, but to us who are being saved it is the power of God. [19] For it is written:

I will destroy the wisdom of the wise,
and the learning of the learned I will set
aside.

[20] Where is the wise one? Where is the scribe? Where is the debater of this age? Has not God made the wisdom of the world foolish? [21] For since in the wisdom of God the world did not come to know God through wisdom, it was the will of God through the foolishness of the proclamation to save those who have faith. [22] For Jews demand signs and Greeks look for wisdom, [23] but we proclaim Christ crucified, a stumbling block to Jews and foolishness to Gentiles, [24] but to those who are called, Jews and Greeks alike, Christ the power of God and the wisdom of God. [25] For the foolishness of God is wiser than human wisdom, and the weakness of God is stronger than human strength.

Responsorial Psalm: Psalms 33:1-2, 4-5, 10-11

R. [(5)]*The earth is full of the goodness of the Lord.*

[1] Exult, you just, in the LORD;
    praise from the upright is fitting.
[2] Give thanks to the LORD on the harp;
    with the ten stringed lyre chant his
        praises.

R. *The earth is full of the goodness of the Lord.*

[4] For upright is the word of the LORD,
    and all his works are trustworthy.
[5] He loves justice and right;
    of the kindness of the LORD the earth is
        full.

R. The earth is full of the goodness of the Lord.

[10] The LORD brings to nought the plans of
nations;
he foils the designs of peoples.
[11] But the plan of the LORD stands forever;
the design of his heart, through all
generations.
R. The earth is full of the goodness of the Lord.

Alleluia: Luke 21:36
R. Alleluia, alleluia.
[36] Be vigilant at all times and pray,
that you may have the strength to stand
before the Son of Man.
R. Alleluia, alleluia.

Gospel: Matthew 25:1-13
Jesus told his disciples this parable: [1] "The Kingdom of heaven will be like ten virgins who took their lamps and went out to meet the bridegroom. [2] Five of them were foolish and five were wise. [3] The foolish ones, when taking their lamps, brought no oil with them, [4] but the wise brought flasks of oil with their lamps. [5] Since the bridegroom was long delayed, they all became drowsy and fell asleep. [6] At midnight, there was a cry, 'Behold, the bridegroom! Come out to meet him!' [7] Then all those virgins got up and trimmed their lamps. [8] The foolish ones said to the wise, 'Give us some of your oil, for our lamps are going out.' [9] But the wise ones replied, 'No, for there may not be enough for us and you. Go instead to the merchants and buy some for yourselves.' [10] While they went off to buy it, the bridegroom came and those who were ready went into the wedding feast with him. Then the door was locked. [11] Afterwards the other virgins came and said, 'Lord, Lord, open the door for us!' [12] But he said in reply, 'Amen, I say to you, I do not know you.' [13] Therefore, stay awake, for you know neither the day nor the hour."

Saturday August 31, 2024
Saturday of the Twenty-first Week in Ordinary Time
First Reading: 1 Corinthians 1:26-31
[26] Consider your own calling, brothers and sisters. Not many of you were wise by human standards, not many were powerful, not many were of noble birth. [27] Rather, God chose the foolish of the world to shame the wise, and God chose the weak of the world to shame the strong, [28] and God chose the lowly and despised of the world, those who count for nothing, to reduce to nothing those who are something, [29] so that no human being might boast before God. [30] It is due to him that you are in Christ Jesus, who became for us wisdom from God, as well as righteousness, sanctification, and redemption, [31] so that, as it is written, *Whoever boasts, should boast in the Lord.*

Responsorial Psalm: Psalms 33:12-13, 18-19, 20-21

R. [12] *Blessed the people the Lord has chosen to be his own.*

[12] Blessed the nation whose God is the LORD,
  the people he has chosen for his own
    inheritance.
[13] From heaven the LORD looks down;
  he sees all mankind.

R. *Blessed the people the Lord has chosen to be his own.*

[18] But see, the eyes of the LORD are upon those
    who fear him,
  upon those who hope for his kindness,
[19] To deliver them from death
  and preserve them in spite of famine.

R. *Blessed the people the Lord has chosen to be his own.*

[20] Our soul waits for the LORD,
  who is our help and our shield,
[21] For in him our hearts rejoice;
  in his holy name we trust.

R. *Blessed the people the Lord has chosen to be his own.*

Alleluia: John 13:34

R. Alleluia, alleluia.
[34] I give you a new commandment:
love one another as I have loved you.
R. Alleluia, alleluia.

Gospel: Matthew 25:14-30

Jesus told his disciples this parable: [14] "A man going on a journey called in his servants and entrusted his possessions to them. [15] To one he gave five talents; to another, two; to a third, one — to each according to his ability. Then he went away. [16] Immediately the one who received five talents went and traded with them, and made another five. [17] Likewise, the one who received two made another two. [18] But the man who received one went off and dug a hole in the ground and buried his master's money. [19] After a long time the master of those servants came back and settled accounts with them. [20] The one who had received five talents came forward bringing the additional five. He said, 'Master, you gave me five talents. See, I have made five more.' ²¹ His master said to him, 'Well done, my good and faithful servant. Since you were faithful in small matters, I will give you great responsibilities. Come, share your master's joy.' ²² Then the one who had received two talents also came forward and said, 'Master, you gave me two talents. See, I have made two more.' ²³ His master said to him, 'Well done, my good and faithful servant. Since you were faithful in small matters, I will give you great responsibilities. Come, share your master's joy.' ²⁴ Then the one who had received the one talent came forward and said, 'Master, I knew you were a demanding person, harvesting where you did not plant and gathering where you did not scatter; ²⁵ so out of fear I went off and buried your talent in the ground. Here it is back.' ²⁶ His master said to him in reply, 'You wicked, lazy servant! So you knew that I harvest where I did not plant and gather where I did not scatter? ²⁷ Should you not then have put my money in the bank so that I could have got it back with interest on my return? ²⁸ Now then! Take the talent from him and give it to the one with ten. ²⁹ For to everyone who has, more will be given and he will grow rich; but from the one who has not, even what he has will be taken away. ³⁰ And throw this useless servant into the darkness outside, where there will be wailing and grinding of teeth.'"

SEPTEMBER 2024
Sunday September 1, 2024

Twenty-second Sunday in ordinary Time, Year B
First Reading: Deuteronomy 4:1-2, 6-8

Moses said to the people: ¹ "Now, Israel, hear the statutes and decrees which I am teaching you to observe, that you may live, and may enter in and take possession of the land which the LORD, the God of your fathers, is giving you. ² In your observance of the commandments of the LORD, your God, which I enjoin upon you, you shall not add to what I command you nor subtract from it. ⁶ Observe them carefully, for thus will you give evidence of your wisdom and intelligence to the nations, who will hear of all these statutes and say, 'This great nation is truly a wise and intelligent people.' ⁷ For what great nation is there that has gods so close to it as the LORD, our God, is to us whenever we call upon him? ⁸ Or what great nation has statutes and decrees that are as just as this whole law which I am setting before you today?"

Responsorial Psalm: Psalms 15:2-3, 3-4, 4-5

R. ^(1a) *The one who does justice will live in the presence of the Lord.*

² Whoever walks blamelessly and does justice;
   who thinks the truth in his heart
      ^{3A} and slanders not with his tongue.

R. *The one who does justice will live in the presence of the Lord.*

^{3B} Who harms not his fellow man,
   nor takes up a reproach against his

neighbor;
4A by whom the reprobate is despised,
     while he honors those who fear the LORD.
R. The one who does justice will live in the
     presence of the Lord.

5 Who lends not his money at usury
     and accepts no bribe against the
         innocent.
Whoever does these things
     shall never be disturbed.
R. The one who does justice will live in the
     presence of the Lord.

Second Reading: James 1:17-18, 21B-22, 27

Dearest brothers and sisters: 17 All good giving and every perfect gift is from above, coming down from the Father of lights, with whom there is no alteration or shadow caused by change. 18 He willed to give us birth by the word of truth that we may be a kind of firstfruits of his creatures.

    21B Humbly welcome the word that has been planted in you and is able to save your souls.

    22 Be doers of the word and not hearers only, deluding yourselves.

    27 Religion that is pure and undefiled before God and the Father is this: to care for orphans and widows in their affliction and to keep oneself unstained by the world.

Alleluia: James 1:18

R. Alleluia, alleluia.

18 The Father willed to give us birth by the
     word of truth
that we may be a kind of firstfruits of his
     creatures.

R. Alleluia, alleluia.

Gospel: Mark 7:1-8, 14-15, 21-23

1 When the Pharisees with some scribes who had come from Jerusalem gathered around Jesus, 2 they observed that some of his disciples ate their meals with unclean, that is, unwashed, hands. 3 —For the Pharisees and, in fact, all Jews, do not eat without carefully washing their hands, keeping the tradition of the elders. 4 And on coming from the marketplace they do not eat without purifying themselves. And there are many other things that they have traditionally observed, the purification of cups and jugs and kettles and beds.— 5 So the Pharisees and scribes questioned him, "Why do your disciples not follow the tradition of the elders but instead eat a meal with unclean hands?" 6 He responded, "Well did Isaiah prophesy about you hypocrites, as it is written:

This people honors me with their lips,
        but their hearts are far from me;
[7] *in vain do they worship me,*
        teaching as doctrines human precepts.

[8] You disregard God's commandment but cling to human tradition." [14] He summoned the crowd again and said to them, "Hear me, all of you, and understand. [15] Nothing that enters one from outside can defile that person; but the things that come out from within are what defile.

[21] "From within people, from their hearts, come evil thoughts, unchastity, theft, murder, [22] adultery, greed, malice, deceit, licentiousness, envy, blasphemy, arrogance, folly. [23] All these evils come from within and they defile."

Monday of the Twenty-second Week in Ordinary Time
First Reading: 1 Corinthians 2: 1-5

[1] When I came to you, brothers, proclaiming the mystery of God, I did not come with sublimity of words or of wisdom. [2] For I resolved to know nothing while I was with you except Jesus Christ, and him crucified. [3] I came to you in weakness and fear and much trembling, [4] and my message and my proclamation were not with persuasive words of wisdom, but with a demonstration of spirit and power, [5] so that your faith might rest not on human wisdom but on the power of God.

Responsorial Psalm: Psalms 119:97, 98, 99, 100, 101, 102

R. [(97)] *Lord, I love your commands.*
[97] How I love your law, O LORD!
        It is my meditation all the day.
R. *Lord, I love your commands.*

[98] Your command has made me wiser than my
                enemies,
        for it is ever with me.
R. *Lord, I love your commands.*

[99] I have more understanding than all my
                teachers
        when your decrees are my meditation.
R. *Lord, I love your commands.*

[100] I have more discernment than the elders,
        because I observe your precepts.
R. *Lord, I love your commands.*

[101] From every evil way I withhold my feet,

that I may keep your words.
R. Lord, I love your commands.

¹⁰² From your ordinances I turn not away,
for you have instructed me.
R. Lord, I love your commands.

Alleluia: cf. Luke 4:18
R. Alleluia, alleluia.
¹⁹ The Spirit of the Lord is upon me;
he has sent me to bring glad tidings to the
poor.
R. Alleluia, alleluia.

Gospel: Luke 4:16-30
¹⁶ Jesus came to Nazareth, where he had grown up, and went according to his custom into the synagogue on the sabbath day. He stood up to read ¹⁷ and was handed a scroll of the prophet Isaiah. He unrolled the scroll and found the passage where it was written:

¹⁸ *The Spirit of the Lord is upon me,*
because he has anointed me
to bring glad tidings to the poor.
He has sent me to proclaim liberty to captives
and recovery of sight to the blind,
to let the oppressed go free,
¹⁹ *and to proclaim a year acceptable to the*
Lord.

²⁰ Rolling up the scroll, he handed it back to the attendant and sat down, and the eyes of all in the synagogue looked intently at him.²¹He said to them, "Today this Scripture passage is fulfilled in your hearing." ²² And all spoke highly of him and were amazed at the gracious words that came from his mouth. They also asked, "Is this not the son of Joseph?" ²³ He said to them, "Surely you will quote me this proverb, 'Physician, cure yourself,' and say, 'Do here in your native place the things that we heard were done in Capernaum.'" ²⁴ And he said, "Amen, I say to you, no prophet is accepted in his own native place. ²⁵ Indeed, I tell you, there were many widows in Israel in the days of Elijah when the sky was closed for three and a half years and a severe famine spread over the entire land. ²⁶ It was to none of these that Elijah was sent, but only to a widow in Zarephath in the land of Sidon. ²⁷ Again, there were many lepers in Israel during the time of Elisha the prophet; yet not one of them was cleansed, but only Naaman the Syrian." ²⁸ When the people in the synagogue heard this, they were all filled with fury. ²⁹ They rose up, drove him out of

the town, and led him to the brow of the hill on which their town had been built, to hurl him down headlong. [30] But he passed through the midst of them and went away.

Memorial of Saint Gregory the Great, Pope & Doctor

First Reading: 1 Corinthians 2:10B-16

Brothers and sisters: [10B] The Spirit scrutinizes everything, even the depths of God. [11] Among men, who knows what pertains to the man except his spirit that is within? Similarly, no one knows what pertains to God except the Spirit of God. [12] We have not received the spirit of the world but the Spirit who is from God, so that we may understand the things freely given us by God. [13] And we speak about them not with words taught by human wisdom, but with words taught by the Spirit, describing spiritual realities in spiritual terms.

[14] Now the natural man does not accept what pertains to the Spirit of God, for to him it is foolishness, and he cannot understand it, because it is judged spiritually. [15] The one who is spiritual, however, can judge everything but is not subject to judgment by anyone.

[16] For "who has known the mind of the Lord, so as to counsel him?" But we have the mind of Christ.

Responsorial Psalm: Psalms 145:8-9, 10-11, 12-13AB, 13CD-14

R. [(17)]*The Lord is just in all his ways.*

[8] The LORD is gracious and merciful,
        slow to anger and of great kindness.
[9] The LORD is good to all
        and compassionate toward all his works.

R. *The Lord is just in all his ways.*

[10] Let all your works give you thanks, O LORD,
        and let your faithful ones bless you.
[11] Let them discourse of the glory of your
                Kingdom
        and speak of your might.

R. *The Lord is just in all his ways.*

[12] Making known to men your might
        and the glorious splendor of your
                Kingdom.
[13AB] Your Kingdom is a Kingdom for all ages,
        and your dominion endures through all
                generations.

R. *The Lord is just in all his ways.*

[13CD] The LORD is faithful in all his words
        and holy in all his works.

14 The LORD lifts up all who are falling
    and raises up all who are bowed down.
R. The Lord is just in all his ways.

Alleluia: Luke 7:16

R. Alleluia, alleluia.

16 A great prophet has arisen in our midst
and God has visited his people.
R. Alleluia, alleluia.

Gospel: Luke 4:31-37

31 Jesus went down to Capernaum, a town of Galilee. He taught them on the sabbath, 32 and they were astonished at his teaching because he spoke with authority. 33 In the synagogue there was a man with the spirit of an unclean demon, and he cried out in a loud voice, 34 "What have you to do with us, Jesus of Nazareth? Have you come to destroy us? I know who you are — the Holy One of God!" 35 Jesus rebuked him and said, "Be quiet! Come out of him!" Then the demon threw the man down in front of them and came out of him without doing him any harm. 36 They were all amazed and said to one another, "What is there about his word? For with authority and power he commands the unclean spirits, and they come out." 37 And news of him spread everywhere in the surrounding region.

Wednesday September 4, 2024

Wednesday of the Twenty- second Week in Ordinary Time

First Reading: 1 Corinthians 3:1-9

Brothers and sisters, 1 I could not talk to you as spiritual people, but as fleshly people, as infants in Christ. 2 I fed you milk, not solid food, because you were unable to take it. Indeed, you are still not able, even now, 3 for you are still of the flesh. While there is jealousy and rivalry among you, are you not of the flesh, and walking according to the manner of man? 4 Whenever someone says, "I belong to Paul," and another, "I belong to Apollos," are you not merely men?

5 What is Apollos, after all, and what is Paul? Ministers through whom you became believers, just as the Lord assigned each one. 6 I planted, Apollos watered, but God caused the growth. 7 Therefore, neither the one who plants nor the one who waters is anything, but only God, who causes the growth. 8 He who plants and he who waters are one, and each will receive wages in proportion to his labor. 9 For we are God's co-workers; you are God's field, God's building.

Responsorial Psalm: Psalms 33:12-13, 14-15, 20-21

*R. (12)Blessed the people the Lord has chosen to
            be his own.*

12 Blessed the nation whose God is the LORD,
the people he has chosen for his own inheritance.

[13] From heaven the LORD looks down;
he sees all mankind.
**R. Blessed the people the Lord has chosen to be
his own.**

[14] From his fixed throne he beholds
all who dwell on the earth,
[15] He who fashioned the heart of each,
he who knows all their works.
**R. Blessed the people the Lord has chosen to be
his own.**

[20] Our soul waits for the LORD,
who is our help and our shield,
[21] For in him our hearts rejoice;
in his holy name we trust.
**R. Blessed the people the Lord has chosen to be
his own.**

Alleluia: Luke 4:18
R. Alleluia, alleluia.
[18] The Lord sent me to bring glad tidings to the
poor
and to proclaim liberty to captives.
R. Alleluia, alleluia.

Gospel: Luke 4:38-44
[38] After Jesus left the synagogue, he entered the house of Simon. Simon's mother-in-law was afflicted with a severe fever, and they interceded with him about her. [39] He stood over her, rebuked the fever, and it left her. She got up immediately and waited on them.

[40] At sunset, all who had people sick with various diseases brought them to him. He laid his hands on each of them and cured them. [41] And demons also came out from many, shouting, "You are the Son of God." But he rebuked them and did not allow them to speak because they knew that he was the Christ.

[42] At daybreak, Jesus left and went to a deserted place. The crowds went looking for him, and when they came to him, they tried to prevent him from leaving them. [43] But he said to them, "To the other towns also I must proclaim the good news of the Kingdom of God, because for this purpose I have been sent." [44] And he was preaching in the synagogues of Judea.

Thursday of the Twenty-second Week in Ordinary Time
First Reading: 1 Corinthians 3:18-23

Brothers and sisters: [18] Let no one deceive himself. If anyone among you considers himself wise in this age, let him become a fool, so as to become wise. [19] For the wisdom of this world is foolishness in the eyes of God, for it is written:

God catches the wise in their own ruses,

[20] and again:

The Lord knows the thoughts of the wise, that
*   they are vain.*

[21] So let no one boast about human beings, for everything belongs to you, [22] Paul or Apollos or Cephas, or the world or life or death, or the present or the future: all belong to you, [23] and you to Christ, and Christ to God.

Responsorial Psalm: Psalms 24:1BC-2, 3-4AB, 5-6
R. [(1)] *To the Lord belongs the earth and all that*
*   fills it.*
[1BC] The LORD's are the earth and its fullness;
        the world and those who dwell in it.
[2] For he founded it upon the seas
        and established it upon the rivers.
R. *To the Lord belongs the earth and all that fills*
*   it.*

[3] Who can ascend the mountain of the LORD?
        or who may stand in his holy place?
[4AB] He whose hands are sinless, whose heart is
                clean,
        who desires not what is vain.
R. *To the Lord belongs the earth and all that fills*
*   it.*

[5] He shall receive a blessing from the LORD,
        a reward from God his savior.
[6] Such is the race that seeks for him,
        that seeks the face of the God of Jacob.
R. *To the Lord belongs the earth and all that fills*

it.

Alleluia: Matthew 4:19
R. Alleluia, alleluia.
[19] Come after me, says the Lord,
and I will make you fishers of men.
R. Alleluia, alleluia.

Gospel: Luke 5:1-11
[1] While the crowd was pressing in on Jesus and listening to the word of God, he was standing by the Lake of Gennesaret. [2] He saw two boats there alongside the lake; the fishermen had disembarked and were washing their nets. [3] Getting into one of the boats, the one belonging to Simon, he asked him to put out a short distance from the shore. Then he sat down and taught the crowds from the boat. [4] After he had finished speaking, he said to Simon, "Put out into deep water and lower your nets for a catch." [5] Simon said in reply, "Master, we have worked hard all night and have caught nothing, but at your command I will lower the nets." [6] When they had done this, they caught a great number of fish and their nets were tearing. [7] They signaled to their partners in the other boat to come to help them. They came and filled both boats so that the boats were in danger of sinking. [8] When Simon Peter saw this, he fell at the knees of Jesus and said, "Depart from me, Lord, for I am a sinful man." [9] For astonishment at the catch of fish they had made seized him and all those with him, [10] and likewise James and John, the sons of Zebedee, who were partners of Simon. Jesus said to Simon, "Do not be afraid; from now on you will be catching men." [11] When they brought their boats to the shore, they left everything and followed him.

Friday September 6, 2024
Friday of the Twenty-second Week in Ordinary Time
First Reading: 1 Corinthians 4:1-5
Brothers and sisters: [1] Thus should one regard us: as servants of Christ and stewards of the mysteries of God. [2] Now it is of course required of stewards that they be found trustworthy. [3] It does not concern me in the least that I be judged by you or any human tribunal; I do not even pass judgment on myself; [4] I am not conscious of anything against me, but I do not thereby stand acquitted; the one who judges me is the Lord. [5] Therefore, do not make any judgment before the appointed time, until the Lord comes, for he will bring to light what is hidden in darkness and will manifest the motives of our hearts, and then everyone will receive praise from God.

Responsorial Psalm: Psalms 37:3-4, 5-6, 27-28, 39-40
R. [39a]**The salvation of the just comes from the Lord.**
[3] Trust in the LORD and do good,
    that you may dwell in the land and be fed
        in security.
[4] Take delight in the LORD,

and he will grant you your heart's
    requests.
R. The salvation of the just comes from the Lord.

[5] Commit to the LORD your way;
    trust in him, and he will act.
[6] He will make justice dawn for you like the
       light;
    bright as the noonday shall be your
       vindication.
R. The salvation of the just comes from the Lord.

[27] Turn from evil and do good,
    that you may abide forever;
[28] For the LORD loves what is right,
    and forsakes not his faithful ones.
Criminals are destroyed
    and the posterity of the wicked is cut off.
R. The salvation of the just comes from the Lord.

[39] The salvation of the just is from the LORD;
    he is their refuge in time of distress.
[40] And the LORD helps them and delivers them;
    he delivers them from the wicked and
      saves them,
    because they take refuge in him.
R. The salvation of the just comes from the Lord.

Alleluia: John 8:12
R. Alleluia, alleluia.
[12] I am the light of the world, says the Lord;
whoever follows me will have the light of life.
R. Alleluia, alleluia.

Gospel: Luke 5:33-39
[33] The scribes and Pharisees said to Jesus, "The disciples of John the Baptist fast often and offer prayers, and the disciples of the Pharisees do the same; but yours eat and drink." [34] Jesus answered them, "Can you make the wedding guests fast while the bridegroom is with them? [35] But the days will come, and when the bridegroom is taken away from them, then they will fast in those days." [36] And he also told them a parable. "No one tears a piece from a new cloak to patch an old one. Otherwise, he will tear the new and the piece from it will not match the old cloak. [37] Likewise, no one pours new wine into old

wineskins. Otherwise, the new wine will burst the skins, and it will be spilled, and the skins will be ruined. [38] Rather, new wine must be poured into fresh wineskins. [39] And no one who has been drinking old wine desires new, for he says, 'The old is good.'"

Saturday September 7, 2024

Saturday of the Twenty-second Week in Ordinary Time
First Reading: 1 Corinthians 4:6B-15

Brothers and sisters: [6B] Learn from myself and Apollos not to go beyond what is written, so that none of you will be inflated with pride in favor of one person over against another. [7] Who confers distinction upon you? What do you possess that you have not received? But if you have received it, why are you boasting as if you did not receive it? [8] You are already satisfied; you have already grown rich; you have become kings without us! Indeed, I wish that you had become kings, so that we also might become kings with you.

[9] For as I see it, God has exhibited us Apostles as the last of all, like people sentenced to death, since we have become a spectacle to the world, to angels and men alike. [10] We are fools on Christ's account, but you are wise in Christ; we are weak, but you are strong; you are held in honor, but we in disrepute. [11] To this very hour we go hungry and thirsty, we are poorly clad and roughly treated, we wander about homeless [12] and we toil, working with our own hands. When ridiculed, we bless; when persecuted, we endure; [13] when slandered, we respond gently. We have become like the world's rubbish, the scum of all, to this very moment.

[14] I am writing you this not to shame you, but to admonish you as my beloved children. [15] Even if you should have countless guides to Christ, yet you do not have many fathers, for I became your father in Christ Jesus through the Gospel.

Responsorial Psalm: Psalms 145:17-18, 19-20, 21
R. [18]*The Lord is near to all who call upon him.*

[17] The LORD is just in all his ways
   and holy in all his works.
[18] The LORD is near to all who call upon him,
   to all who call upon him in truth.
R. *The Lord is near to all who call upon him.*

[19] He fulfills the desire of those who fear him,
   he hears their cry and saves them.
[20] The LORD keeps all who love him,
   but all the wicked he will destroy.
R. *The Lord is near to all who call upon him.*

[21] May my mouth speak the praise of the LORD,
   and may all flesh bless his holy name
      forever and ever.
R. *The Lord is near to all who call upon him.*

Alleluia: John 14:6
R. Alleluia, alleluia.

[6] I am the way and the truth and the life, says
     the Lord;
no one comes to the Father except through
     me.

R. Alleluia, alleluia.

Gospel: Luke 6:1-5

[1] While Jesus was going through a field of grain on a sabbath, his disciples were picking the heads of grain, rubbing them in their hands, and eating them. [2] Some Pharisees said, "Why are you doing what is unlawful on the sabbath?" [3] Jesus said to them in reply, "Have you not read what David did when he and those who were with him were hungry? [4] How he went into the house of God, took the bread of offering, which only the priests could lawfully eat, ate of it, and shared it with his companions?" [5] Then he said to them, "The Son of Man is lord of the sabbath."

Sunday September 8, 2024

Twenty-third Sunday in Ordinary Time, Year B
First Reading: Isaiah 35:4-7A

Thus says the LORD:

[4] Say to those whose hearts are frightened:
     Be strong, fear not!
Here is your God,
     he comes with vindication;
with divine recompense
     he comes to save you.
[5] Then will the eyes of the blind be opened,
     the ears of the deaf be cleared;
[6] then will the lame leap like a stag,
     then the tongue of the mute will sing.
Streams will burst forth in the desert,
     and rivers in the steppe.
[7] The burning sands will become pools,
     and the thirsty ground, springs of water.

Responsorial Psalm: Psalms 146:6-7, 8-9, 9-10
R. [1b] *Praise the Lord, my soul!* or: *Alleluia.*

[6] The God of Jacob keeps faith forever,
     [7] secures justice for the oppressed,
     gives food to the hungry.

The LORD sets captives free.
R. Praise the Lord, my soul! or: **Alleluia.**
[8] The LORD gives sight to the blind;
>   the LORD raises up those who were bowed
>   down.
The LORD loves the just;
>   [9A] the LORD protects strangers.
R. Praise the Lord, my soul! or: **Alleluia.**

[9B] The fatherless and the widow the LORD
>   sustains,
>   but the way of the wicked he thwarts.
[10] The LORD shall reign forever;
>   your God, O Zion, through all generations.
Alleluia.
R. Praise the Lord, my soul! or: **Alleluia.**

Second Reading: James 2:1-5

[1] My brothers and sisters, show no partiality as you adhere to the faith in our glorious Lord Jesus Christ. [2] For if a man with gold rings and fine clothes comes into your assembly, and a poor person in shabby clothes also comes in, [3] and you pay attention to the one wearing the fine clothes and say, "Sit here, please, " while you say to the poor one, "Stand there, " or "Sit at my feet, " [4] have you not made distinctions among yourselves and become judges with evil designs?

[5] Listen, my beloved brothers and sisters. Did not God choose those who are poor in the world to be rich in faith and heirs of the kingdom that he promised to those who love him?

Alleluia: cf. Matthew 4:23

R. Alleluia, alleluia.
[23] Jesus proclaimed the Gospel of the kingdom
and cured every disease among the people.
R. Alleluia, alleluia.

Gospel: Mark 7:31-37

[31] Again Jesus left the district of Tyre and went by way of Sidon to the Sea of Galilee, into the district of the Decapolis. [32] And people brought to him a deaf man who had a speech impediment and begged him to lay his hand on him. [33] He took him off by himself away from the crowd. He put his finger into the man's ears and, spitting, touched his tongue; [34] then he looked up to heaven and groaned, and said to him, "*Ephphatha*!" —that is, "Be opened!"— [35] And immediately the man's ears were opened, his speech impediment was removed, and he spoke plainly. [36] He ordered them not to tell anyone. But the more he ordered them not to, the more they proclaimed it. [37] They were exceedingly astonished and they said, "He has done all things well. He makes the deaf hear and the mute speak."

Memorial of Saint Peter Claver

First Reading: 1 Corinthians 5:1-8

Brothers and sisters: [1] It is widely reported that there is immorality among you, and immorality of a kind not found even among pagans a man living with his father's wife. [2] And you are inflated with pride. Should you not rather have been sorrowful? The one who did this deed should be expelled from your midst. [3] I, for my part, although absent in body but present in spirit, have already, as if present, pronounced judgment on the one who has committed this deed, [4] in the name of our Lord Jesus: when you have gathered together and I am with you in spirit with the power of the Lord Jesus, [5] you are to deliver this man to Satan for the destruction of his flesh, so that his spirit may be saved on the day of the Lord.

[6] Your boasting is not appropriate. Do you not know that a little yeast leavens all the dough? [7] Clear out the old yeast, so that you may become a fresh batch of dough, inasmuch as you are unleavened. For our Paschal Lamb, Christ, has been sacrificed. [8] Therefore, let us celebrate the feast, not with the old yeast, the yeast of malice and wickedness, but with the unleavened bread of sincerity and truth.

Responsorial Psalm: Psalms 5:5-6, 7, 12

R. [9]*Lead me in your justice, Lord.*

[5] For you, O God, delight not in wickedness;
    no evil man remains with you;
        [6] the arrogant may not stand in your sight.
You hate all evildoers.

R. *Lead me in your justice, Lord.*

[7] You destroy all who speak falsehood;
The bloodthirsty and the deceitful
    the LORD abhors.

R. *Lead me in your justice, Lord.*

[12] But let all who take refuge in you
    be glad and exult forever.
Protect them, that you may be the joy
    of those who love your name.

R. *Lead me in your justice, Lord.*

Alleluia: John 10:27

R. Alleluia, alleluia.

[27] My sheep hear my voice, says the Lord;
I know them, and they follow me.

R. Alleluia, alleluia.

Gospel: Luke 6:6-11

[6] On a certain sabbath Jesus went into the synagogue and taught, and there was a man there whose right hand was withered. [7] The scribes and the Pharisees watched him closely to see if he would cure on the sabbath so that they might discover a reason to accuse him. [8] But he realized their intentions and said to the man with the withered hand, "Come up and stand before us." And he rose and stood there. [9] Then Jesus said to them, "I ask you, is it lawful to do good on the sabbath rather than to do evil, to save life rather than to destroy it?" [10] Looking around at them all, he then said to him, "Stretch out your hand." He did so and his hand was restored. [11] But they became enraged and discussed together what they might do to Jesus.

Tuesday September 10, 2024

Tuesday of Twenty-third Week in Ordinary Time
First Reading: 1 Corinthians 6:1-11

Brothers and sisters: [1] How can any one of you with a case against another dare to bring it to the unjust for judgment instead of to the holy ones? [2] Do you not know that the holy ones will judge the world? If the world is to be judged by you, are you unqualified for the lowest law courts? [3] Do you not know that we will judge angels? Then why not everyday matters? [4] If, therefore, you have courts for everyday matters, do you seat as judges people of no standing in the Church? [5] I say this to shame you. Can it be that there is not one among you wise enough to be able to settle a case between brothers? [6] But rather brother goes to court against brother, and that before unbelievers?

[7] Now indeed then it is, in any case, a failure on your part that you have lawsuits against one another. Why not rather put up with injustice? Why not rather let yourselves be cheated? [8] Instead, you inflict injustice and cheat, and this to brothers. [9] Do you not know that the unjust will not inherit the Kingdom of God? Do not be deceived; neither fornicators nor idolaters nor adulterers nor boy prostitutes nor sodomites [10] nor thieves nor the greedy nor drunkards nor slanderers nor robbers will inherit the Kingdom of God. [11] That is what some of you used to be; but now you have had yourselves washed, you were sanctified, you were justified in the name of the Lord Jesus Christ and in the Spirit of our God.

Responsorial Psalm: Psalms 149:1B-2, 3-4, 5-6A AND 9B

R. *(see 4)* *The Lord takes delight in his people.*

[1B] Sing to the LORD a new song
of praise in the assembly of the faithful.
[2] Let Israel be glad in their maker,
let the children of Zion rejoice in their
king.

R. *The Lord takes delight in his people.*

[3] Let them praise his name in the festive
dance,
let them sing praise to him with timbrel

and harp.
⁴ For the LORD loves his people,
and he adorns the lowly with victory.
R. The Lord takes delight in his people.

⁵ Let the faithful exult in glory;
let them sing for joy upon their couches;
⁶ᴬ Let the high praises of God be in their
throats.
⁹ᴮ This is the glory of all his faithful.
Alleluia.
R. The Lord takes delight in his people.

Alleluia: cf. John 15:16
R. Alleluia, alleluia.
¹⁶ I chose you from the world,
That you may go and bear fruit that will last,
says the Lord.
R. Alleluia, alleluia.

Gospel: Luke 6:12-19
¹² Jesus departed to the mountain to pray, and he spent the night in prayer to God. ¹³ When day came, he called his disciples to himself, and from them he chose Twelve, whom he also named Apostles: ¹⁴ Simon, whom he named Peter, and his brother Andrew, James, John, Philip, Bartholomew, ¹⁵ Matthew, Thomas, James the son of Alphaeus, Simon who was called a Zealot, ¹⁶ and Judas the son of James, and Judas Iscariot, who became a traitor.

¹⁷ And he came down with them and stood on a stretch of level ground. A great crowd of his disciples and a large number of the people from all Judea and Jerusalem and the coastal region of Tyre and Sidon ¹⁸ came to hear him and to be healed of their diseases; and even those who were tormented by unclean spirits were cured. ¹⁹ Everyone in the crowd sought to touch him because power came forth from him and healed them all.

Wednesday September 11, 2024

Wednesday of Twenty-third Week in Ordinary Time
First Reading: 1 Corinthians 7:25-31
Brothers and sisters: ²⁵ In regard to virgins, I have no commandment from the Lord, but I give my opinion as one who by the Lord's mercy is trustworthy. ²⁶ So this is what I think best because of the present distress: that it is a good thing for a person to remain as he is. ²⁷ Are you bound to a wife? Do not seek a separation. Are you free of a wife? Then do not look for a wife. ²⁸ If you marry, however, you do not sin, nor does an unmarried woman

sin if she marries; but such people will experience affliction in their earthly life, and I would like to spare you that.

²⁹ I tell you, brothers, the time is running out. From now on, let those having wives act as not having them, ³⁰ those weeping as not weeping, those rejoicing as not rejoicing, those buying as not owning, ³¹ those using the world as not using it fully. For the world in its present form is passing away.

Responsorial Psalm: Psalms 45:11-12, 14-15, 16-17

R. *(11)Listen to me, daughter; see and bend your ear.*

¹¹ Hear, O daughter, and see; turn your ear,
forget your people and your father's
house.
¹² So shall the king desire your beauty;
for he is your lord, and you must worship
him.

R. *Listen to me, daughter; see and bend your ear.*

¹⁴ All glorious is the king's daughter as she
enters;
her raiment is threaded with spun gold.
¹⁵ In embroidered apparel she is borne in to
the king;
behind her the virgins of her train are
brought to you.

R. *Listen to me, daughter; see and bend your ear.*

¹⁶They are borne in with gladness and joy;
they enter the palace of the king.
¹⁷The place of your fathers your sons shall have;
you shall make them princes through all
the land.

R. *Listen to me, daughter; see and bend your ear.*

Alleluia: Luke 6:23AB

R. Alleluia, alleluia.

²³ᴬᴮ Rejoice and leap for joy!
Your reward will be great in heaven.

R. Alleluia, alleluia.

Gospel: Luke 6:20-26

²⁰ Raising his eyes toward his disciples Jesus said:

"Blessed are you who are poor,
    for the Kingdom of God is yours.
21 Blessed are you who are now hungry,
    for you will be satisfied.
Blessed are you who are now weeping,
    for you will laugh.
22 Blessed are you when people hate you,
        and when they exclude and insult you,
        and denounce your name as evil
        on account of the Son of Man.

23 Rejoice and leap for joy on that day! Behold, your reward will be great in heaven. For their ancestors treated the prophets in the same way.

24 But woe to you who are rich,
    for you have received your consolation.
25 But woe to you who are filled now,
    for you will be hungry.
Woe to you who laugh now,
    for you will grieve and weep.
26 Woe to you when all speak well of you,
        for their ancestors treated the false
            prophets in this way."

Thursday September 12, 2024

Thursday of Twenty-third Week in Ordinary Time
First Reading: 1 Corinthians 8:1B-7, 11-13

Brothers and sisters: 1B Knowledge inflates with pride, but love builds up. 2 If anyone supposes he knows something, he does not yet know as he ought to know. 3 But if one loves God, one is known by him.

4 So about the eating of meat sacrificed to idols: we know that *there is no idol in the world*, and that *there is no God but one*. 5 Indeed, even though there are so-called gods in heaven and on earth (there are, to be sure, many "gods" and many "lords"), 6 yet for us there is

one God, the Father,
    from whom all things are and for whom
        we exist,
and one Lord, Jesus Christ,
    through whom all things are and through
        whom we exist.

478

[7] But not all have this knowledge. There are some who have been so used to idolatry up until now that, when they eat meat sacrificed to idols, their conscience, which is weak, is defiled.

[11] Thus, through your knowledge, the weak person is brought to destruction, the brother for whom Christ died. [12] When you sin in this way against your brothers and wound their consciences, weak as they are, you are sinning against Christ. [13] Therefore, if food causes my brother to sin, I will never eat meat again, so that I may not cause my brother to sin.

Responsorial Psalm: Psalms 139:1B-3, 13-14AB, 23-24

R. [(24b)] *Guide me, Lord, along the everlasting way.*

[1B] O LORD, you have probed me and you know
        me;
    [2] you know when I sit and when I stand;
    you understand my thoughts from afar.
[3] My journeys and my rest you scrutinize,
    with all my ways you are familiar.
R. *Guide me, Lord, along the everlasting way.*

[13] Truly you have formed my inmost being;
    you knit me in my mother's womb.
[14AB] I give you thanks that I am fearfully,
        wonderfully made;
    wonderful are your works.
R. *Guide me, Lord, along the everlasting way.*

[23] Probe me, O God, and know my heart;
    try me, and know my thoughts;
[24] See if my way is crooked,
    and lead me in the way of old.
R. *Guide me, Lord, along the everlasting way.*

Alleluia: 1 John 4:12

R. Alleluia, alleluia.
[12] If we love one another,
God remains in us,
and his love is brought to perfection in us.
R. Alleluia, alleluia.

Gospel: Luke 6:27-38

Jesus said to his disciples: [27] "To you who hear I say, love your enemies, do good to those who hate you, [28] bless those who curse you, pray for those who mistreat you. [29] To the person who strikes you on one cheek, offer the other one as well, and from the person who takes your cloak, do not withhold even your tunic. ³⁰ Give to everyone who asks of you, and from the one who takes what is yours do not demand it back. ³¹ Do to others as you would have them do to you. ³² For if you love those who love you, what credit is that to you? Even sinners love those who love them. ³³ And if you do good to those who do good to you, what credit is that to you? Even sinners do the same. ³⁴ If you lend money to those from whom you expect repayment, what credit is that to you? Even sinners lend to sinners, and get back the same amount. ³⁵ But rather, love your enemies and do good to them, and lend expecting nothing back; then your reward will be great and you will be children of the Most High, for he himself is kind to the ungrateful and the wicked. ³⁶ Be merciful, just as also your Father is merciful.

³⁷ "Stop judging and you will not be judged. Stop condemning and you will not be condemned. Forgive and you will be forgiven. ³⁸ Give and gifts will be given to you; a good measure, packed together, shaken down, and overflowing, will be poured into your lap. For the measure with which you measure will in return be measured out to you."

Friday September 13, 2024

Memorial of Saint John Chrysostom, Bishop and Doctor
First Reading: 1 Corinthians 9:16-19, 22B-27

Brothers and sisters: ¹⁶ If I preach the Gospel, this is no reason for me to boast, for an obligation has been imposed on me, and woe to me if I do not preach it! ¹⁷ If I do so willingly, I have a recompense, but if unwillingly, then I have been entrusted with a stewardship. ¹⁸ What then is my recompense? That, when I preach, I offer the Gospel free of charge so as not to make full use of my right in the Gospel.

¹⁹ Although I am free in regard to all, I have made myself a slave to all so as to win over as many as possible. ²²ᴮ I have become all things to all, to save at least some. ²³ All this I do for the sake of the Gospel, so that I too may have a share in it.

²⁴ Do you not know that the runners in the stadium all run in the race, but only one wins the prize? Run so as to win. ²⁵ Every athlete exercises discipline in every way. They do it to win a perishable crown, but we an imperishable one. ²⁶ Thus I do not run aimlessly; I do not fight as if I were shadowboxing. ²⁷ No, I drive my body and train it, for fear that, after having preached to others, I myself should be disqualified.

Responsorial Psalm: Psalms 84:3, 4, 5-6, 12

R. ⁽²⁾ *How lovely is your dwelling place, Lord,*
       mighty God!
³ My soul yearns and pines
       for the courts of the LORD.
My heart and my flesh
       cry out for the living God.
R. *How lovely is your dwelling place, Lord,*
       mighty God!

⁴ Even the sparrow finds a home,
and the swallow a nest
in which she puts her young—
Your altars, O LORD of hosts,
my king and my God!
**R. How lovely is your dwelling place, Lord,
mighty God!**

⁵ Blessed they who dwell in your house!
continually they praise you.
⁶ Blessed the men whose strength you are!
their hearts are set upon the pilgrimage.
**R. How lovely is your dwelling place, Lord,
mighty God!**

¹² For a sun and a shield is the LORD God;
grace and glory he bestows;
The LORD withholds no good thing
from those who walk in sincerity.
**R. How lovely is your dwelling place, Lord,
mighty God!**

Alleluia: 1 John 17:17B, 17A

R. Alleluia, alleluia.
¹⁷ᴮ Your word, O Lord, is truth;
¹⁷ᴬ consecrate us in the truth.
R. Alleluia, alleluia.

Gospel: Luke 6:39-42

³⁹ Jesus told his disciples a parable: "Can a blind person guide a blind person? Will not both fall into a pit? ⁴⁰ No disciple is superior to the teacher; but when fully trained, every disciple will be like his teacher. ⁴¹ Why do you notice the splinter in your brother's eye, but do not perceive the wooden beam in your own? ⁴² How can you say to your brother, 'Brother, let me remove that splinter in your eye,' when you do not even notice the wooden beam in your own eye? You hypocrite! Remove the wooden beam from your eye first; then you will see clearly to remove the splinter in your brother's eye."

Saturday September 14, 2024

Feast of the Exaltation of the Holy Cross
First Reading: Numbers 21:4B-9

⁴ᴮ With their patience worn out by the journey, ⁵ the people complained against God and Moses, "Why have you brought us up from Egypt to die in this desert, where there is no food or water? We are disgusted with this wretched food!"

[6] In punishment the LORD sent among the people saraph serpents, which bit the people so that many of them died. [7] Then the people came to Moses and said, "We have sinned in complaining against the LORD and you. Pray the LORD to take the serpents from us." So Moses prayed for the people, [8] and the LORD said to Moses, "Make a saraph and mount it on a pole, and if any who have been bitten look at it, they will live." [9] Moses accordingly made a bronze serpent and mounted it on a pole, and whenever anyone who had been bitten by a serpent looked at the bronze serpent, he lived.

Responsorial Psalm: Psalms 78:1BC-2, 34-35, 36-37, 38

R. [(See 7b)] *Do not forget the works of the Lord!*

[1BC] Hearken, my people, to my teaching;
      incline your ears to the words of my
         mouth.
[2] I will open my mouth in a parable,
      I will utter mysteries from of old.

R. Do not forget the works of the Lord!

[34] While he slew them they sought him
      and inquired after God again,
[35] Remembering that God was their rock
      and the Most High God, their redeemer.

R. Do not forget the works of the Lord!

[36] But they flattered him with their mouths
      and lied to him with their tongues,
[37] Though their hearts were not steadfast
         toward him,
      nor were they faithful to his covenant.

R. Do not forget the works of the Lord!

[38] But he, being merciful, forgave their sin
      and destroyed them not;
Often he turned back his anger
      and let none of his wrath be roused.

R. Do not forget the works of the Lord!

Second Reading: Philippians 2:6-11

Brothers and sisters:

[6] Christ Jesus, though he was in the form of
      God,
      did not regard equality with God

482

something to be grasped.
⁷ Rather, he emptied himself,
    taking the form of a slave,
    coming in human likeness;
    and found human in appearance,
    ⁸ he humbled himself,
    becoming obedient to death,
    even death on a cross.
⁹ Because of this, God greatly exalted him
    and bestowed on him the name
    that is above every name,
    ¹⁰ that at the name of Jesus
    every knee should bend,
    of those in heaven and on earth and
        under the earth,
    ¹¹ and every tongue confess that
    Jesus Christ is Lord,
    to the glory of God the Father.

Alleluia

R. Alleluia, alleluia.
We adore you, O Christ, and we bless you,
because by your Cross you have redeemed
        the world.
R. Alleluia, alleluia.

Gospel: John 3:13-17

Jesus said to Nicodemus: ¹³ "No one has gone up to heaven except the one who has come down from heaven, the Son of Man. ¹⁴ And just as Moses lifted up the serpent in the desert, so must the Son of Man be lifted up, ¹⁵ so that everyone who believes in him may have eternal life."

¹⁶ For God so loved the world that he gave his only Son, so that everyone who believes in him might not perish but might have eternal life. ¹⁷ For God did not send his Son into the world to condemn the world, but that the world might be saved through him.

Sunday September 15, 2024

Twenty-fourth Sunday in Ordinary Time, Year B
First Reading: Isaiah 50:5-9A

⁵ The Lord GOD opens my ear that I may hear;
and I have not rebelled,
    have not turned back.
⁶ I gave my back to those who beat me,

483

my cheeks to those who plucked my
      beard;
my face I did not shield
      from buffets and spitting.

[7] The Lord GOD is my help,
      therefore I am not disgraced;
I have set my face like flint,
      knowing that I shall not be put to shame.
[8] He is near who upholds my right;
      if anyone wishes to oppose me,
      let us appear together.
Who disputes my right?
      Let that man confront me.
[9A] See, the Lord GOD is my help;
      who will prove me wrong?

Responsorial Psalm: Psalms 116:1-2, 3-4, 5-6, 8-9

R. [9] **I will walk before the Lord, in the land of the
      living.** or: *Alleluia.*
[1] I love the LORD because he has heard
      my voice in supplication,
[2] because he has inclined his ear to me
      the day I called.
**R. I will walk before the Lord, in the land of the
      living.** or: *Alleluia.*

[3] The cords of death encompassed me;
      the snares of the netherworld seized
        upon me;
      [4] I fell into distress and sorrow,
and I called upon the name of the LORD,
      "O LORD, save my life!"
**R. I will walk before the Lord, in the land of the
      living.** or: *Alleluia.*

[5] Gracious is the LORD and just;
      yes, our God is merciful.
[6] The LORD keeps the little ones;
      I was brought low, and he saved me.
**R. I will walk before the Lord, in the land of the
      living.** or: *Alleluia.*

⁸ For he has freed my soul from death,
> my eyes from tears, my feet from
>> stumbling.
⁹ I shall walk before the LORD
> in the land of the living.

R. I will walk before the Lord, in the land of the living. or: *Alleluia.*

Second Reading: James 2:14-18

¹⁴ What good is it, my brothers and sisters, if someone says he has faith but does not have works? Can that faith save him? ¹⁵ If a brother or sister has nothing to wear and has no food for the day, ¹⁷ and one of you says to them, "Go in peace, keep warm, and eat well, " but you do not give them the necessities of the body, what good is it? So also faith of itself, if it does not have works, is dead.

¹⁸ Indeed someone might say, "You have faith and I have works." Demonstrate your faith to me without works, and I will demonstrate my faith to you from my works.

Alleluia: Galatians 6:14

R. Alleluia, alleluia.

¹⁴ May I never boast except in the cross of our
> Lord
through which the world has been crucified
> to me and I to the world.

R. Alleluia, alleluia.

Gospel: Mark 8:27-35

²⁷ Jesus and his disciples set out for the villages of Caesarea Philippi. Along the way he asked his disciples, "Who do people say that I am?" ²⁸ They said in reply, "John the Baptist, others Elijah, still others one of the prophets." ²⁹ And he asked them, "But who do you say that I am?" Peter said to him in reply, "You are the Christ." ³⁰ Then he warned them not to tell anyone about him.

³¹ He began to teach them that the Son of Man must suffer greatly and be rejected by the elders, the chief priests, and the scribes, and be killed, and rise after three days. ³² He spoke this openly. Then Peter took him aside and began to rebuke him. ³³ At this he turned around and, looking at his disciples, rebuked Peter and said, "Get behind me, Satan. You are thinking not as God does, but as human beings do."

³⁴ He summoned the crowd with his disciples and said to them, "Whoever wishes to come after me must deny himself, take up his cross, and follow me. ³⁵ For whoever wishes to save his life will lose it, but whoever loses his life for my sake and that of the gospel will save it."

Memorial of Saints Cornelius, Pope and Cyrian, Bishop and Martyr
First Reading: 1 Corinthians 11:17-26, 33

Brothers and sisters: [17] In giving this instruction, I do not praise the fact that your meetings are doing more harm than good. [18] First of all, I hear that when you meet as a Church there are divisions among you, and to a degree I believe it; [19] there have to be factions among you in order that also those who are approved among you may become known. [20] When you meet in one place, then, it is not to eat the Lord's supper, [21] for in eating, each one goes ahead with his own supper, and one goes hungry while another gets drunk. [22] Do you not have houses in which you can eat and drink? Or do you show contempt for the Church of God and make those who have nothing feel ashamed? What can I say to you? Shall I praise you? In this matter I do not praise you.

[23] For I received from the Lord what I also handed on to you, that the Lord Jesus, on the night he was handed over, took bread [24] and, after he had given thanks, broke it and said, "This is my Body that is for you. Do this in remembrance of me." [25] In the same way also the cup, after supper, saying, "This cup is the new covenant in my Blood. Do this, as often as you drink it, in remembrance of me." [26] For as often as you eat this bread and drink the cup, you proclaim the death of the Lord until he comes.

[33] Therefore, my brothers and sisters, when you come together to eat, wait for one another.

Responsorial Psalm: Psalms 40:7-8A, 8B-9, 10, 17

R. (1 Cor 11:26b) *Proclaim the death of the Lord until*
he comes again.

[7] Sacrifice or oblation you wished not,
   but ears open to obedience you gave me.
[8A] Burnt offerings or sin-offerings you sought
      not;
   then said I, "Behold I come."
R. *Proclaim the death of the Lord until he comes*
again.

[8B] "In the written scroll it is prescribed for me,
[9] To do your will, O my God, is my delight,
   and your law is within my heart!"
R. *Proclaim the death of the Lord until he comes*
again.

[10] I announced your justice in the vast
      assembly;
   I did not restrain my lips, as you, O LORD,
      know.

R. Proclaim the death of the Lord until he comes
again.

[17] May all who seek you
      exult and be glad in you
And may those who love your salvation
      say ever, "The LORD be glorified."
R. Proclaim the death of the Lord until he comes
again.

Alleluia: John 3:16
R. Alleluia, alleluia.
[16] God so loved the world that he gave his only-
      begotten Son,
so that everyone who believes in him might
      have eternal life.
R. Alleluia, alleluia.

Gospel: Luke 7:1-10
[1] When Jesus had finished all his words to the people, he entered Capernaum. [2] A centurion there had a slave who was ill and about to die, and he was valuable to him. [3] When he heard about Jesus, he sent elders of the Jews to him, asking him to come and save the life of his slave. [4] They approached Jesus and strongly urged him to come, saying, "He deserves to have you do this for him, [5] for he loves our nation and he built the synagogue for us." [6] And Jesus went with them, but when he was only a short distance from the house, the centurion sent friends to tell him, "Lord, do not trouble yourself, for I am not worthy to have you enter under my roof. [7] Therefore, I did not consider myself worthy to come to you; but say the word and let my servant be healed. [8] For I too am a person subject to authority, with soldiers subject to me. And I say to one, 'Go,' and he goes; and to another, 'Come here,' and he comes; and to my slave, 'Do this,' and he does it." [9] When Jesus heard this he was amazed at him and, turning, said to the crowd following him, "I tell you, not even in Israel have I found such faith." [10] When the messengers returned to the house, they found the slave in good health.

Tuesday September 17, 2024

Tuesday of Twenty-fourth Week in Ordinary Time
First Reading: 1 Corinthians 12:12-14, 27-31A
Brothers and sisters: [12] As a body is one though it has many parts, and all the parts of the body, though many, are one body, so also Christ. [13] For in one Spirit we were all baptized into one Body, whether Jews or Greeks, slaves or free persons, and we were all given to drink of one Spirit.

    [14] Now the body is not a single part, but many.

[27] Now you are Christ's Body, and individually parts of it. [28] Some people God has designated in the Church to be, first, Apostles; second, prophets; third, teachers; then, mighty deeds; then gifts of healing, assistance, administration, and varieties of tongues. [29] Are all Apostles? Are all prophets? Are all teachers? Do all work mighty deeds? [30] Do all have gifts of healing? Do all speak in tongues? Do all interpret? [31] Strive eagerly for the greatest spiritual gifts.

Responsorial Psalm: Psalms 100:1B-2,3, 4, 5

R. [3] *We are his people: the sheep of his flock.*

[1B] Sing joyfully to the LORD, all you lands;
[2] serve the LORD with gladness;
come before him with joyful song.
R. *We are his people: the sheep of his flock.*

[3] Know that the LORD is God;
he made us, his we are;
his people, the flock he tends.
R. *We are his people: the sheep of his flock.*

[4] Enter his gates with thanksgiving,
his courts with praise;
Give thanks to him; bless his name.
R. *We are his people: the sheep of his flock.*

[5] For he is good, the LORD,
whose kindness endures forever,
and his faithfulness, to all generations.
R. *We are his people: the sheep of his flock.*

Alleluia: Luke 7:16

R. Alleluia, alleluia.

[16] A great prophet has arisen in our midst and God has visited his people.

R. Alleluia, alleluia.

Gospel: Luke 7:11-17

[11] Jesus journeyed to a city called Nain, and his disciples and a large crowd accompanied him. [12] As he drew near to the gate of the city, a man who had died was being carried out, the only son of his mother, and she was a widow. A large crowd from the city was with her. [13] When the Lord saw her, he was moved with pity for her and said to her, "Do not weep." [14] He stepped forward and touched the coffin; at this the bearers halted, and he said, "Young man, I tell you, arise!" [15] The dead man sat up and began to speak, and Jesus gave him to his mother. [16] Fear seized them all, and they glorified God, exclaiming, "A great prophet has arisen in our midst," and "God has visited his people." [17] This report about him spread through the whole of Judea and in all the surrounding region.

Wednesday of Twenty-fourth Week in Ordinary Time
First Reading: 1 Corinthians 12:31-13:13

Brothers and sisters: [31] Strive eagerly for the greatest spiritual gifts.

But I shall show you a still more excellent way.

[1] If I speak in human and angelic tongues but do not have love, I am a resounding gong or a clashing cymbal. [2] And if I have the gift of prophecy and comprehend all mysteries and all knowledge; if I have all faith so as to move mountains, but do not have love, I am nothing. [3] If I give away everything I own, and if I hand my body over so that I may boast but do not have love, I gain nothing.

[4] Love is patient, love is kind. It is not jealous, love is not pompous, it is not inflated, [5] it is not rude, it does not seek its own interests, it is not quick-tempered, it does not brood over injury, [6] it does not rejoice over wrongdoing but rejoices with the truth. [7] It bears all things, believes all things, hopes all things, endures all things.

[8] Love never fails. If there are prophecies, they will be brought to nothing; if tongues, they will cease; if knowledge, it will be brought to nothing. [9] For we know partially and we prophesy partially, [10] but when the perfect comes, the partial will pass away. [11] When I was a child, I used to talk as a child, think as a child, reason as a child; when I became a man, I put aside childish things. [12] At present we see indistinctly, as in a mirror, but then face to face. At present I know partially; then I shall know fully, as I am fully known. [13] So faith, hope, love remain, these three; but the greatest of these is love.

Responsorial Psalm: Psalms 33:2-3, 4-5, 12 AND 22

R. [12] *Blessed the people the Lord has chosen to*
be his own.

[2] Give thanks to the LORD on the harp;
with the ten-stringed lyre chant his
praises.
[3] Sing to him a new song;
pluck the strings skillfully, with shouts of
gladness.
R. *Blessed the people the Lord has chosen to be*
his own.

[4] For upright is the word of the LORD,
and all his works are trustworthy.
[5] He loves justice and right;
of the kindness of the LORD the earth is
full.
R. *Blessed the people the Lord has chosen to be*
his own.

¹² Blessed the nation whose God is the LORD,
>   the people he has chosen for his own
>   inheritance.
²² May your kindness, O LORD, be upon us
>   who have put our hope in you.

R. Blessed the people the Lord has chosen to be
>   ***his own.***

Alleluia: John 6:63C, 68C

R. Alleluia, alleluia.

^{63C} Your words, Lord, are Spirit and life,

^{68C} you have the words of everlasting life.

R. Alleluia, alleluia.

Gospel: Luke 7:31-35

Jesus said to the crowds: ³¹ "To what shall I compare the people of this generation? What are they like? ³² They are like children who sit in the marketplace and call to one another,

'We played the flute for you, but you did not
>   dance.
>   We sang a dirge, but you did not weep.'

³³ For John the Baptist came neither eating food nor drinking wine, and you said, 'He is possessed by a demon.' ³⁴ The Son of Man came eating and drinking and you said, 'Look, he is a glutton and a drunkard, a friend of tax collectors and sinners.' ³⁵ But wisdom is vindicated by all her children."

Thursday September 19, 2024

Thursday of Twenty-fourth Week in Ordinary Time

First Reading: 1 Corinthians 15:1-11

¹ I am reminding you, brothers and sisters, of the Gospel I preached to you, which you indeed received and in which you also stand. ² Through it you are also being saved, if you hold fast to the word I preached to you, unless you believed in vain. ³ For I handed on to you as of first importance what I also received: that Christ died for our sins in accordance with the Scriptures; ⁴ that he was buried; that he was raised on the third day in accordance with the Scriptures; ⁵ that he appeared to Cephas, then to the Twelve. ⁶ After that, he appeared to more than five hundred brothers at once, most of whom are still living, though some have fallen asleep. ⁷ After that he appeared to James, then to all the Apostles. ⁸ Last of all, as to one born abnormally, he appeared to me. ⁹ For I am the least of the Apostles, not fit to be called an Apostle, because I persecuted the Church of God. ¹⁰ But by the grace of God I am what I am, and his grace to me has not been ineffective. Indeed, I have toiled harder than all of them; not I, however, but the grace of God that is with me. ¹¹ Therefore, whether it be I or they, so we preach and so you believed.

Responsorial Psalm: Psalms 118:1B-2, 16AB-17, 28

R. [(1)] *Give thanks to the Lord, for he is good.*

[1B] Give thanks to the LORD, for he is good,
    for his mercy endures forever.
[2] Let the house of Israel say,
    "His mercy endures forever."
R. *Give thanks to the Lord, for he is good.*

[16AB] "The right hand of the LORD is exalted;
    the right hand of the LORD has struck with
        power."
[17] I shall not die, but live,
    and declare the works of the LORD.
R. *Give thanks to the Lord, for he is good.*

[28] You are my God, and I give thanks to you;
    O my God, I extol you.
R. *Give thanks to the Lord, for he is good.*

Alleluia: Matthew 11:28

R. Alleluia, alleluia.
[28] Come to me, all you who labor and are
        burdened,
and I will give you rest, says the Lord.
R. Alleluia, alleluia.

Gospel: Luke 7:36-50

[36] A certain Pharisee invited Jesus to dine with him, and he entered the Pharisee's house and reclined at table. [37] Now there was a sinful woman in the city who learned that he was at table in the house of the Pharisee. Bringing an alabaster flask of ointment, [38] she stood behind him at his feet weeping and began to bathe his feet with her tears. Then she wiped them with her hair, kissed them, and anointed them with the ointment. [39] When the Pharisee who had invited him saw this he said to himself, "If this man were a prophet, he would know who and what sort of woman this is who is touching him, that she is a sinner." [40] Jesus said to him in reply, "Simon, I have something to say to you." "Tell me, teacher," he said. [41] "Two people were in debt to a certain creditor; one owed five hundred days' wages and the other owed fifty. [42] Since they were unable to repay the debt, he forgave it for both. Which of them will love him more?" [43] Simon said in reply, "The one, I suppose, whose larger debt was forgiven." He said to him, "You have judged rightly." [44] Then he turned to the woman and said to Simon, "Do you see this woman? When I entered your house, you did not give me water for my feet, but she has bathed

them with her tears and wiped them with her hair. [45] You did not give me a kiss, but she has not ceased kissing my feet since the time I entered. [46] You did not anoint my head with oil, but she anointed my feet with ointment. [47] So I tell you, her many sins have been forgiven; hence, she has shown great love. But the one to whom little is forgiven, loves little." [48] He said to her, "Your sins are forgiven." [49] The others at table said to themselves, "Who is this who even forgives sins?" [50] But he said to the woman, "Your faith has saved you; go in peace."

Friday of Twenty-fourth Week in Ordinary Time
First Reading: 1 Corinthians 15:12-20

Brothers and sisters: [12] If Christ is preached as raised from the dead, how can some among you say there is no resurrection of the dead? [13] If there is no resurrection of the dead, then neither has Christ been raised. [14] And if Christ has not been raised, then empty too is our preaching; empty, too, your faith. [15] Then we are also false witnesses to God, because we testified against God that he raised Christ, whom he did not raise if in fact the dead are not raised. [16] For if the dead are not raised, neither has Christ been raised, [17] and if Christ has not been raised, your faith is vain; you are still in your sins. [18] Then those who have fallen asleep in Christ have perished. [19] If for this life only we have hoped in Christ, we are the most pitiable people of all.

[20] But now Christ has been raised from the dead, the firstfruits of those who have fallen asleep.

Responsorial Psalm: Psalms 17: 1BCD, 6-7, 8B AND 15

R. [15b] *Lord, when your glory appears, my joy*
will be full.

[1BCD] Hear, O LORD, a just suit;
attend to my outcry;
hearken to my prayer from lips without
deceit.
R. *Lord, when your glory appears, my joy will be*
full.

[6] I call upon you, for you will answer me, O
God;
incline your ear to me; hear my word.
[7] Show your wondrous mercies,
O savior of those who flee
from their foes to refuge at your right hand.
R. *Lord, when your glory appears, my joy will be*
full.

[8B] Hide me in the shadow of your wings,

[15] But I in justice shall behold your face;
>> on waking, I shall be content in your
>> presence.
R. Lord, when your glory appears, my joy will be full.

Alleluia: cf. Matthew 11:25
R. Alleluia, alleluia.
[25] Blessed are you, Father, Lord of heaven and
>> earth;
you have revealed to little ones the
>> mysteries of the Kingdom.
R. Alleluia, alleluia.

Gospel: Luke 8:1-3
[1] Jesus journeyed from one town and village to another, preaching and proclaiming the good news of the Kingdom of God. Accompanying him were the Twelve [2] and some women who had been cured of evil spirits and infirmities, Mary, called Magdalene, from whom seven demons had gone out, [3] Joanna, the wife of Herod's steward Chuza, Susanna, and many others who provided for them out of their resources.

Saturday September 21, 2024

Feast of Saint Matthew, Apostle and Evangelist
First Reading: Ephesians 4:1-7, 11-13
Brothers and sisters: [1] I, a prisoner for the Lord, urge you to live in a manner worthy of the call you have received, [2] with all humility and gentleness, with patience, bearing with one another through love, [3] striving to preserve the unity of the Spirit through the bond of peace: [4] one Body and one Spirit, as you were also called to the one hope of your call; [5] one Lord, one faith, one baptism; [6] one God and Father of all, who is over all and through all and in all.
>> [7] But grace was given to each of us according to the measure of Christ's gift.
>> [11] And he gave some as Apostles, others as prophets, others as evangelists, others as pastors and teachers, [12] to equip the holy ones for the work of ministry, for building up the Body of Christ,[13] until we all attain to the unity of faith and knowledge of the Son of God, to mature manhood, to the extent of the full stature of Christ.

Responsorial Psalm: Psalms 19:2-3, 4-5
R. [5] Their message goes out through all the earth.
[2] The heavens declare the glory of God;
>> and the firmament proclaims his
>> handiwork.
[3] Day pours out the word to day,
>> and night to night imparts knowledge.

R. Their message goes out through all the earth.

⁴ Not a word nor a discourse
   whose voice is not heard;
⁵ Through all the earth their voice resounds,
   and to the ends of the world, their
      message.
R. Their message goes out through all the earth.

Alleluia: cf. *Te Deum*
R. Alleluia, alleluia.
We praise you, O God,
we acclaim you as Lord;
the glorious company of Apostles praise you.
R. Alleluia, alleluia.

Gospel: Matthew 9:9-13
⁹ As Jesus passed by, he saw a man named Matthew sitting at the customs post. He said to him, "Follow me." And he got up and followed him. ¹⁰ While he was at table in his house, many tax collectors and sinners came and sat with Jesus and his disciples. ¹¹ The Pharisees saw this and said to his disciples, "Why does your teacher eat with tax collectors and sinners?" ¹² He heard this and said, "Those who are well do not need a physician, but the sick do. ¹³ Go and learn the meaning of the words, *I desire mercy, not sacrifice*. I did not come to call the righteous but sinners."

Sunday September 22, 2024

Twenty-fifth Sunday in Ordinary Time, Year B
First Reading: Wisdom 2:12, 17-20
The wicked say:
¹² Let us beset the just one, because he is
      obnoxious to us;
   he sets himself against our doings,
reproaches us for transgressions of the law
      and charges us with violations of our
         training.
¹⁷ Let us see whether his words be true;
   let us find out what will happen to him.
¹⁸ For if the just one be the son of God, God will
      defend him
   and deliver him from the hand of his
      foes.
¹⁹ With revilement and torture let us put the

just one to the test
that we may have proof of his gentleness
and try his patience.
[20] Let us condemn him to a shameful death;
for according to his own words, God will
take care of him.

Responsorial Psalm: Psalms 54:3-4, 5, 6 AND 8

R. [(6b)] *The Lord upholds my life.*
[3] O God, by your name save me,
and by your might defend my cause.
[4] O God, hear my prayer;
hearken to the words of my mouth.
R. *The Lord upholds my life.*

[5] For the haughty men have risen up against me,
the ruthless seek my life;
they set not God before their eyes.
R. *The Lord upholds my life.*

[6] Behold, God is my helper;
the Lord sustains my life.
[8] Freely will I offer you sacrifice;
I will praise your name, O LORD, for its
goodness.
R. *The Lord upholds my life.*

Second Reading: James 3:16-4:3

Beloved: [16] Where jealousy and selfish ambition exist, there is disorder and every foul practice. [17] But the wisdom from above is first of all pure, then peaceable, gentle, compliant, full of mercy and good fruits, without inconstancy or insincerity. [18] And the fruit of righteousness is sown in peace for those who cultivate peace.
[1] Where do the wars and where do the conflicts among you come from? Is it not from your passions that make war within your members? [2] You covet but do not possess. You kill and envy but you cannot obtain; you fight and wage war. You do not possess because you do not ask. [3] You ask but do not receive, because you ask wrongly, to spend it on your passions.

Alleluia: cf. 2 Thessalonians 2:14

R. Alleluia, alleluia.
[14] God has called us through the Gospel
to possess the glory of our Lord Jesus Christ.

R. Alleluia, alleluia.

Gospel: Mark 9:30-37

[30] Jesus and his disciples left from there and began a journey through Galilee, but he did not wish anyone to know about it. [31] He was teaching his disciples and telling them, "The Son of Man is to be handed over to men and they will kill him, and three days after his death the Son of Man will rise." [32] But they did not understand the saying, and they were afraid to question him.

[33] They came to Capernaum and, once inside the house, he began to ask them, "What were you arguing about on the way?" [34] But they remained silent. They had been discussing among themselves on the way who was the greatest. [35] Then he sat down, called the Twelve, and said to them, "If anyone wishes to be first, he shall be the last of all and the servant of all." [36] Taking a child, he placed it in their midst, and putting his arms around it, he said to them, [37] "Whoever receives one child such as this in my name, receives me; and whoever receives me, receives not me but the One who sent me."

Monday September 23, 2024

Memorial of Saint Pius of Pietrelcina
First Reading: Proverbs 3:27-34

[27] Refuse no one the good on which he has a
     claim
     when it is in your power to do it for him.
[28] Say not to your neighbor, "Go, and come
     again,
     tomorrow I will give," when you can give
     at once.

[29] Plot no evil against your neighbor,
     against one who lives at peace with you.
[30] Quarrel not with a man without cause,
     with one who has done you no harm.

[31] Envy not the lawless man
     and choose none of his ways:
[32] To the LORD the perverse one is an
     abomination,
     but with the upright is his friendship.

[33] The curse of the LORD is on the house of the
     wicked,
     but the dwelling of the just he blesses;
[34] When dealing with the arrogant, he is stern,

but to the humble he shows kindness.

Responsorial Psalm: Psalms 15:2-3A, 3BC-4AB, 5

R. [(1)]*The just one shall live on your holy*
mountain, O Lord.

[2] He who walks blamelessly and does justice;
who thinks the truth in his heart
[3A] and slanders not with his tongue.

R. *The just one shall live on your holy mountain,*
O Lord.

[3BC] Who harms not his fellow man,
nor takes up a reproach against his
neighbor;
[4AB] By whom the reprobate is despised,
while he honors those who fear the LORD.

R. *The just one shall live on your holy mountain,*
O Lord.

[5] Who lends not his money at usury
and accepts no bribe against the
innocent.
He who does these things
shall never be disturbed.

R. *The just one shall live on your holy mountain,*
O Lord.

Alleluia: Matthew 5:16

R. Alleluia, alleluia.
[16] Let your light shine before others,
that they may see your good deeds and
glorify your heavenly Father.

R. Alleluia, alleluia.

Gospel: Luke 8:16-18

Jesus said to the crowd: [16] "No one who lights a lamp conceals it with a vessel or sets it under a bed; rather, he places it on a lampstand so that those who enter may see the light. [17] For there is nothing hidden that will not become visible, and nothing secret that will not be known and come to light. [18] Take care, then, how you hear. To anyone who has, more will be given, and from the one who has not, even what he seems to have will be taken away."

Tuesday of Twenty-fifth Week in Ordinary Time
First Reading: Proverbs 21:1-6, 10-13

[1] Like a stream is the king's heart in the hand
        of the LORD;
    wherever it pleases him, he directs it.

[2] All the ways of a man may be right in his
        own eyes,
    but it is the LORD who proves hearts.

[3] To do what is right and just
    is more acceptable to the LORD than
        sacrifice.

[4] Haughty eyes and a proud heart—
    the tillage of the wicked is sin.

[5] The plans of the diligent are sure of profit,
    but all rash haste leads certainly to
        poverty.

[6] Whoever makes a fortune by a lying tongue
    is chasing a bubble over deadly snares.

[10] The soul of the wicked man desires evil;
    his neighbor finds no pity in his eyes.

[11] When the arrogant man is punished, the
        simple are the wiser;
    when the wise man is instructed, he gains
        knowledge.

[12] The just man appraises the house of the
        wicked:
    there is one who brings down the wicked
        to ruin.

[13] He who shuts his ear to the cry of the poor
    will himself also call and not be heard.

Responsorial Psalm: Psalms 119:1, 27, 30, 34, 35, 44

R. *(35)Guide me, Lord, in the way of your*
commands.

[1] Blessed are they whose way is blameless,
who walk in the law of the LORD.
R. *Guide me, Lord, in the way of your*
commands.

[27] Make me understand the way of your
precepts,
and I will meditate on your wondrous
deeds.
R. *Guide me, Lord, in the way of your*
commands.

[30] The way of truth I have chosen;
I have set your ordinances before me.
R. *Guide me, Lord, in the way of your*
commands.

[34] Give me discernment, that I may observe
your law
and keep it with all my heart.
R. *Guide me, Lord, in the way of your*
commands.

[35] Lead me in the path of your commands,
for in it I delight.
R. *Guide me, Lord, in the way of your*
commands.

[44] And I will keep your law continually,
forever and ever.
R. *Guide me, Lord, in the way of your*
commands.

Alleluia: Luke 11:28

R. Alleluia, alleluia.
[28] Blessed are those who hear the word of God and observe it.
R. Alleluia, alleluia.

Gospel: Luke 8:19-21

[19] The mother of Jesus and his brothers came to him but were unable to join him because of the crowd. [20] He was told, "Your mother and your brothers are standing outside and they wish to see you." [21] He said to them in reply, "My mother and my brothers are those who hear the word of God and act on it."

Wednesday September 25, 2024

Wednesday of Twenty-fifth Week in Ordinary Time

First Reading: Proverbs 30:5-9

[5] Every word of God is tested;
    he is a shield to those who take refuge in
        him.
[6] Add nothing to his words,
    lest he reprove you, and you will be
        exposed as a deceiver.

[7] Two things I ask of you,
    deny them not to me before I die:
[8] Put falsehood and lying far from me,
    give me neither poverty nor riches;
    provide me only with the food I need;
[9] Lest, being full, I deny you,
    saying, "Who is the LORD?"
Or, being in want, I steal,
    and profane the name of my God.

Responsorial Psalm: Psalms 119:29, 72, 89, 101, 104, 163

R. [(105)] *Your word, O Lord, is a lamp for my feet.*
[29] Remove from me the way of falsehood,
    and favor me with your law.
R. *Your word, O Lord, is a lamp for my feet.*

[72] The law of your mouth is to me more
        precious
    than thousands of gold and silver pieces.
R. *Your word, O Lord, is a lamp for my feet.*

[89] Your word, O LORD, endures forever;
    it is firm as the heavens.
R. *Your word, O Lord, is a lamp for my feet.*

[101] From every evil way I withhold my feet,

that I may keep your words.
R. Your word, O Lord, is a lamp for my feet.

[104] Through your precepts I gain discernment;
therefore I hate every false way.
R. Your word, O Lord, is a lamp for my feet.

[163] Falsehood I hate and abhor;
your law I love.
R. Your word, O Lord, is a lamp for my feet.

Alleluia: Mark 1:15
R. Alleluia, alleluia.
[15] The Kingdom of God is at hand;
repent and believe in the Gospel.
R. Alleluia, alleluia.

Gospel: Luke 9:1-6
[1] Jesus summoned the Twelve and gave them power and authority over all demons and to cure diseases, [2] and he sent them to proclaim the Kingdom of God and to heal the sick. [3] He said to them, "Take nothing for the journey, neither walking stick, nor sack, nor food, nor money, and let no one take a second tunic. [4] Whatever house you enter, stay there and leave from there. [5] And as for those who do not welcome you, when you leave that town, shake the dust from your feet in testimony against them." [6] Then they set out and went from village to village proclaiming the good news and curing diseases everywhere.

Thursday September 26, 2024
Thursday of Twenty-fifth Week in Ordinary Time
First Reading: Ecclesiastes 1:2-11
[2] Vanity of vanities, says Qoheleth,
vanity of vanities! All things are vanity!
[3] What profit has man from all the labor
which he toils at under the sun?
[4] One generation passes and another comes,
but the world forever stays.
[5] The sun rises and the sun goes down;
then it presses on to the place where it
rises.
[6] Blowing now toward the south, then toward
the north,
the wind turns again and again, resuming
its rounds.

[7] All rivers go to the sea,
     yet never does the sea become full.
To the place where they go,
     the rivers keep on going.
[8] All speech is labored;
     there is nothing one can say.
The eye is not satisfied with seeing
     nor is the ear satisfied with hearing.

[9] What has been, that will be;
     what has been done, that will be done.
Nothing is new under the sun.
[10] Even the thing of which we say, "See, this is
        new!"
     has already existed in the ages that
        preceded us.
[11] There is no remembrance of the men of old;
     nor of those to come will there be any
        remembrance
     among those who come after them.

Responsorial Psalm: Psalms 90:3-4, 5-6, 12-13, 14 AND 17BC

R. [1] *In every age, O Lord, you have been our*
        refuge.
[3] You turn man back to dust,
     saying, "Return, O children of men."
[4] For a thousand years in your sight
     are as yesterday, now that it is past,
     or as a watch of the night.
R. *In every age, O Lord, you have been our*
        refuge.

[5] You make an end of them in their sleep;
     the next morning they are like the
        changing grass,
[6] Which at dawn springs up anew,
     but by evening wilts and fades.
R. *In every age, O Lord, you have been our*
        refuge.

[12] Teach us to number our days aright,
     that we may gain wisdom of heart.

13 Return, O LORD! How long?
    Have pity on your servants!
R. In every age, O Lord, you have been our refuge.

14 Fill us at daybreak with your kindness,
    that we may shout for joy and gladness
        all our days.
    17BC Prosper the work of our hands for us!
    Prosper the work of our hands!
R. In every age, O Lord, you have been our refuge.

Alleluia: John 14:6

R. Alleluia, alleluia.
6 I am the way and the truth and the life, says
        the Lord;
no one comes to the Father except through
        me.
R. Alleluia, alleluia.

Gospel: Luke 9:7-9

7 Herod the tetrarch heard about all that was happening, and he was greatly perplexed because some were saying, "John has been raised from the dead"; 8 others were saying, "Elijah has appeared"; still others, "One of the ancient prophets has arisen." 9 But Herod said, "John I beheaded. Who then is this about whom I hear such things?" And he kept trying to see him.

Friday September 27, 2024

Memorial of Saint Vincent de Paul, Priest
First Reading: Ecclesiastes 3:1-11

1 There is an appointed time for everything,
    and a time for everything under the
        heavens.
2 A time to be born, and a time to die;
    a time to plant, and a time to uproot the
        plant.
3 A time to kill, and a time to heal;
    a time to tear down, and a time to build.
4 A time to weep, and a time to laugh;
    a time to mourn, and a time to dance.
5 A time to scatter stones, and a time to gather
        them;

a time to embrace, and a time to be far
from embraces.
[6] A time to seek, and a time to lose;
a time to keep, and a time to cast away.
[7] A time to rend, and a time to sew;
a time to be silent, and a time to speak.
[8] A time to love, and a time to hate;
a time of war, and a time of peace.

[9] What advantage has the worker from his
toil?
[10] I have considered the task that God has
appointed
for the sons of men to be busied about.
[11] He has made everything appropriate to its
time,
and has put the timeless into their hearts,
without man's ever discovering,
from beginning to end, the work which
God has done.

Responsorial Psalm: Psalms 144:1B AND 2ABC, 3-4

R. [(1)] *Blessed be the Lord, my Rock!*
[1B] Blessed be the LORD, my rock,
[2ABC] my mercy and my fortress,
my stronghold, my deliverer,
My shield, in whom I trust.
R. *Blessed be the Lord, my Rock!*

[3] LORD, what is man, that you notice him;
the son of man, that you take thought of
him?
[4] Man is like a breath;
his days, like a passing shadow.
R. *Blessed be the Lord, my Rock!*

Alleluia: Mark 10:45

R. Alleluia, alleluia.
[45] The Son of Man came to serve
and to give his life as a ransom for many.
R. Alleluia, alleluia.

Gospel: Luke 9:18-22

[18] Once when Jesus was praying in solitude, and the disciples were with him, he asked them, "Who do the crowds say that I am?" [19] They said in reply, "John the Baptist; others, Elijah; still others, 'One of the ancient prophets has arisen.'" [20] Then he said to them, "But who do you say that I am?" Peter said in reply, "The Christ of God." [21] He rebuked them and directed them not to tell this to anyone.

[22] He said, "The Son of Man must suffer greatly and be rejected by the elders, the chief priests, and the scribes, and be killed and on the third day be raised."

Saturday September 28, 2024

Saturday of Twenty-Fifth Week in Ordinary Time
First Reading: Ecclesiastes 11:9-12:8

[9] Rejoice, O young man, while you are young
and let your heart be glad in the days of
your youth.
Follow the ways of your heart,
the vision of your eyes;
Yet understand that as regards all this
God will bring you to judgment.
[10] Ward off grief from your heart
and put away trouble from your
presence,
though the dawn of youth is fleeting.

[1] Remember your Creator in the days of your
youth,
before the evil days come
And the years approach of which you will
say,
I have no pleasure in them;
[2] Before the sun is darkened,
and the light, and the moon, and the
stars,
while the clouds return after the rain;
[3] When the guardians of the house tremble,
and the strong men are bent,
And the grinders are idle because they are
few,
and they who look through the windows
grow blind;
[4] When the doors to the street are shut,
and the sound of the mill is low;

505

When one waits for the chirp of a bird,
>> but all the daughters of song are
>>> suppressed;
[5] And one fears heights,
>> and perils in the street;
When the almond tree blooms,
>> and the locust grows sluggish
>> and the caper berry is without effect,
Because man goes to his lasting home,
>> and mourners go about the streets;
[6] Before the silver cord is snapped
>> and the golden bowl is broken,
And the pitcher is shattered at the spring,
>> and the broken pulley falls into the well,
[7] And the dust returns to the earth as it once
>>> was,
>> and the life breath returns to God who
>>> gave it.

[8] Vanity of vanities, says Qoheleth,
>> all things are vanity!

Responsorial Psalm: Psalms 90:3-4, 5-6, 12-13, 14 AND 17

R. [1] *In every age, O Lord, you have been our*
refuge.
[3] You turn man back to dust,
>> saying, "Return, O children of men."
[4] For a thousand years in your sight
>> are as yesterday, now that it is past,
>> or as a watch of the night.
R. *In every age, O Lord, you have been our*
refuge.

[5] You make an end of them in their sleep;
>> the next morning they are like the
>>> changing grass,
[6] Which at dawn springs up anew,
>> but by evening wilts and fades.
R. *In every age, O Lord, you have been our*
refuge.

[12] Teach us to number our days aright,

that we may gain wisdom of heart.

13 Return, O LORD! How long?
Have pity on your servants!

**R. In every age, O Lord, you have been our
refuge.**

14 Fill us at daybreak with your kindness,
that we may shout for joy and gladness
all our days.

17 And may the gracious care of the Lord our
God be ours;
prosper the work of our hands for us!
Prosper the work of our hands!

**R. In every age, O Lord, you have been our
refuge.**

Alleluia: 2 Timothy 1:10

R. Alleluia, alleluia.

10 Our Savior Christ Jesus destroyed death
and brought life to light through the Gospel.

R. Alleluia, alleluia.

Gospel: Luke 9:43B-45

43B While they were all amazed at his every deed, Jesus said to his disciples, 44 "Pay attention to what I am telling you. The Son of Man is to be handed over to men." 45 But they did not understand this saying; its meaning was hidden from them so that they should not understand it, and they were afraid to ask him about this saying.

Sunday September 29, 2024

Twenty-sixth Sunday in Ordinary Time, Year B

First Reading: Numbers 11:25-29

25 The LORD came down in the cloud and spoke to Moses. Taking some of the spirit that was on Moses, the LORD bestowed it on the seventy elders; and as the spirit came to rest on them, they prophesied.

26 Now two men, one named Eldad and the other Medad, were not in the gathering but had been left in the camp. They too had been on the list, but had not gone out to the tent; yet the spirit came to rest on them also, and they prophesied in the camp. 27 So, when a young man quickly told Moses, "Eldad and Medad are prophesying in the camp," 28 Joshua, son of Nun, who from his youth had been Moses' aide, said, "Moses, my lord, stop them." 29 But Moses answered him, "Are you jealous for my sake? Would that all the people of the LORD were prophets! Would that the LORD might bestow his spirit on them all!"

Responsorial Psalm: Psalms 19:8, 10, 12-13, 14

R. *(9a)* ***The precepts of the Lord give joy to the heart.***

[8] The law of the LORD is perfect,
    refreshing the soul;
the decree of the LORD is trustworthy,
    giving wisdom to the simple.
R. *The precepts of the Lord give joy to the heart.*

[10] The fear of the LORD is pure,
    enduring forever;
the ordinances of the LORD are true,
    all of them just.
R. *The precepts of the Lord give joy to the heart.*

[12] Though your servant is careful of them,
    very diligent in keeping them,
[13] yet who can detect failings?
    Cleanse me from my unknown faults!
R. *The precepts of the Lord give joy to the heart.*

[14] From wanton sin especially, restrain your
        servant;
    let it not rule over me.
Then shall I be blameless and innocent
    of serious sin.
R. *The precepts of the Lord give joy to the heart.*

Second Reading: James 5:1-6

[1] Come now, you rich, weep and wail over your impending miseries. [2] Your wealth has rotted away, your clothes have become moth-eaten, [3] your gold and silver have corroded, and that corrosion will be a testimony against you; it will devour your flesh like a fire. You have stored up treasure for the last days. [4] Behold, the wages you withheld from the workers who harvested your fields are crying aloud; and the cries of the harvesters have reached the ears of the Lord of hosts. [5] You have lived on earth in luxury and pleasure; you have fattened your hearts for the day of slaughter. [6] You have condemned; you have murdered the righteous one; he offers you no resistance.

Alleluia: cf. John 17:17B, 17A

R. Alleluia, alleluia.
[17B] Your word, O Lord, is truth;
[17A] consecrate us in the truth.
R. Alleluia, alleluia.

Gospel: Mark 9:38-43, 45, 47-48

[38] At that time, John said to Jesus, "Teacher, we saw someone driving out demons in your name, and we tried to prevent him because he does not follow us." [39] Jesus replied, "Do not prevent him. There is no one who performs a mighty deed in my name who can at the same time speak ill of me. [40] For whoever is not against us is for us. [41] Anyone who gives you a cup of water to drink because you belong to Christ, amen, I say to you, will surely not lose his reward.

[42] "Whoever causes one of these little ones who believe in me to sin, it would be better for him if a great millstone were put around his neck and he were thrown into the sea. [43] If your hand causes you to sin, cut it off. It is better for you to enter into life maimed than with two hands to go into Gehenna, into the unquenchable fire. [45] And if your foot causes you to sin, cut if off. It is better for you to enter into life crippled than with two feet to be thrown into Gehenna. [47] And if your eye causes you to sin, pluck it out. Better for you to enter into the kingdom of God with one eye than with two eyes to be thrown into Gehenna, [48] where 'their worm does not die, and the fire is not quenched.'"

Memorial of Saint Jerome, Priest & Doctor
First Reading: Job 1:6-22

[6] One day, when the angels of God came to present themselves before the LORD, Satan also came among them. [7] And the LORD said to Satan, "Whence do you come?" Then Satan answered the LORD and said, "From roaming the earth and patrolling it." [8] And the LORD said to Satan, "Have you noticed my servant Job, and that there is no one on earth like him, blameless and upright, fearing God and avoiding evil?" [9] But Satan answered the LORD and said, "Is it for nothing that Job is God-fearing? [10] Have you not surrounded him and his family and all that he has with your protection? You have blessed the work of his hands, and his livestock are spread over the land. [11] But now put forth your hand and touch anything that he has, and surely he will blaspheme you to your face." [12] And the LORD said to Satan, "Behold, all that he has is in your power; only do not lay a hand upon his person." So Satan went forth from the presence of the LORD.

[13] And so one day, while his sons and his daughters were eating and drinking wine in the house of their eldest brother, [14] a messenger came to Job and said, "The oxen were ploughing and the asses grazing beside them, [15] and the Sabeans carried them off in a raid. They put the herdsmen to the sword, and I alone have escaped to tell you." [16] While he was yet speaking, another came and said, "Lightning has fallen from heaven and struck the sheep and their shepherds and consumed them; and I alone have escaped to tell you." [17] While he was yet speaking, another messenger came and said, "The Chaldeans formed three columns, seized the camels, carried them off, and put those tending them to the sword, and I alone have escaped to tell you." [18] While he was yet speaking, another came and said, "Your sons and daughters were eating and drinking wine in the house of their eldest brother, [19] when suddenly a great wind came across the desert and smote the four corners of the house. It fell upon the young people and they are dead; and I alone have escaped to tell you." [20] Then Job began to tear his cloak and cut off his hair. He cast himself prostrate upon the ground, [21] and said,

"Naked I came forth from my mother's
            womb,
        and naked shall I go back again.
The LORD gave and the LORD has taken away;
        blessed be the name of the LORD!"

[22] In all this Job did not sin, nor did he say anything disrespectful of God.

Responsorial Psalm: Psalms 17:1BCD, 2-3, 6-7

R. [(6)]*Incline your ear to me and hear my word.*
[1BCD] Hear, O LORD, a just suit;
        attend to my outcry;
        hearken to my prayer from lips without
            deceit.
R. *Incline your ear to me and hear my word.*

[2] From you let my judgment come;
        your eyes behold what is right.
[3] Though you test my heart, searching it in the
            night,
        though you try me with fire, you shall
            find no malice in me.
R. *Incline your ear to me and hear my word.*

[6] I call upon you, for you will answer me, O
            God;
        incline your ear to me; hear my word.
[7] Show your wondrous mercies,
        O savior of those who flee
         from their foes to refuge at your right
            hand.
R. *Incline your ear to me and hear my word.*

Alleluia: Mark 10:45

R. Alleluia, alleluia.
[45] The Son of Man came to serve
and to give his life as a ransom for many.
R. Alleluia, alleluia.

Gospel: Luke 9:46-50

[46] An argument arose among the disciples about which of them was the greatest. [47] Jesus realized the intention of their hearts and took a child and placed it by his side [48] and said to them, "Whoever receives this child in my name receives me, and whoever receives me receives the one who sent me. For the one who is least among all of you is the one who is the greatest."

[49] Then John said in reply, "Master, we saw someone casting out demons in your name and we tried to prevent him because he does not follow in our company." [50] Jesus said to him, "Do not prevent him, for whoever is not against you is for you."

OCTOBER 2024
Tuesday October 1, 2024

Memorial of Saint Theresa of the Child Jesus, Virgin and Doctor
First Reading: Job 3:1-3, 11-17, 20-23

[1] Job opened his mouth and cursed his day.
[2] Job spoke out and said:

[3] Perish the day on which I was born,
   the night when they said, "The child is a
      boy!"

[11] Why did I not perish at birth,
   come forth from the womb and expire?
Or why was I not buried away like an
      untimely birth,
   like babes that have never seen the light?
[12] Wherefore did the knees receive me?
   or why did I suck at the breasts?

[13] For then I should have lain down and been
      tranquil;
   had I slept, I should then have been at
      rest
[14] With kings and counselors of the earth
   who built where now there are ruins
[15] Or with princes who had gold
   and filled their houses with silver.

[17] There the wicked cease from troubling,
   there the weary are at rest.

[20] Why is light given to the toilers,
   and life to the bitter in spirit?

511

²¹ They wait for death and it comes not;
  they search for it rather than for hidden
   treasures,
²² Rejoice in it exultingly,
  and are glad when they reach the grave:
²³ Those whose path is hidden from them,
  and whom God has hemmed in!

Responsorial Psalm: Psalms 88:2-3, 4-5,6,7-8

R. ⁽³⁾*Let my prayer come before you, Lord.*
² O LORD, my God, by day I cry out;
  at night I clamor in your presence.
³ Let my prayer come before you;
  incline your ear to my call for help.
R. Let my prayer come before you, Lord.

⁴ For my soul is surfeited with troubles
  and my life draws near to the nether
   world.
⁵ I am numbered with those who go down into
   the pit;
  I am a man without strength.
R. Let my prayer come before you, Lord.

⁶ My couch is among the dead,
  like the slain who lie in the grave,
Whom you remember no longer
  and who are cut off from your care.
R. Let my prayer come before you, Lord.

⁷ You have plunged me into the bottom of the
   pit,
  into the dark abyss.
⁸ Upon me your wrath lies heavy,
  and with all your billows you overwhelm
   me.
R. Let my prayer come before you, Lord.

Alleluia: Mark 10:45

R. Alleluia, alleluia.
⁴⁵ The Son of Man came to serve
and to give his life as a ransom for many.

R. Alleluia, alleluia.

Gospel: Luke 9:51-56

[51] When the days for Jesus to be taken up were fulfilled, he resolutely determined to journey to Jerusalem, [52] and he sent messengers ahead of him. On the way they entered a Samaritan village to prepare for his reception there, [53] but they would not welcome him because the destination of his journey was Jerusalem. [54] When the disciples James and John saw this they asked, "Lord, do you want us to call down fire from heaven to consume them?" [55] Jesus turned and rebuked them, and they journeyed to another village.

Wednesday October 2, 2024

Memorial of the Holy Guardian Angels
First Reading: Job 9:1-12, 14-16

[1] Job answered his friends and said:

[2] I know well that it is so;
>   but how can a man be justified before
>   God?
[3] Should one wish to contend with him,
>   he could not answer him once in a
>   thousand times.
[4] God is wise in heart and mighty in strength;
>   who has withstood him and remained
>   unscathed?

[5] He removes the mountains before they know
>   it;
>   he overturns them in his anger.
[6] He shakes the earth out of its place,
>   and the pillars beneath it tremble.
[7] He commands the sun, and it rises not;
>   he seals up the stars.

[8] He alone stretches out the heavens
>   and treads upon the crests of the sea.
[9] He made the Bear and Orion,
>   the Pleiades and the constellations of the
>   south;
[10] He does great things past finding out,
>   marvelous things beyond reckoning.

[11] Should he come near me, I see him not;

should he pass by, I am not aware of him;

¹² Should he seize me forcibly, who can say
        him nay?
      Who can say to him, "What are you
        doing?"

¹⁴ How much less shall I give him any answer,
      or choose out arguments against him!
¹⁵ Even though I were right, I could not answer
        him,
      but should rather beg for what was due
        me.
¹⁶ If I appealed to him and he answered my
        call,
      I could not believe that he would hearken
        to my words.

Responsorial Psalm: Psalms 88:10BC-11, 12-13, 14-15

R. *(3) Let my prayer come before you, Lord.*

¹⁰ᴮᶜ Daily I call upon you, O LORD;
      to you I stretch out my hands.
¹¹ Will you work wonders for the dead?
      Will the shades arise to give you thanks?

R. *Let my prayer come before you, Lord.*

¹² Do they declare your mercy in the grave,
      your faithfulness among those who have
        perished?
¹³ Are your wonders made known in the
        darkness,
      or your justice in the land of oblivion?

R. *Let my prayer come before you, Lord.*

¹⁴ But I, O LORD, cry out to you;
      with my morning prayer I wait upon you.
¹⁵ Why, O LORD, do you reject me;
      why hide from me your face?

R. *Let my prayer come before you, Lord.*

Alleluia: Philippians 3:8-9

R. Alleluia, alleluia.

⁸ I consider all things so much rubbish
⁹ that I may gain Christ and be found in him.

R. Alleluia, alleluia.

Gospel: Matthew 18:1-5, 10

[1] The disciples approached Jesus and said, "Who is the greatest in the Kingdom of heaven?" [2] He called a child over, placed it in their midst, [3] and said, "Amen, I say to you, unless you turn and become like children, you will not enter the Kingdom of heaven. [4] Whoever humbles himself like this child is the greatest in the Kingdom of heaven. [5] And whoever receives one child such as this in my name receives me.

[10] "See that you do not despise one of these little ones, for I say to you that their angels in heaven always look upon the face of my heavenly Father.

Thursday October 3, 2024

Thursday of Twenty-sixth Week in Ordinary Time

First Reading: Job 19:21-27

Job said:

[21] Pity me, pity me, O you my friends,
    for the hand of God has struck me!
[22] Why do you hound me as though you were
        divine,
    and insatiably prey upon me?

[23] Oh, would that my words were written
        down!
    Would that they were inscribed in a
        record:
[24] That with an iron chisel and with lead
    they were cut in the rock forever!
[25] But as for me, I know that my Vindicator
        lives,
    and that he will at last stand forth upon
        the dust;
[27] Whom I myself shall see:
    my own eyes, not another's, shall behold
        him,
And from my flesh I shall see God;
    my inmost being is consumed with
        longing.

Responsorial Psalm: Psalms 27:7-8A, 8B-9ABC, 13-14

R. [(13)] *I believe that I shall see the good things of*
        the Lord in the land of the living.
[7] Hear, O LORD, the sound of my call;
    have pity on me, and answer me.

8A Of you my heart speaks; you my glance
        seeks.
R. I believe that I shall see the good things of the
        Lord in the land of the living.

8B Your presence, O LORD, I seek.
9ABC Hide not your face from me;
        do not in anger repel your servant.
You are my helper: cast me not off.
R. I believe that I shall see the good things of the
        Lord in the land of the living.

13 I believe that I shall see the bounty of the
        LORD
    in the land of the living.
14 Wait for the LORD with courage;
        be stouthearted, and wait for the LORD.
R. I believe that I shall see the good things of the
        Lord in the land of the living.

Alleluia: Mark 1:15
R. Alleluia, alleluia.
15 The Kingdom of God is at hand;
repent and believe in the Gospel.
R. Alleluia, alleluia.

Gospel: Luke 10:1-12
1 Jesus appointed seventy-two other disciples whom he sent ahead of him in pairs to every town and place he intended to visit. 2 He said to them, "The harvest is abundant but the laborers are few; so ask the master of the harvest to send out laborers for his harvest. 3 Go on your way; behold, I am sending you like lambs among wolves. 4 Carry no money bag, no sack, no sandals; and greet no one along the way. 5 Into whatever house you enter, first say, 'Peace to this household.' 6 If a peaceful person lives there, your peace will rest on him; but if not, it will return to you. 7 Stay in the same house and eat and drink what is offered to you, for the laborer deserves his payment. Do not move about from one house to another. 8 Whatever town you enter and they welcome you, eat what is set before you, 9cure the sick in it and say to them, 'The Kingdom of God is at hand for you.' 10 Whatever town you enter and they do not receive you, go out into the streets and say, 11 'The dust of your town that clings to our feet, even that we shake off against you.' Yet know this: the Kingdom of God is at hand. 12 I tell you, it will be more tolerable for Sodom on that day than for that town."

Memorial of Saint Francis of Assisi
First Reading: Job 38:1, 12-21; 40:3-5

[1] The LORD addressed Job out of the storm and said:

[12] Have you ever in your lifetime commanded
        the morning
    and shown the dawn its place.
[13] For taking hold of the ends of the earth,
        till the wicked are shaken from its
        surface?
[14] The earth is changed as is clay by the seal,
        and dyed as though it were a garment;
[15] But from the wicked the light is withheld,
        and the arm of pride is shattered.

[16] Have you entered into the sources of the sea,
        or walked about in the depths of the
        abyss?
[17] Have the gates of death been shown to you,
        or have you seen the gates of darkness?
[18] Have you comprehended the breadth of the
        earth?
    Tell me, if you know all:
[19] Which is the way to the dwelling place of
        light,
    and where is the abode of darkness,
[20] That you may take them to their boundaries
        and set them on their homeward paths?
[21] You know, because you were born before
        them,
    and the number of your years is great!

[3] Then Job answered the LORD and said:

[4] Behold, I am of little account; what can I
        answer you?
    I put my hand over my mouth.
[5] Though I have spoken once, I will not do so
        again;
    though twice, I will do so no more.

Responsorial Psalm: Psalms 139:1-3, 7-8, 9-10, 13-14AB

R. (24b)*Guide me, Lord, along the everlasting way.*

¹ O LORD, you have probed me and you know
       me;
    ² you know when I sit and when I stand;
    you understand my thoughts from afar.
³ My journeys and my rest you scrutinize,
    with all my ways you are familiar.

R. *Guide me, Lord, along the everlasting way.*

⁷ Where can I go from your spirit?
    From your presence where can I flee?
⁸ If I go up to the heavens, you are there;
    if I sink to the nether world, you are
       present there.

R. *Guide me, Lord, along the everlasting way.*

⁹ If I take the wings of the dawn,
    if I settle at the farthest limits of the sea,
¹⁰ Even there your hand shall guide me,
    and your right hand hold me fast.

R. *Guide me, Lord, along the everlasting way.*

¹³ Truly you have formed my inmost being;
    you knit me in my mother's womb.
¹⁴ᴬᴮ I give you thanks that I am fearfully,
      wonderfully made;
    wonderful are your works.

R. *Guide me, Lord, along the everlasting way.*

Alleluia: Psalms 95:8

R. Alleluia, alleluia.

⁸ If today you hear his voice,
harden not your hearts.

R. Alleluia, alleluia.

Gospel: Luke 10:13-16

Jesus said to them, ¹³ "Woe to you, Chorazin! Woe to you, Bethsaida! For if the mighty deeds done in your midst had been done in Tyre and Sidon, they would long ago have repented, sitting in sackcloth and ashes. ¹⁴ But it will be more tolerable for Tyre and Sidon at the judgment than for you. ¹⁵ And as for you, Capernaum, 'Will you be exalted to heaven? You will go down to the netherworld.' ¹⁶ Whoever listens to you listens to me. Whoever rejects you rejects me. And whoever rejects me rejects the one who sent me."

Saturday of Twenty-sixth Week in Ordinary Time
First Reading: Job 42:1-3, 5-6, 12-17

[1] Job answered the LORD and said:

[2] I know that you can do all things,
    and that no purpose of yours can be
        hindered.
[3] I have dealt with great things that I do not
        understand;
    things too wonderful for me, which I
        cannot know.
[5] I had heard of you by word of mouth,
    but now my eye has seen you.
[6] Therefore I disown what I have said,
    and repent in dust and ashes.

[12] Thus the LORD blessed the latter days of Job more than his earlier ones. For he had fourteen thousand sheep, six thousand camels, a thousand yoke of oxen, and a thousand she-asses. [13] And he had seven sons and three daughters, [14] of whom he called the first Jemimah, the second Keziah, and the third Kerenhappuch. [15] In all the land no other women were as beautiful as the daughters of Job; and their father gave them an inheritance along with their brothers. [16] After this, Job lived a hundred and forty years; and he saw his children, his grandchildren, and even his great-grandchildren. Then Job died, old and full of years.

Responsorial Psalm: Psalms 119:66, 71, 75, 91, 125, 130

R. [135] *Lord, let your face shine on me.*
[66] Teach me wisdom and knowledge,
    for in your commands I trust.
R. *Lord, let your face shine on me.*

[71] It is good for me that I have been afflicted,
    that I may learn your statutes.
R. *Lord, let your face shine on me.*

[75] I know, O LORD, that your ordinances are just,
    and in your faithfulness you have
        afflicted me.
R. *Lord, let your face shine on me.*

[91] According to your ordinances they still stand

firm:
all things serve you.
R. Lord, let your face shine on me.

125 I am your servant; give me discernment
that I may know your decrees.
R. Lord, let your face shine on me.

130 The revelation of your words sheds light,
giving understanding to the simple.
R. Lord, let your face shine on me.

Alleluia: cf. Matthew 11:25
R. Alleluia, alleluia.
25 Blessed are you, Father, Lord of heaven and
earth,
you have revealed to little ones the
mysteries of the Kingdom.
R. Alleluia, alleluia.

Gospel: Luke 10:17-24
17 The seventy-two disciples returned rejoicing and said to Jesus, "Lord, even the demons are subject to us because of your name." 18 Jesus said, "I have observed Satan fall like lightning from the sky. 19 Behold, I have given you the power 'to tread upon serpents' and scorpions and upon the full force of the enemy and nothing will harm you. 20 Nevertheless, do not rejoice because the spirits are subject to you, but rejoice because your names are written in heaven."

21 At that very moment he rejoiced in the Holy Spirit and said, "I give you praise, Father, Lord of heaven and earth, for although you have hidden these things from the wise and the learned you have revealed them to the childlike. Yes, Father, such has been your gracious will. 22 All things have been handed over to me by my Father. No one knows who the Son is except the Father, and who the Father is except the Son and anyone to whom the Son wishes to reveal him."

23 Turning to the disciples in private he said, "Blessed are the eyes that see what you see. 24 For I say to you, many prophets and kings desired to see what you see, but did not see it, and to hear what you hear, but did not hear it."

Sunday October 6, 2024

Twenty-seventh Sunday in Ordinary Time, Year B
First Reading: Genesis 2:18-24
18 The LORD God said: "It is not good for the man to be alone. I will make a suitable partner for him." 19 So the LORD God formed out of the ground various wild animals and various birds of the air, and he brought them to the man to see what he would call them;

whatever the man called each of them would be its name. [20] The man gave names to all the cattle, all the birds of the air, and all wild animals; but none proved to be the suitable partner for the man.

[21] So the LORD God cast a deep sleep on the man, and while he was asleep, he took out one of his ribs and closed up its place with flesh. [22]The LORD God then built up into a woman the rib that he had taken from the man. When he brought her to the man, [23] the man said:

"This one, at last, is bone of my bones
	and flesh of my flesh;
this one shall be called 'woman,'
	for out of 'her man' this one has been
		taken."
[24] That is why a man leaves his father and mother and clings to his wife, and the two of them become one flesh.

Responsorial Psalm: Psalms 128:1-2,3,4-5, 6

R. (cf. 5) *May the Lord bless us all the days of our lives.*
[1] Blessed are you who fear the LORD,
	who walk in his ways!
[2] For you shall eat the fruit of your
		handiwork;
		blessed shall you be, and favored.
R. *May the Lord bless us all the days of our lives.*

[3] Your wife shall be like a fruitful vine
	in the recesses of your home,
your children like olive plants
	around your table.
R. *May the Lord bless us all the days of our lives.*

[4] Behold, thus is the man blessed
	who fears the LORD.
[5] The LORD bless you from Zion:
	may you see the prosperity of Jerusalem
	all the days of your life.
R. *May the Lord bless us all the days of our lives.*

[6] May you see your children's children.
	Peace be upon Israel!
R. *May the Lord bless us all the days of our lives.*

Second Reading: Hebrews 2:9-11

Brothers and sisters: [9] He "for a little while" was made "lower than the angels," that by the grace of God he might taste death for everyone.

[10] For it was fitting that he, for whom and through whom all things exist, in bringing many children to glory, should make the leader to their salvation perfect through suffering. [11] He who consecrates and those who are being consecrated all have one origin. Therefore, he is not ashamed to call them "brothers."

Alleluia: 1 John 4:12

R. Alleluia, alleluia.

[12] If we love one another, God remains in us
and his love is brought to perfection in us.

R. Alleluia, alleluia.

Gospel: Mark 10:2-16

[2] The Pharisees approached Jesus and asked, "Is it lawful for a husband to divorce his wife?" They were testing him. [3] He said to them in reply, "What did Moses command you?" [4] They replied, "Moses permitted a husband to write a bill of divorce and dismiss her." [5] But Jesus told them, "Because of the hardness of your hearts he wrote you this commandment. [6] But from the beginning of creation, *God made them male and female.* [7] *For this reason a man shall leave his father and mother and be joined to his wife,* [8] *and the two shall become one flesh.* So they are no longer two but one flesh. [9] Therefore what God has joined together, no human being must separate." [10] In the house the disciples again questioned Jesus about this. [11] He said to them, "Whoever divorces his wife and marries another commits adultery against her; [12] and if she divorces her husband and marries another, she commits adultery."

[13] And people were bringing children to him that he might touch them, but the disciples rebuked them. [14] When Jesus saw this he became indignant and said to them, "Let the children come to me; do not prevent them, for the kingdom of God belongs to such as these. [15] Amen, I say to you, whoever does not accept the kingdom of God like a child will not enter it." [16] Then he embraced them and blessed them, placing his hands on them.

Or Mark 10:2-12

[2] The Pharisees approached Jesus and asked, "Is it lawful for a husband to divorce his wife?" They were testing him. [3] He said to them in reply, "What did Moses command you?" [4] They replied, "Moses permitted a husband to write a bill of divorce and dismiss her." [5] But Jesus told them, "Because of the hardness of your hearts he wrote you this commandment. [6] But from the beginning of creation, *God made them male and female.* [7]*For this reason a man shall leave his father and mother and be joined to his wife,* [8] *and the two shall become one flesh.* So they are no longer two but one flesh. [9] Therefore what God has joined together, no human being must separate." [10] In the house the disciples

again questioned Jesus about this. [11] He said to them, "Whoever divorces his wife and marries another commits adultery against her; [12] and if she divorces her husband and marries another, she commits adultery."

Monday October 7, 2024

Memorial of Our Lady of the Rosary
First Reading: Galatians 1:6-12

Brothers and sisters: [6] I am amazed that you are so quickly forsaking the one who called you by the grace of Christ for a different gospel [7] (not that there is another). But there are some who are disturbing you and wish to pervert the Gospel of Christ. [8] But even if we or an angel from heaven should preach to you a gospel other than the one that we preached to you, let that one be accursed! [9] As we have said before, and now I say again, if anyone preaches to you a gospel other than the one that you received, let that one be accursed!

[10] Am I now currying favor with human beings or God? Or am I seeking to please people? If I were still trying to please people, I would not be a slave of Christ.

[11] Now I want you to know, brothers and sisters, that the Gospel preached by me is not of human origin. [12] For I did not receive it from a human being, nor was I taught it, but it came through a revelation of Jesus Christ.

Responsorial Psalm: Psalms 111:1B-2, 7-8, 9 AND 10C

R. [5] *The Lord will remember his covenant for ever.* or: *Alleluia.*

[1B] I will give thanks to the LORD with all my
        heart
    in the company and assembly of the just.
[2] Great are the works of the LORD,
    exquisite in all their delights.

R. [5] *The Lord will remember his covenant for ever.* or: *Alleluia.*

[7] The works of his hands are faithful and just;
    sure are all his precepts,
[8] Reliable forever and ever,
    wrought in truth and equity.

R. [5] *The Lord will remember his covenant for ever.* or: *Alleluia.*

[9] He has sent deliverance to his people;
    he has ratified his covenant forever;
    holy and awesome is his name.
[10C] His praise endures forever.

R. [5] *The Lord will remember his covenant for ever.* or: *Alleluia.*

Alleluia: John 13:34

R. Alleluia, alleluia.
[34] I give you a new commandment:
love one another as I have loved you.

R. Alleluia, alleluia.

Gospel: Luke 10:25-37

[25] There was a scholar of the law who stood up to test Jesus and said, "Teacher, what must I do to inherit eternal life?" [26] Jesus said to him, "What is written in the law? How do you read it?" [27] He said in reply, "You shall love the Lord, your God, with all your heart, with all your being, with all your strength, and with all your mind, and your neighbor as yourself." [28] He replied to him, "You have answered correctly; do this and you will live."

[29] But because he wished to justify himself, he said to Jesus, "And who is my neighbor?" [30] Jesus replied, "A man fell victim to robbers as he went down from Jerusalem to Jericho. They stripped and beat him and went off leaving him half-dead. [31] A priest happened to be going down that road, but when he saw him, he passed by on the opposite side. [32] Likewise a Levite came to the place, and when he saw him, he passed by on the opposite side. [33] But a Samaritan traveler who came upon him was moved with compassion at the sight. [34] He approached the victim, poured oil and wine over his wounds and bandaged them. Then he lifted him up on his own animal, took him to an inn, and cared for him. [35] The next day he took out two silver coins and gave them to the innkeeper with the instruction, 'Take care of him. If you spend more than what I have given you, I shall repay you on my way back.' [36] Which of these three, in your opinion, was neighbor to the robbers' victim?" [37] He answered, "The one who treated him with mercy." Jesus said to him, "Go and do likewise."

Tuesday October 8, 2024

Tuesday of Twenty-seventh Week in Ordinary Time

First Reading: Galatians 1:13-24

Brothers and sisters: [13] You heard of my former way of life in Judaism, how I persecuted the Church of God beyond measure and tried to destroy it, [14] and progressed in Judaism beyond many of my contemporaries among my race, since I was even more a zealot for my ancestral traditions. [15] But when he, who from my mother's womb had set me apart and called me through his grace, was pleased [16] to reveal his Son to me, so that I might proclaim him to the Gentiles, I did not immediately consult flesh and blood, [17] nor did I go up to Jerusalem to those who were Apostles before me; rather, I went into Arabia and then returned to Damascus.

[18] Then after three years I went up to Jerusalem to confer with Cephas and remained with him for fifteen days. [19] But I did not see any other of the Apostles, only James the brother of the Lord. [20] (As to what I am writing to you, behold, before God, I am not lying.) [21] Then I went into the regions of Syria and Cilicia. [22] And I was unknown personally to the churches of Judea that are in Christ; [23] they only kept hearing that "the one who once was persecuting us is now preaching the faith he once tried to destroy." [24] So they glorified God because of me.

Responsorial Psalm: Psalms 139:1B-3, 13-14AB, 14C-15

R. [24b] *Guide me, Lord, along the everlasting way.*

[1B] O LORD, you have probed me and you know

me;

^{2} you know when I sit and when I stand;
  you understand my thoughts from afar.
^{3} My journeys and my rest you scrutinize,
  with all my ways you are familiar.
R. Guide me, Lord, along the everlasting way.

^{13} Truly you have formed my inmost being;
  you knit me in my mother's womb.
^{14AB} I give you thanks that I am fearfully,
    wonderfully made;
  wonderful are your works.
R. Guide me, Lord, along the everlasting way.

^{14C} My soul also you knew full well;
    ^{15} nor was my frame unknown to you
When I was made in secret,
    when I was fashioned in the depths of the
      earth.
R. Guide me, Lord, along the everlasting way.

Alleluia: Luke 11:28
R. Alleluia, alleluia.
^{28} Blessed are those who hear the word of God and observe it.
R. Alleluia, alleluia.

Gospel: Luke 10:38-42
^{38} Jesus entered a village where a woman whose name was Martha welcomed him. ^{39} She had a sister named Mary who sat beside the Lord at his feet listening to him speak. ^{40} Martha, burdened with much serving, came to him and said, "Lord, do you not care that my sister has left me by myself to do the serving? Tell her to help me." ^{41} The Lord said to her in reply, "Martha, Martha, you are anxious and worried about many things. ^{42} There is need of only one thing. Mary has chosen the better part and it will not be taken from her."

Wednesday October 9, 2024

Wednesday of the Twenty-seventh Week in Ordinary Time
First Reading: Galatians 2:1-2, 7-14

Brothers and sisters: ^{1} After fourteen years I again went up to Jerusalem with Barnabas, taking Titus along also. ^{2} I went up in accord with a revelation, and I presented to them the Gospel that I preach to the Gentiles– but privately to those of repute– so that I might not be running, or have run, in vain. ^{7} On the contrary, when they saw that I had been entrusted with the Gospel to the uncircumcised, just as Peter to the circumcised, ^{8} for the one who worked in Peter for an apostolate to the circumcised worked also in me for the

Gentiles, [9] and when they recognized the grace bestowed upon me, James and Cephas and John, who were reputed to be pillars, gave me and Barnabas their right hands in partnership, that we should go to the Gentiles and they to the circumcised. [10] Only, we were to be mindful of the poor, which is the very thing I was eager to do.

[11] And when Cephas came to Antioch, I opposed him to his face because he clearly was wrong. [12] For, until some people came from James, he used to eat with the Gentiles; but when they came, he began to draw back and separated himself, because he was afraid of the circumcised. [13] And the rest of the Jews acted hypocritically along with him, with the result that even Barnabas was carried away by their hypocrisy. [14] But when I saw that they were not on the right road in line with the truth of the Gospel, I said to Cephas in front of all, "If you, though a Jew, are living like a Gentile and not like a Jew, how can you compel the Gentiles to live like Jews?"

Responsorial Psalm: Psalms 117:1BC, 2

**R. Go out to all the world, and tell the Good
            News.**

[1BC] Praise the LORD, all you nations,
        glorify him, all you peoples!

**R. Go out to all the world, and tell the Good
            News.**

[2] For steadfast is his kindness toward us,
        and the fidelity of the LORD endures
            forever.

**R. Go out to all the world, and tell the Good
            News.**

Alleluia: Romans 8:15BC

R. Alleluia, alleluia.

[15BC] You have received a spirit of adoption as
                sons
through which we cry: Abba! Father!

R. Alleluia, alleluia.

Gospel: Luke 11:1-4

[1] Jesus was praying in a certain place, and when he had finished, one of his disciples said to him, "Lord, teach us to pray just as John taught his disciples." [2] He said to them, "When you pray, say:

Father, hallowed be your name,
        your Kingdom come.
        [3] Give us each day our daily bread
        [4] and forgive us our sins
        for we ourselves forgive everyone in debt

to us,
and do not subject us to the final test."

Thursday of the Twenty-seventh Week in Ordinary Time

First Reading: Galatians 3:1-5

[1] O stupid Galatians! Who has bewitched you, before whose eyes Jesus Christ was publicly portrayed as crucified? [2] I want to learn only this from you: did you receive the Spirit from works of the law, or from faith in what you heard? [3] Are you so stupid? After beginning with the Spirit, are you now ending with the flesh? [4] Did you experience so many things in vain?– if indeed it was in vain. [5] Does, then, the one who supplies the Spirit to you and works mighty deeds among you do so from works of the law or from faith in what you heard?

Responsorial Psalm: Luke 1:69-70, 71-72, 73-75

R. [68] *Blessed be the Lord, the God of Israel; he
has come to his people.*

[69] He has raised up for us a mighty savior,
born of the house of his servant David.

R. *Blessed be the Lord, the God of Israel; he has
come to his people.*

[70] Through his holy prophets he promised of
old
[71] that he would save us from our enemies,
from the hands of all who hate us.
[72] He promised to show mercy to our fathers
and to remember his holy covenant.

R. *Blessed be the Lord, the God of Israel; he has
come to his people.*

[73] This was the oath he swore to our father
Abraham:
to set us free from the hands of our
enemies,
[74] free to worship him without fear,
[75] holy and righteous in his sight
all the days of our life.

R. *Blessed be the Lord, the God of Israel; he has
come to his people.*

Alleluia: cf. Acts 16:14B

R. Alleluia, alleluia.
[14B] Open our hearts, O Lord,

to listen to the words of your Son.
R. Alleluia, alleluia.

Gospel: Luke 11:5-13

Jesus said to his disciples: [5] "Suppose one of you has a friend to whom he goes at midnight and says, 'Friend, lend me three loaves of bread, [6] for a friend of mine has arrived at my house from a journey and I have nothing to offer him,' [7] and he says in reply from within, 'Do not bother me; the door has already been locked and my children and I are already in bed. I cannot get up to give you anything.' [8] I tell you, if he does not get up to give him the loaves because of their friendship, he will get up to give him whatever he needs because of his persistence.

[9] "And I tell you, ask and you will receive; seek and you will find; knock and the door will be opened to you. [10] For everyone who asks, receives; and the one who seeks, finds; and to the one who knocks, the door will be opened. [11] What father among you would hand his son a snake when he asks for a fish? [12] Or hand him a scorpion when he asks for an egg? [13] If you then, who are wicked, know how to give good gifts to your children, how much more will the Father in heaven give the Holy Spirit to those who ask him?"

Friday October 11, 2024

Friday of the Twenty-seventh Week in Ordinary Time
First Reading: Galatians 3:7-14

Brothers and sisters: [7] Realize that it is those who have faith who are children of Abraham. [8] Scripture, which saw in advance that God would justify the Gentiles by faith, foretold the good news to Abraham, saying, *Through you shall all the nations be blessed.* [9] Consequently, those who have faith are blessed along with Abraham who had faith.[10] For all who depend on works of the law are under a curse; for it is written, *Cursed be everyone who does not persevere in doing all the things written in the book of the law.* [11] And that no one is justified before God by the law is clear, for *the one who is righteous by faith will live.* [12] But the law does not depend on faith; rather, *the one who does these things will live by them.* [13] Christ ransomed us from the curse of the law by becoming a curse for us, for it is written, *Cursed be everyone who hangs on a tree,*[14] that the blessing of Abraham might be extended to the Gentiles through Christ Jesus, so that we might receive the promise of the Spirit through faith.

Responsorial Psalm: Psalms 111:1B-2, 3-4, 5-6

R. *[5] The Lord will remember his covenant for ever.*
[1BC] I will give thanks to the LORD with all my
          heart
     in the company and assembly of the just.
[2] Great are the works of the LORD,
          exquisite in all their delights.
R. The Lord will remember his covenant for ever.

[3] Majesty and glory are his work,
 and his justice endures forever.
[4] He has won renown for his wondrous deeds;
 gracious and merciful is the LORD.
R. The Lord will remember his covenant for ever.

[5] He has given food to those who fear him;
 he will forever be mindful of his
  covenant.
[6] He has made known to his people the power
  of his works,
 giving them the inheritance of the
  nations.
R. The Lord will remember his covenant for ever.

Alleluia: John 12:31B-32
R. Alleluia, alleluia.
[31B] The prince of this world will now be cast out,
[32] and when I am lifted up from the earth
I will draw all to myself, says the Lord.
R. Alleluia, alleluia.

Gospel: Luke 11:15-26
[15] When Jesus had driven out a demon, some of the crowd said: "By the power of Beelzebul, the prince of demons, he drives out demons." [16] Others, to test him, asked him for a sign from heaven. [17] But he knew their thoughts and said to them, "Every kingdom divided against itself will be laid waste and house will fall against house. [18] And if Satan is divided against himself, how will his kingdom stand? For you say that it is by Beelzebul that I drive out demons. [19] If I, then, drive out demons by Beelzebul, by whom do your own people drive them out? Therefore they will be your judges. [20] But if it is by the finger of God that I drive out demons, then the Kingdom of God has come upon you. [21] When a strong man fully armed guards his palace, his possessions are safe. [22] But when one stronger than he attacks and overcomes him, he takes away the armor on which he relied and distributes the spoils. [23] Whoever is not with me is against me, and whoever does not gather with me scatters.

[24] "When an unclean spirit goes out of someone, it roams through arid regions searching for rest but, finding none, it says, 'I shall return to my home from which I came.' [25] But upon returning, it finds it swept clean and put in order. [26] Then it goes and brings back seven other spirits more wicked than itself who move in and dwell there, and the last condition of that man is worse than the first."

Saturday of the Twenty-seventh Week in Ordinary Time
First Reading: Galatians 3:22-29

Brothers and sisters: [22] Scripture confined all things under the power of sin, that through faith in Jesus Christ the promise might be given to those who believe.

[23] Before faith came, we were held in custody under law, confined for the faith that was to be revealed. [24] Consequently, the law was our disciplinarian for Christ, that we might be justified by faith. [25] But now that faith has come, we are no longer under a disciplinarian. [26] For through faith you are all children of God in Christ Jesus. [27] For all of you who were baptized into Christ have clothed yourselves with Christ. [28] There is neither Jew nor Greek, there is neither slave nor free person, there is not male and female; for you are all one in Christ Jesus. [29] And if you belong to Christ, then you are Abraham's descendants, heirs according to the promise.

Responsorial Psalm: Psalms 105:2-3,4-5, 6-7

R. [8a] *The Lord remembers his covenant for ever.* or: *Alleluia.*

[2] Sing to him, sing his praise,
     proclaim all his wondrous deeds.
[3] Glory in his holy name;
     rejoice, O hearts that seek the LORD!

R. *The Lord remembers his covenant for ever.* or: *Alleluia.*

[4] Look to the LORD in his strength;
     seek to serve him constantly.
[5] Recall the wondrous deeds that he has
          wrought,
     his portents, and the judgments he has
          uttered.

R. *The Lord remembers his covenant for ever.* or: *Alleluia.*

[6] You descendants of Abraham, his servants,
     sons of Jacob, his chosen ones!
[7] He, the LORD, is our God;
     throughout the earth his judgments
          prevail.

R. *The Lord remembers his covenant for ever.* or: *Alleluia.*

Alleluia: Luke 11:28

R. Alleluia, alleluia.
[28] Blessed are those who hear the word of God and observe it.
R. Alleluia, alleluia.

Gospel: Luke 11:27-28

27 While Jesus was speaking, a woman from the crowd called out and said to him, "Blessed is the womb that carried you and the breasts at which you nursed." 28 He replied, "Rather, blessed are those who hear the word of God and observe it."

Sunday October 13, 2024

Twenty-eighth Sunday in Ordinary Time, Year B
First Reading: Wisdom 7:7-11

7 I prayed, and prudence was given me;
    I pleaded, and the spirit of wisdom came
        to me.
8 I preferred her to scepter and throne,
and deemed riches nothing in comparison
        with her,
    9 nor did I liken any priceless gem to her;
because all gold, in view of her, is a little
        sand,
    and before her, silver is to be accounted
        mire.
10 Beyond health and comeliness I loved her,
and I chose to have her rather than the light,
    because the splendor of her never yields
        to sleep.
11 Yet all good things together came to me in
        her company,
    and countless riches at her hands.

Responsorial Psalm: Psalms 90:12-13, 14-15, 16-17

R. (14) *Fill us with your love, O Lord, and we will*
                sing for joy!
12 Teach us to number our days aright,
    that we may gain wisdom of heart.
13 Return, O LORD! How long?
    Have pity on your servants!
R. *Fill us with your love, O Lord, and we will*
                sing for joy!

14 Fill us at daybreak with your kindness,
    that we may shout for joy and gladness
        all our days.
15 Make us glad, for the days when you afflicted
        us,

531

for the years when we saw evil.
***R. Fill us with your love, O Lord, and we will
sing for joy!***

[16] Let your work be seen by your servants
   and your glory by their children;
[17] and may the gracious care of the LORD our
      God be ours;
   prosper the work of our hands for us!
   Prosper the work of our hands!
***R. Fill us with your love, O Lord, and we will
sing for joy!***

Second Reading: Hebrews 4:12-13

Brothers and sisters: [12] Indeed the word of God is living and effective, sharper than any two-edged sword, penetrating even between soul and spirit, joints and marrow, and able to discern reflections and thoughts of the heart. [13] No creature is concealed from him, but everything is naked and exposed to the eyes of him to whom we must render an account.

Alleluia: Matthew 5:3

R. Alleluia, alleluia.
[3] Blessed are the poor in spirit,
for theirs is the kingdom of heaven.
R. Alleluia, alleluia.

Gospel: Mark 10:17-30

[17] As Jesus was setting out on a journey, a man ran up, knelt down before him, and asked him, "Good teacher, what must I do to inherit eternal life?" [18] Jesus answered him, "Why do you call me good? No one is good but God alone. [19] You know the commandments: *You shall not kill; you shall not commit adultery; you shall not steal; you shall not bear false witness; you shall not defraud; honor your father and your mother.*" [20] He replied and said to him, "Teacher, all of these I have observed from my youth." [21] Jesus, looking at him, loved him and said to him, "You are lacking in one thing. Go, sell what you have, and give to the poor and you will have treasure in heaven; then come, follow me." [22] At that statement his face fell, and he went away sad, for he had many possessions.

[23] Jesus looked around and said to his disciples, "How hard it is for those who have wealth to enter the kingdom of God!" [24] The disciples were amazed at his words. So Jesus again said to them in reply, "Children, how hard it is to enter the kingdom of God! [25] It is easier for a camel to pass through the eye of a needle than for one who is rich to enter the kingdom of God." [26] They were exceedingly astonished and said among themselves, "Then who can be saved?" [27] Jesus looked at them and said, "For human beings it is impossible, but not for God. All things are possible for God." [28] Peter began to say to him, "We have given up everything and followed you." [29] Jesus said, "Amen, I say to you, there

is no one who has given up house or brothers or sisters or mother or father or children or lands for my sake and for the sake of the gospel ³⁰ who will not receive a hundred times more now in this present age: houses and brothers and sisters and mothers and children and lands, with persecutions, and eternal life in the age to come."

Or Mark 10:17-27

¹⁷ As Jesus was setting out on a journey, a man ran up, knelt down before him, and asked him, "Good teacher, what must I do to inherit eternal life?" ¹⁸ Jesus answered him, "Why do you call me good? No one is good but God alone. ¹⁹ You know the commandments: *You shall not kill; you shall not commit adultery; you shall not steal; you shall not bear false witness; you shall not defraud; honor your father and your mother*." ²⁰ He replied and said to him, "Teacher, all of these I have observed from my youth." ²¹ Jesus, looking at him, loved him and said to him, "You are lacking in one thing. Go, sell what you have, and give to the poor and you will have treasure in heaven; then come, follow me." ²² At that statement his face fell, and he went away sad, for he had many possessions.

²³ Jesus looked around and said to his disciples, "How hard it is for those who have wealth to enter the kingdom of God!" ²⁴ The disciples were amazed at his words. So Jesus again said to them in reply, "Children, how hard it is to enter the kingdom of God! ²⁵ It is easier for a camel to pass through the eye of a needle than for one who is rich to enter the kingdom of God." ²⁶ They were exceedingly astonished and said among themselves, "Then who can be saved?" ²⁷ Jesus looked at them and said, "For human beings it is impossible, but not for God. All things are possible for God."

Monday October 14, 2024

Monday of Twenty-eighth Week in Ordinary Time
First Reading: Galatians 4:22-24, 26-27, 31–5:1

Brothers and sisters: ²² It is written that Abraham had two sons, one by the slave woman and the other by the freeborn woman. ²³ The son of the slave woman was born naturally, the son of the freeborn through a promise. ²⁴ Now this is an allegory. These women represent two covenants. One was from Mount Sinai, bearing children for slavery; this is Hagar. ²⁶ But the Jerusalem above is freeborn, and she is our mother. ²⁷ For it is written:
Rejoice, you barren one who bore no children;
*   break forth and shout, you who were not*
*   in labor;*
for more numerous are the children of the
*   deserted one*
*   than of her who has a husband.*

³¹ Therefore, brothers and sisters, we are
children not of the slave woman but of the
freeborn woman.
¹ For freedom Christ set us free; so stand

firm and do not submit again to the yoke of
slavery.

Responsorial Psalm: Psalms 113:1B-2, 3-4, 5A AND 6-7

R. *(see 2)* **Blessed be the name of the Lord forever.** or: *Alleluia, alleluia.*

1B Praise, you servants of the LORD,
　　praise the name of the LORD.
2 Blessed be the name of the LORD
　　both now and forever.

R. **Blessed be the name of the Lord forever.** or: *Alleluia, alleluia.*

3 From the rising to the setting of the sun
　　is the name of the LORD to be praised.
4 High above all nations is the LORD;
　　above the heavens is his glory.

R. **Blessed be the name of the Lord forever.** or: *Alleluia, alleluia.*

5A Who is like the LORD, our God,
　　6 who looks upon the heavens and the
　　　　earth below?
7 He raises up the lowly from the dust;
　　from the dunghill he lifts up the poor.

R. **Blessed be the name of the Lord forever.** or: *Alleluia, alleluia.*

Alleluia: Psalms 95:8

R. Alleluia, alleluia.
8 If today you hear his voice,
harden not your hearts.
R. Alleluia, alleluia.

Gospel: Luke 11:29-32

29 While still more people gathered in the crowd, Jesus said to them, "This generation is an evil generation; it seeks a sign, but no sign will be given it, except the sign of Jonah. 30 Just as Jonah became a sign to the Ninevites, so will the Son of Man be to this generation. 31 At the judgment the queen of the south will rise with the men of this generation and she will condemn them, because she came from the ends of the earth to hear the wisdom of Solomon, and there is something greater than Solomon here. 32 At the judgment the men of Nineveh will arise with this generation and condemn it, because at the preaching of Jonah they repented, and there is something greater than Jonah here."

Memorial of Saint Teresa of Avila, Virgin and Doctor
First Reading: Galatians 5:1-6

Brothers and sisters: [1] For freedom Christ set us free; so stand firm and do not submit again to the yoke of slavery.

[2] It is I, Paul, who am telling you that if you have yourselves circumcised, Christ will be of no benefit to you. [3] Once again I declare to every man who has himself circumcised that he is bound to observe the entire law. [4] You are separated from Christ, you who are trying to be justified by law; you have fallen from grace. [5] For through the Spirit, by faith, we await the hope of righteousness. [6] For in Christ Jesus, neither circumcision nor uncircumcision counts for anything, but only faith working through love.

Responsorial Psalm: Psalms 119:41, 43, 44, 45, 47, 48

R. *(41a)* *Let your mercy come to me, O Lord.*

[41] Let your mercy come to me, O LORD,
    your salvation according to your promise.
R. *Let your mercy come to me, O Lord.*

[43] Take not the word of truth from my mouth,
    for in your ordinances is my hope.
R. *Let your mercy come to me, O Lord.*

[44] And I will keep your law continually,
    forever and ever.
R. *Let your mercy come to me, O Lord.*

[45] And I will walk at liberty,
    because I seek your precepts.
R. *Let your mercy come to me, O Lord.*

[47] And I will delight in your commands,
    which I love.
R. *Let your mercy come to me, O Lord.*

[48] And I will lift up my hands to your
        commands
    and meditate on your statutes.
R. *Let your mercy come to me, O Lord.*

Alleluia: Hebrews 4:12
R. Alleluia, alleluia.
[12] The word of God is living and effective,

able to discern reflections and thoughts of
     the heart.
R. Alleluia, alleluia.

Gospel: Luke 11:37-41

[37] After Jesus had spoken, a Pharisee invited him to dine at his home. He entered and reclined at table to eat. [38] The Pharisee was amazed to see that he did not observe the prescribed washing before the meal. [39] The Lord said to him, "Oh you Pharisees! Although you cleanse the outside of the cup and the dish, inside you are filled with plunder and evil. [40] You fools! Did not the maker of the outside also make the inside? [41] But as to what is within, give alms, and behold, everything will be clean for you."

Wednesday October 16, 2024

Wednesday of Twenty-eighth Week in Ordinary Time

First Reading: Galatians 5:18-25

Brothers and sisters: [18] If you are guided by the Spirit, you are not under the law. [19] Now the works of the flesh are obvious: immorality, impurity, licentiousness, [20] idolatry, sorcery, hatreds, rivalry, jealousy, outbursts of fury, acts of selfishness, dissensions, factions, [21] occasions of envy, drinking bouts, orgies, and the like. I warn you, as I warned you before, that those who do such things will not inherit the Kingdom of God. [22] In contrast, the fruit of the Spirit is love, joy, peace, patience, kindness, generosity, faithfulness, [23] gentleness, self-control. Against such there is no law. [24] Now those who belong to Christ Jesus have crucified their flesh with its passions and desires. [25] If we live in the Spirit, let us also follow the Spirit.

Responsorial Psalm: Psalms 1:1-2, 3, 4 & 6

R. (see Jn 8:12) *Those who follow you, Lord, will*
             have the light of life.

[1] Blessed the man who follows not
     the counsel of the wicked
Nor walks in the way of sinners,
     nor sits in the company of the insolent,
[2] But delights in the law of the LORD
     and meditates on his law day and night.
R. Those who follow you, Lord, will have the
     light of life.

[3] He is like a tree
     planted near running water,
That yields its fruit in due season,
     and whose leaves never fade.
     Whatever he does, prospers.
R. Those who follow you, Lord, will have the

light of life.

4 Not so the wicked, not so;
        they are like chaff which the wind drives
            away.
6 For the LORD watches over the way of the
            just,
        but the way of the wicked vanishes.
R. Those who follow you, Lord, will have the
            light of life.

Alleluia: John 10:27
R. Alleluia, alleluia.
27 My sheep hear my voice, says the Lord;
I know them, and they follow me.
R. Alleluia, alleluia.

Gospel: Luke 11:42-46
The Lord said: 42 "Woe to you Pharisees! You pay tithes of mint and of rue and of every garden herb, but you pay no attention to judgment and to love for God. These you should have done, without overlooking the others. 43 Woe to you Pharisees! You love the seat of honor in synagogues and greetings in marketplaces. 44 Woe to you! You are like unseen graves over which people unknowingly walk."

45 Then one of the scholars of the law said to him in reply, "Teacher, by saying this you are insulting us too." 46 And he said, "Woe also to you scholars of the law! You impose on people burdens hard to carry, but you yourselves do not lift one finger to touch them."

Thursday October 17, 2024

Memorial of Saint Ignatius of Antioch, Bishop and Martyr
First Reading: Ephesians 1:1-10
1 Paul, an Apostle of Christ Jesus by the will of God, to the holy ones who are in Ephesus and faithful in Christ Jesus: 2 grace to you and peace from God our Father and the Lord Jesus Christ.

3 Blessed be the God and Father of our Lord Jesus Christ, who has blessed us in Christ with every spiritual blessing in the heavens, 4 as he chose us in him, before the foundation of the world, to be holy and without blemish before him. In love 5 he destined us for adoption to himself through Jesus Christ, in accord with the favor of his will, 6 for the praise of the glory of his grace that he granted us in the beloved.

7 In Christ we have redemption by his Blood, the forgiveness of transgressions, in accord with the riches of his grace 8 that he lavished upon us. In all wisdom and insight, 9 he has made known to us the mystery of his will in accord with his favor that he set forth in him 10 as a plan for the fullness of times, to sum up all things in Christ, in heaven and on earth.

Responsorial Psalm: Psalms 98:1, 2-3AB, 3CD-4, 5-6

R. [2a] *The Lord has made known his salvation.*

[1] Sing to the LORD a new song,
>for he has done wondrous deeds;
His right hand has won victory for him,
>his holy arm.

R. *The Lord has made known his salvation.*

[2] The LORD has made his salvation known:
>in the sight of the nations he has revealed
>>his justice.
[3AB] He has remembered his kindness and his
>>faithfulness
>toward the house of Israel.

R. *The Lord has made known his salvation.*

[3CD] All the ends of the earth have seen
>the salvation by our God.
[4] Sing joyfully to the LORD, all you lands;
>break into song; sing praise.

R. *The Lord has made known his salvation.*

[5] Sing praise to the LORD with the harp,
>with the harp and melodious song.
[6] With trumpets and the sound of the horn
>sing joyfully before the King, the LORD.

R. *The Lord has made known his salvation.*

Alleluia: John 14:6

R. Alleluia, alleluia.

[6] I am the way and the truth and the life, says
>the Lord;
no one comes to the Father except through
>me.

R. Alleluia, alleluia.

Gospel: Luke 11:47-54

The Lord said: [47] "Woe to you who build the memorials of the prophets whom your fathers killed. [48] Consequently, you bear witness and give consent to the deeds of your ancestors, for they killed them and you do the building. [49] Therefore, the wisdom of God said, 'I will send to them prophets and Apostles; some of them they will kill and persecute' [50] in order that this generation might be charged with the blood of all the prophets shed since the foundation of the world, [51] from the blood of Abel to the blood of Zechariah who died between the altar and the temple building. Yes, I tell you, this generation will be charged with their blood! [52] Woe to you, scholars of the law! You have taken away the key of knowledge. You yourselves did not enter and you stopped those trying to enter." [53] When Jesus left, the scribes and Pharisees began to act with hostility toward him and to interrogate him about many things, [54] for they were plotting to catch him at something he might say.

Friday October 18, 2024

Feast of Saint Luke, Evangelist

First Reading: 2 Timothy 4:10-17B

Beloved: [10] Demas, enamoured of the present world, deserted me and went to Thessalonica, Crescens to Galatia, and Titus to Dalmatia. [11] Luke is the only one with me. Get Mark and bring him with you, for he is helpful to me in the ministry. [12] I have sent Tychicus to Ephesus. [13] When you come, bring the cloak I left with Carpus in Troas, the papyrus rolls, and especially the parchments.

[14] Alexander the coppersmith did me a great deal of harm; the Lord will repay him according to his deeds. [15] You too be on guard against him, for he has strongly resisted our preaching.

[16] At my first defence no one appeared on my behalf, but everyone deserted me. May it not be held against them! [17] But the Lord stood by me and gave me strength so that through me the proclamation might be completed and all the Gentiles might hear it.

Responsorial Psalm: Psalms 145:10-11, 12-13, 17-18

R. [12] *Your friends make known, O Lord, the*
glorious splendor of your Kingdom.

[10] Let all your works give you thanks, O LORD,
and let your faithful ones bless you.
[11] Let them discourse of the glory of your
Kingdom
and speak of your might.
R. *Your friends make known, O Lord, the*
glorious splendor of your Kingdom.

[12] Making known to men your might
and the glorious splendor of your Kingdom.
[13] Your Kingdom is a Kingdom for all ages,
and your dominion endures through all
generations.
R. *Your friends make known, O Lord, the*
glorious splendor of your Kingdom.

17 The LORD is just in all his ways
    and holy in all his works.
18 The LORD is near to all who call upon him,
    to all who call upon him in truth.
R. Your friends make known, O Lord, the
        glorious splendor of your Kingdom.

Alleluia: cf. John 15:16

R. Alleluia, alleluia.
16 I chose you from the world,
to go and bear fruit that will last, says the
        Lord.
R. Alleluia, alleluia.

Gospel: Luke 10:1-9

1 The Lord Jesus appointed seventy-two disciples whom he sent ahead of him in pairs to every town and place he intended to visit. 2 He said to them, "The harvest is abundant but the laborers are few; so ask the master of the harvest to send out laborers for his harvest. 3 Go on your way; behold, I am sending you like lambs among wolves. 4 Carry no money bag, no sack, no sandals; and greet no one along the way. 5 Into whatever house you enter, first say, 'Peace to this household.' 6 If a peaceful person lives there, your peace will rest on him; but if not, it will return to you. 7 Stay in the same house and eat and drink what is offered to you, for the laborer deserves payment. Do not move about from one house to another. 8 Whatever town you enter and they welcome you, eat what is set before you, 9 cure the sick in it and say to them, 'The Kingdom of God is at hand for you.'"

Saturday October 19, 2024

Saturday of Twenty-eighth Week in Ordinary Time
First Reading: Ephesians 1:15-23

Brothers and sisters: 15 Hearing of your faith in the Lord Jesus and of your love for all the holy ones, 16 I do not cease giving thanks for you, remembering you in my prayers, 17 that the God of our Lord Jesus Christ, the Father of glory, may give you a spirit of wisdom and revelation resulting in knowledge of him. 18 May the eyes of your hearts be enlightened, that you may know what is the hope that belongs to his call, what are the riches of glory in his inheritance among the holy ones, 19 and what is the surpassing greatness of his power for us who believe, in accord with the exercise of his great might, 20 which he worked in Christ, raising him from the dead and seating him at his right hand in the heavens, 21 far above every principality, authority, power, and dominion, and every name that is named not only in this age but also in the one to come. 22 And he put all things beneath his feet and gave him as head over all things to the Church, 23 which is his Body, the fullness of the one who fills all things in every way.

Responsorial Psalm: Psalms 8:2-3AB,4-5,6-7

R. [7] *You have given your Son rule over the works of your hands.*

2 O LORD, our LORD,
    how glorious is your name over all the
        earth!
    You have exalted your majesty above the
        heavens.
3AB Out of the mouths of babes and sucklings
    you have fashioned praise because of
        your foes.

R. *You have given your Son rule over the works of your hands.*

4 When I behold your heavens, the work of
        your fingers,
    the moon and the stars which you set in
        place—
5 What is man that you should be mindful of
        him,
    or the son of man that you should care
        for him?

R. *You have given your Son rule over the works of your hands.*

6 You have made him little less than the
        angels,
    and crowned him with glory and honor.
7 You have given him rule over the works of
        your hands,
    putting all things under his feet.

R. *You have given your Son rule over the works of your hands.*

Alleluia: John 15:26B, 27A

R. Alleluia, alleluia.

26 The Spirit of truth will testify to me, says the
        Lord,
27A and you also will testify.

R. Alleluia, alleluia.

Gospel: Luke 12:8-12

Jesus said to his disciples: [8] "I tell you, everyone who acknowledges me before others the Son of Man will acknowledge before the angels of God. [9] But whoever denies me before others will be denied before the angels of God.

[10] "Everyone who speaks a word against the Son of Man will be forgiven, but the one who blasphemes against the Holy Spirit will not be forgiven. [11] When they take you before synagogues and before rulers and authorities, do not worry about how or what your defense will be or about what you are to say. [12] For the Holy Spirit will teach you at that moment what you should say."

Sunday October 20, 2024

Twenty-ninth Week Sunday in Ordinary Time, Year B
First Reading: Isaiah 53:10-11

[10] The LORD was pleased
    to crush him in infirmity.

If he gives his life as an offering for sin,
    he shall see his descendants in a long life,
    and the will of the LORD shall be
        accomplished through him.

[11] Because of his affliction
    he shall see the light in fullness of days;
through his suffering, my servant shall
        justify many,
    and their guilt he shall bear.

Responsorial Psalm: Psalms 33:4-5, 18-19, 20, 22

R. [22] *Lord, let your mercy be on us, as we place our trust in you.*

[4] Upright is the word of the LORD,
    and all his works are trustworthy.
[5] He loves justice and right;
    of the kindness of the LORD the earth is
        full.

R. *Lord, let your mercy be on us, as we place our trust in you.*

[18] See, the eyes of the LORD are upon those who
        fear him,
    upon those who hope for his kindness,
[19] To deliver them from death

and preserve them in spite of famine.

R. Lord, let your mercy be on us, as we place our
         trust in you.

[20] Our soul waits for the LORD,
         who is our help and our shield.
[22] May your kindness, O LORD, be upon us
         who have put our hope in you.

R. Lord, let your mercy be on us, as we place our
         trust in you.

Second Reading: Hebrews 4:14-16

Brothers and sisters: [14] Since we have a great high priest who has passed through the heavens, Jesus, the Son of God, let us hold fast to our confession. [15] For we do not have a high priest who is unable to sympathize with our weaknesses, but one who has similarly been tested in every way, yet without sin. [16] So let us confidently approach the throne of grace to receive mercy and to find grace for timely help.

Alleluia: Mark 10:45

R. Alleluia, alleluia.
[45] The Son of Man came to serve
and to give his life as a ransom for many.
R. Alleluia, alleluia.

Gospel: Mark 10:35-45

[35] James and John, the sons of Zebedee, came to Jesus and said to him, "Teacher, we want you to do for us whatever we ask of you." [36] He replied, "What do you wish me to do for you?" [37] They answered him, "Grant that in your glory we may sit one at your right and the other at your left." [38] Jesus said to them, "You do not know what you are asking. Can you drink the cup that I drink or be baptized with the baptism with which I am baptized?" [39] They said to him, "We can." Jesus said to them, "The cup that I drink, you will drink, and with the baptism with which I am baptized, you will be baptized; [40] but to sit at my right or at my left is not mine to give but is for those for whom it has been prepared." [41] When the ten heard this, they became indignant at James and John. [42] Jesus summoned them and said to them, "You know that those who are recognized as rulers over the Gentiles lord it over them, and their great ones make their authority over them felt. [43] But it shall not be so among you. Rather, whoever wishes to be great among you will be your servant; [44] whoever wishes to be first among you will be the slave of all. [45] For the Son of Man did not come to be served but to serve and to give his life as a ransom for many."

Or Mark 10:42-45

[42] Jesus summoned the Twelve and said to them, "You know that those who are recognized as rulers over the Gentiles lord it over them, and their great ones make their authority over them felt. [43] But it shall not be so among you. Rather, whoever wishes to be great among you will be your servant; [44] whoever wishes to be first among you will be the slave of all. [45] For the Son of Man did not come to be served but to serve and to give his life as a ransom for many."

Monday October 21, 2024

Monday of Twenty-ninth Week in Ordinary Time

First Reading: Ephesians 2:1-10

Brothers and sisters: [1] You were dead in your transgressions and sins [2] in which you once lived following the age of this world, following the ruler of the power of the air, the spirit that is now at work in the disobedient. [3] All of us once lived among them in the desires of our flesh, following the wishes of the flesh and the impulses, and we were by nature children of wrath, like the rest. [4] But God, who is rich in mercy, because of the great love he had for us, [5] even when we were dead in our transgressions, brought us to life with Christ (by grace you have been saved), [6] raised us up with him, and seated us with him in the heavens in Christ Jesus, [7] that in the ages to come he might show the immeasurable riches of his grace in his kindness to us in Christ Jesus. [8] For by grace you have been saved through faith, and this is not from you; it is the gift of God; [9] it is not from works, so no one may boast. [10] For we are his handiwork, created in Christ Jesus for good works that God has prepared in advance, that we should live in them.

Responsorial Psalm: Psalms 100:1B-2, 3, 4AB, 4C-5

R. [3b] *The Lord made us, we belong to him.*

[1B] Sing joyfully to the LORD all you lands;
  [2] serve the LORD with gladness;
  come before him with joyful song.
R. *The Lord made us, we belong to him.*

[3] Know that the LORD is God;
  he made us, his we are;
  his people, the flock he tends.
R. *The Lord made us, we belong to him.*

[4AB] Enter his gates with thanksgiving,
  his courts with praise.
R. *The Lord made us, we belong to him.*

[4C] Give thanks to him; bless his name, for he is
  good:
  [5] the LORD, whose kindness endures

forever,
and his faithfulness, to all generations.
R. The Lord made us, we belong to him.

Alleluia: Matthew 5:3
R. Alleluia, alleluia.
[3] Blessed are the poor in spirit;
for theirs is the Kingdom of heaven.
R. Alleluia, alleluia.

Gospel: Luke 12:13-21
[13] Someone in the crowd said to Jesus, "Teacher, tell my brother to share the inheritance with me." [14] He replied to him, "Friend, who appointed me as your judge and arbitrator?" [15] Then he said to the crowd, "Take care to guard against all greed, for though one may be rich, one's life does not consist of possessions."

[16] Then he told them a parable. "There was a rich man whose land produced a bountiful harvest. [17] He asked himself, 'What shall I do, for I do not have space to store my harvest?' [18] And he said, 'This is what I shall do: I shall tear down my barns and build larger ones. There I shall store all my grain and other goods [19] and I shall say to myself, "Now as for you, you have so many good things stored up for many years, rest, eat, drink, be merry!"' [20] But God said to him, 'You fool, this night your life will be demanded of you; and the things you have prepared, to whom will they belong?' [21] Thus will it be for the one who stores up treasure for himself but is not rich in what matters to God."

Tuesday October 22, 2024

Tuesday of Twenty-ninth Week in Ordinary Time
First Reading: Ephesians 2:12-22
Brothers and sisters: [12] You were at that time without Christ, alienated from the community of Israel and strangers to the covenants of promise, without hope and without God in the world. [13] But now in Christ Jesus you who once were far off have become near by the Blood of Christ.

[14] For he is our peace, he made both one and broke down the dividing wall of enmity, through his Flesh, [15] abolishing the law with its commandments and legal claims, that he might create in himself one new person in place of the two, thus establishing peace, [16] and might reconcile both with God, in one Body, through the cross, putting that enmity to death by it. [17] He came and preached peace to you who were far off and peace to those who were near, [18] for through him we both have access in one Spirit to the Father.

[19] So then you are no longer strangers and sojourners, but you are fellow citizens with the holy ones and members of the household of God, [20] built upon the foundation of the Apostles and prophets, with Christ Jesus himself as the capstone. [21] Through him the whole structure is held together and grows into a temple sacred in the Lord; [22] in him you also are being built together into a dwelling place of God in the Spirit.

Responsorial Psalm: Psalms 85:9AB-10, 11-12, 13-14

R. (see 9) *The Lord speaks of peace to his people.*

9AB I will hear what God proclaims;
>   the LORD–for he proclaims peace.

10 Near indeed is his salvation to those who
>   fear him,
>   glory dwelling in our land.

R. *The Lord speaks of peace to his people.*

11 Kindness and truth shall meet;
>   justice and peace shall kiss.

12 Truth shall spring out of the earth,
>   and justice shall look down from heaven.

R. *The Lord speaks of peace to his people.*

13 The LORD himself will give his benefits;
>   our land shall yield its increase.

14 Justice shall walk before him,
>   and salvation, along the way of his steps.

R. *The Lord speaks of peace to his people.*

Alleluia: Luke 21:36

R. Alleluia, alleluia.

36 Be vigilant at all times and pray
that you may have the strength to stand
>   before the Son of Man.

R. Alleluia, alleluia.

Gospel: Luke 12:35-38

Jesus said to his disciples: 35 "Gird your loins and light your lamps 36 and be like servants who await their master's return from a wedding, ready to open immediately when he comes and knocks. 37 Blessed are those servants whom the master finds vigilant on his arrival. Amen, I say to you, he will gird himself, have them recline at table, and proceed to wait on them. 38 And should he come in the second or third watch and find them prepared in this way, blessed are those servants."

Wednesday of Twenty-ninth Week in Ordinary Time

First Reading: Ephesians 3:2-12

Brothers and sisters: 2 You have heard of the stewardship of God's grace that was given to me for your benefit, 3 namely, that the mystery was made known to me by revelation, as I have written briefly earlier. 4 When you read this you can understand my insight into the mystery of Christ, [5] which was not made known to human beings in other generations as it has now been revealed to his holy Apostles and prophets by the Spirit, [6] that the Gentiles are coheirs, members of the same Body, and copartners in the promise in Christ Jesus through the Gospel.

[7] Of this I became a minister by the gift of God's grace that was granted me in accord with the exercise of his power. [8] To me, the very least of all the holy ones, this grace was given, to preach to the Gentiles the inscrutable riches of Christ, [9] and to bring to light for all what is the plan of the mystery hidden from ages past in God who created all things, [10] so that the manifold wisdom of God might now be made known through the Church to the principalities and authorities in the heavens. [11] This was according to the eternal purpose that he accomplished in Christ Jesus our Lord, [12] in whom we have boldness of speech and confidence of access through faith in him.

Responsorial Psalm: Isaiah 12:2-3,4BCD, 5-6

R. [(see 3)] *You will draw water joyfully from the springs of salvation.*

[2] God indeed is my savior;
      I am confident and unafraid.
My strength and my courage is the LORD,
      and he has been my savior.
[3] With joy you will draw water
      at the fountain of salvation.

R. *You will draw water joyfully from the springs of salvation.*

[4BCD] Give thanks to the LORD, acclaim his name;
      among the nations make known his
            deeds,
      proclaim how exalted is his name.

R. *You will draw water joyfully from the springs of salvation.*

[5] Sing praise to the LORD for his glorious
            achievement;
      let this be known throughout all the
            earth.
[6] Shout with exultation, O city of Zion,
      for great in your midst
      is the Holy One of Israel!

R. *You will draw water joyfully from the springs of salvation.*

Alleluia: Matthew 24:42A, 44
R. Alleluia, alleluia.

[42A] Stay awake!

[44] For you do not know when the Son of Man
          will come.

R. Alleluia, alleluia.

Gospel: Luke 12:39-48

Jesus said to his disciples: [39] "Be sure of this: if the master of the house had known the hour when the thief was coming, he would not have let his house be broken into. [40] You also must be prepared, for at an hour you do not expect, the Son of Man will come."

[41] Then Peter said, "Lord, is this parable meant for us or for everyone?" [42] And the Lord replied, "Who, then, is the faithful and prudent steward whom the master will put in charge of his servants to distribute the food allowance at the proper time? [43] Blessed is that servant whom his master on arrival finds doing so. [44] Truly, I say to you, he will put him in charge of all his property. [45] But if that servant says to himself, 'My master is delayed in coming,' and begins to beat the menservants and the maidservants, to eat and drink and get drunk, [46] then that servant's master will come on an unexpected day and at an unknown hour and will punish the servant severely and assign him a place with the unfaithful. [47] That servant who knew his master's will but did not make preparations nor act in accord with his will shall be beaten severely; [48] and the servant who was ignorant of his master's will but acted in a way deserving of a severe beating shall be beaten only lightly. Much will be required of the person entrusted with much, and still more will be demanded of the person entrusted with more."

Thursday October 24, 2024

Thursday of Twenty-ninth Week in Ordinary Time

First Reading: Ephesians 3:14-21

Brothers and sisters: [14] I kneel before the Father, [15] from whom every family in heaven and on earth is named, [16] that he may grant you in accord with the riches of his glory to be strengthened with power through his Spirit in the inner self, [17] and that Christ may dwell in your hearts through faith; that you, rooted and grounded in love, [18] may have strength to comprehend with all the holy ones what is the breadth and length and height and depth, [19] and to know the love of Christ that surpasses knowledge, so that you may be filled with all the fullness of God.

[20] Now to him who is able to accomplish far more than all we ask or imagine, by the power at work within us, [21] to him be glory in the Church and in Christ Jesus to all generations, forever and ever. Amen.

Responsorial Psalm: Psalms 33:1-2, 4-5, 11-12, 18-19

R. [5b] **The earth is full of the goodness of the Lord.**

[1] Exult, you just, in the LORD;
          praise from the upright is fitting.

² Give thanks to the LORD on the harp;
   with the ten-stringed lyre chant his
      praises.
R. *The earth is full of the goodness of the Lord.*

⁴ For upright is the word of the LORD,
   and all his works are trustworthy.
⁵ He loves justice and right;
   of the kindness of the LORD the earth is
      full.
R. *The earth is full of the goodness of the Lord.*

¹¹ But the plan of the LORD stands forever;
   the design of his heart, through all
      generations.
¹² Blessed the nation whose God is the LORD,
   the people he has chosen for his own
      inheritance.
R. *The earth is full of the goodness of the Lord.*

¹⁸ But see, the eyes of the LORD are upon those
      who fear him,
   upon those who hope for his kindness,
¹⁹ To deliver them from death
   and preserve them in spite of famine.
R. *The earth is full of the goodness of the Lord.*

Alleluia: Philippians 3:8-9
R. Alleluia, alleluia.
⁸ I consider all things so much rubbish
⁹ that I may gain Christ and be found in him.
R. Alleluia, alleluia.

Gospel: Luke 12:49-53
Jesus said to his disciples: ⁴⁹ "I have come to set the earth on fire, and how I wish it were already blazing! ⁵⁰ There is a baptism with which I must be baptized, and how great is my anguish until it is accomplished! ⁵¹ Do you think that I have come to establish peace on the earth? No, I tell you, but rather division. ⁵² From now on a household of five will be divided, three against two and two against three; ⁵³ a father will be divided against his son and a son against his father, a mother against her daughter and a daughter against her mother, a mother-in-law against her daughter-in-law and a daughter-in-law against her mother-in-law."

Friday of Twenty-ninth Week in Ordinary Time

First Reading: Ephesians 4:1-6

Brothers and sisters: [1] I, a prisoner for the Lord, urge you to live in a manner worthy of the call you have received, [2] with all humility and gentleness, with patience, bearing with one another through love, [3] striving to preserve the unity of the spirit through the bond of peace; [4] one Body and one Spirit, as you were also called to the one hope of your call; [5] one Lord, one faith, one baptism; [6] one God and Father of all, who is over all and through all and in all.

Responsorial Psalm: Psalms 24:1-2, 3-4AB, 5-6

R. [(see 6)] *Lord, this is the people that longs to see your face.*

[1] The LORD's are the earth and its fullness;
    the world and those who dwell in it.
[2] For he founded it upon the seas
    and established it upon the rivers.

R. Lord, this is the people that longs to see your face.

[3] Who can ascend the mountain of the LORD?
    or who may stand in his holy place?
[4AB] He whose hands are sinless, whose heart is
    clean,
    who desires not what is vain.

R. Lord, this is the people that longs to see your face.

[5] He shall receive a blessing from the LORD,
    a reward from God his savior.
[6] Such is the race that seeks for him,
    that seeks the face of the God of Jacob.

R. Lord, this is the people that longs to see your face.

Alleluia: cf. Matthew 11:25

R. Alleluia, alleluia.

[25] Blessed are you, Father, Lord of heaven and
    earth;
you have revealed to little ones the
    mysteries of the Kingdom.

R. Alleluia, alleluia.

Gospel: Luke 12:54-59

⁵⁴ Jesus said to the crowds, "When you see a cloud rising in the west you say immediately that it is going to rain — and so it does; ⁵⁵ and when you notice that the wind is blowing from the south you say that it is going to be hot — and so it is. ⁵⁶ You hypocrites! You know how to interpret the appearance of the earth and the sky; why do you not know how to interpret the present time?

⁵⁷ "Why do you not judge for yourselves what is right? ⁵⁸ If you are to go with your opponent before a magistrate, make an effort to settle the matter on the way; otherwise your opponent will turn you over to the judge, and the judge hand you over to the constable, and the constable throw you into prison. ⁵⁹ I say to you, you will not be released until you have paid the last penny."

Saturday October 26, 2024

Saturday of Twenty-ninth Week in Ordinary Time

First Reading: Ephesians 4:7-16

Brothers and sisters: ⁷ Grace was given to each of us according to the measure of Christ's gift. ⁸ Therefore, it says:

He ascended on high and took prisoners captive; he gave gifts to men.

⁹ What does "he ascended" mean except that he also descended into the lower regions of the earth? ¹⁰ The one who descended is also the one who ascended far above all the heavens, that he might fill all things.

¹¹ And he gave some as Apostles, others as prophets, others as evangelists, others as pastors and teachers, ¹² to equip the holy ones for the work of ministry, for building up the Body of Christ, ¹³ until we all attain to the unity of faith and knowledge of the Son of God, to mature manhood to the extent of the full stature of Christ, ¹⁴ so that we may no longer be infants, tossed by waves and swept along by every wind of teaching arising from human trickery, from their cunning in the interests of deceitful scheming. ¹⁵ Rather, living the truth in love, we should grow in every way into him who is the head, Christ, ¹⁶ from whom the whole Body, joined and held together by every supporting ligament, with the proper functioning of each part, brings about the Body's growth and builds itself up in love.

Responsorial Psalm: Psalms 122:1-2, 3-4AB, 4CD-5

R. ⁽¹⁾ *Let us go rejoicing to the house of the Lord.*

¹ I rejoiced because they said to me,
    "We will go up to the house of the LORD."
² And now we have set foot
    within your gates, O Jerusalem.

R. *Let us go rejoicing to the house of the Lord.*

³ Jerusalem, built as a city
    with compact unity.
⁴ᴬᴮ To it the tribes go up,

the tribes of the LORD.
R. Let us go rejoicing to the house of the Lord.

4BC According to the decree for Israel,
      to give thanks to the name of the LORD.
5 In it are set up judgment seats,
      seats for the house of David.
R. Let us go rejoicing to the house of the Lord.

Alleluia: Ezekiel 33:11
R. Alleluia, alleluia.
11 I take no pleasure in the death of the wicked
      man, says the Lord,
but rather in his conversion that he may live.
R. Alleluia, alleluia.

Gospel: Luke 13:1-9
1 Some people told Jesus about the Galileans whose blood Pilate had mingled with the blood of their sacrifices. 2 He said to them in reply, "Do you think that because these Galileans suffered in this way they were greater sinners than all other Galileans? 3 By no means! But I tell you, if you do not repent, you will all perish as they did! 4 Or those eighteen people who were killed when the tower at Siloam fell on them — do you think they were more guilty than everyone else who lived in Jerusalem? 5 By no means! But I tell you, if you do not repent, you will all perish as they did!"

6 And he told them this parable: "There once was a person who had a fig tree planted in his orchard, and when he came in search of fruit on it but found none, 7 he said to the gardener, 'For three years now I have come in search of fruit on this fig tree but have found none. So cut it down. Why should it exhaust the soil?' 8 He said to him in reply, 'Sir, leave it for this year also, and I shall cultivate the ground around it and fertilize it; 9 it may bear fruit in the future. If not you can cut it down.'"

Sunday October 27, 2024

Thirtieth Sunday in Ordinary Time, Year B
First Reading: Jeremiah 31:7-9
7 Thus says the LORD:

Shout with joy for Jacob,
      exult at the head of the nations;
      proclaim your praise and say:
The LORD has delivered his people,
      the remnant of Israel.
8 Behold, I will bring them back

from the land of the north;
I will gather them from the ends of the
world,
with the blind and the lame in their
midst,
the mothers and those with child;
they shall return as an immense throng.
[9] They departed in tears,
but I will console them and guide them;
I will lead them to brooks of water,
on a level road, so that none shall
stumble.
For I am a father to Israel,
Ephraim is my first-born.

Responsorial Psalm: Psalms 126:1-2, 2-3, 4-5, 6

R. [3] *The Lord has done great things for us; we
are filled with joy.*

[1] When the LORD brought back the captives of
Zion,
we were like men dreaming.
[2AB] Then our mouth was filled with laughter,
and our tongue with rejoicing.

R. *The Lord has done great things for us; we are
filled with joy.*

[2BC] Then they said among the nations,
"The LORD has done great things for
them."
[3] The LORD has done great things for us;
we are glad indeed.

R. *The Lord has done great things for us; we are
filled with joy.*

[4] Restore our fortunes, O LORD,
like the torrents in the southern desert.
[5] Those that sow in tears
shall reap rejoicing.

R. *The Lord has done great things for us; we are
filled with joy.*

[6] Although they go forth weeping,

carrying the seed to be sown,
They shall come back rejoicing,
 carrying their sheaves.
R. The Lord has done great things for us; we are
  filled with joy.

Second Reading: Hebrews 5:1-6

Brothers and sisters: [1] Every high priest is taken from among men and made their representative before God, to offer gifts and sacrifices for sins. [2] He is able to deal patiently with the ignorant and erring, for he himself is beset by weakness [3] and so, for this reason, must make sin offerings for himself as well as for the people. [4] No one takes this honor upon himself but only when called by God, just as Aaron was. [5] In the same way, it was not Christ who glorified himself in becoming high priest, but rather the one who said to him:

You are my son: this day I have begotten you;

[6] just as he says in another place:

You are a priest forever according to the
  order of Melchizedek.

Alleluia: cf. 2 Timothy 1:10

R. Alleluia, alleluia.
[10] Our Savior Jesus Christ destroyed death
and brought life to light through the Gospel.
R. Alleluia, alleluia.

Gospel: Mark 10:46-52

[46] As Jesus was leaving Jericho with his disciples and a sizable crowd, Bartimaeus, a blind man, the son of Timaeus, sat by the roadside begging. [47] On hearing that it was Jesus of Nazareth, he began to cry out and say, "Jesus, son of David, have pity on me." [48] And many rebuked him, telling him to be silent. But he kept calling out all the more, "Son of David, have pity on me." [49] Jesus stopped and said, "Call him." So they called the blind man, saying to him, "Take courage; get up, Jesus is calling you." [50] He threw aside his cloak, sprang up, and came to Jesus. [51] Jesus said to him in reply, "What do you want me to do for you?" The blind man replied to him, "Master, I want to see." [52] Jesus told him, "Go your way; your faith has saved you." Immediately he received his sight and followed him on the way.

Feast of Saints Simon and Jude, Apostles

First Reading: Ephesians 2:19-22

Brothers and sisters: [19] You are no longer strangers and sojourners, but you are fellow citizens with the holy ones and members of the household of God, [20] built upon the foundation of the Apostles and prophets, with Christ Jesus himself as the capstone. [21] Through him the whole structure is held together and grows into a temple sacred in the Lord; [22] in him you also are being built together into a dwelling place of God in the Spirit.

Responsorial Psalm: Psalms 19:2-3, 4-5

R. *(5a) Their message goes out through all the earth.*

[2] The heavens declare the glory of God,
　　　and the firmament proclaims his
　　　　　handiwork.
[3] Day pours out the word to day,
　　　and night to night imparts knowledge.
R. *Their message goes out through all the earth.*

[4] Not a word nor a discourse
　　　whose voice is not heard;
[5] Through all the earth their voice resounds,
　　　and to the ends of the world, their
　　　　　message.
R. *Their message goes out through all the earth.*

Alleluia: cf. Te Deum

R. Alleluia, alleluia.
We praise you, O God,
we acclaim you as Lord;
the glorious company of Apostles praise you.
R. Alleluia, alleluia.

Gospel: Luke 6:12-16

[12] Jesus went up to the mountain to pray, and he spent the night in prayer to God. [13] When day came, he called his disciples to himself, and from them he chose Twelve, whom he also named Apostles: [14] Simon, whom he named Peter, and his brother Andrew, James, John, Philip, Bartholomew, [15] Matthew, Thomas, James the son of Alphaeus, Simon who was called a Zealot, [16] and Judas the son of James, and Judas Iscariot, who became a traitor.

Tuesday of Thirtieth Week in Ordinary Time
First Reading: Ephesians 5:21-33

Brothers and sisters: [21] Be subordinate to one another out of reverence for Christ. [22] Wives should be subordinate to their husbands as to the Lord. [23] For the husband is head of his wife just as Christ is head of the Church, he himself the savior of the Body. [24] As the Church is subordinate to Christ, so wives should be subordinate to their husbands in everything. [25] Husbands, love your wives, even as Christ loved the Church and handed himself over for her [26] to sanctify her, cleansing her by the bath of water with the word, [27] that he might present to himself the Church in splendor, without spot or wrinkle or any such thing, that she might be holy and without blemish. [28] So also husbands should love their wives as their own bodies. He who loves his wife loves himself. [29] For no one hates his own flesh but rather nourishes and cherishes it, even as Christ does the Church, [30] because we are members of his Body.

[31] *For this reason a man shall leave his father and his mother and be joined to his wife, and the two shall become one flesh.*

[32] This is a great mystery, but I speak in reference to Christ and the Church. [33] In any case, each one of you should love his wife as himself, and the wife should respect her husband.

Responsorial Psalm: Psalms 128:1-2, 3, 4-5

R. [1a] Blessed are those who fear the Lord.

[1] Blessed are you who fear the LORD,
    who walk in his ways!
[2] For you shall eat the fruit of your
        handiwork;
    blessed shall you be, and favored.
R. Blessed are those who fear the Lord.

[3] Your wife shall be like a fruitful vine
    in the recesses of your home;
Your children like olive plants
    around your table.
R. Blessed are those who fear the Lord.

[4] Behold, thus is the man blessed
    who fears the LORD.
[5] The LORD bless you from Zion:
    may you see the prosperity of Jerusalem
    all the days of your life.
R. Blessed are those who fear the Lord.

Alleluia: cf. Matthew 11:25

R. Alleluia, alleluia.

25 Blessed are you, Father, Lord of heaven and
earth;
You have revealed to little ones the
mysteries of the Kingdom.

R. Alleluia, alleluia.

Gospel: Luke 13:18-21

18 Jesus said, "What is the Kingdom of God like? To what can I compare it? 19 It is like a mustard seed that a man took and planted in the garden. When it was fully grown, it became a large bush and '*the birds of the sky dwelt in its branches.*'"

20 Again he said, "To what shall I compare the Kingdom of God? 21 It is like yeast that a woman took and mixed in with three measures of wheat flour until the whole batch of dough was leavened."

Wednesday October 30, 2024

Wednesday of Thirtieth Week in Ordinary Time

First Reading: Ephesians 6:1-9

1 Children, obey your parents in the Lord, for this is right. 2 *Honor your father and mother*. This is the first commandment with a promise, 3 *that it may go well with you and that you may have a long life on earth*. 4 Fathers, do not provoke your children to anger, but bring them up with the training and instruction of the Lord.

5 Slaves, be obedient to your human masters with fear and trembling, in sincerity of heart, as to Christ, 6 not only when being watched, as currying favor, but as slaves of Christ, doing the will of God from the heart, 7 willingly serving the Lord and not men, 8 knowing that each will be requited from the Lord for whatever good he does, whether he is slave or free. 9 Masters, act in the same way towards them, and stop bullying, knowing that both they and you have a Master in heaven and that with him there is no partiality.

Responsorial Psalm: Psalms 145:10-11, 12-13AB, 13CD-14

R. (13c) The Lord is faithful in all his words.

10 Let all your works give you thanks, O LORD,
and let your faithful ones bless you.
11 Let them discourse of the glory of your
Kingdom
and speak of your might.

R. The Lord is faithful in all his words.

12 Making known to men your might
and the glorious splendor of your
Kingdom.
13AB Your Kingdom is a Kingdom for all ages,

and your dominion endures through all
    generations.
R. The Lord is faithful in all his words.

¹³ᴮᶜ The LORD is faithful in all his words
    and holy in all his works.
¹⁴ The LORD lifts up all who are falling
    and raises up all who are bowed down.
R. The Lord is faithful in all his words.

Alleluia: cf. 2 Thessalonians 2:14
R. Alleluia, alleluia.
¹⁴ God has called us through the Gospel
to possess the glory of our Lord Jesus Christ.
R. Alleluia, alleluia.

Gospel: Luke 13:22-30

²² Jesus passed through towns and villages, teaching as he went and making his way to Jerusalem. ²³ Someone asked him, "Lord, will only a few people be saved?" He answered them, ²⁴ "Strive to enter through the narrow gate, for many, I tell you, will attempt to enter but will not be strong enough. ²⁵ After the master of the house has arisen and locked the door, then will you stand outside knocking and saying, 'Lord, open the door for us.' He will say to you in reply, 'I do not know where you are from.' ²⁶ And you will say, 'We ate and drank in your company and you taught in our streets.' ²⁷ Then he will say to you, 'I do not know where you are from. Depart from me, all you evildoers!' ²⁸ And there will be wailing and grinding of teeth when you see Abraham, Isaac, and Jacob and all the prophets in the Kingdom of God and you yourselves cast out. ²⁹ And people will come from the east and the west and from the north and the south and will recline at table in the Kingdom of God. ³⁰ For behold, some are last who will be first, and some are first who will be last."

Thursday October 31, 2024

Thursday of Thirtieth Week in Ordinary Time

First Reading: Ephesians 6:10-20

Brothers and sisters: ¹⁰ Draw your strength from the Lord and from his mighty power. ¹¹ Put on the armor of God so that you may be able to stand firm against the tactics of the Devil. ¹² For our struggle is not with flesh and blood but with the principalities, with the powers, with the world rulers of this present darkness, with the evil spirits in the heavens. ¹³ Therefore, put on the armor of God, that you may be able to resist on the evil day and, having done everything, to hold your ground. ¹⁴ So stand fast with your loins girded in truth, clothed with righteousness as a breastplate, ¹⁵ and your feet shod in readiness for the Gospel of peace. ¹⁶ In all circumstances, hold faith as a shield, to quench all the flaming arrows of the Evil One. [17] And take the helmet of salvation and the sword of the Spirit, which is the word of God.

[18] With all prayer and supplication, pray at every opportunity in the Spirit. To that end, be watchful with all perseverance and supplication for all the holy ones and also for me, [19] that speech may be given me to open my mouth, to make known with boldness the mystery of the Gospel [20] for which I am an ambassador in chains, so that I may have the courage to speak as I must.

Responsorial Psalm: Psalms 144:1B, 2, 9-10

R. *(1b)* **Blessed be the Lord, my Rock!**

[1B] Blessed be the LORD, my rock,
> who trains my hands for battle, my
>> fingers for war.

R. Blessed be the Lord, my Rock!

[2] My mercy and my fortress,
> my stronghold, my deliverer,
My shield, in whom I trust,
> who subdues my people under me.

R. Blessed be the Lord, my Rock!

[9] O God, I will sing a new song to you;
> with a ten stringed lyre I will chant your
>> praise,
[10] You who give victory to kings,
> and deliver David, your servant from the
>> evil sword.

R. Blessed be the Lord, my Rock!

Alleluia: cf. Luke 19:38; 2:14

R. Alleluia, alleluia.

[38] Blessed is the king who comes in the name of
> the Lord.
[14] Glory to God in the highest and on earth
> peace to those on whom his favor
> rests.

R. Alleluia, alleluia.

Gospel: Luke 13:31-35

[31] Some Pharisees came to Jesus and said, "Go away, leave this area because Herod wants to kill you." [32] He replied, "Go and tell that fox, 'Behold, I cast out demons and I perform healings today and tomorrow, and on the third day I accomplish my purpose. [33] Yet I must continue on my way today, tomorrow, and the following day, for it is impossible that a prophet should die outside of Jerusalem.'

³⁴ "Jerusalem, Jerusalem, you who kill the prophets and stone those sent to you, how many times I yearned to gather your children together as a hen gathers her brood under her wings, but you were unwilling! ³⁵ Behold, your house will be abandoned. But I tell you, you will not see me until the time comes when you say, *Blessed is he who comes in the name of the Lord.*"

NOVEMBER 2024
Friday November 1, 2024

Solemnity of All Saints (All Saints Day)
First Reading: Revelation 7:2-4, 9-14

² I, John, saw another angel come up from the East, holding the seal of the living God. He cried out in a loud voice to the four angels who were given power to damage the land and the sea, ³ "Do not damage the land or the sea or the trees until we put the seal on the foreheads of the servants of our God." ⁴ I heard the number of those who had been marked with the seal, one hundred and forty-four thousand marked from every tribe of the children of Israel.

⁹ After this I had a vision of a great multitude, which no one could count, from every nation, race, people, and tongue. They stood before the throne and before the Lamb, wearing white robes and holding palm branches in their hands. ¹⁰ They cried out in a loud voice:

"Salvation comes from our God, who is
     seated on the throne,
   and from the Lamb."

¹¹ All the angels stood around the throne and around the elders and the four living creatures. They prostrated themselves before the throne, worshiped God, ¹² and exclaimed:

"Amen. Blessing and glory, wisdom and
     thanksgiving,
   honor, power, and might
   be to our God forever and ever. Amen."

¹³ Then one of the elders spoke up and said to me, "Who are these wearing white robes, and where did they come from?" ¹⁴ I said to him, "My lord, you are the one who knows." He said to me, "These are the ones who have survived the time of great distress; they have washed their robes and made them white in the Blood of the Lamb."

Responsorial Psalm: Psalms 24:1BC-2, 3-4AB, 5-6

R. ^(see 6) *Lord, this is the people that longs to see
          your face.*

^{1BC} The LORD's are the earth and its fullness;

the world and those who dwell in it.
[2] For he founded it upon the seas
and established it upon the rivers.
**R. Lord, this is the people that longs to see your
face.**

[3] Who can ascend the mountain of the LORD?
or who may stand in his holy place?
[4AB] One whose hands are sinless, whose heart is
clean,
who desires not what is vain.
**R. Lord, this is the people that longs to see your
face.**

[5] He shall receive a blessing from the LORD,
a reward from God his savior.
[6] Such is the race that seeks him,
that seeks the face of the God of Jacob.
**R. Lord, this is the people that longs to see your
face.**

Second Reading: 1 John 3:1-3

Beloved: [1] See what love the Father has bestowed on us that we may be called the children of God. Yet so we are. The reason the world does not know us is that it did not know him. [2] Beloved, we are God's children now; what we shall be has not yet been revealed. We do know that when it is revealed we shall be like him, for we shall see him as he is. [3] Everyone who has this hope based on him makes himself pure, as he is pure.

Alleluia: Matthew 11:28

R. Alleluia, alleluia.
[28] Come to me, all you who labor and are
burdened,
And I will give you rest, says the Lord.
R. Alleluia, alleluia.

Gospel: Matthew 5:1-12A

[1] When Jesus saw the crowds, he went up the mountain, and after he had sat down, his disciples came to him. [2] He began to teach them, saying:

[3] "Blessed are the poor in spirit,
for theirs is the Kingdom of heaven.
[4] Blessed are they who mourn,

for they will be comforted.
⁵ Blessed are the meek,
 for they will inherit the land.
⁶ Blessed are they who hunger and thirst for
  righteousness,
 for they will be satisfied.
⁷ Blessed are the merciful,
 for they will be shown mercy.
⁸ Blessed are the clean of heart,
 for they will see God.
⁹ Blessed are the peacemakers,
 for they will be called children of God.
¹⁰ Blessed are they who are persecuted for the
  sake of righteousness,
 for theirs is the Kingdom of heaven.
¹¹ Blessed are you when they insult you and
  persecute you
 and utter every kind of evil against you
  falsely because of me.
¹²ᴬ Rejoice and be glad,
 for your reward will be great in heaven."

Commemoration of All the Faithful Departed - All Souls Day
First Reading: Wisdom 3:1-9

¹ The souls of the just are in the hand of
  God,
 and no torment shall touch them.
² They seemed, in the view of the foolish,
  to be dead;
 and their passing away was thought
  an affliction
³ and their going forth from us, utter
  destruction.
But they are in peace.
⁴ For if before men, indeed, they be
  punished,
 yet is their hope full of immortality;
⁵ chastised a little, they shall be greatly
  blessed,
 because God tried them
 and found them worthy of himself.

[6] As gold in the furnace, he proved them,
   and as sacrificial offerings he took
      them to himself.
[7] In the time of their visitation they shall
      shine,
   and shall dart about as sparks
      through stubble;
[8] they shall judge nations and rule over
      peoples,
   and the LORD shall be their King
      forever.
[9] Those who trust in him shall understand
      truth,
   and the faithful shall abide with him
      in love:
because grace and mercy are with his
      holy ones,
   and his care is with his elect.

Responsorial Psalm: Psalms 23:1-3A, 3B-4, 5, 6

R. [1] *The Lord is my shepherd; there is nothing*
      I shall want.

or:

Though I walk in the valley of darkness, I
      fear no evil, for you are with me.

[1] The LORD is my shepherd; I shall not
      want.
   [2] In verdant pastures he gives me
      repose;
beside restful waters he leads me;
   [3A] he refreshes my soul.

R. The Lord is my shepherd; there is nothing
      I shall want.

or:

Though I walk in the valley of darkness, I
      fear no evil, for you are with me.

[3B] He guides me in right paths
      for his name's sake.
[4] Even though I walk in the dark valley
      I fear no evil; for you are at my side
with your rod and your staff

that give me courage.
R. The Lord is my shepherd; there is nothing
        I shall want.

or:

Though I walk in the valley of darkness, I
        fear no evil, for you are with me.

[5] You spread the table before me
        in the sight of my foes;
You anoint my head with oil;
        my cup overflows.
R. The Lord is my shepherd; there is nothing
        I shall want.

or:

Though I walk in the valley of darkness, I
        fear no evil, for you are with me.

[6] Only goodness and kindness follow me
        all the days of my life;
and I shall dwell in the house of the LORD
        for years to come.
R. The Lord is my shepherd; there is nothing
        I shall want.

or:

Though I walk in the valley of darkness, I
        fear no evil, for you are with me.

Second Reading: Romans 5:5-11

Brothers and sisters: [5] Hope does not disappoint, because the love of God has been poured out into our hearts through the Holy Spirit that has been given to us. [6] For Christ, while we were still helpless, died at the appointed time for the ungodly. [7] Indeed, only with difficulty does one die for a just person, though perhaps for a good person one might even find courage to die. [8] But God proves his love for us in that while we were still sinners Christ died for us. [9] How much more then, since we are now justified by his Blood, will we be saved through him from the wrath. [10] Indeed, if, while we were enemies, we were reconciled to God through the death of his Son, how much more, once reconciled, will we be saved by his life. [11] Not only that, but we also boast of God through our Lord Jesus Christ, through whom we have now received reconciliation.

Or Romans 6:3-9

Brothers and sisters: [3] Are you unaware that we who were baptized into Christ Jesus were baptized into his death? [4] We were indeed buried with him through baptism into death, so that, just as Christ was raised from the dead by the glory of the Father, we too might live in newness of life.

⁵ For if we have grown into union with him through a death like his, we shall also be united with him in the resurrection. ⁶ We know that our old self was crucified with him, so that our sinful body might be done away with, that we might no longer be in slavery to sin. ⁷ For a dead person has been absolved from sin. ⁸ If, then, we have died with Christ, we believe that we shall also live with him. ⁹ We know that Christ, raised from the dead, dies no more; death no longer has power over him.

Alleluia: Matthew 25:34

R. Alleluia, alleluia.

³⁴ Come, you who are blessed by
        my Father;
inherit the kingdom prepared
for you from the foundation of
        the world.

R. Alleluia, alleluia.

Gospel: John 6:37-40

Jesus said to the crowds: ³⁷ "Everything that the Father gives me will come to me, and I will not reject anyone who comes to me, ³⁸ because I came down from heaven not to do my own will but the will of the one who sent me. ³⁹ And this is the will of the one who sent me, that I should not lose anything of what he gave me, but that I should raise it on the last day. ⁴⁰ For this is the will of my Father, that everyone who sees the Son and believes in him may have eternal life, and I shall raise him on the last day."

Sunday November 3, 2024

Thirty-first Sunday in Ordinary Time, Year B

First Reading: Deuteronomy 6:2-6

Moses spoke to the people, saying: ² "Fear the LORD, your God, and keep, throughout the days of your lives, all his statutes and commandments which I enjoin on you, and thus have long life. ³ Hear then, Israel, and be careful to observe them, that you may grow and prosper the more, in keeping with the promise of the LORD, the God of your fathers, to give you a land flowing with milk and honey.

⁴ "Hear, O Israel! The LORD is our God, the LORD alone! ⁵ Therefore, you shall love the LORD, your God, with all your heart, and with all your soul, and with all your strength. ⁶ Take to heart these words which I enjoin on you today."

Responsorial Psalm: Psalms 18:2-3, 3-4, 47, 51

R. ⁽²⁾ *I love you, Lord, my strength.*

² I love you, O LORD, my strength,
        ³ᴬ O LORD, my rock, my fortress, my
                deliverer.

R. I love you, Lord, my strength.

[3B] My God, my rock of refuge,
    my shield, the horn of my salvation, my
        stronghold!
[4] Praised be the LORD, I exclaim,
    and I am safe from my enemies.
R. I love you, Lord, my strength.

[47] The LORD lives! And blessed be my rock!
    Extolled be God my savior.
[51] You who gave great victories to your king
    and showed kindness to your anointed.
R. I love you, Lord, my strength.

Second Reading: Hebrews 7:23-28

Brothers and sisters: [23] The levitical priests were many because they were prevented by death from remaining in office, [24] but Jesus, because he remains forever, has a priesthood that does not pass away. [25] Therefore, he is always able to save those who approach God through him, since he lives forever to make intercession for them.

[26] It was fitting that we should have such a high priest: holy, innocent, undefiled, separated from sinners, higher than the heavens. [27] He has no need, as did the high priests, to offer sacrifice day after day, first for his own sins and then for those of the people; he did that once for all when he offered himself. [28] For the law appoints men subject to weakness to be high priests, but the word of the oath, which was taken after the law, appoints a son, who has been made perfect forever.

Alleluia: John 14:23

R. Alleluia, alleluia.
[23] Whoever loves me will keep my word,
says the Lord; and my Father will love him
and we will come to him.
R. Alleluia, alleluia.

Gospel: Mark 12:28B-34

[28B] One of the scribes came to Jesus and asked him, "Which is the first of all the commandments?" [29] Jesus replied, "The first is this: *Hear, O Israel! The Lord our God is Lord alone!* [30] *You shall love the Lord your God with all your heart, with all your soul, with all your mind, and with all your strength.* [31] The second is this: *You shall love your neighbor as yourself.* There is no other commandment greater than these." [32] The scribe said to him, "Well said, teacher. You are right in saying, 'He is One and there is no other than he.'

³³ And 'to love him with all your heart, with all your understanding, with all your strength, and to love your neighbor as yourself' is worth more than all burnt offerings and sacrifices." ³⁴ And when Jesus saw that he answered with understanding, he said to him, "You are not far from the kingdom of God." And no one dared to ask him any more questions.

Monday November 4, 2024

Memorial of Saint Charles Borromeo, Bishop

First Reading: Philippians 2:1-4

Brothers and sisters: ¹ If there is any encouragement in Christ, any solace in love, any participation in the Spirit, any compassion and mercy, ² complete my joy by being of the same mind, with the same love, united in heart, thinking one thing. ³ Do nothing out of selfishness or out of vainglory; rather, humbly regard others as more important than yourselves, ⁴ each looking out not for his own interests, but also everyone for those of others.

Responsorial Psalm: Psalms 131:1BCDE, 2,3

R. In you, O Lord, I have found my peace.

^{1BCDE} O LORD, my heart is not proud,
    nor are my eyes haughty;
I busy not myself with great things,
    nor with things too sublime for me.

R. In you, O Lord, I have found my peace.

² Nay rather, I have stilled and quieted
    my soul like a weaned child.
Like a weaned child on its mother's lap,
    so is my soul within me.

R. In you, O Lord, I have found my peace.

³ O Israel, hope in the LORD,
    both now and forever.

R. In you, O Lord, I have found my peace.

Alleluia: John 8:31B-32

R. Alleluia, alleluia.

^{31B} If you remain in my word, you will truly be
        my disciples,
³² and you will know the truth, says the Lord.

R. Alleluia, alleluia.

Gospel: Luke 14:12-14

On a sabbath Jesus went to dine at the home of one of the leading Pharisees. ¹² He said to the host who invited him, "When you hold a lunch or a dinner, do not invite your friends or your brothers or sisters or your relatives or your wealthy neighbors, in case they may invite you back and you have repayment. [13] Rather, when you hold a banquet, invite the poor, the crippled, the lame, the blind; [14] blessed indeed will you be because of their inability to repay you. For you will be repaid at the resurrection of the righteous."

Tuesday of Thirty-first Week in Ordinary Time

First Reading: Philippians 2:5-11

Brothers and sisters: [5] Have among yourselves the same attitude that is also yours in Christ Jesus,

[6] Who, though he was in the form of God,
    did not regard equality with God
    something to be grasped.
[7] Rather, he emptied himself,
    taking the form of a slave,
    coming in human likeness;
    and, found human in appearance,
[8] he humbled himself,
    becoming obedient to death,
    even death on a cross.
[9] Because of this, God greatly exalted him
    and bestowed on him the name
    that is above every name,
[10] that at the name of Jesus
    every knee should bend,
    of those in heaven and on earth and
        under the earth,
[11] and every tongue confess that
    Jesus Christ is Lord,
    to the glory of God the Father.

Responsorial Psalm: Psalms 22:26B-27, 28-30AB, 30E, 31-32

R. [26a] *I will praise you, Lord, in the assembly of*
                your people.
[26B] I will fulfill my vows before those who fear
            him.
[27] The lowly shall eat their fill;
        they who seek the LORD shall praise him:
        "May your hearts be ever merry!"
R. *I will praise you, Lord, in the assembly of your*
        people.

[28] All the ends of the earth
     shall remember and turn to the LORD;
All the families of the nations
     shall bow down before him.
**R. I will praise you, Lord, in the assembly of your
          people.**

[29] For dominion is the LORD's,
     and he rules the nations.
[30AB] To him alone shall bow down
     all who sleep in the earth.
**R. I will praise you, Lord, in the assembly of your
          people.**

[31] To him my soul shall live;
     my descendants shall serve him.
[32] Let the coming generation be told of the LORD
     that they may proclaim to a people yet to
          be born
     the justice he has shown.
**R. I will praise you, Lord, in the assembly of your
          people.**

Alleluia: Matthew 11:28
R. Alleluia, alleluia.
[28] Come to me, all you who labor and are
          burdened,
and I will give you rest, says the Lord.
R. Alleluia, alleluia.

Gospel: Luke 14:15-24
[15] One of those at table with Jesus said to him, "Blessed is the one who will dine in the Kingdom of God." [16] He replied to him, "A man gave a great dinner to which he invited many. [17] When the time for the dinner came, he dispatched his servant to say to those invited, 'Come, everything is now ready.' [18] But one by one, they all began to excuse themselves. The first said to him, 'I have purchased a field and must go to examine it; I ask you, consider me excused.' [19] And another said, 'I have purchased five yoke of oxen and am on my way to evaluate them; I ask you, consider me excused.' [20] And another said, 'I have just married a woman, and therefore I cannot come.' [21] The servant went and reported this to his master. Then the master of the house in a rage commanded his servant, 'Go out quickly into the streets and alleys of the town and bring in here the poor and the crippled, the blind and the lame.' [22] The servant reported, 'Sir, your orders have

been carried out and still there is room.' ²³ The master then ordered the servant, 'Go out to the highways and hedgerows and make people come in that my home may be filled. ²⁴ For, I tell you, none of those men who were invited will taste my dinner.'"

Wednesday of Thirty-first Week in Ordinary Time

First Reading: Philippians 2:12-18

¹² My beloved, obedient as you have always been, not only when I am present but all the more now when I am absent, work out your salvation with fear and trembling. ¹³ For God is the one who, for his good purpose, works in you both to desire and to work. ¹⁴ Do everything without grumbling or questioning, ¹⁵ that you may be blameless and innocent, children of God without blemish in the midst of a crooked and perverse generation, among whom you shine like lights in the world, ¹⁶ as you hold on to the word of life, so that my boast for the day of Christ may be that I did not run in vain or labor in vain. ¹⁷ But, even if I am poured out as a libation upon the sacrificial service of your faith, I rejoice and share my joy with all of you. ¹⁸ In the same way you also should rejoice and share your joy with me.

Responsorial Psalm: Psalms 27:1, 4, 13-14

R. *(1a)* *The Lord is my light and my salvation.*
¹ The LORD is my light and my salvation;
    whom should I fear?
The LORD is my life's refuge;
    of whom should I be afraid?
R. *The Lord is my light and my salvation.*

⁴ One thing I ask of the LORD;
    this I seek:
To dwell in the house of the LORD
    all the days of my life,
That I may gaze on the loveliness of the LORD
    and contemplate his temple.
R. *The Lord is my light and my salvation.*
¹³ I believe that I shall see the bounty of the
      LORD
    in the land of the living.
¹⁴ Wait for the LORD with courage;
    be stouthearted, and wait for the LORD.
R. *The Lord is my light and my salvation.*

Alleluia: 1 Peter 4:14

R. Alleluia, alleluia.
¹⁴ If you are insulted for the name of Christ,

blessed are you,
for the Spirit of God rests upon you.
R. Alleluia, alleluia.

Gospel: Luke 14:25-33

[25] Great crowds were traveling with Jesus, and he turned and addressed them, [26] "If anyone comes to me without hating his father and mother, wife and children, brothers and sisters, and even his own life, he cannot be my disciple. [27] Whoever does not carry his own cross and come after me cannot be my disciple. [28] Which of you wishing to construct a tower does not first sit down and calculate the cost to see if there is enough for its completion? [29] Otherwise, after laying the foundation and finding himself unable to finish the work the onlookers should laugh at him [30] and say, 'This one began to build but did not have the resources to finish.' [31] Or what king marching into battle would not first sit down and decide whether with ten thousand troops he can successfully oppose another king advancing upon him with twenty thousand troops? [32] But if not, while he is still far away, he will send a delegation to ask for peace terms. [33] In the same way, everyone of you who does not renounce all his possessions cannot be my disciple."

Thursday November 7, 2024

Thursday of Thirty-first Week in Ordinary Time

First Reading: Philippians 3:3-8A

Brothers and sisters: [3] We are the circumcision, we who worship through the Spirit of God, who boast in Christ Jesus and do not put our confidence in flesh, [4] although I myself have grounds for confidence even in the flesh.

If anyone else thinks he can be confident in flesh, all the more can I. [5] Circumcised on the eighth day, of the race of Israel, of the tribe of Benjamin, a Hebrew of Hebrew parentage, in observance of the law a Pharisee, [6] in zeal I persecuted the Church, in righteousness based on the law I was blameless.

[7] But whatever gains I had, these I have come to consider a loss because of Christ. [8A] More than that, I even consider everything as a loss because of the supreme good of knowing Christ Jesus my Lord.

Responsorial Psalm: Psalms 105:2-3,4-5, 6-7

R. [(3b)] *Let hearts rejoice who search for the Lord.* or: *Alleluia.*

[2] Sing to him, sing his praise,
     proclaim all his wondrous deeds.
[3] Glory in his holy name;
     rejoice, O hearts that seek the LORD!
R. Let hearts rejoice who search for the Lord. or: *Alleluia.*

[4] Look to the LORD in his strength;
     seek to serve him constantly.
[5] Recall the wondrous deeds that he has

wrought,
 his portents, and the judgments he has
 uttered.
R. Let hearts rejoice who search for the Lord. or: Alleluia.

[6] You descendants of Abraham, his servants,
 sons of Jacob, his chosen ones!
[7] He, the LORD, is our God;
 throughout the earth his judgments
 prevail.
R. Let hearts rejoice who search for the Lord. or: Alleluia.

Alleluia: Matthew 11:28
R. Alleluia, alleluia.
[28] Come to me, all you who labor and are
 burdened,
and I will give you rest, says the Lord.
R. Alleluia, alleluia.

Gospel: Luke 15:1-10
[1] The tax collectors and sinners were all drawing near to listen to Jesus, [2] but the Pharisees and scribes began to complain, saying, "This man welcomes sinners and eats with them." [3] So Jesus addressed this parable to them. [4] "What man among you having a hundred sheep and losing one of them would not leave the ninety-nine in the desert and go after the lost one until he finds it? [5] And when he does find it, he sets it on his shoulders with great joy [6] and, upon his arrival home, he calls together his friends and neighbors and says to them, 'Rejoice with me because I have found my lost sheep.' [7] I tell you, in just the same way there will be more joy in heaven over one sinner who repents than over ninety-nine righteous people who have no need of repentance.

[8] "Or what woman having ten coins and losing one would not light a lamp and sweep the house, searching carefully until she finds it? [9] And when she does find it, she calls together her friends and neighbors and says to them, 'Rejoice with me because I have found the coin that I lost.' [10] In just the same way, I tell you, there will be rejoicing among the angels of God over one sinner who repents."

Friday November 8, 2024

Friday of Thirty-first Week in Ordinary Time
First Reading: Philippians 3:17-4:1
[17] Join with others in being imitators of me, brothers and sisters, and observe those who thus conduct themselves according to the model you have in us. [18] For many, as I have often told you and now tell you even in tears, conduct themselves as enemies of the cross of Christ. [19] Their end is destruction. Their God is their stomach; their glory is in their

"shame." Their minds are occupied with earthly things. [20] But our citizenship is in heaven, and from it we also await a savior, the Lord Jesus Christ. [21] He will change our lowly body to conform with his glorified Body by the power that enables him also to bring all things into subjection to himself.

[1] Therefore, my brothers and sisters, whom I love and long for, my joy and crown, in this way stand firm in the Lord, beloved.

Responsorial Psalm: Psalms 122:1-2, 3-4AB, 4CD-5
R. [(1)] *Let us go rejoicing to the house of the Lord.*
[1] I rejoiced because they said to me,
    "We will go up to the house of the LORD."
[2] And now we have set foot
    within your gates, O Jerusalem.
R. *Let us go rejoicing to the house of the Lord.*

[3] Jerusalem, built as a city
    with compact unity.
[4AB] To it the tribes go up,
    the tribes of the LORD.
R. *Let us go rejoicing to the house of the Lord.*

[4BC] According to the decree for Israel,
    to give thanks to the name of the LORD.
[5] In it are set up judgment seats,
    seats for the house of David.
R. *Let us go rejoicing to the house of the Lord.*

Alleluia: 1 John 2:5
R. Alleluia, alleluia.
[5] Whoever keeps the word of Christ,
the love of God is truly perfected in him.
R. Alleluia, alleluia.

Gospel: Luke 16:1-8
[1] Jesus said to his disciples, "A rich man had a steward who was reported to him for squandering his property. [2] He summoned him and said, 'What is this I hear about you? Prepare a full account of your stewardship, because you can no longer be my steward.' [3] The steward said to himself, 'What shall I do, now that my master is taking the position of steward away from me? I am not strong enough to dig and I am ashamed to beg. [4] I know what I shall do so that, when I am removed from the stewardship, they may welcome me into their homes.' [5] He called in his master's debtors one by one. To the first he said, 'How

much do you owe my master?' [6] He replied, 'One hundred measures of olive oil.' He said to him, 'Here is your promissory note. Sit down and quickly write one for fifty.' [7] Then to another he said, 'And you, how much do you owe?' He replied, 'One hundred measures of wheat.' He said to him, 'Here is your promissory note; write one for eighty.' [8] And the master commended that dishonest steward for acting prudently. For the children of this world are more prudent in dealing with their own generation than the children of light."

Saturday November 9, 2024

Feast of Dedication of the Lateran Basilica in Rome
First Reading: Ezekiel 47:1-2, 8-9, 12

[1] The angel brought me back to the entrance of the temple, and I saw water flowing out from beneath the threshold of the temple toward the east, for the façade of the temple was toward the east; the water flowed down from the southern side of the temple, south of the altar. [2] He led me outside by the north gate, and around to the outer gate facing the east, where I saw water trickling from the southern side. [8] He said to me, "This water flows into the eastern district down upon the Arabah, and empties into the sea, the salt waters, which it makes fresh. [9] Wherever the river flows, every sort of living creature that can multiply shall live, and there shall be abundant fish, for wherever this water comes the sea shall be made fresh. [12] Along both banks of the river, fruit trees of every kind shall grow; their leaves shall not fade, nor their fruit fail. Every month they shall bear fresh fruit, for they shall be watered by the flow from the sanctuary. Their fruit shall serve for food, and their leaves for medicine."

Responsorial Psalm: Psalms 46:2-3, 5-6, 8-9

R. [5] *The waters of the river gladden the city of God, the holy dwelling of the Most High!*

[2] God is our refuge and our strength,
    an ever-present help in distress.
[3] Therefore, we fear not, though the earth be
        shaken
    and mountains plunge into the depths of
        the sea.

R. *The waters of the river gladden the city of God, the holy dwelling of the Most High!*

[5] There is a stream whose runlets gladden the
        city of God,
    the holy dwelling of the Most High.
[6] God is in its midst; it shall not be disturbed;
    God will help it at the break of dawn.

R. *The waters of the river gladden the city of*

>*God, the holy dwelling of the Most*
>*High!*

[8] The LORD of hosts is with us;
>   our stronghold is the God of Jacob.
[9] Come! behold the deeds of the LORD,
>   the astounding things he has wrought on
>   earth.

R. The waters of the river gladden the city of
>   *God, the holy dwelling of the Most*
>   *High!*

Second Reading: 1 Corinthians 3:9C-11, 16-17

Brothers and sisters: [9C] You are God's building. [10] According to the grace of God given to me, like a wise master builder I laid a foundation, and another is building upon it. But each one must be careful how he builds upon it, [11] for no one can lay a foundation other than the one that is there, namely, Jesus Christ.

[16] Do you not know that you are the temple of God, and that the Spirit of God dwells in you? [17] If anyone destroys God's temple, God will destroy that person; for the temple of God, which you are, is holy.

Alleluia: 2 Chronicles 7:16

R. Alleluia, alleluia.

[16] I have chosen and consecrated this house,
>   says the Lord,
that my name may be there forever.

R. Alleluia, alleluia.

Gospel: John 2:13-22

[13] Since the Passover of the Jews was near, Jesus went up to Jerusalem. [14] He found in the temple area those who sold oxen, sheep, and doves, as well as the money-changers seated there. [15] He made a whip out of cords and drove them all out of the temple area, with the sheep and oxen, and spilled the coins of the money-changers and overturned their tables, [16] and to those who sold doves he said, "Take these out of here, and stop making my Father's house a marketplace." [17] His disciples recalled the words of Scripture, *Zeal for your house will consume me.* [18] At this the Jews answered and said to him, "What sign can you show us for doing this?" [19] Jesus answered and said to them, "Destroy this temple and in three days I will raise it up." [20] The Jews said, "This temple has been under construction for forty-six years, and you will raise it up in three days?" [21] But he was speaking about the temple of his Body. [22] Therefore, when he was raised from the dead, his disciples remembered that he had said this, and they came to believe the Scripture and the word Jesus had spoken.

Thirty-second Sunday in ordinary Time, Year B
First Reading: 1 Kings 17:10-16

[10] In those days, Elijah the prophet went to Zarephath. As he arrived at the entrance of the city, a widow was gathering sticks there; he called out to her, "Please bring me a small cupful of water to drink." [11] She left to get it, and he called out after her, "Please bring along a bit of bread." [12] She answered, "As the LORD, your God, lives, I have nothing baked; there is only a handful of flour in my jar and a little oil in my jug. Just now I was collecting a couple of sticks, to go in and prepare something for myself and my son; when we have eaten it, we shall die." [13] Elijah said to her, "Do not be afraid. Go and do as you propose. But first make me a little cake and bring it to me. Then you can prepare something for yourself and your son. [14] For the LORD, the God of Israel, says, 'The jar of flour shall not go empty, nor the jug of oil run dry, until the day when the LORD sends rain upon the earth.'" [15] She left and did as Elijah had said. She was able to eat for a year, and he and her son as well; [16] the jar of flour did not go empty, nor the jug of oil run dry, as the LORD had foretold through Elijah.

Responsorial Psalm: Psalms 146:7, 8-9, 9-10

R. [1b] *Praise the Lord, my soul!* or: *Alleluia.*

[7] The LORD keeps faith forever,
    secures justice for the oppressed,
    gives food to the hungry.
The LORD sets captives free.
R. *Praise the Lord, my soul!* or: *Alleluia.*

[8] The LORD gives sight to the blind;
    the LORD raises up those who were bowed
        down.
The LORD loves the just;
    [9A] the LORD protects strangers.
R. *Praise the Lord, my soul!* or: *Alleluia.*

[9B] The fatherless and the widow he sustains,
    but the way of the wicked he thwarts.
[10] The LORD shall reign forever;
    your God, O Zion, through all generations.
        Alleluia.
R. *Praise the Lord, my soul!* or: *Alleluia.*

Second Reading: Hebrews 9:24-28

24 Christ did not enter into a sanctuary made by hands, a copy of the true one, but heaven itself, that he might now appear before God on our behalf. 25 Not that he might offer himself repeatedly, as the high priest enters each year into the sanctuary with blood that is not his own; 26 if that were so, he would have had to suffer repeatedly from the foundation of the world. But now once for all he has appeared at the end of the ages to take away sin by his sacrifice. 27 Just as it is appointed that human beings die once, and after this the judgment, 28 so also Christ, offered once to take away the sins of many, will appear a second time, not to take away sin but to bring salvation to those who eagerly await him.

Alleluia: Mark 5:3

R. Alleluia, alleluia.

3 Blessed are the poor in spirit,
for theirs is the kingdom of heaven.

R. Alleluia, alleluia.

Gospel: Mark 12:38-44

38 In the course of his teaching Jesus said to the crowds, "Beware of the scribes, who like to go around in long robes and accept greetings in the marketplaces, 39 seats of honor in synagogues, and places of honor at banquets. 40 They devour the houses of widows and, as a pretext, recite lengthy prayers. They will receive a very severe condemnation."

41 He sat down opposite the treasury and observed how the crowd put money into the treasury. Many rich people put in large sums. 42 A poor widow also came and put in two small coins worth a few cents. 43 Calling his disciples to himself, he said to them, "Amen, I say to you, this poor widow put in more than all the other contributors to the treasury. 44 For they have all contributed from their surplus wealth, but she, from her poverty, has contributed all she had, her whole livelihood."

Or Mark 12:41-44

41 Jesus sat down opposite the treasury and observed how the crowd put money into the treasury. Many rich people put in large sums. 42 A poor widow also came and put in two small coins worth a few cents. 43 Calling his disciples to himself, he said to them, "Amen, I say to you, this poor widow put in more than all the other contributors to the treasury. 44 For they have all contributed from their surplus wealth, but she, from her poverty, has contributed all she had, her whole livelihood."

Monday November 11, 2024

Memorial Saint Martin of Tours, Bishop

First Reading: Titus 1:1-9

1 Paul, a slave of God and Apostle of Jesus Christ for the sake of the faith of God's chosen ones and the recognition of religious truth, 2 in the hope of eternal life that God, who does not lie, promised before time began, 3 who indeed at the proper time revealed his word in

the proclamation with which I was entrusted by the command of God our savior, [4] to Titus, my true child in our common faith: grace and peace from God the Father and Christ Jesus our savior.

[5] For this reason I left you in Crete so that you might set right what remains to be done and appoint presbyters in every town, as I directed you, [6] on condition that a man be blameless, married only once, with believing children who are not accused of licentiousness or rebellious. [7] For a bishop as God's steward must be blameless, not arrogant, not irritable, not a drunkard, not aggressive, not greedy for sordid gain, [8] but hospitable, a lover of goodness, temperate, just, holy, and self-controlled, [9] holding fast to the true message as taught so that he will be able both to exhort with sound doctrine and to refute opponents.

Responsorial Psalm: Psalms 24:1B-2, 3-4AB, 5-6

R. [(see 6)]*Lord, this is the people that longs to see your face.*

[1B] The LORD's are the earth and its fullness;
the world and those who dwell in it.
[2] For he founded it upon the seas
and established it upon the rivers.

R. *Lord, this is the people that longs to see your face.*

[3] Who can ascend the mountain of the LORD?
or who may stand in his holy place?
[4AB] He whose hands are sinless, whose heart is clean,
who desires not what is vain.

R. *Lord, this is the people that longs to see your face.*

[5] He shall receive a blessing from the LORD,
a reward from God his savior.
[6] Such is the race that seeks for him,
that seeks the face of the God of Jacob.

R. *Lord, this is the people that longs to see your face.*

Alleluia: Philippians 2:15D, 16A

R. Alleluia, alleluia.
[15D] Shine like lights in the world,
[16A] as you hold on to the word of life.
R. Alleluia, alleluia.

Gospel: Luke 17:1-6

[1] Jesus said to his disciples, "Things that cause sin will inevitably occur, but woe to the one through whom they occur. [2] It would be better for him if a millstone were put around his neck and he be thrown into the sea than for him to cause one of these little ones to sin. [3] Be on your guard! If your brother sins, rebuke him; and if he repents, forgive him. [4] And if he wrongs you seven times in one day and returns to you seven times saying, 'I am sorry,' you should forgive him."

[5] And the Apostles said to the Lord, "Increase our faith." [6] The Lord replied, "If you have faith the size of a mustard seed, you would say to this mulberry tree, 'Be uprooted and planted in the sea,' and it would obey you."

Tuesday November 12, 2024

Memorial of Saint Josaphat, Bishop & Martyr

First Reading: Titus 2:1-8, 11-14

Beloved: [1] You must say what is consistent with sound doctrine, namely, [2] that older men should be temperate, dignified, self-controlled, sound in faith, love, and endurance. [3] Similarly, older women should be reverent in their behavior, not slanderers, not addicted to drink, teaching what is good, [4] so that they may train younger women to love their husbands and children, [5] to be self-controlled, chaste, good homemakers, under the control of their husbands, so that the word of God may not be discredited.

[6] Urge the younger men, similarly, to control themselves, [7] showing yourself as a model of good deeds in every respect, with integrity in your teaching, dignity, [8] and sound speech that cannot be criticized, so that the opponent will be put to shame without anything bad to say about us.

[11] For the grace of God has appeared, saving all [12] and training us to reject godless ways and worldly desires and to live temperately, justly, and devoutly in this age, [13] as we await the blessed hope, the appearance of the glory of the great God and of our savior Jesus Christ, [14] who gave himself for us to deliver us from all lawlessness and to cleanse for himself a people as his own, eager to do what is good.

Responsorial Psalm: Psalms 37:3-4, 18 AND 23, 27 AND 29

R. [39a] *The salvation of the just comes from the Lord.*

[3] Trust in the LORD and do good,
    that you may dwell in the land and be fed
        in security.
[4] Take delight in the LORD,
    and he will grant you your heart's
        requests.

R. *The salvation of the just comes from the Lord.*

[18] The LORD watches over the lives of the
        wholehearted;
    their inheritance lasts forever.

²³ By the LORD are the steps of a man made
         firm,
      and he approves his way.
R. The salvation of the just comes from the Lord.

²⁷ Turn from evil and do good,
      that you may abide forever;
²⁹ The just shall possess the land
      and dwell in it forever.
R. The salvation of the just comes from the Lord.

Alleluia: John 14:23
R. Alleluia, alleluia.
²³ Whoever loves me will keep my word,
and my Father will love him,
and we will come to him.
R. Alleluia, alleluia.

Gospel: Luke 17:7-10
Jesus said to the Apostles: ⁷ "Who among you would say to your servant who has just come in from plowing or tending sheep in the field, 'Come here immediately and take your place at table'? ⁸ Would he not rather say to him, 'Prepare something for me to eat. Put on your apron and wait on me while I eat and drink. You may eat and drink when I am finished'? ⁹ Is he grateful to that servant because he did what was commanded? ¹⁰ So should it be with you. When you have done all you have been commanded, say, 'We are unprofitable servants; we have done what we were obliged to do.'"

Wednesday November 13, 2024

Memorial of Saint Frances Xavier Cabrini

First Reading: Titus 3:1-7
Beloved: ¹ Remind them to be under the control of magistrates and authorities, to be obedient, to be open to every good enterprise. ² They are to slander no one, to be peaceable, considerate, exercising all graciousness toward everyone. ³ For we ourselves were once foolish, disobedient, deluded, slaves to various desires and pleasures, living in malice and envy, hateful ourselves and hating one another.

⁴ But when the kindness and generous love
      of God our savior appeared,
⁵ not because of any righteous deeds we had
         done
      but because of his mercy,
he saved us through the bath of rebirth

and renewal by the Holy Spirit,
⁶ whom he richly poured out on us
    through Jesus Christ our savior,
⁷ so that we might be justified by his grace
    and become heirs in hope of eternal life.

Responsorial Psalm: Psalms 23:1B-3A, 3BC-4, 5, 6

R. [1] *The Lord is my shepherd; there is nothing I*
        shall want.

^{1B} The LORD is my shepherd; I shall not want.
    ² In verdant pastures he gives me repose;
Beside restful waters he leads me;
    ^{3A} he refreshes my soul.
R. *The Lord is my shepherd; there is nothing I*
        shall want.

^{3BC} He guides me in right paths
        for his name's sake.
⁴ Even though I walk in the dark valley
        I fear no evil; for you are at my side
With your rod and your staff
        that give me courage.
R. *The Lord is my shepherd; there is nothing I*
        shall want.

⁵ You spread the table before me
        in the sight of my foes;
You anoint my head with oil;
        my cup overflows.
R. *The Lord is my shepherd; there is nothing I*
        shall want.

⁶ Only goodness and kindness follow me
        all the days of my life;
And I shall dwell in the house of the LORD
        for years to come.
R. *The Lord is my shepherd; there is nothing I*
        shall want.

Alleluia: 1 Thessalonians 5:18

R. Alleluia, alleluia.
¹⁸ In all circumstances, give thanks,

for this is the will of God for you in Christ Jesus.
R. Alleluia, alleluia.

Gospel: Luke 17:11-19

[11] As Jesus continued his journey to Jerusalem, he traveled through Samaria and Galilee. [12] As he was entering a village, ten lepers met him. They stood at a distance from him [13] and raised their voice, saying, "Jesus, Master! Have pity on us!" [14] And when he saw them, he said, "Go show yourselves to the priests." As they were going they were cleansed. [15] And one of them, realizing he had been healed, returned, glorifying God in a loud voice; [16] and he fell at the feet of Jesus and thanked him. He was a Samaritan. [17] Jesus said in reply, "Ten were cleansed, were they not? Where are the other nine? [18] Has none but this foreigner returned to give thanks to God?" [19] Then he said to him, "Stand up and go; your faith has saved you."

Thursday November 14, 2024

Thursday of Thirty-second Week in Ordinary Time
First Reading: Philemon 7-20

Beloved: [7] I have experienced much joy and encouragement from your love, because the hearts of the holy ones have been refreshed by you, brother. [8] Therefore, although I have the full right in Christ to order you to do what is proper, [9] I rather urge you out of love, being as I am, Paul, an old man, and now also a prisoner for Christ Jesus. [10] I urge you on behalf of my child Onesimus, whose father I have become in my imprisonment, [11] who was once useless to you but is now useful to both you and me. [12] I am sending him, that is, my own heart, back to you. [13] I should have liked to retain him for myself, so that he might serve me on your behalf in my imprisonment for the Gospel, [14] but I did not want to do anything without your consent, so that the good you do might not be forced but voluntary. [15] Perhaps this is why he was away from you for a while, that you might have him back forever, [16] no longer as a slave but more than a slave, a brother, beloved especially to me, but even more so to you, as a man and in the Lord. [17] So if you regard me as a partner, welcome him as you would me. [18] And if he has done you any injustice or owes you anything, charge it to me. [19] I, Paul, write this in my own hand: I will pay. May I not tell you that you owe me your very self. [20] Yes, brother, may I profit from you in the Lord. Refresh my heart in Christ.

Responsorial Psalm: Psalms 146:7, 8-9A, 9BC-10

R. [5a] *Blessed is he whose help is the God of Jacob.* or: *Alleluia.*
[7] The LORD secures justice for the oppressed,
    gives food to the hungry.
The LORD sets captives free.
R. *Blessed is he whose help is the God of Jacob.* or: *Alleluia.*

[8] The LORD gives sight to the blind.
The LORD raises up those who were bowed

down;
    the LORD loves the just.
^{9A} The LORD protects strangers.
R. Blessed is he whose help is the God of Jacob. or: *Alleluia.*

^{9BC} The fatherless and the widow he sustains,
    but the way of the wicked he thwarts.
¹⁰ The LORD shall reign forever;
    your God, O Zion, through all generations.
        Alleluia.
R. Blessed is he whose help is the God of Jacob. or: *Alleluia.*

Alleluia: John 15:5

R. Alleluia, alleluia.
⁵ I am the vine, you are the branches, says the
        Lord:
whoever remains in me and I in him will
        bear much fruit.

R. Alleluia, alleluia.

Gospel: Luke 17:20-25

²⁰ Asked by the Pharisees when the Kingdom of God would come, Jesus said in reply, "The coming of the Kingdom of God cannot be observed, ²¹ and no one will announce, 'Look, here it is,' or, 'There it is.' For behold, the Kingdom of God is among you."

²² Then he said to his disciples, "The days will come when you will long to see one of the days of the Son of Man, but you will not see it. ²³ There will be those who will say to you, 'Look, there he is,' or 'Look, here he is.' Do not go off, do not run in pursuit. ²⁴ For just as lightning flashes and lights up the sky from one side to the other, so will the Son of Man be in his day. ²⁵ But first he must suffer greatly and be rejected by this generation."

Friday November 15, 2024

Friday of Thirty-second Week in Ordinary Time
First Reading: 2 John 4-9

[Chosen Lady:] ⁴ I rejoiced greatly to find some of your children walking in the truth just as we were commanded by the Father. ⁵ But now, Lady, I ask you, not as though I were writing a new commandment but the one we have had from the beginning: let us love one another. ⁶ For this is love, that we walk according to his commandments; this is the commandment, as you heard from the beginning, in which you should walk.

⁷ Many deceivers have gone out into the world, those who do not acknowledge Jesus Christ as coming in the flesh; such is the deceitful one and the antichrist. ⁸ Look to yourselves that you do not lose what we worked for but may receive a full recompense. ⁹ Anyone who is so "progressive" as not to remain in the teaching of the Christ does not have God; whoever remains in the teaching has the Father and the Son.

Responsorial Psalm: Psalms 119:1, 2, 10, 11, 17, 18

R. [1b] *Blessed are they who follow the law of the Lord!*

[1] Blessed are they whose way is blameless,
   who walk in the law of the LORD.

R. *Blessed are they who follow the law of the Lord!*

[2] Blessed are they who observe his decrees,
   who seek him with all their heart.

R. *Blessed are they who follow the law of the Lord!*

[10] With all my heart I seek you;
   let me not stray from your commands.

R. *Blessed are they who follow the law of the Lord!*

[11] Within my heart I treasure your promise,
   that I may not sin against you.

R. *Blessed are they who follow the law of the Lord!*

[17] Be good to your servant, that I may live
   and keep your words.

R. *Blessed are they who follow the law of the Lord!*

[18] Open my eyes, that I may consider
   the wonders of your law.

R. *Blessed are they who follow the law of the Lord!*

Alleluia: Luke 21:28

R. Alleluia, alleluia.

[28] Stand erect and raise your heads
because your redemption is at hand.

R. Alleluia, alleluia.

Gospel: Luke 17:26-37

Jesus said to his disciples: [26] "As it was in the days of Noah, so it will be in the days of the Son of Man; [27] they were eating and drinking, marrying and giving in marriage up to the day that Noah entered the ark, and the flood came and destroyed them all. [28] Similarly, as it was in the days of Lot: they were eating, drinking, buying, selling, planting, building; [29] on the day when Lot left Sodom, fire and brimstone rained from the sky to destroy them all. [30] So it will be on the day the Son of Man is revealed. [31] On that day, someone who is on the housetop and whose belongings are in the house must not go down to get them, and likewise one in the field must not return to what was left behind. [32] Remember the wife of Lot. [33] Whoever seeks to preserve his life will lose it, but whoever loses it will save it. [34] I tell you, on that night there will be two people in one bed; one will be taken, the other left. [35] And there will be two women grinding meal together; one will be taken, the other left." [37] They said to him in reply, "Where, Lord?" He said to them, "Where the body is, there also the vultures will gather."

Saturday November 16, 2024

Saturday of Thirty-second Week in Ordinary Time

First Reading: 3 John 5-8

[5] Beloved, you are faithful in all you do for the brothers and sisters, especially for strangers; [6] they have testified to your love before the Church. Please help them in a way worthy of God to continue their journey. [7] For they have set out for the sake of the Name and are accepting nothing from the pagans. [8] Therefore, we ought to support such persons, so that we may be co-workers in the truth.

Responsorial Psalm: Psalms 112:1-2,3-4, 5-6

R. *Blessed the man who fears the Lord.* or: *Alleluia.*

[1] Blessed the man who fears the LORD,
     who greatly delights in his commands.
[2] His posterity shall be mighty upon the earth;
     the upright generation shall be blessed.

R. *Blessed the man who fears the Lord.* or: *Alleluia.*

[3] Wealth and riches shall be in his house;
     his generosity shall endure forever.
[4] Light shines through the darkness for the
          upright;
     he is gracious and merciful and just.

R. *Blessed the man who fears the Lord.* or: *Alleluia.*

[5] Well for the man who is gracious and lends,
     who conducts his affairs with justice;
[6] He shall never be moved;
     the just one shall be in everlasting
          remembrance.

R. *Blessed the man who fears the Lord.* or: *Alleluia.*

Alleluia: cf. 2 Thessalonians 2:14
R. Alleluia, alleluia.
[14] God has called us through the Gospel,
to possess the glory of our Lord Jesus Christ.
R. Alleluia, alleluia.

Gospel: Luke 18:1-8
[1] Jesus told his disciples a parable about the necessity for them to pray always without becoming weary. He said, [2] "There was a judge in a certain town who neither feared God nor respected any human being. [3] And a widow in that town used to come to him and say, 'Render a just decision for me against my adversary.' [4] For a long time the judge was unwilling, but eventually he thought, 'While it is true that I neither fear God nor respect any human being, [5] because this widow keeps bothering me I shall deliver a just decision for her lest she finally come and strike me.'" [6] The Lord said, "Pay attention to what the dishonest judge says. [7] Will not God then secure the rights of his chosen ones who call out to him day and night? Will he be slow to answer them? [8] I tell you, he will see to it that justice is done for them speedily. But when the Son of Man comes, will he find faith on earth?"

Sunday November 17, 2024

Thirty-third Sunday in Ordinary Time, Year B
First Reading: Daniel 12:1-3
[1] In those days, I Daniel, heard this word of the Lord:

"At that time there shall arise
Michael, the great prince,
guardian of your people;
it shall be a time unsurpassed in distress
since nations began until that time.
At that time your people shall escape,
everyone who is found written in the
book.

[2] "Many of those who sleep in the dust of the
earth shall awake;
some shall live forever,
others shall be an everlasting horror and
disgrace.

[3] "But the wise shall shine brightly
like the splendor of the firmament,
and those who lead the many to justice

shall be like the stars forever."

Responsorial Psalm: Psalms 16:5, 8,9-10, 11
R. *(1) You are my inheritance, O Lord!*
5 O LORD, my allotted portion and my cup,
    you it is who hold fast my lot.
8 I set the LORD ever before me;
    with him at my right hand I shall not be
        disturbed.
R. *You are my inheritance, O Lord!*

9 Therefore my heart is glad and my soul
        rejoices,
    my body, too, abides in confidence;
10 because you will not abandon my soul to the
        netherworld,
    nor will you suffer your faithful one to
        undergo corruption.
R. *You are my inheritance, O Lord!*

11 You will show me the path to life,
    fullness of joys in your presence,
    the delights at your right hand forever.
R. *You are my inheritance, O Lord!*

Second Reading: Hebrews 10:11-14, 18
Brothers and sisters: 11 Every priest stands daily at his ministry, offering frequently those same sacrifices that can never take away sins. 12 But this one offered one sacrifice for sins, and took his seat forever at the right hand of God; 13 now he waits until his enemies are made his footstool. 14 For by one offering he has made perfect forever those who are being consecrated.
    18 Where there is forgiveness of these, there is no longer offering for sin.

Alleluia: Luke 21:36
R. Alleluia, alleluia.
36 Be vigilant at all times
and pray that you have the strength to stand
    before the Son of Man.
R. Alleluia, alleluia.

Gospel: Mark 13:24-32
Jesus said to his disciples: 24 "In those days after that tribulation

the sun will be darkened,
    and the moon will not give its light,
^{25} and the stars will be falling from the sky,
    and the powers in the heavens will be
        shaken.

^{26} "And then they will see 'the Son of Man coming in the clouds' with great power and glory, ^{27} and then he will send out the angels and gather his elect from the four winds, from the end of the earth to the end of the sky.

^{28} "Learn a lesson from the fig tree. When its branch becomes tender and sprouts leaves, you know that summer is near. ^{29} In the same way, when you see these things happening, know that he is near, at the gates. ^{30} Amen, I say to you, this generation will not pass away until all these things have taken place. ^{31} Heaven and earth will pass away, but my words will not pass away.

^{32} "But of that day or hour, no one knows, neither the angels in heaven, nor the Son, but only the Father."

Monday November 18, 2024

Monday of Thirty-third Week in Ordinary Time
First Reading: Revelation 1:1-4; 2:1-5

^{1} The revelation of Jesus Christ, which God gave to him, to show his servants what must happen soon. He made it known by sending his angel to his servant John, ^{2} who gives witness to the word of God and to the testimony of Jesus Christ by reporting what he saw. ^{3} Blessed is the one who reads aloud and blessed are those who listen to this prophetic message and heed what is written in it, for the appointed time is near.

^{4} John, to the seven churches in Asia: grace to you and peace from him who is and who was and who is to come, and from the seven spirits before his throne.

I heard the Lord saying to me: ^{1} "To the angel of the Church in Ephesus, write this:

"'The one who holds the seven stars in his right hand and walks in the midst of the seven gold lampstands says this: ^{2} "I know your works, your labor, and your endurance, and that you cannot tolerate the wicked; you have tested those who call themselves Apostles but are not, and discovered that they are impostors. ^{3} Moreover, you have endurance and have suffered for my name, and you have not grown weary. ^{4} Yet I hold this against you: you have lost the love you had at first. ^{5} Realize how far you have fallen. Repent, and do the works you did at first. Otherwise, I will come to you and remove your lampstand from its place, unless you repent."'"

Responsorial Psalm: Psalms 1:1-2, 3, 4 & 6
R. (Rev. 2:17) *Those who are victorious I will feed*
                        from the tree of life.
^{1} Blessed the man who follows not
        the counsel of the wicked

588

Nor walks in the way of sinners,
    nor sits in the company of the insolent,
² But delights in the law of the LORD
    and meditates on his law day and night.
**R. Those who are victorious I will feed from the
    tree of life.**

³ He is like a tree
    planted near running water,
That yields its fruit in due season,
    and whose leaves never fade.
    Whatever he does, prospers.
**R. Those who are victorious I will feed from the
    tree of life.**

⁴ Not so the wicked, not so;
    they are like chaff which the wind drives
        away.
⁶ For the LORD watches over the way of the
        just,
    but the way of the wicked vanishes.
**R. Those who are victorious I will feed from the
    tree of life.**

Alleluia: John 8:12
R. Alleluia, alleluia.
¹² I am the light of the world, says the Lord;
whoever follows me will have the light of life.
R. Alleluia, alleluia.

Gospel: Luke 18:35-43
³⁵ As Jesus approached Jericho a blind man was sitting by the roadside begging, ³⁶ and hearing a crowd going by, he inquired what was happening. ³⁷ They told him, "Jesus of Nazareth is passing by." ³⁸ He shouted, "Jesus, Son of David, have pity on me!" ³⁹ The people walking in front rebuked him, telling him to be silent, but he kept calling out all the more, "Son of David, have pity on me!" ⁴⁰ Then Jesus stopped and ordered that he be brought to him; and when he came near, Jesus asked him, ⁴¹ "What do you want me to do for you?" He replied, "Lord, please let me see." ⁴² Jesus told him, "Have sight; your faith has saved you." ⁴³ He immediately received his sight and followed him, giving glory to God. When they saw this, all the people gave praise to God.

Tuesday of Thirty-third Week in Ordinary Time
First Reading: Revelation 3:1-6, 14-22

[1] I, John, heard the Lord saying to me: "To the angel of the Church in Sardis, write this:

"'The one who has the seven spirits of God and the seven stars says this: "I know your works, that you have the reputation of being alive, but you are dead. [2] Be watchful and strengthen what is left, which is going to die, for I have not found your works complete in the sight of my God. [3] Remember then how you accepted and heard; keep it, and repent. If you are not watchful, I will come like a thief, and you will never know at what hour I will come upon you. [4] However, you have a few people in Sardis who have not soiled their garments; they will walk with me dressed in white, because they are worthy.

[5] "'The victor will thus be dressed in white, and I will never erase his name from the book of life but will acknowledge his name in the presence of my Father and of his angels.

[6] "'Whoever has ears ought to hear what the Spirit says to the churches.'"

[14] "To the angel of the Church in Laodicea, write this:

"'The Amen, the faithful and true witness, the source of God's creation, says this: [15] "I know your works; I know that you are neither cold nor hot. I wish you were either cold or hot. [16] So, because you are lukewarm, neither hot nor cold, I will spit you out of my mouth. [17] For you say, 'I am rich and affluent and have no need of anything,' and yet do not realize that you are wretched, pitiable, poor, blind, and naked. [18] I advise you to buy from me gold refined by fire so that you may be rich, and white garments to put on so that your shameful nakedness may not be exposed, and buy ointment to smear on your eyes so that you may see. [19] Those whom I love, I reprove and chastise. Be earnest, therefore, and repent.

[20] "'Behold, I stand at the door and knock. If anyone hears my voice and opens the door, then I will enter his house and dine with him, and he with me. [21] I will give the victor the right to sit with me on my throne, as I myself first won the victory and sit with my Father on his throne.

[22] "'Whoever has ears ought to hear what the Spirit says to the churches.'"

Responsorial Psalm: Psalms 15:2-3A, 3BC-4AB, 5

R. (Rev. 3: 21) *I will seat the victor beside me on my throne.*

[2] He who walks blamelessly and does justice;
    who thinks the truth in his heart
    [3A] and slanders not with his tongue.

R. *I will seat the victor beside me on my throne.*

[3BC] Who harms not his fellow man,
    nor takes up a reproach against his
      neighbor;

4AB By whom the reprobate is despised,
  while he honors those who fear the LORD.
R. I will seat the victor beside me on my throne.

5 Who lends not his money at usury
  and accepts no bribe against the
    innocent.
He who does these things
  shall never be disturbed.
R. I will seat the victor beside me on my throne.

Alleluia: 1 John 4:10B
R. Alleluia, alleluia.
10B God loved us, and send his Son
as expiation for our sins.
R. Alleluia, alleluia.

Gospel: Luke 19:1-10

1 At that time Jesus came to Jericho and intended to pass through the town. **2** Now a man there named Zacchaeus, who was a chief tax collector and also a wealthy man, **3** was seeking to see who Jesus was; but he could not see him because of the crowd, for he was short in stature. **4** So he ran ahead and climbed a sycamore tree in order to see Jesus, who was about to pass that way. **5** When he reached the place, Jesus looked up and said, "Zacchaeus, come down quickly, for today I must stay at your house." **6** And he came down quickly and received him with joy. **7** When they saw this, they began to grumble, saying, "He has gone to stay at the house of a sinner." **8** But Zacchaeus stood there and said to the Lord, "Behold, half of my possessions, Lord, I shall give to the poor, and if I have extorted anything from anyone I shall repay it four times over." **9** And Jesus said to him, "Today salvation has come to this house because this man too is a descendant of Abraham. **10** For the Son of Man has come to seek and to save what was lost."

Wednesday November 20, 2024

Wednesday of Thirty-third Week in Ordinary Time

First Reading: Revelation 4:1-11

1 I, John, had a vision of an open door to heaven, and I heard the trumpetlike voice that had spoken to me before, saying, "Come up here and I will show you what must happen afterwards." **2** At once I was caught up in spirit. A throne was there in heaven, and on the throne sat **3** one whose appearance sparkled like jasper and carnelian. Around the throne was a halo as brilliant as an emerald. **4** Surrounding the throne I saw twenty-four other thrones on which twenty-four elders sat, dressed in white garments and with gold crowns on their heads. **5** From the throne came flashes of lightning, rumblings, and peals of thunder. Seven flaming torches burned in front of the throne, which are the seven spirits of God. **6** In front of the throne was something that resembled a sea of glass like crystal.

In the center and around the throne, there were four living creatures covered with eyes in front and in back. [7] The first creature resembled a lion, the second was like a calf, the third had a face like that of a man, and the fourth looked like an eagle in flight. [8] The four living creatures, each of them with six wings, were covered with eyes inside and out. Day and night they do not stop exclaiming: "Holy, holy, holy is the Lord God almighty, who was, and who is, and who is to come." [9] Whenever the living creatures give glory and honor and thanks to the one who sits on the throne, who lives forever and ever, [10] the twenty-four elders fall down before the one who sits on the throne and worship him, who lives forever and ever. They throw down their crowns before the throne, exclaiming:

[11] "Worthy are you, Lord our God,
    to receive glory and honor and power,
for you created all things;
    because of your will they came to be and
      were created."

Responsorial Psalm: Psalms 150:1B-2, 3-4, 5-6

R. [(1b)] *Holy, holy, holy Lord, mighty God!*

[1B] Praise the LORD in his sanctuary,
    praise him in the firmament of his
      strength.
[2] Praise him for his mighty deeds,
    praise him for his sovereign majesty.

R. *Holy, holy, holy Lord, mighty God!*

[3] Praise him with the blast of the trumpet,
    praise him with lyre and harp,
[4] Praise him with timbrel and dance,
    praise him with strings and pipe.

R. *Holy, holy, holy Lord, mighty God!*

[5] Praise him with sounding cymbals,
    praise him with clanging cymbals.
[6] Let everything that has breath
    praise the LORD! Alleluia.

R. *Holy, holy, holy Lord, mighty God!*

Alleluia: cf. John 15:16

R. Alleluia, alleluia.

[16] I chose you from the world,
to go and bear fruit that will last, says the
    Lord.

R. Alleluia, alleluia.

Gospel: Luke 19:11-28

[11] While people were listening to Jesus speak, he proceeded to tell a parable because he was near Jerusalem and they thought that the Kingdom of God would appear there immediately. [12] So he said, "A nobleman went off to a distant country to obtain the kingship for himself and then to return. [13] He called ten of his servants and gave them ten gold coins and told them, 'Engage in trade with these until I return.' [14] His fellow citizens, however, despised him and sent a delegation after him to announce, 'We do not want this man to be our king.' [15] But when he returned after obtaining the kingship, he had the servants called, to whom he had given the money, to learn what they had gained by trading. [16] The first came forward and said, 'Sir, your gold coin has earned ten additional ones.' [17] He replied, 'Well done, good servant! You have been faithful in this very small matter; take charge of ten cities.' [18] Then the second came and reported, 'Your gold coin, sir, has earned five more.' [19] And to this servant too he said, 'You, take charge of five cities.' [20] Then the other servant came and said, 'Sir, here is your gold coin; I kept it stored away in a handkerchief, [21] for I was afraid of you, because you are a demanding man; you take up what you did not lay down and you harvest what you did not plant.' [22] He said to him, 'With your own words I shall condemn you, you wicked servant. You knew I was a demanding man, taking up what I did not lay down and harvesting what I did not plant; [23] why did you not put my money in a bank? Then on my return I would have collected it with interest.' [24] And to those standing by he said, 'Take the gold coin from him and give it to the servant who has ten.' [25] But they said to him, 'Sir, he has ten gold coins.' [26] He replied, 'I tell you, to everyone who has, more will be given, but from the one who has not, even what he has will be taken away. [27] Now as for those enemies of mine who did not want me as their king, bring them here and slay them before me.'"

[28] After he had said this, he proceeded on his journey up to Jerusalem.

Thursday November 21, 2024

The Presentation of the Blessed Virgin Mary

First Reading: Revelation 5:1-10

[1] I, John, saw a scroll in the right hand of the one who sat on the throne. It had writing on both sides and was sealed with seven seals. [2] Then I saw a mighty angel who proclaimed in a loud voice, "Who is worthy to open the scroll and break its seals?" [3] But no one in heaven or on earth or under the earth was able to open the scroll or to examine it. [4] I shed many tears because no one was found worthy to open the scroll or to examine it. [5] One of the elders said to me, "Do not weep. The lion of the tribe of Judah, the root of David, has triumphed, enabling him to open the scroll with its seven seals."

[6] Then I saw standing in the midst of the throne and the four living creatures and the elders a Lamb that seemed to have been slain. He had seven horns and seven eyes; these are the seven spirits of God sent out into the whole world. [7] He came and received the scroll from the right hand of the one who sat on the throne. [8] When he took it, the four living creatures and the twenty-four elders fell down before the Lamb. Each of the elders held a harp and gold bowls filled with incense, which are the prayers of the holy ones. [9] They sang a new hymn:

593

"Worthy are you to receive the scroll
and break open its seals,
for you were slain and with your Blood
you purchased for God
those from every tribe and tongue,
people and nation.
[10] You made them a kingdom and priests for
our God,
and they will reign on earth."

Responsorial Psalm: Psalms 149:1B-2, 3-4, 5-6A AND 9B

R. *(Rev. 5:10)* **The Lamb has made us a kingdom of
priests to serve our God.** or: *Alleluia.*

[1B] Sing to the LORD a new song
of praise in the assembly of the faithful.
[2] Let Israel be glad in their maker,
let the children of Zion rejoice in their
king.
R. **The Lamb has made us a kingdom of priests
to serve our God.** or: *Alleluia.*

[3] Let them praise his name in the festive
dance,
let them sing praise to him with timbrel
and harp.
[4] For the LORD loves his people,
and he adorns the lowly with victory.
R. **The Lamb has made us a kingdom of priests
to serve our God.** or: *Alleluia.*

[5] Let the faithful exult in glory;
let them sing for joy upon their couches;
[6A] Let the high praises of God be in their
throats.
[9B] This is the glory of all his faithful.
Alleluia.
R. **The Lamb has made us a kingdom of priests
to serve our God.** or: *Alleluia.*

Alleluia: Psalms 95:8

R. Alleluia, alleluia.
[8] If today you hear his voice,

harden not your hearts.
R. Alleluia, alleluia.

Gospel: Luke 19:41-44

[41] As Jesus drew near Jerusalem, he saw the city and wept over it, [42] saying, "If this day you only knew what makes for peace— but now it is hidden from your eyes. [43] For the days are coming upon you when your enemies will raise a palisade against you; they will encircle you and hem you in on all sides. [44] They will smash you to the ground and your children within you, and they will not leave one stone upon another within you because you did not recognize the time of your visitation."

Friday November 22, 2024

Memorial of Saint Cecilia, Virgin & Martyr
First Reading: Revelation 10:8-11

[8] I, John, heard a voice from heaven speak to me. Then the voice spoke to me and said: "Go, take the scroll that lies open in the hand of the angel who is standing on the sea and on the land." [9] So I went up to the angel and told him to give me the small scroll. He said to me, "Take and swallow it. It will turn your stomach sour, but in your mouth it will taste as sweet as honey." [10] I took the small scroll from the angel's hand and swallowed it. In my mouth it was like sweet honey, but when I had eaten it, my stomach turned sour. [11] Then someone said to me, "You must prophesy again about many peoples, nations, tongues, and kings."

Responsorial Psalm: Psalms 119:14, 24, 72, 103, 111, 131

R. [103a] How sweet to my taste is your promise!

[14] In the way of your decrees I rejoice,
    as much as in all riches.
R. How sweet to my taste is your promise!

[24] Yes, your decrees are my delight;
    they are my counselors.
R. How sweet to my taste is your promise!

[72] The law of your mouth is to me more
        precious
    than thousands of gold and silver pieces.
R. How sweet to my taste is your promise!

[103] How sweet to my palate are your promises,
    sweeter than honey to my mouth!
R. How sweet to my taste is your promise!

[111] Your decrees are my inheritance forever;

the joy of my heart they are.
R. How sweet to my taste is your promise!

 131 I gasp with open mouth
   in my yearning for your commands.
R. How sweet to my taste is your promise!

Alleluia: John 10:27
R. Alleluia, alleluia.
27 My sheep hear my voice, says the Lord;
I know them, and they follow me.
R. Alleluia, alleluia.

Gospel: Luke 19:45-48
45 Jesus entered the temple area and proceeded to drive out those who were selling things, 46 saying to them, "It is written, *My house shall be a house of prayer, but you have made it a den of thieves.*" 47 And every day he was teaching in the temple area. The chief priests, the scribes, and the leaders of the people, meanwhile, were seeking to put him to death, 48 but they could find no way to accomplish their purpose because all the people were hanging on his words.

Saturday November 23, 2024

Saturday of Thirty-third Week in Ordinary Time
First Reading: Revelation 11:4-12
I, John, heard a voice from heaven speak to me: Here are my two witnesses: 4 These are the two olive trees and the two lampstands that stand before the Lord of the earth. 5 If anyone wants to harm them, fire comes out of their mouths and devours their enemies. In this way, anyone wanting to harm them is sure to be slain. 6 They have the power to close up the sky so that no rain can fall during the time of their prophesying. They also have power to turn water into blood and to afflict the earth with any plague as often as they wish.

7 When they have finished their testimony, the beast that comes up from the abyss will wage war against them and conquer them and kill them. 8 Their corpses will lie in the main street of the great city, which has the symbolic names "Sodom" and "Egypt," where indeed their Lord was crucified. 9 Those from every people, tribe, tongue, and nation will gaze on their corpses for three and a half days, and they will not allow their corpses to be buried. 10 The inhabitants of the earth will gloat over them and be glad and exchange gifts because these two prophets tormented the inhabitants of the earth. 11 But after the three and a half days, a breath of life from God entered them. When they stood on their feet, great fear fell on those who saw them. 12 Then they heard a loud voice from heaven say to them, "Come up here." So they went up to heaven in a cloud as their enemies looked on.

Responsorial Psalm: Psalms 144:1, 2, 9-10

R. [1b] *Blessed be the Lord, my Rock!*

[1] Blessed be the LORD, my rock,
> who trains my hands for battle, my
>> fingers for war.

R. *Blessed be the Lord, my Rock!*

[2] My mercy and my fortress,
> my stronghold, my deliverer,
My shield, in whom I trust,
> who subdues my people under me.

R. *Blessed be the Lord, my Rock!*

[9] O God, I will sing a new song to you;
> with a ten stringed lyre I will chant your
>> praise,
[10] You who give victory to kings,
> and deliver David, your servant from the
>> evil sword.

R. *Blessed be the Lord, my Rock!*

Alleluia: cf. 2 Timothy 1:10

R. Alleluia, alleluia.

[10] Our Savior Jesus Christ has destroyed death
and brought life to light through the Gospel.

R. Alleluia, alleluia.

Gospel: Luke 20:27-40

[27] Some Sadducees, those who deny that there is a resurrection, came forward and put this question to Jesus, [28] saying, "Teacher, Moses wrote for us, *If someone's brother dies leaving a wife but no child, his brother must take the wife and raise up descendants for his brother.* [29] Now there were seven brothers; the first married a woman but died childless. [30] Then the second [31] and the third married her, and likewise all the seven died childless. [32] Finally the woman also died. [33] Now at the resurrection whose wife will that woman be? For all seven had been married to her." [34] Jesus said to them, "The children of this age marry and remarry; [35] but those who are deemed worthy to attain to the coming age and to the resurrection of the dead neither marry nor are given in marriage. [36] They can no longer die, for they are like angels; and they are the children of God because they are the ones who will rise. [37] That the dead will rise even Moses made known in the passage about the bush, when he called 'Lord' the God of Abraham, the God of Isaac, and the God of Jacob; [38] and he is not God of the dead, but of the living, for to him all are alive." [39] Some of the scribes said in reply, "Teacher, you have answered well." [40] And they no longer dared to ask him anything.

Feast of Christ the Universal King, Year B
First Reading: Daniel 7:13-14

¹³ As the visions during the night continued, I saw

one like a Son of man coming,
    on the clouds of heaven;
when he reached the Ancient One
    and was presented before him,
¹⁴ the one like a Son of man received dominion,
        glory, and kingship;
    all peoples, nations, and languages serve
        him.
His dominion is an everlasting dominion
    that shall not be taken away,
    his kingship shall not be destroyed.

Responsorial Psalm: Psalms 93:1, 1-2, 5
R. *(1a)* *The Lord is king; he is robed in majesty.*
¹ᴬᴮ The LORD is king, in splendor robed;
    robed is the LORD and girt about with
        strength.
R. *The Lord is king; he is robed in majesty.*

¹ᶜ And he has made the world firm,
    not to be moved.
² Your throne stands firm from of old;
    from everlasting you are, O LORD.
R. *The Lord is king; he is robed in majesty.*

⁵ Your decrees are worthy of trust indeed;
    holiness befits your house,
    O LORD, for length of days.
R. *The Lord is king; he is robed in majesty.*

Second Reading: Revelation 1:5-8
⁵ Jesus Christ is the faithful witness, the firstborn of the dead and ruler of the kings of the earth. To him who loves us and has freed us from our sins by his blood, ⁶ who has made us into a kingdom, priests for his God and Father, to him be glory and power forever and ever. Amen.

⁷ Behold, he is coming amid the clouds,
and every eye will see him,
even those who pierced him.
All the peoples of the earth will lament him.
Yes. Amen.
⁸ "I am the Alpha and the Omega, " says the Lord God, "the one who is and who was and who is to come, the almighty."

Alleluia: Mark 11:9, 10
R. Alleluia, alleluia.
⁹ Blessed is he who comes in the name of the
Lord!
¹⁰ Blessed is the kingdom of our father David
that is to come!
R. Alleluia, alleluia.

Gospel: John 18:33B-37
^{33B} Pilate said to Jesus, "Are you the King of the Jews?" ³⁴ Jesus answered, "Do you say this on your own or have others told you about me?" ³⁵ Pilate answered, "I am not a Jew, am I? Your own nation and the chief priests handed you over to me. What have you done?" ³⁶ Jesus answered, "My kingdom does not belong to this world. If my kingdom did belong to this world, my attendants would be fighting to keep me from being handed over to the Jews. But as it is, my kingdom is not here." ³⁷ So Pilate said to him, "Then you are a king?" Jesus answered, "You say I am a king. For this I was born and for this I came into the world, to testify to the truth. Everyone who belongs to the truth listens to my voice."

Monday November 25, 2024

Monday of Thirty-fourth Week in Ordinary Time
First Reading: Revelation 14:1-3, 4B-5
¹ I, John, looked and there was the Lamb standing on Mount Zion, and with him a hundred and forty-four thousand who had his name and his Father's name written on their foreheads. ² I heard a sound from heaven like the sound of rushing water or a loud peal of thunder. The sound I heard was like that of harpists playing their harps. ³ They were singing what seemed to be a new hymn before the throne, before the four living creatures and the elders. No one could learn this hymn except the hundred and forty-four thousand who had been ransomed from the earth. ^{4B} These are the ones who follow the Lamb wherever he goes. They have been ransomed as the first fruits of the human race for God and the Lamb. ⁵ On their lips no deceit has been found; they are unblemished.

Responsorial Psalm: Psalms 24:1BC-2, 3-4AB, 5-6
**R. ^(see 6)Lord, this is the people that longs to see
your face.**
^{1BC} The LORD's are the earth and its fullness;

the world and those who dwell in it.
² For he founded it upon the seas
    and established it upon the rivers.

R. Lord, this is the people that longs to see your face.

³ Who can ascend the mountain of the LORD?
    or who may stand in his holy place?
⁴ᴬᴮ He whose hands are sinless, whose heart is clean,
    who desires not what is vain.

R. Lord, this is the people that longs to see your face.

⁵ He shall receive a blessing from the LORD,
    a reward from God his savior.
⁶ Such is the race that seeks for him,
    that seeks the face of the God of Jacob.

R. Lord, this is the people that longs to see your face.

Alleluia: Matthew 24:42A, 44

R. Alleluia, alleluia.

⁴²ᴬ Stay awake!
⁴⁴ For you do not know when the Son of Man
    will come.

R. Alleluia, alleluia.

Gospel: Luke 21:1-4

¹ When Jesus looked up he saw some wealthy people putting their offerings into the treasury ² and he noticed a poor widow putting in two small coins. ³ He said, "I tell you truly, this poor widow put in more than all the rest; ⁴ for those others have all made offerings from their surplus wealth, but she, from her poverty, has offered her whole livelihood."

Tuesday November 26, 2024

Tuesday of Thirty-fourth Week in Ordinary Time

First Reading: Revelation 14:14-19

¹⁴ I, John, looked and there was a white cloud, and sitting on the cloud one who looked like a son of man, with a gold crown on his head and a sharp sickle in his hand. ¹⁵ Another angel came out of the temple, crying out in a loud voice to the one sitting on the cloud, "Use your sickle and reap the harvest, for the time to reap has come, because the earth's harvest is fully ripe." ¹⁶ So the one who was sitting on the cloud swung his sickle over the earth, and the earth was harvested.

[17] Then another angel came out of the temple in heaven who also had a sharp sickle. [18] Then another angel came from the altar, who was in charge of the fire, and cried out in a loud voice to the one who had the sharp sickle, "Use your sharp sickle and cut the clusters from the earth's vines, for its grapes are ripe." [19] So the angel swung his sickle over the earth and cut the earth's vintage. He threw it into the great wine press of God's fury.

Responsorial Psalm: Psalms 96:10,11-12, 13

R. [13b] *The Lord comes to judge the earth.*

[10] Say among the nations: The LORD is king.
He has made the world firm, not to be
　　　moved;
　he governs the peoples with equity.
R. *The Lord comes to judge the earth.*

[11] Let the heavens be glad and the earth
　　　rejoice;
　let the sea and what fills it resound;
　　[12] let the plains be joyful and all that is in
　　　them!
Then shall all the trees of the forest exult.
R. *The Lord comes to judge the earth.*

[13] Before the LORD, for he comes;
　for he comes to rule the earth.
He shall rule the world with justice
　and the peoples with his constancy.
R. *The Lord comes to judge the earth.*

Alleluia: Revelation 2:10C

R. Alleluia, alleluia.
[10C] Remain faithful until death,
and I will give you the crown of life.
R. Alleluia, alleluia.

Gospel: Luke 21:5-11

[5] While some people were speaking about how the temple was adorned with costly stones and votive offerings, Jesus said, [6] "All that you see here — the days will come when there will not be left a stone upon another stone that will not be thrown down."

[7] Then they asked him, "Teacher, when will this happen? And what sign will there be when all these things are about to happen?" [8] He answered, "See that you not be deceived, for many will come in my name, saying, 'I am he,' and 'The time has come.' Do not follow them! [9] When you hear of wars and insurrections, do not be terrified; for such things must happen first, but it will not immediately be the end." [10] Then he said to them, "Nation will rise against nation, and kingdom against kingdom. [11] There will be powerful earthquakes, famines, and plagues from place to place; and awesome sights and mighty signs will come from the sky."

Wednesday of Thirty-fourth Week in Ordinary Time
First Reading: Revelation 15:1-4

[1] I, John, saw in heaven another sign, great and awe-inspiring: seven angels with the seven last plagues, for through them God's fury is accomplished.

[2] Then I saw something like a sea of glass mingled with fire. On the sea of glass were standing those who had won the victory over the beast and its image and the number that signified its name. They were holding God's harps, [3] and they sang the song of Moses, the servant of God, and the song of the Lamb:

"Great and wonderful are your works,
    Lord God almighty.
Just and true are your ways,
    O king of the nations.
[4] Who will not fear you, Lord,
    or glorify your name?
For you alone are holy.
    All the nations will come
    and worship before you,
    for your righteous acts have been
      revealed."

Responsorial Psalm: Psalms 98:1, 2-3AB, 7-8, 9

R. *(Rev. 15: 3b)* *Great and wonderful are all your*
    works, Lord, mighty God!

[1] Sing to the LORD a new song,
    for he has done wondrous deeds;
His right hand has won victory for him,
    his holy arm.

R. *Great and wonderful are all your works, Lord,*
    mighty God!

[2] The LORD has made his salvation known:
    in the sight of the nations he has revealed
      his justice.
[3AB] He has remembered his kindness and his
      faithfulness
    toward the house of Israel.

R. *Great and wonderful are all your works, Lord,*
    mighty God!

⁷ Let the sea and what fills it resound,
    the world and those who dwell in it;
⁸ Let the rivers clap their hands,
    the mountains shout with them for joy.
R. Great and wonderful are all your works, Lord,
mighty God!

⁹ Before the LORD, for he comes,
    for he comes to rule the earth;
He will rule the world with justice
    and the peoples with equity.
R. Great and wonderful are all your works, Lord,
mighty God!

Alleluia: Revelation 2:10C
R. Alleluia, alleluia.
¹⁰ᶜ Remain faithful until death,
and I will give you the crown of life.
R. Alleluia, alleluia.

Gospel: Luke 21:12-19
Jesus said to the crowd: ¹² "They will seize and persecute you, they will hand you over to the synagogues and to prisons, and they will have you led before kings and governors because of my name.¹³ It will lead to your giving testimony. ¹⁴ Remember, you are not to prepare your defense beforehand, ¹⁵ for I myself shall give you a wisdom in speaking that all your adversaries will be powerless to resist or refute. ¹⁶ You will even be handed over by parents, brothers, relatives, and friends, and they will put some of you to death. ¹⁷ You will be hated by all because of my name, ¹⁸ but not a hair on your head will be destroyed. ¹⁹ By your perseverance you will secure your lives."

Thursday November 28, 2024

Thursday of the Thirty-fourth Week in Ordinary Time
First Reading: Revelation 18:1-2, 21-23; 19:1-3, 9A
¹ I, John, saw another angel coming down from heaven, having great authority, and the earth became illumined by his splendor. ² He cried out in a mighty voice:

"Fallen, fallen is Babylon the great.
    She has become a haunt for demons.
She is a cage for every unclean spirit,
        a cage for every unclean bird,
        a cage for every unclean and disgusting
            beast."

²¹ A mighty angel picked up a stone like a huge millstone and threw it into the sea and said:

"With such force will Babylon the great city
 > be thrown down,
 > and will never be found again.
²² No melodies of harpists and musicians,
 > flutists and trumpeters,
 > will ever be heard in you again.
No craftsmen in any trade
 > will ever be found in you again.
No sound of the millstone
 > will ever be heard in you again.
²³ No light from a lamp
 > will ever be seen in you again.
No voices of bride and groom
 > will ever be heard in you again.
Because your merchants were the great ones
 > of the world,
 > all nations were led astray by your magic
 > potion."

¹ After this I heard what sounded like the loud voice of a great multitude in heaven, saying:

"Alleluia!
Salvation, glory, and might belong to our
 > God,
² for true and just are his judgments.
He has condemned the great harlot
 > who corrupted the earth with her
 > harlotry.
He has avenged on her the blood of his
 > servants."

³ They said a second time:

"Alleluia! Smoke will rise from her forever
 > and ever."

⁹ Then the angel said to me, "Write this: Blessed are those who have been called to the wedding feast of the Lamb."

Responsorial Psalm: Psalms 100:1B-2,3, 4, 5

R. *(Rev. 19: 9a)* **Blessed are they who are called to**
the wedding feast of the Lamb.

1B Sing joyfully to the LORD, all you lands;
2 serve the LORD with gladness;
come before him with joyful song.

R. Blessed are they who are called to the
wedding feast of the Lamb.

3 Know that the LORD is God;
he made us, his we are;
his people, the flock he tends.

R. Blessed are they who are called to the
wedding feast of the Lamb.

4 Enter his gates with thanksgiving,
his courts with praise;
Give thanks to him; bless his name.

R. Blessed are they who are called to the
wedding feast of the Lamb.

5 For he is good:
the LORD, whose kindness endures
forever,
and his faithfulness, to all generations.

R. Blessed are they who are called to the
wedding feast of the Lamb.

Alleluia: Luke 21:28

R. Alleluia, alleluia.
28 Stand erect and raise your heads
because your redemption is at hand.
R. Alleluia, alleluia.

Gospel: Luke 21:20-28

Jesus said to his disciples: 20 "When you see Jerusalem surrounded by armies, know that its desolation is at hand. 21 Then those in Judea must flee to the mountains. Let those within the city escape from it, and let those in the countryside not enter the city, 22 for these days are the time of punishment when all the Scriptures are fulfilled. 23 Woe to pregnant women and nursing mothers in those days, for a terrible calamity will come upon the earth and a wrathful judgment upon this people. 24 They will fall by the edge of the sword and be taken as captives to all the Gentiles; and Jerusalem will be trampled underfoot by the Gentiles until the times of the Gentiles are fulfilled.

[25] "There will be signs in the sun, the moon, and the stars, and on earth nations will be in dismay, perplexed by the roaring of the sea and the waves. [26] People will die of fright in anticipation of what is coming upon the world, for the powers of the heavens will be shaken. [27] And then they will see the Son of Man coming in a cloud with power and great glory. [28] But when these signs begin to happen, stand erect and raise your heads because your redemption is at hand."

Friday November 29, 2024

Friday of Thirty-fourth Week in Ordinary Time

First Reading: Revelation 20:1-4, 11-21:2

[1] I, John, saw an angel come down from heaven, holding in his hand the key to the abyss and a heavy chain. [2] He seized the dragon, the ancient serpent, which is the Devil or Satan, and tied it up for a thousand years [3] and threw it into the abyss, which he locked over it and sealed, so that it could no longer lead the nations astray until the thousand years are completed. After this, it is to be released for a short time.

[4] Then I saw thrones; those who sat on them were entrusted with judgment. I also saw the souls of those who had been beheaded for their witness to Jesus and for the word of God, and who had not worshiped the beast or its image nor had accepted its mark on their foreheads or hands. They came to life and they reigned with Christ for a thousand years.

[11] Next I saw a large white throne and the one who was sitting on it. The earth and the sky fled from his presence and there was no place for them. [12] I saw the dead, the great and the lowly, standing before the throne, and scrolls were opened. Then another scroll was opened, the book of life. The dead were judged according to their deeds, by what was written in the scrolls. [13] The sea gave up its dead; then Death and Hades gave up their dead. All the dead were judged according to their deeds. [14] Then Death and Hades were thrown into the pool of fire. (This pool of fire is the second death.) [15] Anyone whose name was not found written in the book of life was thrown into the pool of fire.

[1] Then I saw a new heaven and a new earth. The former heaven and the former earth had passed away, and the sea was no more. [2] I also saw the holy city, a new Jerusalem, coming down out of heaven from God, prepared as a bride adorned for her husband.

Responsorial Psalm: Psalms 84:3, 4, 5-6A AND 8A

R. (Rev. 21:3b) *Here God lives among his people.*

[3] My soul yearns and pines
    for the courts of the LORD.
My heart and my flesh
    cry out for the living God.

R. *Here God lives among his people.*

[4] Even the sparrow finds a home,
    and the swallow a nest

in which she puts her young–
Your altars, O LORD of hosts,
   my king and my God!
R. Here God lives among his people.

[5] Blessed they who dwell in your house!
   continually they praise you.
[6A] Blessed the men whose strength you are!
    [8A] They go from strength to strength.
R. Here God lives among his people.

Alleluia: Luke 21:28
R. Alleluia, alleluia.
[28] Stand erect and raise your heads
because your redemption is at hand.
R. Alleluia, alleluia.

Gospel: Luke 21:29-33
[29] Jesus told his disciples a parable. "Consider the fig tree and all the other trees. [30] When their buds burst open, you see for yourselves and know that summer is now near; [31] in the same way, when you see these things happening, know that the Kingdom of God is near. [32] Amen, I say to you, this generation will not pass away until all these things have taken place. [33] Heaven and earth will pass away, but my words will not pass away."

Saturday November 30, 2024

Feast of Saint Andrew, Apostle
First Reading: Romans 10:9-18
Brothers and sisters: [9] If you confess with your mouth that Jesus is Lord and believe in your heart that God raised him from the dead, you will be saved. [10] For one believes with the heart and so is justified, and one confesses with the mouth and so is saved. [11] The Scripture says, *No one who believes in him will be put to shame.* [12] There is no distinction between Jew and Greek; the same Lord is Lord of all, enriching all who call upon him. [13] *For everyone who calls on the name of the Lord will be saved.*

    [14] But how can they call on him in whom they have not believed? And how can they believe in him of whom they have not heard? And how can they hear without someone to preach? [15] And how can people preach unless they are sent? As it is written, *How beautiful are the feet of those who bring the good news!* [16] But not everyone has heeded the good news; for Isaiah says, *Lord, who has believed what was heard from us?* [17] Thus faith comes from what is heard, and what is heard comes through the word of Christ. [18] But I ask, did they not hear? Certainly they did; for

Their voice has gone forth to all the earth,

and their words to the ends of the world.

Responsorial Psalm: Psalms 19:8, 9, 10, 11

R. (10) *The judgments of the Lord are true, and all of them are just.*

or:

(John 6:63) *Your words, Lord, are Spirit and life.*

[8] The law of the LORD is perfect,
    refreshing the soul;
The decree of the LORD is trustworthy,
    giving wisdom to the simple.

R. *The judgments of the Lord are true, and all of them are just.*

or:

Your words, Lord, are Spirit and life.

[9] The precepts of the LORD are right,
    rejoicing the heart;
The command of the LORD is clear,
    enlightening the eye.

R. *The judgments of the Lord are true, and all of them are just.*

or:

Your words, Lord, are Spirit and life.

[10] The fear of the LORD is pure,
    enduring forever;
The ordinances of the LORD are true,
    all of them just.

R. *The judgments of the Lord are true, and all of them are just.*

or:

Your words, Lord, are Spirit and life.

[11] They are more precious than gold,
    than a heap of purest gold;
Sweeter also than syrup
    or honey from the comb.

R. *The judgments of the Lord are true, and all of them are just.*

or:

Your words, Lord, are Spirit and life.

Alleluia: Matthew 4:19

R. Alleluia, alleluia.

[19] Come after me, says the Lord,
and I will make you fishers of men.

R. Alleluia, alleluia.

Gospel: Matthew 4:18-22

[18] As Jesus was walking by the Sea of Galilee, he saw two brothers, Simon who is called Peter, and his brother Andrew, casting a net into the sea; they were fishermen. [19] He said to them, "Come after me, and I will make you fishers of men." [20] At once they left their nets and followed him. [21] He walked along from there and saw two other brothers, James, the son of Zebedee, and his brother John. They were in a boat, with their father Zebedee, mending their nets. He called them, [22] and immediately they left their boat and their father and followed him.

First Sunday of Advent, Year C
First Reading: Jeremiah 33:14-16

[14] The days are coming, says the LORD,
> when I will fulfill the promise
> I made to the house of Israel and Judah.

[15] In those days, at that time,
> I will raise up for David a just shoot;
> he shall do what is right and just in the
>> land.

[16] In those days Judah shall be safe
> and Jerusalem shall dwell secure;
> this is the name they shall call her:
> "The LORD our justice."

Responsorial Psalm: Psalms 25:4-5, 8-9, 10, 14

R. [1b] **To you, O Lord, I lift my soul.**

[4] Yours ways, O LORD, make known to me;
   teach me your paths.

[5] guide me in your truth and teach me,
   for you are God my savior,
   and for you I wait all the day.

R. To you, O Lord, I lift my soul.

[8] Good and upright is the LORD,
   thus he shows sinners the way,

^{9} He guides the humble in justice,
   and teaches the humble his way.

R. To you, O Lord, I lift my soul.
^{10} All the paths of the Lord are kindness and
         constancy
   toward those who keep his covenant and
         his decrees.
^{14} The friendship of the LORD is with those who
         fear him;
   and his covenant, for their instruction.
R. To you, O Lord, I lift my soul.

Second Reading: 1 Thessalonians 3:12-4:2

Brothers and sisters, ^{12} May the Lord make you increase and abound in love for one another and for all, just as we have for you, ^{13} so as to strengthen your hearts, to be blameless in holiness before our God and Father at the coming of our Lord Jesus with all his holy ones. Amen.

^{1} Finally, brothers and sisters, we earnestly ask and exhort you in the Lord Jesus that, as you received from us how you should conduct yourselves to please God—and as you are conducting yourselves—you do so even more. ^{2} For you know what instructions we gave you through the Lord Jesus.

Alleluia: Psalms 85:8

R. Alleluia, alleluia.
^{8} Show us, Lord, your love;
and grant us your salvation.
R. Alleluia, alleluia.

Gospel: Luke 21:25-28, 34-36

Jesus said to his disciples: ^{25} "There will be signs in the sun, the moon, and the stars, and on earth nations will be in dismay, perplexed by the roaring of the sea and the waves. ^{26} People will die of fright in anticipation of what is coming upon the world, for the powers of the heavens will be shaken. ^{27} And then they will see the Son of Man coming in a cloud with power and great glory. ^{28} But when these signs begin to happen, stand erect and raise your heads because your redemption is at hand."

^{34} "Beware that your hearts do not become drowsy from carousing and drunkenness and the anxieties of daily life, and that day catch you by surprise ^{35} like a trap. For that day will assault everyone who lives on the face of the earth. ^{36} Be vigilant at all times and pray that you have the strength to escape the tribulations that are imminent and to stand before the Son of Man."

Monday of the First Week of Advent
First Reading: Isaiah 2:1-5

[1] This is what Isaiah, son of Amoz, saw concerning Judah and Jerusalem.

[2] In days to come,
The mountain of the LORD's house
    shall be established as the highest
        mountain
    and raised above the hills.
All nations shall stream toward it;
    [3] many peoples shall come and say:
"Come, let us climb the LORD's mountain,
    to the house of the God of Jacob,
That he may instruct us in his ways,
    and we may walk in his paths."
For from Zion shall go forth instruction,
    and the word of the LORD from Jerusalem.
[4] He shall judge between the nations,
    and impose terms on many peoples.
They shall beat their swords into plowshares
    and their spears into pruning hooks;
One nation shall not raise the sword against
        another,
    nor shall they train for war again.

[5] O house of Jacob, come,
    let us walk in the light of the LORD!

Responsorial Psalm: Psalms 122:1-2, 3-4B, 4CD-5, 6-7, 8-9
R. Let us go rejoicing to the house of the Lord.
[1] I rejoiced because they said to me,
    "We will go up to the house of the LORD."
[2] And now we have set foot
    within your gates, O Jerusalem.
R. Let us go rejoicing to the house of the Lord.

[3] Jerusalem, built as a city
    with compact unity.
[4AB] To it the tribes go up,
    the tribes of the LORD.

R. Let us go rejoicing to the house of the Lord.

4CD According to the decree for Israel,
to give thanks to the name of the LORD.
5 In it are set up judgment seats,
seats for the house of David.
R. Let us go rejoicing to the house of the Lord.

6 Pray for the peace of Jerusalem!
May those who love you prosper!
7 May peace be within your walls,
prosperity in your buildings.
R. Let us go rejoicing to the house of the Lord.

8 Because of my relatives and friends
I will say, "Peace be within you!"
9 Because of the house of the LORD, our God,
I will pray for your good.
R. Let us go rejoicing to the house of the Lord.

Alleluia: cf. Psalms 80:4
R. Alleluia, alleluia.
4 Come and save us, Lord our God;
let your face shine upon us, that we may be
saved.
R. Alleluia, alleluia.

Gospel: Matthew 8:5-11
5 When Jesus entered Capernaum, a centurion approached him and appealed to him, 6 saying, "Lord, my servant is lying at home paralyzed, suffering dreadfully." 7 He said to him, "I will come and cure him." 8 The centurion said in reply, "Lord, I am not worthy to have you enter under my roof; only say the word and my servant will be healed. 9 For I too am a man subject to authority, with soldiers subject to me. And I say to one, 'Go,' and he goes; and to another, 'Come here,' and he comes; and to my slave, 'Do this,' and he does it." 10 When Jesus heard this, he was amazed and said to those following him, "Amen, I say to you, in no one in Israel have I found such faith. 11 I say to you, many will come from the east and the west, and will recline with Abraham, Isaac, and Jacob at the banquet in the Kingdom of heaven."

Memorial of Saint Francis Xavier, Priest
First Reading: Isaiah 11:1-10

¹ On that day,
A shoot shall sprout from the stump of Jesse,
 and from his roots a bud shall blossom.
² The Spirit of the LORD shall rest upon him:
 a Spirit of wisdom and of understanding,
A Spirit of counsel and of strength,
  a Spirit of knowledge and of fear of the
   LORD,
³ and his delight shall be the fear of the
   LORD.
Not by appearance shall he judge,
 nor by hearsay shall he decide,
⁴ But he shall judge the poor with justice,
 and decide aright for the land's afflicted.
He shall strike the ruthless with the rod of
  his mouth,
  and with the breath of his lips he shall
   slay the wicked.
⁵ Justice shall be the band around his waist,
 and faithfulness a belt upon his hips.

⁶ Then the wolf shall be a guest of the lamb,
 and the leopard shall lie down with the
   kid;
The calf and the young lion shall browse
   together,
 with a little child to guide them.
⁷ The cow and the bear shall be neighbors,
 together their young shall rest;
 the lion shall eat hay like the ox.
⁸ The baby shall play by the cobra's den,
 and the child lay his hand on the adder's
   lair.
⁹ There shall be no harm or ruin on all my
  holy mountain;
 for the earth shall be filled with
   knowledge of the LORD,
 as water covers the sea.

[10] On that day,
The root of Jesse,
   set up as a signal for the nations,
The Gentiles shall seek out,
   for his dwelling shall be glorious.

Responsorial Psalm: Psalms 72:1-2, 7-8, 12-13, 17

R. *(see 7)* *Justice shall flourish in his time, and*
fullness of peace for ever.

[1] O God, with your judgment endow the king,
   and with your justice, the king's son;
[2] He shall govern your people with justice
   and your afflicted ones with judgment.
R. Justice shall flourish in his time, and fullness
of peace for ever.

[7] Justice shall flower in his days,
   and profound peace, till the moon be no
      more.
[8] May he rule from sea to sea,
   and from the River to the ends of the
      earth.
R. Justice shall flourish in his time, and fullness
of peace for ever.

[12] He shall rescue the poor when he cries out,
   and the afflicted when he has no one to
      help him.
[13] He shall have pity for the lowly and the
      poor;
   the lives of the poor he shall save.
R. Justice shall flourish in his time, and fullness
of peace for ever.

[17] May his name be blessed forever;
   as long as the sun his name shall remain.
In him shall all the tribes of the earth be
      blessed;
   all the nations shall proclaim his
      happiness.
R. Justice shall flourish in his time, and fullness

of peace for ever.

Alleluia
R. Alleluia, alleluia.
Behold, our Lord shall come with power;
he will enlighten the eyes of his servants.
R. Alleluia, alleluia.

Gospel: Luke 10:21-24
[21] Jesus rejoiced in the Holy Spirit and said, "I give you praise, Father, Lord of heaven and earth, for although you have hidden these things from the wise and the learned you have revealed them to the childlike. Yes, Father, such has been your gracious will. [22] All things have been handed over to me by my Father. No one knows who the Son is except the Father, and who the Father is except the Son and anyone to whom the Son wishes to reveal him."

[23] Turning to the disciples in private he said, "Blessed are the eyes that see what you see. [24] For I say to you, many prophets and kings desired to see what you see, but did not see it, and to hear what you hear, but did not hear it."

Wednesday of the First Week of Advent
First Reading: Isaiah 25:6-10A
[6] On this mountain the LORD of hosts
>   will provide for all peoples
A feast of rich food and choice wines,
>   juicy, rich food and pure, choice wines.
[7] On this mountain he will destroy
>   the veil that veils all peoples,
The web that is woven over all nations;
>   [8] he will destroy death forever.
The Lord GOD will wipe away
>   the tears from all faces;
The reproach of his people he will remove
>   from the whole earth; for the LORD has
>   spoken.

[9] On that day it will be said:
"Behold our God, to whom we looked to save
>   us!
>   This is the LORD for whom we looked;
>   let us rejoice and be glad that he has
>   saved us!"
[10A] For the hand of the LORD will rest on this

mountain.

Responsorial Psalm: Psalms 23:1-3A, 3B-4, 5, 6

R. *(6cd)* **I shall live in the house of the Lord all the days of my life.**

[1] The LORD is my shepherd; I shall not want.
    [2] In verdant pastures he gives me repose;
Beside restful waters he leads me;
        [3A] he refreshes my soul.
R. **I shall live in the house of the Lord all the days of my life.**

[3B] He guides me in right paths
        for his name's sake.
[4] Even though I walk in the dark valley
        I fear no evil; for you are at my side
With your rod and your staff
        that give me courage.
R. **I shall live in the house of the Lord all the days of my life.**

[5] You spread the table before me
        in the sight of my foes;
You anoint my head with oil;
        my cup overflows.
R. **I shall live in the house of the Lord all the days of my life.**

[6] Only goodness and kindness follow me
        all the days of my life;
And I shall dwell in the house of the LORD
        for years to come.
R. **I shall live in the house of the Lord all the days of my life.**

Alleluia
R. Alleluia, alleluia.
Behold, the Lord comes to save his people;
blessed are those prepared to meet him.
R. Alleluia, alleluia.

Gospel: Matthew 15:29-37

At that time: [29] Jesus walked by the Sea of Galilee, went up on the mountain, and sat down there. [30] Great crowds came to him, having with them the lame, the blind, the deformed, the mute, and many others. They placed them at his feet, and he cured them. [31] The crowds were amazed when they saw the mute speaking, the deformed made whole, the lame walking, and the blind able to see, and they glorified the God of Israel.

[32] Jesus summoned his disciples and said, "My heart is moved with pity for the crowd, for they have been with me now for three days and have nothing to eat. I do not want to send them away hungry, for fear they may collapse on the way." [33] The disciples said to him, "Where could we ever get enough bread in this deserted place to satisfy such a crowd?" [34] Jesus said to them, "How many loaves do you have?" "Seven," they replied, "and a few fish." [35] He ordered the crowd to sit down on the ground. [36] Then he took the seven loaves and the fish, gave thanks, broke the loaves, and gave them to the disciples, who in turn gave them to the crowds. [37] They all ate and were satisfied. They picked up the fragments left over-seven baskets full.

Thursday December 5, 2024

Thursday of the First Week of Advent

First Reading: Isaiah 26:1-6

[1] On that day they will sing this song in the land of Judah:

"A strong city have we;
    he sets up walls and ramparts to protect
        us.
[2] Open up the gates
    to let in a nation that is just,
    one that keeps faith.
[3] A nation of firm purpose you keep in peace;
    in peace, for its trust in you."

[4] Trust in the LORD forever!
    For the LORD is an eternal Rock.
[5] He humbles those in high places,
    and the lofty city he brings down;
He tumbles it to the ground,
    levels it with the dust.
[6] It is trampled underfoot by the needy,
    by the footsteps of the poor.

Responsorial Psalm: Psalms 118:1 and 8-9, 19-21, 25-27A

R. [26a] *Blessed is he who comes in the name of the Lord.* or: *Alleluia.*

[1] Give thanks to the LORD, for he is good,
    for his mercy endures forever.

[8] It is better to take refuge in the LORD
        than to trust in man.
[9] It is better to take refuge in the LORD
        than to trust in princes.
**R. Blessed is he who comes in the name of the
        Lord.** or: ***Alleluia.***

[19] Open to me the gates of justice;
        I will enter them and give thanks to the
            LORD.
[20] This gate is the LORD's;
        the just shall enter it.
[21] I will give thanks to you, for you have
            answered me
        and have been my savior.
**R. Blessed is he who comes in the name of the
        Lord.** or: ***Alleluia.***

[25] O LORD, grant salvation!
        O LORD, grant prosperity!
[26] Blessed is he who comes in the name of the
            LORD;
        we bless you from the house of the LORD.
            [27A] The LORD is God, and he has given us
            light.
**R. Blessed is he who comes in the name of the
        Lord.** or: ***Alleluia.***

Alleluia: Isaiah 55:6
R. Alleluia, alleluia.
[6] Seek the LORD while he may be found;
call him while he is near.
R. Alleluia, alleluia.

Gospel: Matthew 7:21, 24-27
Jesus said to his disciples: [21] "Not everyone who says to me, 'Lord, Lord,' will enter the Kingdom of heaven, but only the one who does the will of my Father in heaven.

[24] "Everyone who listens to these words of mine and acts on them will be like a wise man who built his house on rock. [25] The rain fell, the floods came, and the winds blew and buffeted the house. But it did not collapse; it had been set solidly on rock. [26] And everyone who listens to these words of mine but does not act on them will be like a fool who built his house on sand. [27] The rain fell, the floods came, and the winds blew and buffeted the house. And it collapsed and was completely ruined."

Friday of the First Week of Advent
First Reading: Isaiah 29:17-24

Thus says the Lord GOD:

¹⁷ But a very little while,
  and Lebanon shall be changed into an
    orchard,
  and the orchard be regarded as a forest!
¹⁸ On that day the deaf shall hear
  the words of a book;
And out of gloom and darkness,
  the eyes of the blind shall see.
¹⁹ The lowly will ever find joy in the LORD,
  and the poor rejoice in the Holy One of
    Israel.
²⁰ For the tyrant will be no more
  and the arrogant will have gone;
All who are alert to do evil will be cut off,
  ²¹ those whose mere word condemns a
    man,
Who ensnare his defender at the gate,
  and leave the just man with an empty
    claim.
²² Therefore thus says the LORD,
  the God of the house of Jacob,
  who redeemed Abraham:
Now Jacob shall have nothing to be ashamed
    of,
  nor shall his face grow pale.
²³ When his children see
  the work of my hands in his midst,
They shall keep my name holy;
  they shall reverence the Holy One of
    Jacob,
  and be in awe of the God of Israel.
²⁴ Those who err in spirit shall acquire
    understanding,
  and those who find fault shall receive
    instruction.

Responsorial Psalm: Psalms 27:1, 4, 13-14

R. *(1a)* *The Lord is my light and my salvation.*

[1] The LORD is my light and my salvation;
     whom should I fear?
The LORD is my life's refuge;
     of whom should I be afraid?
R. *The Lord is my light and my salvation.*

[1] One thing I ask of the LORD;
     this I seek:
To dwell in the house of the LORD
     all the days of my life,
That I may gaze on the loveliness of the LORD
     and contemplate his temple.
R. *The Lord is my light and my salvation.*

[13] I believe that I shall see the bounty of the
          LORD
     in the land of the living.
[14] Wait for the LORD with courage;
     be stouthearted, and wait for the LORD.
R. *The Lord is my light and my salvation.*

Alleluia

R. Alleluia, alleluia.
Behold, our Lord shall come with power;
he will enlighten the eyes of his servants.
R. Alleluia, alleluia.

Gospel: Matthew 9:27-31

[27] As Jesus passed by, two blind men followed him, crying out, "Son of David, have pity on us!" [28] When he entered the house, the blind men approached him and Jesus said to them, "Do you believe that I can do this?" "Yes, Lord," they said to him. [29] Then he touched their eyes and said, "Let it be done for you according to your faith." [30] And their eyes were opened. Jesus warned them sternly, "See that no one knows about this." [31] But they went out and spread word of him through all that land.

Saturday December 7, 2024

Memorial of Saint Ambrose, Bishop and Doctor
First Reading: Isaiah 30:19-21, 23-26

Thus says the Lord GOD,
     [19] the Holy One of Israel:

O people of Zion, who dwell in Jerusalem,
     no more will you weep;
He will be gracious to you when you cry out,
     as soon as he hears he will answer you.
[20] The Lord will give you the bread you need
     and the water for which you thirst.
No longer will your Teacher hide himself,
     but with your own eyes you shall see
       your Teacher,
[21] While from behind, a voice shall sound in
      your ears:
     "This is the way; walk in it,"
     when you would turn to the right or to
       the left.

[23] He will give rain for the seed
     that you sow in the ground,
And the wheat that the soil produces
     will be rich and abundant.
On that day your flock will be given pasture
     and the lamb will graze in spacious
       meadows;
[24] The oxen and the asses that till the ground
     will eat silage tossed to them
     with shovel and pitchfork.
[25] Upon every high mountain and lofty hill
     there will be streams of running water.
On the day of the great slaughter,
     when the towers fall,
[26] The light of the moon will be like that of the
      sun
     and the light of the sun will be seven
      times greater
     like the light of seven days.
On the day the LORD binds up the wounds of
      his people,
     he will heal the bruises left by his blows.

Responsorial Psalm: Psalms 147:1-2,3-4, 5-6

R. *(See Isaiah 30:18d)* **Blessed are all who wait for the Lord.**
[1] Praise the LORD, for he is good;
     sing praise to our God, for he is gracious;

it is fitting to praise him.
² The LORD rebuilds Jerusalem;
the dispersed of Israel he gathers.
R. Blessed are all who wait for the Lord.

³ He heals the brokenhearted
and binds up their wounds.
⁴ He tells the number of the stars;
he calls each by name.
R. Blessed are all who wait for the Lord.

⁵ Great is our LORD and mighty in power:
to his wisdom there is no limit.
⁶ The LORD sustains the lowly;
the wicked he casts to the ground.
R. Blessed are all who wait for the Lord.

Alleluia: Isaiah 33:22
R. Alleluia, alleluia.
²² The LORD is our Judge, our Lawgiver, our
King;
he it is who will save us.
R. Alleluia, alleluia.

Gospel: Matthew 9:35-10:1, 5A, 6-8
³⁵ Jesus went around to all the towns and villages, teaching in their synagogues, proclaiming the Gospel of the Kingdom, and curing every disease and illness. ³⁶ At the sight of the crowds, his heart was moved with pity for them because they were troubled and abandoned, like sheep without a shepherd. ³⁷ Then he said to his disciples, "The harvest is abundant but the laborers are few; ³⁸ so ask the master of the harvest to send out laborers for his harvest."

¹ Then he summoned his Twelve disciples and gave them authority over unclean spirits to drive them out and to cure every disease and every illness.

⁵ᴬ Jesus sent out these Twelve after instructing them thus, ⁶ "Go to the lost sheep of the house of Israel. ⁷ As you go, make this proclamation: 'The Kingdom of heaven is at hand.' ⁸ Cure the sick, raise the dead, cleanse lepers, drive out demons. Without cost you have received; without cost you are to give."

Sunday December 8, 2024

Second Sunday of Advent, Year C
First Reading: Baruch 5:1-9
¹ Jerusalem, take off your robe of mourning

and misery;
    put on the splendor of glory from God
            forever:
[2] Wrapped in the mantle of justice from God,
    bear on your head the mitre
    that displays the glory of the eternal
            name.
[3] For God will show all the earth your
            splendor:
        [4] you will be named by God forever
    the peace of justice, the glory of God's worship.
[5] Up, Jerusalem! stand upon the heights;
    look to the east and see your children
gathered from the east and the west
    at the word of the Holy One,
    rejoicing that they are remembered by
            God.
[6] Led away on foot by their enemies they left
            you:
    but God will bring them back to you
    borne aloft in glory as on royal thrones.
[7] For God has commanded
    that every lofty mountain be made low,
    and the age-old depths and gorges,
    be filled to level ground,
    that Israel may advance secure in the
            glory of God.
[8] The forests and every kind of fragrant tree
    have overshadowed Israel at God's
            command;
[9] for God is leading Israel in joy
    by the light of his glory,
    with the mercy and justice for company.

Responsorial Psalm: Psalms 126:1-2, 2-3, 4-5, 6

R. [3] The Lord has done great things for us; we
            are filled with joy.
[1] When the LORD brought back the captives of
            Zion,
    we thought we were dreaming.
[2AB] Then our mouths were filled with laughter;
    and our tongue with rejoicing.

[2BC] Then they said among the nations,
   "The LORD had done great things for
them."
[3] The Lord has done great things for us;
   we are glad indeed.
R. The Lord has done great things for us; we are
            filled with joy.

[4] Restore our fortunes, O LORD,
   like the torrents in the southern desert.
[5] Those who sow in tears
   shall reap rejoicing.
R. The Lord has done great things for us; we are
            filled with joy.

[6] Although they go forth weeping,
   carrying the seed to be sown,
they shall some back rejoicing,
   carrying their sheaves.

R. The Lord has done great things for us; we are
            filled with joy.

Second Reading: Philippians 1:4-6, 8-11

Brothers and sisters: [4] I pray always with joy in my every prayer for all of you, [5] because of your partnership for the gospel from the first day until now. [6] I am confident of this, that the one who began a good work in you will continue to complete it until the day of Christ Jesus. [8] For God is my witness, how I long for all of you with the affection of Christ Jesus. [9] And this is my prayer: that your love may increase ever more and more in knowledge and every kind of perception, [10] to discern what is of value, so that you may be pure and blameless for the day of Christ, [11] filled with the fruit of righteousness that comes through Jesus Christ for the glory and praise of God.

Alleluia: Luke 3:4, 6

R. Alleluia, alleluia.
[4] Prepare the way of the Lord, make straight
         his paths:
[6] all flesh shall see the salvation of God.
R. Alleluia, alleluia.

Gospel: Luke 3:1-6

[1] In the fifteenth year of the reign of Tiberius Caesar, when Pontius Pilate was governor of Judea, and Herod was tetrarch of Galilee, and his brother Philip tetrarch of the region of Ituraea and Trachonitis, and Lysanias was tetrarch of Abilene, [2] during the high priesthood

of Annas and Caiaphas, the word of God came to John the son of Zechariah in the desert. [3] He went throughout the whole region of the Jordan, proclaiming a baptism of repentance for the forgiveness of sins, [4] as it is written in the book of the words of the prophet Isaiah:

"A voice of one crying out in the desert:
'Prepare the way of the Lord,
* make straight his paths.*
[5] *Every valley shall be filled*
* and every mountain and hill shall be made low.*
The winding roads shall be made straight,
* and the rough ways made smooth,*
[6] *and all flesh shall see the salvation of God.'"*

Solemnity of the Immaculate Conception of the Blessed Virgin Mary
First Reading: Genesis 3:9-15, 20

[9] After the man, Adam, had eaten of the tree, the LORD God called to the man and asked him, "Where are you?" [10] He answered, "I heard you in the garden; but I was afraid, because I was naked, so I hid myself." [11] Then he asked, "Who told you that you were naked? You have eaten, then, from the tree of which I had forbidden you to eat!" [12] The man replied, "The woman whom you put here with me — she gave me fruit from the tree, and so I ate it." [13] The LORD God then asked the woman, "Why did you do such a thing?" The woman answered, "The serpent tricked me into it, so I ate it."

[14] Then the LORD God said to the serpent:

"Because you have done this, you shall be
      banned
    from all the animals
    and from all the wild creatures;
on your belly shall you crawl,
    and dirt shall you eat
    all the days of your life.
[15] I will put enmity between you and the
      woman,
    and between your offspring and hers;
he will strike at your head,
    while you strike at his heel."

[20] The man called his wife Eve, because she became the mother of all the living.

Responsorial Psalm: Psalms 98:1, 2-3AB, 3CD-4

R. [1] *Sing to the Lord a new song, for he has*
*   done marvelous deeds.*

¹ Sing to the LORD a new song,
     for he has done wondrous deeds;
His right hand has won victory for him,
     his holy arm.
R. Sing to the Lord a new song, for he has done
        marvelous deeds.

² The LORD has made his salvation known:
     in the sight of the nations he has revealed
         his justice.
³ᴬᴮ He has remembered his kindness and his
         faithfulness
     toward the house of Israel.
R. Sing to the Lord a new song, for he has done
        marvelous deeds.

³ᶜᴰ All the ends of the earth have seen
     the salvation by our God.
⁴ Sing joyfully to the LORD, all you lands;
     break into song; sing praise.
R. Sing to the Lord a new song, for he has done
        marvelous deeds.

Second Reading: Ephesians 1:3-6, 11-12

Brothers and sisters: ³ Blessed be the God and Father of our Lord Jesus Christ, who has blessed us in Christ with every spiritual blessing in the heavens, ⁴ as he chose us in him, before the foundation of the world, to be holy and without blemish before him. In love ⁵ he destined us for adoption to himself through Jesus Christ, in accord with the favor of his will, ⁶ for the praise of the glory of his grace that he granted us in the beloved.

     ¹¹ In him we were also chosen, destined in accord with the purpose of the One who accomplishes all things according to the intention of his will, ¹² so that we might exist for the praise of his glory, we who first hoped in Christ.

Alleluia: cf. Luke 1:28

R. Alleluia, alleluia.
²⁸ Hail, Mary, full of grace, the Lord is with you;
blessed are you among women.
R. Alleluia, alleluia.

Gospel: Luke 1:26-38

²⁶ The angel Gabriel was sent from God to a town of Galilee called Nazareth, ²⁷ to a virgin betrothed to a man named Joseph, of the house of David, and the virgin's name was

Mary. [28] And coming to her, he said, "Hail, full of grace! The Lord is with you." [29] But she was greatly troubled at what was said and pondered what sort of greeting this might be. [30] Then the angel said to her, "Do not be afraid, Mary, for you have found favor with God. [31] Behold, you will conceive in your womb and bear a son, and you shall name him Jesus. [32] He will be great and will be called Son of the Most High, and the Lord God will give him the throne of David his father, [33] and he will rule over the house of Jacob forever, and of his Kingdom there will be no end." [34] But Mary said to the angel, "How can this be, since I have no relations with a man?" [35] And the angel said to her in reply, "The Holy Spirit will come upon you, and the power of the Most High will overshadow you. Therefore the child to be born will be called holy, the Son of God. [36] And behold, Elizabeth, your relative, has also conceived a son in her old age, and this is the sixth month for her who was called barren; [37] for nothing will be impossible for God." [38] Mary said, "Behold, I am the handmaid of the Lord. May it be done to me according to your word." Then the angel departed from her.

Tuesday of the Second Week of Advent
First Reading: Isaiah 40:1-11

[1] Comfort, give comfort to my people,
        says your God.
[2] Speak tenderly to Jerusalem, and proclaim to
            her
        that her service is at an end,
        her guilt is expiated;
Indeed, she has received from the hand of
            the LORD
        double for all her sins.

    [3] A voice cries out:
In the desert prepare the way of the LORD!
        Make straight in the wasteland a highway
            for our God!
[4] Every valley shall be filled in,
        every mountain and hill shall be made
            low;
The rugged land shall be made a plain,
        the rough country, a broad valley.
[5] Then the glory of the LORD shall be revealed,
        and all people shall see it together;
        for the mouth of the LORD has spoken.

[6] A voice says, "Cry out!"

I answer, "What shall I cry out?"
"All flesh is grass,
>and all their glory like the flower of the
>>field.

[7] The grass withers, the flower wilts,
>when the breath of the LORD blows upon
>>it.
>So then, the people is the grass.

[8] Though the grass withers and the flower
>>wilts,
>the word of our God stands forever."

[9] Go up onto a high mountain,
>Zion, herald of glad tidings;
Cry out at the top of your voice,
>Jerusalem, herald of good news!
Fear not to cry out
>and say to the cities of Judah:
>Here is your God!

[10] Here comes with power
>the Lord GOD,
>who rules by his strong arm;
Here is his reward with him,
>his recompense before him.

[11] Like a shepherd he feeds his flock;
>in his arms he gathers the lambs,
Carrying them in his bosom,
>and leading the ewes with care.

Responsorial Psalm: Psalms 96:1-2, 3 AND 10AC, 11-12, 13

R. *(see Isaiah 40:10ab)* **The Lord our God comes with power.**

[1] Sing to the LORD a new song;
>sing to the LORD, all you lands.

[2] Sing to the LORD; bless his name;
>announce his salvation, day after day.

R. The Lord our God comes with power.

[3] Tell his glory among the nations;
>among all peoples, his wondrous deeds.

[10AC] Say among the nations: The LORD is king;
>he governs the peoples with equity.

R. The Lord our God comes with power.

¹¹ Let the heavens be glad and the earth
      rejoice;
   let the sea and what fills it resound;
      ¹² let the plains be joyful and all that is in
      them!
Then let all the trees of the forest rejoice.
R. The Lord our God comes with power.

¹³ They shall exult before the LORD, for he
      comes;
   for he comes to rule the earth.
He shall rule the world with justice
   and the peoples with his constancy.
R. The Lord our God comes with power.

Alleluia
R. Alleluia, alleluia.
The day of the Lord is near;
Behold, he comes to save us.
R. Alleluia, alleluia.

Gospel: Matthew 18:12-14
Jesus said to his disciples: ¹² "What is your opinion? If a man has a hundred sheep and one of them goes astray, will he not leave the ninety-nine in the hills and go in search of the stray? ¹³ And if he finds it, amen, I say to you, he rejoices more over it than over the ninety-nine that did not stray. ¹⁴ In just the same way, it is not the will of your heavenly Father that one of these little ones be lost."

Wednesday of the Second Week of Advent
First Reading: Isaiah 40:25-31
²⁵ To whom can you liken me as an equal?
      says the Holy One.
²⁶ Lift up your eyes on high
      and see who has created these things:
He leads out their army and numbers them,
      calling them all by name.
By his great might and the strength of his
      power
      not one of them is missing!
²⁷ Why, O Jacob, do you say,
      and declare, O Israel,

"My way is hidden from the LORD,
    and my right is disregarded by my God"?

28 Do you not know
        or have you not heard?
The LORD is the eternal God,
        creator of the ends of the earth.
He does not faint nor grow weary,
        and his knowledge is beyond scrutiny.
29 He gives strength to the fainting;
        for the weak he makes vigor abound.
30 Though young men faint and grow weary,
        and youths stagger and fall,
31 They that hope in the LORD will renew their
            strength,
        they will soar as with eagles' wings;
They will run and not grow weary,
        walk and not grow faint.

Responsorial Psalm: Psalms 103:1-2, 3-4, 8 and 10

R. (1) O bless the Lord, my soul!
1 Bless the LORD, O my soul;
        and all my being, bless his holy name.
2 Bless the LORD, O my soul,
        and forget not all his benefits.
R. O bless the Lord, my soul!

3 He pardons all your iniquities,
        he heals all your ills.
4 He redeems your life from destruction,
        he crowns you with kindness and
            compassion.
R. O bless the Lord, my soul!
8 Merciful and gracious is the LORD,
        slow to anger and abounding in kindness.
10 Not according to our sins does he deal with
            us,
        nor does he requite us according to our
            crimes.
R. O bless the Lord, my soul!

Alleluia

R. Alleluia, alleluia.
Behold, the Lord comes to save his people;
blessed are those prepared to meet him.
R. Alleluia, alleluia.

Gospel: Matthew 11:28-30

Jesus said to the crowds: [28] "Come to me, all you who labor and are burdened, and I will give you rest. [29] Take my yoke upon you and learn from me, for I am meek and humble of heart; and you will find rest for yourselves. [30] For my yoke is easy, and my burden light."

Feast of Our Lady of Guadalupe
First Reading: Zechariah 2:14-17

[14] Sing and rejoice, O daughter Zion!
See, I am coming to dwell among you,
   says the LORD.
[15] Many nations shall join themselves to
      the LORD on that day,
   and they shall be his people,
   and he will dwell among you,
   and you shall know that the LORD of
      hosts has sent me to you.
[16] The LORD will possess Judah as his
      portion in the holy land,
   and he will again choose Jerusalem.
[17] Silence, all mankind, in the presence of
      the LORD!
   For he stirs forth from his holy
      dwelling.

Or Revelation 11:19A; 12:1-6A, 10AB

[19A] God's temple in heaven was opened, and the ark of his covenant could be seen in the temple.

[1] A great sign appeared in the sky, a woman clothed with the sun, with the moon under her feet, and on her head a crown of twelve stars. [2] She was with child and wailed aloud in pain as she labored to give birth. [3] Then another sign appeared in the sky; it was a huge red dragon, with seven heads and ten horns, and on its heads were seven diadems. [4] Its tail swept away a third of the stars in the sky and hurled them down to the earth. Then the dragon stood before the woman about to give birth, to devour her child when she gave birth. [5] She gave birth to a son, a male child, destined to rule all the nations with an iron rod. Her child was caught up to God and his throne. [6A] The woman herself fled into the desert where she had a place prepared by God.

^{10AB} Then I heard a loud voice in heaven say: "Now have salvation and power come, and the Kingdom of our God and the authority of his Anointed."

Responsorial Psalm: Judith 13:18BCDE, 19

R. *(15:9d)* **You are the highest honor of our race.**

^{18BCDE} Blessed are you, daughter, by the Most High
> God,
> above all the women on earth;
> and blessed be the LORD God,
> the creator of heaven and earth.

R. **You are the highest honor of our race.**

¹⁹ Your deed of hope will never be forgotten
> by those who tell of the might of God.

R. **You are the highest honor of our race.**

Alleluia

R. Alleluia, alleluia.
Blessed are you, holy Virgin Mary, deserving
> of all praise;
From you rose the sun of justice, Christ our God.
R. Alleluia, alleluia.

Gospel: Luke 1:26-38

²⁶ The angel Gabriel was sent from God to a town of Galilee called Nazareth, ²⁷ to a virgin betrothed to a man named Joseph, of the house of David, and the virgin's name was Mary. ²⁸ And coming to her, he said, "Hail, full of grace! The Lord is with you." ²⁹ But she was greatly troubled at what was said and pondered what sort of greeting this might be. ³⁰ Then the angel said to her, "Do not be afraid, Mary, for you have found favor with God. ³¹ Behold, you will conceive in your womb and bear a son, and you shall name him Jesus. ³² He will be great

and will be called Son of the Most High, and the Lord God will give him the throne of David his father, ³³ and he will rule over the house of Jacob forever, and of his Kingdom there will be no end." ³⁴ But Mary said to the angel, "How can this be, since I have no relations with a man?" ³⁵ And the angel said to her in reply, "The Holy Spirit will come upon you, and the power of the Most High will overshadow you. Therefore the child to be born will be called holy, the Son of God. ³⁶ And behold, Elizabeth, your relative, has also conceived a son in her old age, and this is the sixth month for her who was called barren; ³⁷ for nothing will be impossible for God." ³⁸ Mary said, "Behold, I am the handmaid of the Lord. May it be done to me according to your word." Then the angel departed from her.

Or Luke 1:39-47

[39] Mary set out and traveled to the hill country in haste to a town of Judah, [40] where she entered the house of Zechariah and greeted Elizabeth. [41] When Elizabeth heard Mary's greeting, the infant leaped in her womb, and Elizabeth, filled with the Holy Spirit, [42] cried out in a loud voice and said, "Most blessed are you among women, and blessed is the fruit of your womb. [43] And how does this happen to me, that the mother of my Lord should come to me? [44] For at the moment the sound of your greeting reached my ears, the infant in my womb leaped for joy. [45] Blessed are you who believed that what was spoken to you by the Lord would be fulfilled."

[46] And Mary said:

"My soul proclaims the greatness of the
    Lord;
[47] my spirit rejoices in God my savior."

Friday December 13, 2024

Memorial of Saint Lucy, Virgin & Martyr
First Reading: Isaiah 48:17-19

[17] Thus says the LORD, your redeemer,
    the Holy One of Israel:
I, the LORD, your God,
    teach you what is for your good,
    and lead you on the way you should go.
[18] If you would hearken to my commandments,
    your prosperity would be like a river,
    and your vindication like the waves of
      the sea;
[19] Your descendants would be like the sand,
    and those born of your stock like its
      grains,
Their name never cut off
    or blotted out from my presence.

Responsorial Psalm: Psalms 1:1-2,3,4 & 6

R. *(see John 8:12)* **Those who follow you, Lord, will
      have the light of life.**
[1] Blessed the man who follows not
    the counsel of the wicked
Nor walks in the way of sinners,
    nor sits in the company of the insolent,
[2] But delights in the law of the LORD
    and meditates on his law day and night.

R. Those who follow you, Lord, will have the
light of life.

³ He is like a tree
    planted near running water,
That yields its fruit in due season,
    and whose leaves never fade.
    Whatever he does, prospers.
R. Those who follow you, Lord, will have the
light of life.

⁴ Not so the wicked, not so;
    they are like chaff which the wind drives
    away.
⁶ For the LORD watches over the way of the
    just,
    but the way of the wicked vanishes.
R. Those who follow you, Lord, will have the
light of life.

Alleluia
R. Alleluia, alleluia.
The Lord will come; go out to meet him!
He is the prince of peace.
R. Alleluia, alleluia.

Gospel: Matthew 11:16-19
Jesus said to the crowds: ¹⁶ "To what shall I compare this generation? It is like children who sit in marketplaces and call to one another,¹⁷ 'We played the flute for you, but you did not dance, we sang a dirge but you did not mourn.' ¹⁸ For John came neither eating nor drinking, and they said, 'He is possessed by a demon.' ¹⁹ The Son of Man came eating and drinking and they said, 'Look, he is a glutton and a drunkard, a friend of tax collectors and sinners.' But wisdom is vindicated by her works."

Saturday December 14, 2024

Saturday of the Second Week of Advent
First Reading: Sirach 48:1-4, 9-11
    ¹ In those days,
like a fire there appeared the prophet Elijah
    whose words were as a flaming furnace.
² Their staff of bread he shattered,
    in his zeal he reduced them to straits;

634

[3] By the Lord's word he shut up the heavens
    and three times brought down fire.
[4] How awesome are you, Elijah, in your
       wondrous deeds!
    Whose glory is equal to yours?
[9] You were taken aloft in a whirlwind of fire,
    in a chariot with fiery horses.
[10] You were destined, it is written, in time to
       come
    to put an end to wrath before the day of
       the LORD,
To turn back the hearts of fathers toward
       their sons,
    and to re-establish the tribes of Jacob.
[11] Blessed is he who shall have seen you
    and who falls asleep in your friendship.

Responsorial Psalm: Psalms 80:2AC AND 3B, 15-16, 18-19

R. [(4)] *Lord, make us turn to you; let us see your*
       face and we shall be saved.

[2AC] O shepherd of Israel, hearken,
From your throne upon the cherubim, shine
       forth.
[3B] Rouse your power.

R. *Lord, make us turn to you; let us see your face*
       and we shall be saved.

[15] Once again, O LORD of hosts,
    look down from heaven, and see;
[16] Take care of this vine,
     and protect what your right hand has
       planted,
     the son of man whom you yourself made
       strong.

R. *Lord, make us turn to you; let us see your face*
       and we shall be saved.

[18] May your help be with the man of your right
       hand,
     with the son of man whom you yourself
       made strong.
[19] Then we will no more withdraw from you;
     give us new life, and we will call upon
       your name.

R. Lord, make us turn to you; let us see your face
and we shall be saved.

Alleluia: Luke 3:4, 6
R. Alleluia, alleluia.
[4] Prepare the way of the Lord, make straight
his paths:
[6] All flesh shall see the salvation of God.
R. Alleluia, alleluia.

Gospel: Matthew 17:9A, 10-13
[9A] As they were coming down from the mountain, [10] the disciples asked Jesus, "Why do the scribes say that Elijah must come first?" [11] He said in reply, "Elijah will indeed come and restore all things; [12] but I tell you that Elijah has already come, and they did not recognize him but did to him whatever they pleased. So also will the Son of Man suffer at their hands." [13] Then the disciples understood that he was speaking to them of John the Baptist.

Third Sunday of Advent, Year C
First Reading: Zephaniah 3:14-18A
[14] Shout for joy, O daughter Zion!
Sing joyfully, O Israel!
Be glad and exult with all your heart,
O daughter Jerusalem!
[15] The LORD has removed the judgment against
you
he has turned away your enemies;
the King of Israel, the LORD, is in your midst,
you have no further misfortune to fear.
[16] On that day, it shall be said to Jerusalem:
Fear not, O Zion, be not discouraged!
[17] The LORD, your God, is in your midst,
a mighty savior;
he will rejoice over you with gladness,
and renew you in his love,
he will sing joyfully because of you,
[18A] as one sings at festivals.

Responsorial Psalm: Isaiah 12:2-3, 4, 5-6.
R. [(6)] Cry out with joy and gladness: for among
you is the great and Holy One of Israel.
[2] God indeed is my savior;

636

I am confident and unafraid.
My strength and my courage is the LORD,
and he has been my savior.
³ With joy you will draw water
at the fountain of salvation.
**R. Cry out with joy and gladness: for among you
is the great and Holy One of Israel.**

⁴ Give thanks to the LORD, acclaim his name;
among the nations make known his
deeds,
proclaim how exalted is his name.
**R. Cry out with joy and gladness: for among you
is the great and Holy One of Israel.**

⁵ Sing praise to the LORD for his glorious
achievement;
let this be known throughout all the
earth.
⁶ Shout with exultation, O city of Zion,
for great in your midst
is the Holy One of Israel!
**R. Cry out with joy and gladness: for among you
is the great and Holy One of Israel.**

Second Reading: Philippians 4:4-7

Brothers and sisters: ⁴ Rejoice in the Lord always. I shall say it again: rejoice! ⁵ Your kindness should be known to all. The Lord is near. ⁶ Have no anxiety at all, but in everything, by prayer and petition, with thanksgiving, make your requests known to God. ⁷Then the peace of God that surpasses all understanding will guard your hearts and minds in Christ Jesus.

Alleluia: Isaiah 61:1 (Cited In Luke 4:18)

R. Alleluia, alleluia.
¹ The Spirit of the Lord is upon me,
because he has anointed me
to bring glad tidings to the poor.
R. Alleluia, alleluia.

Gospel: Luke 3:10-18

¹⁰ The crowds asked John the Baptist, "What should we do?" ¹¹ He said to them in reply, "Whoever has two cloaks should share with the person who has none. And whoever has food should do likewise." ¹² Even tax collectors came to be baptized and they said to him, "Teacher, what should we do?" ¹³He answered them, "Stop collecting more than what is

prescribed." [14] Soldiers also asked him, "And what is it that we should do?" He told them, "Do not practice extortion, do not falsely accuse anyone, and be satisfied with your wages."

[15] Now the people were filled with expectation, and all were asking in their hearts whether John might be the Christ. [16] John answered them all, saying, "I am baptizing you with water, but one mightier than I is coming. I am not worthy to loosen the thongs of his sandals. He will baptize you with the Holy Spirit and fire. [17] His winnowing fan is in his hand to clear his threshing floor and to gather the wheat into his barn, but the chaff he will burn with unquenchable fire." [18] Exhorting them in many other ways, he preached good news to the people.

Monday December 16, 2024

Monday of the Third Week of Advent
First Reading: Numbers 24:2-7, 15-17A

[2] When Balaam raised his eyes and saw Israel encamped, tribe by tribe, the spirit of God came upon him, [3] and he gave voice to his oracle:

The utterance of Balaam, son of Beor,
 the utterance of a man whose eye is true,
[4] The utterance of one who hears what God
  says,
 and knows what the Most High knows,
Of one who sees what the Almighty sees,
 enraptured, and with eyes unveiled:
[5] How goodly are your tents, O Jacob;
 your encampments, O Israel!
[6] They are like gardens beside a stream,
 like the cedars planted by the LORD.
[7] His wells shall yield free-flowing waters,
 he shall have the sea within reach;
His king shall rise higher,
 and his royalty shall be exalted.

[15] Then Balaam gave voice to his oracle:

The utterance of Balaam, son of Beor,
 the utterance of the man whose eye is
  true,
[16] The utterance of one who hears what God
  says,
 and knows what the Most High knows,
Of one who sees what the Almighty sees,

638

enraptured, and with eyes unveiled.
17A I see him, though not now;
I behold him, though not near:
A star shall advance from Jacob,
and a staff shall rise from Israel.

Responsorial Psalm: Psalms 25:4-5AB, 6 and 7BC, 8-9

R. (4) *Teach me your ways, O Lord.*

4 Your ways, O LORD, make known to me;
teach me your paths,
5AB Guide me in your truth and teach me,
for you are God my savior.

R. *Teach me your ways, O Lord.*

6 Remember that your compassion, O LORD,
and your kindness are from of old.
7BC In your kindness remember me,
because of your goodness, O LORD.

R. *Teach me your ways, O Lord.*

8 Good and upright is the LORD;
thus he shows sinners the way.
9 He guides the humble to justice,
he teaches the humble his way.

R. *Teach me your ways, O Lord.*

Alleluia: Psalms 85:8

R. Alleluia, alleluia.
8 Show us, LORD, your love,
and grant us your salvation.
R. Alleluia, alleluia.

Gospel: Matthew 21:23-27

23 When Jesus had come into the temple area, the chief priests and the elders of the people approached him as he was teaching and said, "By what authority are you doing these things? And who gave you this authority?" 24 Jesus said to them in reply, "I shall ask you one question, and if you answer it for me, then I shall tell you by what authority I do these things. 25 Where was John's baptism from? Was it of heavenly or of human origin?" They discussed this among themselves and said, "If we say 'Of heavenly origin,' he will say to us, 'Then why did you not believe him?' 26 But if we say, 'Of human origin,' we fear the crowd, for they all regard John as a prophet." 27 So they said to Jesus in reply, "We do not know." He himself said to them, "Neither shall I tell you by what authority I do these things."

First Reading: Genesis 49:2, 8-10

2 Jacob called his sons and said to them:

"Assemble and listen, sons of Jacob,
    listen to Israel, your father.

8 "You, Judah, shall your brothers praise
    —your hand on the neck of your enemies;
    the sons of your father shall bow down to
        you.
9 Judah, like a lion's whelp,
    you have grown up on prey, my son.
He crouches like a lion recumbent,
    the king of beasts—who would dare rouse
        him?
10 The scepter shall never depart from Judah,
    or the mace from between his legs,
While tribute is brought to him,
    and he receives the people's homage."

Responsorial Psalm: Psalms 72:1-2, 3-4AB, 7-8, 17

R. (see 7) *Justice shall flourish in his time, and*
    fullness of peace for ever.
1 O God, with your judgment endow the king,
    and with your justice, the king's son;
2 He shall govern your people with justice
    and your afflicted ones with judgment.
R. *Justice shall flourish in his time, and fullness*
    of peace for ever.

3 The mountains shall yield peace for the
        people,
    and the hills justice.
4AB He shall defend the afflicted among the
        people,
    save the children of the poor.
R. *Justice shall flourish in his time, and fullness*
    of peace for ever.

7 Justice shall flower in his days,

and profound peace, till the moon be no
more.
⁸ May he rule from sea to sea,
and from the River to the ends of the
earth.
**R. Justice shall flourish in his time, and fullness
of peace for ever.**

¹⁷ May his name be blessed forever;
as long as the sun his name shall remain.
In him shall all the tribes of the earth be
blessed;
all the nations shall proclaim his
happiness.
**R. Justice shall flourish in his time, and fullness
of peace for ever.**

Alleluia
R. Alleluia, alleluia.
O Wisdom of our God Most High,
guiding creation with power and love:
come to teach us the path of knowledge!
R. Alleluia, alleluia.

Gospel: Matthew 1:1-17
¹ The book of the genealogy of Jesus Christ, the son of David, the son of Abraham.

² Abraham became the father of Isaac, Isaac the father of Jacob, Jacob the father of Judah and his brothers. ³ Judah became the father of Perez and Zerah, whose mother was Tamar. Perez became the father of Hezron, Hezron the father of Ram, ⁴ Ram the father of Amminadab. Amminadab became the father of Nahshon, Nahshon the father of Salmon, ⁵ Salmon the father of Boaz, whose mother was Rahab. Boaz became the father of Obed, whose mother was Ruth. Obed became the father of Jesse, ⁶ Jesse the father of David the king.

David became the father of Solomon, whose mother had been the wife of Uriah. ⁷ Solomon became the father of Rehoboam, Rehoboam the father of Abijah, Abijah the father of Asaph. ⁸ Asaph became the father of Jehoshaphat, Jehoshaphat the father of Joram, Joram the father of Uzziah. ⁹ Uzziah became the father of Jotham, Jotham the father of Ahaz, Ahaz the father of Hezekiah. ¹⁰ Hezekiah became the father of Manasseh, Manasseh the father of Amos, Amos the father of Josiah. ¹¹ Josiah became the father of Jechoniah and his brothers at the time of the Babylonian exile.

¹² After the Babylonian exile, Jechoniah became the father of Shealtiel, Shealtiel the father of Zerubbabel, ¹³ Zerubbabel the father of Abiud. Abiud became the father of Eliakim, Eliakim the father of Azor, ¹⁴ Azor the father of Zadok. Zadok became the father of Achim, Achim the father of Eliud, ¹⁵ Eliud the father of Eleazar. Eleazar became the father

of Matthan, Matthan the father of Jacob, [16] Jacob the father of Joseph, the husband of Mary. Of her was born Jesus who is called the Christ.

[17] Thus the total number of generations from Abraham to David is fourteen generations; from David to the Babylonian exile, fourteen generations; from the Babylonian exile to the Christ, fourteen generations.

Wednesday December 18, 2024

First Reading: Jeremiah 23:5-8

[5] Behold, the days are coming, says the LORD,
>   when I will raise up a righteous shoot to
>   David;
As king he shall reign and govern wisely,
>   he shall do what is just and right in the
>   land.
[6] In his days Judah shall be saved,
>   Israel shall dwell in security.
This is the name they give him:
>   "The LORD our justice."

[7] Therefore, the days will come, says the LORD,
>   when they shall no longer say, "As the
>   LORD lives,
>   who brought the children of Israel out of
>   the land of Egypt";
[8] but rather, "As the LORD lives,
>   who brought the descendants of the
>   house of Israel
>   up from the land of the north"–
>   and from all the lands to which I
>   banished them;
>   they shall again live on their own land.

Responsorial Psalm: Psalms 72:1-2, 12-13, 18-19

R. (see 7) *Justice shall flourish in his time, and*
>   *fullness of peace for ever.*
[1] O God, with your judgment endow the king,
>   and with your justice, the king's son;
[2] He shall govern your people with justice
>   and your afflicted ones with judgment.
R. *Justice shall flourish in his time, and fullness*
>   *of peace for ever.*

¹² For he shall rescue the poor when he cries
out,
and the afflicted when he has no one to
help him.
¹² He shall have pity for the lowly and the
poor;
the lives of the poor he shall save.
**R. Justice shall flourish in his time, and fullness
of peace for ever.**

¹⁸ Blessed be the LORD, the God of Israel,
who alone does wondrous deeds.
¹⁹ And blessed forever be his glorious name;
may the whole earth be filled with his
glory.
**R. Justice shall flourish in his time, and fullness
of peace for ever.**

Alleluia

R. Alleluia, alleluia.
O Leader of the House of Israel,
giver of the Law to Moses on Sinai:
come to rescue us with your mighty power!
R. Alleluia, alleluia.

Gospel: Matthew 1:18-25

¹⁸ This is how the birth of Jesus Christ came about. When his mother Mary was betrothed to Joseph, but before they lived together, she was found with child through the Holy Spirit. ¹⁹ Joseph her husband, since he was a righteous man, yet unwilling to expose her to shame, decided to divorce her quietly. ²⁰ Such was his intention when, behold, the angel of the Lord appeared to him in a dream and said, "Joseph, son of David, do not be afraid to take Mary your wife into your home. For it is through the Holy Spirit that this child has been conceived in her. ²¹ She will bear a son and you are to name him Jesus, because he will save his people from their sins." ²² All this took place to fulfill what the Lord had said through the prophet:

*²³ Behold, the virgin shall be with child and bear
a son,
and they shall name him Emmanuel,*

which means "God is with us." ²⁴ When Joseph awoke, he did as the angel of the Lord had commanded him and took his wife into his home. ²⁵ He had no relations with her until she bore a son, and he named him Jesus.

First Reading: Judges 13:2-7, 24-25A

[2] There was a certain man from Zorah, of the clan of the Danites, whose name was Manoah. His wife was barren and had borne no children. [3] An angel of the LORD appeared to the woman and said to her, "Though you are barren and have had no children, yet you will conceive and bear a son. [4] Now, then, be careful to take no wine or strong drink and to eat nothing unclean. [5] As for the son you will conceive and bear, no razor shall touch his head, for this boy is to be consecrated to God from the womb. It is he who will begin the deliverance of Israel from the power of the Philistines."

[6] The woman went and told her husband, "A man of God came to me; he had the appearance of an angel of God, terrible indeed. I did not ask him where he came from, nor did he tell me his name. [7] But he said to me, 'You will be with child and will bear a son. So take neither wine nor strong drink, and eat nothing unclean. For the boy shall be consecrated to God from the womb, until the day of his death.'"

[24] The woman bore a son and named him Samson. The boy grew up and the LORD blessed him; [25A] the Spirit of the LORD stirred him.

Responsorial Psalm: Psalms 71:3-4A, 5-6AB, 16-17

R. [(See 8)] *My mouth shall be filled with your praise,*
and I will sing your glory!

[3] Be my rock of refuge,
a stronghold to give me safety,
for you are my rock and my fortress.
[4A] O my God, rescue me from the hand of the
wicked.

R. *My mouth shall be filled with your praise, and*
I will sing your glory!

[5] For you are my hope, O LORD;
my trust, O God, from my youth.
[6AB] On you I depend from birth;
from my mother's womb you are my
strength.

R. *My mouth shall be filled with your praise, and*
I will sing your glory!

[16] I will treat of the mighty works of the LORD;
O God, I will tell of your singular justice.
[17] O God, you have taught me from my youth,
and till the present I proclaim your
wondrous deeds.

R. *My mouth shall be filled with your praise, and*

Alleluia
R. Alleluia, alleluia.
O Root of Jesse's stem,
sign of God's love for all his people:
come to save us without delay!
R. Alleluia, alleluia.

Gospel: Luke 1:5-25

[5] In the days of Herod, King of Judea, there was a priest named Zechariah of the priestly division of Abijah; his wife was from the daughters of Aaron, and her name was Elizabeth. [6] Both were righteous in the eyes of God, observing all the commandments and ordinances of the Lord blamelessly. [7] But they had no child, because Elizabeth was barren and both were advanced in years.

[8] Once when he was serving as priest in his division's turn before God, [9] according to the practice of the priestly service, he was chosen by lot to enter the sanctuary of the Lord to burn incense. [10] Then, when the whole assembly of the people was praying outside at the hour of the incense offering, [11] the angel of the Lord appeared to him, standing at the right of the altar of incense. [12] Zechariah was troubled by what he saw, and fear came upon him.

[13] But the angel said to him, "Do not be afraid, Zechariah, because your prayer has been heard. Your wife Elizabeth will bear you a son, and you shall name him John. [14] And you will have joy and gladness, and many will rejoice at his birth, [15] for he will be great in the sight of the Lord. He will drink neither wine nor strong drink. He will be filled with the Holy Spirit even from his mother's womb, [16] and he will turn many of the children of Israel to the Lord their God. [17] He will go before him in the spirit and power of Elijah to turn the hearts of fathers toward children and the disobedient to the understanding of the righteous, to prepare a people fit for the Lord."

[18] Then Zechariah said to the angel, "How shall I know this? For I am an old man, and my wife is advanced in years." [19] And the angel said to him in reply, "I am Gabriel, who stand before God. I was sent to speak to you and to announce to you this good news. [20] But now you will be speechless and unable to talk until the day these things take place, because you did not believe my words, which will be fulfilled at their proper time." [21] Meanwhile the people were waiting for Zechariah and were amazed that he stayed so long in the sanctuary. [22] But when he came out, he was unable to speak to them, and they realized that he had seen a vision in the sanctuary. He was gesturing to them but remained mute.

[23] Then, when his days of ministry were completed, he went home.

[24] After this time his wife Elizabeth conceived, and she went into seclusion for five months, saying, [25] "So has the Lord done for me at a time when he has seen fit to take away my disgrace before others."

First Reading: Isaiah 7:10-14

[10] The LORD spoke to Ahaz: [11] Ask for a sign from the LORD, your God; let it be deep as the nether world, or high as the sky! [12] But Ahaz answered, "I will not ask! I will not tempt the LORD!" [13] Then Isaiah said: Listen, O house of David! Is it not enough for you to weary men, must you also weary my God? [14] Therefore the Lord himself will give you this sign: the virgin shall conceive and bear a son, and shall name him Emmanuel.

Responsorial Psalm: Psalms 24:1-2, 3-4AB, 5-6

R. *(See 7c and 10b)* **Let the Lord enter; he is the king of glory.**
[1] The LORD's are the earth and its fullness;
    the world and those who dwell in it.
[2] For he founded it upon the seas
    and established it upon the rivers.
R. Let the Lord enter; he is the king of glory.

[3] Who can ascend the mountain of the LORD?
    or who may stand in his holy place?
[4AB] He whose hands are sinless, whose heart is
        clean,
    who desires not what is vain.
R. Let the Lord enter; he is the king of glory.

[5] He shall receive a blessing from the LORD,
    a reward from God his savior.
[6] Such is the race that seeks for him,
    that seeks the face of the God of Jacob.
R. Let the Lord enter; he is the king of glory.

Alleluia

R. Alleluia, alleluia.
O Key of David,
opening the gates of God's eternal Kingdom:
come and free the prisoners of darkness!
R. Alleluia, alleluia.

Gospel: Luke 1:26-38

[26] In the sixth month, the angel Gabriel was sent from God to a town of Galilee called Nazareth, [27] to a virgin betrothed to a man named Joseph, of the house of David, and the virgin's name was Mary. [28] And coming to her, he said, "Hail, full of grace! The Lord is with you." [29] But she was greatly troubled at what was said and pondered what sort of greeting

this might be. [30] Then the angel said to her, "Do not be afraid, Mary, for you have found favor with God. [31] Behold, you will conceive in your womb and bear a son, and you shall name him Jesus. [32] He will be great and will be called Son of the Most High, and the Lord God will give him the throne of David his father, [33] and he will rule over the house of Jacob forever, and of his Kingdom there will be no end."

[34] But Mary said to the angel, "How can this be, since I have no relations with a man?" [35] And the angel said to her in reply, "The Holy Spirit will come upon you, and the power of the Most High will overshadow you. Therefore the child to be born will be called holy, the Son of God. [36] And behold, Elizabeth, your relative, has also conceived a son in her old age, and this is the sixth month for her who was called barren; [37] for nothing will be impossible for God."

[38] Mary said, "Behold, I am the handmaid of the Lord. May it be done to me according to your word." Then the angel departed from her.

Saturday December 21, 2024

First Reading: Songs of Songs 2:8-14

[8] Hark! my lover—here he comes
    springing across the mountains,
    leaping across the hills.
[9] My lover is like a gazelle
    or a young stag.
Here he stands behind our wall,
    gazing through the windows,
    peering through the lattices.
[10] My lover speaks; he says to me,
    "Arise, my beloved, my dove, my
        beautiful one,
    and come!
[11] "For see, the winter is past,
    the rains are over and gone.
[12] The flowers appear on the earth,
    the time of pruning the vines has
        come,
    and the song of the dove is heard in
        our land.
[13] The fig tree puts forth its figs,
    and the vines, in bloom, give forth
        fragrance.
Arise, my beloved, my beautiful one,
    and come!

[14] "O my dove in the clefts of the rock,
    in the secret recesses of the cliff,

Let me see you,
        let me hear your voice,
For your voice is sweet,
        and you are lovely."

Or Zephaniah 3:14-18A

[14] Shout for joy, O daughter Zion!
        Sing joyfully, O Israel!
Be glad and exult with all your heart,
        O daughter Jerusalem!
[15] The LORD has removed the judgment
                against you,
        he has turned away your enemies;
The King of Israel, the LORD, is in your
                midst,
        you have no further misfortune to
                fear.
[16] On that day, it shall be said to Jerusalem:
        Fear not, O Zion, be not discouraged!
[17] The LORD, your God, is in your midst,
        a mighty savior;
He will rejoice over you with gladness,
        and renew you in his love,
He will sing joyfully because of you,
        [18A] as one sings at festivals.

Responsorial Psalm: Psalms 33:2-3, 11-12, 20-21

R. [(1a; 3a)] *Exult, you just, in the Lord! Sing to him*
        a new song.
[2] Give thanks to the LORD on the harp;
        with the ten-stringed lyre chant his
                praises.
[3] Sing to him a new song;
        pluck the strings skillfully, with shouts of
                gladness.
R. Exult, you just, in the Lord! Sing to him a new
        song.

[11] But the plan of the LORD stands forever;
        the design of his heart, through all
                generations.
[12] Blessed the nation whose God is the LORD,

the people he has chosen for his own
      inheritance.

R. Exult, you just, in the Lord! Sing to him a new song.

[20] Our soul waits for the LORD,
      who is our help and our shield,
[21] For in him our hearts rejoice;
      in his holy name we trust.

R. Exult, you just, in the Lord! Sing to him a new song.

Alleluia

R. Alleluia, alleluia.
O Emmanuel, our King and Giver of Law:
come to save us, Lord our God!
R. Alleluia, alleluia.

Gospel: Luke 1:39-45

[39] Mary set out in those days and traveled to the hill country in haste to a town of Judah, [40] where she entered the house of Zechariah and greeted Elizabeth. [41] When Elizabeth heard Mary's greeting, the infant leaped in her womb, and Elizabeth, filled with the Holy Spirit, [42] cried out in a loud voice and said, "Most blessed are you among women, and blessed is the fruit of your womb. [43] And how does this happen to me, that the mother of my Lord should come to me? [44] For at the moment the sound of your greeting reached my ears, the infant in my womb leaped for joy. [45] Blessed are you who believed that what was spoken to you by the Lord would be fulfilled."

Sunday December 22, 2024

Fourth Sunday of Advent, Year C
First Reading: Micah 5:1-4A
Thus says the LORD:

[1] You, Bethlehem-Ephrathah,
      too small to be among the clans of Judah,
from you shall come forth for me
      one who is to be ruler in Israel;
whose origin is from of old,
      from ancient times.
      [2] Therefore the Lord will give them up,
         until the time
      when she who is to give birth has borne,
and the rest of his kindred shall return

to the children of Israel.
³ He shall stand firm and shepherd his flock
    by the strength of the LORD,
    in the majestic name of the LORD, his God;
and they shall remain, for now his greatness
    shall reach to the ends of the earth;
    ⁴ᴬ he shall be peace.

Responsorial Psalm: Psalms 80:2-3, 15-16, 18-19.

R. ⁽⁴⁾ *Lord, make us turn to you; let us see your*
    face and we shall be saved.

² O shepherd of Israel, hearken,
    from your throne upon the cherubim,
        shine forth.
³ Rouse your power,
    and come to save us.

R. Lord, make us turn to you; let us see your face
    and we shall be saved.

¹⁵ Once again, O LORD of hosts,
    look down from heaven, and see;
take care of this vine,
    ¹⁶ and protect what your right hand has
        planted
    the son of man whom you yourself made
        strong.

R. Lord, make us turn to you; let us see your face
    and we shall be saved.

¹⁸ May your help be with the man of your right
        hand,
    with the son of man whom you yourself made
        strong.
¹⁹ Then we will no more withdraw from you;
    give us new life, and we will call upon
        your name.

R. Lord, make us turn to you; let us see your face
    and we shall be saved.

Second Reading: Hebrews 10:5-10

Brothers and sisters: ⁵ When Christ came into the world, he said:

"Sacrifice and offering you did not desire,
> but a body you prepared for me;
> > ^{6} in holocausts and sin offerings you took
> > > no delight.
^{7} Then I said, 'As is written of me in the scroll,
> behold, I come to do your will, O God.'"

^{8} First he says, "Sacrifices and offerings, holocausts and sin offerings, you neither desired nor delighted in." These are offered according to the law. ^{9} Then he says, "Behold, I come to do your will." He takes away the first to establish the second. ^{10} By this "will," we have been consecrated through the offering of the body of Jesus Christ once for all.

Alleluia: Luke 1:38
R. Alleluia, alleluia.
^{38} Behold, I am the handmaid of the Lord.
May it be done to me according to your
> word.
R. Alleluia, alleluia.

Gospel: Luke 1:39-45
^{39} Mary set out and traveled to the hill country in haste to a town of Judah, ^{40} where she entered the house of Zechariah and greeted Elizabeth. ^{41} When Elizabeth heard Mary's greeting, the infant leaped in her womb, and Elizabeth, filled with the Holy Spirit, ^{42} cried out in a loud voice and said, "Blessed are you among women, and blessed is the fruit of your womb. ^{43} And how does this happen to me, that the mother of my Lord should come to me? ^{44} For at the moment the sound of your greeting reached my ears, the infant in my womb leaped for joy. ^{45} Blessed are you who believed that what was spoken to you by the Lord would be fulfilled."

Monday December 23, 2024

First Reading: Malachi 3:1-4, 23-24
> ^{1} Thus says the Lord GOD:
Lo, I am sending my messenger
> to prepare the way before me;
And suddenly there will come to the temple
> the LORD whom you seek,
And the messenger of the covenant whom
> > you desire.
> Yes, he is coming, says the LORD of hosts.
^{2} But who will endure the day of his coming?
> And who can stand when he appears?
For he is like the refiner's fire,

or like the fuller's lye.
³ He will sit refining and purifying silver,
    and he will purify the sons of Levi,
Refining them like gold or like silver
    that they may offer due sacrifice to the
        LORD.
⁴ Then the sacrifice of Judah and Jerusalem
    will please the LORD,
    as in the days of old, as in years gone by.

²³ Lo, I will send you
    Elijah, the prophet,
Before the day of the LORD comes,
    the great and terrible day,
²⁴ To turn the hearts of the fathers to their
        children,
    and the hearts of the children to their
        fathers,
Lest I come and strike
    the land with doom.

Responsorial Psalm: Psalms 25:4-5AB, 8-9, 10 AND 14

R. *(see Luke 21:28)* ***Lift up your heads and see; your redemption is near at hand.***
⁴ Your ways, O LORD, make known to me;
    teach me your paths,
^{5AB} Guide me in your truth and teach me,
    for you are God my savior.
R. *Lift up your heads and see; your redemption is near at hand.*

⁸ Good and upright is the LORD;
    thus he shows sinners the way.
⁹ He guides the humble to justice,
    he teaches the humble his way.
R. *Lift up your heads and see; your redemption is near at hand.*

¹⁰ All the paths of the LORD are kindness and
        constancy
    toward those who keep his covenant and
        his decrees.

¹⁴ The friendship of the LORD is with those who
 fear him,
 and his covenant, for their instruction.
**R. Lift up your heads and see; your redemption
 is near at hand.**

Alleluia
R. Alleluia, alleluia.
O King of all nations and keystone of the
 Church:
come and save man, whom you formed from
 the dust!
R. Alleluia, alleluia.

Gospel: Luke 1:57-66
⁵⁷ When the time arrived for Elizabeth to have her child she gave birth to a son. ⁵⁸ Her neighbors and relatives heard that the Lord had shown his great mercy toward her, and they rejoiced with her. ⁵⁹ When they came on the eighth day to circumcise the child, they were going to call him Zechariah after his father, ⁶⁰ but his mother said in reply, "No. He will be called John." ⁶¹ But they answered her, "There is no one among your relatives who has this name." ⁶² So they made signs, asking his father what he wished him to be called. ⁶³ He asked for a tablet and wrote, "John is his name," and all were amazed. ⁶⁴ Immediately his mouth was opened, his tongue freed, and he spoke blessing God. ⁶⁵ Then fear came upon all their neighbors, and all these matters were discussed throughout the hill country of Judea. ⁶⁶ All who heard these things took them to heart, saying, "What, then, will this child be?" For surely the hand of the Lord was with him.

Tuesday December 24, 2024

First Reading: 2 Samuel 7:1-5,8B-12, 14A, 16
¹ When King David was settled in his palace, and the LORD had given him rest from his enemies on every side, ² he said to Nathan the prophet, "Here I am living in a house of cedar, while the ark of God dwells in a tent!" ³ Nathan answered the king, "Go, do whatever you have in mind, for the LORD is with you." ⁴ But that night the LORD spoke to Nathan and said: ⁵ "Go, tell my servant David, 'Thus says the LORD: Should you build me a house to dwell in?

^{8B} "'It was I who took you from the pasture and from the care of the flock to be commander of my people Israel. ⁹ I have been with you wherever you went, and I have destroyed all your enemies before you. And I will make you famous like the great ones of the earth. ¹⁰ I will fix a place for my people Israel; I will plant them so that they may dwell in their place without further disturbance. Neither shall the wicked continue to afflict them as they did of old, ¹¹ since the time I first appointed judges over my people Israel. I will give you rest from all your enemies. The LORD also reveals to you that he will

establish a house for you. [12] And when your time comes and you rest with your ancestors, I will raise up your heir after you, sprung from your loins, and I will make his Kingdom firm. [14A] I will be a father to him, and he shall be a son to me. [16] Your house and your Kingdom shall endure forever before me; your throne shall stand firm forever.'"

Responsorial Psalm: Psalms 89:2-3, 4-5, 27 AND 29

R. [(2)] *For ever I will sing the goodness of the Lord.*

[2] The favors of the LORD I will sing forever;
      through all generations my mouth shall
        proclaim your faithfulness.
[3] For you have said, "My kindness is
        established forever";
      in heaven you have confirmed your
        faithfulness.

R. *For ever I will sing the goodness of the Lord.*

[4] "I have made a covenant with my chosen
        one,
      I have sworn to David my servant:
[5] Forever will I confirm your posterity
      and establish your throne for all
        generations."

R. *For ever I will sing the goodness of the Lord.*

[27] "He shall say of me, 'You are my father,
      my God, the rock, my savior.'
[29] Forever I will maintain my kindness toward
        him,
      and my covenant with him stands firm."

R. *For ever I will sing the goodness of the Lord.*

Alleluia

R. Alleluia, alleluia.
O Radiant Dawn,
splendor of eternal light, sun of justice:
come and shine on those who dwell in
      darkness and in the shadow of death.
R. Alleluia, alleluia.

Gospel: Luke 1:67-79

[67] Zechariah his father, filled with the Holy Spirit, prophesied, saying:

[68] "Blessed be the Lord, the God of Israel;
for he has come to his people and set
them free.
[69] He has raised up for us a mighty Savior,
born of the house of his servant David.
[70] Through his prophets he promised of old
[71] that he would save us from our enemies,
from the hands of all who hate us.
[72] He promised to show mercy to our fathers
and to remember his holy covenant.
[73] This was the oath he swore to our father
Abraham:
[74] to set us free from the hand of our
enemies,
free to worship him without fear,
[75] holy and righteous in his sight
all the days of our life.
[76] You, my child, shall be called the prophet of
the Most High,
for you will go before the Lord to prepare
his way,
[77] to give his people knowledge of salvation
by the forgiveness of their sins.
[78] In the tender compassion of our God
the dawn from on high shall break upon
us,
[79] to shine on those who dwell in darkness
and the shadow of death,
and to guide our feet into the way of
peace."

Tuesday December 24, 2024

The Nativity of the Lord – Vigil Mass
First Reading: Isaiah 62:1-5

[1] For Zion's sake I will not be silent,
for Jerusalem's sake I will not be quiet,
until her vindication shines forth like the
dawn
and her victory like a burning torch.

[2] Nations shall behold your vindication,
and all the kings your glory;

you shall be called by a new name
pronounced by the mouth of the LORD.
³ You shall be a glorious crown in the hand of
the LORD,
a royal diadem held by your God.
⁴ No more shall people call you "Forsaken,"
or your land "Desolate,"
but you shall be called "My Delight,"
and your land "Espoused."
For the LORD delights in you
and makes your land his spouse.
⁵ As a young man marries a virgin,
your Builder shall marry you;
and as a bridegroom rejoices in his bride
so shall your God rejoice in you.

Responsorial Psalm: Psalms 89:4-5, 16-17, 27, 29

R. ⁽²ᵃ⁾ *For ever I will sing the goodness of the Lord.*

⁴ I have made a covenant with my chosen one,
I have sworn to David my servant:
⁵ Forever will I confirm your posterity
and establish your throne for all
generations.

R. For ever I will sing the goodness of the Lord.

¹⁶ Blessed the people who know the joyful
shout;
in the light of your countenance, O LORD,
they walk.
¹⁷ At your name they rejoice all the day,
and through your justice they are exalted.

R. For ever I will sing the goodness of the Lord.

²⁷ He shall say of me, "You are my father,
my God, the rock, my savior."
²⁹ Forever I will maintain my kindness toward
him,
and my covenant with him stands firm.

R. For ever I will sing the goodness of the Lord.

Second Reading: Acts 13:16-17, 22-25

¹⁶ When Paul reached Antioch in Pisidia and entered the synagogue, he stood up, motioned with his hand, and said, "Fellow Israelites and you others who are God-fearing,

listen. [17] The God of this people Israel chose our ancestors and exalted the people during their sojourn in the land of Egypt. With uplifted arm he led them out of it. [22] Then he removed Saul and raised up David as king; of him he testified, 'I have found David, son of Jesse, a man after my own heart; he will carry out my every wish.' [23] From this man's descendants God, according to his promise, has brought to Israel a savior, Jesus. [24] John heralded his coming by proclaiming a baptism of repentance to all the people of Israel; [25] and as John was completing his course, he would say, 'What do you suppose that I am? I am not he. Behold, one is coming after me; I am not worthy to unfasten the sandals of his feet.'"

Alleluia

R. Alleluia, alleluia.
Tomorrow the wickedness of the earth will
        be destroyed:
the Savior of the world will reign over us.
R. Alleluia, alleluia.

Gospel: Matthew 1:1-25

[1] The book of the genealogy of Jesus Christ, the son of David, the son of Abraham.

[2] Abraham became the father of Isaac, Isaac the father of Jacob, Jacob the father of Judah and his brothers. [3] Judah became the father of Perez and Zerah, whose mother was Tamar. Perez became the father of Hezron, Hezron the father of Ram, [4] Ram the father of Amminadab. Amminadab became the father of Nahshon, Nahshon the father of Salmon, [5] Salmon the father of Boaz, whose mother was Rahab. Boaz became the father of Obed, whose mother was Ruth. Obed became the father of Jesse, [6] Jesse the father of David the king.

David became the father of Solomon, whose mother had been the wife of Uriah. [7] Solomon became the father of Rehoboam, Rehoboam the father of Abijah, Abijah the father of Asaph. [8] Asaph became the father of Jehoshaphat, Jehoshaphat the father of Joram, Joram the father of Uzziah. [9] Uzziah became the father of Jotham, Jotham the father of Ahaz, Ahaz the father of Hezekiah. [10] Hezekiah became the father of Manasseh, Manasseh the father of Amos, Amos the father of Josiah. [11] Josiah became the father of Jechoniah and his brothers at the time of the Babylonian exile.

[12] After the Babylonian exile, Jechoniah became the father of Shealtiel, Shealtiel the father of Zerubbabel, [13] Zerubbabel the father of Abiud. Abiud became the father of Eliakim, Eliakim the father of Azor, [14] Azor the father of Zadok. Zadok became the father of Achim, Achim the father of Eliud, [15] Eliud the father of Eleazar. Eleazar became the father of Matthan, Matthan the father of Jacob, [16] Jacob the father of Joseph, the husband of Mary. Of her was born Jesus who is called the Christ.

[17] Thus the total number of generations from Abraham to David is fourteen generations; from David to the Babylonian exile, fourteen generations; from the Babylonian exile to the Christ, fourteen generations.

[18] Now this is how the birth of Jesus Christ came about. When his mother Mary was betrothed to Joseph, but before they lived together, she was found with child

through the Holy Spirit. [19] Joseph her husband, since he was a righteous man, yet unwilling to expose her to shame, decided to divorce her quietly. [20] Such was his intention when, behold, the angel of the Lord appeared to him in a dream and said, "Joseph, son of David, do not be afraid to take Mary your wife into your home. For it is through the Holy Spirit that this child has been conceived in her. [21] She will bear a son and you are to name him Jesus, because he will save his people from their sins." [22] All this took place to fulfill what the Lord had said through the prophet:

[23] *Behold, the virgin shall conceive and bear*
> *a son,*
and they shall name him Emmanuel,

which means "God is with us." [24] When Joseph awoke, he did as the angel of the Lord had commanded him and took his wife into his home. [25] He had no relations with her until she bore a son, and he named him Jesus.

Or Matthew 1:18-25

[18] Now this is how the birth of Jesus Christ came about. When his mother Mary was betrothed to Joseph, but before they lived together, she was found with child through the Holy Spirit. [19] Joseph her husband, since he was a righteous man, yet unwilling to expose her to shame, decided to divorce her quietly. [20] Such was his intention when, behold, the angel of the Lord appeared to him in a dream and said, "Joseph, son of David, do not be afraid to take Mary your wife into your home. For it is through the Holy Spirit that this child has been conceived in her. [21] She will bear a son and you are to name him Jesus, because he will save his people from their sins." [22] All this took place to fulfill what the Lord had said through the prophet:

[23] *Behold, the virgin shall conceive and bear*
> *a son,*
and they shall name him Emmanuel,

which means "God is with us." [24] When Joseph awoke, he did as the angel of the Lord had commanded him and took his wife into his home. [25] He had no relations with her until she bore a son, and he named him Jesus.

Tuesday December 24, 2024

The Nativity of the Lord – Mid Night Vigil Mass
First Reading: Isaiah 9:1-6
[1] The people who walked in darkness
> have seen a great light;
upon those who dwelt in the land of gloom
> a light has shone.

² You have brought them abundant joy
        and great rejoicing,
as they rejoice before you as at the harvest,
        as people make merry when dividing
                spoils.
        ³ For the yoke that burdened them,
        the pole on their shoulder,
and the rod of their taskmaster
        you have smashed, as on the day of
                Midian.
        ⁴ For every boot that tramped in battle,
        every cloak rolled in blood,
        will be burned as fuel for flames.
⁵ For a child is born to us, a son is given us;
        upon his shoulder dominion rests.
They name him Wonder-Counselor, God-
                Hero,
        Father-Forever, Prince of Peace.
⁶ His dominion is vast
        and forever peaceful,
from David's throne, and over his kingdom,
        which he confirms and sustains
by judgment and justice,
        both now and forever.
The zeal of the LORD of hosts will do this!

Responsorial Psalm: Psalms 96: 1-2, 2-3, 11-12, 13

R. *(Luke 2:11)* **Today is born our Savior, Christ the Lord.**
¹ Sing to the LORD a new song;
        sing to the LORD, all you lands.
^{2A} Sing to the LORD; bless his name.
R. Today is born our Savior, Christ the Lord.

^{2B} Announce his salvation, day after day.
        ³ Tell his glory among the nations;
        among all peoples, his wondrous deeds.
R. Today is born our Savior, Christ the Lord.

¹¹ Let the heavens be glad and the earth
                rejoice;
        let the sea and what fills it resound;
        ¹² let the plains be joyful and all that is in them!

Then shall all the trees of the forest exult.
R. Today is born our Savior, Christ the Lord.

[13] They shall exult before the LORD, for he
            comes;
        for he comes to rule the earth.
He shall rule the world with justice
        and the peoples with his constancy.
R. Today is born our Savior, Christ the Lord.

Second Reading: Titus 2:11-14

Beloved: [11] The grace of God has appeared, saving all [12] and training us to reject godless ways and worldly desires and to live temperately, justly, and devoutly in this age, [13] as we await the blessed hope, the appearance of the glory of our great God and savior Jesus Christ, [14] who gave himself for us to deliver us from all lawlessness and to cleanse for himself a people as his own, eager to do what is good.

Alleluia: Luke 2:10-11

R. Alleluia, alleluia.
[10] I proclaim to you good news of great joy:
[11] today a Savior is born for us,
Christ the Lord.
R. Alleluia, alleluia.

Gospel: Luke 2:1-14

[1] In those days a decree went out from Caesar Augustus that the whole world should be enrolled. [2] This was the first enrollment, when Quirinius was governor of Syria. [3] So all went to be enrolled, each to his own town. [4] And Joseph too went up from Galilee from the town of Nazareth to Judea, to the city of David that is called Bethlehem, because he was of the house and family of David, [5] to be enrolled with Mary, his betrothed, who was with child.

[6] While they were there, the time came for her to have her child, [7] and she gave birth to her firstborn son. She wrapped him in swaddling clothes and laid him in a manger, because there was no room for them in the inn.

[8] Now there were shepherds in that region living in the fields and keeping the night watch over their flock. [9] The angel of the Lord appeared to them and the glory of the Lord shone around them, and they were struck with great fear. [10] The angel said to them, "Do not be afraid; for behold, I proclaim to you good news of great joy that will be for all the people. [11]For today in the city of David a savior has been born for you who is Christ and Lord. [12] And this will be a sign for you: you will find an infant wrapped in swaddling clothes and lying in a manger." [13] And suddenly there was a multitude of the heavenly host with the angel, praising God and saying:

¹⁴ "Glory to God in the highest
    and on earth peace to those on whom his
      favor rests."

The Nativity of the Lord – Mass at Dawn
First Reading: Isaiah 62:11-12

¹¹ See, the LORD proclaims
    to the ends of the earth:
say to daughter Zion,
    your savior comes!
Here is his reward with him,
    his recompense before him.
    ¹² They shall be called the holy people,
    the redeemed of the LORD,
and you shall be called "Frequented,"
    a city that is not forsaken.

Responsorial Psalm: Psalms 97:1, 6, 11-12
R. A light will shine on us this day: the Lord is
      born for us.
¹ The LORD is king; let the earth rejoice;
    let the many isles be glad.
⁶ The heavens proclaim his justice,
    and all peoples see his glory.
R. A light will shine on us this day: the Lord is
      born for us.

¹¹ Light dawns for the just;
    and gladness, for the upright of heart.
¹² Be glad in the LORD, you just,
    and give thanks to his holy name.
R. A light will shine on us this day: the Lord is
      born for us.

Second Reading: Titus 3:4-7

Beloved: ⁴ When the kindness and generous love of God our savior appeared, ⁵ not because of any righteous deeds we had done but because of his mercy, He saved us through the bath of rebirth and renewal by the Holy Spirit, ⁶ whom he richly poured out on us through Jesus Christ our savior, ⁷so that we might be justified by his grace and become heirs in hope of eternal life.

Alleluia: Luke 2:14
R. Alleluia, alleluia.
[14] Glory to God in the highest,
and on earth peace to those
on whom his favor rests.
R. Alleluia, alleluia.

Gospel: Luke 2:15-20
[15] When the angels went away from them to heaven, the shepherds said to one another, "Let us go, then, to Bethlehem to see this thing that has taken place, which the Lord has made known to us." [16] So they went in haste and found Mary and Joseph, and the infant lying in the manger. [17] When they saw this, they made known the message that had been told them about this child. [18] All who heard it were amazed by what had been told them by the shepherds. [19] And Mary kept all these things, reflecting on them in her heart. [20] Then the shepherds returned, glorifying and praising God for all they had heard and seen, just as it had been told to them.

Wednesday December 25, 2024

The Nativity of the Lord – Mass During the Day
First Reading: Isaiah 52:7-10
[7] How beautiful upon the mountains
   are the feet of him who brings glad
      tidings,
announcing peace, bearing good news,
   announcing salvation, and saying to Zion,
   "Your God is King!"

[8] Hark! Your sentinels raise a cry,
   together they shout for joy,
for they see directly, before their eyes,
   the LORD restoring Zion.
   [9] Break out together in song,
   O ruins of Jerusalem!
For the LORD comforts his people,
   he redeems Jerusalem.
[10] The LORD has bared his holy arm
   in the sight of all the nations;
all the ends of the earth will behold
   the salvation of our God.

Responsorial Psalm: Psalms 98:1,2-3, 3-4,5-6
**R. [3c] All the ends of the earth have seen the
      saving power of God.**
[1] Sing to the LORD a new song,

662

for he has done wondrous deeds;
his right hand has won victory for him,
    his holy arm.
**R. All the ends of the earth have seen the saving
        power of God.**

[2] The LORD has made his salvation known:
        in the sight of the nations he has revealed
            his justice.
[3] He has remembered his kindness and his
            faithfulness
        toward the house of Israel.
**R. All the ends of the earth have seen the saving
        power of God.**

[3] All the ends of the earth have seen
        the salvation by our God.
[4] Sing joyfully to the LORD, all you lands;
        break into song; sing praise.
**R. All the ends of the earth have seen the saving
        power of God.**
[5] Sing praise to the LORD with the harp,
        with the harp and melodious song.
[6] With trumpets and the sound of the horn
        sing joyfully before the King, the LORD.
**R. All the ends of the earth have seen the saving
        power of God.**

Second Reading: Hebrews 1:1-6

Brothers and sisters: [1] In times past, God spoke in partial and various ways to our ancestors through the prophets; [2] in these last days, he has spoken to us through the Son, whom he made heir of all things and through whom he created the universe,

[3] who is the refulgence of his glory,
        the very imprint of his being,
        and who sustains all things by his mighty
            word.
When he had accomplished purification
        from sins,
        he took his seat at the right hand of the
            Majesty on high,
[4] as far superior to the angels

as the name he has inherited is more
    excellent than theirs.

[5] For to which of the angels did God ever say:

You are my son; this day I have begotten
    you?
Or again:

I will be a father to him, and he shall be a
    son to me?

[6] And again, when he leads the firstborn into the world, he says:

Let all the angels of God worship him.

Alleluia
R. Alleluia, alleluia.
A holy day has dawned upon us.
Come, you nations, and adore the Lord.
For today a great light has come upon the
    earth.
R. Alleluia, alleluia.

Gospel: John 1:1-18
[1] In the beginning was the Word,
    and the Word was with God,
    and the Word was God.
[2] He was in the beginning with God.
[3] All things came to be through him,
    and without him nothing came to be.
What came to be [4] through him was life,
    and this life was the light of the
        human race;
[5] the light shines in the darkness,
    and the darkness has not overcome
        it.

[6] A man named John was sent from God. [7] He came for testimony, to testify to the light, so that all might believe through him. [8] He was not the light, but came to testify to the light. [9] The true light, which enlightens everyone, was coming into the world.

¹⁰ He was in the world,

and the world came to be through
him,
but the world did not know him.

¹¹ He came to what was his own,

but his own people did not accept
him.

¹² But to those who did accept him he gave power to become children of God, to those who believe in his name, ¹³ who were born not by natural generation nor by human choice nor by a man's decision but of God.

¹⁴ And the Word became flesh

and made his dwelling among us,
and we saw his glory,
the glory as of the Father's only Son,
full of grace and truth.

¹⁵ John testified to him and cried out, saying, "This was he of whom I said, 'The one who is coming after me ranks ahead of me because he existed before me.'" ¹⁶ From his fullness we have all received, grace in place of grace, ¹⁷ because while the law was given through Moses, grace and truth came through Jesus Christ. ¹⁸ No one has ever seen God. The only Son, God, who is at the Father's side, has revealed him.

Or John 1:1-5, 9-14

¹ In the beginning was the Word,

and the Word was with God,
and the Word was God.

² He was in the beginning with God.

³ All things came to be through him,

and without him nothing came to be.
What came to be ⁴ through him was life,
and this life was the light of the
human race;

⁵ the light shines in the darkness,

and the darkness has not overcome
it.

⁹ The true light, which enlightens
everyone,
was coming into the world.

¹⁰ He was in the world,

and the world came to be through

him,
but the world did not know him.
¹¹ He came to what was his own,
but his own people did not accept
him.

¹² But to those who did accept him he gave power to become children of God, to those who believe in his name, ¹³ who were born not by natural generation nor by human choice nor by a man's decision but of God.

¹⁴ And the Word became flesh
and made his dwelling among us,
and we saw his glory,
the glory as of the Father's only Son,
full of grace and truth.

Thursday December 26, 2024

Feast of Saint Stephen, First Martyr
First Reading: Acts 6:8-10; 7:54-59

⁸ Stephen, filled with grace and power, was working great wonders and signs among the people. ⁹ Certain members of the so-called Synagogue of Freedmen, Cyrenians, and Alexandrians, and people from Cilicia and Asia, came forward and debated with Stephen, ¹⁰ but they could not withstand the wisdom and the spirit with which he spoke. ⁵⁴ When they heard this, they were infuriated, and they ground their teeth at him. ⁵⁵ But he, filled with the Holy Spirit, looked up intently to heaven and saw the glory of God and Jesus standing at the right hand of God, ⁵⁶ and he said, "Behold, I see the heavens opened and the Son of Man standing at the right hand of God." ⁵⁷ But they cried out in a loud voice, covered their ears, and rushed upon him together. ⁵⁸ They threw him out of the city, and began to stone him. The witnesses laid down their cloaks at the feet of a young man named Saul. ⁵⁹ As they were stoning Stephen, he called out "Lord Jesus, receive my spirit."

Responsorial Psalm: Psalms 31:3CD-4, 6 AND 8AB, 16BC AND 17

R. ⁽⁶⁾ *Into your hands, O Lord, I commend my spirit.*

^{3CD} Be my rock of refuge,
a stronghold to give me safety.
⁴ You are my rock and my fortress;
for your name's sake you will lead and
guide me.

R. *Into your hands, O Lord, I commend my spirit.*

⁶ Into your hands I commend my spirit;
you will redeem me, O LORD, O faithful

God.

^{8AB} I will rejoice and be glad because of your
          mercy.
R. Into your hands, O Lord, I commend my spirit.

^{16BC} Rescue me from the clutches of my enemies
          and my persecutors.
¹⁷ Let your face shine upon your servant;
     save me in your kindness.
R. Into your hands, O Lord, I commend my spirit.

Alleluia: Psalms 118:26A, 27A

R. Alleluia, alleluia.
^{26A} Blessed is he who comes in the name of the
          LORD:
^{27A} the LORD is God and has given us light.
R. Alleluia, alleluia.

Gospel: Matthew 10:17-22

Jesus said to his disciples: ¹⁷ "Beware of men, for they will hand you over to courts and scourge you in their synagogues, ¹⁸ and you will be led before governors and kings for my sake as a witness before them and the pagans. ¹⁹ When they hand you over, do not worry about how you are to speak or what you are to say. You will be given at that moment what you are to say. ²⁰ For it will not be you who speak but the Spirit of your Father speaking through you. ²¹ Brother will hand over brother to death, and the father his child; children will rise up against parents and have them put to death. ²² You will be hated by all because of my name, but whoever endures to the end will be saved."

Feast of Saint John, Apostle and Evangelist
First Reading: 1 John 1:1-4
Beloved:

¹ What was from the beginning,
     what we have heard,
     what we have seen with our eyes,
     what we looked upon
     and touched with our hands
     concerns the Word of life —
² for the life was made visible;
     we have seen it and testify to it
     and proclaim to you the eternal life

that was with the Father and was made
visible to us —
[3] what we have seen and heard
we proclaim now to you,
so that you too may have fellowship with
us;
for our fellowship is with the Father
and with his Son, Jesus Christ.

[4] We are writing this so that our joy may be complete.

Responsorial Psalm: Psalms 97:1-2,5-6,11-12
R. [(12)] *Rejoice in the Lord, you just!*
[1] The LORD is king; let the earth rejoice;
let the many isles be glad.
[2] Clouds and darkness are around him,
justice and judgment are the foundation
of his throne.
R. Rejoice in the Lord, you just!

[5] The mountains melt like wax before the
LORD,
before the LORD of all the earth.
[6] The heavens proclaim his justice,
and all peoples see his glory.
R. Rejoice in the Lord, you just!

[11] Light dawns for the just;
and gladness, for the upright of heart.
[12] Be glad in the LORD, you just,
and give thanks to his holy name.
R. Rejoice in the Lord, you just!

Alleluia: *Te Deum*
R. Alleluia, alleluia.
We praise you, O God,
we acclaim you as Lord;
the glorious company of Apostles praise you.
R. Alleluia, alleluia.

Gospel: John 20:1A AND 2-8

1A On the first day of the week, 2 Mary Magdalene ran and went to Simon Peter and to the other disciple whom Jesus loved, and told them, "They have taken the Lord from the tomb, and we do not know where they put him." 3 So Peter and the other disciple went out and came to the tomb. 4 They both ran, but the other disciple ran faster than Peter and arrived at the tomb first; 5 he bent down and saw the burial cloths there, but did not go in. 6 When Simon Peter arrived after him, he went into the tomb and saw the burial cloths there, 7 and the cloth that had covered his head, not with the burial cloths but rolled up in a separate place. 8 Then the other disciple also went in, the one who had arrived at the tomb first, and he saw and believed.

Saturday December 28, 2024

Feast of the Holy Innocents, Martyrs
First Reading: 1 John 1:5-2:2

Beloved: 5 This is the message that we have heard from Jesus Christ and proclaim to you: God is light, and in him there is no darkness at all. 6 If we say, "We have fellowship with him," while we continue to walk in darkness, we lie and do not act in truth. 7 But if we walk in the light as he is in the light, then we have fellowship with one another, and the Blood of his Son Jesus cleanses us from all sin. 8 If we say, "We are without sin," we deceive ourselves, and the truth is not in us. 9 If we acknowledge our sins, he is faithful and just and will forgive our sins and cleanse us from every wrongdoing. 10 If we say, "We have not sinned," we make him a liar, and his word is not in us.

1 My children, I am writing this to you so that you may not commit sin. But if anyone does sin, we have an Advocate with the Father, Jesus Christ the righteous one. 2 He is expiation for our sins, and not for our sins only but for those of the whole world.

Responsorial Psalm: Psalms 124:2-3, 4-5, 7CD-8

R. (7) *Our soul has been rescued like a bird from*
            the fowler's snare.

2 Had not the LORD been with us —
When men rose up against us,
    3 then would they have swallowed us alive,
When their fury was inflamed against us.
R. *Our soul has been rescued like a bird from the*
            fowler's snare.

4 Then would the waters have overwhelmed
            us;
The torrent would have swept over us;
    5 over us then would have swept the raging
            waters.
R. *Our soul has been rescued like a bird from the*
            fowler's snare.

7CD Broken was the snare,
    and we were freed.
8 Our help is in the name of the LORD,
    who made heaven and earth.
**R. Our soul has been rescued like a bird from the
                fowler's snare.**

Alleluia: cf. *Te Deum*
R. Alleluia, alleluia.
We praise you, O God,
we acclaim you as Lord;
the white robed army of martyrs praise you.
R. Alleluia, alleluia.

Gospel: Matthew 2:13-18

13 When the magi had departed, behold, the angel of the Lord appeared to Joseph in a dream and said, "Rise, take the child and his mother, flee to Egypt, and stay there until I tell you. Herod is going to search for the child to destroy him." 14 Joseph rose and took the child and his mother by night and departed for Egypt. 15 He stayed there until the death of Herod, that what the Lord had said through the prophet might be fulfilled, *Out of Egypt I called my son.*

16 When Herod realized that he had been deceived by the magi, he became furious. He ordered the massacre of all the boys in Bethlehem and its vicinity two years old and under, in accordance with the time he had ascertained from the magi. 17 Then was fulfilled what had been said through Jeremiah the prophet:

18 *A voice was heard in Ramah,*
    sobbing and loud lamentation;
Rachel weeping for her children,
    and she would not be consoled,
    since they were no more.

Sunday December 29, 2024

Feast of The Holy Family of Jesus, Mary and Joseph
First Reading: Sirach 3:2-6, 12-14
2 God sets a father in honor over his
            children;
        a mother's authority he confirms
            over her sons.
3 Whoever honors his father atones for
        sins,
        and preserves himself from them.

When he prays, he is heard;
⁴ he stores up riches who reveres his
mother.
⁵ Whoever honors his father is gladdened
by children,
and, when he prays, is heard.
⁶ Whoever reveres his father will live a
long life;
he who obeys his father brings
comfort to his mother.

¹² My son, take care of your father when
he is old;
grieve him not as long as he lives.
¹³ Even if his mind fail, be considerate of
him;
revile him not all the days of his life;
¹⁴ kindness to a father will not be
forgotten,
firmly planted against the debt of
your sins
—a house raised in justice to you.

Or 1 Samuel 1:20-22, 24-28

²⁰ In those days Hannah conceived, and at the end of her term bore a son whom she called Samuel, since she had asked the LORD for him. ²¹ The next time her husband Elkanah was going up with the rest of his household to offer the customary sacrifice to the LORD and to fulfill his vows, ²² Hannah did not go, explaining to her husband, "Once the child is weaned, I will take him to appear before the LORD and to remain there forever; I will offer him as a perpetual nazirite."

²⁴ Once Samuel was weaned, Hannah brought him up with her, along with a three-year-old bull, an ephah of flour, and a skin of wine, and presented him at the temple of the LORD in Shiloh. ²⁵ After the boy's father had sacrificed the young bull, Hannah, his mother, approached Eli and said:

²⁶ "Pardon, my lord! As you live, my lord, I am the woman who stood near you here, praying to the LORD. ²⁷ I prayed for this child, and the LORD granted my request. ²⁸ Now I, in turn, give him to the LORD; as long as he lives, he shall be dedicated to the LORD." Hannah left Samuel there.

Responsorial Psalm: Psalms 128:1-2, 3, 4-5.

R. *(cf. 1)* **Blessed are those who fear the Lord and
walk in his ways.**
¹ Blessed is everyone who fears the LORD,

who walks in his ways!
² For you shall eat the fruit of your handiwork;
      blessed shall you be, and favored.
**R. Blessed are those who fear the Lord and walk
      in his ways.**

³ Your wife shall be like a fruitful vine
      in the recesses of your home;
your children like olive plants
      around your table.
**R. Blessed are those who fear the Lord and walk
      in his ways.**

⁴ Behold, thus is the man blessed
      who fears the LORD.
⁵ The LORD bless you from Zion:
      may you see the prosperity of Jerusalem
      all the days of your life.
**R. Blessed are those who fear the Lord and walk
      in his ways.**

Or Psalms 84:2-3, 5-6, 9-10.
R. *(cf. 5a)* **Blessed are they who dwell in your
      house, O Lord.**
² How lovely is your dwelling place, O LORD of
      hosts!
    ³ My soul yearns and pines for the courts
      of the LORD.
My heart and my flesh cry out for the living
      God.
**R. Blessed are they who dwell in your house, O
      Lord.**
⁵ Happy they who dwell in your house!
      Continually they praise you.
⁶ Happy the men whose strength you are!
      Their hearts are set upon the pilgrimage.
**R. Blessed are they who dwell in your house, O
      Lord.**

⁹ O LORD of hosts, hear our prayer;
      hearken, O God of Jacob!
¹⁰ O God, behold our shield,

and look upon the face of your anointed.
R. Blessed are they who dwell in your house, O
Lord.

Second Reading: Colossians 3:12-21

Brothers and sisters: [12] Put on, as God's chosen ones, holy and beloved, heartfelt compassion, kindness, humility, gentleness, and patience, [13] bearing with one another and forgiving one another, if one has a grievance against another; as the Lord has forgiven you, so must you also do. [14] And over all these put on love, that is, the bond of perfection. [15] And let the peace of Christ control your hearts, the peace into which you were also called in one body. And be thankful. [16] Let the word of Christ dwell in you richly, as in all wisdom you teach and admonish one another, singing psalms, hymns, and spiritual songs with gratitude in your hearts to God. [17] And whatever you do, in word or in deed, do everything in the name of the Lord Jesus, giving thanks to God the Father through him.

[18] Wives, be subordinate to your husbands, as is proper in the Lord. [19] Husbands, love your wives, and avoid any bitterness toward them. [20] Children, obey your parents in everything, for this is pleasing to the Lord. [21] Fathers, do not provoke your children, so they may not become discouraged.

Or Colossians 3:12-17

Brothers and sisters: [12] Put on, as God's chosen ones, holy and beloved, heartfelt compassion, kindness, humility, gentleness, and patience, [13] bearing with one another and forgiving one another, if one has a grievance against another; as the Lord has forgiven you, so must you also do. [14] And over all these put on love, that is, the bond of perfection. [15] And let the peace of Christ control your hearts, the peace into which you were also called in one body. And be thankful. [16] Let the word of Christ dwell in you richly, as in all wisdom you teach and admonish one another, singing psalms, hymns, and spiritual songs with gratitude in your hearts to God. [17] And whatever you do, in word or in deed, do everything in the name of the Lord Jesus, giving thanks to God the Father through him.

Or 1 John 3:1-2, 21-24

Beloved: [1] See what love the Father has bestowed on us that we may be called the children of God. And so we are. The reason the world does not know us is that it did not know him. [2] Beloved, we are God's children now; what we shall be has not yet been revealed. We do know that when it is revealed we shall be like him, for we shall see him as he is.

[21] Beloved, if our hearts do not condemn us, we have confidence in God [22] and receive from him whatever we ask, because we keep his commandments and do what pleases him. [23] And his commandment is this: we should believe in the name of his Son, Jesus Christ, and love one another just as he commanded us. [24] Those who keep his commandments remain in him, and he in them, and the way we know that he remains in us is from the Spirit he gave us.

Alleluia: Colossians 3:15A, 16A
R. Alleluia, alleluia.
[15A] Let the peace of Christ control your hearts;

R. Alleluia, alleluia.

Or cf. Acts 16:14B

R. Alleluia, alleluia.

14B Open our hearts, O Lord,
to listen to the words of your Son.

R. Alleluia, alleluia.

Gospel: Luke 2:41-52

41 Each year Jesus' parents went to Jerusalem for the feast of Passover, 42 and when he was twelve years old, they went up according to festival custom. 43 After they had completed its days, as they were returning, the boy Jesus remained behind in Jerusalem, but his parents did not know it. 44 Thinking that he was in the caravan, they journeyed for a day and looked for him among their relatives and acquaintances, 45 but not finding him, they returned to Jerusalem to look for him. 46 After three days they found him in the temple, sitting in the midst of the teachers, listening to them and asking them questions, 47 and all who heard him were astounded at his understanding and his answers. 48 When his parents saw him, they were astonished, and his mother said to him, "Son, why have you done this to us? Your father and I have been looking for you with great anxiety." 49 And he said to them, "Why were you looking for me? Did you not know that I must be in my Father's house?" 50 But they did not understand what he said to them. 51 He went down with them and came to Nazareth, and was obedient to them; and his mother kept all these things in her heart. 52 And Jesus advanced in wisdom and age and favor before God and man.

Monday December 30, 2024

Sixth Day in the Octave of Christmas

First Reading: 1 John 2:12-17

12 I am writing to you, children, because your sins have been forgiven for his name's sake.

13 I am writing to you, fathers, because you know him who is from the beginning.

I am writing to you, young men, because you have conquered the Evil One.

14 I write to you, children, because you know the Father.

I write to you, fathers, because you know him who is from the beginning.

I write to you, young men, because you are strong and the word of God remains in you, and you have conquered the Evil One.

15 Do not love the world or the things of the world. If anyone loves the world, the love of the Father is not in him. 16 For all that is in the world, sensual lust, enticement for the eyes, and a pretentious life, is not from the Father but is from the world. 17 Yet the world and its enticement are passing away. But whoever does the will of God remains forever.

Responsorial Psalm: Psalms 96:7-8A, 8B-9, 10

R. *(11a)Let the heavens be glad and the earth rejoice!*

⁷ Give to the LORD, you families of nations,
>   give to the LORD glory and praise;
>   ^{8A} give to the LORD the glory due his name!

R. *Let the heavens be glad and the earth rejoice!*

^{8B} Bring gifts, and enter his courts;
>   ⁹ worship the LORD in holy attire.
Tremble before him, all the earth.

R. *Let the heavens be glad and the earth rejoice!*

¹⁰ Say among the nations: The LORD is king.
He has made the world firm, not to be
>   moved;
>   he governs the peoples with equity.

R. *Let the heavens be glad and the earth rejoice!*

Alleluia

R. Alleluia, alleluia.
A holy day has dawned upon us.
Come, you nations, and adore the Lord.
Today a great light has come upon the earth.
R. Alleluia, alleluia.

Gospel: Luke 2:36-40

³⁶ There was a prophetess, Anna, the daughter of Phanuel, of the tribe of Asher. She was advanced in years, having lived seven years with her husband after her marriage, ³⁷ and then as a widow until she was eighty-four. She never left the temple, but worshiped night and day with fasting and prayer. ³⁸ And coming forward at that very time, she gave thanks to God and spoke about the child to all who were awaiting the redemption of Jerusalem.

³⁹ When they had fulfilled all the prescriptions of the law of the Lord, they returned to Galilee, to their own town of Nazareth. ⁴⁰ The child grew and became strong, filled with wisdom; and the favor of God was upon him.

Tuesday December 31, 2024

The Seventh Day in the Octave of Christmas
First Reading: 1 John 2:18-21

¹⁸ Children, it is the last hour; and just as you heard that the antichrist was coming, so now many antichrists have appeared. Thus we know this is the last hour. ¹⁹ They went out from us, but they were not really of our number; if they had been, they would have remained with us. Their desertion shows that none of them was of our number. ²⁰ But you have the

anointing that comes from the Holy One, and you all have knowledge. [21] I write to you not because you do not know the truth but because you do, and because every lie is alien to the truth.

Responsorial Psalm: Psalms 96:1-2,11-12,13

R. *(11a) Let the heavens be glad and the earth rejoice!*

[1] Sing to the LORD a new song;
   sing to the LORD, all you lands.
[2] Sing to the LORD; bless his name;
   announce his salvation, day after day.

R. *Let the heavens be glad and the earth rejoice!*

[11] Let the heavens be glad and the earth
      rejoice;
   let the sea and what fills it resound;
   [12] let the plains be joyful and all that is in
      them!
Then shall all the trees of the forest exult
   before the LORD.

R. *Let the heavens be glad and the earth rejoice!*

[13] The LORD comes,
   he comes to rule the earth.
He shall rule the world with justice
   and the peoples with his constancy.

R. *Let the heavens be glad and the earth rejoice!*

Alleluia: John 1:14A, 12A

R. Alleluia, alleluia.

[14A] The Word of God became flesh and dwelt
      among us.
[12A] To those who accepted him
he gave power to become the children of
      God.

R. Alleluia, alleluia.

Gospel: John 1:1-18

[1] In the beginning was the Word,
   and the Word was with God,
   and the Word was God.
[2] He was in the beginning with God.
[3] All things came to be through him,

and without him nothing came to be.
What came to be [4] through him was life,
> and this life was the light of the human
> > race;
> [5] the light shines in the darkness,
> and the darkness has not overcome it.

[6] A man named John was sent from God. [7] He came for testimony, to testify to the light, so that all might believe through him. [8] He was not the light, but came to testify to the light. [9] The true light, which enlightens everyone, was coming into the world.

[10] He was in the world,
> and the world came to be through him,
> but the world did not know him.
[11] He came to what was his own,
> but his own people did not accept him.

[12] But to those who did accept him he gave power to become children of God, to those who believe in his name, [13] who were born not by natural generation nor by human choice nor by a man's decision but of God.

[14] And the Word became flesh
> and made his dwelling among us,
> and we saw his glory,
> the glory as of the Father's only-begotten
> > Son,
> full of grace and truth.

[15] John testified to him and cried out, saying, "This was he of whom I said, 'The one who is coming after me ranks ahead of me because he existed before me.'" [16] From his fullness we have all received, grace in place of grace, [17] because while the law was given through Moses, grace and truth came through Jesus Christ. [18] No one has ever seen God. The only-begotten Son, God, who is at the Father's side, has revealed him.

For comments, corrections, requests and other pieces of information that may help us serve you better, please contact:

Facebook: www.facebook.com/catholiclectionary
Twitter: https://twitter.com/catholiclector